# MANAGERIAL DECISION ANALYSIS

**The Irwin Series in Quantitative Analysis for Business**

**Consulting Editor:**
Robert B. Fetter
*Yale University*

# MANAGERIAL DECISION ANALYSIS

DANNY SAMSON
University of Melbourne

1988
IRWIN
Homewood, Illinois 60430

Acquisitions editor: *Richard T. Hercher*
Production editors: *Margaret S. Haywood and Ethel Shiell*
Copyediting coordinator: *Merrily D. Mazza*
Production manager: *Irene H. Sotiroff*
Artist: *Benoit Design*
Compositor: *Better Graphics*
Typeface: *10/12 Times Roman*
Printer: *Arcata Graphics/Kingsport*

ISBN 0-256-06162-9

Library of Congress Catalog Card No. 87-82172

*Printed in the United States of America*

1 2 3 4 5 6 7 8 9 0 K 5 4 3 2 1 0 9 8

# Preface

As the decisions that managers must make become increasingly complex, the need for powerful analytic frameworks and methodologies for supporting those decisions increases. This book is a compilation of knowledge about the prescriptive styled application of the paradigm of decision analysis (decision making under uncertainty) to managerial problems. It describes the philosophy, process, and methods of decision analysis. The motivation for writing it was a strong belief in the usefulness of decision analysis and the resultant desire to broaden and increase the set of people who can benefit from it, both in business and in educational institutions.

*Managerial Decision Analysis* has been developed while teaching courses in decision analysis to undergraduates, MBA, Executive MBA, and various executive programs. In many of these courses the curriculum was broad, with decision analysis forming only a part of a program which contained a variety of modeling approaches. In these experiences it soon became clear that many managers and potential managers found decision analysis to be much more interesting and useful than other topics in management science. The reasons for this revolve about the fact that the decision analysis framework is comprehensive, powerful, and flexible. The comprehensiveness lies in the completeness of the approach: it's ability to model problem structure, preferences, and uncertainty. The power of the approach lies in the quality of the insight that it produces. The flexibility of decision analysis is its ability to address so many different problems and different aspects of those problems.

These qualities reflect the fact that decision analysis developed with important contributions from a variety of fields, including economics, engineering, psychology, mathematics, and statistics.

Decision analysis is much more than a mathematical construct, in contrast to some of the better known management science models. It has evolved over the past few decades from its origins as statistical decision theory to the point where, as a result of its usefulness, it is increasingly attracting the attention of managers and students of management. However, the development of this paradigm is not complete, and a number of challenges to inprove the effectiveness of decision analysis remain. This volume presents decision analysis 'warts and all', but in doing so, I hasten to add that taken together, the warts constitute only a minor ailment, and the patient is expected to live and flourish for a long time! Indeed, it is not clear if some of the warts are attached to decision analysis itself, or to those of us whose decision behavior is inconsistent and capricious in relation to prescriptively appealing, systematic axioms and principles.

This book focuses less than some others on the basics of probability theory and more on the important modeling and implementation issues of supporting managerial decisions with rigorous analysis. The treatment is generally not mathematical, requiring only a knowledge of algebra.

*Managerial Decision Analysis* has a number of distinctive features. Complete chapters are included on sensitivity analysis, behavioral aspects of decision analysis, implementation issues, decision support systems, and complementary decision aids, which reflect more recent developments in the field. These chapters build on a basic foundation of the elements of decision analysis, which constitutes approximately the first half of the book. A further distinctive feature of this volume is the inclusion of a decision analysis software package and associated documentation, called ARBORIST[1], that is bringing decision analysis squarely into the computer age. This microcomputer based software can be used in a number of ways. It's primary purpose is as a tool to formulate and solve decision tree models. As such it can be used in decision analysis courses from Day 1 and can be embedded throughout the course, in problem solving and illustration of concepts. Some instructors will prefer to use it to illustrate key points, rather than require it to be generally used. It is also an excellent vehicle through which the manager/computer interface can be examined, including the way each contributes to decision support processes. On the other hand, for those who do not have computers available but still wish to study decision analysis in depth, the text was written such that it can be used independently of the software.

This book was designed to be used in many different courses and programs. It can be used as an upper level undergraduate text in Quantitative Analysis or Business Decision Making courses. Similarly, in MBA programs, it should make a useful contribution to courses in Quantitative Methods and Managerial Decision Making. It should be particularly appropriate for the focus of executive MBA programs, because of the real world orientation.[2] In addition, there is increasing attention being paid to management and decision making in a number of other professional fields, including medicine, law, engineering, and architecture. A course in managerial decision analysis can be very effective in those curricula. A number of suggested course designs are provided in the instructor's guide.

---

[1] ARBORIST is a product of Texas Instruments, Incorporated

[2] Examples, problems and case studies in this text have been included for discussion purposes rather than to illustrate either effective or ineffective decision making or management.

A multidisciplinary field such as decision analysis can make great contributions in providing insights about complex managerial problems, and its development would have been impossible without a number of outstanding contributions. Many people have made strong contributions to the development of modern decision analysis, and it is appropriate to acknowledge in particular the excellent work of Ronald Howard, Ralph Keeney, Howard Raiffa, and Robert Schlaifer, whose writings have strongly influenced my approach in this volume.

I am grateful to Howard Thomas for getting me interested, challenged, and stimulated by the field of decision analysis over the past 10 years. His influence on my view of the field, both as my PhD supervisor and later as a colleague, has been very substantial. This volume benefited greatly from the detailed reviews of the manuscript which were provided at various stages by a number of professors, including:

Donald N. Stengel—*California State University, Fresno*
R.K. Sarin—*UCLA*
Barbara Mandis—*University of Northern Iowa*
Craig W. Kirkwood—*Arizona State University*
Colin E. Bell—*University of Iowa*
Richard G. Newman—*Indiana University, Northwest*
Donald R. Plane—*Rollins College*
Peter H. Farquhar—*Carnegie-Mellon University*
Wayne Winston—*Indiana University*
David L. Olson—*Texas A&M University*
Howard Raiffa—*Harvard University*
and Editor Robert Fetter—*Yale University*

Naturally, there were as many different views about how the material should be organized as there were reviewers. Some interesting design issues arose. For example, should the material on behavioral aspects of decision analysis be integrated with the chapters on methods for assessing probability and utility? Some instructors prefer to teach the fundamental principles first, generate enthusiasm about them, and then present the evidence of biases and assessment difficulties later. Others argued strongly for integration of the concepts of prescription and description. My choice was to adopt the first of these views because it provides the maximum flexibility to instructors. Instructors who wish to integrate these concepts to a greater extent than is done in the book can easily do so through the way that they order lectures, reading assignments, and problems.

Although there are many possible ways to organize material, my conclusion on this issue was that the expected utility of the book was highly sensitive to total content per se, and somewhat less sensitive to the way it is organized, so long as a sensible organization was chosen. Hence a top priority was to start with the basic principles of decision analysis philosophy and methods, and go all the way towards distilling recent research results in the field, while still providing the flexibility for instructors to choose their own menu of topics to be covered, and their own order. A course in decision analysis can be designed to proceed from Chapter 1 straight through to Chapter 15, which is how I generally teach it. I expect that only a few instructors will wish to deviate from a design which begins with Chapter 1 through to 5. After Chapter 5, instructors can choose from essentially stand-alone chapters on utility, sensitivity analysis, simulation in decision analysis, probability revision, information value, behavioral aspects, decision support systems, and complementary decision aids. Indeed, depending on the nature of the audience, the time constraints, and the depth of coverage desired, instructors may wish to choose a menu of topics which includes various components from these chapters. My thanks go to Lisa Jones for her superb word processing work and to Dean McDonald for proofreading and contributing to the editing of this volume and the instructor's manual. My publisher, Richard D. Irwin, and particularly my editor, Dick Hercher, provided an excellent basis of support. This book could not have been completed without the encouragement of my wife, Jeanette, my children, and my parents. Finally, I wish to acknowledge the supportive environment provided by the University of Illinois, where this book was conceived and begun, and the University of Melbourne, where it was completed.

Most first editions of books contain various types of errors despite the best efforts of authors and editors. I will be pleased to hear of any that you find, as well as your more general comments on it.

**Danny Samson**

# Contents

CHAPTER ONE

# Introduction to Decision Modeling

## OUTLINE



## OBJECTIVES

After completing this chapter, you should be able to:

1. Define the analysis process in the context of management problems.
2. Define what a decision is in a managerial context.
3. Understand the various sources of complexity that can make managerial decision making complex.
4. Distinguish problems, models, and decisions.
5. Describe the complexity in a variety of managerial decisions in the fields of financial, marketing, and production/operations management.
6. Discuss the various definitions and interpretations of decision analysis.
7. Outline the philosophy of decision modeling in terms of providing insight and decision support.
8. Describe the concepts of decomposition.
9. Contrast aided and unaided decision processes.

# INTRODUCTION

## About This Book

This book is about analyzing decisions. In both our personal and professional lives we face many problems that require solution, and these problems often involve making decisions.[1] The process of management can be viewed as a series of decisions, and we can judge the relative quality of managers and management systems by examining the quality of the decisions that they make.

Decision processes and the analysis that can be done to support decisions revolve around three elements: problems, conceptual frameworks, and techniques. Our focus in this book is on decision analysis, which is both a conceptual framework and a set of techniques that managers are finding useful in dealing with complex problems. The objective of decision analysis is to improve the quality of decisions that managers make. This book requires no complex mathematics, only algebra in most parts, but it goes a long way toward providing an understanding of both managerial decision processes and how the methods and frameworks of decision analysis can be used to improve decision making.

This chapter is about managerial problems, decision making, and decision modeling in general, and provides a brief introduction to the decision analysis framework. Chapter 2 gives a detailed description of decision analysis as both a philosophy and set of procedures. These procedures are designed to help managers make rational and logical decisions to resolve the complex problems they face. Chapters 3 to 15 focus on individual aspects and elements of decision analysis.

## Types of Decisions

Some decisions require detailed thought and analysis, and others do not. For example, each morning when we wake up we do not analyze in detail what to do first. The alternatives might be: (*a*) have breakfast, (*b*) get dressed, (*c*) brush hair. We make these decisions thousands of times without careful thought.

Other personal decisions do warrant careful thought and perhaps analysis; for example, buying a new house or changing jobs. These decisions are not trivial and may have some or all of the following characteristics:

1. They involve significant, long-lasting impacts.
2. The decision maker has many alternatives to choose from.
3. They affect other people as well as the decision maker.

---

[1] A **problem** is a doubtful or difficult situation, and a **decision** is the process of resolving such a situation.

4. The consequences may be uncertain.
5. They involve multiple dimensions of value.

These types of complexity may also be present in managerial decisions. As an example, consider a marketing manager who is thinking about launching a new product. If he makes the major investment that such a launch requires, there will be long-lasting effects on the company in terms of cash flow, market share, employment opportunities, and other dimensions of value. Managers usually have to choose between a number of different ways to launch products. Since they cannot see into the future, the degree of success of a new product launch is likely to be uncertain at the time when they must choose a course of action. Also, they may not have sole decision-making responsibility, and even if they do, they may wish to consider the impact of their choices on various other groups of people, both within and outside the company. Many such decisions are difficult because of their complexity.

If the decision is both important and complex enough then it is often worthwhile trying to formally analyze it, if time permits. Sometimes, both in our professional and personal lives we may wish to think carefully about something but cannot because of time constraints. For example, suppose you are playing a tennis match and the stakes are high (in terms of pride or money or both). During an important point you have the opportunity to play a deep approach shot and rush the net. Many alternatives exist in terms of topspin versus underspin, down the line versus cross court, etc. As the ball approaches you there is no time to calculate percentage success rates and carefully analyze the situation in the same way as you could analyze a decision to change jobs or move house. However you may have done some previous thinking and have a prespecified strategy or at least some heuristics (rules of thumb) you can use, such as "when in doubt, attack his backhand." Although you may not have done a formal analysis, these heuristics become a set of decision rules that can guide your actions.

We learn by experience that some situations warrant formal decision analysis and some do not. Very often we need not perform formal analyses of decisions because the solution to a problem is obvious; in other words, it is clearly evident without analysis that one course of action is better than all possible others. In other situations, rational analyses are not appropriate because decisions may involve elements (such as love) which simply defy rational decomposition and analysis. Rational decision making becomes particularly important in the context of management, where complex decision situations exist and high-quality decision analyses can prove very valuable. Consider the U.S. automobile companies in Detroit. Was their response to the Japanese assault on U.S. markets in the 1970s a demonstration of good decision making? Another interesting example is that of the many utility companies who built nuclear generating plants over the past 20 years. With hindsight, we can say that they misestimated the demand for electricity and the difficulties of nuclear power technology in most cases. Did they make bad decisions or were they all just unlucky? These kinds of decisions are made by the executives of organizations and are very complex. The magnitude and complexity of these decisions make it worthwhile to allocate substantial resources to carefully analyze them. The rest of this book is devoted to the application of decision analysis to such managerial situations.

## DECISION MAKING AND DECISION MODELS

Ronald Howard, one of the pioneers in the field of decision analysis, has written: "Decision making is what you do when you don't know what to do" (Howard 1980). Particularly in a managerial context, the problems we face are becoming increasingly complex, and our intuitive (unaided) decision processes are less and less able to address the complexity adequately. These complex problems can generally be effectively dealt with, and our decisions can be effectively supported by analysis.

The major purposes of decision models are to **support** our decisions and **provide insight** about our decision problems. In this sense they are prescriptive rather than descriptive. For the product launch problem described above, a purely intuitive approach is perhaps not a wise strategy, because there are important things to be learned from analysis. Decision analysis involves the **decomposition** of the elements of a decision to allow detailed separate study of those elements. Decision analysts do not propose to replace intuitive processes with purely analytic processes, but rather to merge or mold together analytic and intuitive modes so that the analysis supports the intuition.

Simple and easily solved decision problems do not require decision analysis. In such cases, our cognitive processes are usually able to achieve good solutions to problems through the holistic or intuitive approach. In general it is the complex problem that can most usefully be aided by analytic models. Figure 1–1 shows the analytic process as the following series of steps:

Step 1: Formulate the problem, defining its scope and time horizon. Is the solution obvious? If not, proceed to step 2.

Step 2: Construct the model, noting any assumptions and abstractions that are made in doing so. For all real problems that we model, the intricacies of those problems usually force us to make simplifying assumptions. Although this may at first be viewed as a shortcoming of decision models, it is actually a strength! There is much insight to be gained about the problem by starting with a very simple model and then refining it in a number of stages.

**FIGURE 1–1** The Analysis Process

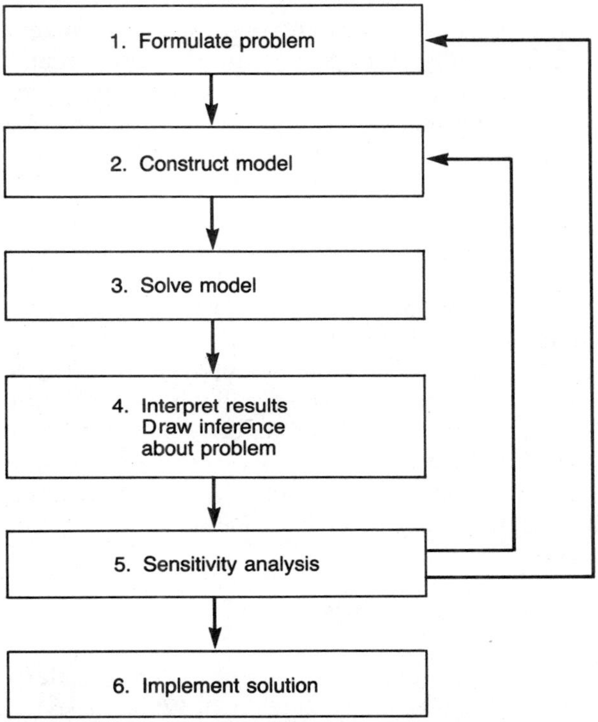

1. Formulate problem
2. Construct model
3. Solve model
4. Interpret results
   Draw inference
   about problem
5. Sensitivity analysis
6. Implement solution

Step 3: Solve the model by manipulating it to obtain solution values for variables and identify optimal strategies. We emphasize that because of the abstractions and assumptions originally made, the solution to the model is distinct from the solution to the original problem.

Step 4: Review the original assumptions, and interpret the model solution in that light. Draw inferences about the solution to the problem based on the solution of the model and these assumptions.

Step 5: Conduct a sensitivity analysis to challenge the assumptions that were originally made. Consider whether more insight can be gained through redefining and refining the model, and if so, return to step 2. In the light of what has been learned from the modeling process, consider whether the problem needs to be respecified, and if so, return to step 1.

Step 6: Implement the solution to the problem, using the insights gained from the analysis.

This process is not typically one in which decision makers and analysts follow a straightforward path through the steps, but rather one where much lateral thinking is done involving many jumps from one step to another. For example, sensitivity analysis can and often should actually be conducted as an integral part of every step. Note that although the analysis of decision problems is aimed at achieving definite answers, *many practitioners achieve more benefit from the analysis process itself than from the answers that are produced*. The analysis process forces them to think very hard about the problem in a systematic manner.

### Types of Models

Many different kinds of models exist. Decision analysts construct models of decision situations. The form of these models is in terms of mathematical symbols and equations, decision diagrams, etc. Engineers construct pilot plant models of chemical processes, models of machines, cars, bridges, dams, buildings, harbors and other structures that may be simply small-scale versions of the real thing. The aim of all these models, whether mathematical models such as decision analyses or physically real models such as chemical process pilot plants, is to provide **information** for **decision-making** purposes.

## THE NATURE OF DECISION ANALYSIS

In its narrowest form, decision analysis has been considered a set of statistical techniques (statistical decision theory). While these techniques play an important analytic role, most practitioners and academics now take a much broader view of decision analysis, recognizing its contribution to the phases of problem identification and measurement.

A second view of decision analysis is that it is but one of a variety of available decision models. Management scientists or decision scientists (persons who develop decision models and use them to solve problems) use many modeling approaches, and their choice of a particular approach is often guided by their desire to fit a model that has similar features to a problem. For example, if a problem has a definable objective and some constraints that can all be expressed as linear combinations of decision variables, and uncertainty is not an important element, then linear programming might be an appropriate model. Alternatively, if a problem involves random arrivals into a service system, then queueing analysis can be used. Decision analysis is most useful for nonprogrammed decisions. These are typically ill-structured problems involving uncertainty and multiple dimensions of value.

A third, even broader, view of decision analysis is taken by many, which is that decision analysis is "a philosophy, articulated by a set of logical axioms, and a methodology and collection of systematic procedures, based upon those axioms, for responsibly analyzing the complexities inherent in decision problems'' (Keeney 1982). On a different level, decision analysis can be defined as ''a formalization of common sense for decision problems which are too complex for informal use of common sense.''[2]

Felsen (1979) has commented on human information processing limitations. He states that our human computing power is modest, our information storage ability is slow and unreliable, and that we can effectively deal with only a small number of dimensions (variables). These arguments provide the justification for the use of decision-aiding models and decision-support technologies. The human brain can be very effective at making lateral thinking connections and creating images of problems and their possible solutions. Most of us are, however, limited to thinking in terms of three or four dimensions only and therefore need to decompose complex problems and analyze them in component parts. The decision analysis approach provides a common sense, efficient decomposition procedure. Both as a philosophy and as a formalization of common sense, decision analysis provides a framework and a thinking algorithm for decision making.

According to this broad view, decision analysis is more than just another mathematical tool for analyzing resource allocation problems. Indeed when choosing a modeling approach for a problem, you do not need to choose between decision analysis and other methods such as linear programming and dynamic programming because, in its broadest perspective, decision analysis can be considered as a meta-decision approach or philosophy encompassing each of these other approaches. Linear programming requires the additional specific assumptions of linearity and no uncertainty (i.e., it could be considered a special or particular form of decision analysis or is at least consistent with decision analysis under these assumptions). Likewise, dynamic programming is consistent with decision analysis and is appropriate for multistage decisions where a certain principle of optimality can be invoked.

Decision analysis often requires the use of subsidiary models that may be in any of a variety of forms. A marketing manager who is considering a new product launch problem may decompose the problem and model it using decision analysis as the overall conceptual framework. The overall decision analysis may be supported by a number of other models. Linear programming may be used to help choose an advertising program mix. Financial models may be used to forecast cash flows. Statistical models may be used to determine market shares. The results and insights that are outputs of these subsidiary models can become *inputs* of the overall decision analysis

[2] Both these definitions are due to Ralph Keeney, who has been a major contributor to the field.

model. Apart from the powerful techniques embodied in decision analysis, its real strength is as a flexible integrating framework.

Whichever view of the hierarchy of models is taken, it is a well-documented fact that decision analysis has been helpful to many organizations (Ulvila and Brown 1982). It is increasingly included in business school curricula and used in business. As organizations face more and more complex problems, and decisions become more and more involved in these complexities, the usefulness of formal decision-making frameworks seems likely to increase. Our distant ancestors who lived in caves would have had very little need for formal decision models because their lives and hence their decisions were relatively simple. The decisions confronting modern-day organizations (and hence their managers) are much more complex than our ancestors could have imagined. Extrapolating to the future, if societal issues continue to increase in complexity, we will need to rely on models to aid us in more and more of our decisions. Organizations already find it necessary to process vast amounts of information and use computers to aid in the task. New fields of study are rapidly developing (such as Decision Support Systems and Artificial Intelligence) which merge the creative abilities of our human brains with the logic systems and information processing abilities of computers and link decision models to vast data bases. Of course, many of our decisions can still be made intuitively (hopefully using common sense) or through a decision analysis (as a formalized common sense approach).

Decision models in general, and decision analysis in particular, are useful *prescriptive* decision support aids and are not intended to be *descriptive*. The primary thrust of decision analysis is to guide and prescribe decision behaviors, and over 20 years of intense experience has shown that decision analysis can successfully aid decision processes. Decision analysis does not generally attempt to describe decision behavior, and in fact, decision analysis is not generally considered a powerful descriptive device.

Decision analysis is also known by the term *decision making under uncertainty*. This is because it is a particularly useful approach when the problem involves risk. The terms *risk* and *uncertainty* have been treated by economists for many decades as distinguishable entities. The principal difference in the definition of these terms is that *risk* has been defined as a set of possible consequences whose probabilities are known, whereas *uncertainty* has been defined as a set of possible consequences with unknown probabilities. This distinction is unnecessary for the purposes of decision analysis. Our approach is to treat chance events as if their probabilities can be subjectively assessed. The subjective approach to probability (which is an important part of decision analysis) does not directly treat the issue of whether probabilities are completely known or unknown, but rather defines probabilities as degrees of belief in the likelihood of an occurrence.

## RELEVANT PROBLEM TYPES

What types of problems can be addressed with the support of decision analysis? First, we can classify decision problems along the dimension of "the degree to which they are programmed." Decisions that are programmed are routine, repetitive, and usually straightforward. They do not generally require a great deal of managerial skill. For example, consider the process of insuring your car. From the insurer's viewpoint, its decision to accept you or not (as a policyholder) is routine. Hence insurance companies design rules and regulations that can be implemented by clerks.

Nonprogrammed decisions are unique and complex, and hence cannot be easily made in an intuitive manner. These types of decisions are the ones that can be effectively supported by decision analysis. For example, consider the strategic planning process a corporation must face. These problems are usually one of a kind, involving many types of complexity. To begin with, nonprogrammed problems are usually ill-structured. For the insurance company referred to above, the alternative actions are well defined. It must either underwrite (accept) the risk or not and set the insurance premium according to well-documented rules. In contrast, for a strategic management decision, possible courses of action have to be created, conflicting objectives must be considered, and competitive elements and sources of uncertainty must be accounted for. Nonprogrammed decisions require skilled managers who can use common sense to solve problems, and where these problems are complex, decision analysis as a form of formalized common sense can be a powerful tool.

Decision analysis can be used on any kind of nonprogrammed problem an organization faces, including decision problems in production, marketing, finance, personnel management, and strategic management. Let us examine in more detail some of the more important types of managerial decisions in the fields of production, marketing, and finance.

## PRODUCTION DECISIONS

A production system converts inputs (also called factors of production) into outputs. Inputs are in the form of labor, land, capital, materials, and energy. Outputs are primarily products and services, but also include profit, growth, employment, economic, and political factors.

Many decisions involving a production system are complex and therefore difficult to structure and to make. Such decisions may involve process design, aggregate planning, and facilities planning.

### Process Design

The production system an organization uses can take many forms. It may be possible to organize a system as a flow shop (assembly line) or as a job shop, or as a mixed system having some elements of both of these system types. The order of operations in a factory and the flow of materials and information must be designed. The same types of decisions must be made for complex service systems such as hospitals and airports. Choices between different production technologies must also be made in the design process.

### Aggregate Planning

The aggregate planning decisions of how and what to produce and in what quantities and orders must be made over a long time horizon in many production systems. Consider an automobile plant where production must be planned many months in advance to facilitate the purchase of raw materials and the organization of the labor force and machinery. Aggregate planning is usually performed over a 12-month time horizon, and may involve a difficult choice between a number of competing alternative plans.

### Facilities Planning

Facilities planning decisions involve examining and possibly changing the production capacity and product mix of the organization. For example, all organizations at some time must decide whether to build a new facility or refurbish an old one. Let us briefly consider the complexity involved in the decision to build a new production system such as a factory or hospital. The first step in the analysis is usually demand forecasting, or the determination of whether or not there is a real and continuing need for the system modification or expansion. Forecasting often involves dealing with considerable uncertainty. This step is followed by the generation and evaluation of alternatives, including an economic analysis and a consideration of qualitative and strategic factors. A choice is then made based at least partially on the results of the analysis.

## MARKETING DECISIONS

Marketing involves much more than just sales and advertising. Marketing decisions are often closely related to production decisions. Important marketing decisions may involve product design, price, and distribution system design.

### Product Design

Product design may strongly influence sales, hence the choice of an appropriate design is a very important decision. This decision is often complex because of the uncertainty in the relationship between product design and sales, and also because product design decisions must also account for production system factors.

### Price

The price of a product or service usually affects both sales and profit. The important decision of setting a price involves competitive market aspects (which may be uncertain) and the relationship between price and quantity, which may not be known exactly.

Decisions between alternatives may therefore be complex and usually have a strong effect on financial performance. Thus they warrant careful consideration. Formal processes of analysis through the construction of decision models can aid this decision process.

### Distribution System Design

The manner in which a product or service is distributed to customers may strongly affect its sales. Many different distribution system designs are available, and complex decisions face the organization in making these choices. The distribution system decision cannot usually be made in isolation of all other decisions, because the system should be appropriate to the product design and price. Decisions of how to advertise are also part of this system design process.

## FINANCIAL DECISIONS

The financial management of an organization includes the management of capital and of cash flow. Important classes of problems include capital budgeting and working capital management.

### Capital Budgeting

Decisions that involve the allocation of funds within an organization are termed capital budgeting decisions. They are obviously closely linked to both production and marketing decisions. In its most general form, the capital budget decision process considers both sources and uses of funds.

Many complex factors affect profitability, taxation, retained earnings, and other key variables. Capital budget decisions have impacts on shareholders, debtors, employees, suppliers, and customers. They often commit the company to a course of action over a long time horizon into an uncertain future environment. The complexity of such decisions is often very great.

### Working Capital Management

The decisions involving the maintenance of liquidity and current asset and liability management can also involve many sources of complexity. For example, purchasing and inventory policy alternatives may involve uncertainty in availability and cost of funds.

In both types of financial decisions described above, the complexity involved in the process makes the decisions difficult to make intuitively. In such cases, sound quantitative analysis has an important role to play. Intuitive judgment can be supported by structured rational models.

Decision analysis has also been used by many public bodies, governments, and agencies to set policies and standards and assist in unique decision situations. We briefly sketch here some examples of where decision analysis has been applied. These examples have been described by Ulvila and Brown (1982) and Keeney and Raiffa (1976).

---

## EXAMPLE 1–1

## An Option Purchase Decision

In 1974, AIL was offered the rights to the defense market for a flight safety system. AIL had to make a relatively quick decision. There were three major sources of uncertainty associated with whether or not the agreement would be licensed, and whether or not two defense contracts would result for AIL. The alternative to buying an option on the rights was to wait until some of these uncertainties were resolved and perhaps then seek a sublicense. Ulvila and Brown (1982) described five important elements that contributed to the success of this analysis:

1. A simple decision tree was used that did not have too many details on it.
2. The initial structure and analysis were refined using sensitivity analysis techniques. In sensitivity analyses, changes in decision elements are made and the effects of these changes are observed.
3. Subsidiary models were used. For example, cash flow models and probability models can be very useful in determining inputs to the decision tree.

4. Many expert opinions were solicited from various AIL staff, so that the decision was a team effort.
5. The decision analysts kept close contact with top management to ensure that the decision structure under consideration was realistic.

---

## EXAMPLE 1–2

### Electric Power Generation

Communities must decide on their electric power needs and make commitments that have long time horizons. The alternatives involve fossil fuel (coal/oil) burning plants or nuclear power plants, or not expanding their generating capacity and facing shortages, or purchasing electric power. Many uncertainties exist with respect to construction and operating costs and the future cost of imported electricity (electricity purchased from outside the system). Power plants have long operating lives and may affect the environment for much longer periods after they cease operation. These decisions involve a choice of power generating capacity and technology with uncertain economic effects. Keeney and Raiffa (1976) suggest that many other dimensions of value are also important, including the health of residents who live in the region and the effect on business, farms, and local politics. Tradeoffs between dimensions of value that are fundamentally different (such as kilowatts, dollars, and health) are particularly difficult. The decision-making process is a complex one involving many levels of government and many different government agencies, utilities, and various community groups. All of these groups have different ways of looking at (structuring) the problem and different preference structures.

---

## EXAMPLE 1–3

### Location of an Airport

Over the past 20 years many large cities around the world have grown significantly both in size and population. As a result, their major international airports located originally on the edge of the populated area are now surrounded by residential or industrial developments and have expanded to the point where further expansion is either impossible or very expensive. These cities must make decisions about further expansion of these airports versus building or upgrading of other airports to meet continually increasing demands. This problem has been faced by many governments in places like Tokyo, Sydney, London, Paris, and many American cities, and many different approaches have been taken. Keeney and Raiffa (1976) report on an airport location decision in Mexico City where present facilities could be expanded and modernized or a new airport could be built. As with all such decisions, the situation is dynamic in that the problem of increasing demand has a multiyear time horizon, and airport capacity must be provided to meet this demand in discrete "lumps." Alternative actions must therefore be defined in terms of both their nature and their timing. In the case of Mexico City, Keeney and Raiffa identified a number of dimensions of value relevant to the decision including:

*a.* Costs (federal government).
*b.* Airport capacity (airlines, military, other users).
*c.* Safety (airlines, users, residents).
*d.* Noise levels (residents, users).
*e.* Access time (users).
*f.* Displacement of people (residents).

We note that these dimensions of value which define objectives and preference structures have different impacts on different groups (as noted above in brackets). Tradeoffs must be made across these conflicting objectives and between and within each of these impacted groups. This type of decision is both complex and non-programmed.

---

To conclude this section, we note that a large and increasing number of organizations are systematically using decision analysis to aid their decision processes. Ulvila and Brown (1982) have listed applications in Ford Motor Co., Honeywell, Pillsbury, Southern Railway, Union Texas Petroleum, ITT, and the Federal Aviation Administration. There are a large number of professional decision analysis consultants who work either as outside consultants and are called in by organizations to help solve problems, or who work in-house in large organizations (as internal consultants). The examples described above are typical of what is now the very large number of applications of decision analysis, both in business and government.

## THE HISTORY OF DECISION ANALYSIS

People have been making decisions for many thousands of years using common sense, heuristics, or intuitive methods. Only during this century has a theory of decision making emerged as a decision support procedure. The earliest significant contributions to the development of decision analysis in its current form were by Bernoulli (1738), Ramsay (1931), DeFinetti (1937), and von Neumann and Morganstern (1947). These early developments were related to two central elements of decision analysis: utility theory and subjective probability. In the 1950s Wald (1950) and Savage

(1954) played major roles in the development of statistical decision th which was and still is the theoretical basis of decision analysis.

In the 1960s many important contributions were made whereby statistical decision theory was applied to problems in economics. Measurement problems were confronted and the techniques of applied statistical decision theory were applied to managerial problems. The term *decision analysis* was used to describe this rapidly developing discipline, and many applications occurred in business and government. Four very good books were published in the 1960s, by Pratt et al. (1965), Raiffa (1968), Raiffa and Schlaifer (1968), and Schlaifer (1969). Taken together, these books still give an excellent treatment to most aspects of decision analysis even though a great deal of development has occurred in the past two decades in a number of directions:

*a.* A large number of experiential applications have occurred, and many of these have been written up in books and journals. This body of experience has given decision analysis researchers and practitioners a deep understanding of the nature of real decision processes and how decision analysis interventions can improve the quality of decisions.

*b.* Better measurement and assessment procedures are continually being developed in risk and multiobjective preference modeling and in modeling uncertainty.

*c.* Improved problem structuring procedures have been developed, and over the past two decades decision analysis has been found to be increasingly useful for semistructured and unstructured problems, in contrast to the initial applications, which were mainly on well-structured problems.

*d.* Behavioral decision analysis has developed as a field of study of its own, relating actual decision behavior to those behaviors that are prescribed by decision analysis axioms and models.

All of these developments are discussed in detail in later chapters. In concluding this chapter, we note that decision analysis has developed as a result of contributions from many fields of study, including statistics, engineering, economics, psychology, and management. It has now been widely applied to problems as diverse as corporate planning decisions and medical diagnostics. It is not limited in its sphere of application to any one field or type of problem, although its potential usefulness is greatest for complex problems involving uncertain elements. Our primary focus in this volume is the application of decision analysis to problems faced by managers.

## SUMMARY

Decisions are becoming increasingly complex as uncertainty, multiple objectives, multiple decision makers or interest groups, larger impacts, and longer time horizons are involved. It is useful to decompose complex decisions into related elements, and decision analysis provides a framework for doing so. As a philosophy or paradigm, decision analysis aims to support our intuitive decision-making processes and abilities and ultimately help us make more effective decisions. The decision models we construct are usually based on abstractions from reality. They help us to focus on all of the stages of problem solving, from problem formulation through solution and implementation. Indeed there is often more to be learned about the problem from the process of analysis than from the answers the analysis yields.

## FURTHER READING

Many useful studies describe the analytic process in general and decision analysis in particular. Articles by Keeney (1982), Howard (1980), and Ulvila and Brown (1982) are particularly well written and not technical in nature. More detailed accounts of decision making under uncertainty are given by Raiffa (1968), Schlaifer (1969), and Keeney and Raiffa (1976).

## REFERENCES

BERNOULLI, D. 1738. "Exposition of a New Theory on the Measurement of Risk," reprinted in *Econometrica* 22 (1954), pp. 23–36.

DEFINETTI, B. 1964. "La Prevision: Ses Lois Logiques, Ses Sources Subjectives." In *Studies in Subjective Probability,* ed. H. E. Kyburg and H. E. Smokler. New York: John Wiley & Sons.

FELSEN, J. 1979. *Decision Making Under Uncertainty*. New York: CBS Publishing.

HOWARD, R. A. 1980. "An Assessment of Decision Analysis." *Operations Research* 28, no. 1 (January), pp. 4–27.

KEENEY, R. L. 1982. "Decision Analysis: An Overview." *Operations Research* 30, no. 5 (September), pp. 803–38.

KEENEY, R. L., and H. RAIFFA. 1976. *Decisions with Multiple Objectives*. New York: John Wiley & Sons.

PRATT J. W., H. RAIFFA, and R. O. SCHLAIFER. 1965. *Introduction to Statistical Decision Theory*. New York: McGraw-Hill.

RAIFFA, H. 1968. *Decision Analysis*. Reading, Mass.: Addison-Wesley Publishing.

RAMSAY, F. P. 1964. "Truth and Probability." In *Studies in Subjective Probability,* ed. H. E. Kyburg and H. E. Smokler. New York: John Wiley & Sons.

SAVAGE, L. J. 1954. *The Foundations of Statistics*. New York: John Wiley & Sons.

SCHLAIFER, R. O. 1969. *Analysis of Decisions under Uncertainty*. New York: McGraw-Hill.

ULVILA, J. W., and R. V. BROWN. 1982. "Decision Analysis Comes of Age." *Harvard Business Review,* September, pp. 130–41.

VON NEUMANN, J., and O. MORGANSTERN. 1947. *Theory of Games and Economic Behavior*. Princeton, N.J.: Princeton University Press.

WALD, A. 1950. *Statistical Decision Functions*. New York: John Wiley & Sons.

## PROBLEMS

1. What elements can make a decision complex?
2. Think of a complex decision that you have been involved in (probably a decision that was difficult to make). Why was it a difficult decision? What were the specific elements of complexity in that decision?
3. Suppose you are the manager of a company that is considering making and marketing a new product. It is a blood pressure monitor that looks like a wristwatch and gives a continuous display of blood pressure. The inventor of the product has offered you the manufacturing license (for a fee). What decisions need to be made? What are the main alternatives associated with these decisions? If you do buy the manufacturing license, what uncertainties will you face, and how can you reduce these uncertainties?
4. Suppose you are a company president and must decide where to locate a new plant that your company needs to meet future demand. The short listed alternatives are Los Angeles, Houston, or Seoul (South Korea). What are the major elements of such a decision?
5. How will you evaluate your next job move? If you had a number of alternative positions offered to you, what criteria would be important in evaluating each alternative? How would you trade off among these criteria to make a choice? Can you imagine any uncertain factors that would impinge on the decision?
6. Decision analysis can be used in the health industries to examine many different problems. In medical diagnostics and treatment decisions, there is often a great deal of uncertainty about which procedures should be followed in any particular case because observed symptoms do not clearly indicate which disease a patient has. Although one clear objective is to cure the patient, difficult decisions must be made involving trade-offs of probability of cure, side effects, patient discomfort, and cost. All doctors and patients must weigh the likelihoods and impacts of various alternatives, although very few perform formal, logical analyses. To support their decisions, doctors and patients may be able to gain insight about the attractiveness of various courses of action through using decision tree structures and expressing their uncertainties about outcomes as probabilities.

   In pairs, take the role of doctor and patient (with a serious disease) and discuss possible actions for dealing with it. What types of complexity are involved?

7. Keeney and Raiffa (1976) describe the problem of heroin addiction in New York City. This problem needs to be managed by the city, and the mayor must decide on one or a combination of a number of options.

   As with most public policy decisions, the many impacted groups have different preference structures. There are also some uncertain quantities. Keeney and Raiffa suggest that the mayor of New York would like to: lessen the number of addicts, lessen the cost of having these addicts, improve the quality of life of both addicts and nonaddicts, reduce organized crime, preserve civil rights and liberties, decrease youth alienation, and further his political ambitions.

   This decision is complex, involving many dimensions of value, uncertainties, and multiple interest groups. Formal (decision analysis) problem structuring and quantitative analysis can help sort out the apparent messy nature of this problem. In such instances the potential of decision analytic procedures is high in the stages of problem structuring, evaluation, and implementation. It can be used as a forum for communication and expression of opinion as well as a means of justification and support for choosing a particular strategy.

   Individually, or as a group exercise, generate alternative actions for dealing with this problem and discuss each one with respect to the mayor's objectives. As mayor, how would you decide?
8. Assume that you are the manager of the research and development division of a major manufacturing organization. You have a fixed budget and 300 technical people in your research and development division, plus support and administration staff. Define some of the problems and classes of decisions that you must manage. Include in your answer a discussion of resource allocation processes, choice of research projects, and organization of people and equipment. For each of the decisions, define the available alternatives, the major sources of uncertainty, and the criteria on which the decisions would be made.
9. You are the director of manufacturing at a company that makes consumer goods. Give examples of three types of decisions that you expect to have to make, and categorize these as strategic, involving long time horizons and high stakes, or tactical. For each of these decisions give examples of alternative actions, sources of uncertainty, and decision criteria.
10. You are the general manager of a company that manufactures a new kind of car battery. Your production manager wants the battery to be designed to fulfill the technical specifications and be easy to manufacture at minimum cost and high quality. Your marketing manager wants the battery to be designed to appeal to customers

and generate maximum sales. As general manager you must resolve the conflict between your functional managers. On what basis should the product design decisions be made?

11. *The Wall Street Journal* (March 8, 1985) reported that the Chrysler Corporation has decided not to acquire or build another car assembly plant in the United States as it had previously planned due to the strong U.S. dollar and the lifting of import restraints on Japanese cars. What would be some of the major factors involved in making decisions of this type. Estimate the time horizon for such a facilities planning decision. Given that exchange rates can fluctuate substantially and that trade relationships can change between countries such as Japan and the United States, how can decisions be made with respect to new facilities with lives of many years that involve a great deal of uncertainty in factors such as prices, costs, exchange rates, and trade relations? Can these decisions be supported by models?

12. A manufacturing company has a press which stamps out metal parts. These parts are key components of its manufacturing and assembly system. The press is one of the most expensive pieces of equipment in the facility. On Monday morning it suffered a major breakdown. Repair is expensive and time consuming. Time is of the essence because a major contract would be adversely affected by long periods of downtime. The company's alternatives include repairing the existing machine, replacing it with a reconditioned unit, buying a new machine of the same design, or buying a more modern electronically controlled machine. The existing machine has been in place for 15 years, breaks down fairly regularly, and requires two operators. The new generation of presses for performing this task can be automatically fed and do not require a full-time operator. How would the decision to repair or replace this machine be made? How would the alternatives be evaluated? What are the sources of uncertainty? How would you make a decision?

CHAPTER TWO

# The Decision Analysis Approach

## OUTLINE



## OBJECTIVES

After completing this chapter, you should be able to:

1. Clearly describe the decision analysis process, in terms of its stages.
2. Decompose descriptions of problems into clearly defined decision variables and chance event variables.
3. Draw simple decision trees.
4. Describe the role of quantitative assessment and data in decision tree models.
5. Discuss the application of decision rules to decision trees.
6. Explain the nature and importance of sensitivity analysis.

## INTRODUCTION

This chapter provides an overview of decision analysis. We begin by describing the process as a series of stages and describing the major features of each stage. This is followed by a case study description of a decision which was supported by the use of decision analysis.

Decision analysis is both a decision-making *philosophy* and a formalized *process* of analysis. We can learn a lot about the underlying philosophy by studying the process in detail. The process generally involves the following stages:

1. **Problem identification** and decision model structuring.
2. **Assessment** of the likelihood and magnitude of impacts.
3. Use of a **decision criterion** to model the process of choice.
4. **Sensitivity analysis** to determine the robustness of solutions to assumptions.
5. **Implementation** of the preferred strategy.

There is now a substantial body of evidence, in the form of published studies, showing that the systematic approach of decomposing a problem and going through these stages helps managers to deal with the complexity that a modern organization must manage.

Let us examine each of these stages in more detail.

## PROBLEM IDENTIFICATION AND MODEL STRUCTURING

The first element that needs careful consideration is the problem itself. Have we correctly recognized the problem or are we just treating some symptoms?

---

### EXAMPLE 2–1

### Manufacturing Company Performance

Suppose that for a manufacturing company, the return on investment (ROI) has not reached expectations in a particular year. Was the performance really poor or were the ROI goals set too high? If financial performance was poor, was it because sales were low (a marketing problem), because production costs were too high, because of poor financing methods, or some combination of these three? The observed symptom which was below target ROI could have been caused by problems in any one of the firm's three major systems: production, marketing, or finance. We often need to do some detective work to develop a good understanding of the real problem based on some observed symptoms. A decision needs to be made to resolve the poor profit performance problem.

---

Many problems are really complex intertwined combinations of subproblems, particularly in medium-sized or large organizations. Let us reconsider the above example of a manufacturer. Assume that for some reason product quality becomes inconsistent or falls. Other things being equal, this production problem would be likely to lead to a marketing problem such as reduced sales orders. The marketing department might want to respond by cutting prices and instructing the production department to change product specifications to reduce cost, possibly causing a further decline in quality.

Problems triggered by seemingly minor events can snowball into major headaches unless they are systematically analyzed. The emphasis of such analysis should be *decision* and *action* oriented. We should ask: "What is the problem and what are we going to do about it?" In thinking about what to do, we are forced to confront the problem and identify it.

## Specification of Objectives

As part of the problem identification process, the decision maker's objectives must be known. This involves at least an understanding of what is the desired direction of movement from the current situation and often includes a more precise specification of goals. We must ask the following questions: (*a*) What are our dimensions of value? (*b*) What specific goals (on these dimensions) do we expect to achieve? (*c*) If there are multiple dimensions of value, what trade-offs are we prepared to make?

These objectives are necessary for us to evaluate the alternative actions. For the manufacturing example, some dimensions of value could be profit contribution, market share, sales, product quality, and corporate image. These objectives may not be considered equally important, and management must consider the trade-off relationships between them. This important issue and methods for making trade-offs and evaluating alternatives are considered in more detail in a later chapter.

## Definition of a Time Horizon

The impact of a decision is partly a function of the time horizon associated with it. The time horizon is the time period over which the consequences of the decision will occur. For the manufacturing example, the time horizon would be the period over which the cash flows (revenues and costs), market share, sales, and quality would be affected. Time horizons can be very short, as in a simple gambling situation with small stakes, or long, as in a factory location decision that may have impacts lasting many years.

## Alternative Actions

One of the most important steps in the problem-solving process is to list a set of alternative possible actions. In an organizational context, this creative process must be performed by managers. It cannot be performed by computers, except where they have been programmed to respond to sets of cues, and this can only be done for relatively simple problems. The creative process of generating alternatives requires both knowledge of the problem and its environment as well as the ability to think laterally. For the manufacturing company listed above, three basic alternatives were seen to be possible: (*a*) reduce prices holding other things equal; (*b*) reduce prices and costs; (*c*) increase quality.

## Uncertain Consequences

The second phase of model structuring is to qualitatively assess the impacts and consequences of each alternative action, particularly the uncertain consequences. This involves listing the sources of uncertainty relevant to the problem. For the manufacturer, some relevant sources of uncertainty were: (*a*) price elasticity of demand (this measures the sensitivity of demand to changes in price); (*b*) the nature of the cost-quality relationship; (*c*) the nature of the quality-demand relationship. Since the company is considering a price reduction (aimed at boosting sales), one of the key factors is the demand elasticity. Unless there is a good deal of experience to call on from past situations when various prices were charged, there is likely to be some uncertainty about the consequences (in terms of demand quantity) of a price change. Similarly, the cost-quality and quality-demand relationships are relevant factors in this decision but are not known with certainty.

## Decision Tree Diagrams

A decision tree is a useful aid for diagrammatically representing the decision situation. Decision trees contain only two kinds of elements. By convention, squares are used to represent decision nodes. These are points at which the decision maker has control and must exercise choice. Circles are used to represent chance event nodes. These are points where the decision maker does not have control and where chance or "nature" determines an outcome.

## EXAMPLE 2–2

### A Machine Purchase Decision

Figure 2–1 is a simple decision tree showing a decision node where a person is considering whether or not to test one or both of two machines that he is considering buying and modifying for his production process. He must decide immediately how many tests to order. The tests are expensive, but the results would provide valuable information about the feasibility and cost of modifying the machines. Note that the lines on a decision tree (such as Figure 2–1) which connect various nodes to each other denote the consequences and relationships between events.

**FIGURE 2–1** Decision Tree for the Machine Test Example

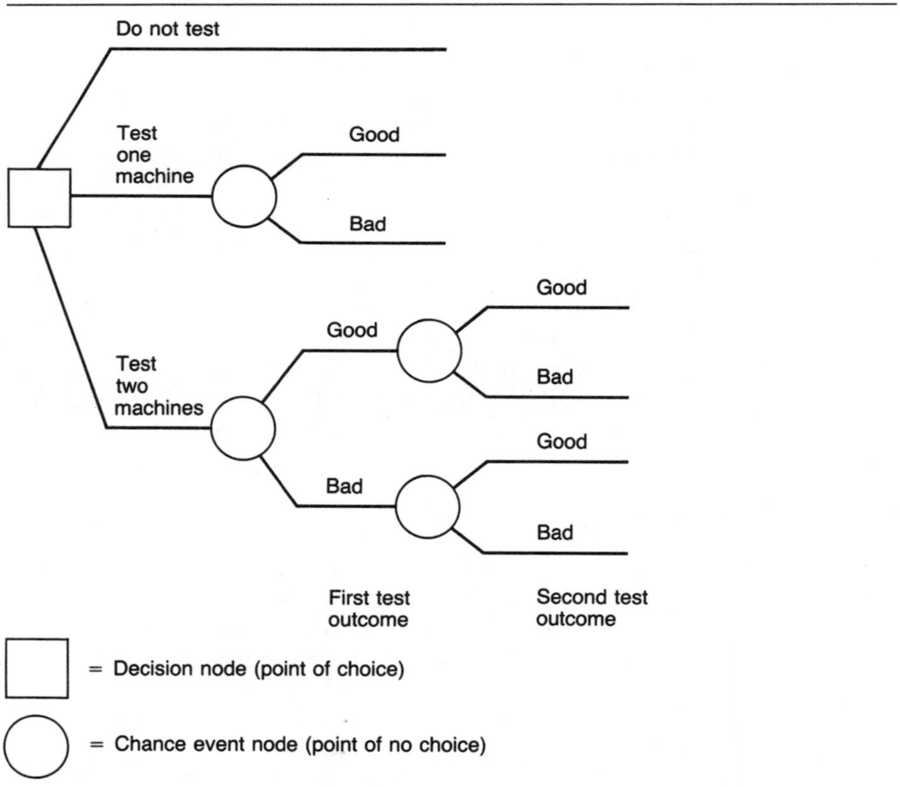

A decision tree is a pictorial diagram of events. The two types of events, namely decision events and chance events, are arranged so as to represent the order in which they might occur. This is a very important point: to have value, a decision tree must not only have the proper elements on it represented correctly as decision or chance event nodes, but they should also be sensibly ordered.

There is, however, more than just one possible structure that may represent a decision. Alternative views of a complex problem may lead to the construction of a number of decision trees to represent it. The debate about which decision tree best represents the problem is normally itself one that provides insight about the problem. Decision trees are a useful mechanism for achieving a focused view of the problem.

It is also possible to draw a single tree in a number of different ways that may look different but are structurally equivalent. Note that when chance event nodes and decision nodes are directly connected they generally cannot be combined or reordered without altering the meaning of the tree. However, when nodes of the same type, either chance event or decision nodes, are directly connected, they can be combined or reordered. Figure 2–2 is structurally equivalent to Figure 2–1, showing that when two chance event nodes are directly connected on a decision tree, they can be combined into one with a subsequent restructuring of the branches. For the machine testing example, the outcomes are equally well represented by Figure 2–1 and Figure 2–2. Indeed if the order of the "good" and "bad" outcomes does not matter, but only the numbers of "good" and "bad" outcomes are relevant, then the "test two machines" chance event node could be shown as:

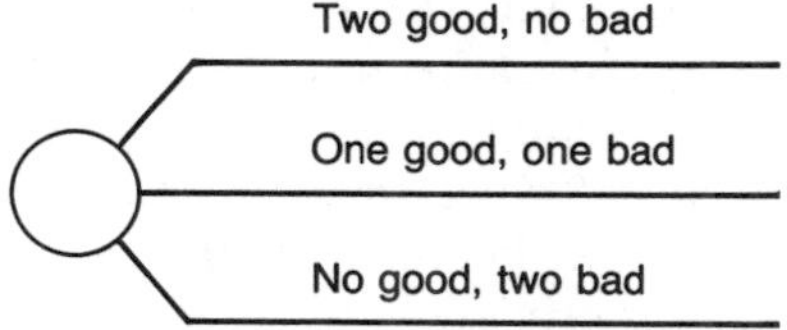


By combining the "first is good, second is bad" and the "first is bad, second is good" branches from Figure 2–2 into one branch, the tree has become somewhat simpler, but we must take care to note that the "one good, one bad" outcome is a compound event consisting of two basic events. This point is critical to correctly calculating or assessing the likelihoods of the various outcomes.

At this stage we have already covered enough ground to consider what the process of decision analysis can teach us about its philosophy. First, we must structure the decision situation by deciding that we have control over some elements (called decision variables) and no control over other elements (called chance events or sources of uncertainty). In this sense we visualize a decision as a game against nature, whereby we make a move (by

**FIGURE 2–2** Another Decision Tree for the Machine Test Example

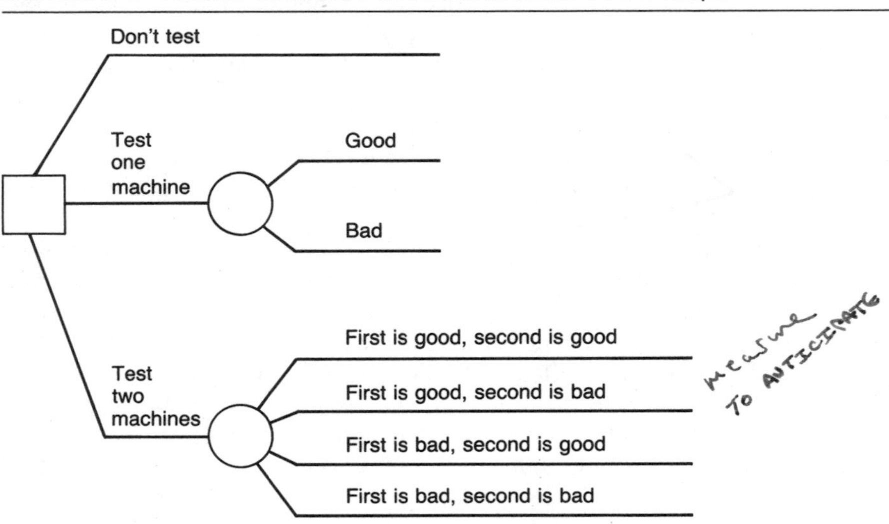


setting a decision variable) and nature responds (by choosing one of the branches emanating from a chance event node). Although we cannot control the outcome of a chance event, we can anticipate the possibilities before the fact, represent those chance possibilities on the decision tree, and take them into account in our decision making. Looking ahead, this will mean measuring the uncertainty (using probabilities) and also accounting for the impacts (such as gaining or losing amounts of money) of each chance event. *Decision analysis is synonymous with the term "decision making under uncertainty" because a central element of both the process and the philosophy is the explicit recognition and measurement of sources of uncertainty in the decision-making process.*

In identifying the decision nodes and sources of uncertainty (chance event nodes), we must classify all decision elements as one type or the other. How then should we handle a decision situation where we believe we have partial control over a relevant variable? For example, suppose you are in a partnership and must consult with your partners on a decision. Your position is that you have some control over the decision but not all. A second scenario is a contracting or negotiation situation. Suppose you are arguing about the size of an out-of-court settlement with another party. You have some input and hence partial control over whether there will be a settlement, and if so how much it will be. This partial control difficulty can nearly always be resolved by taking the relevant decision element and **decomposing** it further. For the court settlement negotiation (a class of problem discussed at length later), decision analysis has been successfully applied through decomposing the negotiation process into a series of decision nodes (my actions, offers, and counteroffers) and chance event nodes (the other party's actions, offers, and counteroffers). The strength of using decision analysis in this instance is that through laying out the alternatives and chance events we can choose a strategy based on our **anticipation** and **calculations** of the other party's actions. More generally, we can usually not control all the elements of a decision, but we can always try to account for all relevant decision elements. We can decompose complex decision situations and represent them as decision trees comprising sets of decision nodes and chance event nodes. This structuring process is often a very creative and rewarding experience for the decision maker, for just by logically laying out the decision elements we can learn a great deal about the problem.

Let us return to the manufacturing company example described earlier and formulate a decision tree. Three alternatives were generated, and these are shown on the first (left) node of Figure 2–3. The subsequent chance event nodes are also shown on Figure 2–3. Although a decision maker may believe that Figure 2–3 is a reasonable first-pass representation, in any real decision situation there are likely to be many subleties and details that can be incorporated on a tree as refinements. We must consider whether such refinements are important enough to warrant their inclusion on the tree or whether they should be left off the tree. An important feature of a tree is its clarity. If efforts at refining a tree cause it to become overly complex (a bush rather than a tree!) then one of the major purposes of decision tree modeling has been defeated. If too many details are included on the tree, then the main issues will be diluted. Therefore in implementing decision tree analyses, we must start with a clear, simple representation and add only those refinements that are central to the decision.

It is important for us to realize that there is usually not a black and white situation with respect to decision trees. For most problems there is not a single correct tree structure such that all other structures are wrong. However, there are degrees of quality of representativeness. The quality of a particular structure is based mainly on how the decision maker views it in terms of its ability to represent and encapsulate the important decision elements. For any problem, it is possible to draw good (representative) decision trees or bad (poorly representative) trees. Experience has taught us that for any problem it is worth trying a number of different structures and comparing them.

## Discrete and Continuous Variables

Decision trees can only have a finite number of branches on them, however continuous variables (that have an infinite number of possible outcomes) must often be represented. For example on Figure 2–3, all of the chance

**FIGURE 2-3** Decision Tree for a Manufacturing Company Decision

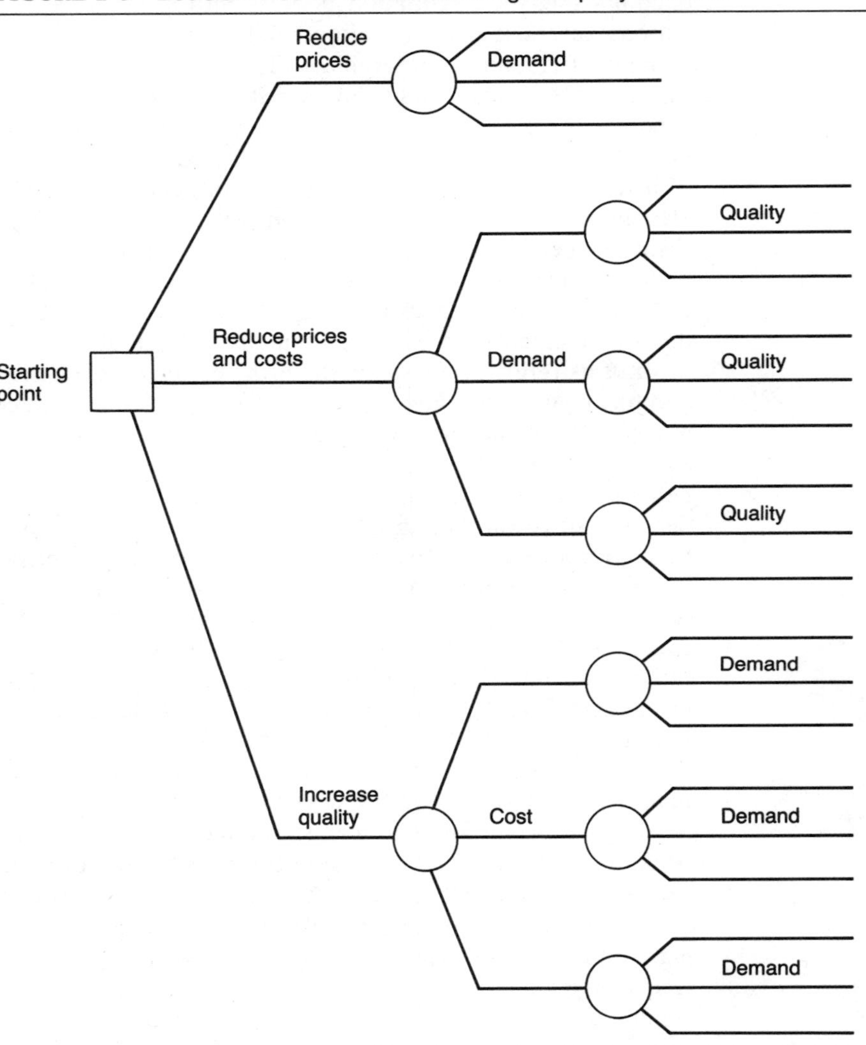


Note that on the middle and bottom branch there are chance event nodes in immediate sequence. This structure does not imply sequential change in demand then quality (middle branch) or in cost then demand (bottom branch). In each case, it represents a view that both chance variables may change as a result of the stated action without implying that these changes are sequential or simultaneous. Chance event nodes in immediate sequence can be combined or reordered without loss of equivalence.

event nodes represent uncertain quantities that are continuous variabl‹ however they are represented by only three possible levels. It is oftε reasonable to make this kind of approximation, or else to use some other finite number of levels. When a variable is continuous in nature or is discrete with a large number of possible outcome states, the decision analyst must choose a sensible number of distinct levels with which to represent it, one level per branch, on a decision tree. For example if market share is an uncertain quantity, expected to be within the range of 10% to 20%, it may be reasonable to use three representative levels: 12%, 15%, and 18% on the branches of a decision tree chance event node. If a finer degree of detail is required, a possible representation is to have five branches: 11%, 13%, 15%, 17%, and 19%. A variety of representations is possible. The chosen representation should be the one that would contribute most to producing insight about the problem, subject to the constraint of not overly cluttering the decision tree with unnecessary detail.

## Decision Tree Structuring Guidelines

We can specify some structural guidelines for the construction of decision tree models. We begin by defining the problem, describing it as a situation. The next step is to list some viable alternative actions. On a decision tree, these actions define the branches which emanate from the first (left) decision node. Next comes a definition of important sources of uncertainty. It is also useful to specify a set of objectives, not because they are directly a part of the tree structure, but because this specification process helps with problem identification and model structuring generally.

The first-pass decision tree can now begin to take shape with the initial actions and sources of uncertainty defined and positioned in representative order. Subsequent possible actions and chance event outcomes should then be defined and grafted onto the tree. At any time during this process, the decision maker should feel free to review and revise the tree by adding or deleting branches or nodes, or reordering them to improve the clarity of the representation. In this way a decision tree can be grown from the initial left-side "root" node. Special attention should be focused on being consciously creative and thinking laterally in generating alternatives, because it is too easy for us to naturally explore a single avenue to its logical end and forget about other decision tree branches altogether!

Three other guidelines should be used when constructing decision trees. The first is that the branches emanating from every decision node and chance event node should be complete in describing all possible occurrences, and should be distinctly defined so that exactly one of them will represent any possible occurrence. The second is that it is usually sensible to order all nodes chronologically, that is, to lay out the decision tree so as to represent the natural order and timing of events that can occur. The third is to use the structural equivalence principles, where desired, to redraw decision trees in equivalent forms, where this action improves the quality of representation as perceived by the decision maker. These principles allow for chance event nodes that are not separated by a decision node, or vice versa, to be combined or reordered.

With the recent advent of high-quality computer software such as the package supplied with this volume, it is feasible to include more branches and more detail on decision trees than if they are to be constructed and manipulated by hand. However, the same guiding principle applies whether one is using pencil and paper, or keyboard and computer screen: start simple with the most important elements, then sequentially add and refine as desired.

To summarize, the decision structuring stage of decision analysis involves problem identification, specifying objectives, defining a time horizon, generating alternatives, and identifying sources of uncertainty. Although these elements of problem structuring have been described separately, they typically are strongly related. The decision structuring process may also involve the construction of a decision tree as a graphic representation. It is usually best to start with a simple tree structure and then go through a series of refining processes, where the decision model is made more sophisticated as its quality of representation (of the problem) is increased. This is a process of structural sensitivity analysis, where we consider relaxing certain of the original simplifying assumptions, and determine how much extra insight we could gain about the problem through doing so.

## ASSESSMENT OF CONSEQUENCES AND LIKELIHOODS

In this second stage of decision analysis, numerical data are collected and generated so that the previously specified alternatives can be evaluated. Two types of data are needed, namely the data on the impacts of various strategies and the probabilistic data that describe the relative likelihoods of various outcome branches emanating from chance event nodes.

### Assessment of Consequences

This assessment process involves assigning values to each endpoint on the decision tree for each dimension of value. For the manufacturing example represented by the decision tree on Figure 2–3, an assessment must be made for each dimension of value, such as cash flows, market share, sales, and product quality, for each endpoint of the tree. Since we have listed four dimensions of value, and Figure 2–3 has 21 endpoints, this assessment task can be time consuming and arduous. However, it is a necessary and useful part of thinking the problem through. For more complex decision trees, many hundreds or even thousands of assessments may be needed, but fortunately these complex trees often contain branches that are similar to others, or structural patterns that allow particular assessments to be used in more than one place on the tree. If the assessment task is complex, then we can assume a preference structure function and assess the parameters of that function. Business decisions often involve money only. Alternatively in some instances we may need to rate and weight a number of dimensions of value.

A question often asked about decision analysis is, "How do we generate the data required for the tree?" For some decision situations, some or even most of the data may be hard, or relatively objective in its nature and source. On the other hand, particularly when we confront problems and decision situations with which we have little experience, there are often no past events from which we can directly collect and apply data. In such cases we may either modify and adjust indirectly relevant data, or else generate subjective estimates on the basis of virtually no relevant past data.

For our manufacturing example, as for many other decision situations, there may not be a single person who is best able to supply all the necessary data about impacts and consequences. The company's marketing experts may be best able to supply data about sales (as a function of price and quality), and the production engineers are likely to be most capable of estimating costs as a function of specified quality. In general, the use of experts to supply data in decision analysis (as in all branches of quantitative analysis) is an important part of achieving a high-quality model. Since no single person is usually an expert in all the aspects of a complex problem, the model builder must communicate with a number of other people. This communication is usually not confined to the data collection phase of decision analysis, but includes the process of obtaining inputs about problem identification and model structuring from all interested parties. Hence, decision analysts must possess certain communication skills, particularly the ability to investigate and explain a problem and to lead another person to focus on an issue and express an opinion about it. Since numbers must ultimately be placed on the decision tree, we must also be skilled at the process of translating our opinions into quantitative measures. Human beings are known to have inherent biases in their assessment processes, and it is important that assessments be interpreted in the light of any possible biases that exist. This important topic of behavioral decision analysis, the study of our human assessment processes and their biases, is discussed at length in a later chapter.

## Assessment of Probabilities

Hand in hand with the assessment of consequences, we must assess probabilities, the likelihoods of those consequences which are uncertain. Information sources for probability assessments can be of many types. First, it is sometimes possible to calculate probabilities where we know or are prepared to assume the probability of simple events (for example, the probability of heads is 0.5 on a fair coin toss) and can then calculate probabilities for more complex events that are combinations of these simple events. Probabilities can also be calculated if we are able to assume that an uncertain quantity can be described by a known probability distribution. In the manufacturing example, we need to assess demand levels, quality, and costs of achieving various qualities, and for each of these we must assess probability values. These quantities are all uncertain and in decision analysis, *probability is the language of uncertainty* that must be used to describe them.

The first step in an assessment process is to define the measures and scales to be used. For example, in the case of a manufacturer, demand levels must be estimated, and we would normally use units of sales (for example, number of items, tons, or gallons). For costs and revenues we have the measure of monetary units with which we are all familiar. Some other quantities are more elusive in their scale. Quality is an example of a parameter that can be measured in many ways. We can use physical or chemical properties when measuring product quality, such as the percentages of carbon or tungsten in steel, the amount of nitrogen or sulphur in crude oil or coal, or the thickness of a coat of paint. We can also measure quality by performance characteristics, such as the speed of a machine or the frequency of breakdowns. Alternatively we can measure the quality of a product by the number and nature of complaints we get from customers.

We must achieve a sensible measurement scale for each relevant quantity in the decision (whether this quantity is known or uncertain), and for those quantities that are assumed uncertain, we must make probabilistic statements about specific values or ranges for those variables.

We often learn a lot from the assessment process, not just about the assessments themselves but about the quality of the model structure. Our thinking about assessments and variable values will frequently lead us to think of ways to improve the representative quality and structure of the decision model. This is perfectly legitimate and indeed is highly desirable. The probabilities we assess for the various possible outcomes of uncertain quantities are written on their appropriate branches on decision trees. They are then used, along with the measures of magnitude of outcomes (monetary and/or nonmonetary) to compare the desirability of various decision alternatives. The assessment phase is an integral and important part of decision analysis.

## DECISION CRITERIA

Once the problem is identified, the decision tree structured, and the relevant quantitative assessments made, what should we do with the model? How can we best gain insight about the task we set out to perform, which is to make a good decision? We must choose a preferred strategy. This process comprises a detailed comparison of competing alternatives on every decision node on the tree and a noting of our preference, such as: "If I were to arrive at this decision node, my preferred choice would be to go in that particular direction." We can specify such preferences for decision nodes because we have control at those points on the tree. We cannot make such statements for chance event nodes, because even though we probably have preferences for chance outcomes, by definition we cannot control chance events. To identify a preferred decision strategy, we normally specify a decision rule, which represents the decision maker's preference (choice) function.

Many different kinds of evaluation rules (decision criteria) exist. They reflect the different kinds of objectives that decision makers may have. We can model forms of pessimism or optimism, we can play the averages, or we can model risk-aversion or risk-seeking preferences. These different criteria are helpful in generally teaching us about our decision behavior and in helping us gain insight about particular decisions. A variety of decision rules are needed because different situations and different decision makers call for various evaluation approaches.

---

## EXAMPLE 2–3

### Insurance Purchase Decisions

Consider the example of personal lines of insurance such as automobile, household, or health insurance. We often purchase insurance as individuals or families even though we know that the insurance company profits from our business and finances its operation by charging us more than the expected value (the average) of our possible claims. By purchasing insurance we are likely to be losing money in the long run, yet most of us still do it, and even after careful thought, we will not rush away and cancel our policies. We buy insurance because we just can't afford to play the averages due to our inability to bear the risk (that is, finance the fluctuations about the average that can and do occur). Some of us are probably pessimistic about the possibility of a major auto accident or theft of our vehicle, a house fire, or the cost of a serious health problem, or if we are not pessimistic, many of us are averse to risk. Our risk aversion is such that we are prepared to pay substantial premiums to obtain indemnification from an insurer.

How can insurers afford to take on all these risks? They have the law of averages, often called the law of large numbers, on their side. The uncertainty that insurers face is relatively low because of this averaging out effect. Hence in terms of decision criteria, we cannot afford, as individuals, to play the averages, but the insurers can. Insurers can do this as long as they have a large number of independent, individually small risks, such as is the case with auto, household, or health insurance. When it comes to insuring jumbo jets, nuclear power stations, and supertankers, even large insurance companies cannot afford to play the averages on any single risk because of the potentially large claims. For such large risks, insurance companies exhibit risk aversion by sharing their risks with other companies.

---

We can conclude from this example that sometimes it is reasonable to play the averages, and sometimes it is not.

Returning to our consideration of decision tree alternatives, and particularly the choice of a preferred strategy, we can *operationalize* these concepts of playing the averages and risk aversion. To choose a strategy that best plays the averages, we calculate the expected value at each chance event node as the probability weighted average of its consequences and the value at a decision node as the value of the highest of its expected consequences. If we are averse to uncertainty (or indeed if we tend to seek it) then we can adjust the expected value by a risk premium.

---

## EXAMPLE 2–4

### Insurance of the Hunk Diamond

Doctor William Hunk, a well-known archeologist, is even more famous as a result of his discovery of a very large diamond. Its market value has been estimated at \$800,000. Doctor Hunk was worried about the possibility of its theft, and sought an insurance price quotation. He believed that there was a 1 in 20 chance of it being stolen in any given year (that is, a probability of 0.05). The insurance company quoted him an annual premium of \$75,000 which was rather a large hunk of his archeological salary. He drew a decision tree to represent his decision, which we reproduce as Figure 2–4. Dr. Hunk calculated the expected cost of not insuring as:

$$\begin{aligned}\text{Expected cost} &= (0.05 \times \$800{,}000) + (0.95 \times \$0)\\ &= \$40{,}000\end{aligned}$$

This expected loss was much less than the insurance premium, hence the expected value rule suggests that he should not insure. However deep down, he had a gut-feel or intuitive desire to insure the diamond anyway, even at the seemingly high premium. Why did the decision tree analysis run counter to his intuitive preferences? The answer is that the expected value rule was not appropriate in this instance for Dr. Hunk. We generally can not afford to play the averages unless the law of large numbers is acting or unless we can fairly easily afford to absorb the downside risks

**FIGURE 2–4** Dr. Hunk's Insurance Decision Tree

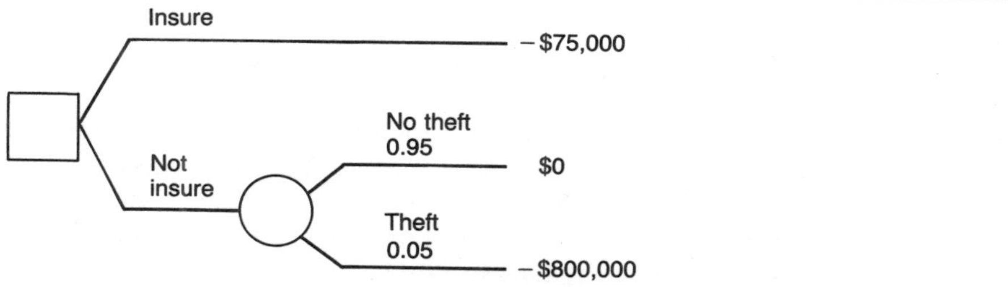


The "insure" branch has an expected cost of $75,000 which we show as a negative cash flow. The "not insure" branch has an expected (average) cost that is the probability weighted average of the possible outcomes. Since there is a 0.95 chance of zero loss and a 0.05 chance of $800,000 loss, the expected loss is given as:

$$(0.95 \times \$0) + (0.05 \times \$800{,}000) = \$40{,}000$$

On an expected value basis, the insurance is expensive relative to not insuring.

involved in a decision. Dr. Hunk was prepared to pay more than the expected cost of the risk because of his aversion to that risk. If we wish to model Dr. Hunk's decision criterion, we need a richer decision criterion than the expected value rule. A risk preference modeling method, known as expected utility analysis, is able to account for and measure various personal attitudes towards risk.

To summarize, once the decision is structured and represented as a decision tree diagram, we make quantitative assessments and must then determine our preferred strategy. To this end, we represent our preference structures with decision rules. Many such rules exist, and their aim is to help us to make a rational choice.

## SENSITIVITY ANALYSIS

Sensitivity analysis is the process of examining the assumptions and parameters of the model and checking on the robustness of the solution to those assumptions. Many people describe sensitivity analysis as "what if analysis" where we probe the implications of alternative conditions to those that we originally assumed.

Once the decision is structured, the assessments made, and a decision rule applied, a thorough sensitivity analysis should be performed. However this does not mean that we should not be questioning the assumptions of the model continuously as part of the whole decision analysis process. We should. In any complex problem there are dozens of factors that lead to the determination of a preferred strategy, and in a sensitivity analysis we reexamine the way these elements interact and question the credibility of our analysis.

We can check the sensitivity of the solution to model structure or parameter values. We can do one-off sensitivity analysis where all assumptions except one are held constant, or we can simultaneously allow more than one assumption to be varied. Although sensitivity analysis is usually described as a stage of decision analysis to be performed after a decision rule is applied to a structured model, we should perform decision analyses with a focus on continuously considering the effect that our assumptions have on the solution. This view of sensitivity analysis is one of *embedding* it in the very fabric of each stage of the analysis. Our continuous sensitivity monitoring leads to increases in both efficiency and effectiveness in the decision modeling process.

---

## EXAMPLE 2–5

### Hunk Diamond Revisited

Let us briefly revisit the Hunk Diamond example (Figure 2–4). This decision tree is a very simple one, yet even so, we made a number of assumptions in structuring it that can be questioned. First, we can question the tree structure. Did the decision tree adequately represent the problem? Were there any other relevant alternatives or sources of uncertainty that should have been considered? For example, what about the possibility that the diamond is lost or stolen, but that our insurance claim is not paid? This can occur either because the insurer disputes the legitamacy of the claim or because the company goes into liquidation during the policy period. Are these complications (or any others) important enough to warrant their inclusion on the decision tree? They certainly can be accounted for in the model if we so desire (try it!). On the branch labeled "Insure" in Figure 2–4, we can simply add a chance event node that indicates that there is a chance that the claim will be paid or not.

A second form of sensitivity analysis regards numerical parameter values. For every number on the tree that played a part in the calculation of a preferred strategy, we can check the effect of changing that number on the solution. It is useful to determine which numbers were critical to the solution and which were not, so that we can better understand the driving forces acting in the problem. For example on Figure 2–4 we assumed a probability of theft of 0.05. It is likely that there is considerable uncertainty about the accuracy of this estimate (yes, there can be uncertainty about uncertainty in this sense). This uncertainty is due to our lack of both experience and relevant data about this event. It is important for us to know whether the preferred strategy is sensitive to this number. If it is, then we need to carefully rethink that probability number and perhaps make further attempts to collect data or in some other way arrive at an accurate estimate. If the solution is insensitive to a particular decision tree input, then we need not spend as much time and money making sure that we have got it absolutely right.

In general the key sensitivity question is: "Does our preferred strategy change as we change our assumptions?" As our belief about the theft probability changes from 0.05 (say down to 0.01 or up to 0.10) does it significantly change our willingness to insure? Of course we are all different, but most of us would find this a critical factor. Hence we need to get this number right to make an informed decision. Here we are considering what is the true value of this probability under certain conditions, and not the fact that Dr. Hunk can change this probability (for example, by locking the diamond away rather than displaying it).

A third form of sensitivity analysis is sensitivity to decision criteria. Does our choice of a decision criterion affect the preferred strategy indicated by the model? For example if we used a decision rule based on risk aversion, did we assume a correct degree of risk aversion, and if not, is the solution sensitive to this assumption?

These sensitivity analysis issues are an important part of the decision analysis process, and we reemphasize that they should be considered as an integral part of every step of the analysis.

---

## IMPLEMENTATION

As with all decision and management science approaches, the model produces insight and information to assist the decision maker in solving a problem. Once a strategy has been chosen it must be implemented, which involves monitoring and controlling the decision elements.

More generally, in studying decision analysis, we are very interested in practical problems that may occur as a part of implementing the decision analysis itself. Like all modeling approaches, decision analysis has some difficulties associated with it. These include assessment and measurement difficulties. Also, as a relatively new approach, decision analysis is not yet widely known or accepted as a useful decision support mechanism in all organizations. It is generally possible however, to anticipate and to manage such implementation difficulties. Decision analysis can produce substantial benefits. It supports managerial decision processes by: (*a*) Providing a mechanism by which managers can directly shed light on problems. (*b*) Being a rational, logical thinking algorithm. (*c*) Being a medium for communication.

## SUMMARY: THE CONTRIBUTION OF DECISION ANALYSIS TO DECISION MAKING

This chapter has presented the basic ideas of decision analysis. Decision analysis was defined both as a philosophy and a process designed to support managerial judgment. As decision makers, it is difficult for us to grasp all of the important elements of complex problems in an intuitive manner, and decision analysis provides a structural framework for formalizing our common sense decision processes. This is done by decomposing these complex decisions into distinct elements. The process normally involves the steps of problem identification, model structuring, assessment of consequences and likelihoods, application of a decision rule, sensitivity analysis, and ultimately, implementation of the chosen strategy. Like all decision and management science processes, decision analysis aims to aid managerial judgment and choice processes and certainly not to replace them.

Decision analysis can also be a thinking algorithm for the manager. In this sense it provides a framework for structuring and decomposing decisions and communicating the elements of a decision to others. For managerial systems to function properly, effective communication is paramount, and modern organizations (both private and public sector) are made up of many decision makers. Even if there is ultimately only one decision maker, a number of expert opinions may be required from other people in or outside the organization. Through the process of decision model structuring, the decision maker can identify exactly what the information needs are and how information should be integrated into the decision process.

The decision tree itself can be a valuable communication and structuring aid. Almost all practicing managers can recall experiences where they have spent many hours in meetings with others in their organization. Many times the effectiveness of these meetings is low because the participants have difficulty communicating about the problem or else cannot agree on a problem definition. In many of these cases, the use of decision analysis can increase the effectiveness of the decision process as a common sense structuring device people can use to gain a focus on important issues.

Decision analysis is a modeling approach, abstracted and distinct from the real world problem. The process of structuring, assessing, and using a decision rule provides a preferred strategy indication on the decision tree. The identification of a preferred strategy has great value to decision makers, once they test its robustness to the model's assumptions through sensitivity analysis. We reemphasize, however, that even if it were not possible for decision analysis to provide an evaluation of competing alternatives through the use of a decision rule, there would still be much insight to be gained from the model structuring phase. Indeed there are many decisions we must make as managers which initially appear complex and fuzzy. For some of these nonprogrammed problems, a decision rule does not need to be formally applied once the problem is properly structured because the preferred or dominant strategy becomes obvious.

With respect to model quality, the same is true for decision analysis as for any other model. We know that in general a poor-quality model produces little insight and may indeed be misleading. We must also remember that the phrase "garbage in, garbage out" applies to decision analysis models as well as computer programs and most other systems. Hence it is not enough just to use a decision-aiding approach. We must use it correctly, and this requires taking great care with model quality.

## CASE STUDY

### Should We Settle or Go to Court?

Midwestern Utility Company was in dispute with a local county taxing body over the correct amount of tax to be paid by the utility for the power plant it operated in that county. The basic issue was whether the bulk of the power generating equipment at the plant was special purpose equipment (and hence not subject to tax) or standard equipment for a facility of its kind, in which case the equipment in question would be included in the tax base. Tax was assessed at a rate of 2% of the book value of the facility. This dispute had been going on for eight years, ever since the plant had been built. The amount of the dispute was $19 million in present value terms, including past taxes claimed to be due by the county and potential future taxes over the life of the plant.

The county had recently offered to settle the issue if Midwestern would pay $12 million in back taxes by exempting Midwestern from future taxes on the equipment. Midwestern knew that the issue would end up in court unless the matter was settled in a timely manner. If the matter did go to court, it would surely end up, on appeal from one side or the other, in the state Supreme Court.

Two further complications existed in this decision. First there was the so-called CWIP issue, which was a second point of conflict between Midwestern and the county. CWIP, or construction work in progress, did not have a clearly defined value, and the county had valued the company's CWIP at a very high value resulting in a $250,000 difference in the company's and the county's calculation of due taxes. The second complication was that the county was a small one; so small indeed that Midwestern's taxes represented a major portion of its revenue. Hence if the county did not receive the $19 million at issue, it would probably have to raise its tax rate in the future to generate enough revenue to cover its expenditures. This would of course adversely affect Midwestern's cash flows associated with this plant, and as one Midwestern executive expressed it, "If we win, we lose!" The company president, Jack Thomas, asked Robert (Bob) Carlson, the company's chief tax accountant, to analyze the problem and recommend a strategy. Bob Carlson was a competent young man with an accounting degree from a good university. He was an experienced certified public accountant. There was very little in the tax code that Bob did not know about. He also knew that this was a fairly complex decision problem and that he needed help in analyzing it. He particularly wanted to do a good job on this problem because he had just applied for a promotion. Bob contacted a friend who was a decision science professor at a nearby university and asked if he could help sort things out.

Phil Phillips, the decision science professor, listened to Bob's description of the problem. Together they decided that the CWIP issue was an unneccessary complication. Although it would be feasible to have the CWIP issue settled in court as well as the major equipment issue, Bob was concerned that in the process of adjudicating the two issues simultaneously, the judge (or ultimately the supreme court justices) would award one issue to each side. Midwestern did not want to take the chance of winning

**FIGURE 2–5** The Initial Decision Tree

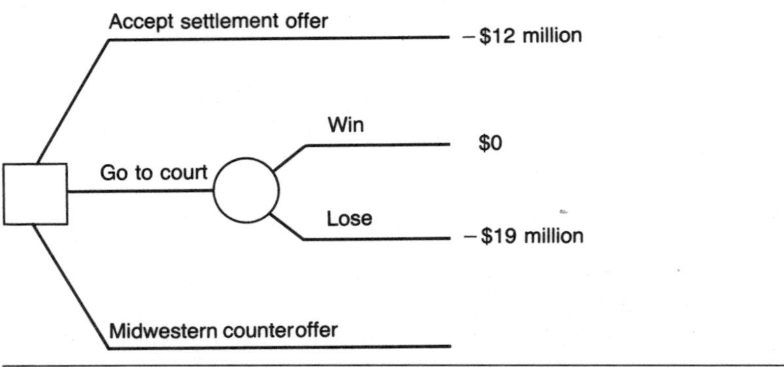


CWIP and losing the major equipment issue because of the relative size of the monetary impacts. Hence the decision was made to keep the two issues separate and settle them individually with the county, either in or out of court. Phil and Bob drew a decision tree for the equipment issue, which is reproduced as Figure 2–5. The first tree they drew showed three major alternatives. In addition to the alternatives identified initially (namely settle or go to court), Phil asked about the possibility of Midwestern making a counteroffer. He suggested that Bob telephone the county clerk and try and squeeze a couple more million out of them. Bob explained that a counteroffer could be made but that it would have to be relayed from Midwestern's lawyer to theirs. Bob also explained that the court process would not just be a win or lose situation and that shades of grey existed. In particular, the equipment that was the subject of the dispute was composed mainly of two components: (*a*) coal-fired boilers; (*b*) steam power generators. It was thought that a partial judgment was a distinct possibility. This meant that some equipment could be judged as standard (hence subject to tax) and some would be judged as special purpose.

A second factor that was not on the initial decision tree was the uncertainty about whether the county would raise tax rates if they lost a substantial tax source like the one being disputed. Bob thought it was quite likely but decided to investigate the matter more thoroughly. Phil also suggested that Bob ask the company attorney for his opinions about the likelihood of winning or losing the case, should it proceed to the court system. Bob said that he would need a couple of days to get the information, and he and Phil got back together later that week.

When they met again, Phil and Bob reviewed the new information Bob had collected. They modified the decision tree to the one shown on Figure 2–6. The new tree reflects a more refined consideration of the situation. Bob had investigated the possibility of a partial court victory and had found that the only likely outcome would yield a present value of tax cost of $8 million. He also found out that the county would entertain the possibility of raising the tax rate for one year only if it suffered a total loss in the case. Bob estimated the tax rate increase needed to provide the county with additional revenue to make up for the unexpected loss and calculated that Midwestern's resultant increased tax burden would be $3 million. Bob had met with Jack Thomas, the company president, who had agreed in principle to a counteroffer of $8

**FIGURE 2–6** Midwestern's Decision Tree

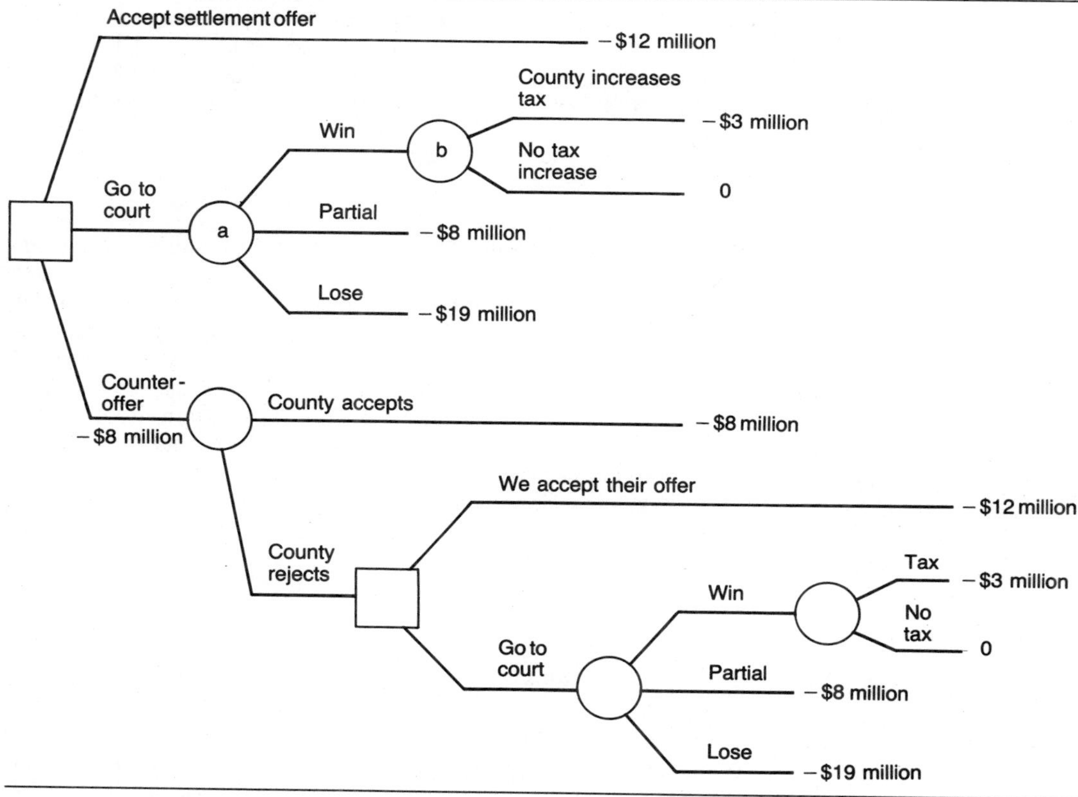


million if the board of directors approved it. Phil and Bob decided that if their counteroffer was rejected, they could still retreat to a position of either accepting the county's original offer or going to court. The original offer had been made in writing and was good for another 10 days from the day of Phil and Bob's second meeting.

Phil and Bob next turned their attention to the likelihood of various occurrences. Bob had met several times with Midwestern's lawyer, Natalie Cooper, about the likelihoods of various court outcomes. Natalie had difficulty putting a number on it because although she felt that Midwestern had an excellent case, the majority of these types of cases were judged in favor of the taxing bodies. She was strongly encouraged by the county's willingness to settle a $19 million suit for $12 million and assessed probabilities of:

| | |
|---|---|
| Win big | 0.5 |
| Win partial | 0.2 |
| Lose | 0.3 |

After their discussions, Bob and Natalie decided to call another lawyer in as a consultant because they felt that Natalie might have been too close to the situation.

Bob also knew that Natalie was considered by many to be a born optimist, and although she was an excellent contract lawyer, she had little experience in this type of tax matter. At Natalie's suggestion he contacted a large East Coast law firm, and they referred him to an attorney, Sarah Ballestrat, who specialized in this type of case. She went over all the details with Bob and agreed that Natalie had been optimistic about Midwestern's chances of winning big in court, but only a little. Mrs. Ballestrat's probabilities were:

| | |
|---|---|
| Win big | 0.4 |
| Win partial | 0.4 |
| Lose | 0.2 |

Compared to Natalie's assessments, Mrs. Ballestrat thought that a partial judgment was much more likely.

Bob also decided, after investigating the past behavior of this and other similar counties, that a one-year tax rate increase was very likely if the county sustained a large loss. He assigned a 0.9 probability to the tax increase branch. At this point Phil asked Bob a number of questions about the structure of the decision tree. Phil wanted to know if any other alternative actions might be open to Midwestern. Bob couldn't think of any, except that the amount to be counteroffered was a variable and could be set at any value from zero to $12 million. Bob thought that a counteroffer of $4 million or perhaps $5 million was more appropriate than the $8 million which the company president had suggested. However as Bob explained it: "He's the president and I'm not, so the counteroffer is $8 million."

## Making a Choice

Bob said that he felt good about the decision tree structure except that they had two different sets of probabilities associated with the court outcome. He had some minor reservations about the way the discounted cash flows had been calculated, but when he and Phil used some different discount rates and assumptions, they discovered there was very little sensitivity in the calculated cash flows to these assumptions. This made Bob much more confident about the decision analysis. He and Phil decided to double check with Natalie whether the county's original settlement offer would still be available as an option for Midwestern after a counteroffer was made and rejected. Natalie assured them that their assumption was correct.

Now Bob had to decide on a preferred strategy and prepare a presentation of his analysis and recommendations to the company president and board of directors. He noted that the top branch on Figure 2-6 was clean and simple but the price tag was $12 million. By "clean and simple" he meant that Midwestern would avoid the drawn out process of going to court. This would save him, Natalie, and a number of others in the corporation a lot of time. When Phil asked Bob to put a value on all this time, Bob estimated that it might be as much as $150,000 if the case went to the state Supreme Court (which was likely if no prior settlement was reached).

Phil and Bob decided to begin their evaluation process by calculating the expected value of each branch on the tree. On the "go to court" branch the expected value of winning big was −$2.7 million. Of course all the cash flows were shown as negative on the tree because they were all cash outflows. The expected value of −$2.7 million was the probability weighted average of the cash flow consequences:

$$0.9 \times -\$3 \text{ million} + 0.1 \times \$0 = -\$2.7 \text{ million}$$

Bob noted that number (−$2.7 million) on the tree at chance event node *b* on Figure 2–6, even though he pointed out that −$2.7 million was not an actual cash flow (that is, it would not actually occur) but was rather a representative expectation of two other cash flows. To calculate the expected value of the chance event node *a* on Figure 2–6 associated with the court outcome, they tried both sets of probabilities:

For Natalie:

$$\text{Expected cash flow} = 0.5 \times -2.7 + 0.2 \times -8 + 0.3 \times -19$$
$$= -\$8.65 \text{ million}$$

For Mrs. Ballestrat:

$$\text{Expected cash flow} = 0.4 \times -2.7 + 0.4 \times -8 + 0.2 \times -19$$
$$= -\$8.08 \text{ million}$$

In fact, although the probabilities assessed by the attorneys seemed quite different, the expected values of the outcomes were quite similar for both sets of assessments. Phil pointed out that the riskiness of the outcomes was somewhat larger for Natalie's assessments since she placed higher likelihood on the two extreme outcomes and less likelihood on the "partial win" branch. Bob wrote the average of the two expected values (−$8.36 million) on the tree. See Figure 2–7, where the expected values are shown in boxes.

On the counteroffer branch of Figure 2–7, decision node 2 has an expected value of −$8.36 million because the "go to court" option is identical to that on the branch

**FIGURE 2–7** Midwestern's Decision Tree

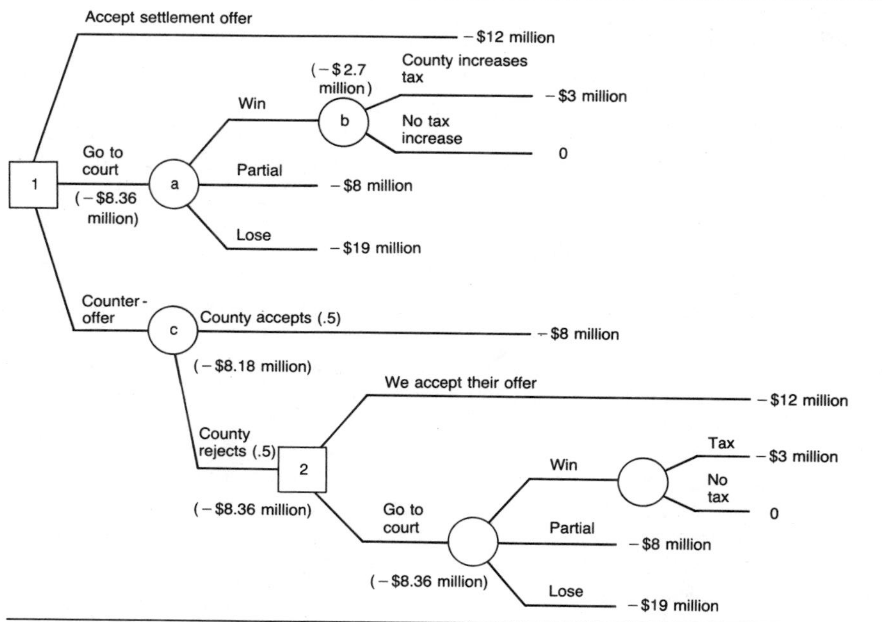

above and looking forward from decision node 2, the preferred strategy is to choose the option with the lowest expected loss. Bob was unsure about the likelihood that the county would accept an offer of $8 million, but Phil pointed out that for an expected value analysis this factor did not seem to be critical. If the probability of the counteroffer being accepted was zero, then the expected value at chance event node *c* was −$8.36 million, and if that probability was set at one, then the expected value at (*c*) was −$8 million, i.e., not very different in relative terms. Natalie thought that the counteroffer acceptance likelihood was 0.5 and hence the expected value was:

$$0.5 \times -8 + 0.5 \times -8.36 = -8.18 \text{ (\$ million)}$$

When they considered Figure 2–7 and particularly the expected values they had calculated, Bob pointed out that there seemed to be almost no advantage to making a counteroffer in expected value terms, and this seemed unreasonable. If that were the case, he suggested that they make a smaller counteroffer, but Natalie thought that the likelihood of acceptance of a counteroffer which was less than $8 million was quite low.

Phil pointed out that the use of an expected value decision rule ignored the risk associated with various strategies, and to illustrate his point he drew risk profiles for the "go to court" and "counteroffer" branches. These profiles (see Figure 2–8) show the probabilities of various outcomes represented as the height of the bars on a graph. Phil used Natalie's probabilities to illustrate his point.

Phil showed that by not making a counteroffer, the chances of an extreme outcome ($0 or −$19 million) were much larger (as can be seen from the risk profiles). There was, in a sense, nothing to lose by making a counteroffer, and some significant gains were possible.

## Implementation: The Outcome

When Bob presented the analysis to the board of directors of Midwestern, they all agreed that a counteroffer seemed to be worth making. Phil and Natalie attended the meeting, and various board members asked Phil questions about the assumptions and calculations. Natalie was closely questioned about the sensitivity of the likelihood that the county would accept a counteroffer in the amount offered. After Natalie explained that the county was obviously willing to negotiate (since they had made the original settlement offer) she stated that she thought a very low counteroffer would not be accepted. She thought that a $6 million or $7 million counteroffer would have a 0.2 acceptance likelihood and that anything lower would certainly be rejected outright by the county.

After a lengthy discussion, the board agreed that the advantages of settling out of court were significant in terms of minimizing their tax liability, avoiding the risk of a large court loss (which would cost $19 million), and reducing the administrative and legal staff's load which would be significant if the issue went right through the court system. The board looked long and hard at what the best counteroffer strategy was and decided to offer $7 million. This offer was subsequently made. It was rejected by the county, but it led to a series of negotiations between the two parties that ultimately led to an out-of-court settlement of $8.5 million, which Midwestern was very satisfied with.

**FIGURE 2–8** Risk Profiles of Decision Alternatives

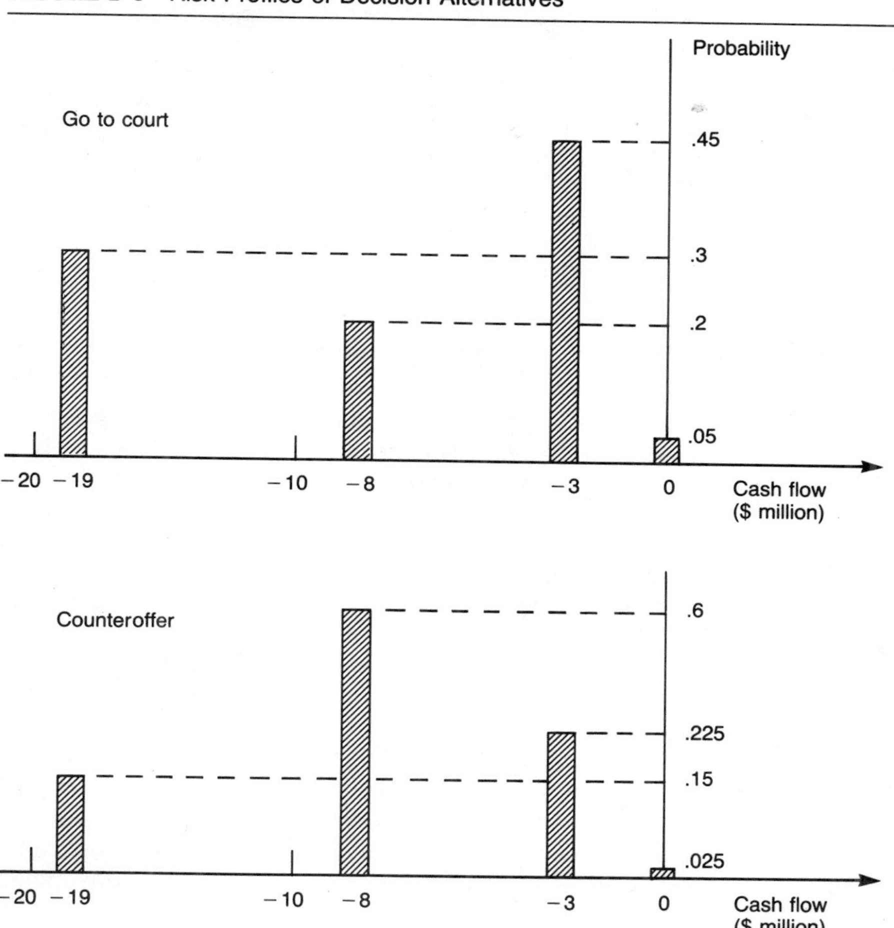


After it was all over, Phil and Bob got together again and discussed the decision process. Bob noted that after all his analytic efforts (with Phil's help), the board decided on a different counteroffer figure to the one on the decision tree. Phil responded that the decision analysis had served their purposes very well. Using decision analysis, they had structured and restructured the problem until they were happy with the representation. They had obtained and used expert information. They had found a way to logically evaluate their options both in terms of expected value and associated risks. Finally, they had used the decision tree as a communication medium in making the problem clear to the real decision makers, the board of directors. Even though the board had chosen a different counteroffer amount from the one on Figure 2–7, Phil and Bob agreed they had gained a lot of insight about the problem from the decision analysis. Phil explained that decision analysis was a mechanism for formalizing their common sense. He said that for simple problems, formal analysis was not needed, but as problems become more complex, the advantages of such analyses rapidly increase.

In retrospect, Phil and Bob decided that the counteroffer branch on their tree should perhaps have had a few more decision branches, representing alternative counteroffer amounts. They thought that they should have anticipated that a counteroffer might open up a negotiation process that would lead to an acceptable out-of-court settlement. "Well, I guess we didn't produce a perfect decision model" concluded Phil, "but what we did produce was certainly enough to stimulate the board of directors to make a good decision."

## SUMMARY: GOOD DECISIONS AND GOOD DECISION ANALYSIS

In summarizing this chapter, let us consider what a good decision and what a good decision analysis is. A good decision cannot simply be defined as one that led to a good outcome, a happy ending. This is because many factors (chance events) may be out of the control of the decision makers. To illustrate, in the Midwestern Utility Case, if the numbers had been different, a sensible decision might have been to go to court, in which case a happy or unhappy ending might have been defined as the winning or losing of the court case.

Generally, it is possible to have well made decisions and simultaneously have good or bad outcomes of various chance events. We cannot measure decision quality purely by the outcome.

The quality of a decision should be measured in a similar way to the quality of a decision analysis. Was the decision properly considered? Were the sources of complexity appropriately accounted for? If the problem was difficult, was it systematically decomposed? Was the right degree of detail and level of effort used in modeling the decision, including structuring, assessing, and choosing a strategy? If we are satisfied with the answers to these questions, then we can usually say that the quality of the decision process was high, even if a high-quality decision sometimes leads to an unfortunate outcome.

In thinking about decision making, we must proceed on the common sense basis of assuming that most of the time, good decision processes are likely to lead to better outcomes than poor decision processes. We also assert (confidently) that rational, systematic decision analysis methodologies provide useful inference which support and contribute to the making of good decisions. The basis for these assumptions and assertions is the combined experiences of many decision analysts. Ultimately, the value of a decision analysis must be strongly related to the quality of insight that it generates, and whether or not the resulting decision strategy was improved by introducing an analysis process.

## FURTHER READING

A number of useful general articles and books have been written in the field of decision analysis. Articles by Howard (1980), Grayson (1973), Keeney (1982), Bodily (1981), Magee (1964), Brown (1970), and Hammond (1967) give useful accounts of various aspects of decision analysis. More generally, books by Brown, Kahr, and Peterson (1974), Moore and Thomas (1976), Schlaiffer (1969), Raiffa (1968), Huber (1980), and Holloway (1979) present general descriptions of decision analysis and applications. Winkler (1972) also has written a very insightful volume focusing mainly on the probability-related aspects of decision analysis.

## REFERENCES

Bodily, S. 1981. "When Should You Go to Court?" *Harvard Business Review,* May–June, p. 103.

Brown, R. V. 1970. "Do Managers Find Decision Theory Useful?" *Harvard Business Review* 48, pp. 78–89.

Brown, R. V., A. S. Kahr, and C. Peterson. 1974. *Decision Analysis for the Manager*. New York: Holt, Rinehart & Winston.

Grayson, C. J. 1973. "Management Science and Business Practice." *Harvard Business Review,* July–August, p. 41.

Hammond, J. S., III. 1967. "Better Decisions with Preference Theory." *Harvard Business Review,* November, p. 123.

Holloway, C. 1979. *Decision Making Under Uncertainty*. Englewood Cliffs, N.J.: Prentice-Hall.

Howard, R. A. 1980. "An Assessment of Decision Analysis." *Operations Research* 28, pp. 4–27.

Huber, G. P. 1980. *Managerial Decision Making*. Glenview, Ill.: Scott Foresman.

Keeney, R. L. 1982. "Decision Analysis: An Overview." *Operations Research* 30, no. 5 (September), pp. 803–38.

McGee, J. F. 1964. "Decision Trees for Decision Making." *Harvard Business Review,* July, p. 126.

Moore, P. G., and H. Thomas. 1976. *The Anatomy of Decisions*. New York: Penguin Books.

Raiffa, H. 1968. *Decision Analysis*. Reading, Mass.: Addison-Wesley Publishing.

Schlaifer, R. O. 1969. *Analysis of Decisions Under Uncertainty*. New York: McGraw-Hill.

Winkler, R. L. 1972. *Introduction to Bayesian Inference and Decision*. New York: Holt, Rinehart & Winston.

## PROBLEMS

1. List the stages of decision analysis and briefly outline each one.
2. Is the process of decision analysis likely to be approximately the same for all decision problems? If not, what differences might occur across different kinds of problems?
3. Is decision analysis able to contribute to all types of problems equally well, or are programmed and nonprogrammed problems different in this context?
4. What are the aims and major uses of decision analysis?
5. Do the steps of decision analysis need to be performed in a once-through, straightforward manner or do some problems require flexibility in the analysis process?
6. In decision structuring and decision tree diagramming, variables must be categorized as either decision variables or uncertain quantities. Think of an example of a variable that at first doesn't seem to fit either category (i.e., the decision maker has partial control), and then decompose that variable into decision and chance event variables.
7. Explain the role of decision rules in determining a preferred strategy on a decision tree.
8. Is there any benefit to be derived from the decision structuring phase of decision analysis, or is the value of an analysis solely associated with the numerical assessment and analysis that follows the structuring phase?
9. What are subjective probabilities?
10. What is the nature and usefulness of sensitivity analysis?
11. Consider the product launch decision described in Chapter 1. Formally structure this problem and draw a decision tree. Are different structures possible?
12. A publisher has received a proposal for a book from an unknown author. The book seems to have potential, and the publisher must decide whether or not to spend about $2,000 having the proposal professionally reviewed. If the reviews are positive, he would negotiate a contract with the author and commit the company to produce the book. After it is finished he would have to decide on an initial print volume. Sales quantity is the major source of uncertainty, and the aim of the first printing is to produce enough copies so as to not need a reprint for about two years, but not so many as to be left with a warehouse full of stock if sales are slower than expected.

    Structure the publisher's decision problem as a decision tree.
13. Figure 2–9 shows a decision tree model for a new technology purchase decision. The manager who was responsible for the operation had to choose between keeping an existing technology and

FIGURE 2–9

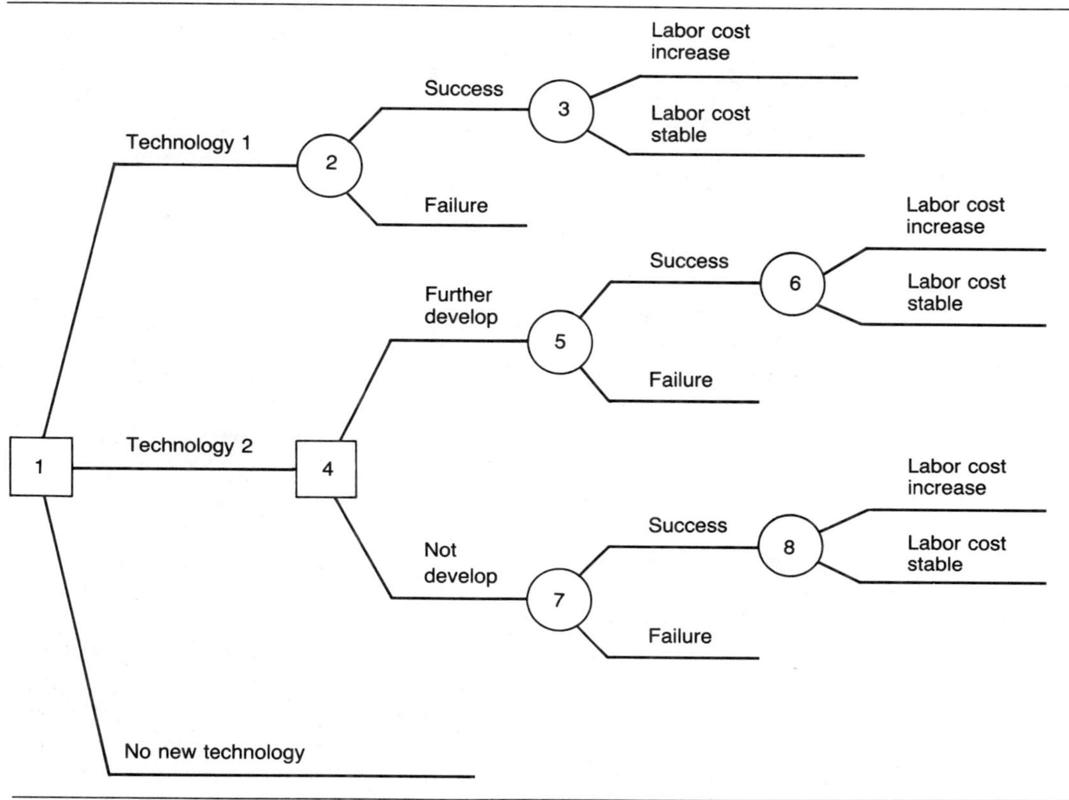


implementing one of two new technologies in part of a production system. Convert the decision tree (Figure 2–9) into structural equivalent forms by:

*a.* Combining nodes 2 and 3.
*b.* Combining nodes 5 and 6.
*c.* Combining nodes 7 and 8.
*d.* Combining nodes 1 and 4.

Can nodes 2 and 3 be reordered?

14. Referring to Figure 2–9, is an equivalent structure to this tree one which has the secondary decision (node 4) coming after (to the right of) the success/fail node? Construct a tree so that Technology 2 is found to be successful or unsuccessful before the decision of whether or not to further develop it is taken. If these trees are not equivalent, explain their difference.

15. Referring to Figure 2–9, the manager decided that if he chose either of the new technologies and it failed, he would subsequently be able to choose the other new technology. Modify Figure 2–9 to represent this multistage situation.
16. Referring to Figure 2–9, the manager also wanted to account for uncertainty in demand for the product, because the substantial investment in new technology would be more worthwhile if demand was high rather than low. He decided that this uncertain quantity should be represented at three levels, high, medium, and low demand. Incorporate this modification on the decision tree (Figure 2–9).
17. What are the data requirements of a decision tree model? What specific quantitative data elements would be required by the decision tree in Figure 2–9? How many assessments would be required by the tree described in problem 16, above?
18. A manager of a research and development department was interested in funding only a subset of projects that had been proposed to her:
    *a.* If she was considering a set of *up to* three possible projects, how many alternatives does she have in terms of combinations of projects that could be funded?
    *b.* What if she has five projects?
    *c.* She has a budget and is considering that of the projects she funds, it is feasible to fund each one at three levels, high, medium, and low. How many combinations of projects and funding levels are there with three projects? With five projects?
19. Referring to the R&D management problem (problem 18, above), what role can a decision tree model play when there are a large number of distinct alternatives? Describe the structure and complexity of a decision tree with all possible combinations of five projects, three levels of possible funding, and two chance events, namely project success/failure and payback period (for successful projects).
20. An inventor has been offered a substantial sum of money for an electronic product. The money was offered by an acquaintance who wants to develop the product commercially. The inventor has the choice of accepting the money or applying for a patent herself. She knows from past experience that the granting of a patent is not automatic, and she may be unsuccessful even though she believes the idea to be original.

    If she obtains a patent herself rather than sells the rights to the product idea, she could try to develop the product design further or approach a large manufacturer and attempt to strike a deal that would be of mutual benefit.

If her patent application is unsuccessful, she could go ahead with the product development anyway, or even without a patent, she could approach a commercial manufacturer.

The inventor believed that there were some risks involved in the process. These were particularly that her ideas might be stolen by some person or organization and commercialized without proper credit or benefit being given to the inventor.

Structure a decision tree showing the alternative actions and sources of uncertainty open to the inventor.

21. Cardio Technologies Inc. (CTI) is a well-known manufacturer of heart pacemakers. Their devices are surgically implanted in patients with certain types of heart disorders and provide an electrical signal or pacing for the heart muscles. Their newest, most advanced model, the CT50, has been on the market for six months, and a serious problem has arisen. Of the 250 units implanted in the first month after the CT50 was released, 12 units have failed and had to be replaced (at CTI's expense) because of low battery power. Fortunately these failures do not represent widespread health threats to patients because the lowering of pacemaker output is very gradual and would in nearly all cases be detected at regular checkups before a serious problem occurred. CTI is uncertain as to whether only a small proportion of CT50s are faulty or whether all units will fail during the four-year warranty period. It has already initiated negotiations with the battery supplier who refused to accept liability for the 12 failures (or any future such events). A total of 1,800 units have been implanted, and 3,000 more have been manufactured and are at various stages of distribution all over the world.

    CTI is very concerned about the 12 failures and future possible failures. It is considering the possibility of making this information public and offering to replace all currently implanted model CT50 units with another CTI model. This could be an expensive action (depending on how many patients took up the offer) and might also damage the company's image as a high-quality producer in the industry.

    On the other hand, if CTI can prove that the battery caused the fault, then the battery manufacturer would be responsible for the costs. Given this supplier's initial reaction, CTI is not sure whether any money could be recovered from the supplier unless legal action were taken. CTI is considering delaying or not making its public announcement until more data is collected on failure rates.

    Define the problem. List the alternative actions and sources of uncertainty. Draw a representative decision tree.

22. This exercise requires a computer and ARBORIST. Structure the

decision tree shown as Figure 2–7 using ARBORIST. This process requires the definition of the various nodes and branches, and the associated payoffs. Roll back the tree using the expected value calculation procedure within ARBORIST.

Comment on the usefulness of ARBORIST, relative to doing a decision tree analysis by hand. Suppose you wanted to add a branch somewhere on the tree or change some of the probabilities or payoffs. Once a decision tree is set up and on file, is it easier to perform modifications, refinements, and recalculation by hand or with ARBORIST?

---

## Case Study

### Exo Health

The Exo Health company manufactured and distributed high-tech health monitoring products. Their product lines included digital readout thermometers, pulse, and blood pressure kits. In addition they manufactured programmable exercise bikes and weight machines that electronically monitored and fed back medical data to the user. Exo Health had grown through continuously introducing new products. It marketed its products to health clubs, through catalog sales, and to department stores.

Recently, the company was approached by an inventor who had developed a new product that could be worn on the wrist and would continuously monitor blood pressure. The technological breakthrough was an ultrasensitive detecting sensor. Exo Health was interested in the concept. It had been successfully marketing conventional blood pressure equipment for some time that was a little difficult for the layman to use, and this new product could be very attractive for those people who needed to monitor their blood pressure. The inventor wanted $1 million in cash and 5% of all sales revenue in exchange for the exclusive license to manufacture. He gave Exo Health two days to decide after which he intended to approach another (competing) company.

The president of Exo Health and the vice presidents of manufacturing and marketing immediately met to consider the proposal. The inventor had left them with a prototype. The prototype worked very well on only two of the three executives and would not register a blood pressure for the third. They thought that this might be because the pressure waves might be weaker in his arm. The question was: "How many people would the device work on, and could it be modified to work on everybody?" The Exo Health executives decided that even if it could be made to work properly on everybody that its manufacturing cost would be high. They estimated about $65 each, but without having more details they thought their estimate could be wrong by as much as $15 either way. They were also uncertain about demand. "If the manufacturing cost is $65," said the president, "it will sell for $110 or $115, and that price tag means our market will be pretty small." The vice president said that for people who really need continuous blood pressure monitoring, medical insurance funds would encourage such purchases and probably pay for them because of their preventative effect. If so, the demand could be much larger than if they were generally not covered by medical insurance.

"OK," said the president. "So if we buy the rights, within 18 months we may be competing with cheaper, lower quality imports, so how can we justify the million dollar up-front cost?" The marketing vice president said that he was confident that the inventor would be open to a lower offer of about $500,000. He also argued that this new product would reduce sales of conventional blood pressure kits, but he wasn't sure by how much. He felt strongly that if he was going to lose market share in conventional blood pressure units, that he would like to lose it to another product that Exo Health marketed, rather than to H. B. Danforth or some other competitor. "There's always a chance," said the vice president of manufacturing, "that this thing will only work on say one person in two or even three, so no company will manufacture it. We will have to decide on the offer before we know if we can modify it to work on everybody. If we decide not to go with it, maybe Danforth or Zero-One (another competitor) will, in which case we'll be very sorry if its a big success."

Structure the decision problem facing Exo Health. Define the problem, the alternative actions open to it, and the sources of uncertainty. Construct a decision tree to represent the problem.

## CASE STUDY

### Universal Airlines[1]

In June of 1986, the executives of Universal Airlines had a difficult decision to make. Their pilots had been on strike for just over a month, and the dispute had just been settled. In three days, flights would begin again, and Universal would be flying a full schedule within a week. The executives were considering what actions to take to regain their market share.

The alternatives they considered were:

*a.* A massive advertising campaign.
*b.* A low-pricing strategy.
*c.* A discount coupon offer.

At a meeting conducted by the company president and attended by four senior vice presidents, the VP of marketing, Dave Harding, had been pushing hard for a massive advertising campaign. His arguments had not really impressed John (Jack) Fredericks, the company president or anyone else at the meeting. Dave was insistent

---

[1] Part of this case study is adapted from a situation described by L. Digman, *Interfaces*, April 1980, pp. 97–101.

that revenue could be generated purely through a media blitz that would "repair any damage done to our image as a result of the strike." The consensus was more that the company image had not been damaged much, and further that people generally knew the strike was over. Jeffrey Johnson, the senior VP of Flight Operations, wanted to know whether advertising would add to people's general awareness in an effective manner.

"I know that advertising will generate some sales, but just how much additional business will we get from the $6 million you want to spend?" asked Johnson. Harding replied that past experience suggested that initial additional revenues would be $2 million to $4 million, and the repeat business resulting from those passengers would eventually be anything from two to three times the initial figures. "We are looking at between $4 million to $12 million of additional revenue," said Harding, "and this translates almost one-to-one into profit contribution since we'll be flying a full schedule anyway, and marginal or variable costs are very low under these conditions." Fredericks agreed that the advertising campaign might well be cost/benefit effective under these circumstances, but that the other options should be explored.

At this point the discussion moved on to the subject of pricing policy. Jeff Johnson suggested that both travellers and travel agents were price sensitive and that a temporary price cut of 20% or more would bring back all the lost market and more. Johnson admitted that the price cut might be matched by some of Universal's competitors, or even worse, start a price war in the industry. He estimated that such a price cut would increase average load factors during the first month of operations from 35% to at least 50% and maybe 55%. Further results would depend on the reactions of competitors. If they matched the price cuts (presumed to occur after a month) then Universal's load factors would drop to an average of 45%, and prices would take a year to slide back up to current values. If competitors reacted by dropping prices moderately but not to match those of Universal, then load factors would be virtually unaffected. It was concluded that a good deal of uncertainty existed with respect to this action. There was no real way of predicting what actions would be taken by Universal's major competitors. The feeling at the meeting was quite negative as a result of this uncertainty.

A third option which surfaced was the use of flight coupons. More specifically, this strategy involved the distribution of coupons for 50% off a future flight for all Universal passengers who travel in the first month after the strike. Dave Harding stated that such an action would surely attract passengers to Universal's flights, but how many? He also raised the question of whether competitors would follow suit, and how possible competitive reactions would affect load factors.

After over an hour of discussion of the various issues, Jack Fredericks stood up and said it was time to structure the discussion. He pointed out that three basic alternatives existed and that each had uncertain consequences. Further, certain of the alternatives could be carried out in combination. The only combination he ruled out was a price cut plus discount coupon combination.

Suppose you were an observer at the Universal meeting. Draw a decision tree that models the structure of the problem facing the company. Try to include all relevant structural elements but do not place numbers on the tree.

If you were going to try and evaluate each option and calculate the probabilities of various consequences, what information would you need?

CHAPTER THREE

# Decision Model Structuring

## OUTLINE



## OBJECTIVES

After completing this chapter, you should be able to:

1. Structure decision trees for a variety of managerial problems.
2. Discern the differences and qualities of alternate decision tree representations of a problem.
3. Describe the role of subsidiary models and expert judgments.
4. Discuss the power of decision analysis as a managerial decision support philosophy and set of methods.
5. Debate a managerial problem using the decision analysis philosophy and structure.
6. Help a manager with a problem by structuring a decision analysis model of it.
7. Discuss the philosophy behind the decision analysis methodology in multistage decision trees.

## INTRODUCTION

This chapter focuses on decision model structuring, particularly on the use of decision trees to represent managerial decisions. We will examine ways in which problems can be decomposed into elements that can be represented as decision tree models. In looking at a variety of decision trees and the processes by which they are constructed, the purpose of this chapter is to provide insight about a critically important stage of decision analysis, namely model construction.

Achieving a high-quality model structure is of paramount importance, for this stage of the process sets the foundation for the whole analysis. Subsequent stages of decision analysis, including the assessment of data and decision strategy evaluation, relate directly to the model structure. There is little to be gained from having accurate data and an excellent evaluation process if the model structure is poor. On the other hand, a high-quality model structure can itself produce important insights about the problem. Further, when well-structured models are combined with appropriate data and strategy evaluation rules, decision analysis can be very powerful in supporting decision processes.

Since decision models are representations of real decision problems, our first thought may be to make as few simplifying assumptions as possible, thus ensuring that the model is realistic. Is it then reasonable to ask: "The fewer the assumptions, the better (more realistic) the model?" The answer to this question comes from an examination of the purpose of decision modeling. In Chapter 1 it was argued that the aim of modeling is to **provide insight** about decisions, hence models should generally be structured so as to provide as much insight as possible within practical constraints.

The ultimate aim of decision modeling is to **produce better decisions** (through the provision of insight about those decisions). It does not necessarily follow that fewer assumptions are better than more assumptions. A more realistic model (with fewer assumptions) is usually a more complex model, perhaps with too much detail clouding the important central issues. On the other hand, a model with too many assumptions is likely to be abstract and too different from the problem to provide meaningful insight. Once a problem is identified, an important skill in decision modeling is to strike the correct balance and **choose the correct level of detail**. The decisions relating to what to include and what to exclude (assume away) in the model are critical to its value as a decision aid.

The decision analysis approach is one of decomposition; hence a sensible procedure is to systematically isolate and categorize key elements of the problem and then choose a subset of those elements for inclusion in the model. *Fortunately we do not have to live and die by the first model that we construct for any problem. We can construct a number of different models and make judgments about which ones seem most suitable*. This process of structural sensitivity analysis can be performed many times (or even continuously) during the course of an analysis.

Two very important aspects of a model or modeling process are **quality** and **applicability.** In a very interesting article on the use of models in decision making, Ansoff and Hayes (1973) define model quality in terms of **power** (the amount of nontrivial inference produced) and **elegance** (whereby a minimum of analytic tools provides a lot of power). They define model applicability in terms of **relevance** (modeling problems of importance to the manager), **validity** (confidence that the inferences gained from the model will occur in the real world), **potential for use** (likelihood of being accepted as a basis for action), and **cost-effectiveness** (where the resultant improvements exceed the cost of the modeling process). Ansoff and Hayes point out that difficulties can occur in organizations because of the primary preferences of model builders for quality and the primary preferences of managers for applicability. These conflicts have severely reduced the potential application of many management science approaches in the past. There is much to be learned from this conflict when designing a decision analysis model. We note that there is little benefit for managers from building high-quality models if they are not applicable to real problems. There is also little benefit to be had from building models that are suitably applicable but of low quality. Hence the modeling process involves making model structuring decisions that may themselves be complex, so as to ensure that levels of both quality and applicability are high.

It is often necessary to make trade-off decisions across these dimensions when structuring models. For decision analysis models, high model quality can generally best be achieved by initially choosing a moderate level of detail. We can then modify and refine the model in a number of steps. High levels of applicability can best be achieved by ensuring that the manager or management group who are the ultimate decision makers remain intimately connected with the decision analyst (model builder) through every phase of that analysis. For example consider the Airport Development at Mexico City problem, where the decision analysis process has been well documented. For this instance, Keeney and Raiffa (1976) describe a modeling process whereby a very large number of alternatives (over 100) was sequentially reduced to a short list of five. At each screening step, a more detailed analysis of the alternatives was conducted. This very sensible procedure was coupled with a continuous set of consultations between analysts and decision makers.

In summary, experienced analysts tell us always to keep in mind the aim of decision modeling. Decision modeling is not an end in itself but a means toward better decision making. To do so involves producing models that are neither too simplistic nor overly complex. In decision analysis, our goals are to provide an understanding of the problem and the various strategies or alternatives available. It takes practice to achieve these goals.

## STRUCTURING: DEFINITION OF PROBLEMS AND DECOMPOSITION INTO DECISION ELEMENTS

To consider how best to analyze a problem through decomposing it and constructing a decision model, we must first examine what a problem actually is. A good working definition is that a problem is the occurrence, existence, or anticipation of an undesirable state or event. The inclusion of the term *anticipation* is important because a good manager not only manages undesirable or crisis events as they occur, but can often anticipate their development ahead of time.

What then are the ways we can recognize and deal with problems, and how can our processes of problem management be supported by decision analysis? Managers usually identify the existence or development of problems in one of a number of possible ways:

1. By observing or being told about the actions of people such as subordinates, competitors, suppliers, or customers.
2. Through comparing a situation or anticipated state or event with a desired state and noting a discrepancy. For example we can often forecast ahead of time that quarterly or yearly sales or profits will be above or below prespecified target levels.
3. By predicting future behavior within the organization or in its environment and deducing that unless action is taken to change the present course of events, an undesirable situation will occur.

This list of problem identification processes is not exhaustive, as there is in general a wide variety of such processes. Regardless of which mechanism precipitates the awareness of a problem, our minds naturally turn toward analyzing a set of symptoms to identify their cause and also to a consideration of how we can deal with the problem. Both of these processes, problem identification and analysis, require considerable thought, and when the problem is complex, then the process of analysis can often help. Formal analytic processes such as decision analysis can help our intuitive processes of deductive reasoning and our creative problem-solving abilities through ensuring that our thinking is **systematic** in nature. Decision analysis also supports problem resolution (decision making) with a set of useful aiding mechanisms such as decision trees, probability assessment techniques, and utility function representations. It is important to note that a systematic approach to problem solving and decision making does not preclude the use of creativity. Indeed, the systematic consideration of decision elements can foster processes of lateral thinking and creative problem solving.

The decision analysis process begins with the structuring phase. This phase involves defining various decision elements and their interrelationships. These decision elements were introduced in Chapter 2 as alternative actions (open to the decision maker), sources of uncertainty, and the time horizon over which the decision elements have an effect.

## Example 3–1

### Development of a New Jet Engine

A manufacturer of aircraft engines has developed a radical new type of jet engine. It has been brought to the prototype stage, and on the test bed, the prototype has been found to be fuel efficient, but unfortunately it is noisy. The new engine's specifications are such that it is mainly suitable for civil aviation uses, with some limited potential for military applications. The senior executives of the company realized that this potentially profitable new product was at a critical point in its development.

They were anxious to get it to the market and to make it available to a variety of aircraft manufacturers who were, at the time, designing a number of new aircraft types. It would be very timely to announce an excellent new engine concept because there were, in the industry, a number of new planes being developed that would potentially be able to use it. Long delays would ensure that these opportunities would be lost.

On the other hand, the process of publicizing this engine (and therefore its new design principle) would allow a number of competitors to engage immediately in competitive design processes. Until now, the project had been kept highly confidential, and the managers believed that no one else was working on a similar design.

If the decision was made to go public with the engine now, some aircraft manufacturers would be reticent to place orders because of the noise problem. Others would not be so concerned. The market would be somewhat limited for the engine in its current state because many airports around the world had noise restrictions in force. There was a great advantage in keeping the technological lead, and one school of thought was to keep quiet about the engine and work on solving the noise problem.

The company's chief engineer outlined two major strategies for dealing with the engine noise. The first was to make a relatively minor investment of about $800,000 in trying to modify the engine using conventional technology. The second alternative involved a major investment, about $5 million, in using the same new design concept, but in altering some of the design parameters substantially. The engineer estimated that the likelihood and magnitude of possible noise reduction was higher with the second approach but left it to senior management to wrestle with the problem of what to do with the new product.

The benefits from being able to offer the marketplace a high fuel efficient engine were related to the cost of fuel. This cost was relatively low in late 1986 when the decision had to be made, however there was uncertainty about future fuel prices.

The senior executive in charge of the new development listed some potential actions the company could immediately take:

1. Make a public announcement now.
2. Attempt a minor redesign (costing $800,000).
3. Attempt a major redesign (costing $5 million).
4. Stop the project development.

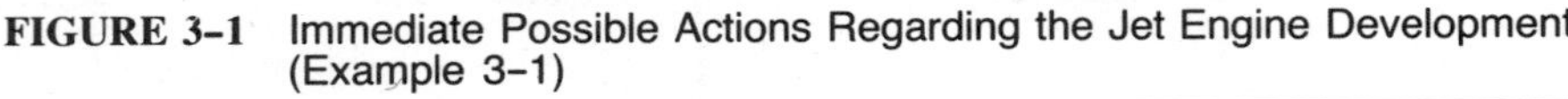

**FIGURE 3–1** Immediate Possible Actions Regarding the Jet Engine Development (Example 3–1)

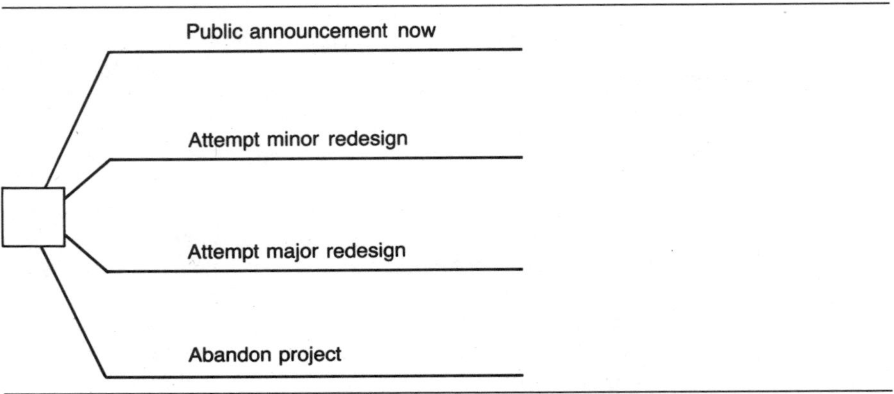


After a thorough process of thinking about what other options were available, the executive decided that this list was complete in covering all feasible immediate alternatives, and he began to draw a decision tree. See Figure 3–1.

The executive then called on the chief engineer and two other senior managers to assist him with the rest of the structure. They debated the immediate possible consequences of each proposed alternative and placed them on the tree. See Figure 3–2.

Figure 3–2 shows that the executive was uncertain about the degree to which competitors would produce similar engine designs, should he announce the engine immediately. He represented this uncertainty as a chance event node with three possible outcomes. Following that he represented his uncertainty about sales in a similar manner. He showed on the tree that if a minor investment was undertaken, the result could be success in solving the noise problem, partial improvement, or failure. If a major redesign effort were undertaken, the possible outcomes were either complete success or complete failure. He put chance event nodes representing his uncertainty about sales on these other branches, where appropriate. In doing so he noted that the actual ranges of high sales to low sales could be quite different at various "sales" chance event nodes. The possible ranges of sales depended on what came before each chance event node on the tree. For example if redesign success was achieved, "high sales" would be much higher than if he made an immediate public announcement and many competitive designs occurred.

The executive looked at the tree critically and thought about how it might have been incomplete. He asked his colleagues to help him identify what he had implicitly assumed.

He made a list of assumptions as follows:

1. Only the four listed immediate actions were available to him.
2. The most important sources of uncertainty were as shown on the tree.
3. No future action alternatives existed that were relevant to the analysis.
4. If either redesign process was undertaken, competitive designs would not be an important factor.

**FIGURE 3–2** Growing the Jet Engine Development Decision Tree

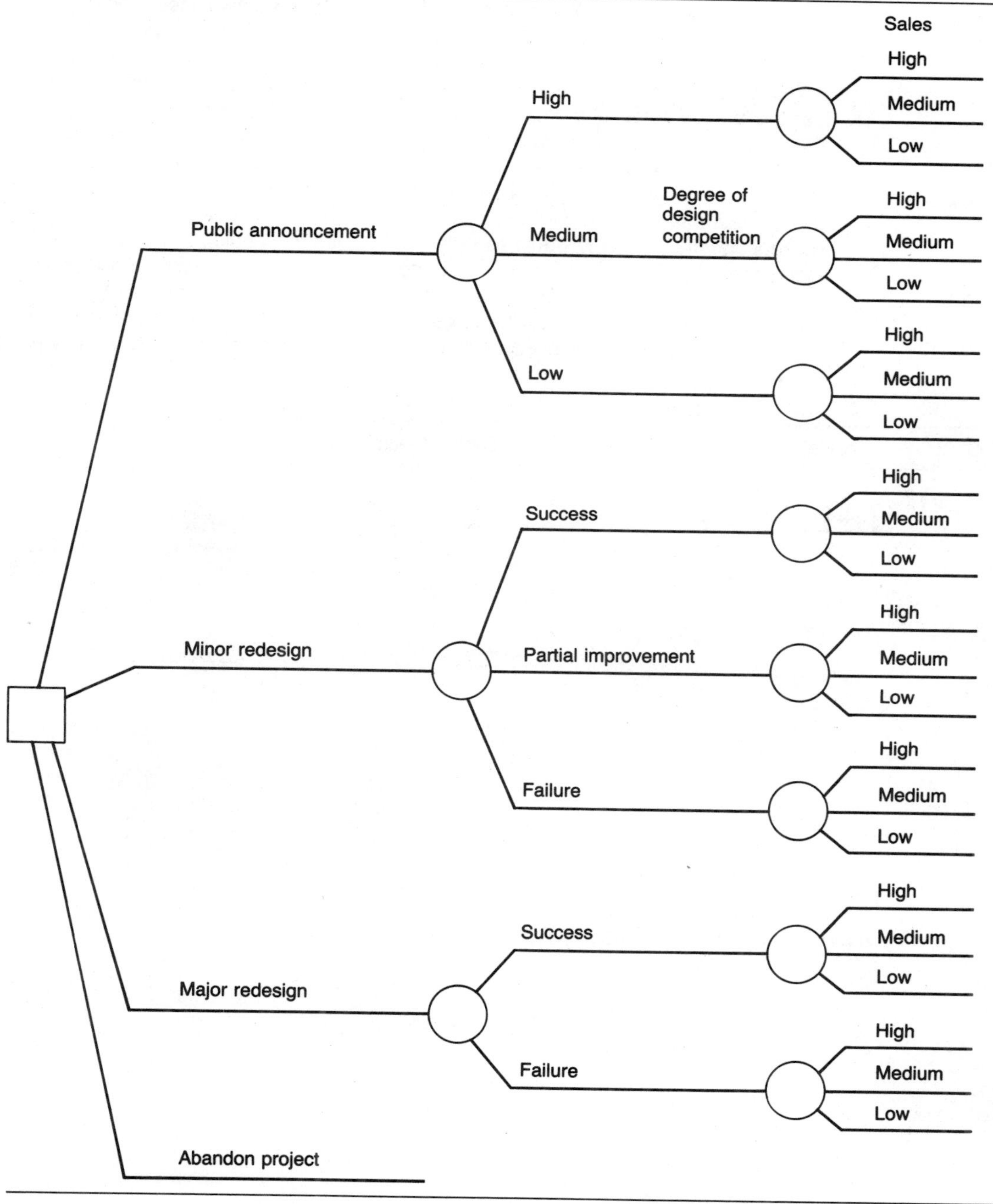

After careful thought the group chose some further important issues to incorporate in the model. They wanted to refine the tree to make it more realistic and considered a number of ways of doing so. Their list of the additional features that they wanted to account for on the tree was as follows: First, if they undertook either redesign, they could subsequently decide to publicly announce or abandon the project after the redesign effort outcome was known. Second, there were two more feasible immediate actions open to them. These were combinations of basic existing alternatives, involving an immediate public announcement combined with either redesign effort. Third, where there was competition it was important to recognize that the company might or might not ultimately have the best designed engine. To encapsulate this factor, they defined a variable called "our relative design quality." This uncertainty ultimately would be reflected in sales and could have been implicitly accounted for in the "sales" chance event node, however, the group chose to show it on the tree as a separate source of uncertainty, coming before (to the left of) "sales." Figure 3–3 shows a representation of the refined decision tree. This structural representation does not show all the branches, particularly where repetitive patterns could

**FIGURE 3–3** A Refined Decision Tree for the Jet Engine Decision

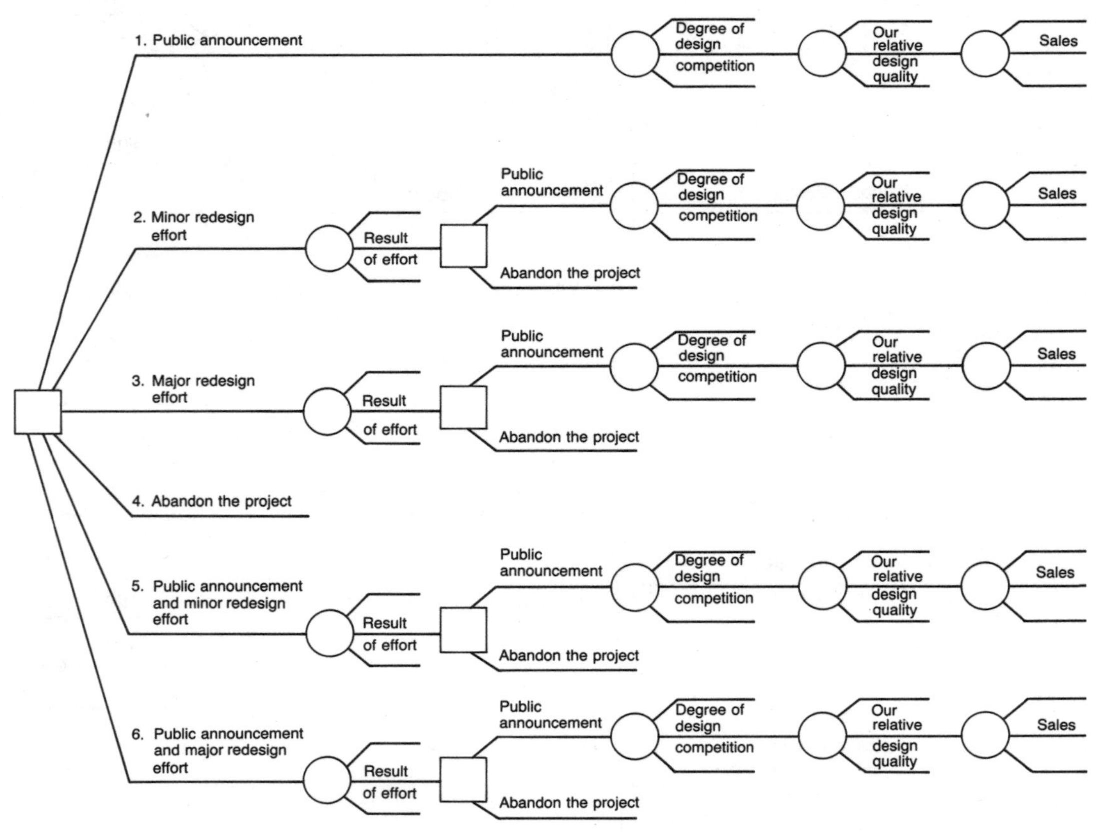

**FIGURE 3–4** Decision Tree Showing a Modification to Branch 2 for the Jet Engine Development

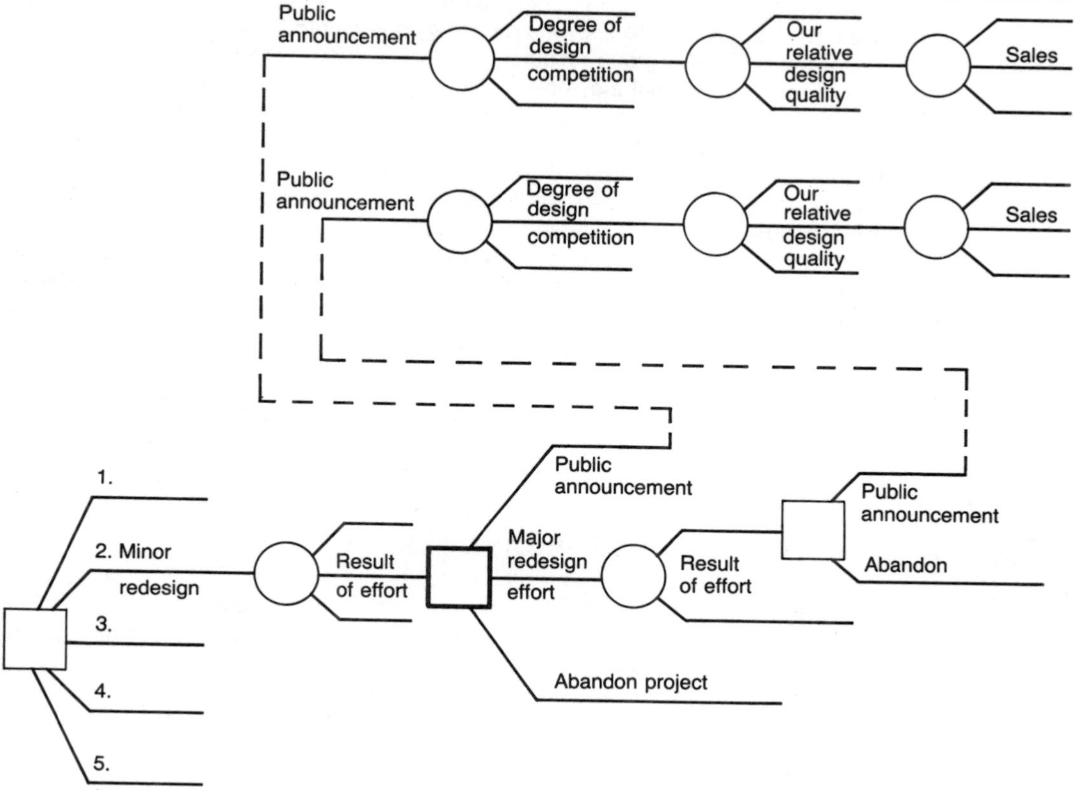

NOTE: Branches 1, 3, 4, and 5 are identical to those in Figure 3–3.

exist. On such a structural tree, certain branches are left off the tree to keep it simple enough to represent on one page. A tree representation that showed each and every branch cannot always be effectively shown on a single page. Structural decision trees provide a summary of the structure without showing all the detail. For this decision tree, the construction of a complete tree, showing all branches, would be time consuming because of the many sets of repeated nodes and branches. Try it! Decision tree computer software, such as the package supplied with this volume, can make this task much easier.

The group decided that they were now reasonably satisfied with the structure (Figure 3–3) and began to make some assessments of probabilities for the chance events and cash flows to assign to the end of each branch. They did draw the tree out in full as a large chart. As they were discussing various likelihoods of events, the chief engineer suddenly realized they had made some assumptions that were not recognized as such. They had implicitly assumed that it was not feasible to simultaneously undertake both redesign efforts, with or without a public announcement. Also they had assumed away the possibility of trying the redesign efforts sequentially. After lengthy discussion it was decided not to complicate the tree with all the possible new combinations because most were infeasible. All of them were screened out at this stage, except the possibility of doing the major redesign if the minor redesign effort failed. Branch 2 in Figure 3–3 was modified as in Figure 3–4.

At this stage the group reflected on what they had accomplished so far. They unanimously agreed that they now understood the problem much better than before they started the decision analysis. Two members of the group claimed to be ready to choose a decision strategy, however the chief engineer was keen on taking the process further by quantifying all the cash flows and likelihoods. All in all, it was felt that the decision had been well modeled. As one member of the group expressed it: "We could have chosen a course of action using only our intuition. Having done the analysis, we are now much better placed to make a choice, although we might still be unlucky with those chance events. They are out of our control, but at least now we know the possibilities of various outcomes occurring, much better than before we did the analysis."

---

## SINGLE- AND MULTIPLE-STAGE DECISIONS

Decisions with varying numbers of decision elements naturally require decision tree models with varying degrees of complexity. In this section we will examine three types of decision analysis models:

*a*. Single-stage decision models.
*b*. Two-stage decision models.
*c*. Other multiple-stage models.

### Single-Stage Decision Models

In cases where there is only one source of uncertainty and one decision variable, the appropriate decision tree must look like either Figure 3–5 or Figure 3–6. In the case of Figure 3–5 the uncertain quantity is resolved before the decision maker must commit to the choice of an action. Decisions like this are relatively simple and require little support from models. An example of this kind of decision would occur in a French restaurant where the food is not precooked, but is prepared after orders are taken. Once orders are taken, the raw materials are processed to meet those orders. It is, of course, an advantage to have the uncertainty resolved before the decision of how many meals of which type need be made.

Compare Figure 3–5 with Figure 3–6. In the latter case the decision must be made before the uncertainty is resolved, and whatever action is chosen at decision node *A*, the decision maker must live with the consequences he cannot control at chance event nodes *B*, *C*, or *D*.

**FIGURE 3–5** A Single-Stage Decision Tree with Chance Event Node First

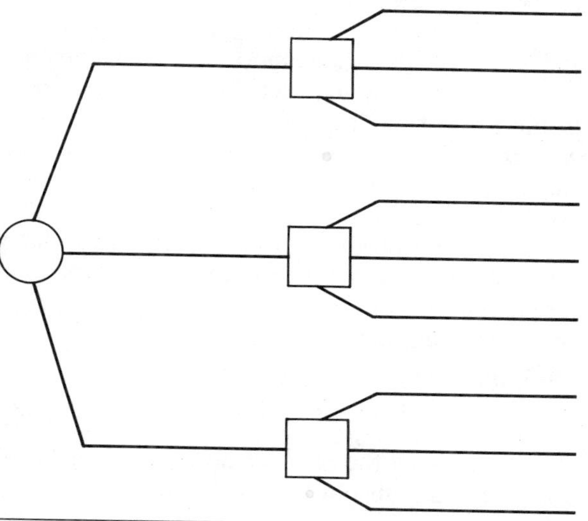

**FIGURE 3–6** A Single-Stage Decision Tree with Decision Node First

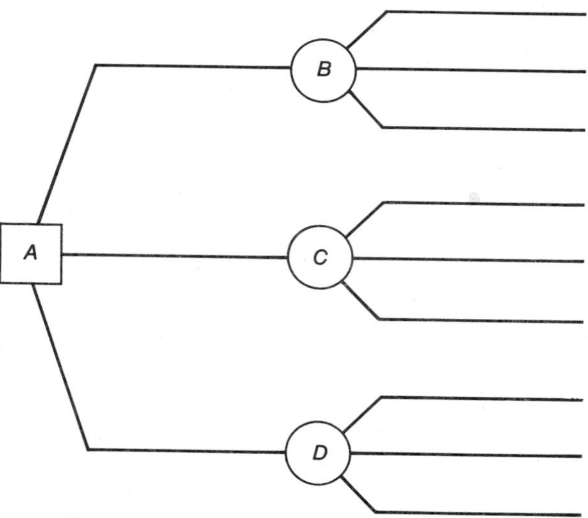

In Figure 3–6, the decision maker can only control his destiny so far as which chance event node he encounters. This type of decision is commonly faced by all of us, both in business and personal decision making. Let us contrast the example of the French restaurant with that of a baker who bakes bread only one time per day. Each morning he must decide how many loaves to prepare for sale even though demand for his bread is not known with certainty at the time of baking.

The baker must choose a production quantity $Q$, and the demand $D$ may be more than or less than $Q$ or (ideally) exactly equal to $Q$. Let us examine a simple example that commonly occurs where $Q$ and $D$ are discrete variables, and where price $P$ and production cost $C$ are invariant with volume produced or sold. We also assume the existence of a probability distribution on the uncertain quantity $D$, known as $P(D)$. Let us assume that any product not sold within the specified single time horizon must be thrown away (that is, has no salvage value).

If $Q < D$ then profit $X$ is given by $X = P - C \times Q$.

This is the case where all the product that is made gets sold. If $Q > D$ then excess product remains unsold and profit is given by

$$\begin{aligned} \text{Profit } X &= P - C \times D - C \times Q - D \\ &= P \times D - C \times Q \end{aligned}$$

Since decisions like this must often be made repeatedly (the baker faces the bread production quantity decision every day), it is often useful to play the averages and maximize the **expected value** of profit.

The expected profit in this case is given by:

$$\text{Expected profit } E(X) = \sum_i P \times D_i \times P(D_i) - C \times Q$$

---

## Example 3–2

### The Baker's Problem

A baker produces various types of breads, pies, and cakes for sale each day. He must decide how many chocolate cakes to produce on a daily basis given that his history of sale (upon which he bases his sales forecast) over the past 100 days is:

| *Number of Cakes Demanded* | *Frequency* |
|---|---|
| 0 | 10 |
| 1 | 20 |
| 2 | 40 |
| 3 | 30 |
| | 100 |

This daily demand probability distribution is therefore

$$Pr(0) = 0.1$$
$$Pr(1) = 0.2$$
$$Pr(2) = 0.4$$
$$Pr(3) = 0.3$$

He believes that past demand was fully representative of future demand.

Cakes have a variable cost of \$3 and sell for \$7. All cakes not sold on the day of baking must be thrown away. Let us calculate expected profit for values of $Q$ in the range zero to three.

$$\text{For } Q = 0,\ E(X) = \$0$$
$$\text{For } Q = 1,\ E(X) = 0 + 7(0.9) - 3 = \$3.3$$
$$\text{For } Q = 2,\ E(X) = 0 + 7(0.2) + 14(0.7) - 6 = \$5.2$$
$$\text{For } Q = 3,\ E(X) = 0 + 7(0.2) + 14(0.4) + 21(0.3) - 9 = \$4.3$$

To maximize his expected profit, the baker should make two cakes each day. Of course only 40% of the time will he meet demand exactly. On other days he will either make too many or too few cakes. Note that the expected profit of \$5.20 can never be exactly realized on any given day but is a probability-weighted average of the range of possible outcomes. However it is reasonable to expect that over some large number of days, $n$, that aggregate profit will be approximately $\$5.2 \times n$, and this approximation grows relatively more accurate as $n$ increases.

---

We note as a practical point that for a problem like the one faced by the baker, the monetary stakes are relatively low, and a carefully conceived decision analysis is perhaps not justified in such instances. Most bakers make their batch size decisions based on very informal, intutitive-styled processes. However problems of similar form often occur in other business situations, where the stakes are much higher and the effort of conducting a decision analysis is well justified.

## Single-Stage Decisions and Decision Tables

Figure 3–7 shows a decision tree for the cake production example (Example 3–2).

Since there are only two decision elements, $Q$ and $D$, the decision can be represented as a table (see Table 3–1). Table 3–1 shows the same information as Figure 3–7. However as the number of possible states in a problem gets larger, the decision tree gets bushier quickly and becomes a messy form of representation, whereas the tabular form does not. Consider a situation where 10 levels of the decision variable and the chance event are possible. Using a decision tree format, 100 (10 × 10) end points must be constructed. This is an arduous task. Such a decision tree cannot possibly be shown

**FIGURE 3–7** The Cake Production Decision Tree, Example 3–2

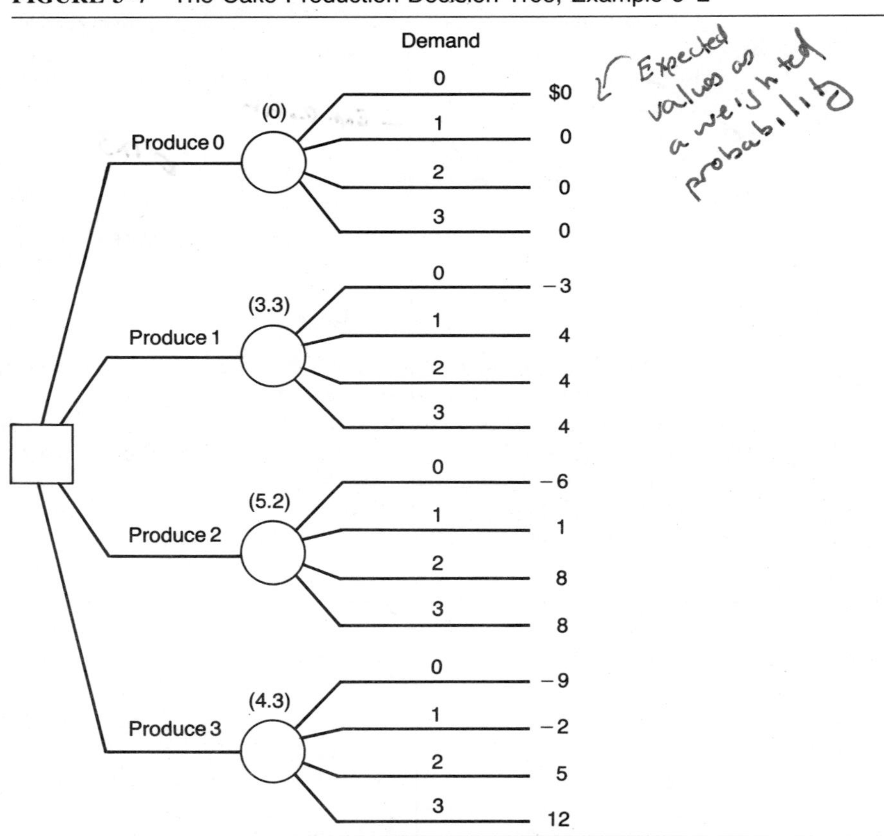


NOTE: Net cash flows are shown at the endpoints of the tree. Expected values are calculated as probability-weighted averages of those cash flows.

**TABLE 3–1** Payoffs and Expected Values for the Cake Example

| *Decision Variable* | *State of Nature (D)* 0 | 1 | 2 | 3 | *Expected Value* |
|---|---|---|---|---|---|
| Q = 0 | 0.0 | 0.0 | 0.0 | 0.0 | 0.0 |
| Q = 1 | −3.0 | 4.0 | 4.0 | 4.0 | 3.3 |
| Q = 2 | −6.0 | 1.0 | 8.0 | 8.0 | 5.2 |
| Q = 3 | −9.0 | −2.0 | 5.0 | 12.0 | 4.3 |
| Probability | 0.1 | 0.2 | 0.4 | 0.3 | |

clearly on a single page. However, we can neatly construct a table with 10 columns and 10 rows on a single page. In fact, for single-stage decision problems of this size (10 × 10) the most convenient solution procedure is to develop a formula and use a programmable calculator or computer to do the repetitive calculations required. These types of calculations can easily be programmed using a language like BASIC or FORTRAN or else a spreadsheet software package, if warranted.

Single-stage decisions can be conveniently structured and represented either as decision trees or decision tables. Although there is relatively little complexity in such structures, there can be considerable complexity in:

*a.* Deciding that a particular decision problem can be adequately represented as a single-stage model.
*b.* Making a choice between alternatives.

As a result of these factors, we should not assume that single-stage decision trees or tables represent easy decisions to make just because there is only one decision variable and one source of uncertainty. This point is illustrated by the following example.

---

## EXAMPLE 3–3

### A Marketing Problem

As marketing manager of a large metal fabrication business, you must make a choice on the price of one of your products, which has recently been redesigned. The product has been substantially improved in quality as a result of new technology. You have decided to raise the price from \$4 by either \$1 or \$2, but are uncertain about how these price increases would affect sales, and ultimately profits.

FIGURE 3–8 Decision Tree for the Marketing Problem, Example 3–3

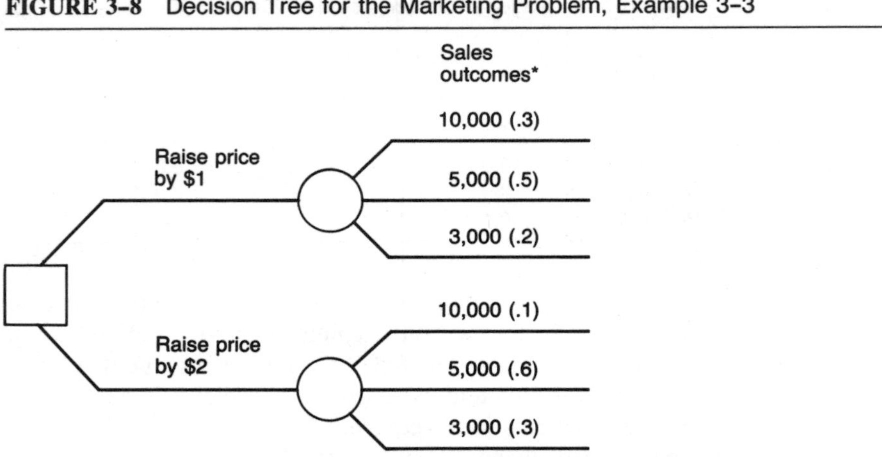


* Figures shown in thousands are numbers sold. Probabilities of outcomes are shown in brackets.

You have constructed a decision tree (Figure 3–8) which best represents your feelings about the problem, including assessments of the uncertain quantity, sales. Which option do you choose? Even though Figure 3–8 is a relatively simple decision tree structure, this decision may be a difficult one to make. It is not clear that choosing a strategy that maximizes expected numbers of sales is a suitable criterion. Since the price will be different across the two possible actions, maximizing expected number of sales is not the same as maximizing expected sales revenue. Expected profit maximization is a different criterion again.

---

For this example it is clear that even though the problem can be adequately represented as a simple, single-stage structure, its resolution, that is, choosing and implementing a decision strategy, may not be straightforward.

## Two-Stage Decision Models

Additional complexity is involved when there are multiple sources of uncertainty and more than one decision variable. In these decision situations we must still define the domain for each decision variable and the probabilities for each uncertain quantity (as for single-stage decision problems). However before going into the detailed numerical expression of variable values, we must choose the set of relevant decision elements and their juxtaposition in the model.

**FIGURE 3–9** The Two-Stage Decision Tree

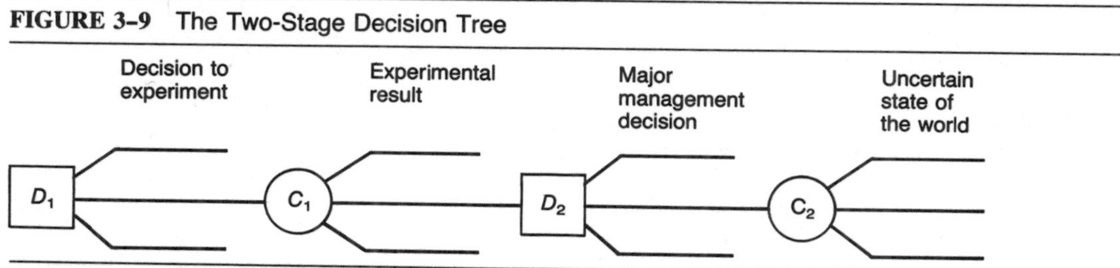


Note that not all branches and nodes are shown on this structural representation. Also, the assumption that three branches emanate from various nodes is made for convenience sake. Any number of branches can exist in general, although it is often convenient to discretize continuous variables into three levels.

Let us at first consider a particular form of multistage decision model called a two-stage decision. Generalization to other multistage decisions will follow. A particular two-stage decision tree (shown as Figure 3–9) is a very important form of decision model because of the problems it can be used to represent. It is rich in both power and applicability. However, note that Figure 3–9 is certainly not the only class of problem that can be represented as a two-stage decision tree.

There are many managerial problems that are indeed two-stage problems of the form of Figure 3–9. These generally involve any situation in which information may be collected (for example, in a survey) and used to help make a decision. In such cases the decision node shown on Figure 3–9 as $D_1$ represents the decision of whether or not to collect information. For example, if a market survey is being considered, how many people or items should be surveyed? The various alternatives can be defined and then represented by the branches emanating from node $D_1$. Given that a survey is undertaken, there is, a priori, uncertainty about the survey or sample result. This uncertainty cannot be resolved until after the survey data is collected and analyzed. At the time the survey is being considered, the result is, of course, unknown and is represented as an uncertain quantity (node $C_1$) on Figure 3–9. The survey result does become known however, before the decision point $D_2$ is reached so that decision $D_2$ will be made with the availability of the information from the survey. It is reemphasized that although this survey information would be available before node $D_2$ is reached in the actual decision situation, the decision to conduct a survey (node $D_1$) must be made before this uncertainty is resolved.

Once decision $D_2$ is made, the state of the world which is uncertain, namely decision element $C_2$, becomes resolved, and the consequences and payoffs become known.

## EXAMPLE 3–4

### Boston Beer Company

The Boston Beer Company produces and markets two main beer products, principally in Massachusetts. The company was considering a geographical expansion program to distribute its major product to the Midwest (principally Chicago) initially, and later to the West Coast as well. There was uncertainty about the degree of acceptance that the product would receive in these new areas, and management was considering the viability of the expansion plan and some alternate ways to deal with the uncertainty.

The important uncertain quantity was market share. It was very difficult to forecast what the ultimate market share would be for an East Coast beer in the Midwest and Southwest marketing regions, particularly because previous attempts to expand by other East Coast companies had resulted in very mixed results with some products quickly becoming national market leaders and others, failures. Industry analysts claimed that consumer taste patterns and preferences were different in various regions of the country. A study of other companies' attempts to geographically diversify did not shed much light on the situation in terms of reducing management's uncertainty about market share. Boston's senior vice president of marketing, John Preston, suggested that one of three possibilities be undertaken: "As I see it, we could in theory go ahead with substantial investments in distribution networks and advertising expenditures in our Midwest region, but there is a great deal of risk in doing so. The risk is simply that our beer won't sell very well in places like Chicago. It doesn't matter if we do or don't understand the reasons behind high or low sales in Midwest sales centers because the only important factor is the sales themselves.

"On the other hand, the other extreme option is to scrap the idea of taking our beers national and instead concentrate more on achieving higher sales in local markets. That would be a pity in my opinion because we do have a very well-conceived expansion plan.

"Both of these options seem unattractive to me, and I am not prepared to commit myself to a decision either way just now. We are fighting against the uncertainty of what our ultimate sales will be. We know almost exactly what sales levels must be achieved to make this expansion worthwhile, but we just don't know whether we will achieve them.

"We can of course collect information and hopefully reduce our uncertainty as a result. I see two major forms of possible action. The first is to commission point of purchase comparison tests and survey a sample of consumers. A fairly comprehensive market survey in, say, two cities would cost us about $175,000. Is it worth spending that amount of money to reduce our uncertainty? And what do we get for our investment? Let's remember that it's a once-up expense, and the only return on the investment is the survey result. That survey result may be useful in helping us make a decision, or it may not. Simply put, the result may be a borderline one, in which case

**FIGURE 3–10** A Two-Stage Decision Tree Representation of the Boston Beer Example

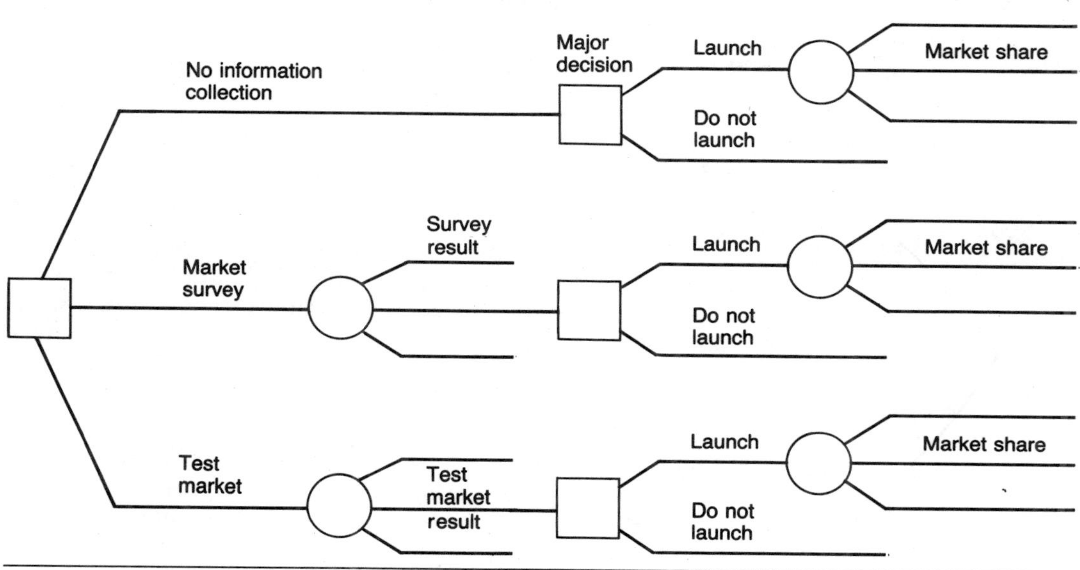


we'll be no better placed to make a decision than we are now. Or else the result may just confirm our present beliefs about prospective market share, in which case we'll go ahead with the plan anyway, and we'll sleep a little better than if we don't have a survey result to reassure us. But if the survey doesn't change our minds about the decision, how can we spend nearly $200,000 just to confirm our expectations? My final point on the matter of the survey is that because its only a sample taste preference test its results will be imperfect in a statistical sense.

"A second option is to set up a test market in one or maybe two cities or towns. This option would be much more expensive than a simple survey, but we will get a much more reliable information base from a test market than from a survey. Of course either of these things will take some time, about six months for the test market and four to six weeks for the survey.

"Even if we conduct an extensive test market program, there will still be some uncertainty about our ultimate market share if we decide to go ahead."

Mr. Preston has outlined a two-stage decision problem. The first stage is the decision of whether or not to collect information, and if so, how to do it and what information to collect. The second, and more important decision is whether to go ahead with the major expansion plan. The decision tree in Figure 3–10 shows these possibilities.

The tree structure of a two-stage decision clearly shows the relationships between the decision elements, however the information, decision elements, and relationships are quite subtle and require further consideration. In considering using decision analysis to support such a decision as in the Boston Beer example, we need to know a number of things:

*a.* What are the information inputs of the model?
*b.* What are the outputs of the model?
*c.* How do the outputs enhance our understanding of the problem and lead to a better decision process and a better decision?

Let us begin with the information inputs. These are in the form of cash flow estimates (costs, benefits, profits, etc.) and probabilistic statements about the outcomes of the uncertain consequences. Cash flow estimates often need to be highly subjective, and subjective probabilities (expressions of the degree of belief in the likelihood of a chance event) may need to be used for probability calculations. These model inputs are very important because they strongly affect model outputs; hence they need careful attention.

Information outputs from the model provide insights about the consequences and attractiveness of the various options. This attractiveness or utility of each option relates not just to simple cost and benefit but also to the risk associated with each of the various alternatives, which can be expressed in the form of risk profiles (see Chapter 2).

Without the aid of a model, the decision maker is in the state of knowledge expressed above by Mr. Preston. He can conceive of some alternatives but doesn't have a good mechanism to properly structure and evaluate them carefully or to creatively consider new options.

How would you make a decision without the aid of a decision model, if you were in Mr. Preston's position? Most people would use their experience from other (hopefully similar) situations, their intuition, and the seat of their pants. The model provides a solid basis for decomposition and analysis and is also likely to motivate a further consideration of new or modified alternatives. For example in the Boston Beer example, can some form of survey be obtained for less than $175,000? Suppose only $50,000 could be spent on a survey, or perhaps $100,000? How does the level of quality of the information generated by the survey vary with the size of the survey budget? In Chapter 11 we will formally compare the **benefits** of various levels of information with the **costs** to highlight the economic aspects of this two-stage decision situation. The Boston Beer example demonstrates that it is possible to capture the logic of a two-stage decision in a model that includes an initial information collection decision.

## Other Multiple-Stage Models

Decision trees have been used to model a wide variety of decision problems. These problems range from the strategic in nature to tactical/operational and cover every aspect of management. Their usefulness extends to many other fields such as legal and medical. Decision analysts have had experience with problems of many different types and levels of complexity. In many cases these problems have been reduced and simplified in their representations as models; however, some extremely complex decision trees have been drawn, having a very large number of nodes and branches.

The decision analysis approach and the decision tree structuring process are very flexible, requiring only that decision elements be categorized as decision variables or sources of uncertainty. Within this famework, decision trees theoretically can be of any shape or size, meaning that the number and configuration of nodes and branches are not bound in any manner. There are however, practical limits on the size of decision tree models, and further, there is generally a decreasing marginal benefit associated with the construction of very large, very complex structures. The practical limits associated with constructing large decision trees are very high because computer software is now available that allows the construction of decision trees with thousands of nodes. In the vast majority of management decisions, these limits will never be reached. Even for very complex decisions, it usually makes good sense to assume away some of the less important elements and concentrate on accurately modeling a subset of more important key elements. This is a very sensible modeling procedure, at least as a first pass. Secondary effects and details can always be added after the central model is successfully established, or they can be brought in to the analytic process through sensitivity analyses. Another practical difficulty with large decision trees is the magnitude and complexity of the probability assessment process. In summary, let us reemphasize that the decision tree modeling approach is flexible in terms of model size and configuration, allowing for both a wide variety of applications and for its use as a tool in the creative process of model construction.

## OTHER LINKED DECISION SUPPORT MODELS

The decision analysis model used to represent a particular decision problem may be linked to, or supported by, one or more other models. These linkages may be direct, for example, a computerized decision tree or decision analysis system may be linked to a forecasting model so that some outputs of the forecasting model directly input to the decision analysis model. Although we can forecast that the incidence of such direct linkages will increase with the increasing development of integrated software packages, more frequent linkages currently occur between decision analysis and other models that are not direct couplings of this type.

Practitioners very frequently use more than one modeling approach to support a decision process. If the main or meta-model which is used to represent the decision is a decision analysis model, then subsidiary models that provide inputs to the meta-decision model can take a variety of forms.

These models might be used to support the decision analysis in a number of different ways, including the structuring, assessment, and sensitivity analysis phases of decision analysis. In the structuring phase, subsidiary or support models can screen a large number of possible options or alternative actions to produce subsets that are further evaluated in the decision analysis. Subsidiary models are also very useful in providing information for the quantitative assessment phase of the decision analysis. In many instances it may be reasonable to construct an elaborate subsidiary model just to calculate an estimate of a probability or consequence payoff that becomes or contributes to the estimation of a single number on a decision tree. In the sensitivity analysis phase of decision analysis, it may be useful to use subsidiary models to examine the effects of changes in particular variables, or indeed to help gauge the possible variability of parameters from their previously assumed values.

Let us briefly consider what types of models are likely to be used as subsidiary models in a managerial decision analysis process. These can be thought of in the context of a decision tree model where the umbrella model of the decision in aggregate is supported and receives inputs from other models that individually deal with only a part of the problem. We will consider models in three classes:

1. Optimal resource allocation models.
2. Statistical (data analytic) models.
3. Other models.

The class, consisting of optimal resource allocation models, covers operational research and other mathematical approaches such as those found in the finance, management science, and economic literatures. This category broadly covers the topics of mathematical programing models such as linear programing, inventory, queueing, and Markov models, as well as some other financial, economic, and econometric modeling approaches.[1] These models might deal with anything from the operations of a complete national economy to the capital budget of a small corporate division or business unit. The three following examples show how very different types of models may provide useful inputs to a decision model.

[1] For further details of these models see H. Bierman, C. P. Bonini, and W. H. Hausman, *Quantitative Analysis for Business Decisions* (Homewood, Ill.: Richard D. Irwin, 1986.)

## EXAMPLE 3–5

### A Macroeconomic Model

The return on investment of a particular foreign venture a company is making is dependent on the gross national product (GNP) of that foreign country over a multiyear time horizon. This GNP is considered as an uncertain quantity in the decision analysis, and to forecast various possible future GNP states and associated probabilities, complex macroeconomic models need to be used. The macroeconomic model produces GNP estimates that become inputs to the decision model. Figure 3–11 shows two subsidiary models that could supply data for the decision tree. One of these provides a probability distribution of GNP, and the other uses GNP data to

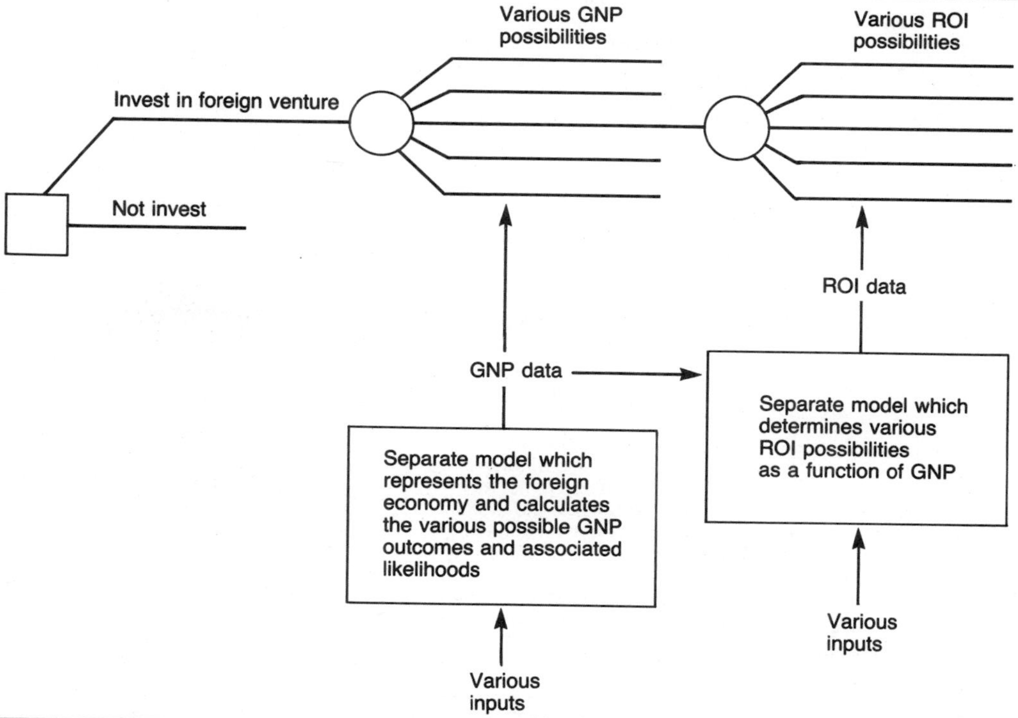

**FIGURE 3–11** Use of Subsidiary Models to Support a Decision Analysis of an Investment Problem

provide probability distributions of return on investment (ROI), which are conditional upon certain GNP outcomes.

---

## EXAMPLE 3–6

### A Linear Program Model

A large petrochemical plant was generating cash for a multinational corporation. A very important tax planning decision had to be made, which was strongly affected by the future profitability of the plant. The profitability of the plant was in turn, strongly

**FIGURE 3–12** Use of a Subsidiary Model to Support a Tax Strategy Decision Analysis Model

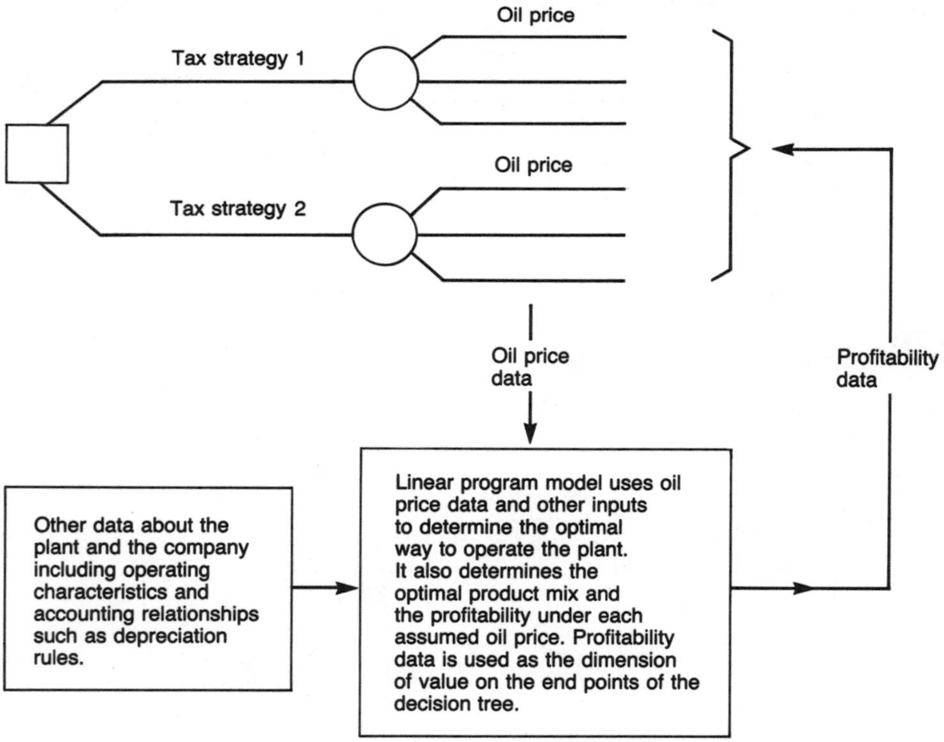

NOTE: Different tax strategies may involve the choice of one or more depreciation methods for equipment affecting the time pattern of tax payments.

affected by world oil prices, and a large linear program was used to determine the optimal operating characteristics of the plant for a given set of oil prices. The tax planning decision model made considerable use of the linear program as a subsidiary model. The linear program was run a number of times with different oil price inputs. It provided an important linkage between the uncertain oil prices and the tax decision. A detailed explanation of how such a linear program could be used is given in Figure 3-12.

---

Examples 3-5 and 3-6 illustrate the use of models of two kinds of systems (an economy and a petrochemical plant). In both cases these system models provided important data for the decision model. Statistical models are also often useful in providing estimates of key numbers that become inputs to a decision model. Regression analysis models and other forecasting procedures can be used not only to provide best estimates for a parameter, but also to indicate levels of variance or uncertainty. For example, the standard error of an estimate as calculated using a statistical technique may be used as one form of input to a subjective probability assessment procedure.

---

## EXAMPLE 3-7

### An Investment Strategy Decision

A portfolio management consultant was designing an investment strategy for a corporate client who had asked to be presented with between three and five alternatives to choose from. The choice would ultimately be made using a decision analysis model as an aid.

The decision analysis model related the investment decision to a number of other important factors such as the operating and financing decisions of the firm. To achieve the goal of producing a short list of good alternative strategies, the consultant made use of mean-variance analysis and stochastic dominance criteria. These techniques allow for efficient ranking of investment strategies and were used to screen out a number of strategies which should not have been included on a short list.

---

A myriad of other models may supply information relevant to a decision analysis model. Hence we can often use a decision analysis approach to support a strategic or operational decision, where the decision analysis approach is the central or umbrella model and a number of other models and techniques provide input to the central model.

Some further examples are:

1. A statistical model relating advertising expenditure and media mix to advertising effectiveness. Advertising cost might itself be or contribute to a cash flow on a decision tree, and advertising effectiveness might be an input to a sales estimate.
2. A queueing theory model can be used to relate the capacity of a service system to its level of service and cost. Such models would provide useful information to decision analysis models in system design and capacity planning problems.
3. An engineering model relating the size and capacity of a bridge to its optimal construction design and cost could be a useful subsidiary model in urban planning decision models.

Models need not be abstract in nature. For example, a pilot scale or prototype model of a factory or production system, chemical process, or building structure might be constructed (possibly at great expense) for the sole purpose of providing information for a decision analysis. These are called iconic models. In such a case, the net value of the model could be taken into account as part of the decision analysis using the two-stage decision tree approach (described earlier in this chapter). These two-stage models are treated in more detail in Chapters 10 and 11.

## SUBSIDIARY MODELS, DECISION AIDS, AND EXPERT OPINIONS

Subsidiary models play a very important role in many real decision analyses, but should be distinguished in our thinking from two other important model inputs, namely decision aids and expert opinions. Decision aids are procedures aimed to assist decision makers in structuring and assessment tasks. For example, a wide variety of procedures has been designed to facilitate the subjective assessment of probabilities. These aids have usually been designed specifically to lead to assessments with minimum biases. These decision aids are not models because they do not in themselves represent problems or systems; however, they do play a very important role in the provision of high-quality assessments and inputs in decision analysis models.

Expert opinions are another very important form of input in decision analysis models. These opinions may themselves be based on the output of subsidiary models or have been elicited with the assistance of decision aids. The opinion of a technical research scientist on the viability of a new chemical process, or the belief of a marketing expert about sales of a new product are examples of expert opinion.

**FIGURE 3–13** Use of Decision Analysis as an Umbrella Meta-Approach

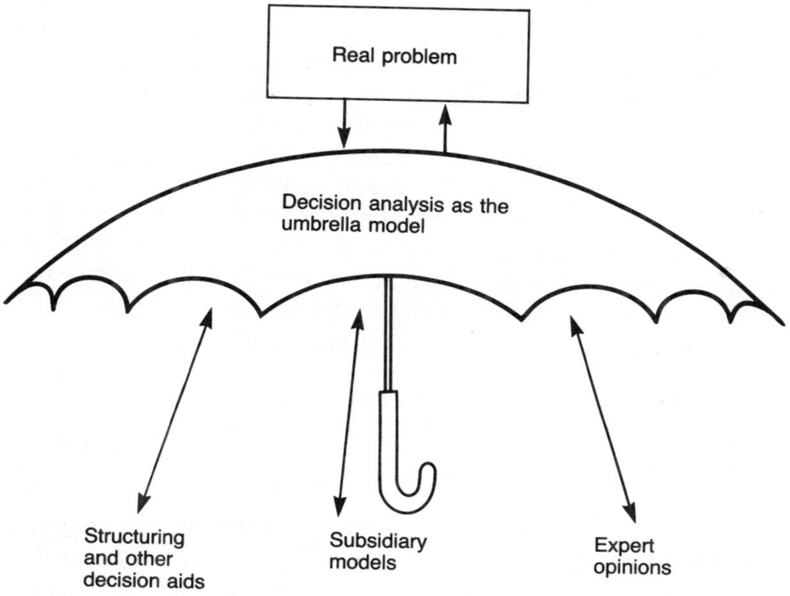

Decision analysis models can be of many possible forms, including single stage or multistage, stand alone or part of a linked system of models. Complex decision problems are often modeled using the decision analysis approach as a meta-model or umbrella framework linking other models, aids, and expert inputs (see Figure 3–13). Through this sort of approach, even very complex problems can be decomposed into elements, even though these elements may be strongly related. Figure 3–13 shows how the pieces of a complex decision analysis can be fitted together effectively when the central element is a decision analysis umbrella model through which many other analytical elements and inputs can be related.

## SUMMARY

The most important contribution of decision analysis in problem formulation and model construction is its provision of a framework through which to define problems. Consider this framework a lens through which the decision maker can focus on the important decision elements of alternative actions, sources of uncertainty, and time horizon. The decision analysis approach stimulates a logical and systematic decision process, yet provides enough flexibility so as not to stifle creative inputs and problem solutions.

Decision trees are used as representations of decision problems. They represent the situation that the decision maker envisages in terms of controlled variables (decision variables), uncontrolled variables (sources of uncertainty), and the time horizon. The structured ordering of the decision and chance event nodes is also an important part of the model.

Special cases of single-stage and two-stage models were examined in this chapter. Each of these can be applied to a variety of decision problems. The single-stage decision is conceptually simple, but even so may represent decisions that are very difficult to make. The two-stage decision tree model is particularly useful when a major decision is preceded by a decision to collect information or experiment in some manner.

The final important concept in this chapter is that of linking decision analysis models to other types of models. Many different kinds of models are frequently used to provide inputs to or support the structuring, assessment, and evaluation phases of decision analysis.

## FURTHER READING

When considering the process and philosophy of model building, two key sources of valuable information should be central to any reading list. These are by Herbert Simon (1977) and by Newell and Simon (1972). A third very useful source is by Ackoff and Emery (1972). These volumes do not focus specifically on decision analysis; however, between them they give an excellent coverage of systems thinking and put the modeling process into context as part of a system of management.

A significant number of further treatments of decision analysis structuring issues and examples have been published. These include books by Raiffa (1968), Schlaifer (1969), Moore and Thomas (1976), and Keeney and Raiffa (1976) referenced in earlier chapters.

A number of useful articles pertaining to the role of decision analysis models in management have appeared in the *Harvard Business Review* including those by Brown (1970), McGee (1964), and Bodily (1981).

## REFERENCES

Ackoff, R. L., and R. Emery. 1972. *On Purposeful Systems*. Hawthorne, N.Y.: Aldine Publishing.

Ansoff, H. I., and R. L. Hayes. 1973. "The Role of Models in Corporate Decision Making," in M. Ross (ed) OR72, North Holland.

Bodily, S. 1981. "When Should You Go To Court." *Harvard Business Review*, May-June, p. 103.

Brown, R. V. 1970. "Do Managers Find Decision Theory Useful." *Harvard Business Review* 48, pp. 78–89.

Keeney, R. L., and H. Raiffa. 1976. *Decisions with Multiple Objective: Preferences and Value Tradeoffs*. New York: John Wiley & Sons, Chapter 8.

McGee, J. F. 1964. "Decision Trees for Decision Making." *Harvard Business Review,* July, p. 126.

Moore, P. G., and H. Thomas. 1976. *The Anatomy of Decisions*. New York: Penguin Books.

Newell, A., and H. A. Simon. 1972. *Human Problem Solving*. Englewood Cliffs, N.J.: Prentice Hall.

Raiffa, H. 1968. *Decision Analysis*. Reading, Mass.: Addison-Wesley Publishing.

Schlaifer, R. O. 1969. *Analysis of Decisions Under Uncertainty*. New York: McGraw-Hill.

Simon, H. A. 1977. *The New Science of Management Decisions*. Englewood Cliffs, N.J.: Prentice-Hall.

## PROBLEMS

1. Briefly investigate a recent merger, acquisition, or takeover bid described in the financial press. Consider the decision process that the organization's top management experienced. Attempt to reconstruct such a process. If you are considering a takeover, then separately structure the decision facing the company proposing the takeover and the decision facing the company that is potentially being taken over. In your structuring process, consider the motivation for takeover as well as the various decision elements involved. Classify the possible decision elements as alternative actions or sources of uncertainty. For the target company, what strategies are open to it, and what sources of uncertainty relate to each strategy?
2. In 1984, General Motors announced that it was going to build a new Saturn car plant, somewhere in the United States. Over the following few months, a large number of state governments put many proposals to GM, wooing them with promises of tax reduction or exemption, labor force stability, and low-cost land and utilities. For the state governments, securing this plant would be a major political and economic plus, given the employment and economic stimulation it would provide. Consider two decisions made by GM. The first is the decision to make a major investment in a new car and manufacturing facility. The second is where to locate it. Are these decisions completely separable (should they be made independently of each other)? Structure each decision by considering the major decision elements of each one.

3. A large farm machinery manufacturer is considering the purchase of an expensive multifunction automatic assembly machine. The flexible purpose machine was in essence a set of connected robots that could both finish and assemble special purpose units such as tractor gearboxes. The machine was very expensive, but if it worked well, it would substantially increase productivity. A number of uncertain factors included the performance of the machine in terms of its output rate, reliability, and product quality. Management was not sure how much time and money they would have to spend (above and beyond the purchase price) on integrating the machine into their production system. They were also unsure about how their labor unions would react to the machine. Labor reaction could be totally favorable, in which case cooperation in starting up and using the machine would occur. On the other hand, an unfavorable labor reaction would lead to damaging productivity decreases. Further, if the machine worked well, some benefit would come from the possibility of introducing similar machines in other similar plants owned by the company.

   As an alternative to this high-tech strategy the company considered doing nothing or else making some minor investments in machinery and delaying the major investment commitment until information could be collected that would reduce some of the uncertainties.

   List the decision elements (alternative actions, sources of uncertainty), and structure a decision tree that includes them. Is there only one correct tree, or can you think of more than one possible representation that may be feasible? For each source of uncertainty you listed, what would be the types of information you could try to collect to reduce your uncertainty?

4. A small software company has developed a product containing a large number of mathematical programs, including statistical, operations research, econometric, and decision modeling capabilities. The company knows that such an integrated package is also being developed by at least two other companies, and is planning its marketing strategy. The first decision it is considering is whether to go to market immediately with the product in its present form or to develop it further. If developed further, two options are available:
   *a.* Given six months the system could be made much more user friendly than it presently is and the few bugs that currently exist in the system could be eliminated.
   *b.* Given twelve months, the analytic models in the system could be linked to the spreadsheet, database, and report writing software that is also being developed in-house.

   A second strongly related decision is how to market the product. The small company is financed mainly by venture capital and debt.

The resources are therefore limited. Some people in the company believe that because the company has little experience in sales and distribution, the product should be sold to an organization like IBM or a large publishing/software house establishing a profit sharing/licensing agreement. Others in the company believe that the product is so good that it will sell itself and prefer an in-house marketing strategy. They did not want to sell out and needlessly share their profits with another company just because they lacked marketing experience.

Analyze the alternative actions open to the company and the risks (sources of uncertainty) associated with each alternative. List the decision elements, and draw one or more decision trees to represent the problem.

5. A New York-based delicatessen imports and sells fresh oysters. Oysters are sold by the dozen, and deliveries arrive only three times a week. They can be sold to the public only on the day of delivery or the day after.

   The oysters cost \$5 per dozen and sell for \$10 per dozen. There is also a fixed charge of \$10 per delivery no matter how many oysters are ordered. The store owner is trying to decide how many to order and estimates demand (over each two-day period between deliveries) at:

| | | | |
|---|---|---|---|
| 10 | dozen with | probability | 0.1 |
| 12 | " | " | 0.2 |
| 14 | " | " | 0.2 |
| 16 | " | " | 0.25 |
| 18 | " | " | 0.15 |
| 20 | " | " | 0.1 |

   *a.* Draw a decision tree and a decision table showing the relevant profits of each order amount/demand combination.

   *b.* Suppose that the importing agent offers to accept back from the delicatessen unsold oysters at \$2 per dozen. Does this change the rankings of the alternative order amounts based on expected profit calculations?

6. For the oyster problem (above), construct a formula that describes expected profit in terms of cost, price, demand, and probability of demand. Include the value of possible returns to the importing agent as a factor in the formula.

7. An architect who recently started his own business is considering the purchase of an automated drafting system. He can purchase a system with three possible drafting capacities. His payoffs for having any of these systems will depend on the demand for drafting

services he can generate over the next few years. The costs for each system are shown below along with the architect's probabilities that demand will match the capacity of each one.

| | *Total Cost* | *Demand Level Probability* |
|---|---|---|
| Small system | $10,000 | 0.4 |
| Medium system | $14,000 | 0.3 |
| Large system | $20,000 | 0.3 |

If working at capacity, each system will generate net cash flow at a yearly rate of 50% of its total cost. If a system is chosen that is smaller than that demanded, it would work at capacity. If a system is chosen that is larger than needed, revenue from the system would be only as much as would be produced by the appropriate sized smaller system. The architect decided to count cash flow for three years and use a zero discount rate.

*a.* Construct a decision tree and a payoff table for this problem. Calculate the expected profit contribution for each alternative.

*b.* Is an expected value decision criterion appropriate for this type of decision in the same way as it was for the oyster problem (problem 5)? Give reasons for your answer.

*c.* Draw risk profiles for each alternative action. If you were highly averse to risk, would you make a different decision than if you were not averse to risk?

8. Refer to the architect's problem (above). After constructing the basic decision model the architect decided to investigate the effect of some of his key assumptions.

*a.* The first was the assumption of a three-year cash flow horizon that he used as a best estimate. The architect realized that this estimate might be inaccurate and that the equipment might have a longer economically useful life or indeed become obsolete in less than three years. He reworked the problem by assuming two-year and four-year cash flow horizons to see how such alternative assumptions would affect his decision. Calculate his expected profit under these alternative assumptions. The architect then reasoned that since the cash flow horizon was uncertain, he could assign probabilities to its possible values and did so as follows:

2 years of cash flow has 0.1 probability
3 years of cash flow has 0.6 probability
4 years of cash flow has 0.3 probability

Calculate the expected profit contribution of each drafting system including the uncertainty about cash flow horizon.

*b*. The architect was also concerned about whether he had overestimated his ability to obtain work and keep the drafting systems busy. In particular he felt that he might have underestimated the probability that demand would match the small-system capacity. Rework the problem (with the three-year cash flow horizon only) with some increased probabilities of small-system demand level. Assume that as the probability of small-system demand increases, the probabilities of medium- and large-system demands fall by equal amounts. Find the breakeven point whereby small-system demand probability increases by enough to make its expected profit the highest.

9. Harry's Hire Company rented over 50 different types of machinery and other items, mostly to the general public and to tradesmen on a daily rental basis. Harry had started small and grown to the point where he had over $500,000 invested in stock. One day his store manager told him that the demand for paint spraying equipment was often higher than their stock, and customers who telephoned or came in to the rental office often had to be turned away.

   Harry had become very sensitive to the issue of cost and profit effectiveness recently as the rentals industry in the region had just had two new market entrants and competition was heating up. He had recently analyzed sales for much of his stock and sold off a number of items that had low demand and were generating virtually no profit. These included his fleet of six ride-on lawnmowers and 10 snow ploughs.

   He had estimated the marginal cost of each item of his inventory including finance (investment) costs, maintenance costs, and storage costs. There were currently five spray painting machines, which had a marginal variable daily cost of $2 each, assuming they were continuously used.

   His sales records indicated that the number of units rented over the past 270 days were:

| *Units Rented* | *Frequency* |
|---:|---:|
| 0 | 15 |
| 1 | 22 |
| 2 | 56 |
| 3 | 65 |
| 4 | 48 |
| ALL 5 | 64 |

He wondered how many times out of the 64 days, when all five were rented, that more than five would have rented if he had had them in stock. The daily rental on a spray painter was $20 (10 times its marginal cost). Harry did not want to miss out on satisfying any demand, but on the other hand, did not want to have any more units than was justifiable on a profit basis.

He decided to take a marginal approach and consider buying one or two more units. He asked his assistant how often, when all five existing units were rented, did more people request spray painters. His assistant said that when all five units were out: "It seemed like half the time somebody wants one and we can't supply and on half of those occasions there is actually more than an extra unit needed because at least two people ask for spray painters and we're out."

*a.* Harry deduced (from his sales records and from his assistant's statement) the complete probability distribution of demand. Calculate this distribution. Use this distribution to calculate the expected value of buying one or two more machines.

*b.* After Harry had decided what to do about the spray painters, his assistant pointed out that many people who rented sprayers also rented extension ladders, planks, and wallpaper strippers. Of those who asked for sprayers and were turned away, none came back a day or two later or made future reservations, and none of them rented anything else. After sampling a number of sales dockets, Harry estimated that the additional profit from any person renting a sprayer averaged $15. He wasn't sure whether this should be accounted for in his paint sprayer decision (because the additional profit was on other items). Should this factor be taken into account? Give reasons for your point of view. How does this factor affect the decision?

10. Consider the single-stage decision tree problem given in Example 3–2. Does a single-stage decision tree representation adequately cover all the factors in this decision? When the baker discussed the problem of optimal production quantities with his wife (who had an MBA from a leading business school), she gave him an explanation along the following lines:

"An important assumption in this model is the **direction of influences** of the variables. It was assumed above that profit is affected by the decision variable $Q$, the random variable $D$ and the known constant values of $P$, $C$, and $P(D)$. These input variables to the profit equation were assumed to be independent of each other (that is, they were assumed to have no affect on each other). Although this model may seem entirely reasonable at first, let us further consider some possible relationships between these parameters.

Consider a case where the production quantity $Q$ has an effect on $P(D)$. For example, if you stop making cakes altogether, would $P(D)$ stay the same over time? The likelihood is that demand would soon fall off. Potential customers would stop demanding the product after repeatedly being told that none was available. You would lose business and perhaps goodwill, leading to potential losses of sales in other product lines.

"By similar reasoning, if you choose to produce a larger number of cakes than appears optimal (such as four), would the extra cakes (displayed in the window) generate extra demand in comparison to the situation where only two cakes were produced?

"It does appear that the simple model as outlined above may not completely encompass all such situations. Could we modify it to account for such secondary influences as the effect of $Q$ on $P(D)$, and if so, how could it be done?"

More generally, the baker's wife noted that an important point arising from the cake example above is that during the process of and after we have constructed a model, no matter how simple it is, we should very carefully consider the assumptions we made, both explicit and implicit. So-called secondary effects, such as the longer-term influence of $Q$ on $P(D)$, can be very important and failure to account for them can lead to a poor decision. The important lesson to be learned from this exercise is that model structure should never be taken for granted, but rather should be closely examined. Structural sensitivity analysis is a central element of decision analysis. The baker wondered whether there were any real problems that could reasonably be represented as single-stage decisions. Express a view about this, illustrating your answer with an example.

11. You are faced with the following decision. A rich uncle has left you \$100,000 in his will. You are considering only two possible alternatives, one of which is a risk-free investment with a return of 12% per year, and the other is an investment in a stock portfolio venture that you have estimated will return 5% with probability 0.3, 10% with probability 0.4, and 20% with probability 0.3. Which do you choose?

    Of course there is no right or wrong answer to this question because the decision involves personal preference. Even though it is a relatively simple single-stage decision with only one source of uncertainty, many people find such choices difficult.

    Now suppose a third choice becomes available. This option has the possibilities of 3% return with probability 0.4, 10% return with probability 0.2, 15% return with probability 0.3, and 30% return with probability 0.1. Which option do you prefer now? The comparison of options literally involves comparing probability distributions, and the conceptual difficulties involved in this process lead us to use rules such as expected value as discussed earlier. Explain your choice.

12. Consider a decision faced by Professor Bob Ambivalent who recently left his job at the University of Chicago to take up a position in a foreign country. Professor Ambivalent is of two minds about whether he should sell his house in Chicago. The problem is complex because his future is uncertain. He may or may not like living overseas and may want to return to the United States after a short period, or perhaps a long period. If and when he does return to the United States, he is uncertain about whether it will be to Chicago, either to work at his old job or at another location within driving distance of his current house. Bob and his wife are also considering having another child, in which case the current house would be too small anyway. Mrs. Ambivalent said that even if they don't ever come back to live in the house, it could be rented and might turn out to be a good investment. On the other hand, Bob knew that if they didn't sell the house they couldn't afford to buy another when they arrived overseas and would have to live in a rented house themselves. He wasn't convinced that real estate in Chicago would be a good investment in the medium or long term but had been advised that good capital gains would probably occur in the next 18–24 months.

    Bob and his wife agreed that the decision was a hard one because of the many decision elements and their interrelationships. It was also a very important decision for them because their house was their biggest financial asset, and the decision could affect their lives for many years.

    Bob and Rita (Mrs. Ambivalent) discussed the various possibilities at length before Bob finally said, "We're just going around in circles and need to get a handle on the decision." Bob felt a need to simplify the decision and introduce some structure to their thinking. "We have an immediate decision," he said, "to sell or keep the house. If we don't sell it right now, we can always change our minds and sell it later, say in a year or two. By then we'll know whether we want to come back and live in Chicago or not. If we sell the house we could invest the money and get a good return with little risk, whereas it's a gamble to just keep it as an investment. Nobody knows what's going to happen to housing prices." Bob was familiar with decision trees and began to sketch one (shown as Figure 3–14).

**FIGURE 3–14** Mr. and Mrs. Ambivalent's Initial Decision Tree

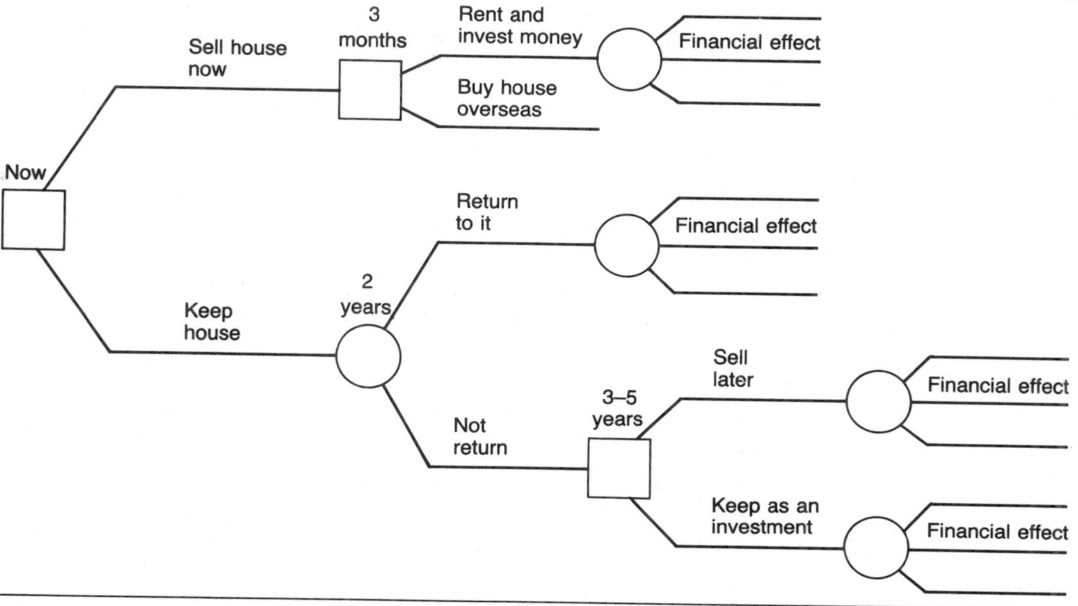


Rita said that the diagram helped her see things more clearly, but that she didn't want to live in a rented house for more than a year, or at the most two. Bob agreed with her but suggested that before they started making preference statements and choices, they should review their options. "The decision tree diagram is a simplified representation of the real thing in many ways," said Bob. "I have assumed certain dates for various things to happen, such as, in two years we will either return to live in the house or not. In fact we may return earlier or later than that, or not at all, but two years is a representative possibility. Time is a continuous variable, and I have just assumed some likely dates associated with various decision points. The financial effects of our decisions are uncertain in all cases, except if we sell the house and invest all the money in risk-free assets, which we won't do. Those uncertain effects are shown at the end of each branch on the tree. Also, it's possible that in two years or so we will want to come back to Chicago and live in the house, but I can't be sure of getting a job close enough to it." Rita said that it made sense to keep it if it was likely they would return to the vicinity in two or three years, but Bob qualified this by saying that this was only so if the housing market went up at least a little during that period. He pointed out that if the house didn't appreciate in value, they would be sorry if they didn't sell it because they could get 15–20% return on their investments through buying bonds. "The rent will just pay the mortgage, taxes, and expenses, so if prices don't go up, it's a poor investment. In that case we could get a 50% return over three years in the bond market and buy a much nicer house if we do return," explained Bob.

"Yes, I can see the pluses and minuses of keeping the house, but how can we know when these various things will happen, what will happen to housing prices, and whether we will return?" asked Rita. "I think we had better think about this on a year-by-year basis. Also, how can we account for my dislike for renting houses? I don't mind doing it for a short period, but now that we've owned our own home, I don't want to rent for long. We'll need a bigger place anyway if we have another baby."

Bob responded by saying that the problem was complex, and he couldn't cram everything onto a decision tree, but he would try again. "OK, let's take it year by year," he said. Figure 3–15 shows his year 1 decision tree diagram.

After drawing the tree with only a one-year time horizon (shown as Figure 3–15), Bob tried to expand it by adding on to each branch the possible actions and uncertain events that could occur in year 2.

Although the idea of constructing a multiperiod year-by-year tree was a good one in theory, Bob and Rita soon found out that it was impossible in practice. A decision tree showing all possibilities over

**FIGURE 3–15** Decision Tree for Year 1 Only for the House Sale Decision

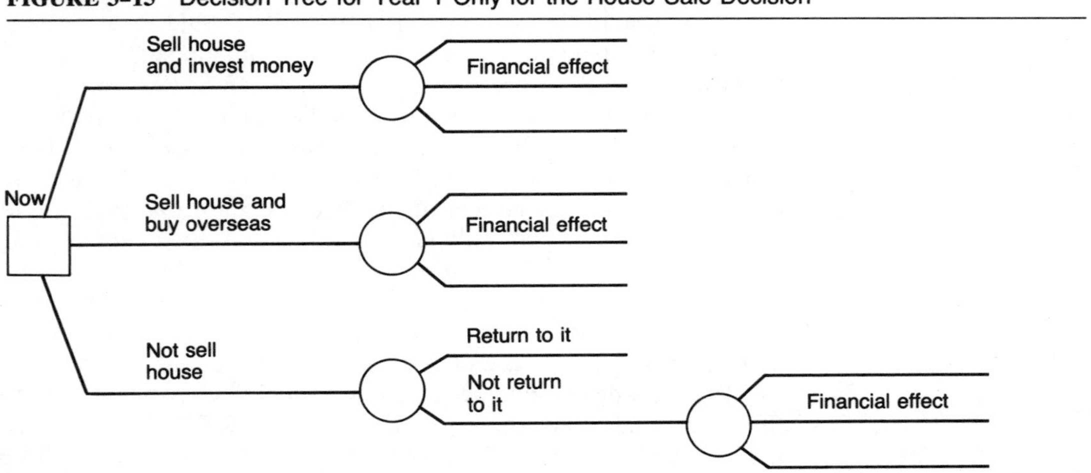

just two years looks more like a bushy mess than a tree (try constructing one for yourself!) Attempting to construct a year-by-year decision tree over a five-year period would have proved to be a frustrating and fruitless task for Mr. and Mrs. Ambivalent. However the process of constructing Figure 3–15 did provide them with some insight about the decision, and about their original decision tree (shown as Figure 3–14). They realized that a lot could be gained by using a relatively simple decision tree, such as Figure 3–14, and examining the effects of altering the assumptions they made in its construction. There is generally much to be gained from relaxing or changing various assumptions (abstractions from reality) that are inherent in the model and observing the results of those changes. For example, Bob assumed that if they did return to live in the house, it might be in two years. It is useful to know what the effect on the model would be if this two-year assumption were changed to some other value, such as six months, one year, three years, or five years. This type of sensitivity analysis involves changing a single parameter in the model while keeping the rest of the decision tree structure the same. The parametric sensitivity analysis is useful once a suitable decision tree structure is established.

Bob and Rita also considered some structural sensitivity analysis. For example, on their original decision tree (Figure 3–14) Bob had not explicitly included the complicating factor of the house becoming too small if the Ambivalent's decided to have another baby. Bob began to think about restructuring the tree to include this possibility because if they returned to the house in one or two years and then shortly afterward decided to have a baby (and move to a bigger house), perhaps it would be more sensible to sell it now. He began including this factor on the tree and restructuring it when he remembered having previously had plans drawn up for an addition to the house.

*a.* How could decision analysis aid the Ambivalents in their decision? To answer compare the process described above with an unaided (intuitive) one.

*b.* If Bob approached you, as a friend or colleague, and asked for your advice, what further refinements in model structuring would you recommend?

13. Use ARBORIST to solve problem 5 (above).
14. Use ARBORIST to solve problem 7 (above).
15. Structure the decision facing Harry's Hire Company (problem 9, above) using ARBORIST. In which ways was ARBORIST able to be a useful part of the decision analysis process?
16. Figure 3–10 shows a decision tree representation for the Boston Beer example.

*a*. Does this decision tree adequately represent all of the factors involved in the problem? Critically evaluate the quality of this decision tree as a representation of the problem.
*b*. What sources of complexity might exist that are not addressed by the decision tree (Figure 3–10)?
*c*. What additional elements could be encompassed in the decision tree model? How would you include them in the model?
*d*. What are the benefits from using a decision analysis approach in this kind of decision?

17. Figure 3–3 represents a refined decision tree for the jet engine decision. How can a manager who starts with a simple representation such as Figure 3–1, and then grows and refines it to Figure 3–2 and Figure 3–3, know when to stop including more and more elements on a decision tree?

---

## Case Study

# Atlanta Photo Finishers (A)

Atlanta Photo Finishers (APF) began as a single store in Westgate Mall shopping center, a large suburban shopping center in Atlanta. Its owner/operator, Richard Doleson had struck a very good bargain and took over a lease from an ailing dry cleaning business. The deal included many of the shop fittings. He installed an automatic photo processing machine (Grummer model G440) imported from West Germany. It produced extremely high-quality prints and was very reliable, although replacement parts had been a problem initially.

The success of the business in Westgate Mall led to the purchase of three more stores in Atlanta, all of which were fully owned by Mr. Doleson. With four stores, it was worthwhile for him to advertise in the daily Atlanta newspapers and on local TV. APF's policy was to provide a high-quality product with a guarantee of "ready in 45 minutes or free." The capacity and reliability of the processing machines had ensured that free processing had only been provided on two occasions per month per store (on average). APF charged significantly more for its product than low-priced competitors such as K mart, and an analysis of credit card sales receipts had shown that there was a lot of repeat business. To attract new customers, particularly after opening a new store, Mr. Doleson offered free sets of second prints and a sweepstakes-style competition for customers, with photographic equipment and free developing as prizes.

In March 1986 his accountant and friend Robert (Bob) Willis had suggested that the business was very well cashed up and ready for further expansion.

Mr. Doleson analyzed the Atlanta area in terms of present population, demand for his product, the competitive situation, and possibilities for future growth, and concluded that the Atlanta market was or soon would be saturated with fast photo finishers (FPFs). He could identify only one more possible site for a fifth store in Atlanta and felt that profitability there might not be as high as in other stores because of the location. Further, the position was such that some of the potential business from this fifth store might reduce sales from two of his other APF sites. Bob and Richard agreed that the potential was there for profit, but probably less than in the other stores. They also realized that in the longer term, business growth would have to be outside Atlanta, and quite possibly outside Georgia.

Richard knew that the German machine he used was not being used anywhere else in the country, and he had deliberately kept very quiet about the machine's excellent cost effectiveness and reliability when talking to other people in the industry. He and Bob talked at length about the possibilities of expansion outside Atlanta, and they decided that there were two major possibilities:

1. Expanding APF-owned stores.
2. Setting up a franchise system.

There were many factors Richard knew he would have to consider. He also wanted to make the right decision about the potential fifth store in Atlanta, knowing that its profitability was uncertain to a greater extent than his other stores and that it might even cost two of his other stores some of their sales.

Bob advised him that if he wanted to raise some money in the form of debt to finance an expansion outside Atlanta (say three or four stores in another city, as a first step), he could do so almost immediately, but if the fifth outlet in Atlanta was opened, then it would be about 12 months before the company's liquid asset position would be suitable to attract debt financing at good rates. Bob also suggested that Richard should consider taking on one or more partners to finance an expansion, otherwise the expansion would be limited in pace by growth through reinvestment (and leveraged by limited debt financing).

On the other hand, franchising appeared to be an attractive alternative, in that the franchisees provided capital and bore much of the risk associated with individual store locations. Richard laughingly commented to Bob: "I could be the Colonel Sanders of fast photo finishing." Richard pointed out that franchising meant that he would have less risk on his shoulders but also less return, in that he would probably earn a small share of sales or net profits from such a system. He pointed out that if he franchised, his management skills, which he felt were the key to his past success, would not easily be transferred. Bob replied that even if he expanded and retained some or all of the ownership, his hands-on management activity of each branch would be severely diluted. "Suppose you borrow some money and/or take on a partner and in five years you have 20 stores in four or five states," said Bob. "Your role will be strategic management, and top-level decision making. If you want to expand, whether by franchise, debt-financed, or equity-financed ownership, your days of close supervision of branch operations are over."

Richard said that there were a number of things he was uncertain about. The first was the effect of the various expansion strategies on cash flow and profit. He reasoned that if he raised some money through a loan or by selling some shares in the business, he could open about three new branches very quickly and then decide whether or not to try to float a national franchise system. Alternatively, he could set up a franchise system almost immediately. He was uncertain about how quickly such a system would grow given the stiff competition in the major cities.

Richard was also uncertain about how his relationship with Grummer Corporation would develop. "I currently have an excellent relationship with Grummer. They will soon be taking orders for their new model G660 and are also looking for significant U.S. sales in the next few years. If we can expand rapidly and broadly there are two possibilities. The first is that I will be able to get a very good discount by making a bulk purchase of their machines. The second is that I could become Grummer's sole U.S. importing agent, gaining control of their U.S. operation. This would also allow me to get excellent prices and service on the machines in my own store. These factors will significantly affect the profitability of my stores and my competitive position in any new markets I enter. Whether we expand by franchise or partially debt financed ownership, the deal I make with Grummer will be a key factor in my profitability and competitiveness. If I can get a 30% discount or more by buying about 15 G660 processors, then APF branches will be the lowest cost competitors in most markets. This, in combination with our high-quality product, should be a formula for real success."

## CASE QUESTION

Construct a decision tree model representing the problem described above.

*a.* What assumptions were made in this modeling process?
*b.* How could the model help in the resolution of the problem?

## CASE STUDY

### Superior Power and Gas Company (A)

Superior Power and Gas Company generates electricity and distributes gas and electricity to nearly 3 million people in an industrial northern state. A decision must soon be made that will have far reaching consequences for many years to come in the company. The decision concerning the future of the Parkville nuclear plant at the time (late 1985) had become a major headache for the company. It was substantially over budget and substantially behind its construction schedule.

The nuclear power industry grew significantly in the 1950s and 1960s and was spurred on by the energy crisis of the mid 1970s. By 1985 there were 120 commercial power reactors operating. The early 1980s had been a very bad period for the industry. Over 100 reactor orders had been cancelled and most plants under construction were experiencing delays, construction and regulation problems, and huge cost overruns. For example, Seabrook 1 and 2 were originally projected at a cost of \$970 million. Seabrook 1 was budgeted in 1985 at \$4.5 billion. Washington Power

Supply System was bankrupted by its nuclear plant construction program. Many plants were abandoned after very substantial investments had been made in them, for example Midland after it was 85% complete and Marble Hill after 50%.

Nuclear plants are complex and difficult to construct. For example, a coal fired plant may have 200 critical pipe hangers, and a nuclear plant may have over 5,000. Construction and safety standards required in nuclear plants are very much higher than in other facilities.

In 1972 a decision was made to install two reactors at Parkville costing roughly $550 million each including generating equipment. The first was due on line in 1982 and was planned to provide sufficient generating capacity until 1986 when the second would come on line. The second reactor was planned to bring the company's capacity to the point where three small, old coal fired plants could be phased out. As early as 1977 it was realized that projected demand levels for the 1980s and beyond would not eventuate, and plans for the second reactor were scrapped (essentially wasting $52 million in feasibility studies and preliminary site preparation and construction costs).

Reactor 1 was continued. In the early 1980s expensive design modifications caused substantial delays. The Nuclear Regulatory Commission (NRC) was insisting on high standards and tolerances that were rigidly enforced. The reactor system was now at a point where $2.1 billion had been spent, and the company's best estimate was for a total cost of $4.2 billion and a September 1987 start up! Management generally agreed that in retrospect they had made a poor decision to go nuclear, had chosen an inexperienced general contractor, and had grossly misestimated the complexity and cost of the construction process. It was little comfort to them to know that many other utilities around the country were in similar positions.

The present difficulties had been developing for a considerable time, and Superior's senior management had, with the agreement of the State Regulatory Commission, called in a consultant to assist them. The consultant had been called in to evaluate the future actions of Superior specifically with respect to Parkville. The company had received a lot of adverse publicity over the past six months, and both the local media and the public were pressuring the State Regulatory Commission to force Superior's shareholders to bear much of the burden of the plant costs rather than include them in the rate base (i.e., electricity prices).

The consultant arranged an initial strategy meeting to suggest and consider future options for the Parkville site.

The strategy meeting (held on Monday, November 11, 1985) was attended by the company president, three senior vice presidents, the Parkville site project manager, and two partners from the consulting company. One of the consultants, David Short, opened the meeting by saying that the consultants' report would become part of the public record, and would probably have some bearing on the State Regulatory Commission's attitude towards the next rate hearing. He explained that there was no intent to investigate past decisions or lay blame on anybody for the present situation, but simply to look to the future. He asked what the options were for Parkville.

The company president outlined a number of alternatives. "We could shut down the whole thing on virtually 24-hours' notice," he said. "Of course many of the contracts have cancellation penalty provisions, which would have to be paid, but if we were to shut down, let's remember that the average daily construction cost right now is $2.1 million, so I don't want to waste too much time. If a complete abandonment of the project is justified, we could survive financially, and, who knows, in 5 or 10 years we may use the site for coal or nuclear based power generation. That would depend on demand, which is highly uncertain over that time horizon. The current economic climate leads us to project a sharp decline in industrial demand over the next four years. If that turns around, Parkville could be needed by the early 1990s. Shutting down the plant and then starting up later would be very expensive. We might be better off finishing the containment building and reactor and leaving the generators if we choose to shutdown.

"Of course a second alternative is to press on. We are doing better now than we were this time last year and we have established a good relationship with the NRC. Since Rabel Pleck resigned last June, Mike Decker (the new site manager) has established an excellent management team and, we feel, much better control. There is still a problem with forecasting both the total completion cost and the demand for power 10 years away. Just last week, for example, we realized that we had to redesign the pipe system in the reactor vessel because of stress fracturing problems that other similar reactors are having in operation. We are still recovering from the shock of the NRC announcement, but our early estimate is about $30 or $40 million in extra cost." "You can probably nearly double that," said Mike Decker, "if past experience means anything."

David Short then asked a number of questions and understood from the answers that if demand in the 1990s was as low as some industry analysts were projecting, it would be much cheaper not to start up the plant when it was finished in 1987, but to import small amounts of power from the grid as needed. It was agreed that even if the plant was successfully completed on time and at a cost close to the latest budget, the company might not be able to justify operating it until about 1993 on the basis of projected demand levels. "Of course everything is relative, and this depends on the cost of our coal-based power and imports," said the senior vice president of operations, Fred N. Burdge.

David Short then raised the question of scrapping the nuclear technology but still developing Parkville as a coal fired plant.

"Yes," said Mr. Burdge, "we could convert to coal but there again we are up against great conversion and construction costs, and the problem of the new acid rain legislation." The state government was about to begin a process of legislation applying to coal fired plants that could require new stringent emission standards. "At this stage we just don't know how tough they are going to get, but insiders tell us that things may well be very much more stringent for new plants than existing ones. That could mean expensive scrubbers and other air and water cleaning processes or even that new coal fired plants are virtually out of the question altogether," said Mr. Burdge.

"You are limiting your thinking to local or midwest coal, which is high in sulfur content," said Mr. Decker. "What about other, better-grade, cleaner coals that are available, admittedly at higher cost?" "As an alternative to making a commitment to coal right now, we could wait and see what the preliminary legislation looks like, and try and have some say in it," said Mr. Burdge. "Over the next nine months while the legislation process proceeds, we could do a preliminary design and feasibility study within the company of a coal conversion."

Mr. Short asked if the wait-and-see idea on the coal legislation would mean continuing the nuclear plant construction or stopping. He was told that either was possible, but that it was probably not worth stopping because over that period the nature of the current contracts was such that little would be saved by stopping, but much would be lost if construction were halted and a later decision made to continue with nuclear power. He also asked about an immediate commitment to convert to coal. "Would you build in scrubbers or not?"

Mr. Burdge explained that choices were available. The company could design to current emission standards and add on the necessary extras later, or modify the design to include scrubbers but not spend any money on them until the legislation issue was settled.

Mike Decker made some concluding comments about the state of gloom prevailing in the company. He said that everyone was upset about Parkville, and had been for some time, but that at least they were now going to seriously consider its future and commit themselves to a positive decision. He reasoned that they might well have to bury some past mistakes and admit that a lot of the money that had been sunk into the project would never be recovered.

David Short said that he would need a day or so to structure the problem as he saw it initially and would be back shortly, seeking further information and opinions from various people. He and his colleague started mapping out what they saw as the major options available to the company.

## CASE QUESTION

Draw a decision tree to represent the problem. What further data would be required to make a choice?

CHAPTER FOUR

# Probability Assessment

## OUTLINE



## OBJECTIVES

After completing this chapter, you should be able to:

1. Discuss the importance of explicitly recognizing uncertainty (using probability) in decision analysis models.
2. Define uncertain quantities in managerial problems as probabilistic (chance event) variables in decision analysis models.
3. Use a variety of methods for subjectively assessing probability distributions for uncertain quantities.
4. Discuss the notions of objective and subjective probability.
5. Use the basic rules of probability to define and combine probability values as required on decision trees.
6. Discuss the concepts of probability as the language of uncertainty, and define conditional and joint probability concepts.
7. Discuss the particular assessment and decision-making aspects of rare events.
8. Construct probability distributions in various forms, for continuous and discrete variables.

## INTRODUCTION

This chapter is concerned with the assessment of probabilities that describe the likelihood of chance events. Once a decision tree is structured, it is very useful to quantify these likelihoods using a probability scale. The expression of probabilities is very helpful in allowing the decision analyst to identify a preferred decision strategy. The concept of making judgments about event likelihoods, and expressing them as probabilities, is simple yet very powerful. The **simplicity** of probability is in its definition: as a measurement scale, in the range zero to one, it is simply a representation of the degree of likelihood of occurrence for a defined event. The **power** of probability in decision trees is in having a numerical measure that is easy to understand and that efficiently communicates information about likelihood. Probabilities are also useful as a direct input component to our most robust decision rules, which are expected value rules.[1] Probabilities are therefore an important part of decision analysis.

In dealing with probabilistic concepts we must be aware of a number of issues, including various possible interpretations of probability, assessment techniques, and human information processing biases. The first two of these issues are examined in detail in this chapter, and the question of biases is treated in Chapter 13.

Decision analysis purports to successfully account for uncertainty in decision modeling. In order to accomplish this, it is imperative that the decision maker has a good **understanding** of probabilistic concepts and has developed some **skills** in probability assessment. Readers who are unfamiliar with the basic definitions, concepts, and rules of probability, including joint probability, conditional probability, and the rules of addition and multiplication should read the appendix at the end of this chapter.

## OBJECTIVE AND SUBJECTIVE INTERPRETATIONS OF PROBABILITY

There are a number of different viewpoints that can be taken about probability. It is important to remember that probability is an abstract concept. Uncertainty (as measured by probability) cannot be touched, smelled, tasted, seen, or heard, yet either formally or informally we all deal with it nearly every day. Many people never deal with probability in any formal manner, yet they still make decisions involving uncertain quantities. The informal treatment of probability (or at least of uncertainty) generally involves a heuristic process of considering the likelihood of an event and integrating it into the decision process.

---

[1] Expected values are probability weighted averages of values.

---

## EXAMPLE 4–1

### A Truck Driver Decision

Consider an interstate truck driver who has just made a delivery and is considering dropping in at a particular dock to see if a return load is available. He would probably consider the following elements:

1. The cost of going to the dock.
2. The benefit derived from going to the dock if a load is available.

Can he make a good decision based on these two factors alone? Suppose that the dock is out of his way and the total cost of going there to check the load board is $50. If a load is available that suits him (in terms of load size and destination) his operating profit will be $200. Should he risk $50 to possibly make $200? What additional information would be useful in order to make a good decision about whether to go to the dock or not?

---

It would be most useful if the truck driver knew something about the **likelihood** of a suitable load being available. If we put ourselves in the position of the truck driver, would we go to the dock if:

1. A load was very unlikely to be available?
2. A load was highly likely to be available?

From this example we can see that *the likelihood of key events can be of critical importance in decision processes*. Further, cost and profit are decision elements measured in terms of money whereas likelihood is not. How then can we estimate, interpret, and integrate probability concepts into our decision processes? There are two major interpretations of probability. The first interpretation of probability is objective and relates to the process of calculating probabilities using relative frequency data or statistical techniques. The second interpretation is subjective, defined to include all objective factors as well as less tangible factors such as the expertise of decision makers. Subjective probabilities represent the degree of belief of the decision maker. The distinction between objective and subjective processes of estimating and interpreting applies to both probabilistic and point estimate assessment.

**Subjective probability** in decision analysis is judgmental, in that various inputs such as those based on data, calculated probability distribution-based elements, and degree of belief can all be encompassed in the probabilities placed on decision trees. The relative weighting given to different sources of information that may contribute to a probabilistic estimate depends on the availability and reliability of those information sources, and these weightings are generally a matter of judgment. Some probability estimates are dominated by data based evidence. For example the likelihood of an insured driver making a claim on his auto insurance policy may be based on relative frequency information from a large data base. Some probabilities may be based on calculated or modeled deductions. For example, the probability of winning in a number lottery, where the player chooses eight numbers and must include a particular set of 5 from a set of 40, can be calculated. Often, we have neither good, appropriate data nor can we calculate a probability that we need for a decision tree. In such cases, expert opinions in the form of subjective assessments may be the dominant element of a probability estimate. For example, a new product technology, unlike any other, may or may not become a marketing success. If there are no similar experiences to call upon, then the degree of belief of people who have knowledge about the product and the market become the critical input to the probability estimate.

In decision analysis we must often model decisions that have ramifications extending well into the future. Our uncertainty is often a result of our inability to know the future. To make plans and decisions, we produce forecasts, both of future events and of the probabilities of those events. In these forecasts, the events and their probabilities may again be based mainly on calculation, data, and extrapolation, or mainly subjective judgment. Let us compare and contrast sales forecasts made by two companies, as follows:

---

## Example 4–2

### Sales Forecasting at King Gee

A marketing manager at King Gee Pants wished to forecast sales for 35 product lines of overalls, jeans, shorts, trousers, and shirts. He used an extrapolative forecasting procedure that isolated and measured the trend and seasonal effects in sales for each product over the past 10 years. The extrapolation to produce future sales forecasts merely involved the continuation of the past average trend and seasonal differences. This process was performed on a computer using the past sales data in a mathematical formula to calculate the future sales predictions.

## EXAMPLE 4–3

### Sales Forecasting at Avon International

Avon International sells many different cosmetic and personal hygiene products to regions in Europe, Australasia, Africa, and South America. These products are usually also sold in the United States and are often released there a few months before they are included in foreign catalogs. Avon International needs to forecast sales for each geographic region for each product line so that production and shipping arrangements can be made. Underestimation of demand usually means long delays in supplying customers. Overestimation means that production and shipping costs are incurred as a loss. How then should Avon estimate sales? For example, how many thousand cases of a particular perfume will sell in Europe? For new products (which are regularly introduced) there is no local sales history, and experience has shown that very little can be learned from U.S. sales about the success or failure of a product overseas.

The sales forecasting process at Avon involved a group of about six experienced marketing managers sitting in conference and attempting to estimate sales based on factors that include product design and quality, market size, market competition, economic forecasts, and price.

The integration of these factors was generally done on an intuitive, subjective basis, and although there was often disagreement and debate, the Avon group always produced a sales forecast.

---

Let us contrast the King Gee and Avon forecasting procedures. The King Gee process was relatively analytic and objective in that the feelings and beliefs about sales of the marketing manager were not inputs to the model. On the other hand the Avon process was relatively subjective because the beliefs of the assessors were the main basis of the forecasts. In the Avon process there was little hard data, either calculated or based on historical fact, that could be used.

It is important to note that within the decision analysis paradigm there is usually no such thing as a purely objective measurement or assessment. For example, in the King Gee forecasting process, decisions requiring judgment (hence subjective input) were made about the form of the forecasting model and the relevance of various data sets. Also, extrapolative models, such as the one used by King Gee, assume steady state (that is, the market did not and will not change its underlying structure during the forecast period), and the acceptance of such assumptions also requires judgment. Although a mathematical (and hence seemingly objective) method was used by King Gee, it was surrounded by a number of judgments about its use, design, and result.

We often judge the suitability of a model by the result it produces. If a forecasting model produces a result that seems ridiculous, we question the validity of the model to a greater extent than we would if the result was close to our expectations. This process of judging the result is also very much a subjective one.

We reemphasize that probabilities can be calculated or based solely on past data. For most situations, these types of estimates are inputs to a subjective process. At King Gee, for example, the model output forecasts were examined and used in conjunction with statements like "the economy seems to be turning down right now, but the downturn is not reflected in the model." This subjective process had a large objective component but was certainly not purely objective.

For probabilistic assessment, just as for point estimate assessment, there is sometimes a great deal of objective input in an assessment, and sometimes virtually none.

---

## EXAMPLE 4–4

### Weather Forecasting

Consider the uncertain quantity: "the probability that it will rain tomorrow where I live." How could we assess this probability? Many methods are available, for example:

1. Meteorological models are based on atmospheric conditions and movements including measurement of temperature, barometric pressure, cloud cover, moisture, and other factors. Very complex computerized models are used to generate weather forecasts, and these forecasts can include estimates of probabilities of rain.
2. A very different approach is to use relative frequency information. For example, we could consider the past 50 years of weather data and count up the number of times it has rained on days with tomorrow's date.
3. A third distinct method would be to informally analyze the current weather situation and other factors and make a purely subjective assessment.

All three of these approaches have some value. A fourth approach is to combine information from all practically useful sources, including structural models, relative frequency information, and subjective judgment. This general subjective approach is inherent in decision analysis. With respect to weather forecasting, a decision maker who must account for the weather in his decisions (for example, a farmer) could use structural models and forecasts, relative frequency information, and any other sources to assess parameters such as the probability of rain. In such a process, many subjective judgments must be made, not only as expressions of the general degree of belief or intuitive feelings of the decision maker or expert. Subjective judgments must also be made regarding the validity, calibration, and accuracy of structural models and relative frequency data. This point can be illustrated by considering the probability of a hard frost in central Florida during a particular winter. This probability could be estimated using long-term forecasts produced by the National Weather Service. Alternatively, relative frequency data is available for over 100 years. This estimate of the probability of a hard frost is of great importance to orange growers, orange juice companies, and orange juice commodity traders. Is there a way of **objectively** providing an accurate estimate of this probability? Most subjectivists (people who subscribe to the subjective interpretation of probability) would argue that there is not, on the basis that the forecasts based on structural models and relative frequency data involved various judgments in themselves. In the case of relative frequency data, should we use all of the past 100 years or just the past 10 or 20 years, or some other scheme? Is the recent data to be given the same weight in the forecast as the less recent data? In the case of the structural model, assumptions involving subjective elements were made about structural form and the use of data. Subjectivists argue that all assessment processes are subjective, but fully recognize that hard data generated by models and relative frequency sources may have an important role to play in our assessment process.

---

## EXAMPLE 4–5

### Child Support Enforcement

The State of Illinois Department of Public Aid and many other state agencies are charged with the task of administering and enforcing a system of child support payments, primarily by fathers who are living apart from their children.

In an effort to target groups who are likely (and also groups who are unlikely) to regularly pay their obligated amounts, a study was done relating probability of payment to various characteristics of a case. Case characteristics such as age, address, employment status, and type, were used to explain payment probability using a regression model. The model was used to predict payment probability for any case based on a set of case characteristics. This objective process became an important part of the judgmental process made by caseworkers and interviewers who recommend what action should be taken (court, delay, administrative hearing) for that case.

This is an example where a model plays a major role in probabilistic assessment. There is however, an important subjective element used to interpret the model output in deriving a final estimate and choosing a decision strategy because the model does not measure all relevant factors and because the model design was itself chosen as part of a process of judgment.

---

These arguments can be summarized by reference to Figures 4–1 and 4–2. Figure 4–1 shows an objective estimation process. One appealing characteristic of such processes is their ability to consistently reproduce results. Given a set of inputs, an objective process can be understood in terms of the structured way it converts inputs to outputs.

A subjective process is shown in Figure 4–2. Such a process is not necessarily capable of being mathematically structured or programmed because it involves judgment and intuition. It may include one or more objective processes within it, however it subjectively interprets the output of objective processes and combines these with opinion, intuition, and relevant judgments to produce estimates and forecasts. One shortcoming of subjective processes is that inaccuracies and biases occur in these procedures of combining and processing information from various sources.

**FIGURE 4–1** Representation of an Objective Process

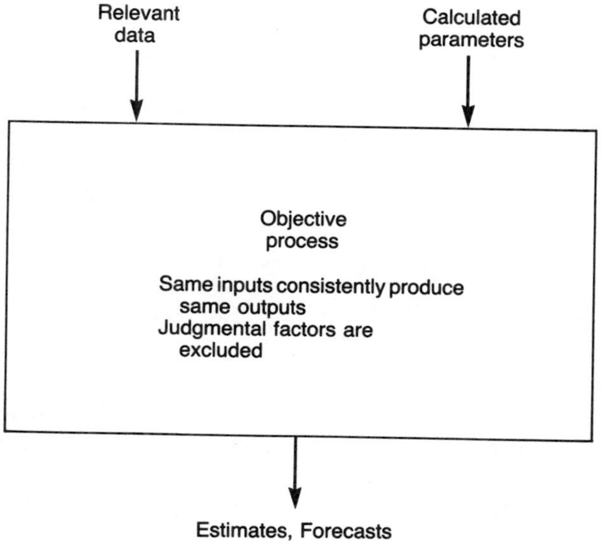

**FIGURE 4–2** Representation of a Subjective Process

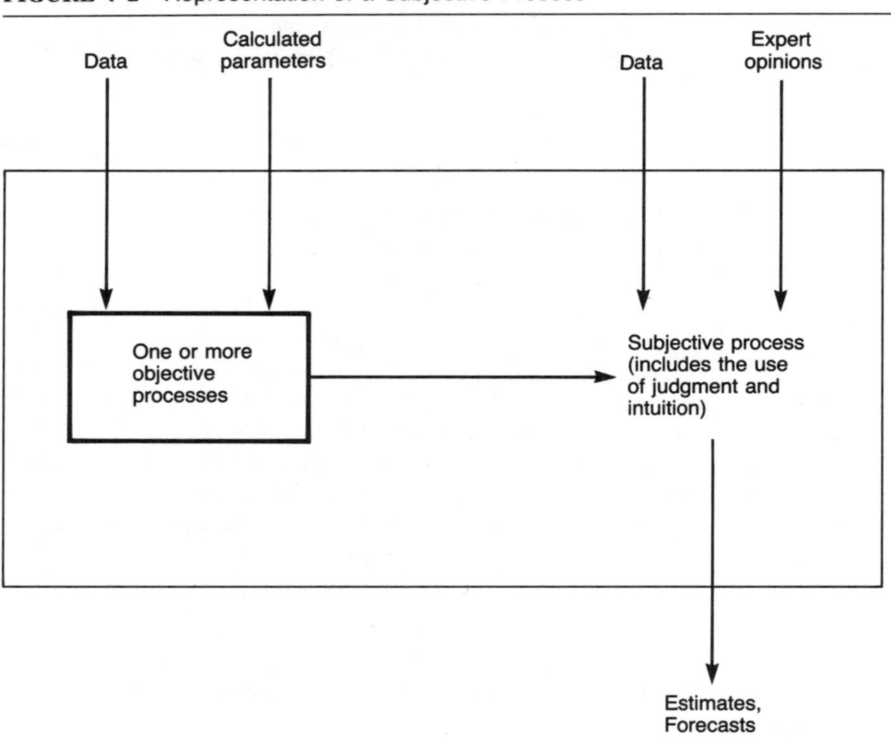


Objective processes are often thought of as exact and subjective processes as inexact or fuzzy. Although there is a lot of truth to these common conceptions, they do not represent the whole truth in terms of what is important in decision-making processes. For example, expert opinions may be a very valuable source of information for a forecast even though they are subjective.

Subjective probabilities and assessment procedures are imperfect, however the alternative to using expert opinions and other subjective inputs in decision making is to ignore the subjective element. Like problem solving and decision making, subjective probability assessment is an art, not a science, yet we can be scientific about calibrating our subjective assessment processes so as to minimize biases. There are at least two ways of reducing the biases that exist in subjective processes:

1. Use objective rules and aids to supplement, guide, and calibrate subjective processes. A very good example is the use of a probability

rule called Bayes Theorem for combining probabilistic sources of information.

2. Training in subjective assessment procedures has been demonstrated to produce better (that is, less biased) assessments.

---

## EXAMPLE 4–6

### Marina Development[2]

A state government was considering the development of a Marina in a popular resort region. The governor instructed the relevant department to conduct a feasibility study. An important criterion for the development was that it would pay for itself, that is, taxpayers' money would not be used. Hence the construction would be financed primarily by bonds and would only go ahead if there was a very high likelihood of at least breaking even. The director of the responsible state agency was faced with the task of estimating the demand for boating berths at the proposed marina. Specifically, he had commissioned a preliminary design for a marina with 220 berths, and at a current market rate, had calculated that breakeven would occur (in terms of revenue matching the sum of capital and operating costs) if 175 of these berths were rented. He was very interested in knowing the probability that 175 or more berths would be rented, and asked his assistant, Paul Skirvin, to collect any relevant information and help him with the assessment.

Paul noted that the required revenue was 175 × 52 revenue weeks per year. It was expected that most rentals would be permanent (52 weeks per year) but that demand for berths in summer would be higher than in winter because many people took their summer vacations in this region. Paul decided to separately analyze the demand for permanent berths and for summer peak season berths. He started by contacting the operators of the two marinas nearest to the proposed development site. They were 25 and 40 miles away, respectively. He found that the demand for berths was considerably higher than current supply in the general area. One of the marina managers told him they had 350 berths permanently rented and a waiting list of 100 names. Over and above that, the manager said that many inquiries came in from boat owners who could not even be put on the waiting list because it was full. The manager of the other marina was less optimistic, but Paul thought that he was being cagey because he perceived the new development as a competitive threat.

Paul asked each of the managers what they thought of the chances of renting 175 berths, and the responses were "8 out of 10" and "probably, but not definitely."

---

[2] This example is disguised to preserve the confidentiality of those involved in the decision.

He got a somewhat different picture when he talked to the owners of the local boating dealerships. These people were all very optimistic about the new development, saying that the demand for boating berths was so high that 220 berths were not nearly enough and that the government should reconsider its design and provide 400 or more berths. Paul recognized that this group of businessmen also had a vested interest in the marina development decision, as such a new facility would boost the demand for boats and accessories. He finally contacted the president of the local boat-owners club, and asked him about the demand for mooring berths in the area. The president was also optimistic, and said that he had at least a hundred members of his club who would jump at the chance of a permanent berth. He also said that there were more than twice as many boat owners who did not live in the county but who would keep their boats moored at the proposed site if berths were available.

On the question of demand over the period from May 1 to September 30, the club president told Paul that the sky was the limit. Paul asked for a copy of the boat club's mailing list (400 members), and the club president obliged him.

From all the information he had gathered, Paul thought the chance that at least 175 berths would be rented was very high, at least 19 out of 20, or 0.95, and he reported this back to his boss. He also reported that for the five summer months, the marina was almost sure to be full. The director said that he was satisified that demand would be high enough to warrant going ahead with the project. He was also glad that demand seemed strong enough that the development would not substantially affect any local businesses (other marinas) in a harmful way. Indeed a good deal of spinoff revenue would be created in the local area. He reported the findings to the governor. The green light was given to go ahead and commission the detailed design phase of the project. At the same time, the director decided to survey the members of the local boat club and see how many of them would like to reserve a berth.

---

From the foregoing examples and discussion we can conclude that sometimes the process of obtaining a probabilistic estimate about an uncertain quantity can be quite structured and dominated by objective factors, and sometimes the estimates are based mainly on opinion and raw judgment, which in turn may be based on information which is difficult to quantify. Yet as managers we must confront this assessment task as part of our decision process. Most practicing managers do not employ formal methods for accounting for uncertain quantities in their decisions, and in decision analysis we formalize this common sense, heuristic approach.

Another important aspect of probabilistic assessment evident in Example 4–6 was that of biases. Whenever we solicit opinions or judgments from specialists or experts we should be aware of possible biases in their responses. These biases may be unconscious, meaning that the expert is really trying to give his best estimate but is poorly calibrated or influenced by factors so as to give a poor estimate. It is also possible that biases may be intentional because the expert wishes to influence the decision. Such may have been the case in Example 4–6 where both the local marina operators and the local boat dealers had strong financial interests riding on the government's development decision.

In the next section of this chapter we consider some subjective assessment procedures in detail and how they lead to probabilities or probability distributions that can be used in decision processes.

## THE SUBJECTIVE PROBABILITY ASSESSMENT PROCESS

There are many methods available for assessing probabilities. If an uncertain quantity or event is important, then we should try to assess the appropriate probabilities even if there is little hard data available. Examples of such events are:

*a.* The target company's acceptance or rejection of a takeover bid that your company intends to make.
*b.* The extent of success of a new technology in a new application area.
*c.* The future price of a commodity.
*d.* Whether or not a competitor will initiate a price war.
*e.* The onset of another energy crisis and oil shortage.
*f.* The future growth of an economy.
*g.* The possibility of global nuclear war.
*h.* The possible purchase of a house at an auction for less than a specified amount.

Although it may be possible to do some useful objective analysis with some of these examples, there is a major element of assessing the probabilities of these events that is subjective.

Subjective assessment processes generally defy analytic or mathematical modeling and involve the **human** processing of information to arrive at an opinion or conclusion. To get a firsthand feel for subjective processes, put yourself in the position of needing to assess the probabilities of each of the example events mentioned above. As you consider each one, monitor your thought processes and note the important elements.

In an excellent paper published in *Management Science,* Spetzler and Stael von Holstein (1975) classified assessment techniques as:

*a.* Probability methods, where probabilities are assessed for certain values of an uncertain quantity or event. (For example, what is the probability that the Dow Jones Averages will reach 3,000 by the year 1995?)
*b.* Value methods, where values are assessed for certain probability statements. (For example, what is your median estimate of the rate of inflation over the next year?)

*c.* Probability value methods, where probabilistic statements are made about various points on a value scale. (For example, choose a low, medium, and high value of the national rate of unemployment in five years' time, and assess their likelihoods.)

Assessment techniques can be direct or indirect. Direct techniques involve a process of asking questions that have numerical answers (either probabilities, values, or both). Indirect methods involve betting on alternatives and adjusting the competing alternatives until a state of indifference occurs, so that a probability can be deduced from the judgment.

Let us consider a few specific assessment methods.

**Method 1: Indirect Assessment Aids.** A number of possible aids can be used to assist in the visualization of probability. For example, a pointer can be positioned along a bar or ruler to represent the relative likelihood of an event as the proportion of the bar to one side of the pointer.

An alternative method is to use a probability wheel whereby sections of a wheel are of two different colors. The proportions of these colors are adjusted so that the likelihood of a pointer on this wheel ending up on one color or the other is the same as the probability of some event.

**Method 2: Betting Techniques.** An assessor can be asked which of two events he would prefer to bet on. For example, "Would you rather bet that our profits next year will be more or less than $5 million?" Relative likelihoods can be inferred by introducing odds into the betting situations. Alternatively, reference events can be used, such as, "Would you rather bet on profits of over $5 million next year or the possibility of getting consecutive heads with two tosses of a coin?" This class of betting techniques allows for the deduction of the assessor's probabilities.

**Method 3: Fixed Probability Techniques.** Schlaifer (1969) suggests a method of fixing a probability scale (in the usual range of zero to one) and dividing it into equal-sized intervals. The values of the uncertain quantities are then assigned to the fixed fractiles. For example, he suggests a method of equiprobable groups where for an uncertain quantity, 10 equiprobable values must be assessed. For each probability sector, a representative value is chosen. This method can be used to assess probability distributions for continuous variables as discrete approximations. For example, Table 4–1 shows a set of estimates for the percent of voters who will vote Democrat in an upcoming state election. These are cumulative probabilities.

Note that in Table 4–1 there are 10 equally likely values associated with the 10 probability ranges. The values are known (Schlaifer 1969) as bracket medians, and if the uncertain quantity is continuous (as is generally the case of a percentage scale) then each bracket median represents a range.

**TABLE 4–1** Estimates of the Percent of Voters Who Will Vote Democrat

| *Probability Range* | *Democrat (percent)* |
|---|---|
| 0–0.1 | ≤31 |
| 0.1–0.2 | ≤39 |
| 0.2–0.3 | ≤44 |
| 0.3–0.4 | ≤48 |
| 0.4–0.5 | ≤52 |
| 0.5–0.6 | ≤55 |
| 0.6–0.7 | ≤58 |
| 0.7–0.8 | ≤62 |
| 0.8–0.9 | ≤66 |
| 0.9–1.0 | ≤75 |

**FIGURE 4–3** Cumulative Distribution of the Percent Democrat Vote

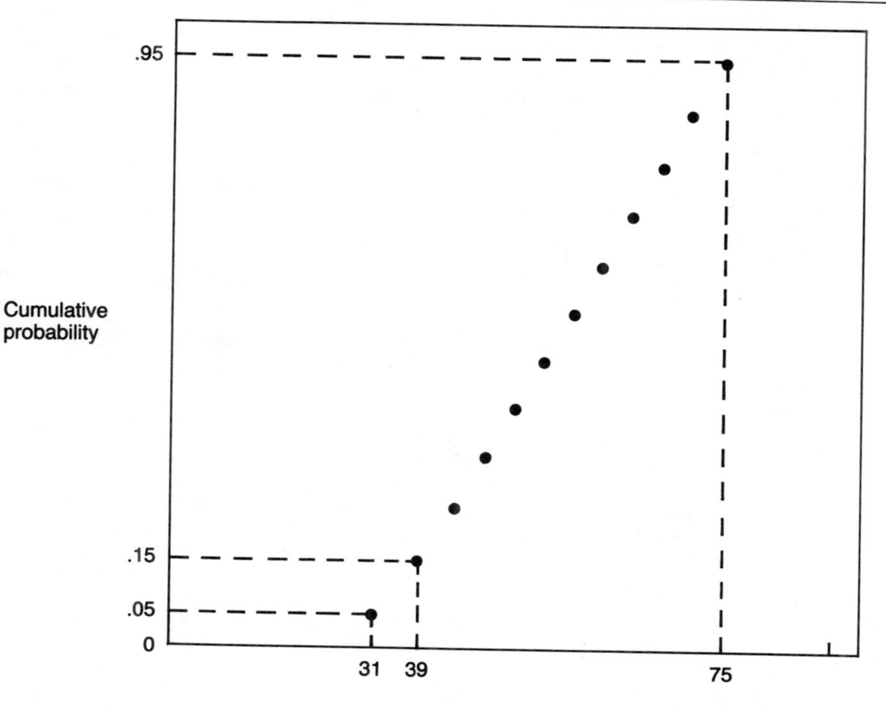

Data in this form can be interpreted and transformed to other forms of representation. The 10 equally likely values in Table 4–1 are ordered and can be used to construct a cumulative distribution. On a cumulative distribution diagram, each value from Table 4–1 would be plotted against the fractile at the center of its corresponding probability range. For example, the probability range 0.7–0.8 was assigned a value of 62%. The 62% value is assigned as the 75th fractile inferring the probability that 62% or less of voters vote Democrat is 0.75. Similarly, the probability of 48% of voters voting Democrat is 0.35. See Figure 4–3.

**Method 4: Fixed Value Techniques.** For an uncertain quantity, a representative set of values can be defined and probabilities assessed for each value. Consider the data in Table 4–2 which show a set of assessments for percent of GNP growth over a three-year period. Figure 4–4 shows a cumulative probability distribution for this data.

In Table 4–2 the uncertain quantity was split into 10 equal-width ranges covering the expected range of possible outcomes. Growth of less than −4% or more than 16% is considered impossible according to the data set. Probabilities are then set to reflect the assessor's beliefs in the various ranges.

It is not necessary to use 10 groupings for either the fixed probability (Method 3) or fixed value (Method 4) techniques. If a coarser set of assessments is satisfactory, then five ranges may be adequate in some circumstances. It is often convenient to represent uncertain quantities as having only three possible outcome levels, namely high, medium, and low. These could be set according to the equiprobable method (where we seek high, medium, and low values so that they are equally likely), or we could set representative high, medium, and low values and then assess a probability for each one.

As a practical note, if an uncertain quantity is represented by 10 levels on a decision tree that has a large number of elements (nodes), then the tree may come to resemble a bush. In other words if we wish to distinguish finely

**TABLE 4–2** Probability Distribution of GNP Growth

| *Percent GNP Growth over Three Years* | *Probability* |
|---|---|
| −4 to −2 | 0.05 |
| −2 to 0 | 0.08 |
| 0 to 2 | 0.15 |
| 2 to 4 | 0.18 |
| 4 to 6 | 0.23 |
| 6 to 8 | 0.16 |
| 8 to 10 | 0.09 |
| 10 to 12 | 0.03 |
| 12 to 14 | 0.02 |
| 14 to 16 | 0.01 |

**FIGURE 4–4** Cumulative Distribution of Percent of GNP Growth

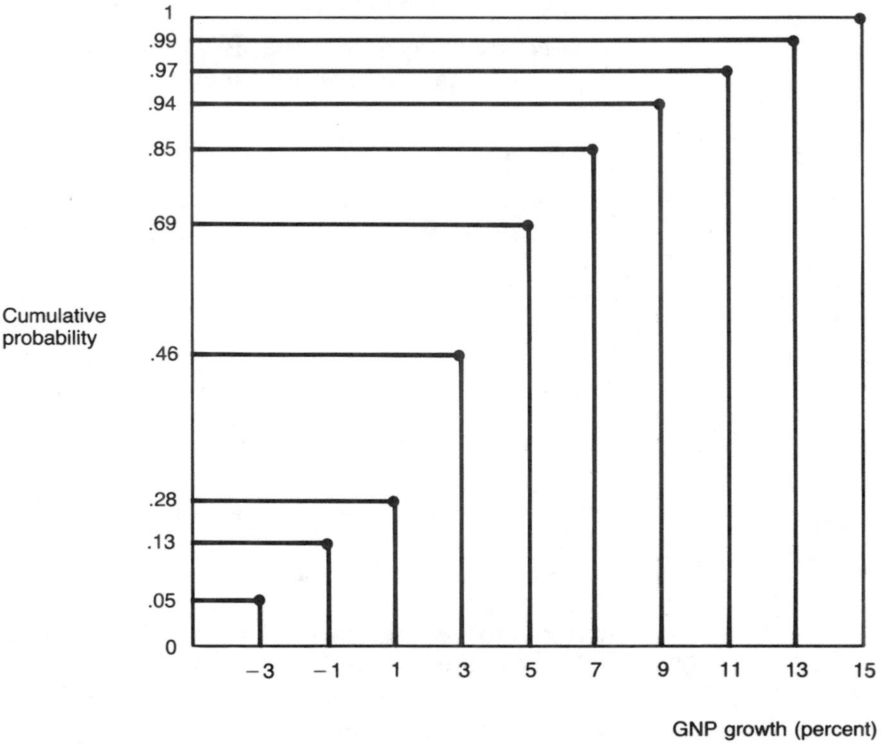

(using many levels) rather than coarsely (using few levels) on an uncertain quantity, we must be prepared to accept the consequences of a more detailed decision tree and a correspondingly larger assessment task. Trade-offs must be made between the increased accuracy of finer measurement (more branches) and the accompanying difficulty of manipulating a more cumbersome decision tree. The choice of degree of detail is up to the decision maker.

**Method 5: Graphical Representation.** For some decision makers, direct graphical representation of their state of uncertainty is possible. For example, consider the uncertainty associated with the price of gold at some future date. We could try and draw a graph of this uncertain quantity, either as a continuous variable or discrete approximation. Rather than consider bets on various alternatives or specify numbers, some people naturally prefer to draw diagrams and can specify probability distributions in any of a number of graphical forms:

*a.* Cumulative distribution functions.
*b.* Probability density functions.
*c.* Bar graphs, column graphs, pie graphs.

Alternatively we may wish to specify a known mathematical distribution form (for example, the Normal distribution) and subjectively estimate its parameters.

**Method 6: Specific Fractile Specification Techniques.** It is possible to assess directly any set of fractiles for an uncertain quantity. An effective method is to assess the 1% and 99% fractiles, followed by the median (50% fractile), followed by the quartiles (25% and 75% fractiles). A cumulative distribution curve can be drawn using these five points. Method 3 is really a specific case of method 6 in which the assessed fractiles are probabilistically equidistant.

## EFFECTIVENESS OF ASSESSMENTS

Since there are a variety of classes of assessment methods available (see the preceding section), an important issue is that of which method is best both in general and for specific assessment tasks. Further, it is useful to know how we can improve our assessment processes and accuracy.

With regard to the first issue, a good deal of research, mainly in the form of controlled laboratory studies, has compared various methods. There does not seem to be an overall best general method, because the need for assessment aid varies greatly from person to person. As a general rule, *the preferences of the decision maker should be followed in terms of which assessment process is most appealing*. Some assessors prefer to draw bar graphs or look at probability wheels and feel ill at ease with the idea of directly assessing fractiles. Others are very comfortable with direct fractile assessment and do not see any value in using graphs, wheels, or other indirect methods.

No clear picture emerges in terms of which assessment procedure is best in general. We note that the suitability of various methods is also related to the nature of the uncertain quantity. Whereas an assessor may prefer to use a fixed value method for one uncertain quantity, it can be reasonable for that same assessor to want to draw bar graphs or use a direct fractile procedure for another uncertain quantity.

Huber (1974) has written a very good paper summarizing much of the body of knowledge in the area of subjective assessment. He suggests the following ways of improving the accuracy of subjective judgments:

1. Training of assessors.
2. Using several assessors.
3. Using an appropriate assessment procedure.

The first factor, training of assessors, refers to knowledge of probability and statistics, knowledge of natural biases, and experience in subjective assessment. Research studies have shown that expertise and experience improve assessments (Samson and Thomas 1986).

The second factor, using several assessors, involves the elicitation of probabilities by a number of people and the subsequent aggregation of those assessments. On average, this aggregation lowers the impact of random error and capricious estimates. Many methods of aggregation exist. Consider Example 4–6 in which the probability distribution of demand for marina berths was an important decision element. If a number of people had given their opinions on this uncertain quantity, then how might they be aggregated? Perhaps the simplest procedure would be to take arithmetic averages, possibly weighted according to the perceived expertise of each assessor. If it can be arranged (as is usually possible in an organizational setting), it is often productive to have the assessors interact with each other. In such cases it is possible that they will move towards a consensus view, although that is certainly not a guaranteed outcome. At the least, a properly directed exchange of views can occur whether the interaction is direct (as in a meeting of assessors) or indirect (as in the Delphi procedure).

The third factor is the use of an appropriate assessment procedure. The actual elicitation techniques (discussed earlier) are part of a broader process of assessment. Huber describes this process in terms of *motivation, structuring, encoding,* and *checking*. The methods listed earlier referred only to the encoding phase, in which information is processed by the assessor to produce a set of quantitative estimates. The motivation phase involves informing the assessors that their judgments are important inputs to a decision, and that they should give their unbiased opinions. Structuring refers to the process of defining the uncertain quantity in a meaningful manner. The step which follows or is integrated with the actual encoding process is called the checking step and refers to ensuring that the quantitative estimates really do reflect the assessor's degree of belief about the uncertain quantities.

---

## Example 4–7

### Market Share Assessment at Boston Beer

The Boston Beer company was very interested in expanding from an East Coast operation to some Midwest and later on some West Coast markets. They had designed an effective marketing strategy and were considering collecting survey information or running a test market. Their Senior Vice President of Marketing, John

Preston, had been concerned about committing substantial financial resources to attacking the new markets in the light of uncertainty about sales. He called on a friend who was experienced in analyzing decisions to assist in establishing some measure of the uncertainty, so that he could evaluate the benefits that might be derived from the survey or test market. His friend, David Auger, suggested they go through a process of trying to establish a probability distribution for sales. David suggested they begin by carefully defining the uncertain quantity itself. He asked whether the critical variable was sales in the first six months or year after entering the new markets, or sales after about five years, when market share would hopefully be established at some more or less equilibrium value. Mr. Preston responded that he was more interested in knowing what sort of steady state market share could be established. He argued that sales in the first year were important but that it would take at least two years before Boston Beer would establish a substantial market share. Their dialogue went as follows:

**DAVID AUGER (DA):** So you believe, John, that the variable of real interest is sales in year 3, that is the period from 24 to 36 months after market entry. OK, then. Given the Midwest marketing plan you have designed, let's start by looking at some really extreme outcomes. Suppose that Boston Beer products really take off, and the program is a huge success. What would be your estimate of sales in year 3 in the Midwest marketing region? Should we be speaking in terms of dollars or gallons?
**JOHN PRESTON (JP):** Rather than considering dollars or gallons, I'd feel better talking about market share in percentage terms. We can then easily convert to gallons from our estimates of market size, and to dollars from our knowledge of prices. To answer your question, I believe that the best we could do would be a 3% share of the whole Midwest beer market.
**DA:** Well, I don't want to influence your opinions. After all I'm only the person with procedural expertise in probability assessment. Three percent seems like a pretty low market share to me. Of course you are the person with the knowledge about beer markets. All I know about beer is that there are very few brands I don't like. Are you sure you can't envision any circumstances in which that year 3 market share could get above 3%?
**JP:** You're quite right, actually. I was being quietly conservative and probably shouldn't be. Yes, it is possible that market share could reach 4% or even 5%, but that's really unlikely. I think that given our limited resources for production growth, our product quality, and marketing plan, any more than 5% is impossible. A share of 5% is unlikely but might be achieved if everything works out just right.
**DA:** Well, let's not worry about likelihoods just yet. First we want to define the parameters and establish boundary values on them. Focus for a minute on a worst-case scenario. What's the least possible market share you could envision? I suppose you can't do worse than zero market share.
**JP:** That's true, but even if the whole exercise turns out to be a disaster, we'll have a fair bit of beer shipped out to warehouses in places like Chicago and St. Louis by that time, and we'll sell it at a reduced price rather than bring it back. So market share would be greater than zero even if we drop out of all the markets. Say about ½%.
**DA:** But do you really want to consider a market liquidation effect like that? I thought we were interested in assessing a steady state or ongoing market share, and although you would sell off your inventory, you're really describing a steady state share of zero, aren't you? In other words, total failure is possible.

**JP:** Yes, I'm afraid it certainly is, which is why I want to get some better information.
**DA:** So far now we are defining a best case as 5% share in year 3 and a worst case of zero share, apart from dumping inventory in a cut-and-run situation. Let's try a couple of different assessment techniques and see where they get us. First of all, let's try dividing your range into 10 bands. This diagram might help. (See Figure 4–5.) Now for each band we want to define a probability. For example, what is the chance of achieving market share of above 4%?
**JP:** Pretty unlikely, say about a 1 in 10 chance.
**DA:** So bands *I* and *J* as I've labelled them (see Figure 4–5) have a total probability of 0.1. What about the range 0% to 1%?
**JP:** Unfortunately, I think there is roughly a one in four chance of an unsuccessful campaign in which market share would not reach 1%. Actually its probably a little higher, say 0.3 probability.
**DA:** Let's now look at some of the values in between 1% and 4%. If we split this range into two, from 1% to 2.5% and from 2.5% to 4%, can you tell me which of these ranges is more likely in your opinion?
**JP:** I'd prefer to think of three ranges, 1% to 2%, 2% to 3%, and 3% to 4%, if it's OK.
**DA:** Fine.
**JP:** My best guess is that 2% to 3% will be most likely, probably as likely as the other two ranges 1% to 2% and 3% to 4% put together.
**DA:** In that case we can say the following, referring to the lettered sections on the graph:

$$\begin{aligned} P(I \text{ or } J) &= 0.1 \\ P(A \text{ or } B) &= 0.3 \\ P(C \text{ or } D \text{ or } E \text{ or } F \text{ or } G \text{ or } H) &= 0.6 \\ P(C \text{ or } D) &= P(D \text{ or } E \text{ or } F \text{ or } G) \\ &= 0.3 \end{aligned}$$

How do you feel about those ranges 1% to 2% and 3% to 4%?
**JP:** They are very close to equally likely in my opinion.
**DA:** I'll write the probabilities on the graph and draw vertical columns to represent their height. (See Figure 4–6.) Right now we are working with only five levels of value. We can split each of these into two later. Just check our progress so far. Have we captured your overall beliefs about market share? For example, it's a little unusual to see a bimodal distribution as you have here. Is that what you intended? Do you want to change anything?
**JP:** Actually, I know that bimodal distributions don't naturally occur all that often. Most people almost automatically use the Gaussian (normal) distribution for all

**FIGURE 4–5** Division of the Uncertain Quantity, Market Share, into Ten Equal-Width Intervals

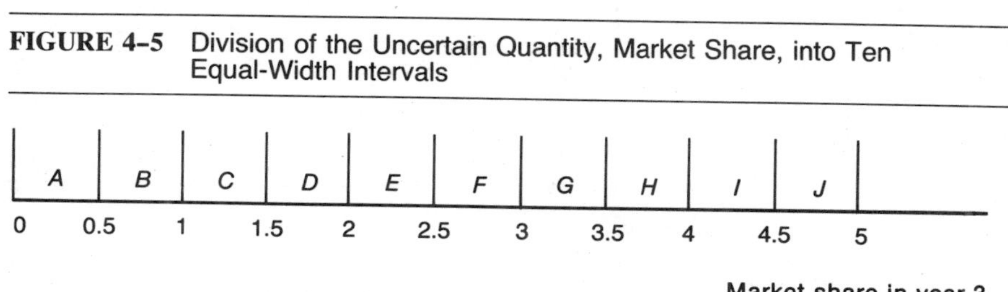

**FIGURE 4–6** Initial Assessment of Probabilities

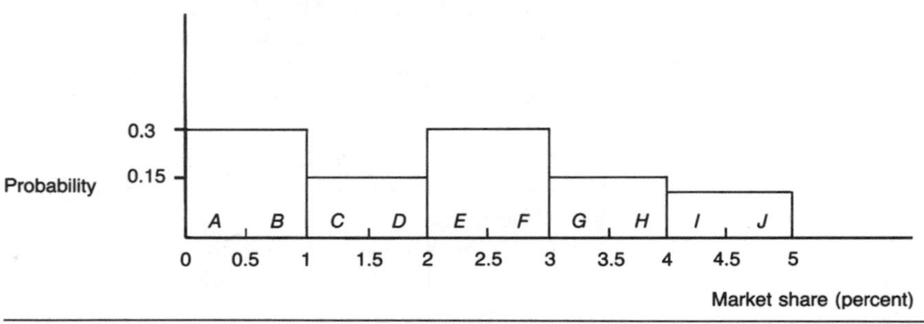


probability work, and I can remember a statistics professor being critical of that practice. In this case I think a bimodal distribution is correct because there is a substantial chance of a flop, which would give us a market share of zero or very close. If it's not a flop, then a market share of about 3% is more likely than 1% or 2%.

**DA:** Are you happy with the relative heights of the columns (see Figure 4–6) as representations of likelihood?

**JP:** No, let's reduce the "*A* or *B*" block a little, say to 0.25.

**DA:** OK, that's fine. Now, the probabilities have to add to one. Do you want me to reduce the "*A* or *B*" block so that the relative heights are like this? (See Figure 4–7.) In that case I'll just rescale the numbers so that the probabilities add to one and the relativities stay the same.

**JP:** No, I also want to add some height to the "*G* or *H*" column, changing it from 0.15 to 0.2. Yes, that's much better. See, I think that if it's not a flop, then we will probably (although not definitely) achieve at least a 2% share. I think those numbers represent my beliefs exactly.

**DA:** Fine. Remember that nothing is signed and sealed here, and you can make any changes you want at any time. Let's look at some of the columns and see if there's any point in splitting them to get finer divisions in the distribution. For example, take

**FIGURE 4–7** Revised Probability Distribution

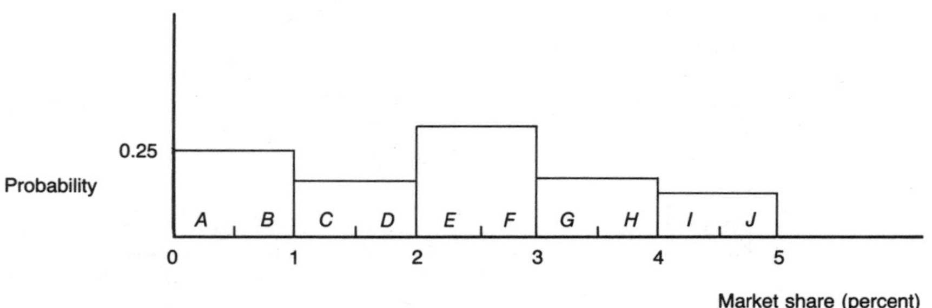


NOTE: The probabilities do not sum to one on this figure. Rescaling or further adjustment is necessary.

the "$A$ or $B$" column which has a total probability of 0.25. Given that the outcome is $A$ or $B$, how do you think $A$ and $B$ compare in terms of their likelihood?

**JP:** It's the bimodal thing again. The flop mode is $A$, and a $B$ result of 0.5% to 1% is quite unlikely. Let's split it so that $p(A) = 0.2$ and $p(B) = 0.05$. In fact, let's look at $C$ and $D$ as well. I think $B$ is as likely as $C$. I am happy with $p(A)$ at 0.2. I want $p(B)$ equal to $p(C)$ and $p(D)$ a little above $p(C)$. How about this:

$$\begin{aligned} p(A) &= 0.2 \\ p(B) &= 0.05 \\ p(C) &= 0.05 \\ p(D) &= 0.1 \end{aligned}$$

No, let's change $p(D)$ to 0.08 and $p(B)$ and $p(C)$ each to 0.06. That's good.

**DA:** OK, I have changed the graph to show that. (See Figure 4–8.) By the way, notice that on Figure 4–8 we have some narrow and some wide blocks. We need to be careful not to be misled by the probabilities here in terms of their representation on the graph. Probabilities are represented on this sort of graph as the area under the curve or line. When all blocks in a histogram are of equal width, then the heights of the blocks properly represents the probabilities. This is not the case on Figure 4–8. For example the "$E$ and $F$" block has a total probability of 0.3. Compare it to the $A$ block (with probability 0.2). If I had made the "$E$ and $F$" block higher than $A$, we might be misled into thinking that $p(E) = p(F) = 0.3$. In fact, we can only say that $p(E) + p(F) = 0.3$. Have a look at $E$ and $F$. What do you think of them relative to each other?

**JP:** They should stay the same. Actually, I now see that we are dealing with a continuous variable as if it existed in discrete chunks, and that's not right.

**DA:** We can always take care of that later, and we will in just a minute. We'll do it by either using more and more columns, splitting existing columns, or else by smoothing a curve through the column tops.

**JP:** Good, because I think there is a definite mode about 2.6% or 2.7%, and now (see Figure 4–8) we are showing a flat peak on the "$E$ or $F$" block.

**DA:** We will take care of that. Let's finish getting the sections roughed out first. Look at sections $G$ and $H$. How do they compare with each other?

**JP:** After section $F$, we are in a decreasing tail of the distribution. So if $p(G$ or $H)$ is 0.20, then I would say $p(G) = 0.12$ and $p(H) = 0.08$. It seems a little silly giving such precise numbers when my uncertainty about market share is so high.

**FIGURE 4–8** Further Revision

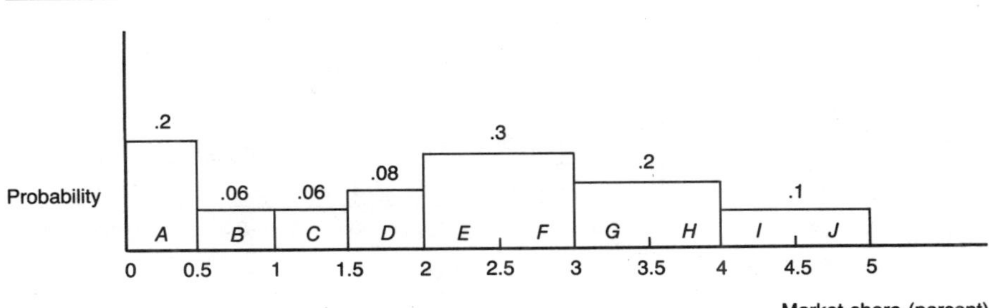

**DA:** Don't worry. The process of assigning numbers to something subjective often seems strange at first, but all we are doing is measuring your beliefs. You have an excellent understanding of what's going on, so please continue.

**JP:** Well, sections *I* and *J* should be about $p(I) = 0.05$ and $p(J) = 0.03$. I know that doesn't add to 0.1 as it should, but I want to leave a little chance for the possibility of more than 5% market share. It's been in the back of my mind that a market share of above 5% is remotely possible, and 0.02 seems about right. That's one chance in 50, isn't it?

**DA:** Yes. OK, let's plot the column graph again. (See Figure 4–9.) I'll show the area to the right of 5% as being the range 5% to 6% for now. I also want to translate this to a cumulative distribution. (See Figure 4–10.) See how the cumulative distribution plots the probability of market share being less than any specified value. The height of each column on the original graph translates into the slope of the corresponding sections on the cumulative probability plot.

**JP:** Yes, and now we can draw a smooth curve through those discontinuous graphs to recognize that we are dealing with a continuous variable. (See Figures 4–11 and 4–12.) Which graph shall I use?

**DA:** It doesn't really matter. Use the one you feel most comfortable with. As you know, they contain the same information in different forms. First though, take a minute to check your graph and the implications of the probability statements, both in absolute terms and also relative to each other. For example, you are saying that a market share above 4% is pretty unlikely. A probability of 0.1 is a 1 in 10 chance.

**JP:** That's what I believe. Actually, I think we are basically there, and this is what I need for my decision tree. Since the tree requires discrete levels of market share and their probabilities, there's no real need to draw a smooth curve, but let's try it anyway. (See Figure 4–11.) I'll do it on the original graph. Yes, that looks just right.

**DA:** OK, now let's use a different method to check a few points on your probability distribution. Forget about the process we have just been through for a moment, and we will put these graphs away. I would like you to directly assess for me the 1% and 99% fractiles of the distribution. In other words, what are the plausible but unlikely lowest and highest values?

**JP:** Well, it's still zero at the low end and 5 or 5½ at the high end.

**FIGURE 4–9** Final Market Share Assessments

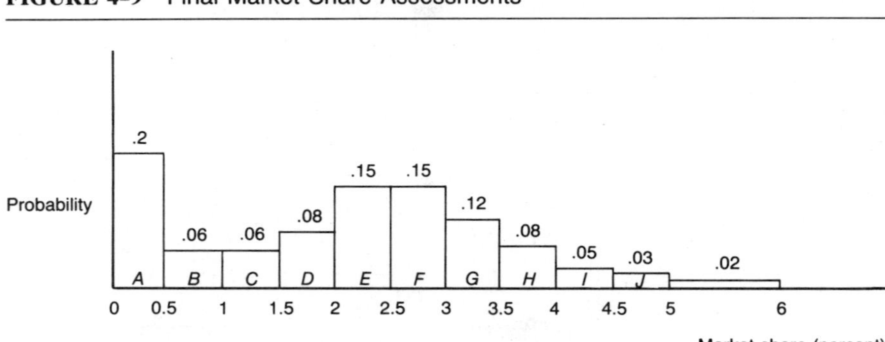

**FIGURE 4–10** Cumulative Distribution of Market Share (percent)

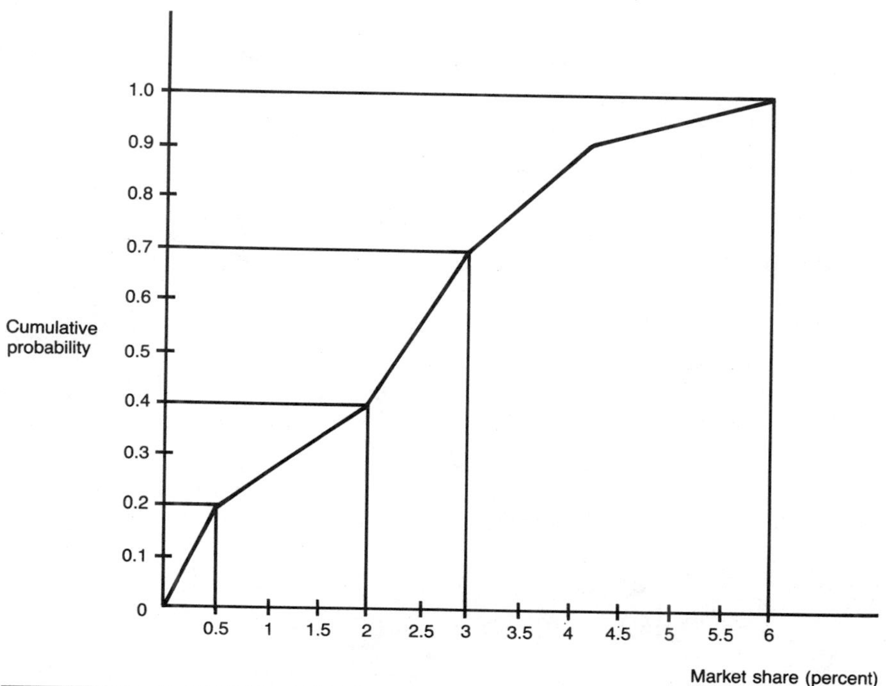


**FIGURE 4–11** Continuous Approximation to the Assessed Probability Distribution

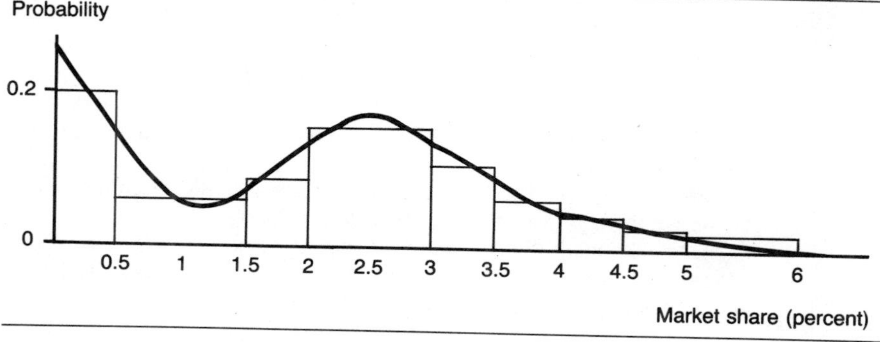

**FIGURE 4–12** Continuous Curve Approximation to the Assessed Cumulative Distribution

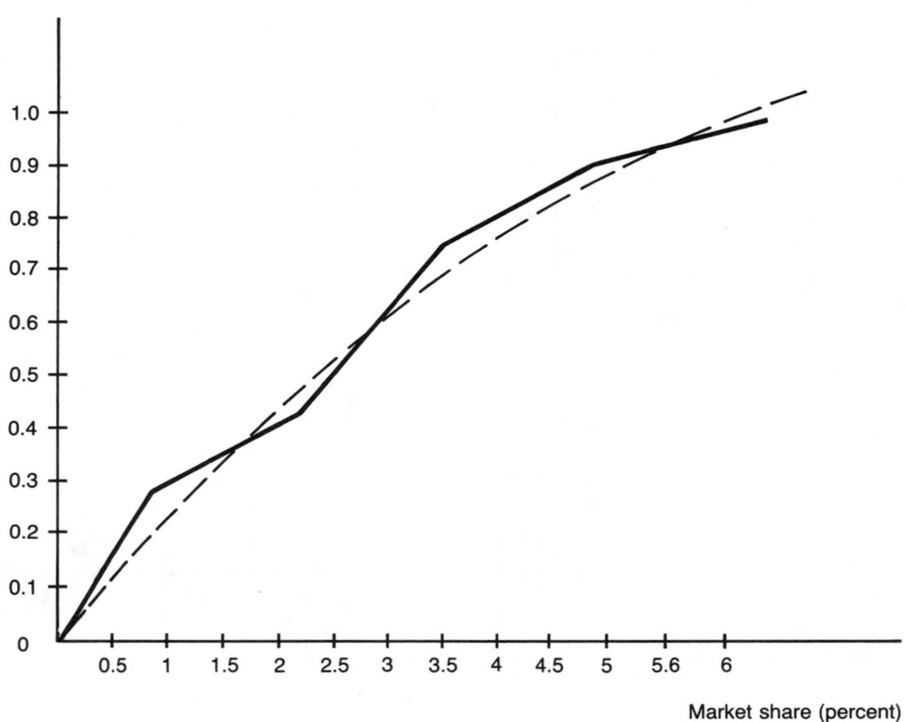


**DA:** Now please assess the median, which is the 50% fractile. Given that market share in year 3 is likely to be in the range zero to 5½ or so, what is the value of market share that is equally likely to be above or below the true answer?
**JP:** I think that it has to be about 2.5% market share. It's an even bet as to whether market share ends up above or below 2½%.
**DA:** Now, if I tell you that it is below 2½% market share, what is your lower quartile, that is 25% fractile? Also, what is your upper quartile (75% fractile)?
**JP:** Lower quartile: about 1%, and upper quartile of 3%, or a little above.
**DA:** Let's compare your direct estimates of these quartiles with the distribution we already have.
**JP:** Let's see. The fractile estimates are actually all pretty close or even very close to what we previously had (Figure 4–12).
**DA:** Good. If there had been some discrepancies, we would have needed to recheck things and iron them out. I think we now have a distribution that we can confidently use on our decision tree!

The Boston Beer example demonstrates how an interview process can effectively lead to the construction of a subjective probability distribution. One further important point is with respect to the definition of the uncertain quantity. The decision maker/probability assessor needs to be familiar with the uncertain quantity and clear about its definition. In the Boston Beer example, it could have been feasible to measure performance in terms of profit rather than market share. However, it was decided to decompose profit into revenue and cost, and consider only the market share component of revenue as the relevant source of uncertainty. This is an important issue in general, in decision analysis modeling. It is useful to keep in mind that we can usually decompose further where appropriate, or else combine variables. We should decompose to a level that allows for the best assessment result and maximizes the eventual quality of insights that the model produces.

## EXTREME PROBABILITIES: A SPECIAL CASE

Extremely large probabilities (very close to one) or extremely small (very close to zero) introduce special assessment difficulties. Events that have extreme probabilities often introduce additional difficulty and complexity in decision making because it is not easy to treat them in a conventional manner. For events having probabilities that are extremely large, complementary events exist with extremely small probabilities. These rare events warrant further study because problems that involve rare events are becoming increasingly frequent and important in societal and managerial decision problems.

---

### EXAMPLE 4–8

### Nuclear Power Plant Regulation

The Nuclear Regulatory Commission in the United States and many other similar bodies overseas are vitally interested in the safety of nuclear power plants. One type of event that is of particular concern is a major catastrophe that would lead to a meltdown, causing widespread damage to life and property and releasing nuclear particles into the environment. Regulatory agencies must make decisions involving trade-offs between money (spent on safety equipment and procedures) and level of safety. In structuring and making these decisions it is important to be able to effectively measure safety. One measure is the probability of an accident. In nuclear power plants we can define $P$ as the probability of a serious accident (involving a major release of harmful substances). Values of $P$ have been estimated in the range $10^{-4}$ to as low as $10^{-9}$ per reactor per year. In other words, the probability of a major accident at any reactor in any given year may be in the range 0.000000001 to 0.0001. Fortunately, these catastrophic events are forecast as being rare. It is important to ask the questions:

1. How can rare-event probabilities be assessed?
2. How can we make decisions involving rare events?

---

Let us firstly define rare events as those with probabilities of less than 1/50 (0.02). With respect to assessment procedures, let us consider two kinds of rare events, namely **statistically** rare events and **probabilistic** rare events. We define probabilistic rare events as events having small probability of occurrence per unit time. Statistically rare events have a small probability of occurrence over a total sample space. Consider the possibility of a valve or pipe failing while operating in an oil refinery, or perhaps a car tire blowing out under normal operating conditions on a given day. Each of these events has a low probability, but these probabilities can be reasonably accurately estimated using relative frequency information. An oil company may have data based on many thousands of valves, and data may be available based on literally millions of tires (although missing information may be a difficulty in this instance). These examples are of **probabilistic** rare events, where individual units have very low probabilities but over a large number of existing units, frequencies of occurrence are not extremely low. Although it is unlikely that any individual will experience a tire blowout on a given day, it is safe to assume that quite a few occur each day around the country. Hence if the information can be gathered, probabilities for probabilistic rare events can be estimated based on past data.

Let us contrast this example with the **statistically** rare event of a nuclear plant meltdown. There is no well-documented history of a complete meltdown even though there is a history of a few thousand reactor years of operation. Although we can learn from the Chernobyl incident, major design differences mean that there is little direct inference that can be drawn from Chernobyl regarding the likelihood of a meltdown in the United States. In this instance, the relative frequency approach has only a little information to offer. Regulators wish to determine just how rare this event is, and their estimate will have a very real bearing on decision making.

Another example is the possibility of a major accident involving an LNG tanker in New York harbor. To prepare for such an emergency and to regulate shipping in the harbor, it is useful to estimate the probability of this event. Again, this is a statistically rare event having no history, hence the probability is difficult to estimate. Would you estimate $10^{-10}$ per ship per trip, or a higher or lower value?

A number of different approaches have been taken to try and get a handle on rare event probabilities. Perhaps the most prominent is that of **decomposition.** In an analogous manner to that in which decisions are decomposed, events can be decomposed into subevents. We can try to classify the possible mechanisms by which an event could occur and separately assess probabilities for each mechanism. Consider the possibility of a dam wall failure leading to the uncontrollable release of water. Since all dam designs and locations are unique, we cannot easily use relative frequency information from one dam site and apply it to another. A decomposition approach involves the identification of specific events leading up to the failure event. Examples of subevents might be earthquake, structural failure (concrete degradation), equipment malfunction (flood gate control equipment malfunction), sabotage, and accidental impact (by an airplane). This is not an exhaustive list, but merely a set of examples of how an event may be decomposed. Further analysis and decomposition of each subevent may lead to a structure that allows for the separate consideration and probabilistic assessment of elements of a rare event. The rules of probability manipulation can then be used to estimate the likelihood for the event. Although it has not yet been clearly demonstrated that such decompositions do improve rare event probability estimates, there is little doubt that the decomposition process fosters careful thinking about the event, just as decision analysis fosters careful (formalized common sense) thinking about decisions. Preliminary evidence indicates that the quality of the decomposition strongly affects the accuracy of the estimate.

We do have concrete decision aids useful for decomposing rare events and achieving probability estimates for them. The most important of these are fault trees and event trees. These are similar to decision trees except that they focus on decomposing a single (rare) event. Fault trees show the events that lead to the critical event. In the instance of a nuclear power plant meltdown, a fault tree would lay out the details of the systems that would need to fail to cause the meltdown. A fault tree shows the actual sequence of events leading to a failure.

An event tree is like a decision tree, but without decision nodes. It is a decomposition of an event sequence which explores the ramifications of some initiating event. In contrast, a fault tree shows the component events which must happen in sequence or combination to cause the major fault. Each of these forms of representation is a structured decomposition. The point of such decompositions is to consider the subevents and assess probabilities for them, then to deduce a probability for the rare event of interest, using the addition and multiplication rules of probability. To summarize, fault and event trees are powerful, useful methods, similar to decision trees, for assessing rare event probabilities.

Once a rare event probability is estimated, how can we account for it in decision making? Consider the case of LNG tanker accident in New York harbor. Let us suppose that best estimates of accident probabilities are $10^{-6}$

per ship per trip. As a regulator, how would you integrate this very small number with the very large impact of the accident in terms of potential injury and damages? Is the risk of accident worth the gain? The answer is obviously yes because ships do regularly transport LNG in the harbor. If the probability were $10^{-4}$ or $10^{-2}$, would society make a different judgment and prohibit LNG shipping in New York harbor? It becomes obvious that in the case of rare events, there is difficulty in conceptualizing the event and its probability, as well as in establishing an acceptable decision rule.

Low probability, high-impact events are becoming increasingly common as technology advances and production systems become larger and more complex. Hence decision makers need to establish procedures for dealing with these events. Decision analytic methods of event decomposition appear to be a promising avenue of investigation. The formal systematic framework of decision analysis is a useful one for decisions involving the acceptability of risk.

As mentioned above, part of the difficulty with rare events is our inability to conceptualize and measure differences in probability that are very small in absolute terms. Let us contrast a rare event with one that is not rare. Consider an event for which you have subjectively assessed a probability of 0.4. Let us imagine that it is a sales estimate for your company. If a colleague were to ask you just how precise your estimate was, would you claim that you meant to say 0.4 and not 0.39 or 0.41? The answer is probably that you could not discriminate in subjective terms at the level of 0.01 of error on the probability scale. Most of us would feel strongly about distinguishing between 0.4 and 0.3 (or 0.5) but not between 0.4 and 0.39 (or 0.41).

Let us now consider the debate over the safety of nuclear power plants. The extremes of this debate have been roughly a low estimate of $10^{-9}$ per reactor year and a high estimate of $10^{-4}$ per reactor year. The difference between these two estimates in absolute terms is *very small* compared to the difference between 0.4 and 0.39:

$$\begin{aligned} 10^{-4} - 10^{-9} &= 0.0001 - 0.000000001 \\ &= 0.000099999 \\ 0.4 - 0.39 &= 0.01 \end{aligned}$$

Although in **absolute** terms the 0.4–0.39 difference is much larger than $10^{-4}$–$10^{-9}$, in **relative** terms the former expression is very much smaller. In relative terms the $10^{-9}$ and $10^{-4}$ estimates differ by a factor of 100,000!

For statistically rare events another problem is the use of information to update estimates. In the case of the LNG accident in NY harbor, let us assume that an estimate of $10^{-6}$ per ship per year is deemed to be acceptable. Do we lower this estimate if no accidents occur over a time period? Do we raise it when an accident occurs, and if so, by how much? Although a statistical method exists for combining probabilistic sources of information and accounting for evidence, it requires a prior distribution reflecting the decision makers' beliefs about the uncertainty of the estimate. Since we are uncertain about the probability of an LNG accident, is it realistic to consider a range of probability and perhaps a probability distribution of probability? These somewhat abstract concepts are certainly valid in a statistical sense but are difficult to conceptualize and of limited power as decision aids for most practical applications. Certainly for rare events it is unreasonable to use probability wheels and graphs. These aids are generally most useful when probabilities are in the range 0.1 to 0.9.

## SUMMARY

Probabilistic assessment is an important part of decision analysis. The probability statements are usually key inputs to the decision model and thus warrant careful efforts in their assessment.

In some instances, relative frequency information or statistical models are useful in determining probabilities. Whether or not objective information is available, there is a subjective element present in probabilistic assessment.

Skill in subjective probability assessment can be developed through training in assessment skills, through developing statistical expertise, and through understanding human information processing biases.[3]

A number of methods for encoding probabilities are available including the use of assessment aids such as probability wheels and graphs. Direct assessment procedures include fixed probability and fixed value assessments and direct fractile estimates. It is not possible to generally state that one of these methods is superior to others. The preferred method is normally the choice of the assessor and based on the characteristics of the problem. The conceptual difficulties associated with probabilistic thinking become exacerbated in the context of rare events. Rare events pose difficulties in both their probability assessment and integration in decision models.

In essence, the subjective assessment process involves quantifying, on a scale of zero to one, a degree of belief about the likelihood of an event. Research has shown that this process is subject to error, just as point estimate forecasts are. Despite the imperfections in human assessment processes, in decision making it is usually better to try to explicitly account for uncertainty than to ignore it.

To complete this summary, we quote from Spetzler and Stael von Holstein (1975) who give the following encoding principles:

> The uncertain quantity should be important to the decision, as determined by a sensitivity analysis.

[3] These issues are discussed further in Chapter 13.

The quantity should be defined for the subject as an unambiguous state variable. If the subject believes the outcome of the quantity can be affected to some extent by his decision, then the problem needs restructuring to eliminate this effect.

The level of detail required from the encoding process depends on the importance of the quantity and should be determined by sensitivity analysis before the interview. It may sometimes be sufficient to elicit only a few points on the distribution.

The quantity should be well structured. The subject may think of the quantity as conditional on other quantities; accordingly, conditionalities should consciously be considered and brought into the structure because our minds deal ineffectively in combining uncertain quantities. Mental acrobatics should be minimized.

The quantity should be clearly defined. A good test of this quality is to ask whether a clairvoyant could reveal the value of the quantity by specifying a single number without requesting clarification. To cite an example, it is not meaningful to ask for the "price of wheat in 1974," because the clairvoyant would need to know the quantity, kind of wheat, at what date, at which Exchange, and the buying or selling price. However, "the closing price of durum wheat on June 30, 1975 at the Chicago Commodity Exchange" would be a well-defined quantity.

The quantity should be described by the analyst on a scale that is meaningful to the subject. For example, in the oil industry, the subject—depending on his occupation—may think in terms of gallons, barrels, or tank cars. The wrong choice of scale may cause the subject to spend more effort on fitting his answers to the scale than on evaluating his uncertainty. It is important, therefore, to choose a unit with which the subject is comfortable; after the encoding, the scale can be changed to fit the analysis. As a rule, let the subject choose the scale if there is no obvious scale.

## FURTHER READING

For those readers who require a more in-depth treatment of this subject, a number of excellent sources are available. Most modern statistics texts offer some material on the subjective concept of probability, however these treatments are often brief.

A series of excellent articles have appeared in statistical and other journals over the past 25 years. These include two very good articles by Winkler (1967). Slovic and Lichtenstein have published a lengthy article (1971) comparing Bayesian and Regression approaches of information processing. Articles by Huber (1974) and Spetzler and Stael von Holstein (1975) are very good and have already been referred to in this chapter. In addition, Hogarth (1975) has written on the cognitive processes aspect of subjective probability assessment.

Books dealing with decision analysis also offer useful insights into subjective probability assessment. In addition to those of Raiffa (1968) and Schlaifer

(1970), which are referenced in earlier chapters, a volume by Lindley (1973) contains a number of useful insights. Bunn's more recent book (1984) covers some of the issues in assessment, including fault and event trees.

## REFERENCES

BUNN, D. W. 1984. *Applied Decision Analysis*. New York: McGraw-Hill.

HOGARTH, R. B. 1975. "Cognitive Processes and the Assessment of Subjective Probability Distributions." *Journal of the American Statistical Association* 70, pp. 271–89.

HUBER, G. P. 1974. "Methods for Quantifying Subjective Probabilities and Multiattribute Utilities." *Decision Sciences* 5, pp. 430–58.

LINDLEY, D. 1973. *Making Decisions*. New York: John Wiley & Sons.

SAMSON, D.A., and H. THOMAS. 1986. "Assessing Probability Distributions by the Fractile Method: Evidence from Managers." OMEGA 14, no 5, pp. 401–7.

SCHLAIFER, R.O. 1969. *Analysis of Decisions Under Uncertainty*. New York: McGraw-Hill.

SLOVIC, P., and S. LICHTENSTEIN. 1971. "Comparison of Bayesian and Regression Approaches to the Study of Information Processing in Judgment." *Organizational Behavior and Human Performance* 6, pp. 649–744.

SPETZLER, C. S., and C. A. S. STAEL VON HOLSTEIN. 1975. "Probability Encoding in Decision Analysis." *Management Science* 22, pp. 340–58.

WINKLER, R. L. 1967. "The Assessment of Prior Distributions in Bayesian Analysis." *Journal of the American Statistical Association* 62, pp. 776–800.

WINKLER, R. L. 1967. "The Quantification of Judgment: Some Methodological Suggestions." *Journal of the American Statistical Association,* 62, pp. 1105–1120.

## PROBLEMS

1. Consider the following quantities:
   *a.* Your yearly salary 10 years from now.
   *b.* The number of books you will refer to or read over the next year.
   Was your initial reaction to think of a best point estimate or to think in terms of a range of possibilities? Suppose that these quantities were important to a decision you must make. Explain the difference between using a point estimate (ignoring uncertainty) and explicitly considering the quantities as uncertain. Could these different processes affect the decision?
2. For each of the uncertain quantities in problem 1 above, use the methods of fixed probabilities and of fixed values independently to

**TABLE 4–3** Fixed Probability Assessment Table

| *Cumulative Probability* | *Representative Value* |
|---|---|
| 0–0.1 | |
| 0.1–0.2 | |
| 0.2–0.3 | |
| 0.3–0.4 | |
| 0.4–0.5 | |
| 0.5–0.6 | |
| 0.6–0.7 | |
| 0.7–0.8 | |
| 0.8–0.9 | |
| 0.9–1.0 | |

assess probability distributions. For the fixed probability method, find 10 equiprobable values as in Table 4–3. For the fixed value method, start by defining the upper and lower possible bounds on each quantity. Divide the defined range into 10 equal-width bands and assign probabilities to each band. The 10 probabilities must sum to one. If the lower bound is $X_L$ and the upper bound is $X_H$ then Table 4–4 shows the 10 bands that should be defined.

3. For each uncertain quantity in problems 1 and 2 (above), use the five-point fractile technique to assess a cumulative probability distribution. This technique involves the following steps.
   *a.* Assess a lower bound (defined as the 0.01 fractile, and an upper bound (defined as the 0.99 fractile). These values should be located so that there is only a 1% chance that in each case the true value of the uncertain quantity is more extreme than the fractile.
   *b.* Assess the median of the distribution, that is the 0.5 fractile.
   *c.* Assess the interquartile values, that is, the 0.25 and 0.75 fractiles.

   Plot these distributions on separate graphs with the quantity value on the horizontal axis and the cumulative probability scale on the vertical axis.

**TABLE 4–4** Fixed Value Assessment Table

| *Value* | *Probability* |
|---|---|
| $X_L$ to $(.9X_L + .1X_H)$ | |
| $(.9X_L + .1X_H)$ to $(.8X_L + .2X_H)$ | |
| $(.8X_L + .2X_H)$ to $(.7X_L + .3X_H)$ | |
| $(.7X_L + .3X_H)$ to $(.6X_L + .4X_H)$ | |
| $(.6X_L + .4X_H)$ to $(.5X_L + .5X_H)$ | |
| $(.5X_L + .5X_H)$ to $(.4X_L + .6X_H)$ | |
| $(.4X_L + .6X_H)$ to $(.3X_L + .7X_H)$ | |
| $(.3X_L + .7X_H)$ to $(.2X_L + .8X_H)$ | |
| $(.2X_L + .8X_H)$ to $(.1X_L + .9X_H)$ | |
| $(.1X_L + .9X_H)$ to $X_H$ | |

4. On the graphs constructed as part of problem 3 above, plot the data that formed the assessments you made in problem 2. Use the bracket medians to locate points. You should have three cumulative probability graphs for each uncertain quantity. How different were the distributions produced using the various methods? Do the distributions have the properties you desire, such as central tendency, symmetry (or perhaps asymmetry)? You may need to use differencing techniques to translate the cumulative distributions to column graphs. If you are not satisfied with any of the distributions you have assessed, make appropriate revisions until you feel that the distributions do reflect your beliefs about the uncertain quantities.
5. Did the process of formally eliciting probability distributions enhance your understanding of the uncertain quantities? Explain your answer and suggest the apparent strengths and weaknesses of each method. Would you be prepared to use these distributions and others like them in decision-making processes? Explain your answer in terms of the benefits of subjective assessment of probabilities versus alternative approaches.
6. Is a computer capable of subjectivity in general and subjective assessment of probabilities in particular? Define and contrast the subjective and relative frequency approaches to probability assessment.
7. Use the data in Table 4–1 to construct a probability distribution of the assessed percentage of voters who will vote Democrat. How would this information be useful in an election campaign? Compare it with the usual form of election poll information.
8. Use the data in Table 4–2 to construct a histogram of assessed percent of GNP growth over three years.
9. Consider the event: "A manned space flight will successfully land on Mars in the next five years." Without decomposing this event into subevents, assess a probability for the event as defined. Now consider two different ways of decomposing the event by thinking of suitable structures, such as the chain of events that would have to precede a manned space flight to Mars. Assess probabilities for these subevents, and use the rules of probability to calculate a probability for the main event.
10. This question is related to, but distinct from problem 9 (above). Consider the number of years, $N$, between now and when a successful manned space flight to Mars occurs. This is an uncertain quantity. Assess a five-point fractile distribution for this uncertain quantity. Follow this with a 10-interval, fixed probability distribution assessment. Check for consistency between your methods.
11. This question relates to problem 10 above. Structure the process into a series of steps or stages that must occur before a manned

space flight to Mars occurs. For each step assess a probability distribution over time using a convenient method. Combine these distributions to get a composite distribution that you can use to compare with the results of problem 10. Was the decomposition helpful?

12. Assess a cumulative probability distribution for the uncertain quantity: "The number of MBA graduates in the United States this year." Compare your distribution with those of your colleagues and attempt to converge towards a consensus, or group representation of this probability distribution.
13. Construct a simple decision tree using ARBORIST. Use the probability wheel assessment aid within ARBORIST to experiment with this assessment procedure. To what extent can such aids help the judgmental assessment procedure?
14. Consider the uncertain quantity "damage to your car over the next 12 months." If you do not have a car, consider some other item of value that you have.
    *a.* What is your estimate of the probability that your car will be damaged or stolen over the next 12 months?
    *b.* If it is damaged or stolen, what is the highest likely amount of loss that could occur, and what is the lowest? Use the concepts of 99% and 1% fractiles to estimate these extremes. What is the median value?
    *c.* Use this data, and further estimates as needed, to construct a probability distribution for the total amount of insurance claims that you expect to make over the next year, assuming that you have full insurance on your car against damage and theft.
    *d.* Once you have assessed this distribution, calculate its expected value and compare this with the insurance premium you pay.
    *e.* What conclusions can you draw from the comparison of the expected value of your claims distribution and the premium you pay?
15. Assess five-point fractile distributions using the methods outlined in this chapter. In each case begin with the 1% and the 99% fractiles followed by the median (50% fractile), followed by the quartile (25% and 75%) fractiles.
    *a.* The percentage of your class colleagues who believe that there will be a nuclear war on this planet during the next 10 years.
    *b.* The percentage of your class colleagues who believe that there will be a nuclear war on this planet during the next 50 years.
    *c.* The percentage of your coffee-drinking class colleagues who usually use a sweetener (of any type) in their coffee.
    *d.* The percentage of your class colleagues who consider themselves beer drinkers.

*e*. The percentage of your class colleagues who believe in capital punishment.
*f*. The percentage of your class colleagues who are in favor of the legalization of marijuana smoking.
*g*. The latitude of Melbourne, Australia.
*h*. The number of MBA graduates in the United States per year.
*i*. The shortest distance by road from New York to Los Angeles.

For these uncertain quantities make your assessments using your current state of knowledge. Do not investigate sources of information that would change that state of knowledge.

16. Put yourself in the position of responsibility for the risk management function for the city of New York. You have been asked to consider whether this city should take out insurance against liability claims (against the city) made by people who attend the upcoming concert by a famous British rock-and-roll group. Expected attendance is between 300,000 and 750,000 people. The last two concerts of this nature in Central Park produced a number of injuries, all of which were attended to by on-site paramedics, with no resulting liability suits against the city. You have had three insurance companies quote for full coverage against this liability. The quotes were \$50,000, \$70,000, and \$150,000. Administrators organizing the event have identified a number of possible instances that might result in loss, such as injuries caused due to a blackout of the lighting system, injuries caused by a light tower falling over or somebody falling from a light tower, and injuries caused by fighting. Although no previous concerts resulted in lawsuits, your brief is to consider whether the city should insure against the possibility of a liability claim.
    *a*. Use a five-point fractile assessment procedure to translate your state of knowledge/uncertainty into a probability distribution. The uncertain quantity in this case is the total cost to the city of any possible claims.
    *b*. Construct a continuous probability distribution of loss amount.
    *c*. Based on your assessments would you take out insurance given that the lowest premium is \$50,000? State the reasons for your decision.

# APPENDIX

## A PROBABILITY PRIMER

Probability is the language with which we measure and describe uncertainty. Hence a basic understanding of the concepts of probability is fundamental to the study and use of decision analysis. This appendix, in conjunction with Chapter 4, should be studied by anyone who is not familiar with probabilistic concepts. We begin with a brief introduction to set theory as a useful framework from which to approach the field of probability. The style of this presentation is not to give formal proofs and definitions but to provide information in a concise form that will provide the basic understanding necessary to facilitate the use of probabilistic concepts in decision analysis. The reader who requires a more formal or detailed treatment should consult any of a variety of business statistics texts.[1]

## SET THEORY

A *set* is a collection of things, called *elements*. Sets are usually described by either a rule (such as the set of all odd numbers) or by the elements comprising that set (such as the names of all people enrolled in a particular course).

A *sample space* describes the set of all possible results from a random occurrence. For example, when two dice are tossed, the sample space of outcomes showing on the tops of the dice is the set: (2, 3, 4, 5, 6, 7, 8, 9, 10, 11, 12).

An *event* is an occurrence, defined in terms of a subset of a sample space. For example we can define the event: "toss a pair of dice and get an odd-numbered outcome." This event is associated with the subset of outcomes (3, 5, 7, 9, 11) and occurs if any of the elements in the subset occurs.

The *union* of two sets is itself a set containing all the elements in one *or* the other (or both) of the two sets. For example, the union of sets defined as the readers of *The Wall Street Journal* and the readers of the *New York Times* is the set of readers of one or other (or both of these) papers.

---

[1] There are dozens of books covering an introduction to concepts of probability and statistics. Three good texts are P. Newbould, *Statistics for Business and Economics* (New York: Prentice-Hall, 1984); W. Mendenhall and J. E. Reinmuth, *Statistics for Management and Economics* (New York: Duxbury Press, 1978); and R. Pfaffenberger and J. Patterson, *Statistical Methods in Business and Economics* (Homewood, Ill.: Richard D. Irwin, 1987).

**FIGURE A–1** Union and Intersection of Two Sets

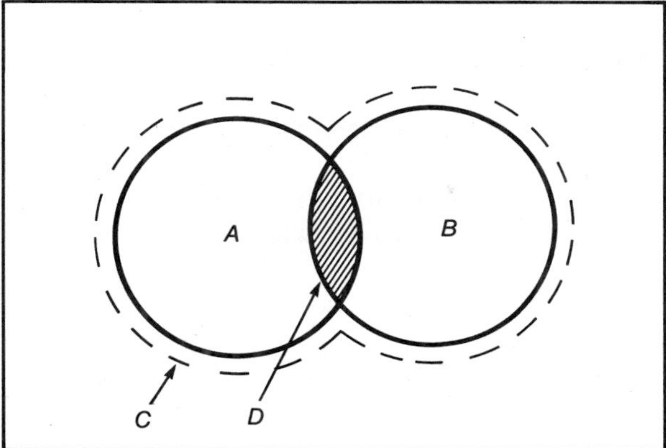


The box is the universal set (set of all things). Set *A* is the circle showing the readers of *The Wall Street Journal*. Set *B* is the circle showing the readers of the *New York Times*. Set *C* is the union of sets *A* and *B*, written $A \cup B$. Set *C* is shown as the dotted line. Set *D* is the intersection of sets *A* and *B*, written $A \cap B$ and is shown as a shaded area.

The *intersection* of two sets is itself a set containing elements that are in both of the original sets. In the newspaper example above, the intersection of the set of readers of *The Wall Street Journal* and the set of readers of the *New York Times* is the set of readers of both papers.

It is often convenient to represent sets in diagram form. Figure A–1 shows the sets involved in the newspaper example.

If two sets have no elements in their intersection they are *mutually exclusive*. The same can be said for events as for sets. If two or more events have no outcomes in common, they are mutually exclusive. If two or more events (subsets) together contain all the outcomes (elements) of a sample space (set), they are *collectively exhaustive*.

## PROBABILITY

Probability can be simply defined in terms of events. We define the probability, $P(E)$, of an event, $E$, as the likelihood of $E$ occurring:

$$P(E) = \frac{\text{Number of ways } E \text{ can occur}}{\text{Total number of equally likely outcomes in the sample space}}$$

This definition is not valid when outcomes are not equally likely. For example, reconsider the tossing of two dice and the event: "The outcome is a 3." How many elements are in the sample space? Each die has six possible outcomes hence there are $6 \times 6 = 36$ possible combinations of outcomes of the two. The numerator of the above probability definition is the number of ways that the outcome 3 can occur, and there are two ways, namely, a 2 and a 1, and a 1 and a 2. It is important to note that these are two distinct outcomes. They are a combination of two random events, each die outcome being independent of the other.

The definition of probability given above is limited to a specific class of events. More generally, probability is defined as being the likelihood of a specified event. This can be primarily a (subjective) degree of belief, or perhaps an estimate based on historical evidence.

## MANIPULATION OF PROBABILITIES

Probabilities must be equal to or fall in the range between zero and one. Two important basic rules of probabilities are:

**The Addition Rule**

$$P(A \cup B) = P(A) + P(B)$$

if $A$ and $B$ are mutually exclusive. For example, in dealing with the toss of two dice, if

$$A = (3), \qquad P(A) = \frac{2}{36}$$

and

$$B = (12), \qquad P(B) = \frac{1}{36}$$

then

$$A \cup B = (3, 12) \text{ and } P(A \cup B) = \frac{3}{36}$$

We must modify this rule if the sets $A$ and $B$ are not mutually exclusive. In the dice example, if

$$A = (2,3)$$

and

$$B = (2,12)$$

then

$$P(A) = P(2) + P(3) = \frac{1}{36} + \frac{2}{36} = \frac{3}{36}$$

$$P(B) = P(2) + P(12) = \frac{1}{36} + \frac{1}{36} = \frac{2}{36}$$

It is logically incorrect in this case to state that

$$P(A \cup B) = P(A) + P(B)$$
$$= \frac{3}{36} + \frac{2}{36} = \frac{5}{36}$$

Why? This is because both sets ($A$ and $B$) contain the outcome 2 and hence in the union calculation the probability of a 2 occurrence is double counted. This would be the case for all outcomes that are in both sets (that is, in the intersection of the two sets).

We may more generally state the addition rule

$$P(A \cup B) = P(A) + P(B) - P(A \cap B)$$

By subtracting the probability of outcomes in the intersection we avoid the double counting effect. Where $A$ and $B$ are mutually exclusive, their intersection is the empty (null) set, having no elements.

**The Multiplication Rule.** To define the multiplication rule we need two more definitions:

First, *conditional probability* is the likelihood of an event occurring given that some other event has or has not occurred. We write $P(A/B)$, the probability of ($A$ given $B$), to signify the conditional probability of $A$ occurring given that $B$ occurs or has occurred. Note that $P(A/B)$ and $P(B/A)$ are not the same thing.

Second, two events, $A$ and $B$, are *probabilistically independent* if

$$P(A/B) = P(A)$$

and

$$P(B/A) = P(B)$$

These equations literally state that event independence exists when the likelihood of one event occurring is unaffected by the occurrence or not of the other event. For example, the likelihood of rain at a particular instant in New York and in Singapore could be said to be independent events. Although this could be argued as not strictly true, these events are very close to independent. Knowing that it has or has not rained in Singapore would hardly change a rain probability prediction in New York, and vice versa. However, if we consider Minneapolis and St. Paul, the likelihood of rain in these cities is certainly not independent. Their close proximity means that the knowledge that it did or did not just rain in Minneapolis is likely to affect a rain probability forecast in St. Paul, and vice versa.

We can say

$$P(\text{Rain in Singapore/Rain in New York}) = P(\text{Rain in Singapore})$$

and

$$P(\text{Rain in New York/Rain in Singapore}) = P(\text{Rain in New York})$$

But it would not be reasonable to assume the same independence for a pair of cities that are near each other:

$$P(\text{Rain in Minneapolis/Rain in St. Paul}) \neq P(\text{Rain in Minneapolis})$$
$$P(\text{Rain in St. Paul/Rain in Minneapolis}) \neq P(\text{Rain in St. Paul})$$

We can now use the notions of independence and conditional probability to define the probability multiplication rule.

For events which are independent

$$P(A \text{ and } B) = P(A) \times P(B)$$

For events which are dependent

$$\begin{aligned} P(A \text{ and } B) &= P(A/B) \times P(B) \\ &= P(B/A) \times P(A) \end{aligned}$$

The addition and multiplication rules are important for manipulating the probabilities on decision trees.

## PROBABILITY DISTRIBUTIONS

A probability distribution describes the likelihoods of a complete set of events in a sample space. Probability distributions can take on many forms. They can describe random variables, which may be discrete or continuous in nature, using formulae. The binomal, Poisson, and normal distributions are common examples of probability distributions defined by algebraic formulae. Each of these structured distribution forms, and a host of others, may be useful in certain situations in modeling the likelihoods of outcomes of a random variable.

A probability distribution can be defined simply as a set of probabilities for a set of events covering all of the sample space. For example, in the toss of two dice:

$$P(2) = \frac{1}{36}$$
$$P(3) = \frac{2}{36}$$
$$P(4) = \frac{3}{36}$$
$$P(5) = \frac{4}{36}$$
$$P(6) = \frac{5}{36}$$
$$P(7) = \frac{6}{36}$$
$$P(8) = \frac{5}{36}$$

$$P(9) = \frac{4}{36}$$

$$P(10) = \frac{3}{36}$$

$$P(11) = \frac{2}{36}$$

$$P(12) = \frac{1}{36}$$

$$\Sigma = \frac{36}{36}$$

*Cumulative probability distributions* contain the same basic information as probability distributions, except in cumulative form. A cumulative distribution for the two-dice example is:

$$P(2) = \frac{1}{36}$$

$$P(3) = \frac{3}{36}$$

$$P(4) = \frac{6}{36}$$

$$P(5) = \frac{10}{36}$$

$$P(6) = \frac{15}{36}$$

$$P(7) = \frac{21}{36}$$

$$P(8) = \frac{26}{36}$$

$$P(9) = \frac{30}{36}$$

$$P(10) = \frac{33}{36}$$

$$P(11) = \frac{35}{36}$$

$$P(12) = \frac{36}{36}$$

Cumulative probabilities describe the likelihood of a variable taking on a value less than or equal to the specified one.

CHAPTER FIVE

# Choosing between Alternatives

## OUTLINE



## OBJECTIVES

After completing this chapter, you should be able to:

**1.** Apply the nonprobabilistic decision rules to any single-stage decision model, noting their associated insights and limitations.
**2.** Use the expected value decision rule to roll back any complete decision tree.
**3.** Discuss the implications and limitations of the expected value approach.
**4.** Judge whether the expected value approach is a good or poor representation for a decision maker's choice process in any decision model.
**5.** Discuss the nature and value of insights and inferences produced by decision analysis in terms of decision process, understanding the problem, and guiding choice.
**6.** Draw conclusions based on mean-variance comparisons, and note the assumptions and limitations of the mean-variance approach.
**7.** Explain the dominance approach, and compare whole probability distributions (risk profiles).
**8.** Judge which situations warrant formal modeling of decision criteria and which are more suited to the use of heuristics.

# INTRODUCTION

This chapter provides descriptions and evaluations of various rules that can be applied to decision analysis models in order to identify the best course of action. We will outline a number of different kinds of rules and suggest which are best, which are worst, and why. The key issues in choosing a decision rule to apply to a decision model are the rule's accuracy as a representation of the decision maker's preferences and the quality of prescriptive insight that will be gained from its use. Once a managerial decision problem has been structured and the quantitative information is at hand, the time has come to determine the best strategy. A decision strategy is the statement of a set of preferred actions. Strategies may be conditional upon the actions of others or upon the resolution of uncertain quantities. An example of a decision strategy is:

"Let's test market our beer in localities X, Y, and Z for six months. If we achieve a market share equal to or above 4% on average, we will enter those new markets. If the test market results are generally poor (market share equal to or less than 1%), we will not enter any new markets. If market share in the test regions is mediocre (share between 1% and 4%) we will invest in test marketing some other locations."

Let us note some features of this decision strategy that can be applied in general. First, it is **complete.** By this, we mean that it involves an initial action and a set of subsequent actions (conditional upon a chance event) that cover **all** possible eventualities. Second, it is **action oriented.** The decision model was structured such that various actions were evaluated and the resulting decision strategy is a **plan of action.** Third, a **time element** is involved. Planned actions can be immediate or at some time in the future. The pattern of uncertainty resolution and choice between alternatives is built in to the decision analysis model structure and must be appropriately reflected in the decision strategy.

This chapter focuses on the process of choosing a decision strategy for an established decision model. Once the decision maker has a decision tree that represents the problem well, information is collected and assessments are made of the relevant probabilities and payoffs. At this point the model can be used to produce inferences about the problem. This is not to say that there is nothing to be learned from the problem structuring and assessment phases of decision analysis. These phases are particularly helpful in generating an understanding of the problem. However, it is at the choice stage where the problem is generally resolved in the sense that a decision strategy is identified based on inference gained from the decision model.

Many methods are available for making choices and determining decision strategies. These can conveniently be categorized as *formal rules* or *heuristics* (informal rules often termed *rules of thumb*).

Formal rules include very simple decision criteria or can become quite complex as we include more and more refinements and factors of importance in them. They include nonprobabilistic rules (rules which do not take account of event likelihoods), probabilistic rules involving single dimensions of value, and risk adjusting rules. In this chapter we will discuss non-probabilistic rules as well as probabilistic rules involving single dimensions of value. More complex formal rules (involving the utility concept) are given special treatment in Chapters 6 and 7.

This chapter also considers heuristic methods of decision making.

## NONPROBABILISTIC RULES

A number of rules for choosing between alternatives exist that take no account of the likelihood of various outcomes and events. These include the maxi-max, maxi-min and mini-max regret decision criteria.

### The Maxi-Max Decision Rule

This criterion involves a choice of the action that can lead to the best possible outcome, regardless of anything else. It is a strategy that an optimist might follow. Let us consider how this rule works in the following example.

---

EXAMPLE 5–1

## Doncaster Battery Company (A)

The Doncaster Battery Company is faced with a decision to commit its production resources to one of three strategies. The demand for the various products the company makes is uncertain, and the three production strategies are the best of a much larger number of options initially considered. It is expected that the demand patterns will result in one of four possible events. The management team at Doncaster Battery has calculated the payoffs associated with each action-consequence pair. (See Table 5–1.)

Table 5–1 is a payoff table showing the profit contribution ($000) of each action-consequence pair. The maxi-max decision rule suggests that strategy 2 should be undertaken because it is the one with the highest payoff potential. That payoff is $700,000, and occurs only if the demand pattern (which is uncertain at the time of decision) turns out to be Event 3. Note that this rule does not account for the likelihood of events. It also does not account for the other payoffs of the optimal strategy (which in this case is strategy 2). These other payoffs may be extremely poor indeed, and the

**TABLE 5–1** Doncaster Battery Forecast Profit Contributions ($000)

| | Demand Pattern | | | |
|---|---|---|---|---|
| | *Event 1* | *Event 2* | *Event 3* | *Event 4* |
| Strategy 1<br>Level Production* | 400 | 320 | 540 | 600 |
| Strategy 2<br>Chase Demand, Overtime | 250 | 350 | 700 | 550 |
| Strategy 3<br>Partial Second Shift | 600 | 280 | 150 | 400 |

* Level production means keeping the same production rate all year. If demand is seasonal, then at various times substantial finished goods inventories may occur. Strategy 2 involves matching production to seasonal demand, keeping low inventory. Strategy 3 requires a second shift to be added during the peak demand period for about 10 weeks.

**TABLE 5–2** A Modified Payoff Table for Doncaster Battery

| | *Event 1* | *Event 2* | *Event 3* | *Event 4* |
|---|---|---|---|---|
| Strategy 1 | 400 | 320 | 540 | 600 |
| Strategy 2 | Bankruptcy | Bankruptcy | 700 | Bankruptcy |
| Strategy 3 | 600 | 280 | 150 | 400 |

maxi-max rule does not change its recommended choice. For example, consider Table 5–2.

Table 5–2 has been constructed so as to be identical to Table 5–1, except that for strategy 2, all events except event 3 lead to bankruptcy. The maxi-max rule still suggests that strategy 2 is the best one because it still has the highest of the maximum payoffs over all the strategies. It is easy to understand why this rule is termed **optimistic.** The decision maker who follows this rule is hoping for a favorable event and is prepared to act on the presumption of a favorable event, while ignoring other possible consequences. To summarize, the maxi-max rule compares the best payoff of each strategy and guides the decision maker to choose the strategy having the highest of these payoff maxima. It boils down simply to finding the strategy with the best potential outcome, regardless of other factors.

---

The maxi-max rule is of limited direct usefulness because there are few situations in which it is appropriate to go for broke and choose a strategy with the possibility of achieving the best outcome, regardless of all other factors. However, it is useful to consider what the best possible outcome is when making decisions under uncertainty, and the maxi-max rule is therefore one that can provide insight about a problem. Many executives, when making a difficult decision, want to know: ''What is the best possible result that we can achieve?'' The maxi-max rule identifies the decision strategy which can lead to that chance outcome.

Executives also often wish to know what is the worst thing that can happen to them in choosing a strategy. Further, they may wish to know which strategy leads to the least-worst chance outcome. Another non-probabilistic decision rule called maxi-min is appropriate in that circumstance.

## The Maxi-Min Decision Rule

The maxi-min criterion considers the worst payoff of each strategy and selects the best strategy as the one with the highest of these minimum outcomes. In other words, if we assume that the chance event produces the most unfavorable outcome for any strategy, then maxi-min chooses such as to maximize over these worst outcomes. In the Doncaster Battery example (Table 5–1) the minimum payoffs of the various strategies were:

| | |
|---|---|
| Level production, Strategy 1: | 320 |
| Chase demand, overtime, Strategy 2: | 250 |
| Partial second shift, Strategy 3: | 150 |

The highest of these minima is the $320 figure associated with strategy 1. The maxi-min criterion can obviously lead to a very different recommended choice from the maxi-max rule. Note that both rules are based on comparisons of extreme outcomes. In the maxi-max case, extreme best outcomes for each strategy are compared, and in the maxi-min case, extreme worst outcomes for each strategy are compared. Just as the maxi-max rule is consistent with an optimistic outlook over the range of the uncertain quantity, the maxi-min rule infers a pessimistic outlook.

## The Mini-Max Regret Decision Rule

The mini-max regret criterion is different from the purely pessimistic maxi-min and optimistic maxi-max rules in its philosophy. Whereas the maxi-max and maxi-min rules are **prospective** in terms of looking forward through time to the outcome resolution, the mini-max regret rule is **retrospective** in its outlook. Suppose the general manager of Doncaster Battery said: ''I am concerned about making a decision that I will regret later. After the decision is made and the outcome is known, I'll be kicking myself if I have made the wrong choice. Which strategy is likely to cause me least regret?''

Let us answer that question by defining regret formally. Regret (which can be defined for any action-consequence pair) is the amount of difference between the payoff for that pair and the best payoff for that chance event. Hence to calculate regret amounts, the first thing that must be identified is the **best strategy for each chance event.** In Table 5–1, these best strategies are:

Strategy 3 given Event 1
Strategy 2 given Event 2
Strategy 2 given Event 3
Strategy 1 given Event 4

Given any chance event, you would in retrospect have no regret if you had chosen the corresponding best strategy as shown immediately above. For each chance event, your regret for any other strategy is then defined as the difference between the payoffs of the "no regret" strategy and the strategy that was actually chosen. The regret information can be summarized on a regret table. Table 5–3 shows the regrets for the Doncaster Battery example. It is derived from Table 5–1 using the following steps:

1. For each column of payoffs (associated with a particular outcome) assign zero regret to the row with the highest payoff.
2. For each other element of that column, the regret value for any strategy is the difference between its payoff and the highest payoff of that column.

In Table 5–3 note the maximum regret that could occur for any strategy by looking along the rows. The maximum regret values are:

Strategy 1: 200
Strategy 2: 350
Strategy 3: 550

The mini-max regret rule recommends selection of the strategy that has the lowest value of maximum regret. In this instance, strategy 1 would be selected.

In summary, it is possible to make choices according to rules that do not account for event likelihoods. Although it is useful to know about these rules, the decision analysis philosophy generally aims towards explicitly recognizing and accounting for uncertainty. Hence, these rules tend to be useful in special cases only and are rarely used in real decision problems. Their examination does introduce a number of useful concepts. First, we note that the use of different choice criteria can lead to different preferred strategy indications. Second, it is apparent that concepts such as optimism, pessimism, and regret can be operationalized and quantified. Some of these

**TABLE 5–3** A Regret Table for Doncaster Battery Company

| | *Event 1* | *Event 2* | *Event 3* | *Event 4* |
|---|---|---|---|---|
| Strategy 1 | 200 | 30 | 160 | 0 |
| Strategy 2 | 350 | 0 | 0 | 50 |
| Strategy 3 | 0 | 70 | 550 | 200 |

rules may not be reasonable in themselves for use in many real decision processes, but can form the basis of more complex, more realistic choice criteria.

These rules also can be useful in providing insights about the problem, even when they do not accurately represent the decision maker's preferences. Even though a decision maker may wish to take probabilities into account, it is often useful to know what the implications are of optimistic, pessimistic, and regret rules. Hence these nonprobabilistic rules do have a role to play in decision analysis, on occasion, in providing insights about decisions even if they are not used to directly determine a preferred decision strategy.

## RULES INVOLVING PROBABILITY

In most real decisions involving uncertainty, there are two types of decision elements that should normally be considered. The first is the **value** associated with various alternatives and outcomes. Value may be measured in terms of money (as is the case in many business decisions) or else in terms of other dimensions. This value element was the only type of element considered in the previous section of this chapter which dealt with nonprobabilistic rules.

The second decision element is the **likelihood** of uncertain events. To account for this element, we have defined a measurement scale, called probability, which has been discussed at some length in an earlier chapter.

### The Expected Value Rule

Probabilistic decision rules account in some way for both likelihoods and values associated with various alternative actions. The most common probabilistic rule is the expected value rule. Under this rule, the desirability of a decision strategy is the **expected value** of its possible outcomes.

Hence for actions, $A_i$, where

$$i = 1 \text{ to } n,$$

we define outcomes, $O_j$,

$$(j = 1 \text{ to } m)$$

that can occur having values $V_{ij}$ and probabilities $p_{ij}$. The expected value of a particular action $A_i$ is

$$EV_i = \sum_{\text{all } j} p_{ij} \times V_{ij}.$$

The expected value decision criterion suggests that the decision maker should choose the action $A_i$, which has the most preferred expected value

(value of $EV_i$). To use this rule we must, for every alternative action, multiply all the relevant outcome values by their probabilities and add these products. The resultant expected values are then simply compared to see which is best. Note that the number of actions, $n$, and outcomes, $m$, may vary across nodes on a decision tree.

---

## EXAMPLE 5–2

### Doncaster Battery Company (B)

The general manager of Doncaster Battery (see Example 5–1) wanted to take into account the probabilities of the various chance events involved in his decision as well as the values (profit contributions). He assessed a set of probabilities for each of the four chance events as:

| *Event* | *1* | *2* | *3* | *4* |
|---|---|---|---|---|
| Probability | 0.2 | 0.4 | 0.3 | 0.1 |

The expected values for each strategy are:

$$\begin{aligned} EV\text{ (strategy 1)} &= 0.2 \times 400 + 0.4 \times 320 + 0.3 \times 540 + 0.1 \times 600 \\ &= 430 \\ EV\text{ (strategy 2)} &= 0.2 \times 250 + 0.4 \times 350 + 0.3 \times 700 + 0.1 \times 550 \\ &= 455 \\ EV\text{ (strategy 3)} &= 0.2 \times 600 + 0.4 \times 280 + 0.3 \times 150 + 0.1 \times 400 \\ &= 317. \end{aligned}$$

These expected values are in the same units of measure as the values themselves, in this case in thousands of dollars (see Table 5–1). Note that the expected values are exactly what they pertain to be, namely **expectations,** and that they are not real values that may occur as outcomes but merely **probability weighted averages** of values. For this example, if the decision maker was going to base his decision on an expected value rule, then strategy 2 should be selected, as it has the most preferred expected value of profit contribution.

---

A most preferred strategy may be defined as having the highest expected value, as would be expected if profit is the payoff variable. Alternatively we may be wishing to find the strategy such that the most preferred choice has the lowest expected value. A common example is cost minimization where payoffs are measured in dollar terms but represent costs rather than profits. Expected values need not be associated with monetary values, but rather can be calculated for any scale of measure. Many managerial decisions have monetary values as a major dimension of value, however, it is often useful and necessary to consider other types of values. To further illustrate the expected value concept, consider the following example of a manufacturing manager who is choosing between alternative production system designs.

## EXAMPLE 5-3

### Zinco Productions (A)

Zinco Productions was a small division of a large chemical conglomerate organization. Its general manager, Bob Schroer, had a decision to make about replacing part of his production process. The division produced only one product, zinc oxide, a white powder used mainly in various types of creams and paints. The total world market for this product had shrunk substantially over recent years as cheaper chemicals replaced zinc oxide in many of the products that it had traditionally been used for. While a large number of zinc oxide plants had closed down around the country, Zinco had remained profitable, and Mr. Schroer foresaw a period where total demand would stabilize and profitability would increase. He had been able to stay competitive during difficult times because of the high quality of his product and because of his ability to keep costs down in the manufacturing facility.

Mr. Schroer had been carefully monitoring his costs and noted that a substantial portion of them were related to the cost of electric power. Electric rates were expected to rise sharply in future years, and he gave thought to replacing part of his production process with a new, electronically controlled system which would be much more energy efficient. The cost of the new system almost exactly balanced the cost of future energy savings. The critical factor in Mr. Schroer's mind in this instance was how the new process might affect his product quality.

Product quality was measured in terms of particle size and proportion of impurities, with the latter being by far the more important and more difficult factor to control. With the old process, impurities were currently 0.15% and there was a 50:50 chance that this could be decreased to 0.12% in the near future through the implementation of new operating procedures (using existing equipment).

To Mr. Schroer's knowledge, the new process was untried in zinc oxide plants, and he was uncertain about its effect on product quality. He discussed this matter with his suppliers and process engineers and then assessed the following probability distribution for new process product quality.

| *Impurities* | *Probability* |
|---|---|
| 0.08% | 0.05 |
| 0.10% | 0.15 |
| 0.12% | 0.2 |
| 0.14% | 0.4 |
| 0.16% | 0.2 |
| | $\Sigma$ = 1.0 |

The expected value of quality with the new process was:

$$\begin{aligned}\text{Expected quality} &= 0.08\% \times 0.05 + 0.10\% \times 0.15 + 0.12\% \times 0.2 \\ &\quad + 0.14\% \times 0.4 + 0.16\% \times 0.2 \\ &= 0.131\%\end{aligned}$$

The expected value of the old process was:

$$\begin{aligned}\text{Expected quality} &= 0.15\% \times 0.5 + 0.12\% \times 0.5 \\ &= 0.135\%\end{aligned}$$

Since Mr. Schroer obviously preferred a minimum of impurities, the expected value rule indicates that the new process is preferable. This difference in expected values was quite small.

---

From this example we can see that the expected value rule can be applied to any measure of value, whether it be monetary or nonmonetary. When the measure is money, the expected value rule is known as expected monetary value (EMV).

## Expected Value Rules in Multiple-Stage Decisions

The expected value rule can be used as a decision criterion in multiple-stage decisions, through the use of the following rollback procedure:

> On a decision tree, work from right to left, beginning with each of the final outcomes and their associated values. In doing so, determine the expected value of nodes as follows:
>
> *a.* For decision nodes, the expected value at the node is the *most preferred expected value* of all immediately subsequent nodes or branches.
>
> *b.* For chance event nodes, the expected value is the *probability weighted average* of the value of all immediately subsequent nodes or branches.

This procedure can be used to implement the expected value rule for any decision tree, no matter how large and complex its structure may be. This rollback procedure is a systematic calculation of expected values from right to left on the decision tree. A useful additional procedure is to cross out those branches emanating from decision nodes that do not have the best expected value. If this is done as part of the rollback, then the optimal strategy can easily be read from a decision tree as that which involves the branches that are not crossed out.

The next example follows from Example 5–3, Zinco Productions (A).

---

## EXAMPLE 5–4

### Zinco Productions (B)

Just as Mr. Schroer was considering the equipment replacement problem, two events occurred that forced him to rethink the decision. The first was a machinery breakdown that occurred elsewhere in the production process which temporarily closed down the system. Mr. Schroer realized that this was an ideal time to introduce the new process, if it were to be introduced at all. Therefore, he felt that the decision needed to be made immediately. The second new factor was that he received a letter from his zinc supplier announcing a possible change in the nature of this raw material. The letter said that there was a possibility that the old zinc product would be discontinued and that a new product consisting of larger zinc granules would replace it. Mr. Schroer consulted his chief production engineer and drew a decision tree in order to help clarify his problem. The decision tree reflects the fact that the changed product specifications the zinc supplier had advised of would differentially affect the zinc oxide quality (as measured by percentage of impurities) depending on whether or not the new electronically controlled equipment was installed. Mr. Schroer realized he could always react to this change in raw material specifications (should it occur) by changing supplier. His alternative actions and assessments of various outcomes and their possibilities are all shown on Figure 5–1.

He needed to make a number of probabilistic assessments associated with the uncertain quantities in this decision and decided to use a three-outcome structure for the uncertain events of chance event nodes $C_5$, $C_6$, $C_7$, and $C_8$ (Figure 5–1). For each of these he presumed a low, medium, and high possible outcome, having prespecified probabilities of 0.2, 0.6, and 0.2 respectively for each one. He then subjectively assessed quality values representing his beliefs about each outcome. He reviewed his assessments by comparing the estimates both across and within the various branches and nodes. He also carefully considered these assessments relative to those he had previously made (see Example 5–1) which are shown as nodes $C_3$ and $C_4$ on Figure 5–1. He contacted the zinc supplier and asked exactly what were the chances that they would make the change in zinc granule size. They had replied that the probability was 0.75.

**FIGURE 5–1** Mr. Schroer's Decision Tree*

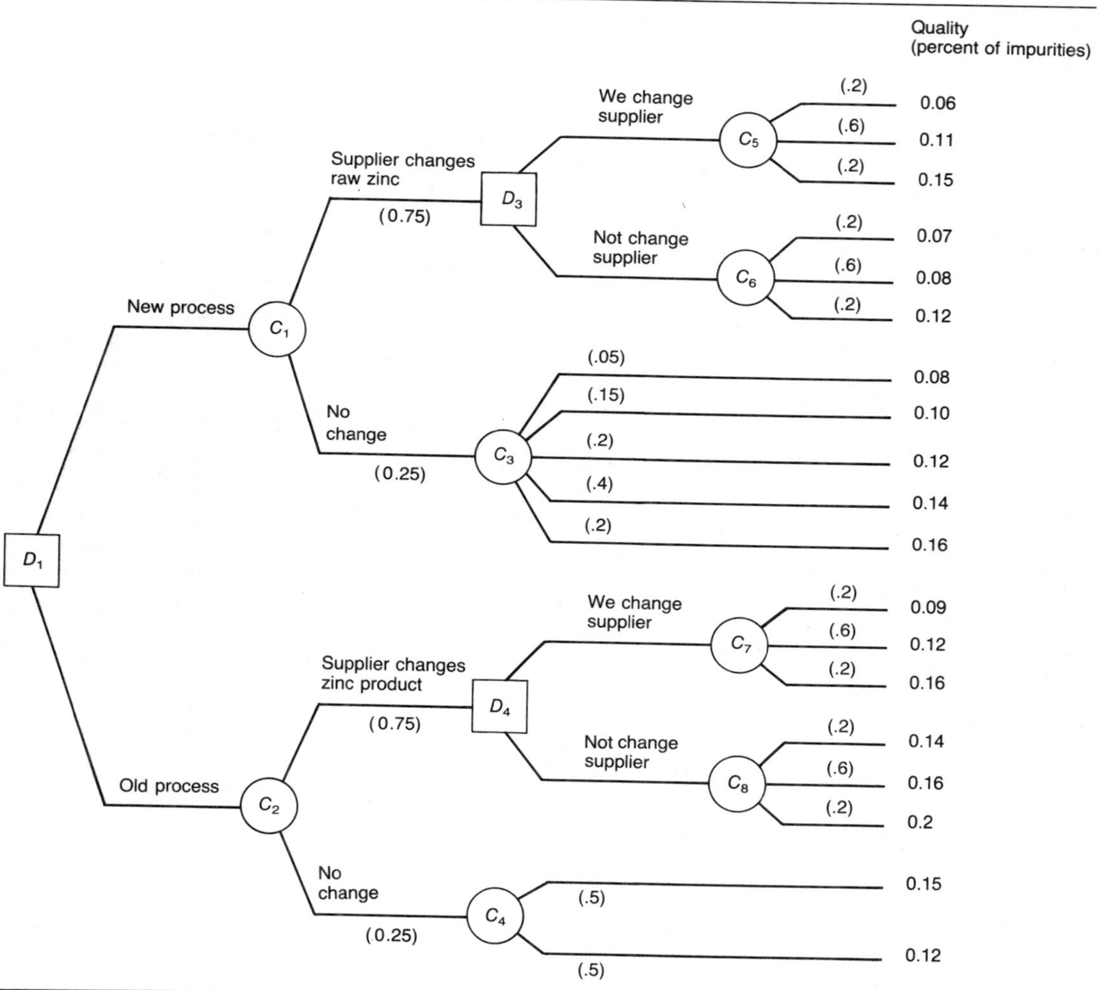


* Chance events $C_5$, $C_6$, $C_3$, $C_7$, $C_8$, and $C_4$ all describe uncertainty about quality.

The decision tree structure reflected the fact that Mr. Schroer felt that the "old versus new" process decision had to be made virtually immediately. He knew that the decision would be affected by the subsequent events involving raw material supply.

He then rolled back the decision tree. Figure 5–2 shows the expected values associated with various nodes. Note that less impurity is preferred to more in applying the expected value rule. Mr. Schroer also crossed out branches emanating from

**FIGURE 5–2** Mr. Schroer's Decision Tree, Rolled Back Using an Expected Value Criterion

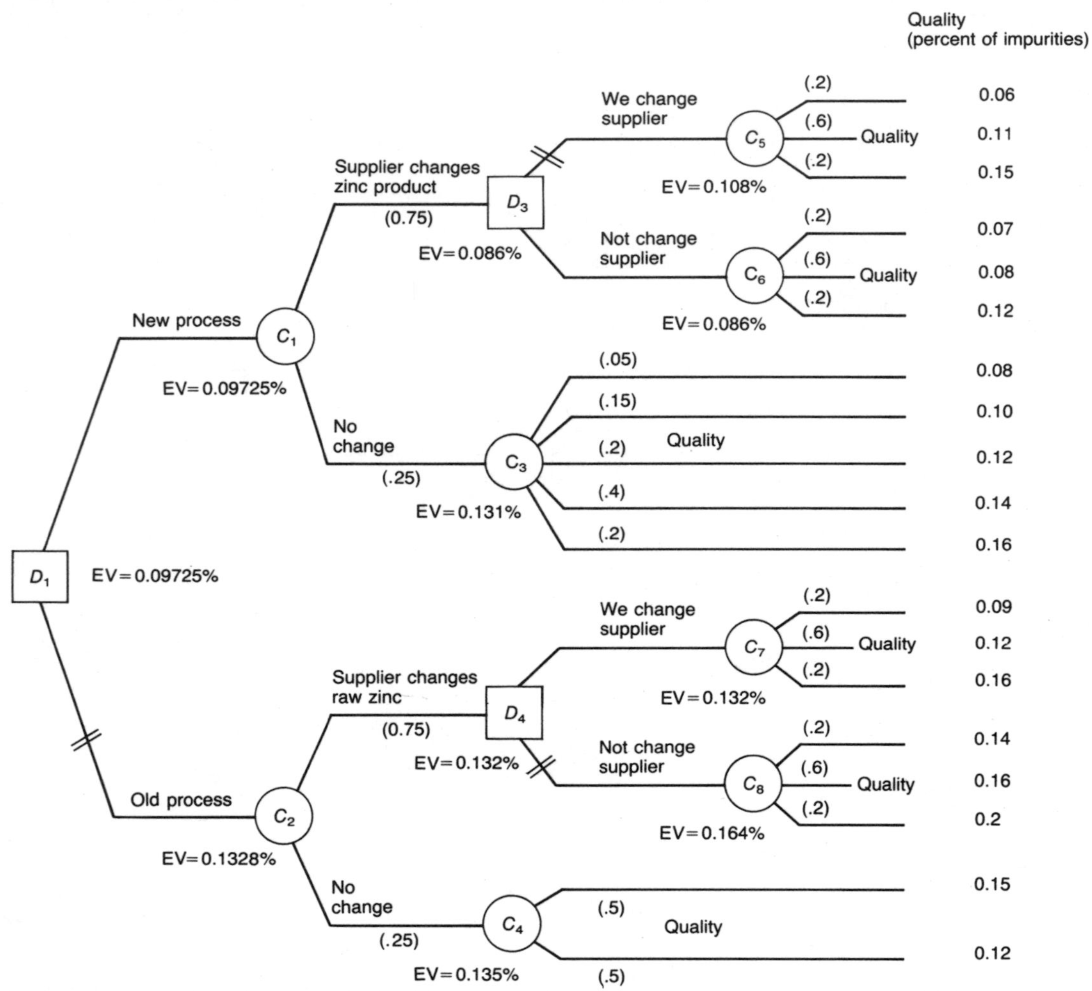


decision nodes that were not preferred, by putting two small strokes through those branches. The expected value rule indicated a clear difference between the new and the old process. This was particularly the case if the supplier made the product specification change, which appeared likely. If this change was made, the old process produced low-quality (high-percent impurity) zinc oxide. The strategy indicated by the decision analysis was to adopt the new process and if the supplier changed his product, to not change suppliers. Mr. Schroer also realized that the new process combined so well with the new zinc raw material (in terms of zinc oxide quality) that he decided to contact his zinc supplier and strongly encourage the change.

He also made a mental note to consider changing supplier if the current supplier did not change its zinc specification. He reasoned that if the current supplier had the potential to change to a raw zinc that would reduce his impurities, then there might be an alternative supplier already producing the zinc with those specifications. He asked the site purchasing manager to investigate. Irrespective of how the raw material supply picture resolved itself, he was now confident that the new electronically controlled process was superior in terms of the quality of product that would result. He double checked his analysis process and implemented his decision.

---

## Limitations of the Expected Value Approach

The expected value rule is powerful, and therefore popular, however, it has a number of limitations. These limitations should lead us to question its usefulness in certain situations. Even with these limitations, expected value is a very powerful decision rule, but it is very good practice to keep the limitations in mind when applying the rule.

**Limitation 1.** The use of an expected value to represent a probability distribution means that information is lost in the sense that the expected value is merely a summary statistic representing the distribution. Are there instances where some of the lost information in the probability distribution (information not fully represented by the expected value) may be relevant to the decision? The answer to this question is a definite yes! For example, we may be interested in the degree of uncertainty associated with various options. A well-known measure of the degree of spread about the mean is the standard deviation. In Example 5–3, Mr. Schroer might have been averse to risk, in which case he would have wanted to compare the risk profiles (see Chapter 2) of the options, or their standard deviations. In such an instance he might then have found that the alternative with the best (in this example, lowest) expected value did not have the best standard deviation. **Trade-offs** would then have to be made. In summary, the expected value rule is appropriate only when the decision maker wishes to gain insight about how best to play the averages and is not concerned about the spread of real outcomes about those averages.

When it is not reasonable merely to play the averages, but nevertheless, desirable to account for probabilities, more complex decision rules are required. This is the subject of Chapter 6.

**Limitation 2.** Expected value rules assume a linear preference function. This limitation is technically related to limitation 1, however it manifests itself differently. Limitation 1 was concerned with the general lack of the expected value rule to account for a decision maker's attitude (e.g., aversion) towards risk. This limitation concerns his preference towards certain levels of value. For example in Figure 5–2 we see that a quality of 0.06% is a possible consequence of chance event $C_5$. This level of very high quality does not appear anywhere else on the tree. Let us presume that if that very high quality were achieved, Mr. Schroer could sell his product as High Grade Zinc Oxide and command a much higher price than if quality were worse than 0.06% impurity. The expected value rule as applied in Example 5–3 does not account for this type of decision element, as it is based on a linear preference scale. Deviations from this linear scale of value can occur as both curvilinear preference functions or discontinuities, and we should check to see whether the linearity assumption is a good approximation as part of the process of interpreting the results.

A related point is with respect to the use of quality as a measure of value in this decision. Since Mr. Schroer's decision was a business decision and the aim of his decision was presumably to meet some monetary goals, was it reasonable to make decisions on the basis of quality? Mr. Schroer knew that the cost of each of the decision options was identical, and he used quality as a measure of value without explicitly specifying the relationship between quality and his monetary goals. A fundamental question he probably should have thought about was whether quality had any intrinsic value or whether it was useful only as a surrogate variable for profits. If he were to dispense with quality as a measure of value and translate the outcomes into monetary amounts, then he would at least have the potential to eliminate the effects of nonlinearities in the quality-profit relationship.

Nevertheless, the expected value rule is based on the assumption that preference is a linear function of some dimension of value, and we note that the preference functions of managers for monetary amounts are themselves generally nonlinear over all but very narrow ranges. This issue of assumed linearity of value/preference is distinct from but related to the issue of aversion or preference for risk.

**Limitation 3.** Single dimensions of value can be treated by the expected value criterion, however trade-offs between different criteria are not accounted for by this rule. For example, if both money and quality each had intrinsic value in Example 5–3, then it is likely that trade-offs would need to be made as part of the decision process. These types of trade-offs are not addressed by the expected value rule as defined in this chapter and hence must be separately analyzed (see Chapter 7). We are assuming that only a single criterion of value exists when we apply the expected value rule as outlined in this chapter. This is unrealistic for many business problems.

**Limitation 4.** Is the philosophy of expected value appropriate to the decision? Unlike the other limitations discussed above, this one refers to the general nature of the expected value criterion itself. Limitations 1, 2, and 3 above questioned the validity and applicability of the rule in certain types of decisions and demonstrated its inability to effectively account for certain elements which may be present in a decision. This fourth limitation questions the rationale, given a set of probabilities and values, for treating them in the particular way defined by the expected value rule. The answer to this question is twofold. First, there *are* compelling theoretical reasons for using an expected value rule. Second it is appealing, indeed almost a natural strategy, to think of weighted averages in some decision situations (such as gambling). However, we should keep in mind that the expected value rule is merely an *abstract concept* that represents a play-the-average strategy, and hence its role should be limited to that of a decision criterion. There are circumstances where the concept of expectation is not an appropriate basis for evaluating alternatives. It must be used only to model and provide inference about real choice processes, and generally not to replace them.

## Expected Opportunity Loss (EOL)

A particular form of expected value is the expected opportunity loss. For any alternative this is the expected value of regret associated with that action.

---

## Example 5–5

### Doncaster Battery Company (C)

The regret values for the Doncaster Battery problem are shown in Figure 5-3. A set of probabilities for each outcome was defined in Example 5-2. These data sets can easily be combined to yield expected regret values as follows:

$$\begin{aligned}
\text{Strategy 1: Expected regret} &= 200 \times 0.2 + 30 \times 0.4 + 160 \times 0.3 + 0 \times 0.1 \\
&= 100 \\
\text{Strategy 2: Expected regret} &= 350 \times 0.2 + 0 \times 0.4 + 0 \times 0.3 + 50 \times 0.1 \\
&= 75 \\
\text{Strategy 3: Expected regret} &= 0 \times 0.2 + 70 \times 0.4 + 550 \times 0.3 + 200 \times 0.1 \\
&= 213
\end{aligned}$$

The EOL rule states that the most preferred strategy is the one with the most preferred expected regret (EOL value). In this case, strategy 2 is preferred because it has the lowest EOL. This EOL value of 75 (again, units are $000) is lower by 25 than the EOL of strategy 1, and lower by 138 than the EOL of strategy 3.

---

**FIGURE 5–3** Regret Values for Doncaster Battery Company

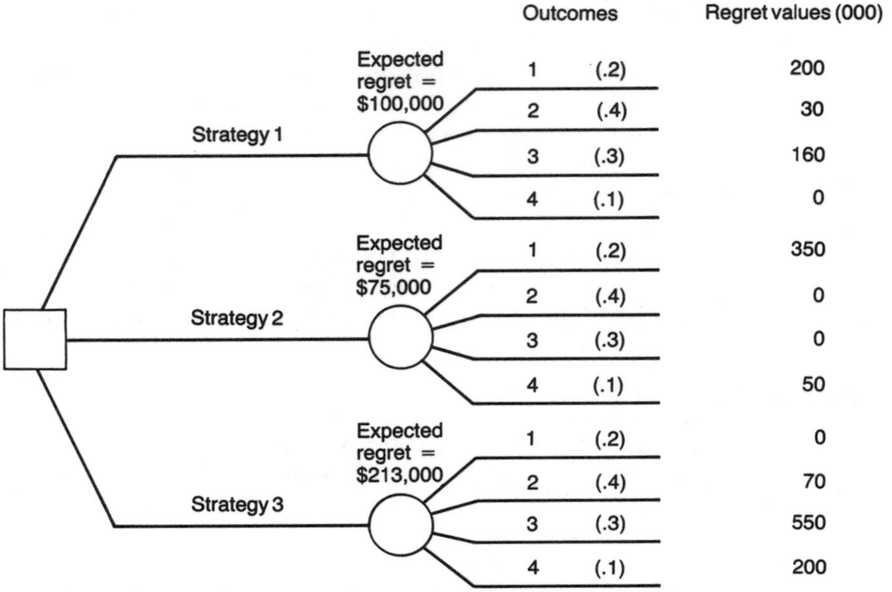

Compare the results of Example 5–5 (the EOL rule) and Example 5–2 (the corresponding EMV example). We can immediately note that the EOL and EMV rules produced exactly the same preference rankings of alternatives, and further, that the differences between the calculated EMV and EOL values are identical. This is indeed not coincidence, but a result of having used the same information in the EMV and EOL calculations. This relationship between EMV and EOL values applies to all examples because all of the regret values (used in EOL computations) are calculated by making the same linear transformation (subtractions of column minima) from the original payoff table. EMV (maximization) and EOL (minimization) rules are essentially the same rule, simply incorporating a linear transformation between them. There are a few instances where it may be handy to calculate EOL values, particularly if the decision maker is thinking in terms of values of regret as against pure monetary values such as cash flows. For large, multistage decision trees, EOL can become complex to interpret, and general practice in decision analysis is to use EMV.

## MEAN-VARIANCE RULES AND STOCHASTIC DOMINANCE

Sometimes it is appropriate to use probabilistic rules that involve more than just the expected value of an uncertain quantity. For example, as mentioned earlier, a decision maker who is sensitive to the degree of risk associated with various strategies may calculate standard deviations or variances as well as expected values and use both these parameters (mean and variance) either to screen options or as a basis of ultimate choice.

---

## EXAMPLE 5–6

### Private Investor

A private investor is considering investing in a foreign country which he believes will experience substantial growth over the next few years. His investment strategies in stocks have been to choose a small number of blue-chip corporations and design a portfolio based on them. Accordingly he has obtained data for the 10 largest companies in the foreign country and calculated the mean and variance of returns from their stock, taking into account price movements and dividends. His raw data are shown in Table 5–4. This data is also represented in Figure 5–4.

The investor considers himself to be a risk-averse wealth maximizer and hence wishes to obtain the highest mean return *and* suffer the lowest variance. However he realizes that it is often a fact of life that stocks with high expected returns also have high variability of returns. He notes that some stocks can immediately be deleted from

**TABLE 5–4** Mean and Variance Values for Ten Stocks

| *Company* | *Expected Return* | *Variance of Return* |
|---|---|---|
| 1 | 8 | 15 |
| 2 | 12 | 22 |
| 3 | 4 | 7 |
| 4 | 16 | 40 |
| 5 | 9 | 30 |
| 6 | 8 | 12 |
| 7 | 12 | 30 |
| 8 | 13 | 17 |
| 9 | 10 | 20 |
| 10 | 10 | 29 |

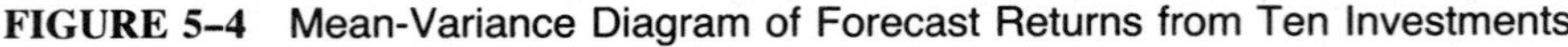

**FIGURE 5–4** Mean-Variance Diagram of Forecast Returns from Ten Investments

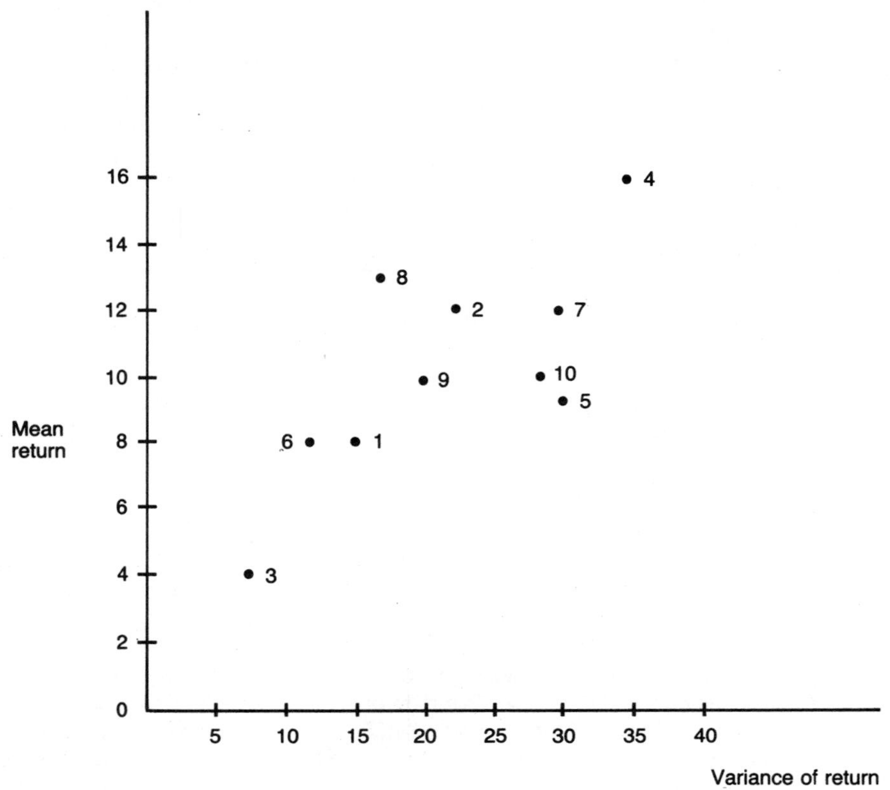


his list of candidates because their mean-variance performance is inferior to others on the list. He reasoned as follows:

1. Company 1 has the same expected return as company 6 but a higher variance, hence company 1 is mean-variance dominated by company 6 and can be eliminated.
2. Similarly, company 7 is dominated by company 2, and company 10 is dominated by company 9.
3. Companies 5 and 7 have the same variance, but company 5 has the lower expected return of the two, hence it is mean-variance dominated and can be screened out.

These instances of dominance relate to separate individual preference for higher values of mean return and lower values of return variance. In addition, companies 2 and 9 can be screened out because in each case company 8 has a higher mean and lower variance. The nondominated companies (3, 4, 6, and 8) form an "efficient portfolio" from which a choice can be made depending on the decision makers' preferences and trade-off rates for mean and variance of return.

The mean-variance measure can be first used as a screening device and then further used to design an efficient portfolio. This particular decision problem is treated in detail in the literature of financial management.[1]

---

Mean-variance analysis is particularly appropriate in situations where the probability distributions of the uncertain quantities are fully described by their mean and variance. The normal distribution is an important example where this holds true. In many instances, the mean and variance of a distribution do not completely describe it, and thus it may be preferable to attempt to compare those distributions directly, rather than compare their means, variances, and perhaps other summary statistics such as median, mode, skewness, and kurtosis (peakedness). Where complete distributions are compared, the principles of **stochastic dominance** can be applied. Let us examine a set of dominance rules in the context of an example.

---

## EXAMPLE 5–7

### Weefind Oil and Gas Corporation

A simulation model produced probability distributions of return on investment for an oil exploration company. At each proposed drilling site, two basic strategies were possible:

Strategy A: Drill one hole and use the results from this operation to decide whether or not to drill another, and if so, where.
Strategy B: Drill two holes at the same time (approximately one mile apart).

Strategy A had the advantage of allowing the decision makers to use the information from the first drilling operation to make relatively well-informed decisions

[1] See, for example, Van Horne (1979).

**FIGURE 5–5** Decision Model Representation for the Weefind Oil Example

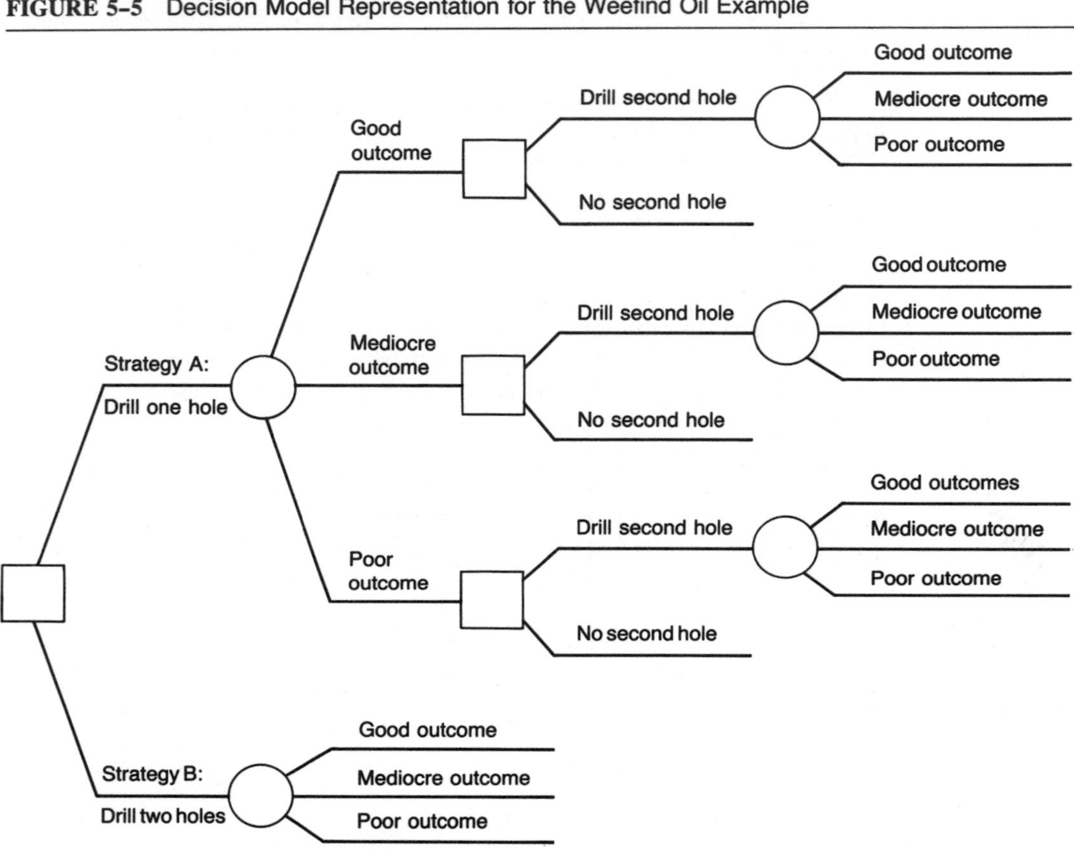


on the second hole. Strategy B was much cheaper to implement, since frequently, two holes were eventually drilled anyway and substantial cost savings occurred if they were drilled at about the same time. Figure 5–5 shows the basic structure of this decision.

Based on their knowledge of the geology of the area and various cost and revenue factors, the analysts within Weefind had structured a fairly complex model which calculated probabilities of various returns on investment. The first site, an offshore field near Galveston, yielded the results shown in Figure 5–6.

From Figure 5–6 it is entirely reasonable to conclude that strategy B is superior to strategy A at this site because the ROI of strategy B is certain to be higher than that of A.

**FIGURE 5–6** Probability Distributions of Return on Investment for Oil Exploration Strategies in Texas

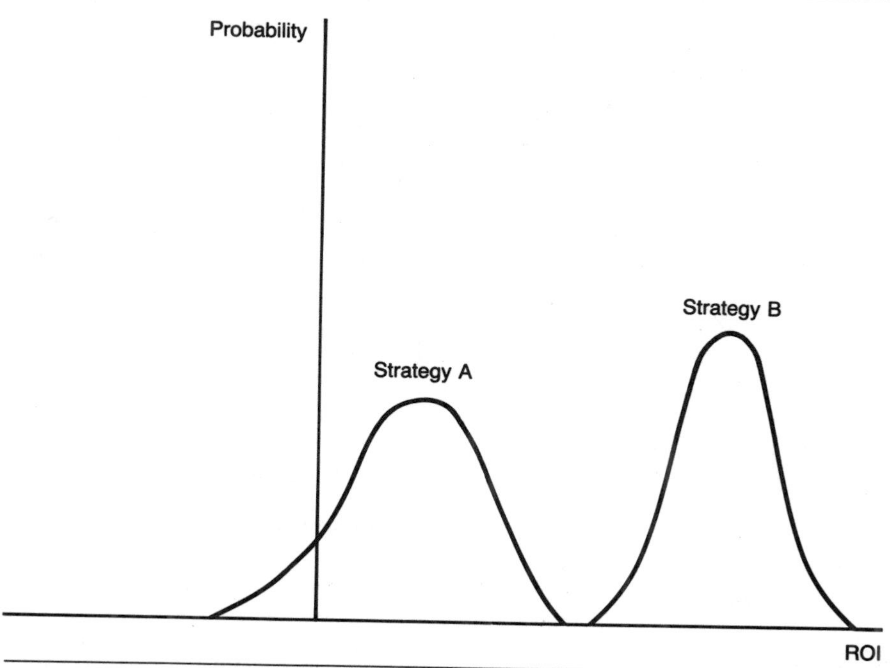


Figure 5–7 shows the probability distributions for a second site (in Oklahoma). In this second instance the probability density distributions do intersect, and we cannot say (as we did for site 1) that one strategy is certain to produce a higher ROI than the other. However we can say that *for all ROI values,* strategy A is *more likely* to exceed that value than strategy B. Note that for the Texas site, we concluded that one alternative dominated the other with certainty. This **deterministic** result is in contrast to that of the Oklahoma site, which is **probabilistic.** Indeed, we note that when the probability density functions do cross and the cumulative probability distributions of competing alternatives do not cross, a condition for **first-order stochastic dominance** exists. For both the deterministic dominance and the first-order stochastic dominance, rankings can be stated without any knowledge of the decision maker's attitude towards risk. Deterministic and first-order stochastic dominance rules can be applied by any decision maker who prefers higher values of ROI to lower values (or vice versa) over the whole range.

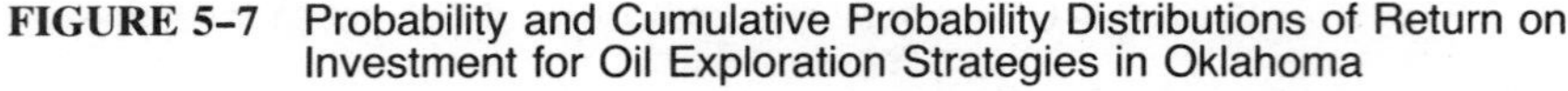


**FIGURE 5–7** Probability and Cumulative Probability Distributions of Return on Investment for Oil Exploration Strategies in Oklahoma

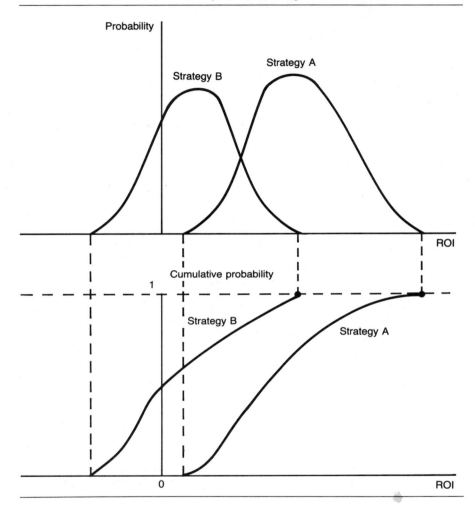

Now consider the probability distributions of a third site the company has leased (in California). The probability distributions for the two drilling strategies are shown in Figure 5–8.

At the California site, first-order stochastic dominance cannot be applied. Notice that strategy B entails more uncertainty than strategy A, including both higher chances of lower ROI and higher chances of higher ROI. For decision makers who are averse to risk, a second law of stochastic dominance can sometimes be applied.

**FIGURE 5–8** Probability and Cumulative Probability Distributions for Oil Exploration Strategies in California

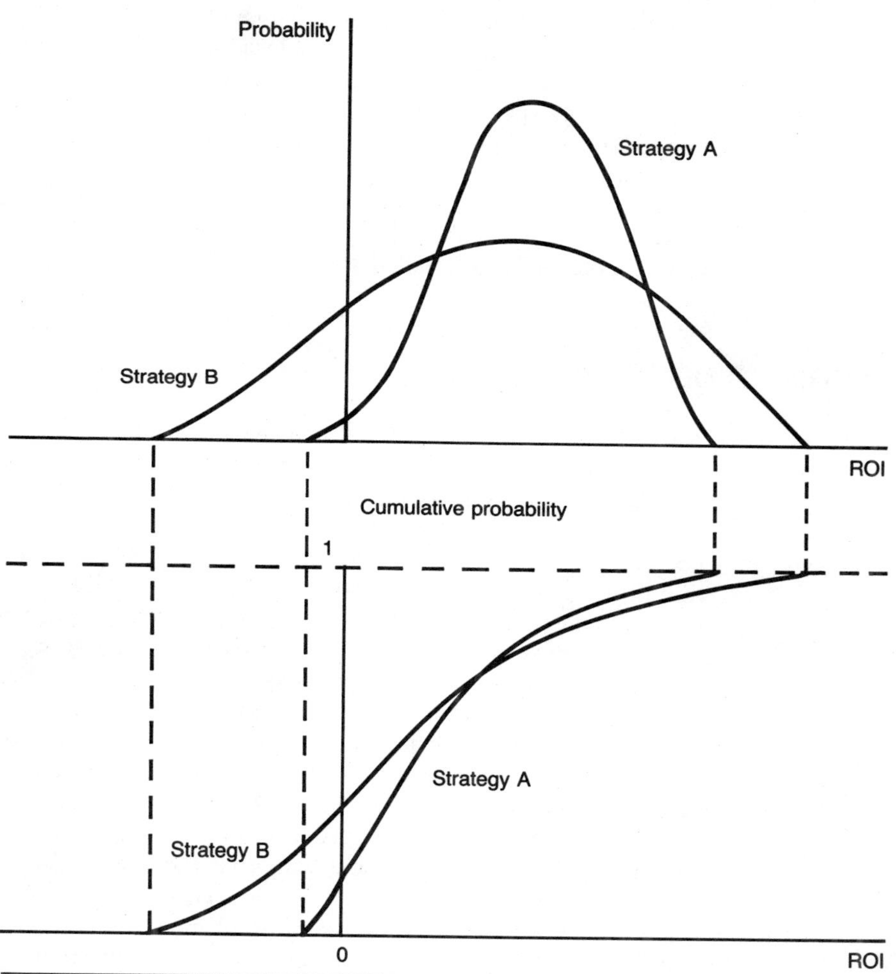


This more complex rule takes account of both the decision maker's preference for higher rather than lower values of ROI as well as preference for less rather than more risk, but can be difficult to implement.

In many instances distribution pairs such as those shown above do not exhibit any of these forms of dominance and as a result cannot be ranked using these methods. Although it is feasible to consider higher-order stochastic dominance rules, these higher-order rules are more complex and difficult to conceptualize and hence less likely to produce useful inferences. The important advantage of stochastic dominance rules is that they do not require exact specification of a decision maker's preference function, but only of some of its general properties (such as preference for wealth, or risk aversion). For cases where these rules fail to produce a ranking of alternatives, and where it seems useful in any case for the decision maker to specify more details about his preferences, expected utility rules can be used (see Chapter 6 for a detailed treatment).

## HEURISTIC DECISION RULES

All of the decision criteria defined and illustrated above are *exact* in the sense that once a decision problem is defined and quantified, there is no subjective element involved in applying the decision rule. These decision rules are all *highly programmed,* and moreover can all be expressed mathematically. In practice we often confront problems where the exact specification of the problem and its quantification are not necessary or not possible. Many managers have neither the time nor the desire to continually *optimize,* but rather make decisions through a process of **satisficing.**

This satisficing process can involve not only the choice phase of decision making but, perhaps more importantly, the search and evaluation phases. The satisficing process involves the use of approximate, limited, simple models. The search is for a solution that meets some minimum standard (that is *"good enough,"* rather than *"the best"*).

The concept of heuristic processes is to some extent related to that of satisficing. Heuristic approaches involve the search for satisfactory solutions (or even good solutions). Once a good solution is found, a further search for the absolute best possible solution is normally not carried out in a heuristic process. Consider the contrast between such a soft, subjective process and the hard, optimizing, objectivity of a linear programming algorithm. Heuristic approaches can adopt hunches and intuition in searching for problem solutions, as well as rules-of-thumb (see Chapter 1 for an example). They can also involve shortcuts in process rather than methodical, systematic searches.

Examples of heuristics from everyday life are:

When in doubt, play the backhand side of the court (from Chapter 1).
If the highway looks clogged from point X, take the alternative bypass road.

If the boss slams his office door when he arrives in the morning, stay out of his way.

Similarly, heuristics can often be used in monetary or business decision situations. For example:

Customer X's urgent requests take priority, but customer Y's do not.
Never buy stock during periods of high international tension.
Don't try to squeeze every dollar out of your best client.
In decision tree analysis, always use an expected value decision rule as a first pass.
Never hire a salesman who doesn't wear a suit to his interview.
Don't trust a person who never looks you in the eye.

These examples are not prescribed as consistently good or even usable heuristics, and on close examination most readers would probably question the general usefulness of at least one of them.

For the manager it is useful to consider whether to adopt a heuristic approach or a more formal approach for a particular decision. Many factors enter into this choice including the importance of the decision and its nature. Some problems do not easily lend themselves to formal methods of analysis, and in such cases heuristic methods may not only be cheaper and easier to use but may outperform the formal models. As mentioned earlier, sometimes there is just not enough time to undertake a formal modeling procedure. Heuristic rules are usually relatively easy to implement.

On the other hand, heuristic rules are usually set in place to suggest actions based on specific cues or events. Hence when circumstances change, rules that might previously have been good enough may lead to poor performance, whereas systematic modeling and monitoring procedures may have reacted better to these changes in circumstance. As with formal modeling procedures such as decision analysis, we must ask the following questions about heuristics:

1. Is the solution or heuristic robust or sensitive to changes in the system or environment?
2. Is the heuristic really good enough or is a more refined analytical process warranted?

## SUMMARY

A variety of decision rules exist. Simple rules that ignore the likelihood of chance outcomes can be formulated, however they appear to be neither prescriptively appealing nor descriptively valid. Rules based on expected value concepts (probability weighted averages) are prescriptively appealing and are also powerful as decision aids in terms of producing inference about preferences. However, expected value rules also have a number of associated limitations, and their potential applicability should be carefully considered as part of each decision modeling process for which they are considered. Even though these limitations exist, expected value rules are very powerful and usually are a good starting point in the choice phase of a decision analysis.

Mean-variance analysis and stochastic dominance rules are more comprehensive than expected value rules in the sense that they incorporate more information about the uncertain quantities into the decision. However, they do not always lead to the identification of a preferred strategy or a set of rankings and as a result tend to be more useful as screening devices.

Heuristics represent an alternative approach to decision analysis, being relatively informal and often part of a satisficing philosophy and process.

Ultimately it's a case of choosing a methodology which is appropriate to the problem. All of the decision rules described in this chapter can usefully contribute to the insight to be gained from decision models in appropriate circumstances. *The expected value rule is the decision analyst's stock in trade choice rule*, however the selection of a choice criterion usually is a case of which rule best represents the preference system of the decision maker and the nature of the problem. This can be interpreted in both a *prescriptive* sense (which rule *should* the decision maker use as a guide?) or a *descriptive* sense (which rule best *represents* the decision maker's actual choice behavior).

From a practical perspective the amount of effort involved in using any of the rules described in this chapter is usually only a small fraction of the total effort involved in the decision analysis. In such cases it is worth applying a number of different rules and choice processes, as a great deal of insight about the problem can be gained from doing so.

## FURTHER READING

For those readers who wish to read further about various aspects of choosing between alternatives, a number of good sources exist. Books on decision analysis by Brown, et al. (1984) and Holloway (1979) give general treatments and examples of choice procedures. Cooke and Slack (1984) consider choice methods in a broader context and offer a valuable set of insights into decision making.

Many good books and articles relating to specific topics have been published. Three excellent books which address issues in decision making such as satisficing versus optimizing are by Simon (1957), March and Simon (1958), and Cyert and March (1963). Although many more recent treatments exist, these books give classic treatments to topics in organizational decision processes and are well worth reading.

The topics of mean-variance analysis and stochastic dominance are also much written about. Mean-variance analysis is described by Van Horne (1979), and nearly all standard finance theory textbooks. A particularly clear presentation, in the context of risk management decisions, is given by Doherty (1985).

Articles on stochastic dominance tend to be technical in nature, and the following sources give an explanation of the concepts in detail: Hadar and Russell (1969), Hanoch and Levy (1969), Porter and Carey (1974), and Eilon and Tilley (1975).

On the subject of heuristics, a very good readable article is by Weist (1966) in the *Harvard Business Review*. Other articles by Hinkle and Kuehn (1967) and Simon and Newell (1958) are also relevant.

## REFERENCES


BROWN, R. V., A. S. KAHR, and C. PETERSON. 1974. *Decision Analysis for the Manager*. New York: Holt, Rinehart, Winston.

COOKE, S., and N. SLACK. 1984. *Making Management Decisions*. Englewood Cliffs, N.J.: Prentice-Hall.

COPELAND, T. E., and J. F. WESTON. 1979. *Financial Theory and Corporate Policy*. Reading, Mass.: Addison-Wesley Publishing.

CYERT, R., and J. G. MARCH. 1963. *Behavioral Theory of the Firm*. Englewood Cliffs, N.J.: Prentice-Hall.

DOHERTY, N. A. 1985. *Corporate Risk Management*. New York: McGraw-Hill.

EILON, S., and R. TILLEY. 1975. "Stochastic Dominance for Ranking Ventures." *Omega* 3, pp. 177–84.

HADAR, J., and W. R. RUSSELL. 1969. "Rules for Ordering Uncertain Prospects." *American Economic Review* 49 (March), pp. 25–34.

HANOCH, J., and H. LEVY. 1969. "The Efficiency Analysis of Choices Involving Risk." *Review of Economic Studies* 36, pp. 335–46.

HINKLE, C. L., and A. A. KUEHN. 1967. "Heuristic Models: Mapping the Maze for Management." *California Management Review* 10, no. 1, pp. 59–68.

HOLLOWAY, C. A. 1979. *Decision Making Under Uncertainty*. Englewood Cliffs, N.J.: Prentice-Hall.

MARCH, J. G., and H. A. SIMON. 1958. *Organizations*. New York: John Wiley & Sons, p. 139.

PORTER, R. B., and K. CAREY. 1974. "Stochastic Dominance as a Risk Analysis Criterion." *Decision Sciences* 5, pp. 10–21.

SIMON, H. A., 1957. *Administrative Behavior*. New York: Macmillan.

SIMON, H. A., and A. NEWELL. 1958. "Heuristic Problem Solving: The Next Advance in Operations Research." *Operations Research* 6, no. 3, pp. 281–300.

VAN HORNE, J. 1979. *Financial Management and Policy*. Englewood Cliffs, N.J.: Prentice-Hall.

WEIST, J. D. 1966. "Heuristic Programs for Decision Making." *Harvard Business Review*, September/October, pp. 129–43.

## PROBLEMS

1. In what circumstances would a decision not be sensitive to the particular choice criterion used? Give an example and contrast it with an example where different decision rules lead to different rankings of alternatives.
2. It can be argued that nonprobabilistic rules ignore a very important element of decisions and hence have little or no usefulness in decision analysis. Is this true? Illustrate your response with at least one example.
3. Explain the purpose of decision rules in terms of producing inferences and aiding versus replacing managerial judgments.
4. What are the important characteristics of the following major classes of decision rules: nonprobabilistic rules, expected value, mean-variance, stochastic dominance. In your answer, define both the power and limitations of each.
5. Bob Butter, owner of Best Brakes (a brake and muffler business) was considering the expansion of his business from one facility to two. He had three basic options: to not expand, to buy an existing business, or to lease a building and open a new facility. If he expanded, his profitability would be strongly affected by both the level of future rents in the area in which he wanted to locate his facility and by the decision of a large truck rental company who were also considering placing a facility in the area. Bob expected to get a major contract from this company if they did so. Bob defined four possibilities:

   Outcome 1: Rents increase sharply, truck business occurs.
   Outcome 2: Rents increase sharply, truck business does not occur.
   Outcome 3: Rents increase slowly, truck business occurs.
   Outcome 4: Rents increase slowly, truck business does not occur.

   He analyzed his profitability and deduced the net present value associated with each action-consequence set (NPVs are in $000).[2]

[2] NPV, meaning net present value, is a method for evaluating strategies based on discounting future cash flows to determine their present value equivalent.

| | Outcome 1 | Outcome 2 | Outcome 3 | Outcome 4 |
|---|---|---|---|---|
| Do not expand | 280 | 280 | 280 | 280 |
| Buy existing business | 490 | 120 | 600 | 140 |
| Open new business | 480 | 80 | 520 | 130 |
| Probability | 0.4 | 0.2 | 0.3 | 0.1 |

He also assessed joint probability values as shown in the table.

*a.* Use maxi-max and maxi-min rules on the data that Bob produced. Do they lead to the same rankings of alternatives?

*b.* Construct a regret table and use the mini-max regret criterion to rank the alternatives.

*c.* Calculate the expected NPV of each option.

*d.* Calculate the expected regret of each option (also known as expected opportunity loss) and compare these rankings with those in part *c*.

*e.* If Bob was risk averse, how might he act, and is his risk aversion adequately accounted for by any of the above decision rules?

*f.* Is mean-variance analysis appropriate in this problem? Explain your answer.

6. A magazine-stand owner was reviewing his operation. In examining how many copies of a particular magazine to order, he pulled up his records to help him. His problem was to balance the cost of ordering too many magazines with the lost sales he would experience if he ordered too few. He considered a monthly business magazine and noted the sales history over the past 20 months as follows:

| Sales | Frequency |
|---|---|
| 0 | 0 |
| 1 | 0 |
| 2 | 1 |
| 3 | 3 |
| 4 | 4 |
| 5 | 6 |
| 6 | 3 |
| 7 | 3 |

He noted that his average sales were close to five per month. He currently paid $1.50 for the magazine and sold it at his magazine stand for the regular retail price of $2.00. Unsold magazines were worthless at the end of the month.

*a.* Construct a payoff table and a decision tree.

*b.* Use EMV to determine the best payoff. Is the best strategy under EMV the same as the expected sales?
*c.* Is your answer to part *b* above likely to be true in all situations?
*d.* Construct a regret table and determine the best strategy under EOL.
*e.* If the magazine-stand owner could negotiate a return credit for unsold magazines, how might this affect his decision?
*f.* Suppose he was able to return his unsold magazines for 30 cents each. What would be the optimal EMV strategy?
*g.* Suppose he could return his magazines for full credit. What would be the optimal EMV strategy?

7. A seminar organizer had to pay an outside speaker $10,000 for a keynote address at a particular seminar. He wanted to set the price for attendance so as to maximize his monetary return. He estimated that over the range of possible prices he could charge, demand would be as follows:

| *Price = $125* | | | *Number of attendees* | | |
|---|---|---|---|---|---|
| | *80* | *90* | *100* | *110* | *120* |
| Probability | 0.1 | 0.3 | 0.4 | 0.1 | 0.1 |

| *Price = $150* | | | *Number of attendees* | | |
|---|---|---|---|---|---|
| | *70* | *80* | *90* | *100* | *110* |
| Probability | 0.1 | 0.3 | 0.4 | 0.1 | 0.1 |

| *Price = $175* | | | *Number of attendees* | | |
|---|---|---|---|---|---|
| | *60* | *70* | *80* | *90* | *100* |
| Probability | 0.2 | 0.2 | 0.3 | 0.2 | 0.1 |

*a.* Determine his best pricing strategy under EMV.
*b.* Is the solution to part *b*, above, the same as his best strategy if he wished to maximize his probability of breaking even? Would this be the case in general?
*c.* The organizer originally assumed that he would not have to bear any variable costs associated with the seminar. However, he was subsequently told that the cost of providing coffee, a text book, and some lecture notes would be $30 per attendee. Recalculate the EMV analysis, taking the variable cost into account.

**FIGURE 5–9** A Computer System Acquisition Decision

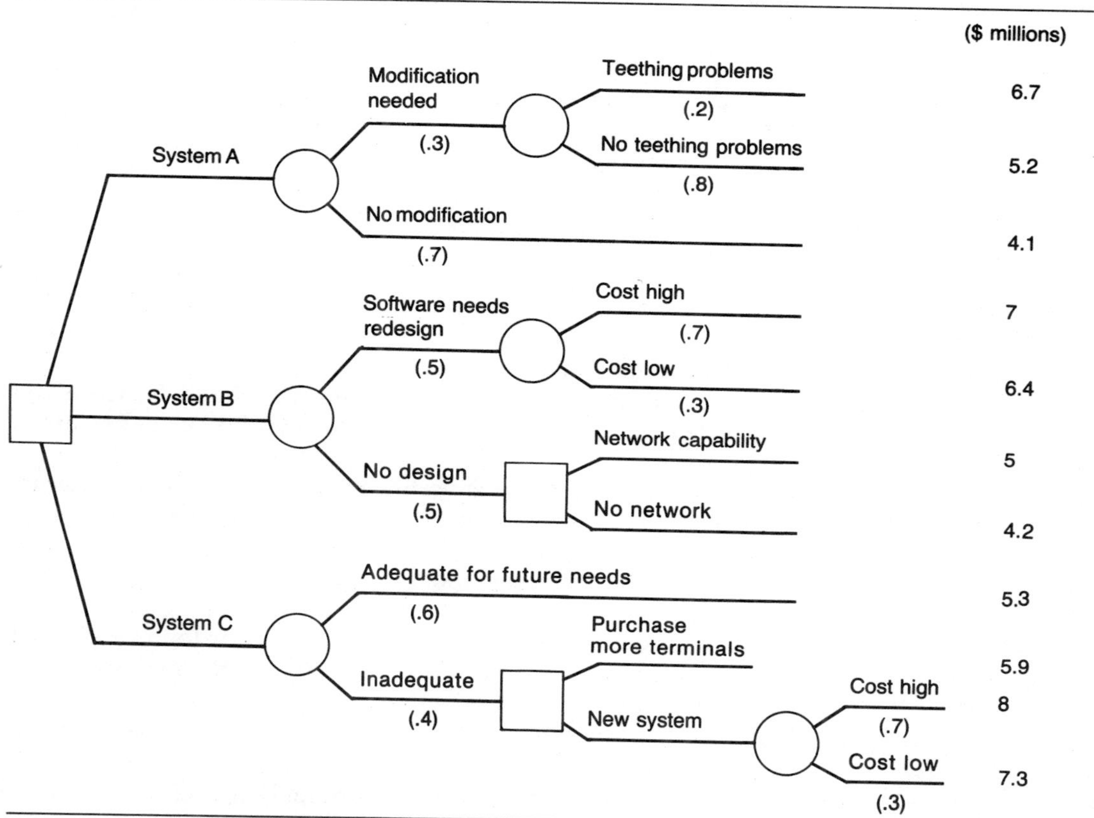


8. Roll back the decision tree shown by Figure 5–9, using EMV. Write a statement of the optimal strategy, and construct a risk profile of that strategy. Figure 5–9 is concerned with a problem faced by a bank that is choosing a new computer system. The monetary amounts on the decision tree are total costs for achieving an operational system.
9. An investment fund manager has charted the returns of a number of investment funds she is interested in. She wrote a simple computer program to access the relevant data from her data base and calculate means and variances of these funds. The results were as follows:

| *Fund* | *Mean Return* | *Variance of Return* |
|---|---|---|
| 1 | 14 | 7 |
| 2 | 14 | 9 |
| 3 | 8 | 14 |
| 4 | 10 | 11 |
| 5 | 16 | 16 |
| 6 | 9 | 14 |
| 7 | 16 | 9 |
| 8 | 9 | 13 |
| 9 | 8 | 14 |

*a*. Plot the mean and variance data. Are any alternatives dominated by others?
*b*. Which fund would you choose and why?

10. This exercise refers to the data in problem 9, above. Suppose you were able to invest half of your available funds in each of two of the listed investments.
    *a*. Assuming that these investments had independent returns, would you generally prefer to diversify rather than put all your eggs in one basket? Why?
    *b*. What would the mean and variance be of a 50:50 portfolio of funds 1 and 7?
    *c*. How would the mean and variance of this portfolio be affected if funds 1 and 7 had returns that were positively correlated? What if they were negatively correlated?
11. Describe a business situation in which it is appropriate to use a heuristic.
12. How would a manager know when to apply a decision rule to a decision tree, or to stop the analysis once the tree is structured and data is assessed?
13. Decision rules such as EMV have limitations. Why would we use EMV when we could use processes such as stochastic dominance rules to compare whole probability distributions?
14. What are the pros and cons of optimizing (determining the very best strategy) relative to satisficing? Describe some situations in which it is reasonable to do each of these.
15. Use ARBORIST to model the Doncaster Battery Company (B) problem, Example 5–2. Roll back the decision tree and print a risk profile for the best strategy.
16. Use ARBORIST to solve the decision tree for Mr. Schroer, Figure 5–2, in the Zinco (B) example. Print a risk profile for the optimal strategy.
17. Solve problem 7, above, using ARBORIST.
18. Solve problem 8, above, using ARBORIST. Use the rollback procedure (Figure 5–9) and use ARBORIST to print a risk profile.

19. James Alexander was the new manufacturing manager of the Penguin Confectionery Company, a relatively small food processing company. The main processing unit in which raw materials were combined had a critical component requiring a three-month lead time for replacement purposes. This meant that if no spares of this component were kept in stock, a breakdown would completely stop the production process for three months while a new one was obtained. To avoid this, past practice in the company had always been to keep two spare components in the storeroom. Mr. Alexander decided to see whether this was the most cost effective policy for him. He began by examining the number of components replaced over the past 10 years. The probability of a breakdown on any day was calculated from past data as 1 in 50 (0.02). Breakdowns were independent through time, hence Mr. Alexander used the Poisson probability distribution to calculate the breakdown distribution over 90 days as follows:

$$P(N \text{ breakdowns}) = \frac{e^{-\lambda}\lambda^N}{N!}$$

where

$$\lambda = 90/50 = 1 \cdot 8$$

and

$$N = \text{Number of breakdowns}$$

The distribution is given by:

| *Number of Breakdowns in 90 days* | *Probability* |
|---|---|
| 0 | 0.165 |
| 1 | 0.297 |
| 2 | 0.268 |
| 3 | 0.161 |
| 4 | 0.072 |
| 5 | 0.026 |
| 6 | 0.008 |
| 7 | 0.003 |
| | $\Sigma = 1$ |

He then examined the costs associated with storing various numbers of components. The interest costs associated with holding a component for a quarter was $3,000. The fixed cost associated with shutting down the process and then starting it up again was $10,000. In his initial analysis he assumed away the cost of lost production due to shutdowns based on the fact that the company stored enough finished goods so that a shutdown would not cause a great disruption in the distribution system.

*a.* Use the nonprobabilistic rules described in this chapter to identify the optimum inventory policy for this component.

*b.* Use an expected value analysis to determine the optimal policy. Was the company's existing policy optimal in expected value terms?

20. Refer to problem 19, above. Mr. Alexander wished to account for the days in which the eonfectionery processing system was shut down due to the inability of his storeroom to supply spares of the critical component. If we denote the daily cost of a shutdown as $\$x$, above and beyond the fixed cost of shutting down and starting up (which was \$10,000) how can this be taken into account in an expected value analysis?

21. Referring to problems 19 and 20, above, what would be the optimal policy if $x$, the daily shutdown cost, was \$100? What if it was \$1,000?

22. This problem refers to problems 19 and 20, above. The company was thinking of increasing its production capacity by installing, in parallel with the existing processing unit, a second production system. The component in question would be part of the new process which would be identical to the existing process. If the new system had the same projected breakdown rates for this component as the old system, what would be the optimal spares policy based on an expected value analysis? What would the optimal policy be if there were three processing units in parallel? Assume that breakdowns in the various processing units are independent of each other but identically distributed. How would you solve this problem both with and without the assumption of a daily downtime cost of \$500?

---

## CASE STUDY

### James Jones Art Auctions (A)

James Jones wholly owned and directed a small art auction company. He held monthly auctions in his auction rooms, selling paintings and other forms of art that usually brought prices in the range \$10,000 to \$200,000. In the past he had not been able to attract sellers of really high-quality paintings (in the million dollar range and up). He had recently been negotiating with a potential seller who wished to sell a total of three paintings. All three of the paintings were lesser-known works of very famous masters, and James saw this opportunity as one in which he could both make some money, and also establish a reputation for himself as an auctioneer/dealer in paintings of the highest quality. If he was successful in this venture, James thought that he would be able to enter a new and very profitable class of business, namely that of artworks in the $500,000 and up category.

The deal he had been negotiating was fairly complex. The seller was Klaus Heinegen, a local businessman. Mr. Heinegen needed cash to finance an expanding new aspect of his manufacturing business. His cash needs were spread over a three-month period as follows:

| | |
|---|---|
| January | $500,000 |
| February | $700,000 |
| March | $2,000,000 |

To generate this cash, Mr. Heinegen had suggested to James that one painting be included in each of his three successive auctions. Mr. Heinegen had insisted that James drop his usual auction fee from 12% (of the reserve price) to 10%. It was also agreed that James would incur the advertising costs associated with each painting. Table 5-5 shows the details of each painting:

James estimated the probability of sale for each painting, taking into account the painting, current trends in the art world and the economy, and the reserve prices. His estimates were:

| *Painting* | *Probability of Sale* |
|---|---|
| Gauguin | 0.8 |
| Rembrandt | 0.7 |
| Picasso | 0.8 |

The contract between James and Mr. Heinegen stipulated that after each auction, James was not obliged to accept the next painting and commit $60,000 in advertising. On the other hand, Mr. Heinegen was obliged to give James the option of selling a second painting (either the Rembrandt or the Picasso) if he was successful with painting 1, and similarly was obliged with a third painting if James was successful with whichever painting he chose to auction in February.

James knew that even if he sold the Gauguin, which was by no means a certainty, he would take a loss because the fee would be less than the advertising expenses. However, it was obvious that a little profit was involved with the Rem-

**TABLE 5–5** Data on the Paintings

| | *Artist* | *Sale Date* | *Reserve Price ($)* | *Advertising Expenses ($)* |
|---|---|---|---|---|
| Painting 1 | Gauguin | January* | 550,000 | 60,000 |
| Painting 2 | Rembrandt | {February/ | 1,000,000 | 60,000 |
| Painting 3 | Picasso | March} | 2,500,000 | 60,000 |

* If he sold the Gauguin at his January auction, James would be allowed to choose which painting to include in the February auction and which to leave until March.

brandt, and a substantial gain was to be made if he sold the Picasso. Further, he thought that if he sold all three paintings, he would as a result, enhance his reputation and gain access to further profitable business that might eventuate in profit with a present value of up to $150,000. He looked at the sales agreement before him and pondered the various aspects of this decision. He had never before spent $60,000 on advertising a single painting.

## CASE QUESTIONS

Draw a decision tree representing James' decision situation. Consider the project, initially, in isolation of the benefits associated with future business that it may generate. Use the EMV criterion to roll back the tree and state the resultant strategy. Construct a probability distribution of the net cash flows associated with this strategy and draw a risk profile.

1. James wanted to know what the affect on the decision would be of changing his probability estimate for the likelihood of sale of the Picasso. If he changed this figure from 0.8 to 0.6, does the optimal strategy (using the EMV rule) change?
2. How might James consider the value (of up to $150,000) of the future benefits associated with the deal as a result of further business that would be generated if he sold all three paintings?

CHAPTER SIX

# The Expected Utility Decision Criterion

## OUTLINE



## OBJECTIVES

After completing this chapter, you should be able to:

1. Describe how the expected utility approach encompasses decision makers' attitudes towards risk.
2. Assess unidimensional utility functions and describe various assessment methods.
3. Use utility functions in applying the expected utility rule to decision trees.
4. Judge when it is appropriate to use the expected utility rule rather than expected value.
5. Discuss the concept of risk aversion and how it can be modeled.
6. Debate the purpose and use of mathematical representations for utility functions.
7. Interpret the results of the application of an expected utility rule.

## INTRODUCTION

This chapter describes and develops a comprehensive decision rule, called expected utility, which can be used to model the individual preference set of a decision maker. This powerful decision rule can encompass multiple dimensions of value and nonlinear attitudes toward risk, yet it can be applied to decision trees using the same simple rollback procedure as the expected value rule.

The expected utility approach is a very important part of decision analysis. It is a means by which we can encapsulate another form of complexity in the analysis. Whereas expected monetary value (EMV) is a good decision rule to use in many instances, there are some decisions, particularly those unique, strategic situations involving high stakes, where the expected utility approach provides more useful insights and inferences.

For routine, repetitive decisions, or those involving gains and losses that are not very large relative to a company's assets, expected value rules are often all that are needed. Expected value rules are appropriate for many operational decisions such as inventory control and statistical quality control. For such cases it is usually valid to assume a linear preference function. For high-stakes strategic decisions, real preference functions are often nonlinear, and it is useful to model them as such, using the expected utility approach.

In earlier chapters, particularly Chapter 5, a number of different decision criteria were examined. Although each of these was capable of producing some insights for the decision maker, they all suffered from various limitations. The expected utility decision criterion, which is the subject of this chapter, is considerably more comprehensive than any of the formal rules presented earlier and generally does not suffer from those same limitations. Before examining the expected utility rule, let us briefly review the rules which were introduced in Chapter 5:

1. Maxi-max, maxi-min, and mini-max regret are all nonprobabilistic rules based purely on comparisons of the values (payoffs) associated with various decision strategies. These rules ignore the likelihoods of the chance outcomes.
2. Expected value rules, including expected monetary value (EMV) and expected opportunity loss (EOL), are more comprehensive than the nonprobabilistic rules, however they incorporate a number of limiting assumptions as detailed in Chapter 5. These include the use of an expected value to represent a range of values (the lost information concept), the assumption of a linear preference function (risk neutrality), and the limitation of being able to address only single dimensions of value.

3. Mean-variance rules are limited in that they are based on the presumption of either a particular form of preference function or else that the normal distribution can be used to represent the uncertain quantities.
4. Stochastic dominance rules do not require the specification of a particular set of preferences but merely some properties of the preference function. However, this criterion basically involves the direct comparison of complete probability distributions and is not always able to produce a set of rankings of alternatives.

The expected utility approach is different from all the other approaches because it is more general and more comprehensive in nature. Indeed the expected value and mean-variance rules are *merely special cases* of the expected utility approach where particular preference function forms have been assumed. The expected utility rule involves the complete specification by the decision maker of a preference function, known as a utility function. A utility function specifies the relationship between a set of states of some dimension of value (such as money, quality, market share) and the degree of utility corresponding to that state. Figure 6–1 shows some examples of utility function graphs. From Figure 6–1 we can make a number of observations. Utility functions need not be of any particular shape or form. In Figure 6–1a, preference (utility) is shown to generally increase as wealth increases, however preference functions generally need not do so. Wide variations are possible in terms of the shape of preference functions. In Figure 6–1b, the preference function has a maximum, indicating that the doctor believes that there is a best state, and preference decreases as movement away from this optimal state occurs.

Utility functions in Figure 6–1 are expressed in terms of single dimensions only. Hence it is presumed, for example in Figure 6–1c, that although the production manager probably has preferences for many dimensions of value, he is able to express his preference for quality as an independent function. We note that it may be necessary to specify the levels of other variables for which a particular utility function such as Figure 6–1c holds true. Utility is a measure of preference for various values of a variable. It measures the *relative strength of desirability* that the decision maker has for those values.

If we can successfully measure the preference function of a decision maker, those preferences can be used to produce powerful insights as part of decision analysis models. This approach presumes that decision makers have, within them, a set of preferences that are at least reasonably stable across time and across decision contexts.

This chapter covers both the theoretical aspects and some of the practical elements of utility theory, limited to representations of single dimen-

**FIGURE 6–1** Some Examples of Utility Functions

a. Utility function of a company president for wealth.

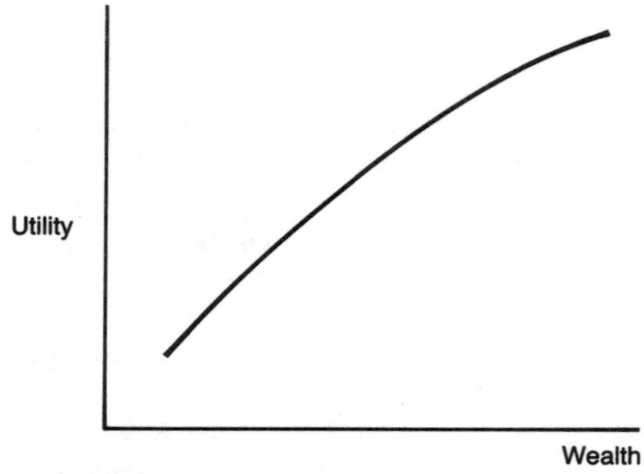

b. Utility function of a doctor for blood cholesterol levels in his patients.

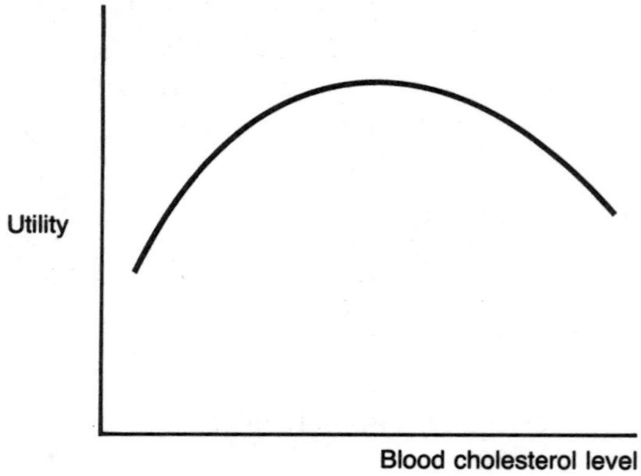

c. Utility function of a production manager for quality of product.

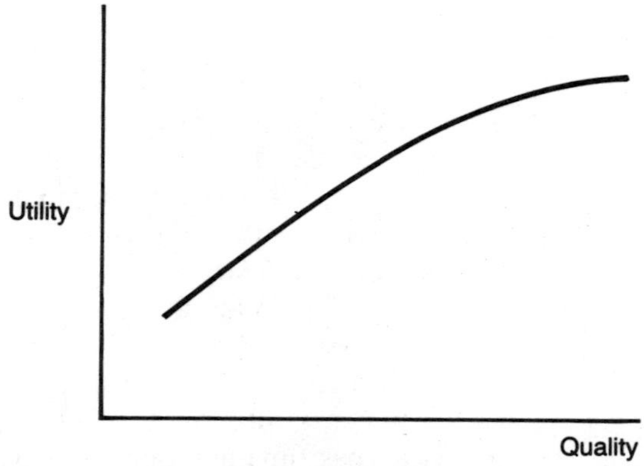

sions of value. Chapter 7 is devoted to extending the concept to account for multiple dimensions of value. Chapter 13 gives a more detailed coverage of many of the behavioral issues related to this aspect of decision analysis.

## THE UNDERLYING THEORY OF EXPECTED UTILITY

Although utility theory has been documented in its present form for four decades (von Neumann and Morgenstern 1947), there are still many unresolved issues and a raging debate among distinguished scholars both about its theoretical basis (see, for example, Hagen and Wenstop 1984) and about its usefulness in decision analysis (Schoemaker 1982). These issues are discussed further in Chapter 13. Despite the fact that the theory has imperfections in its ability to describe decision behavior, there is no doubt that it is *very appealing in a prescriptive sense*. It is also generally considered to be a very useful approach for modeling decision-maker preferences.

The underlying theory of expected utility is a set of axioms. These axioms are presented in the Appendix at the back of this chapter. A decision maker who follows this specific set of preference relations (the axioms) will be an expected utility maximizer. The vast majority of readers will consider the axioms to be very reasonable, describing the preference system of a logical, rational person. This is the heart of the prescriptive appeal of the expected utility criterion.

The unidimensional utility function can have any dimension of value as its domain. Utility functions often have money as their domain, however other dimensions such as quality, timeliness, efficiency, or productivity could be appropriate to particular problems.

## UTILITY ASSESSMENT PROCEDURES

Many different techniques exist for establishing unidimensional utility functions. We will focus on techniques that establish utility functions through the use of judgments made by decision makers on hypothetical decisions. An alternative approach is to observe actual decision-making behavior and deduce utilities from this revealed preference data. This latter method is difficult to implement because real decisions are often too complex to be decomposed into easily analyzed unidimensional value terms.

Hypothetical decisions used to derive utility functions normally involve uncertainty. Decision makers are typically asked to express preference, or lack of preference (indifference) if it exists, between pairs of specified gambles or between a gamble and a certain outcome. Hence their judgments, and the resultant utility functions based on these judgments, take into account both strength of preference for various outcome states and preference or aversion for varying degrees of uncertainty.

Before the actual judgments are elicited, it is recommended that the decision maker go through a process of motivation and preanalysis. This process integrates the utility function and its assessment phase as part of the decision analysis. Just as the preanalysis phase of a decision analysis involves the identification of the problem and realization that a formalized approach such as decision analysis is warranted, the decision maker should be properly motivated to identify a utility function. He should also spend some time thinking generally about the nature and properties of his preference pattern.

## The Five-Point Assessment Method

A well-known utility assessment method (known as the five-point assessment method) is outlined below:

Step 1: (This is the preanalysis step.) Note that the preference function for the dimension of value may be nonlinear. If the preference set is linear then a simple expected value rule is appropriate. Indeed, the expected value rules defined in Chapter 5 are merely special cases of expected utility rules where the utility function is a straight line. *The realization that the decision maker's preferences are nonlinear is the main motivation for establishing a utility function.* Think about the properties of the utility function, particulary its slope and curvature.

Step 2: Define the extreme values of the domain. This range should cover all of the outcomes on the decision tree.

Step 3: Construct the gamble:

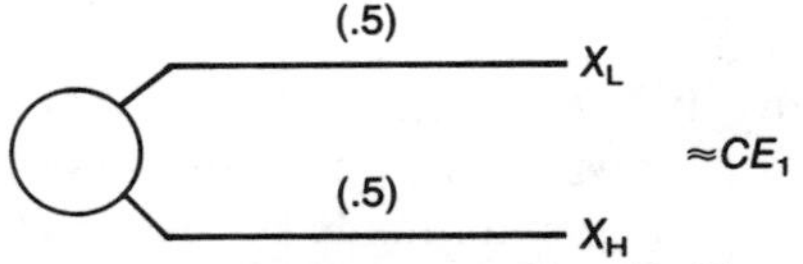


The symbol ≈ denotes a condition of indifference.

In this gamble $X_L$ is the minimum point on the defined domain and $X_H$ is the maximum. Assess a certainty equivalent (CE) for this gamble. A certainty equivalent is the certain amount that would be equal in expected utility terms to the gamble. The value of the CE is such that you are indifferent between it and the gamble.

By definition

$$U(CE) = \text{Expected utility (gamble)}$$

It is convenient to define

$$U(X_L) = 0$$
$$U(X_H) = 1$$

In this instance the decision maker assesses $CE_1$ and we know

$$\begin{aligned} U(CE_1) &= 0.5\ U(X_L) + 0.5\ U(X_H) \\ &= 0.5 \times 0 + 0.5 \times 1 \\ &= 0.5 \end{aligned}$$

The judgment of a certainty equivalent allows the point to be plotted on the preference function (see Figure 6–2).

Step 4: Construct the gambles:

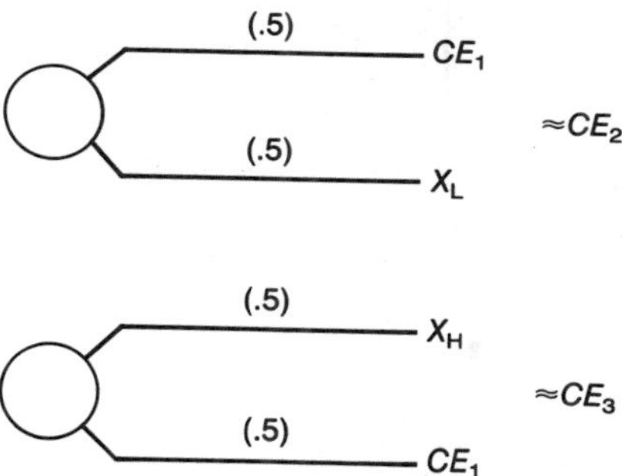


Separately assess certainty equivalents for these gambles, $CE_2$ and $CE_3$ respectively. We can say that:

$$\begin{aligned} U(CE_2) &= 0.5\ U(CE_1) + 0.5\ U(X_L) \\ &= 0.25 \end{aligned}$$

and

$$\begin{aligned} U(CE_3) &= 0.5\ U(CE_1) + 0.5\ U(X_H) \\ &= 0.75 \end{aligned}$$

These points can also be plotted on a utility graph (see Figure 6–2).

Step 5: Draw a curve through the five points on the utility graph.

Step 6: Check the assessments and the graph for consistency. If the graph is not reasonably smooth, then check the assessments and make some more assessments by designing some further gambles.

Using the utility function, once it is assessed, is a relatively straightforward matter. The assessed consequences (payoffs on the decision tree) in

**FIGURE 6–2** A Utility Assessment Procedure

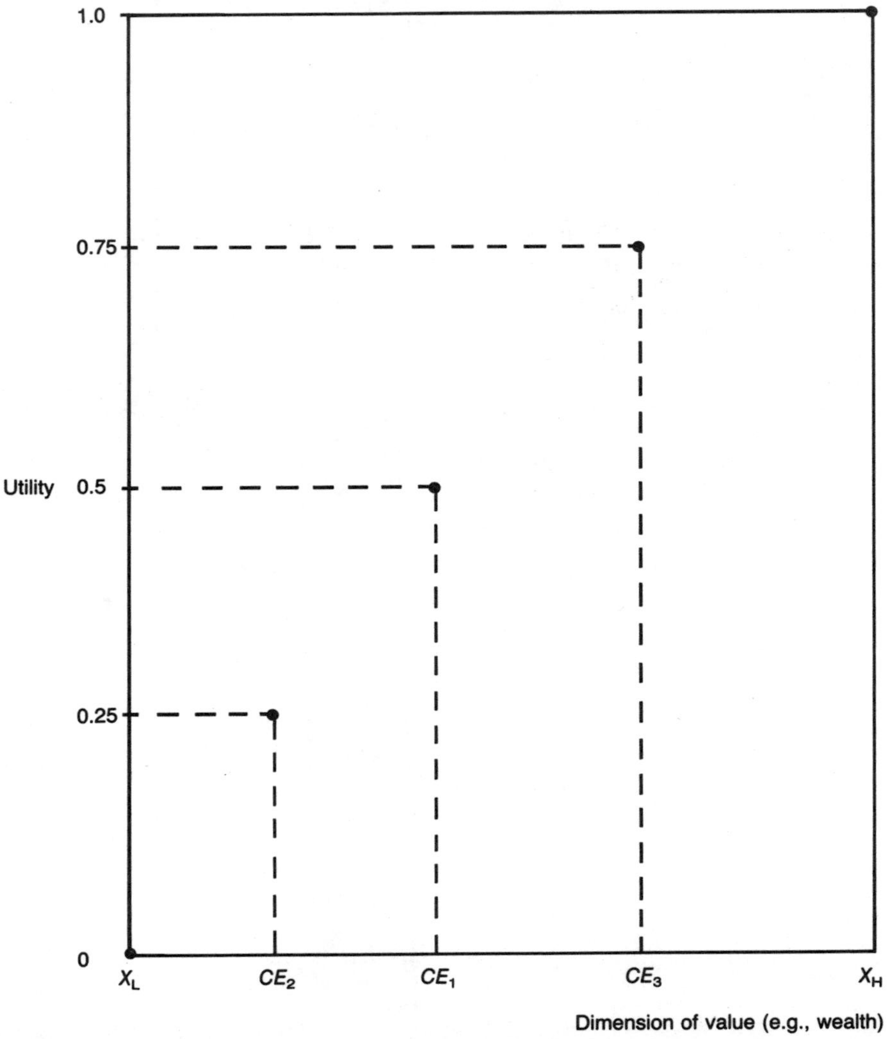

the decision model are replaced by corresponding utilities, and the expected value rule is applied to those utilities. This may simply involve a single set of calculations for a single-stage decision model, or a rollback procedure for a multistage decision tree. The important point to note is that by using expected utilities, actual values on a decision tree are replaced by a utility measure that incorporates the decision maker's preference set over those values!

---

## EXAMPLE 6–1

### Your Utility Function for Personal Wealth

Figure 6–3 is a graph on which we will represent your utility for wealth. The wealth scale ranges from \$0 to \$200,000. The utility scale, $U$, is set to range from a minimum

**FIGURE 6–3** Your Utility Function for Wealth

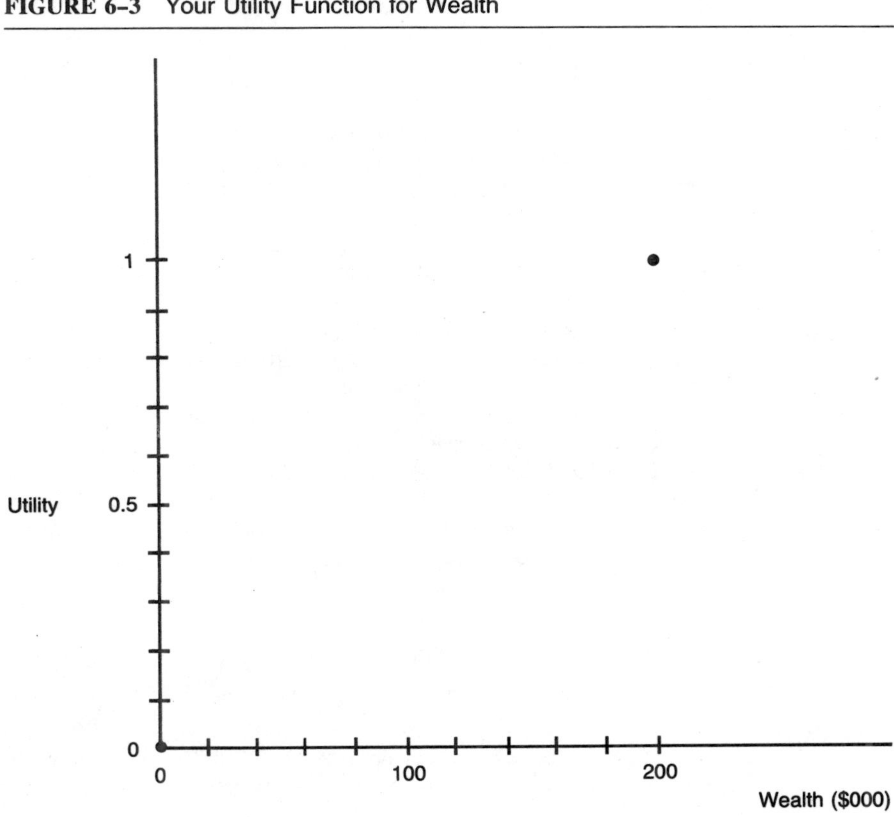

of zero (at zero wealth) to a maximum of one (at a wealth level of $200,000). Hence we define

$$U(\$0) = 0$$
$$U(\$200{,}000) = 1$$

Note that the actual numerical scale of the utility range is arbitrary, and the above-scale definitions were made for the sake of convenience only. Any other pair of definitions would serve the same purpose, as long as they preserved the desired property: $U(\$200{,}000) > U(\$0)$. In effect, any linear transformation (adding and multiplying the utility scale by constant values) can be applied to a utility function without changing its properties, so long as the multiplicative constant is positive.

Consider Figure 6–3. It relates wealth to utility. Utility should be interpreted to mean *strength of preference*, desirability, or the relative state of 'happiness' associated with various wealth levels. Let us now use the five-point assessment method to establish your utility function in the range zero to $200,000.

The first step is to construct the gamble

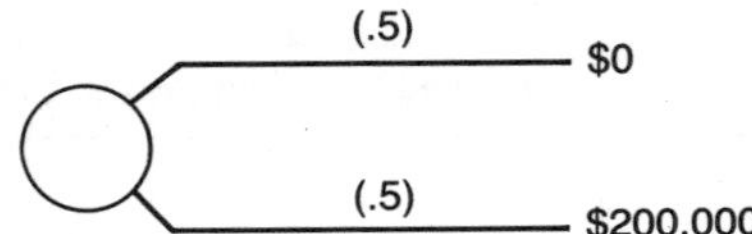


and assess your certainty equivalent to it. If it is difficult to pull this number out of thin air, you may wish to home in on your point of indifference by postulating various trial certainty equivalents (CE) and considering whether you prefer the trial value or the gamble. For example, do you prefer the above gamble, or $100,000 for certain? Remember that we are dealing with states of wealth here, not cash flows. If you preferred the $100,000 to the gamble, try another (lower) trial CE in an attempt to find your point of indifference. Would you prefer $70,000 for certain, or face the gamble? After a series of trials, you should come to the point where you have a lot of difficulty choosing between the CE and the gamble, simply because you are indifferent, preferring neither one nor the other.

We emphasize that there is *not* a correct answer to a CE question in an objective sense, as it is a subjective matter of individual preference. In assessing CE values and utility functions, you are not trying to calculate something correctly, but merely trying to represent a part of your inner self, namely your preference function. Formalizing and modeling this preference function as a utility function helps decision analysis to more realistically represent your decision process!

Returning to Figure 6–3, suppose your point of indifference to the original gamble was $60,000. Then we can say

$$\begin{aligned} U(\$60{,}000) &= 0.5\ U(\$0) + 0.5\ U(\$200{,}000) \\ &= 0.5 \times 0 + 0.5 \times 1 \\ &= 0.5 \end{aligned}$$

Plot *your* certainty equivalent at the 0.5 utility level. Now go on and construct further gambles, establishing enough points on Figure 6–3 to smooth a curve through

**FIGURE 6–4** Two Risky Investments

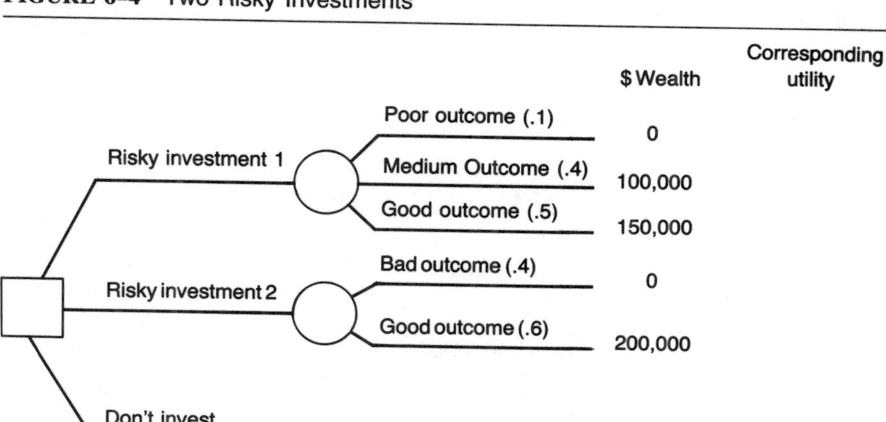


them. A total of at least five points, including the two end points, should be established.

You can then use your utility function on decision models, to include your preference function in the model, replacing monetary values on a decision tree by their corresponding utilities, and using the expected value rollback procedure to determine the optimal strategy under expected utility.

For example, if someone has offered you the chance of investing all your assets and going into a high-risk business with a 10% chance of making you bankrupt and a 40% chance of finishing up with $100,000 and a 50% chance of finishing up with $150,000, you can determine the expected utility of this gamble using your utility function (Figure 6–3). You can then compare this expected utility with the expected utility of not investing or with other opportunities. Use your utility function to determine the expected utility of the two risky investments shown by Figure 6–4. Presume that you have an initial wealth of $110,000. Look at Figure 6–3 where you have plotted your utility function. Note the corresponding utilities for the various wealth amounts on Figure 6–4 and calculate the expected utilities for the two risky investments. What ranking of decision alternatives does the expected utility rule imply? Now compare this with the EMV rankings:

EMV (risky investment 2) = $120,000
EMV (risky investment 1) = $115,000
EMV (don't invest) = 110,000

If your expected utility rankings were different from the EMV rankings, we must conclude that your personal preferences were not well modeled by the linear (EMV) function, hence the motivation and justification for using the more comprehensive expected utility approach!

## EXAMPLE 6–2

### Doncaster Battery Company (D)

The utility function shown on Figure 6–5 represents that of the owner of the Doncaster Battery Company. Apart from the profit contributions shown on Table 5–1, the company had $200,000 in equity. Hence total wealth is considered to be $200,000 more than the figures in Table 5–1.

The general manager of the company wanted to account for risk in his decision

**FIGURE 6–5** A Utility Function for Doncaster Battery Company

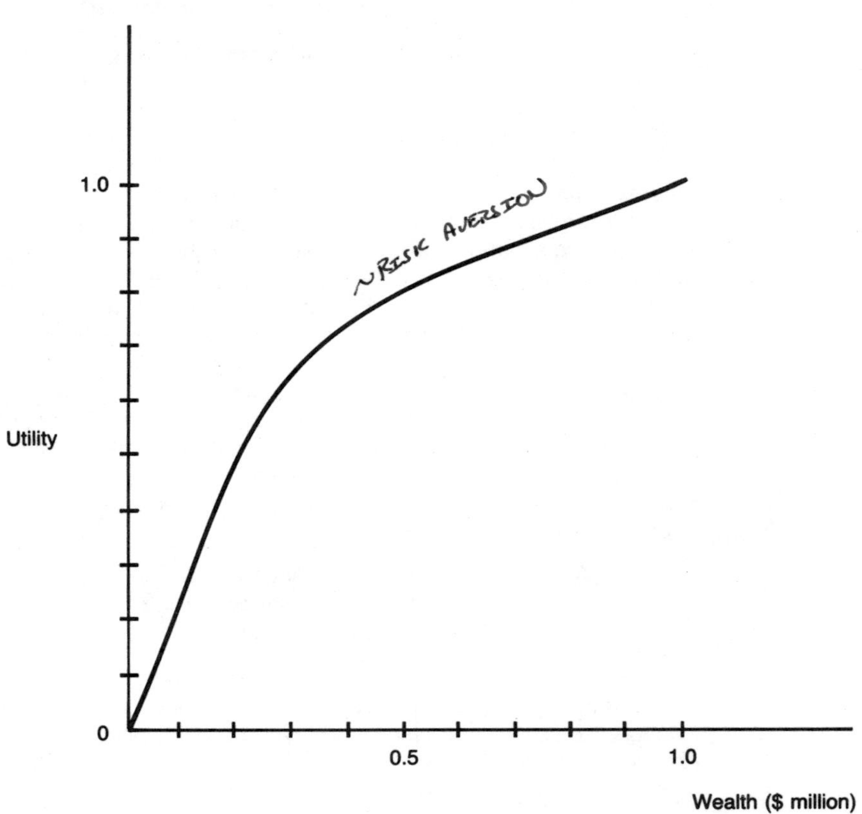

**TABLE 6–1** Utilities for the Doncaster Battery Problem

| | *Outcome* | | | |
|---|---|---|---|---|
| | *1* | *2* | *3* | *4* |
| Strategy 1 | 0.86 ($400,000) | 0.82 ($320,000) | 0.92 ($540,000) | 0.94 ($600,000) |
| Strategy 2 | 0.78 ($250,000) | 0.84 ($350,000) | 0.96 ($700,000) | 0.92 ($550,000) |
| Strategy 3 | 0.94 ($600,000) | 0.80 ($280,000) | 0.70 (150,000) | 0.76 ($400,000) |
| Probability | 0.2 | 0.4 | 0.3 | 0.1 |

(Example 5–2). He calculated the expected utilities by noting the utility values that correspond to the profit contributions as shown in Table 6–1 (plus other equity). These utilities can be read off the graph (Figure 6–5).

Numbers in parentheses in Table 6–1 are the profit contributions. The expected utilities are the probability weighted averages of the utility values:

Strategy 1:

$$\begin{aligned} EU &= 0.2 \times 0.86 + 0.4 \times 0.82 + 0.3 \times 0.92 + 0.1 \times 0.94 \\ &= 0.87 \end{aligned}$$

Strategy 2:

$$\begin{aligned} EU &= 0.2 \times 0.78 + 0.4 \times 0.84 + 0.3 \times 0.96 + 0.1 \times 0.92 \\ &= 0.872 \end{aligned}$$

Strategy 3:

$$\begin{aligned} EU &= 0.2 \times 0.94 + 0.4 \times 0.8 + 0.3 \times 0.7 + 0.1 \times 0.76 \\ &= 0.794 \end{aligned}$$

The probabilities used in these calculations come from Example 5–2. Note the utilities that were read from the graph were expressed as having two significant digits. Hence the strategy 2 expected utility of 0.872 should be rounded off to be 0.87. This is the same expected utility as for strategy 1. The question arises as to why the expected utilities are so close to identical for these two strategies when the expected values were different ($430,000 and $455,000 for strategies 1 and 2 respectively). The difference in expected values of $25,000 is a little over 5% of the total. The expected utility criterion has evaluated strategy 1 higher than strategy 2 relative to the expected values. This is because of the nature of the utility function and the relative riskiness of these two strategies. The curvature of the utility function (Figure 6–5) is such that it expresses a degree of *risk aversion*. Note that there is a decreasing marginal utility for wealth on this utility function. The rate of increase in utility (per unit wealth) decreases as wealth level increases. Under conditions of risk aversion, a riskier strategy, having more of its consequences closer to the extremes of the domain has a lower expected utility.

---

To illustrate this point, calculate the expected utility (from Figure 6-5) of a 50:50 gamble on wealth levels $0 and $1 million. Since $0 has an assigned utility of zero utiles (units of utility) and $1 million has an assigned utility of one utile on Figure 6–5, this gamble has an expected utility of 0.5. The expected value of this gamble is $500,000. Now consider an alternative strategy to taking the gamble, which is to achieve a wealth state of $500,000 with certainty. From Figure 6–5, the expected utility can be read from the graph as 0.81. The certain consequence had a much higher expected utility than the gamble even though the expected monetary values were the same. This is because of the risk aversion, which is inherent in, and represented by, this utility function.

Turning to the Doncaster Battery example, the payoffs associated with strategy 2 are much more spread than those of strategy 1. In other words, strategy 2 has relatively more uncertainty associated with it. Preferences or aversion for these differential degrees of risk are accounted for by the expected utility criterion (but not by the expected value criterion). In this example strategy 2 had the higher expected value, but when the riskiness of the two strategies is accounted for (by the expected utility method), strategies 1 and 2 turn out to be about equally desirable.

As a result of performing the expected utility analysis, the decision maker would have gained considerable insight about the decision. His own expressed risk aversion and wealth preferences are such that an expected monetary value rule (as in Example 5–2) was not totally adequate as a decision aid. Although one of the alternative actions (strategy 2) had a higher expected monetary value, its inherent riskiness was such that *overall,* it was found to be about equally desirable with strategy 1. The increased riskiness of strategy 2 is expressed by the risk profiles shown in Figure 6–6. Note that the columns in the risk profile of strategy 2 are generally more spread than those for strategy 1.

Undimensional utility functions can be used for monetary domains such as wealth or for other measures of value, as in the following Zinco Productions (C) example. They can be usefully applied to personal decisions involving our own assets or other values, or else to managerial problems when we, as managers, must make decisions involving corporate or public assets or values.

We should note in passing that it is only reasonable to use these straightforward assessment methods when utility functions are monotonically increasing or monotonically decreasing over the relevant range. For example with reference to the figure below, there is *no* sensible indifference value in

**FIGURE 6–6** Risk Profiles for Doncaster Battery Company

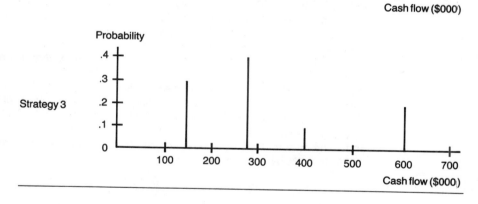

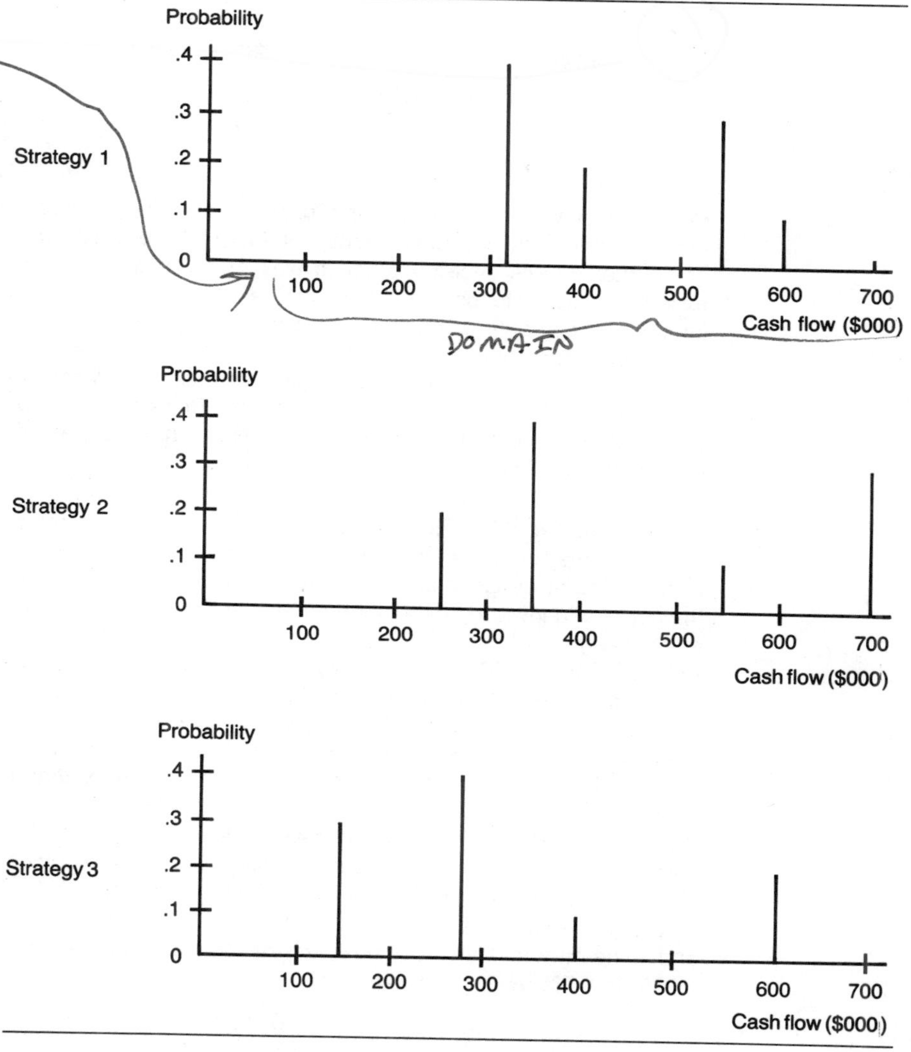

the range between two extreme cholesterol levels that would be a natural CE for the gamble.

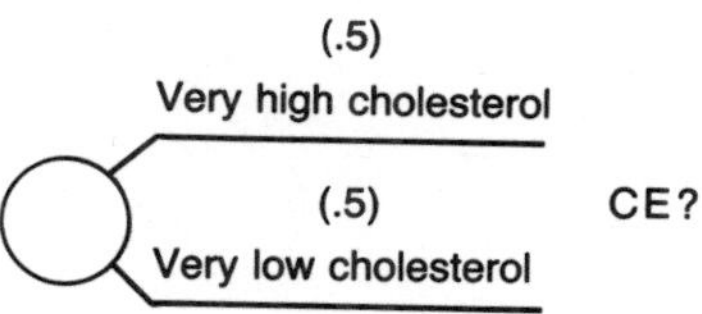

## EXAMPLE 6–3

### Zinco Productions (C)

Bob Schroer was responsible for a decision regarding processing equipment and material supply in a zinc oxide production facility. (See Zinco Productions (A) and (B) in Chapter 5.) His decision problem was modeled as Figure 5–2. After using an expected value criterion to roll back his decision tree, he noted that his preference function for percentage impurities was not linear. He thought that it might be both curved and also contain a discontinuity.

To help him assess his utility function, he called in a local management consulting firm run by three brothers, called Decisions, Decisions, and Decisions, Inc. One of the brothers, Don Decision, helped Mr. Schroer through the utility function assessment phase as follows:

**DON DECISION (DD):** So you have realized that your preferences for various levels of impurity may be nonlinear. I can see from your decision tree that the highest level of impurity you envisage is 0.2% and the lowest is 0.06%. Let's define those levels as the upper and lower bounds of the domain and assign them utilities of one and zero respectively.

**BOB SCHROER (BS):** OK, but I want you to know that I also think there is what you would call a discontinuity in my utility function. If I can achieve a level of impurities of 0.06%, then I can sell my product as special high grade and substantially improve my profit picture. But if the impurities are worse than 0.06%, even 0.065%, then we couldn't do that. So 0.06% or better is very much better than slightly worse than 0.06% for that reason.

**DD:** Yes, it sounds like you do have a discontinuous function, and that's quite unusual. I don't see such utility functions often. There are a number of ways to treat it. I'll tell you what we will do. Since your discontinuity is at one end of the range of values on your decision tree, we will redefine our range of interest to exclude the value 0.06% and come back to it later. For now, let's define the range (of impurities) of interest as 0.07% to 0.2%, and we'll assign utilities as:

$$U(0.07\%) = 1$$
$$U(0.2\%) = 0$$

I'll put them on the graph right now (Figure 6–7). Don't worry about 0.06% for now. Suppose you had a decision to make involving a 50:50 gamble between 0.07% and 0.2% shown as:

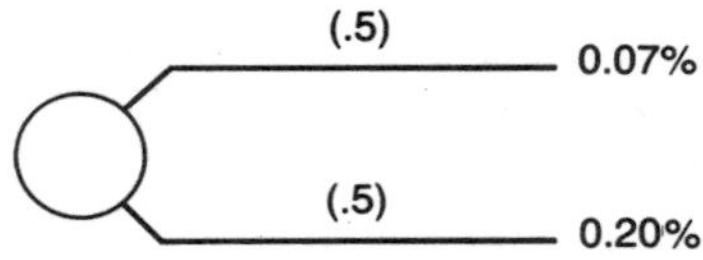

**FIGURE 6–7** Definition of a Utility Scale

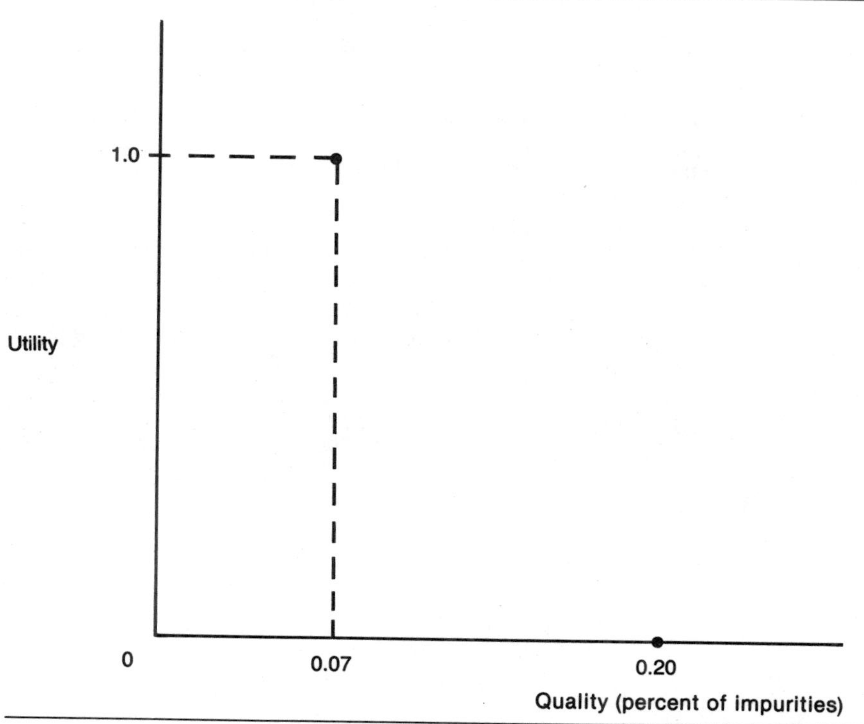


Is there a certainty equivalent to this gamble you can identify? In other words, what would be the value you would accept with certainty that would be equally desirable to facing this risk?

**BS:** I'm not sure, maybe about 0.15% or 0.17%.

**DD:** Let's see if we can be specific. Look at this decision tree:

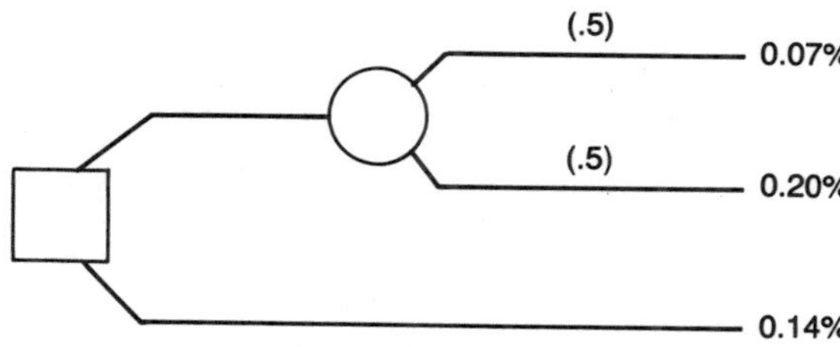


Which value would you choose?

**BS:** Oh, that's easy, I'd go for the 0.14% because I am averse to the downside risk of 0.2%. I can see now what nonlinear preferences mean. In pure and simple expected value terms, the gamble option has an *expected* impurity level of

$$0.5 \times 0.07\% + 0.5 \times 0.2\% = 0.135\%$$

So, based purely on expected value, the gamble is superior to the 0.14% certain outcome.

**DD:** Suppose I make the certain outcome on that tree 0.18%. What would you choose?

**BS:** Well, for my purposes 0.18% is not really all that much better than 0.2%, so I'd gamble and hope for the best.

**DD:** Suppose for the gamble that the certainty alternative you could choose was 0.16%.

**BS:** I'd go with the 0.16%. I see now that you are helping me to *converge* on my certainty equivalent for that gamble. Actually I would take a certain 0.16% to the gamble, but I would prefer the gamble to 0.17%. What should we do? I think my certainty equivalent is halfway in between.

**DD:** Then I can write an expected utility indifference equation

$$0.5\ U(0.07\%) + 0.5\ U(0.2\%) = U(0.165\%)$$

**BS:** Yes, that looks good. Even though on a linear scale 0.165% is closer to 0.2% than it is to 0.07%, my profitability is such that I really would want to avoid a gamble that would result in 0.2%. Anything close to 0.2% or higher would be just about considered as a bad batch.

**DD:** Let's plot the point $U(0.165\%) = 0.5$. Now consider a 50:50 gamble between 0.07% and 0.165%.

**BS:** Again I'd prefer a certain result that is worse than the weighted average of those two. Say 0.13%.

**DD:** We can write

$$\begin{aligned} U(0.13\%) &= 0.5\ U(0.07\%) + 0.5\ U(0.165\%) \\ &= 0.75 \end{aligned}$$

Let's plot that point on the graph (see Figure 6–8). Now we have four points. There is not really all that much point in identifying another point between 0.165% and 0.2%. I think we could do a reasonable job of drawing the curve in between 0.07% and 0.2% with what we now have (Figure 6–8). Let's extrapolate the curve to 0.06% and note that at that value the curve discontinues to some higher value of utility because of your increased profit opportunities. To get a measure for that extra utility, suppose you had a 50:50 gamble on the values 0.06% and 0.2%:

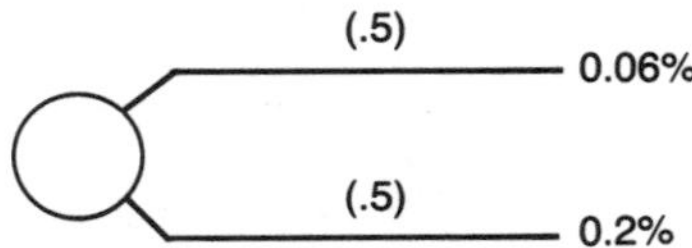


What is your certainty equivalent?

**BS:** For that gamble my certainty equivalent is 0.12%. That's the value I would accept with certainty in exchange for the gamble. You can see I have a strong preference for 0.06% by comparing this result with the first gamble we did.

**DD:** That's right. Our first one showed

$$0.5\ U(0.07\%) + 0.5\ U(0.2\%) = U(0.165\%)$$

**FIGURE 6–8** Utility Function for Percent of Impurities

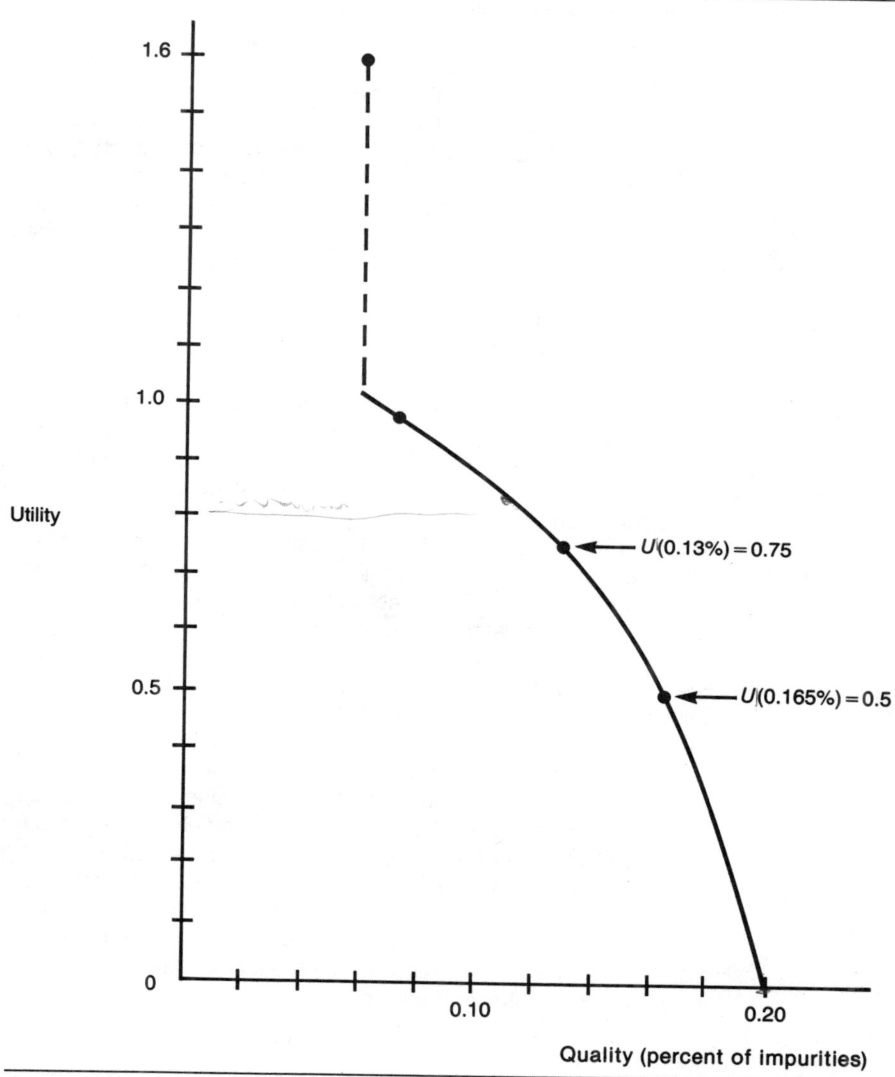


Now we have

$$0.5\ U(0.06\%) + 0.5\ U(0.2\%) = U(0.12\%)$$

We can read the utilities for 0.12% and 0.2% off the graph. They are 0.8 and zero, respectively. So solving the equation, the utility of 0.06% must work out to 1.6 utiles. Now let's check some of the results for consistency.

**BS:** Yes, the utility function looks very interesting. Not only does it show that as percentage impurities increase, my utility decreases, but it shows my utility decreasing at an increasing rate. That's good.

**DD:** OK. Now let's apply the expected utility criterion to the decision problem. Taking your original decision tree (Figure 5–1), I'll write the corresponding utility (from Figure 6–8) next to the quality figures. Now we'll roll back the tree as before, but this time we'll use the expected utilities instead of the raw quality estimates. By doing this we are taking into account not only the quality estimates, but also your stated preferences or desirability for those quality states.

**BS:** That's a very powerful tool, but I have two questions. First, when using expected utilities do we roll back the tree in the same way as for expected values? Second, how sensitive is the solution to any inaccuracies that may exist in the utility function?

**DD:** I certainly agree that it's a powerful approach to aiding decision makers. That's because it's *comprehensive* in accounting for *uncertainty* (through the use of probabilities), *forecast payoffs,* which in this instance happen to be measured by product quality, and *decision maker preferences and risk attitude.* In answer to your first question, the rollback procedure for expected utility is identical to the expected value analysis you have already done except that you are using utilities instead of values. I'm sure you remember there are just two components of the rollback procedure. Move from right to left on the tree so that at decision nodes you choose the most preferred option (and cross out the rest). At chance event nodes you calculate the expected value as the probability-weighted average of the values. In this case the values are the utilities. Remember also that utilities have no meaning themselves as numbers but are related to *real* measures that we value through the utility functions (like Figure 6–8).

**BS:** Good. Now, is the result robust to errors in the utility function? Suppose my utility function changes tomorrow.

**DD:** Well, if you know that your function changes significantly, you could always assess it again and redo the analysis. But your question brings up another deeper issue. To be honest, we are still struggling a little in terms of being confident about utility functions capturing the complex decision behavior and preferences of decision makers. There is no doubt that they go a long way in this. That is, they represent important aspects of decision behavior. They also represent a logical, rational approach, and to many of us, are representative of how we would *like* to behave in ideal conditions. Most human beings are, however, irrational and capricious as decision makers. So I can argue that the hypothetical judgments we make that are used to establish a utility function may not really capture my true preferences. If that's the case, the resulting utility function should not be thought of as a deadly accurate model but rather as a guide.

**BS:** Can I think of it as something that gives me an understanding of my preferences and also as a mechanism and guide for applying my preferences to the decision problem? In other words, I can learn as much from the utility function assessment and application process as from the bottom-line answer.

**DD:** Yes, I think that's often the case. You certainly shouldn't think of it as the gospel truth because of the biases and inaccuracies that can creep in. Please don't get me wrong. I have seen many applications of decision analysis that included expected utility analyses. It is a very powerful approach and can often be very insightful.

**BS:** How about the assessment method? You mentioned the existence of a number of methods. I had some difficulty judging a certainty equivalent for a 50:50 gamble on 0.07% or 0.20% because it's not the kind of decision I make in reality.

**DD:** That's a very good point. Indeed a number of assessment biases can creep in, and some assessment methods are better than others, depending on the nature of the problem and the decision maker. I usually like to structure the gambles to be similar to those in the decision problem, or at least in the decision maker's experience base.

---

## Other Utility Assessment Methods

A variety of other utility assessment methods exist. Most are based on the comparison of two gambles which we call $A$ and $B$ (Figure 6–9a).

A special case of this paired gamble comparison that we have already met is when either $x$ or $y$ is 0 (or 1) in which case we are comparing an uncertain event (often called a lottery) to a certainty equivalent. In the cases involving certainty equivalents, we can specify all the parameters except one in the set $A_1$, $A_2$, $x$, $B$, and make a judgment on the other that will satisfy the indifference relation. See Figure 6–9b. Whichever way the judgment is made, the result that is used (referring to Figure 6–9b) to identify the utility function is

$$x\ U(A_1) + (1 - x)\ U(A_2) = U(B)$$

**FIGURE 6–9** Gambles Used to Elicit Utility Functions

a. Paired gamble indifference

Gamble A

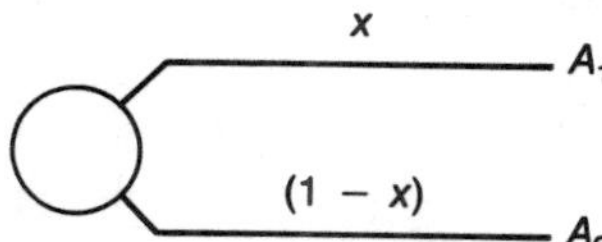


≈

Gamble B

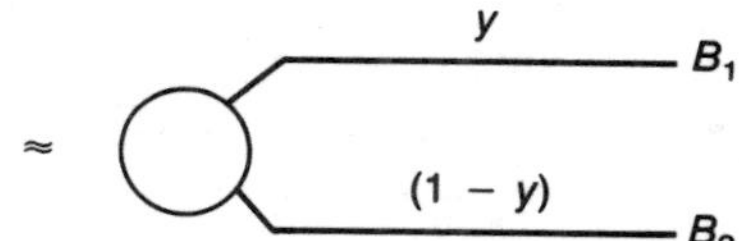


b. Certainty equivalent value of a gamble

Gamble A

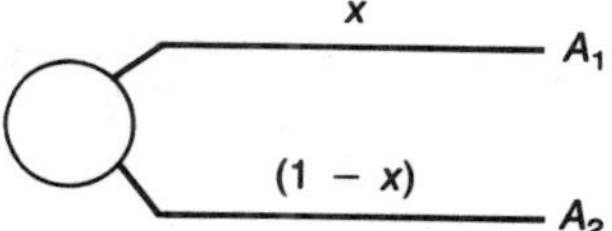


Certain consequence

$\approx B$

More generally (referring to the paired gamble case of Figure 6–9a)

$$x\ U(A_1) + (1 - x)\ U(A_2) = y\ U(B_1) + (1 - y)\ U(B_2)$$

The method used above to establish Mr. Schroer's utility function also chained the gambles. That is, the result of one judgment on a gamble was used to frame subsequent gambles. In theory this is entirely reasonable, but in practice it means that random errors in judgment or, systematic biases, may be propagated.

Not all methods involve chaining. For example in Figure 6–9b values of $A_1$ and $A_2$ could be specified, and a number of judgments could be made on $B$ as the value of $x$ is varied (or vice versa). These gambles would not be chained together in the sense that the judgments made are not used in subsequent gambles. These issues are further discussed in Chapter 13. For the reader who requires a more detailed treatment, Farquhar (1984) has comprehensively reviewed and classified a large variety of utility assessment procedures.

The experience of a substantial number of decision analysts has led to a conventional wisdom about utility function assessment expressed below as a set of guidelines.

1. Construct the gambles so that the judgments and comparisons are generally similar to the differences between alternatives in the decision problem. Don't use 50:50 gambles to establish a utility function if the decision mainly involves extreme probabilities. Don't try to judge a certainty equivalent over a very large range of values if the decision involves only a small range. Since judgments (and resulting utility functions) are sensitive to the framing of the gamble, it generally makes good sense to consider utility functions as context dependent or task specific. This is a practical point based on empirical research results which does not stem from the basic theory of utility. The theory itself does not address the biases that occur when it is used, and these practices are aimed at reducing the magnitude of those biases.

2. Use a variety of methods. To understand the magnitude of the judgmental inaccuracies in the process, use a second method to check the established utility function. Jst as when checking subjective probability estimates, it is wise to check the assessments using at least two assessment procedures.

3. Recognize that the relatively poor descriptive validity of the theory leads to inaccuracies in representation. Ultimately, it does not matter whether it's the theory at fault for not encompassing human decision behavior, or the decision maker's fault for not behaving in accordance with the set of axioms. What is important is that in cases where the axioms do not represent the decision behavior well, the utility function is not generally an accurate representation. It may represent the basic preference pattern quite

well but not be accurate enough to be a good device for predicting behavior. *Its power is in presenting a theory of rational choice which can be made operational, albeit imperfectly.* Hence like all other modeling approaches, the expected utility rule should be used as a decision aid, to guide actual judgment and provide insight to support judgment, and never to replace it.

Indeed the work done by behavioral decision analysts which shows that many decision makers behave in irrational or capricious ways, does not weaken the position of normative decision analysis. *On the contrary, the fact that people are naturally poor decision makers provides a strong motivation for formalizing common sense.*

Consider a world where the majority of people are intuitively very good decision makers. This is certainly not the situation on our earth, but let's think of it as another planet. On this other planet, people are able to digest and assimilate complex sets of information. They are able to deal in an unaided manner with the complicating factors of uncertainty, nonlinear preferences, multiple goals, and group decisions. Do they need to study the 'science' of decision analysis? Obviously not. Do we earthlings have abilities similar to these aliens, or are we generally capricious and somewhat limited in our intuitive information-processing abilities?

To summarize the arguments made so far in this chapter, the expected utility approach is a component of decision analysis that formalizes our intuition about risk preference and incorporates it into decision models. As with any quantitative analysis there is a possibility of specification inaccuracies in expected utility models; however, the insights to be gained purely from the specification and analysis process are usually extremely useful.

## MATHEMATICAL REPRESENTATIONS OF UTILITY FUNCTIONS

Many different kinds of mathematical formulae exist that represent utility function curves such as Figure 6–5. It is often convenient to fit mathematical functions to utility curves. This is because mathematical functions are concise, exact forms of expression, whereas graphs drawn by hand such as Figure 6–5 are not. In this section we examine three families of mathematical utility functions.

### Exponential Utility Function

The exponential utility function is defined as

$$U(x) = -e^{-kx} \qquad [6\text{–}1]$$

where

$x$ is the dimension of value (usually assumed to be wealth)
$k$ is a constant
$e$ is the exponential constant ($e = 2.71828$)

Another form of this function is

$$U(x) = \frac{1}{k}(1 - e^{-kx}) \qquad [6\text{–}2]$$

These two expressions of the exponential utility function are equivalent since utility functions are unique up to a positive linear transformation. This means that if a utility function is changed by addition of a constant value and multiplication by a positive constant value, its properties are exactly preserved. Figure 6–10 shows examples of the exponential utility function. In Figure 6–10, line *A*, being further from the diagonal EMV line, represents a utility function with a higher degree of risk aversion than line *B*.

**FIGURE 6–10** Exponential Utility Function

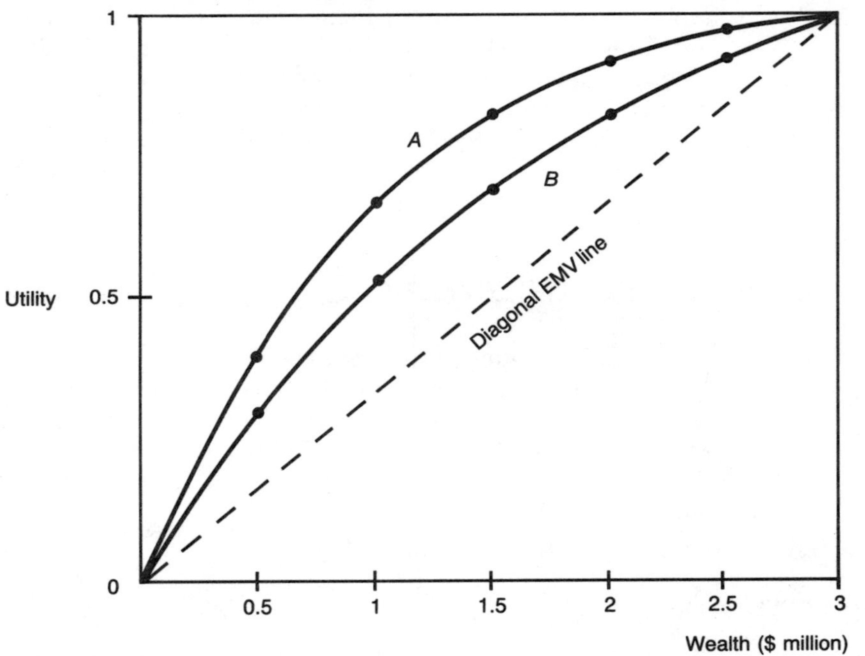


NOTE: Line *A*: $U(X) = (1 - e^{-1\times 10^{-6}X}) / 0.95$
Line *B*: $U(X) = (1 - e^{-5\times 10^{-7}X}) / 0.77$

## Logarithmic Utility Function

The logarithmic utility function is given by

$$U(x) = \log (x + b) \tag{6–3}$$

where $b$ is a constant.

Figure 6–11 shows examples of the logarithmic function.

## Quadratic Utility Function

The quadratic utility function is given by

$$U(x) = a + bx - cx^2 \tag{6–4}$$

where $a$, $b$, and $c$ are constants.

Figure 6–12 shows examples of this function.

The graphs of these mathematical representations may appear to be quite similar, although those readers who are more mathematically inclined

**FIGURE 6–11** Logarithmic Utility Function

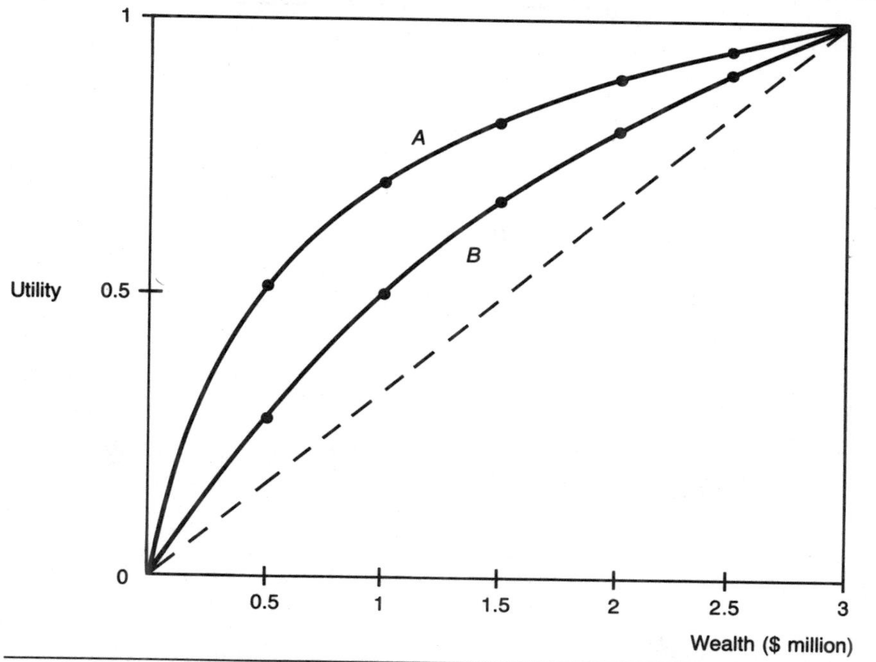


NOTE: Line $A$: $U(X) = 1/3.48Ln(X + 10^5) - 3.3$
Line $B$: $U(X) = 1/1.425\ Ln(X + 9.5 \times 10^5) - 9.66$

**FIGURE 6–12** Quadratic Utility Functions

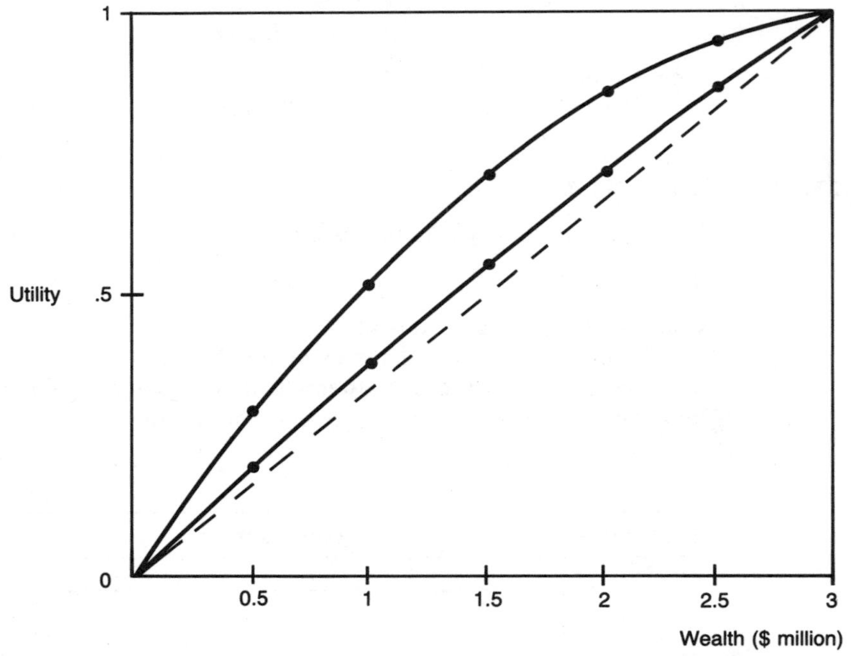


NOTE: Line *A*: $U(X) = (X - 1.5 \times 10^{-8}X^2) / 2.865 \times 10^6$
Line *B*: $U(X) = (X - 5 \times 10^{-8}X^2) / 2.55 \times 10^6$

know that the shapes of these graphs (Figures 6–10, 6–11, and 6–12) are fundamentally different. Note that each of these functions has a similar shape to Figure 6–5. As with Figure 6–5, the decreasing marginal utility is shown by a characteristically concave graph shape on all of Figures 6–10, 6–11, and 6–12.

## Risk Aversion

To illustrate the important *differences* between these functions, we formally define a measure of *risk aversion* (RA) as

$$RA = \frac{-U''(x)}{U'(x)} \qquad [6\text{–}5]$$

where $U''(x)$ is the second derivative of $U(x)$ and $U'(x)$ is the first derivative of $U(x)$.

A number of other different definitions of risk aversion have been proposed, however the one given by Equation [6–5] is most commonly used. It is useful to calculate the risk-aversion functions of the three mathematical functions given above, in order to draw inference about their differences. First however, let us note that the risk-aversion function, Equation [6–5], actually does measure the degree of aversion to uncertainty in a utility function. The numerator of the risk-aversion function $U''(x)$ measures the curvature (rate of change of slope) of the function. More curvature means more risk aversion. Figure 6–13 shows three utility functions. Line *A* is straight and hence represents a function where preference (utility) is proportional to wealth. Line *B* is curved (concave) and represents a risk-averse preference pattern. Line *C* is even more curved than line *B* and hence represents a greater degree of risk aversion (shown as a greater degree of curvature). We can say in general

$$RA(\text{Line } C) > RA(\text{Line } B) > RA(\text{Line } A)$$

Since Line *A* is straight: $RA(\text{Line } A) = 0$

**FIGURE 6–13** Utility Functions Showing Different Degrees of Risk Aversion

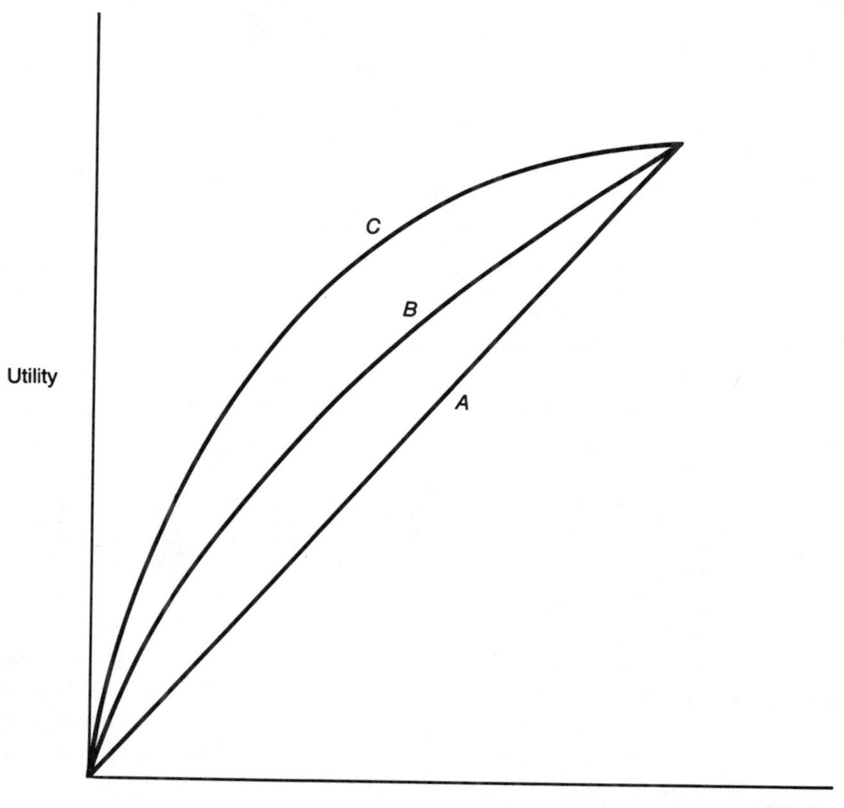


NOTE: Lines with higher curvature represent more risk-averse preference patterns.

**FIGURE 6–14** Utility Functions Showing Different Degrees of Risk Seeking (risk proneness)

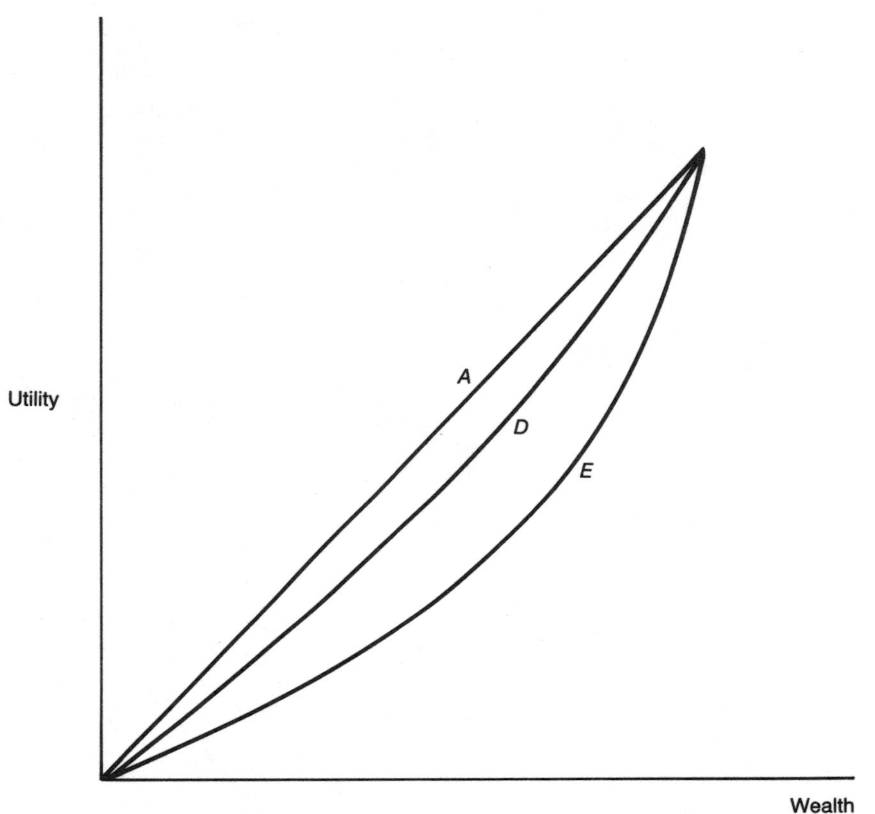


NOTE: Lines with higher curvature represent more risk-seeking preference patterns.

Note that the converse would apply to risk proneness where convex curves (see lines *D* and *E* on Figure 6–14) represent various degrees of risk proneness.

The denominator of Equation [6–5] is the slope of the utility function. Its inclusion in the risk-aversion formula has the effect of scaling the risk-aversion value, so that even though the utility scale is arbitrary, numerical values of risk aversion have real meaning. Hence risk aversion is the *ratio of curvature to slope* of the utility function. The negative sign in Equation [6–5] is included in the formula to make this risk-aversion measure positive and increasing as risk aversion increases.

A person who is risk averse would refuse an actuarially fair bet and indeed would generally pay to avoid such a bet. Suppose for example that an investment opportunity requires a \$1,000 investment and has a 50:50 chance of yielding \$0 or \$2,000. This is an actuarially fair gamble because the expected outcome of the uncertain event equals the certain investment. A risk-averse person would not invest. A risk-neutral person would be indifferent to it. A risk-prone (also known as risk-seeking) person would invest. In highlighting the concept of attitude towards risk in this manner, we note that it is not reasonable generally to classify people as risk averse, neutral, or prone in their decision behavior. Indeed any individual may well exhibit all three characteristics in various decision contexts. Preference functions can have convex, concave, and straight sections.

For the exponential utility function as given by Equation [6–1]

$$\begin{aligned} U(x) &= -e^{-kx} \\ U'(x) &= k\, e^{-kx} \\ U''(x) &= -k^2\, e^{-kx} \\ RA &= k \end{aligned}$$

For the function as given by Equation [6–2]

$$\begin{aligned} U(x) &= 1/k\,(1 - e^{-kx}) \\ U'(x) &= e^{-kx} \\ U''(x) &= -k\, e^{-kx} \\ RA &= k \end{aligned}$$

From this we note that if linear transformations are applied to utility functions, their risk aversion, as defined by Equation [6–5], is unaltered.

For the exponential utility function, the parameter of the function, $k$, is the measure of risk aversion (RA).

Consider the logarithmic utility function

$$\begin{aligned} U(x) &= \log\,(x + b) \\ U'(x) &= \frac{1}{x + b} \\ U''(x) &= \frac{-1}{(x + b)^2} \\ RA &= \frac{1}{x + b} \end{aligned}$$

Whereas for the exponential utility function the RA function was constant, this is not so for the logarithmic function. For the logarithmic function, RA decreases as $x$ (wealth) increases. To many people this property of *decreasing risk aversion* is a representative and desirable one. Many of us feel we would be less risk averse (in other words generally less worried about uncertainty) if our level of wealth was higher.

For the quadratic utility function

$$U(x) = a + bx - cx^2$$
$$U'(x) = b - 2cx$$
$$U''(x) = -2c$$
$$RA = \frac{2c}{b - 2cx}$$

We could redefine the quadratic function without changing its properties by linear transformation to

$$U(x) = x - dx^2$$

In that case

$$U'(x) = 1 - 2dx$$
$$U''(x) = -2d$$
$$RA = \frac{2d}{1 - 2dx}$$

The important feature of this function is that as $x$ (level of wealth) increases, risk aversion also increases. Although there is no such thing as a *generally* desirable utility function or functional property, this property of increasing risk aversion seems, a priori, to be one which would not apply to many people's wealth preference pattern.

Three utility function forms have been described in this section. Many other functional forms exist. (See, for example, Keeney and Raiffa 1976.) Some of these are more complex than the three that are described above, in the sense that they have more parameters. Indeed it is feasible to define functions that are simple additive combinations of the functions described above. As with all mathematical function-fitting processes, more complex functions having more parameters can incorporate more modeling features, and generally fit better, if they are sensibly chosen. However, unless there is a real need to use complex functions, simple functions should be used because they are easier to fit, compute, and manipulate.

---

## EXAMPLE 6–4

### Developing Corporate Utility Functions

A well-documented decision analysis application was published by C. S. Spetzler in 1968. Spetzler's aim was to establish utility functions that would be representative for a corporation. Spetzler described a useful set of properties for a prescriptive utility function to be:

1. Continuous and twice differentiable.
2. Leading to a risk aversion (RA) which satisfies $RA \geq 0$.
3. RA should be constant or monotonically decreasing over the range.

He fitted the following logarithmic function to data that he collected from managers

$$U(x) = A + B \log(x + C)$$

where

$x$ is the dimension of value
$A, B, C$ are constants.

---

Figure 6–15 is a typical example of data with a curve of best fit. Note that not all of the points fall exactly on the line. This may be because the logarithmic function does not exactly describe the preference pattern, because the utility approach does not encompass all of the elements of the preference pattern, or because of (relatively small) judgmental inconsistencies made by the decision maker.

Mathematical utility functions can be fitted by obtaining only enough judgments to identify the function parameters. For example consider the exponential utility function

$$U(x) = -e^{-kx}$$

If a certainty equivalent to a gamble

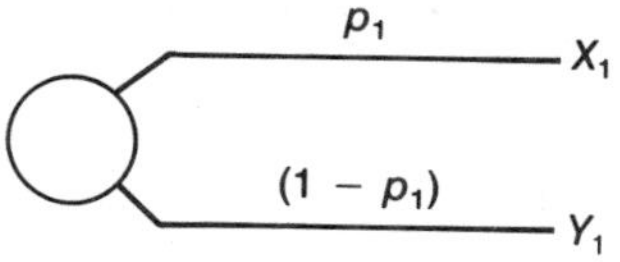

$p_1$ → $X_1$
$(1 - p_1)$ → $Y_1$

is judged to be $CE_1$, then we get

$$U(CE_1) = p_1\ U(X_1) + (1 - p_1)\ U(Y_1)$$

For the exponential function

$$-e^{-kCE_1} = p_1\ (-e^{-kX_1}) + (1 - p_1)(-e^{-kY_1}) \qquad [6\text{–}6]$$

This equation can be solved relatively easily for a value of $k$, either by trial and error or by algorithmic search (e.g., using a computer routine).

Computer programs exist for fitting mathematical utility functions by solving equations such as Equation [6–6]. One of the earliest powerful decision analysis computer packages was designed by Schlaifer (1971). This

**FIGURE 6–15** A Utility Function Fitted to a Typical Set of Assessment Data

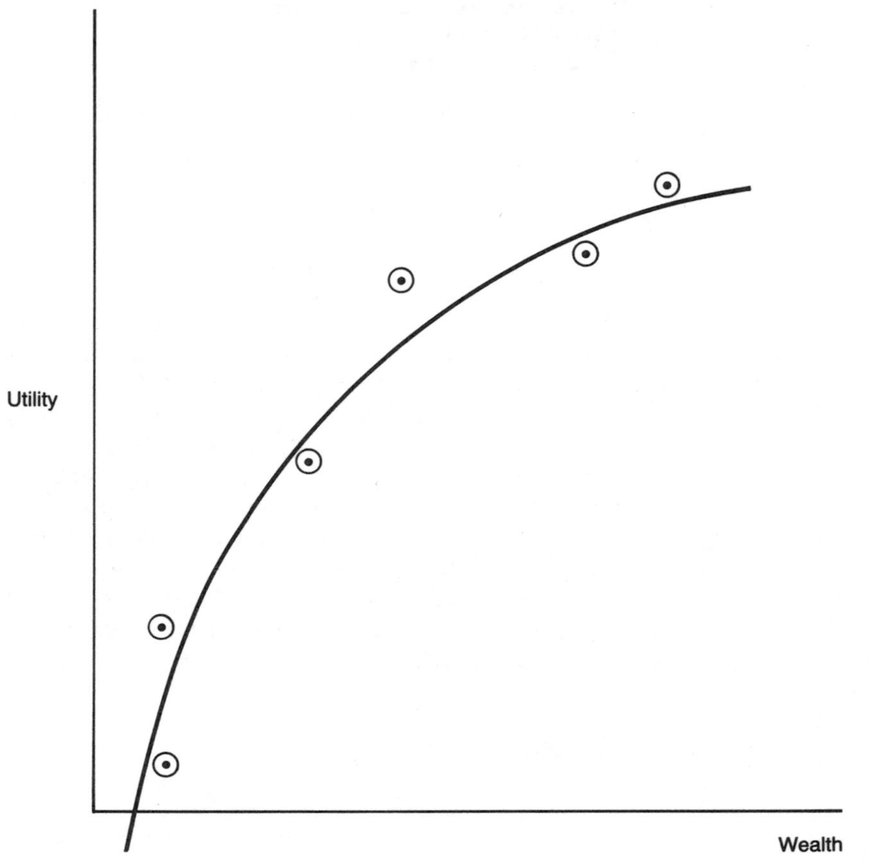


package and others that followed it allow the user to compute a number of useful things including utility function parameters, such as in Equation [6–6], and probability estimates. Similar procedures can be followed for fitting other forms of mathematical utility functions.

## EMPIRICAL EVIDENCE

Utility theory and the preference function modeling approach it encompasses has been found to be lacking as a descriptive approach. Details of some of the problems associated with fitting and using utility functions are given in Chapter 13. These problems can be summarized as follows:

*a.* Biases and inconsistencies exist in the judgments made by decision makers.

*b.* The expected utility approach sometimes fails to describe decision behavior, even though from a prescriptive viewpoint it is very appealing.

A number of directions of research effort in decision analysis are under way as attempts to increase the usefulness of utility theory. These include processes of documentation of biases, searches for better fitting procedures, and attempts to modify and enrich the theory.

## Documentation of Biases

Two very informative publications, Hershey et al. (1982) and Kahneman and Tversky (1981) have shown that decision makers consistently violate the axioms of utility theory when making real-life decisions. See Chapter 13 for a detailed discussion. Hershey et al. point to the context dependencies of utility functions, stating that certain factors affect the judgment of decision makers in ways that are not predicted or explained by utility theory.

In summary, utility theory, as a prescriptive method, does not exactly describe preference patterns for many people. However as a theory of rational choice there is much to be gained through using it as a modeling procedure.

## Better Fitting Procedures

A number of procedural strategies exist for improving the quality of utility functions as representations of decision-maker preferences. For example, Hershey et al. (1982) suggested that choices should be presented in terms of final wealth positions. This suggestion raises the important issue of definition of the domain of the utility function. In strictest terms, the domain of a utility function should be final wealth positions, however it is often convenient to express desirability for other measures such as cash flows, net present value, market share, or earnings per share. Hershey et al. argue that because of context dependencies and inconsistencies, which arise as a result of the framing of decisions, these measures should be translated into corresponding wealth positions.

Further, we note the value of looking at the broader perspective that comes from considering the effect of a decision in the context of wealth rather than other measures such as cash flow. Financial managers generally know that investment opportunities should not just be considered in isolation but rather be considered as additions to an existing or future portfolio. Similarly, in decision analysis the translation of cash flows into final wealth positions broadens the context in which the decision is framed and adds value to the model. Hence it is argued that unless decisions are minor in their impact, they generally should be considered as part of a *portfolio* rather than in *isolation*. This argument is nothing more than an argument for *strategic thinking* for important decisions. The incorporation of wealth as a dimension of value (rather than cash flows) aids the process of understanding the strategic implications of a decision. For decisions where the impacts are very small relative to total wealth, one should question whether an expected utility analysis or indeed a decision analysis is warranted.

A second process for improving the usefulness of utility functions is to find improved fitting procedures for mathematical utility functions. Consider the basic procedure given by Equation [6–6]. This equation allows a utility function parameter to be deduced on the basis of just one judgment. The errors in the judgment of $CE_1$ will be directly reflected in errors in the parameter value. These errors may be random or systematic in nature, or a combination. Random errors can be reduced by a process of averaging out.

Suppose that the underlying certainty equivalent of a decision maker for a gamble is $CE_i$. The decision maker may not specify this amount exactly, but may specify $(CE_i + e_i)$ where $e_i$ is an error term. It is possible to fit mathematical utility functions to a set of judgments so as to minimize an error function. This error function may be the sum of absolute values of error or sum of squares. This methodology is similar in nature to that of linear regression, where a model form is specified, and a least-squares criterion of best fit is applied. However with utility theory there is relatively little basis, a priori, on which to presume a particular functional form. The fitting procedure can itself be used to confirm assumptions about utility function form, through a process of comparing the magnitude of errors associated with best fits of various functional forms.

## Modifying and Enriching the Theory

As a result of the fairly poor descriptive power of the expected utility decision rule, some decision analysts are striving to change the form of the theory or else propose alternatives. For example, Prospect theory is an alternative approach described in Chapter 13. Other researchers have attempted to use more complex forms of utility representations to more fully encompass decision behavior. For example, utility functions have been proposed with domains that are expressed as streams of cash flows through time. Others have incorporated measures of regret (see Chapter 5) as well as payoff or wealth amounts. Although these more complex representations generally do fit better to decision behavior, they are more difficult to fit in terms of parameter estimation and, being less simple, are less prescriptively appealing.

Ultimately, we should consider the value of the expected utility approach in terms of what we learn from using it. Can its use help us make better decisions? The answer to this question is a definite yes, but this is not so much because a decision maker who strictly follows the expected utility rule strategies will continually make the right decisions. Indeed, the assessment biases mean that accuracy of representation cannot be guaranteed. Rather, the usefulness of the expected utility rule is very much like the more general usefulness of the decision analysis approach. Both provide a systematic, conceptually sensible basis for gaining insights about decisions.

---

## EXAMPLE 6–5

### Risk Management at Boston Utility Service Company (BUSC)[1]

Boston Utility Service Company is a public utility with approximately $1.5 billion in yearly sales. It was concerned about the risk that it carried in the categories of property (plant and equipment), business interruption, and liability. To this end a decision analysis consultant was called in to help the company determine its attitude towards risk and to help translate this attitude into operating policy. The company had insurance policies with deductible amounts that had been kept very low even as the company grew. The decision analyst expressed the idea that the company should have a consistent risk policy to be implemented in both its investment decisions and in managing its own downside risks and potential losses. To understand and synthesize a statement of the corporate risk philosophy, the analyst interviewed the company president, two senior vice presidents, and seven vice presidents. As part of these interviews the analyst asked a series of questions (requiring judgments about gambles) of those executives as shown in Figure 6–16. From this, a picture emerged of the overall attitude toward risk of the company's top level decision makers. The executives were all generally risk averse when large gambles were involved, but were willing to play the averages (using an expected monetary value) for relatively small amounts. For losses they were generally happy to bear some risk. Figure 6–17 shows the form of the utility function for the company. It was interesting to note that there seemed to be a target level at or near the "present wealth" level where risk aversion was predominant for higher wealth levels and risk seeking or neutrality existed at lower levels. Note that when dealing with a group decision-making process, there are often likely to be differences between group members, and an averaging, consensus, or smoothing process should occur.

As a result of the study, a number of benefits occurred. First, the company's executives heightened both their awareness and understanding of general issues involving risky decisions. Second, the group members communicated effectively (both through the analyst and directly) and became sensitive to the attitudes towards

---

[1] This example is drawn from Samson (1987). To preserve confidentiality, the name of the company has been changed.

**FIGURE 6–16** Hypothetical Gambles Used to Assess a Utility Function

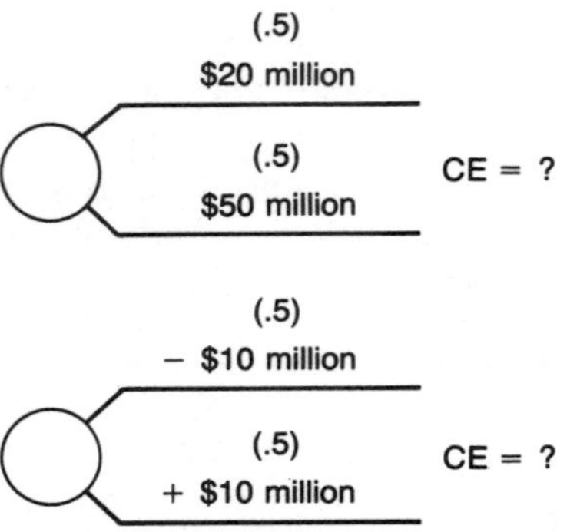


NOTE: Corporate executives were asked to assess their certainty equivalent values to these gambles.

**FIGURE 6–17** Utility Functions Can Change Their Curvature (as shown by this function fitted to a corporate vice president's assessments)

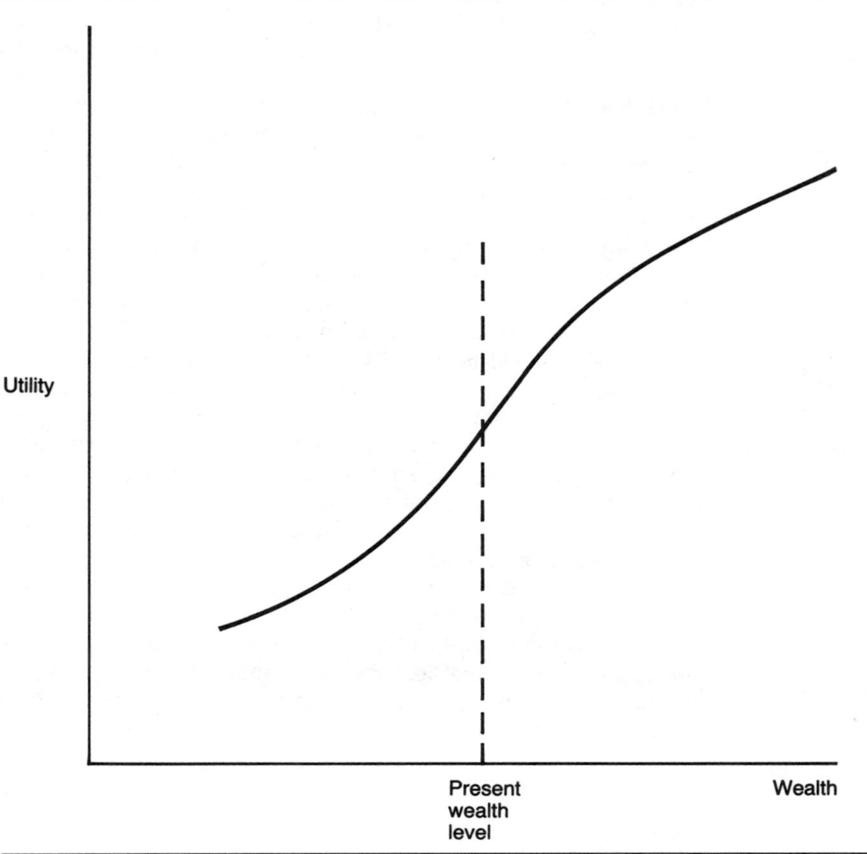

risk of their colleagues. Third, the corporate risk philosophy was treated as a statement of company policy and was used to communicate that policy to key operating staff. Fourth, it was realized that the company had both the financial capacity and desire to retain certain risks, which were at that time being transferred to insurance companies. As a result, new insurance policies were negotiated with subtantially higher deductible amounts and lower premiums.

## EXAMPLE 6–6

### Solar Technics

The Solar Technics Company was a small research and development oriented company which held the manufacturing rights to a patented device for controlling solar heating systems. They were considering selling these rights, either now or later, to another firm that had the resources to manufacture the product. Solar was also considering keeping these rights and subcontracting out the fabrication and assembly of the product. They were concerned about the future of this product which depended strongly on the future of solar heating systems in general. Factors that were hard to predict entered into this future, such as world oil and gas prices and technological advancements which might result in their product's obsolescence. They structured the problem as a decision tree (see Figure 6–18). Figure 6–18 shows the present value of cash flows. These cash flows were discounted to present values and in the case of "manufacture ourselves," were summed over the assumed life of the product.

**FIGURE 6–18** Solar Technics Decision Tree

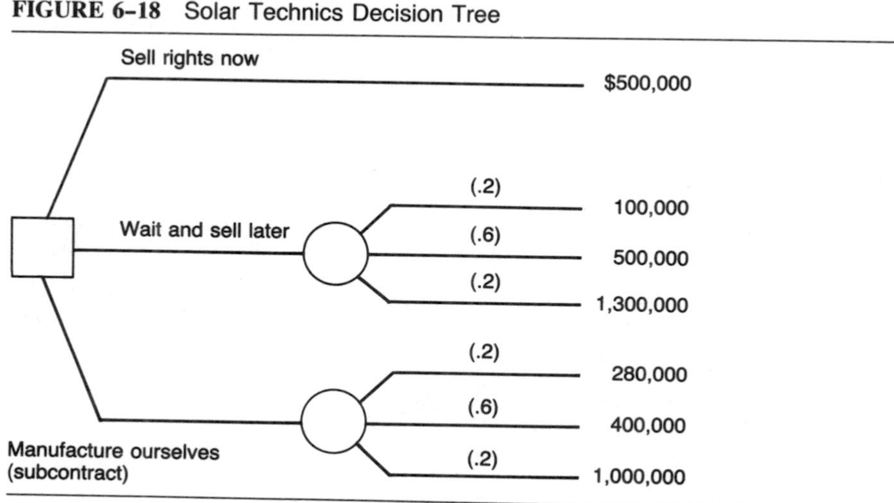

Expected values indicated that the most attractive option was to "sell later"

$$
\begin{aligned}
\text{Expected value (sell rights now)} &= \$500{,}000 \\
\text{Expected value (sell rights later)} &= 0.2 \times \$100{,}000 + 0.6 \times \$500{,}000 \\
&\quad + 0.2 \times \$1{,}300{,}000 \\
&= \$580{,}000 \\
\text{Expected value (manufacture ourselves)} &= 0.2 \times \$280{,}000 + 0.6 \times \$400{,}000 \\
&\quad + 0.2 \times \$1{,}000{,}000 \\
&= \$496{,}000
\end{aligned}
$$

Although the "sell later" option had a higher expected value, it was recognized that it also had substantially higher uncertainty (spread of cash flows around the expected value) associated with it. Rachel Catrino, the company president and owner, had recently attended an advanced management education program and wanted to see what she could gain by going through an expected utility analysis. She assessed certainty equivalent values for gambles generally similar to those shown on the decision tree. She realized from this exercise that she was risk averse and fitted a number of mathematical formulae to her certainty equivalence data points. The exponential function fitted quite well with a parameter value of $k = 5 \times 10^{-6}$

$$U(x) = -e^{-5 \times 10^{-6} x}$$

Rachel contemplated the implications of accepting an exponential function representation. She knew that it implied constant risk aversion, and after some consideration, decided that this property was quite a reasonable one for her. For example, she felt that her decisions and her risk attitude would not change if she suddenly inherited a few million dollars.

She then evaluated the expected utility of each alternative in her decision

$$
\begin{aligned}
\text{Expected utility (sell now)} &= -e^{-5 \times 10^{-6} \times 5 \times 10^{5}} \\
&= -0.082 \\
\text{Expected utility (sell later)} &= 0.2(-e^{-5 \times 10^{-6} \times 10^{5}}) \\
&\quad + 0.6(-e^{-5 \times 10^{-6} \times 5 \times 10^{5}}) \\
&\quad + 0.2(-e^{-5 \times 10^{-6} \times 1.3 \times 10^{6}}) \\
&= -0.169 \\
\text{Expected utility (manufacture ourselves)} &= 0.2(-e^{-5 \times 10^{-6} \times 2.8 \times 10^{5}}) \\
&\quad + 0.6(-e^{-5 \times 10^{-6} \times 5 \times 10^{5}}) \\
&\quad + 0.2(-e^{-5 \times 10^{-6} \times 10^{6}}) \\
&= -0.1315
\end{aligned}
$$

These utilities correspond to certainty equivalents (CE) of

$$
\begin{aligned}
\text{CE (sell now)} &= \$500{,}000 \\
\text{CE (sell later)} &= \$353{,}000 \\
\text{CE (manufacture ourselves)} &= \$405{,}000
\end{aligned}
$$

Rachel noted that in *expected value* terms the rank order of options was (from best to worst):

1. Sell later.
2. Sell now.
3. Manufacture ourselves.

When she took her risk aversion into account using *expected utility,* a change occurred in these rank orders to:

1. Sell now.
2. Manufacture ourselves.
3. Sell later.

The "sell later" option, which had the highest expected value, also had the highest uncertainty. Hence for this option the *risk premium,* which is the difference between the expected value and the certainty equivalent, was relatively high.

She then checked to see how sensitive these results were to her assessed utility function. She was confident that she had the correct functional form but wished to check the sensitivity of the results to the degree of risk aversion.

She knew that if she increased the value of $k$ (the utility function parameter for the exponential function is the measure of risk aversion), the "sell now" option would become relatively *more* attractive in the expected utility analysis because it was the least uncertain. Of more interest to her was the effect on the ranking of alternatives of decreasing the degree of risk aversion.

She decided to recalculate the expected utilities with a 10% reduction in the degree of risk aversion. Rachel thought that there was some chance that her value of $k$ might be wrong by as much as 10% but most likely not by much more.

When $k$ was reduced by 10% to $4.5 \times 10^{-6}$ she obtained the following results:

| *Option* | *Expected Utility* | *Certainty Equivalent* | *Rank* |
|---|---|---|---|
| Sell now | −0.105 | $500,000 | 1 |
| Sell later | −0.1913 | $367,000 | 3 |
| Manufacture ourselves | −0.158 | $410,000 | 2 |

Rachel noted that reducing the degree of risk aversion by 10% did not change the preference rankings, although it did narrow the gap between the certainty equivalent of the best option, "sell now" and the other options that involved more uncertainty.

She decided to explore the sensitivity analysis more fully. In particular she wanted to know just how much the degree of risk aversion would have to change in the model to result in a different set of rankings. She knew that if the value of $k$ was reduced by enough, the "sell later" alternative would be ranked above the "sell now" option. Ultimately if $k = 0$, (the no risk-aversion case) the certainty equivalents are equal to the expected values. Rachel wrote a small computer program to calculate the certainty equivalent values over a range of values of $k$. This program saved her from doing a number of repetitive calculations by hand. Figure 6–19 shows the certainty equivalent values for each option as a function of $k$. From this, Rachel concluded that the option that was high in expected value and risk, "sell later," only became the best ranked option if $k \leq 1.2 \times 10^{-6}$. She went back over her utility function assessments and decided that she was considerably more risk averse than this.

To make her decision, she took a step back from her detailed analysis and reconsidered the problem as a whole. From the decision analysis she had learned a

**FIGURE 6–19** Correlation of Certainty Equivalent with Degree of Risk Aversion for Solar Technics

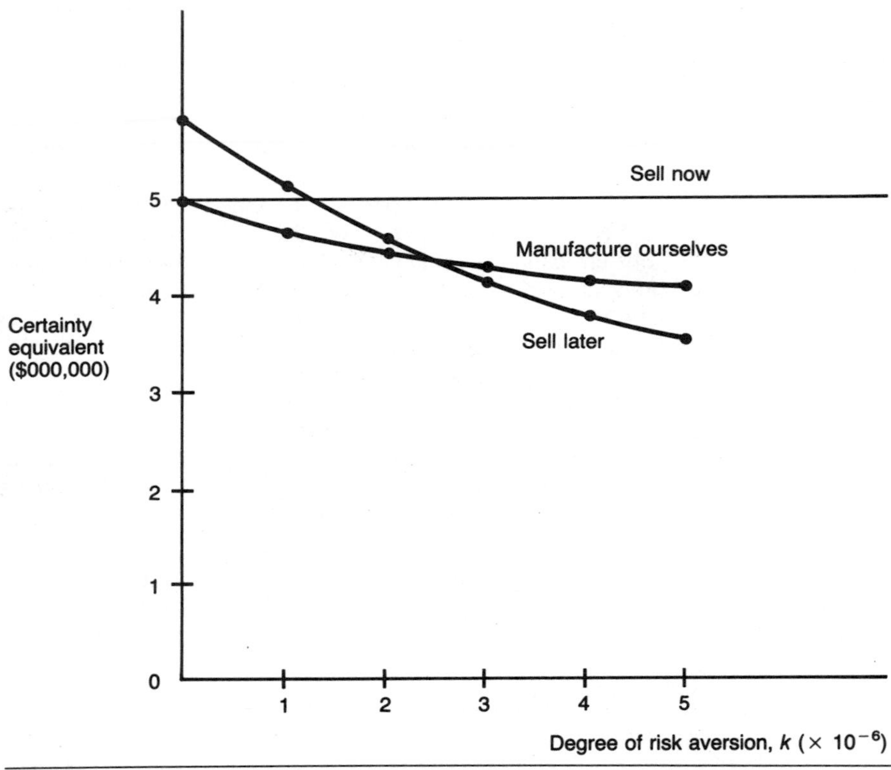


lot about the decision and about her own attitude toward risk. She reconsidered the assessments she had made on Figure 6–18 and decided that they were as accurate as she could make them. Finally she thought carefully about whether the decision tree was complete. Were there any other feasible alternative actions? She could not think of any. Since both her instincts and the decision analysis/expected utility analysis indicated that the "sell now" option was the most attractive, she chose to do so, and made the necessary arrangements.

## SUMMARY

The expected utility decision criterion is a powerful prescriptive approach. It encompasses the preference pattern of the decision maker including the attitude toward risk. Utility functions can have monetary measures as their domain (for example, final-period wealth) or can be used to represent preference patterns for nonmonetary dimensions of value.

This chapter focuses on unidimensional utility functions, although the theory can be usefully extended to encompass multiple dimensions of value (see Chapter 7).

The expected utility rule is generally considered to be prescriptively appealing as a rational basis for yielding insights about decisions. Although the rule provides powerful prescriptive insights, it does not do so well as a descriptive model. In actual decision-making applications, we observe people who consistently violate the axioms of expected utility.

Many methods exist for assessing utility functions. They can be deduced from observing a person's decision behavior or constructed using the results of a series of hypothetical gamble decisions. When establishing a utility function, a variety of methods should be used to ensure that a consistent, coherent representation is established.

Mathematical functions can be fitted to preference patterns. A variety of functions are available, having different properties and resultant implications about risk-aversion functions.

Whether graphical or mathematical representations of utility functions are used, the expected utility decision rule is useful in establishing an understanding of decision-maker preferences and providing inferences for decision-making purposes.

## FURTHER READING

Much has been written about the theory of utility and its application. The early and traditional treatment that should be read is the von Neumann and Morgenstern (1947) book in which the basics of utility theory are developed. A second excellent source of both the concepts and mechanics of expected utility is Raiffa's (1968) book. His chapters on utility make very good reading.

More recently, a number of useful articles have been written that will give the reader a deeper appreciation of specific aspects of expected utility if read in conjunction with this chapter and Chapter 13. These are by Farquhar (1984) on the subject of utility assessment, and by Hershey et al. (1982), Schoemaker (1982), and Kahneman and Tversky (1981).

For an appreciation of the technical issues as well as the conceptual basis of the decision analysis/expected utility approach, Keeney and Raiffa (1976) has become something of a handbook. The early chapters of this book provide the motivation and justification for the approach, and the later chapters contain the technical information. Their Chapter 4 is a useful addition to this reading list, focusing on unidimensional utility.

## REFERENCES

FARQUHAR, P. 1984. "Utility Assessment Methods." *Management Science* 30 (November), pp. 1283–1300.

HAGEN, O., and F. WENSTOP. 1984. *Progress in Utility and Risk Theory*. Holland: D. Reidel Publishing.

HERSHEY, J. C., H. C. KUNREUTHER, and P. J. H. SCHOEMAKER. 1982. "Sources of Bias in Assessment Procedures for Utility Functions." *Management Science* 28, no. 8, August.

KAHNEMAN, D., and A. TVERSKY. 1979. "Prospect Theory: An Analysis of Decisions under Risk." *Econometrica* 47, no. 2, p. 263.

KEENEY, R., and H. RAIFFA. 1976. *Decisions With Multiple Objectives: Preferences and Value Tradeoffs*. New York: John Wiley & Sons.

RAIFFA, H. 1968. *Decision Analysis*. Reading, Mass: Addison-Wesley Publishing.

SAMSON, D. A. 1987. "Corporate Risk Philosophy for Improved Risk Management." *Journal of Business Research* 15, pp. 107–22.

SCHLAIFER, R. O. 1971. *Computer Programs for Elementary Decision Analysis*. Boston: Division of Research, Harvard Business School.

SCHOEMAKER, P. J. H. 1982. "The Expected Utility Model: Its Variants, Purposes, Evidence and Limitations." *Journal of Economic Literature* 20, pp. 529–63.

SPETZLER, C. S. 1968. "The Development of a Corporate Risk Policy for Capital Investment Decisions." *IEEE Systems Science and Cybernetics* SSC–4, pp. 279–300.

VON NEUMANN, J., and O. MORGENSTERN. 1947. *Theory of Games and Economic Behavior*. 2nd. ed. Princeton, N.J: Princeton University Press.

## PROBLEMS

1. How does the expected utility decision criterion aid the decision modeling process?
2. What is the difference between expected value and expected utility?
3. Explain the concept and measure of risk aversion. How does it relate to utility functions?
4. What procedural guidelines might help a decision maker to accurately assess a utility function?
5. Utility functions have been described as "context bounded." Discuss this viewpoint.
6. There is strong evidence that many people violate the axioms of expected utility. Does this mean that people are generally irrational in their decision making or that the theory is weak?
7. Refer to the Midwestern Utility example in Chapter 2. Figure 2–7 shows the decision tree model for the tax problem that Midwestern faced. Since two competing options had expected values that were very close, it was decided to conduct an expected utility analysis. The president of Midwestern assessed his certainty equivalent values to a set of gambles as follows:

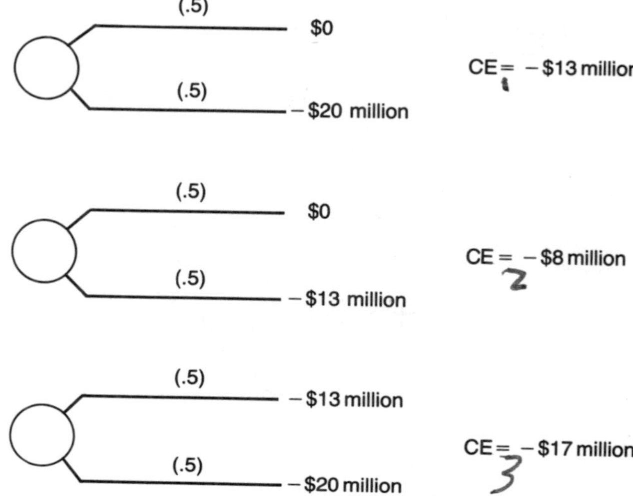


Construct a utility function (using graph paper) and use the preferences to roll back the decision tree and determine the decision model strategy. Compare the expected utility solution with the expected value solution.

8. Review the problem faced by an architect in Chapter 3, problem 7. The architect assessed a utility function by considering the following gambles:

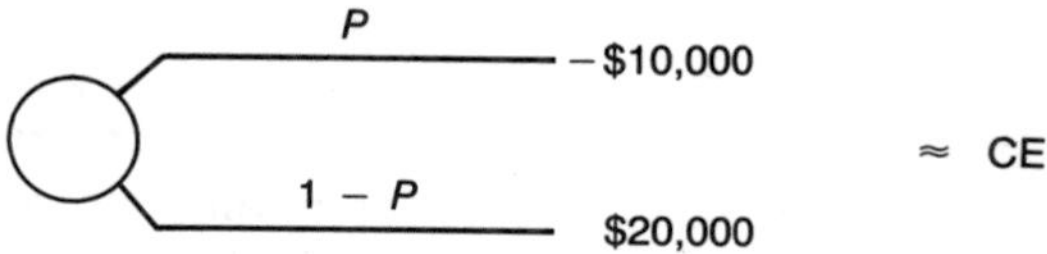


For various values of *P*, corresponding values of *CE* were assessed as follows:

| *P* | *CE* |
|---|---|
| 0.2 | $ 10,000 |
| 0.5 | $ 1,000 |
| 0.8 | $ −7,000 |

Use the expected utility method to determine a preferred strategy and compare this to the expected value solution.

9. In problem 5, Chapter 5, Bob Butter was considering a very important decision regarding the expansion of his business. His utility

**FIGURE 6–20** Bob Butter's Utility Function

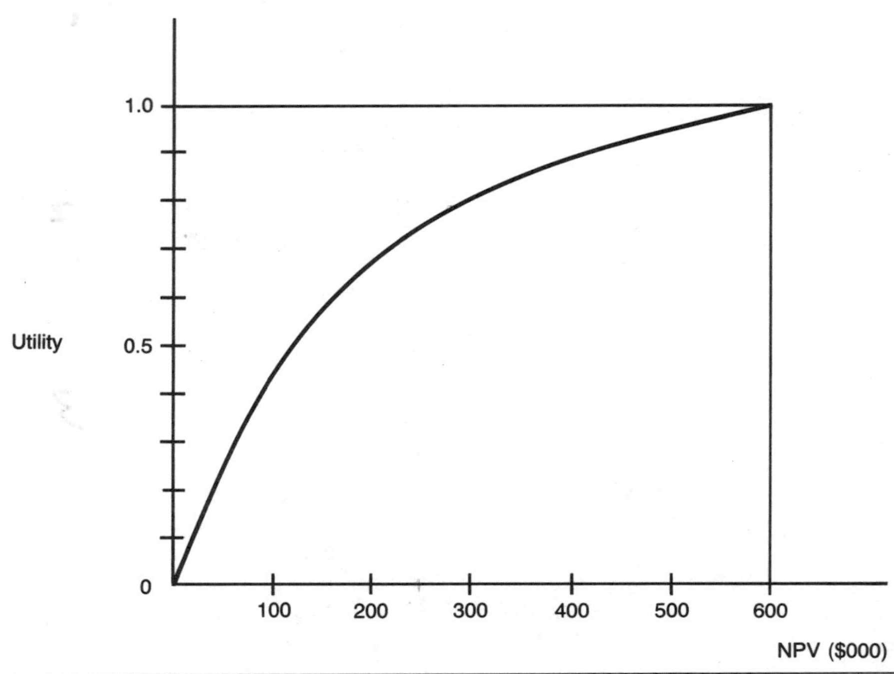


function is shown on Figure 6–20. Use the expected utility rule to deduce what might be an appropriate strategy for Bob.

10. Use the utility function (Figure 6–8) established by Bob Schroer in Zinco Productions (B) to roll back the decision tree (Figure 5–2) that was constructed in Zinco Productions (A). What is the decision strategy? Is the expected utility solution different from the expected value solution, and if so, why?
11. Use the utility function (Figure 6–21) to apply the expected utility rule to problem 8, Chapter 5. Compare the expected value and expected utility results.
12. Can ARBORIST be used for the application of the expected utility criterion? Given that the expected utility rollback procedure is the same as the general expected value procedure, can ARBORIST be used with utility values being placed on the decision tree? Redo problem 11 above, using ARBORIST.

**FIGURE 6–21** A Utility Function for Cost

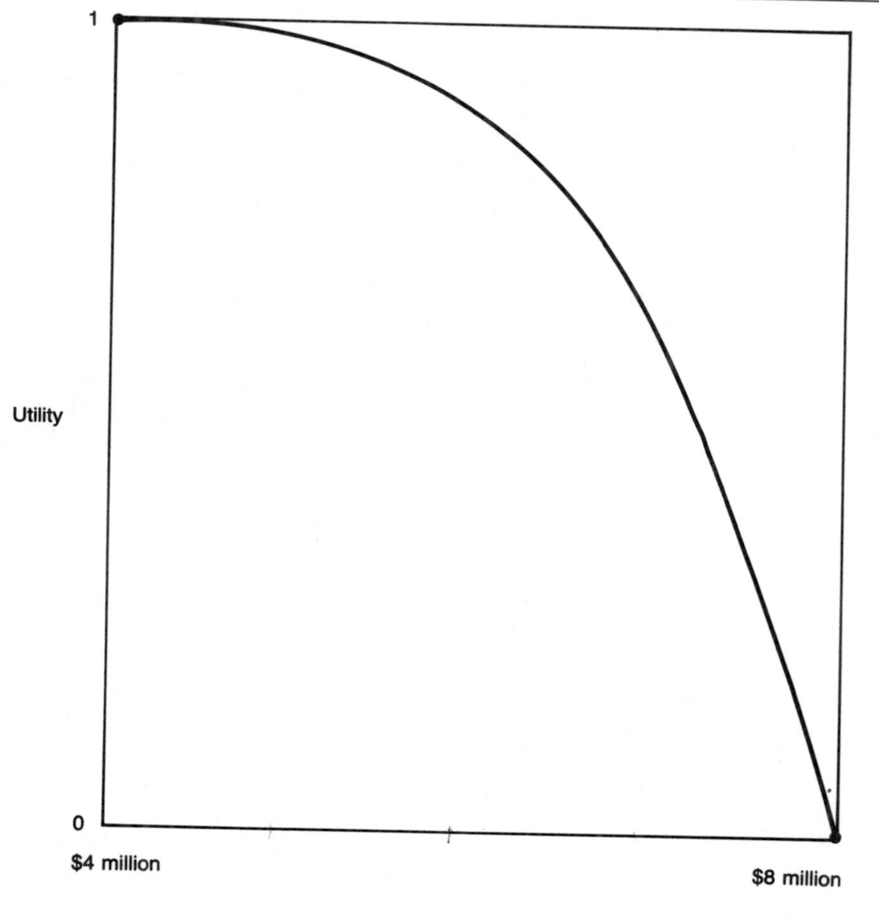


13. The risk manager of a restaurant chain was reviewing the insurance arrangements the company had against possible losses to equipment and buildings resulting from theft, fire, and other similar sources of loss to property. The risk manager consulted with a number of people both within and outside the company and reviewed the loss records of the company. He then produced a forecast for yearly total loss as follows:

| *Dollars of Total Loss per Year* | *Probability* |
|---|---|
| 0– 50,000 | 0.02 |
| 50,000–100,000 | 0.04 |
| 100,000–150,000 | 0.08 |
| 150,000–200,000 | 0.13 |
| 200,000–250,000 | 0.18 |
| 250,000–300,000 | 0.20 |
| 300,000–350,000 | 0.15 |
| 350,000–400,000 | 0.10 |
| 400,000–450,000 | 0.06 |
| 450,000–500,000 | 0.04 |

The insurance premium for next year for this loss had been quoted by an insurance broker at $290,000.

*a.* Calculate the expected loss. Use bracket medians.

*b.* The risk manager used an exponential utility function to measure the degree of risk aversion in an expected utility model. The parameter of that exponential utility function was $1.5 \times 10^{-6}$. Apply the expected utility rule to determine the certainty equivalent of not taking out insurance. Compare this with the insurance premium, and draw a conclusion about the attractiveness of insuring against this loss.

*c.* What is the value of the parameter of the exponential utility function that would make the "insure" alternative equivalent, in expected utility terms, to the "not insure" alternative?

14. Refer to problem 13, above. The insurance broker contacted the risk manager to tell him of an alternate form of insurance that would be available. Specifically, if the restaurant company bore the first $150,000 of loss liability, the reduction in premium would be $120,000. Compare this new alternative with the existing alternatives in problem 13, of fully insuring or not insuring. Draw risk profiles and cumulative loss distributions for each of these three alternative strategies. Discuss the fact that the two parties to such a contract are likely to have different probability distributions of loss.

15. A manager wished to fit a mathematical utility function to help him in his decision modeling. He constructed a gamble with 0.5 probability of a $2 million gain and a 0.5 probability of a $1 million gain. This chance event was very similar to that for a business opportunity that he faced. The alternative to that opportunity was an uncertain gain comprised of a 0.5 probability of $1.8 million, a 0.3 probability of $1.2 million, and a 0.2 probability of $0.7 million.

    *a.* The certainty equivalent that he assessed for the 0.5/0.5 split of $2 million/$1 million was $1.35 million. Fit an exponential utility function to this risk attitude and determine the value of the risk-aversion parameter.

*b.* Fit a logarithmic utility function to this risk attitude.
*c.* Fit a quadratic utility function to this risk attitude.
*d.* For each of these utility functions as fitted, which alternative is indicated as preferable: the 0.5/0.5 split of $2 million/$1 million or the 0.5/0.3/0.2 split of $1.8 million/$1.2 million/$0.7 million?
*e.* Was the choice sensitive to the form of utility function chosen?
*f.* Do you expect your answer to part (e) to be generally true? State your reasons.

---

## CASE STUDY

### James Jones Art Auctions (B)

James Jones was considering a complex business deal, in which he would contract to advertise (at his own expense) and subsequently auction, up to three paintings belonging to Klaus Heinegen. After having a friend help him to structure a decision tree for his problem, James felt that the modeling approach was somewhat limited in the insight that it produced. He told his friend, a recent MBA graduate from Stanford University, that he had learned a lot from the modeling process but wasn't satisfied with the use of a simple expected value rule:

**JAMES JONES (JJ):** The solution the expected value rule produces is fine, and I can understand the problem much better now that we have dissected it so carefully. But when we put it back together and used expected value, we assumed that I can afford to take certain risks and play the averages, but I can't. This is a big decision for me, and the stakes are high.
**FRIEND:** Look, I know how to take that into account as part of the decision model. We will identify your preference pattern over the range of monetary values in question. What's the best and worst you could do in this deal?
**JJ:** If I advertise and don't sell a painting, I will be in the hole for $60,000. About the same if I sell the first but not the second. On the other hand, I can make a commission of over $400,000 if I sell them all, less $180,000 expenses. That's a net profit of $220,000.
**FRIEND:** OK. You also mentioned a possible benefit of up to $150,000 from related future business. Let's establish your preference pattern over the cash flow range, $ – 100,000 to $400,000. That will adequately cover it. Since you have estimated sale probabilities in the region of 0.7 and 0.8, giving combinations for all paintings in the range 0.3–0.6 we'll construct gambles like that. In fact, let's use 50:50 gambles. You can probably relate very well to them.
First, suppose you faced a 50:50 gamble on stakes of $400,000 or $ – 100,000. You have a choice of facing this gamble or avoiding it altogether. What would you do?

**JJ:** I don't know, it's a very close thing. I guess I'd rather not take the chance.
**FRIEND:** How much would you pay to avoid the gamble?
**JJ:** At most $25,000. Yes, that is the point where I'd rather face the gamble than pay more than $25,000.
**FRIEND:** I can see why you were not comfortable playing the averages. By the way, remember that these cash flows are in addition to your other wealth and prospective earnings.
**JJ:** Exactly, that's why I am averse to the gamble. A loss of $100,000 would really hurt.
**FRIEND:** Well, now consider a 50:50 gamble between $25,000 and $400,000. What would be your certainty equivalent?
**JJ:** I'd say $150,000.
**FRIEND:** So you would prefer $155,000 to the gamble, but you would prefer the gamble to $145,000. Is that correct?
**JJ:** Yes.
**FRIEND:** Now, if you faced a gamble of $25,000 or $−100,000 with equal likelihoods, what would you pay with certainty to avoid it?
**JJ:** In this case, I think that my certainty equivalent would be equal to the expected value or close to it. I will say $−40,000. I would pay $40,000 to avoid such a gamble but not more.
**FRIEND:** All right, you have shown almost a risk neutrality in the range of losses and a risk aversion in the range of gains. Let's plot your utility function and run a few consistency checks. Then we'll replace the monetary figures on the decision tree with your utility values. That will allow us to see whether the incorporation of your preference pattern changes the optimal strategy the model produces.

## CASE QUESTION

Construct Mr. Jones's utility function and redo the analysis from James Jones Art Auctions (A) in Chapter 5. Compare the expected value and expected utility solutions in terms of the insights to be gained by modeling this decision.

## APPENDIX

### The Axioms of Decision Analysis/ Expected Utility

Pratt, Raiffa, and Schlaifer (1964 and 1965) give a formal statement of the axioms of expected utility, and the reader who is interested in the detail and technical treatment should refer to those sources.[1] We give here two sets of axioms, of which the first set is for expected utility only. *These axioms lead to the result that a decision maker who follows these "rational behavior" axioms should be an "expected utility maximizer."*

We define outcome sets, $O_i$, in the context of these axioms to mean sets of possible payoffs, $P_i$, which have specified probabilities, $p_i$. We also define the symbols $>$ meaning "is preferred to" and $\sim$ meaning "indifference between."

We further define outcome sets $O_i$ here as simple lotteries, so that $O_i(P_1, p, P_2)$ represents a $p$ probability of a payoff $P_1$ and a $1-p$ probability of a payoff $P_2$.

**Axiom A** (Preference Existence)
For every pair of payoffs, $P_j$ and $P_k$, preferences exist so that $P_j > P_k$ or $P_j \sim P_k$ or $P_j < P_k$.

**Axiom B** (Transitivity)
If $O_i > O_j$ and $O_j > O_k$ then $O_i > O_k$ and if $O_i \sim O_j$ and $O_j \sim O_k$ then $O_i \sim O_k$.

**Axiom C** (Outcome Set Comparison)
If $P_j > P_k$, then:

$$O_1(P_j,p_1,P_k) = O_2(P_j,p_2,P_k) \text{ if } p_1 = p_2$$

and

$$O_1(P_j,p_1,P_k) > O_2(P_j,p_2,P_k) \text{ if } p_1 > p_2$$

**Axiom D** (Existence of Utility)
A number, $N_i$, can be expressed by the decision maker for every payoff, $P_i$, so that for a simple outcome involving an upper payoff $P_U$ and a lower payoff $P_L$:

$$P_i \sim O(P_L,N_i,P_U)$$

$N_i$ is the indifference probability value and is a measure of utility.

**Axiom E** (Probability Specification)
For every relevant event, $E$, a probability $p(E)$ can be specified so that there is indifference between:

*a.* obtaining $P_U$ if $E$ occurs and $P_L$ if $E$ does not, and
*b.* $O(P_U,p(E),P_L)$

---

[1] J. W. Pratt, H. Raiffa, and R. O. Schlaifer, *Introduction to Statistical Decision Theory*, (New York: McGraw-Hill, 1964). Also see J. W. Pratt, H. Raiffa, and R. O. Schlaifer, "The Foundations of Decision Under Uncertainty: An Elementary Exposition," *Journal of the American Statistical Association*, 59, 1965, pp. 353–75.

**Axiom F** (Substitution)
If a decision $D_1$ requires a choice between $O_1$ and $O_2$, and if $O_2 \sim O_3$ then $D_2 \sim D_1$ where $D_2$ requires a choice between $O_1$ and $O_3$.

**Axiom G** (Conditional Preference Equivalence)
If $O_1$ and $O_2$ are both possible only if event $E$ occurs, then the preference ordering of $O_1 > O_2$ or $O_1 \sim O_2$ or $O_1 < O_2$ does not change with knowledge of whether or not $E$ occurs.

The second set of axioms is drawn from Keeney (1982) and is consistent with the first. However, this second set covers decision analysis as a complete paradigm, whereas the first set covers the expected utility component only. This set is expressed in an intuitive, nonmathematical form.

Keeney has formulated axioms as follows:

**AXIOM 1a** (Generation of Alternatives). At least two alternatives can be specified.

**AXIOM 1b** (Identification of Consequences). Possible consequences of each alternative can be identified.

**AXIOM 2** (Quantification of Judgment). The relative likelihoods (i.e., probabilities) of each possible consequence that could result from each alternative can be specified.

**AXIOM 3** (Quantification of Preference). The relative desirability (i.e., utility) for all the possible consequences of any alternative can be specified.

**AXIOM 4a** (Comparison of Alternatives). If two alternatives would each result in the same two possible consequences, the alternative yielding the higher chance of the preferred consequence is preferred.

**AXIOM 4b** (Transitivity of Preferences). If one alternative is preferred to a second alternative and if the second alternative is preferred to a third alternative, then the first alternative is preferred to the third alternative.

**AXIOM 4c** (Substitution of Consequences). If an alternative is modified by replacing one of its consequences with a set of consequences and associated probabilities (i.e., a lottery) that is indifferent to the consequence being replaced, then the original and the modified alternatives should be indifferent.[2]

---

[2] R. L. Keeney, "Decision Analysis: An Overview," *Operations Research* 30, no. 5, 1982, p. 830.

CHAPTER SEVEN

# Multiattributed Utility Functions

## OUTLINE



## OBJECTIVES

After completing this chapter, you should be able to:

1. Describe how some decisions involve multiple dimensions of value that need to be accounted for.
2. Discuss the multiattribute utility model approach for modeling this aspect of decision complexity.
3. Use additive multiattribute models, including scale definitions and appropriately assessing rates and weights.
4. Clearly relate the role of the multiattribute utility approach to other aspects of decision analysis.
5. Judge when it is reasonable to assume mutual utility independence in modeling, and note the limitations inherent in assuming this property.
6. Describe additive and linear additive scoring rules, and note the relationship between them and utility-based decision models.
7. Interpret the results of multiattribute utility analyses in terms of the insights produced for the decision maker.
8. Structure a high-quality set of attributes for decision problems where such analysis is appropriate.

## INTRODUCTION

This chapter is about multiattributed utility functions, which are useful components of decision analysis models, when the decision involves multiple dimensions of value. If a decision involves only a single dimension of value, such as money, then an expected value rule (for example, expected monetary value, or EMV, Chapter 5) or unidimensional utility rule (Chapter 6) is appropriate. For some decisions, an important part of the problem is multiple dimensions of value, and these can be modeled by utility functions with a multiattributed domain. In decision trees, *utilities* are treated in the same way as monetary or nonmonetary *values,* whether those utilities have unidimensional domains or are multiattribute. In either case the utility values are placed on the endpoints of decision trees, and the usual rollback procedure can be applied.

The usefulness of multiattributed utility functions is in encompassing this additional type of complexity into a decision analysis model. We can encapsulate a multiple set of $N$ dimensions of value ($DV$) into a single measure $U$, defined as:

$$U(DV_1, DV_2, DV_3 . . . DV_N)$$

By assuming and fitting a reasonable structure to this function, we can combine a set of separate dimensions of value into a single measure, $U$, which can be placed straight onto a decision tree! The power of this modeling procedure is this ability to include in a model, our complex, multidimensional preference set, and hence provide understanding of how our preferences interface the other important decision elements.

In earlier chapters, methods for modeling choice processes were described as useful aids to the decision maker. These rules ranged from quite simple (for example, maxi-max) to more complex (unidimensional expected utility). As we progressively considered more complex rules, we found that they became more comprehensive in terms of the set of decision elements they encompassed. The most simple nonprobabilistic rules (maxi-max, maxi-min) determined decision strategy by searching for extreme payoffs. Expected value rules (for example, EMV) used probabilities to determine weighted average payoffs. Expected utility rules also accounted for the decision maker's preference pattern.

In Chapter 6, only unidimensional expected utility was considered. Many managerial decisions involve multiple conflicting objectives. These multiple objectives are themselves a substantial source of complexity in decision making and need to be addressed by decision-aiding processes. In this chapter we will examine a number of procedures for analyzing decision problems where this element of complexity (more than one dimension of value) is present. We will begin by extending a previous example into the domain of multiattributes, then consider multiple dimension utility functions in more detail.

## A MULTIATTRIBUTE PROBLEM

### EXAMPLE 7–1

#### Zinco Productions (D)

Refer to Example 6–3, Zinco Productions (C). Bob Schroer had considered his strategy with respect to installing some new equipment in the zinc oxide plant that he managed. This decision was based purely on the effects of various alternatives on product quality. He had measured product quality by the percentage of impurities in the zinc oxide product. The decision was made simple by the fact that the cost of the new equipment almost exactly balanced the projected savings in energy costs resulting from the new process. Hence money was not a consideration in the decision, and Mr. Schroer based his analysis and choice purely on product quality.

After he made his decision, Mr. Schroer telephoned the engineering contractor who was to supply the new production process equipment to give them the good news. They replied that the original informal quote for the project would have to be changed. One of the major pieces of equipment involved was a large electronically controlled centrifuge imported from West Germany. The recent strength of the deutsche mark meant that the cost of this centrifuge would be 30% higher than originally expected. The centrifuge was the most expensive piece of equipment involved, accounting for 50% of the total project cost. Mr. Schroer learned that the project cost would now be about 15% more than was originally suggested. Continued strength of the mark was expected relative to local currency, and no other centrifuge manufacturer was able to supply this highly specialized piece of equipment.

Mr. Schroer was taken aback by this information. He sat down to review the situation. When the net cost of the project in dollar terms was zero, he had been able to carefully analyze the decision based on quality considerations alone. At that time, he felt that the problem was pretty complex, and he was pleased at having been able to analyze it and come to a point where he was happy with a decision.

He now realized that a substantial new complication existed. He could no longer base his comparisons of alternative strategies on a single dimension of value (product quality) as he had done before. He now had to choose a strategy knowing that there were monetary implications as well as product quality considerations. More specifically, it appeared as if the option with the best quality outcome was the costly option.

Mr. Schroer realized that he had to make a decision involving trade-offs across two very different dimensions of value, namely money and quality. He needed to specify the nature of his preference relationships across these dimensions. He had refined his model from originally dealing with *expected quality,* to *expected utility of quality.* He now needed to modify his utility function from the form *U* (quality), to the form *U*(money, quality).

## MULTIDIMENSIONAL UTILITY FUNCTIONS

The simplest kind of multidimensional utility function is the two-attribute case. Problems that involve more than two attributes of value are similar in kind to two-dimensional utility problems but present more complexity as a function of their size. The Zinco Productions (D) example, above, involved only two attributes that were relatively easy for the decision maker to identify. In other cases, the process of attribute definition (which generally should precede the utility function structuring and analysis phases) is not so easy.

### Identifying Attributes

In all problems involving multiple dimensions of value, the first task in the analysis process is to clearly define those dimensions of value. In doing so we answer the question: "What things of value are affected by this decision?"

The structure of a system of attributes can exist at a number of levels. This argument is very similar in nature to the argument made in Chapters 1 and 2 about the level of detail or disaggregation in decision analysis models.

It is possible to define decision and management science models so that they lack detail and leave out important features. The quality of inference may be reduced as a result. On the other hand, if a model is too detailed, it is possible to become lost in a sea of description and trivia and miss the decision trees for the forest. Decision trees can turn into bushy messes or even swamps if judgment in this regard is not good.

The same principles can be applied to multiple attribute systems. There should be enough attributes to produce a high-quality analysis, but not too many as to make the analytic task impractically large. The set of attributes should also adequately cover but not double count the important aspects of the problem. This balance is not hard to achieve with a little practice.

Keeney and Raiffa (1976) provide a good discussion of this issue. They suggest that a set of attributes should be complete, operational, decomposable, nonredundant, and of minimum size.

### Attributes and Objectives

In the context of management, many studies have been conducted of corporate and public objectives. Many books and articles have been written about objectives and about management by objectives.

Whereas we define attributes as "dimensions of value" in a model, an objective can be defined as "an aim or end of action" (Granger 1964). Objectives are, in a sense, more specific than attributes because they often define specific levels along dimensions of value. For example, an attribute may be "market share" whereas an objective may be "to increase market share *X%* by time *Y*." Alternative definitions exist, for example, some people define objectives as general aims and use the term *goal* to define specific levels of an objective. Although these relatively minor differences in definition exist, objectives and attributes can be viewed as being very similar. They both are expressions of the aims and states of desirability for decision makers. A number of findings regarding objectives are useful to our study of multiple criteria utility functions in decision analysis.

Granger (1964, p. 64) argues for the importance of total corporate planning, beginning with the question, "What are our overall objectives?" This is essentially the same problem as that of attribute definition in decision analysis. Granger argues that objectives must be clear in their definition, balanced, and valid. He also suggests that objectives should:

1. Guide action.
2. Allow for measurement and control.
3. Be ambitious and challenging.
4. Be realistic with respect to organizational constraints.
5. Relate to objectives at other levels of the organization.

The literature on objectives of two and three decades ago usefully argued for the *formal definition of sets of objectives to aid in planning and decision making*. However the definition of a list of objectives is not enough to facilitate good decision making. The conversion of lists of objectives into multiattribute utility functions allows them to be formally included in a decision analysis, and hence usefully incorporated into decision-aiding models.

The properties of a good set of utility function attributes, which are listed above, correspond closely to what could be defined as a good set of characteristics for organizational objectives. These similarities make it feasible for an organization, or part thereof, to translate its list of objectives into a utility function that can then be integrated into its decision processes. Thus in an organizational setting, multiattribute utility functions (as representations of the preferences of the organization) provide us with a mechanism for *operationalizing our system of objectives*. The process of specification of a utility function is very productive in this context because it forces decision makers to define attributes and preference structures, and ultimately to be specific (in a quantitative manner) about trade-offs between objectives.

## EXAMPLE 7–2

# A Government Housing Development Project

A state government was considering various designs for a housing project to provide low rental apartments in an inner suburb of a large city. The area being considered contained a number of houses and small apartment blocks, some of which had been condemned. Some of the land was already owned by the government. A task force was established to address the problem, and a decision analysis framework was adopted.

Five alternative strategies were identified:

1. Do nothing.
2. Purchase all land in the area and re-let to low-income families.
3. Purchase all land in the area and rent on the open market.
4. Purchase all land and renovate/replace buildings for renting to low-income families.
5. Purchase all land and renovate/replace buildings for the open market.

The relevant attributes (dimensions of value) of the utility function were first determined to be:

*a.* Monetary effects.
*b.* Social service.
*c.* Effects on the local housing market.
*d.* Aesthetic value.

Each of these attributes was then carefully defined and decomposed. For example "monetary effects" would accrue to the government, to current residents, to new residents, and to developers. The main monetary decision variable was the net cost of each alternative to the government. These monetary effects were defined as uncertain and were treated as an uncertain quantity in the decision analysis.

The "aesthetics" attribute was decomposed into two elements:

*a.* Aesthetics for residents.
*b.* Aesthetics for nonresidents.

It was recognized that these two groups would have different interests, principally a much greater involvement by residents and their strong interest in aesthetics inside the buildings as well as outside.

The decision makers felt the original four attributes were well defined except that they wanted to decompose "aesthetics" into two parts. They chose a simple structure for their utility function form, where the individual attributes are considered to contribute in an additive manner only to the total utility score. This functional form assumes away various possible second-order effects and interactive dependencies, however it is simple to use and very robust. It involves giving each attribute a general importance weighting factor, $k$, and scoring each decision alternative on each attribute.

The final utility function form was a simple additive form

$$U = k_1\left(\begin{array}{c}\text{Net monetary}\\ \text{benefit}\end{array}\right) + k_2\left(\begin{array}{c}\text{Social}\\ \text{services}\end{array}\right) + k_3\left(\begin{array}{c}\text{Housing market}\\ \text{impact}\end{array}\right) + k_4\left(\begin{array}{c}\text{Aesthetics for}\\ \text{residents}\end{array}\right) + k_5\left(\begin{array}{c}\text{Aesthetics for}\\ \text{nonresidents}\end{array}\right)$$

The utility functions and attribute weights ($k$ values) were assessed using the techniques outlined earlier in this and the preceding chapter. The outputs of the model (expected utilities) did not point to a clear winner or best strategy. However the analysis *process* did lead to an informed, focused discussion of issues. Having done the analysis, the decision makers took a holistic approach to actually making the decision. The analysis had made them acutely aware of the trade-offs across strategies. They did not try to use the model to choose a best strategy, but rather discussed the issues and trade-offs until it became relatively clear as to what their preferences were. After a lengthy discussion they were able to eliminate three of the five strategies. This allowed them to focus directly on comparing the remaining two. They referred back to their utility analysis, refined their judgments and came to a decision.

---

To summarize, we should ask the question: What did the decision analysis/expected utility framework provide in terms of decision support? The answer can best be derived by comparing the process described above with a hypothetical unaided decision process. An unaided process would have involved the definition of alternatives and their evaluation, hopefully (but not necessarily) in a systematic manner. *The unaided decision process may well have proceeded in an ad hoc manner.* Without a model and a decision framework or structure it is likely that a holistic approach would have been used that was not supported by a rational analysis. Discussion of each of the alternatives would probably not have involved a systematic evaluation of each one, but rather an incomplete set of simple comparisons that would not logically lead to a firm conclusion. The decision might have been made based primarily on a "gut-feel" basis, meaning a holistic, intuitive process.

Relative to the unaided process, the multiobjective utility analysis represents a substantially more thorough (systematic) approach.

We should not exclude the intuitive, subjective input, but rather recognize its importance through the formal integration of subjective factors into the model. Other approaches are possible, for example cost-benefit analysis. Although cost-benefit analysis is not really a multiobjective approach, it does encompass nonmonetary objectives by attempting to place a monetary equivalent value on them. Hence in a cost-benefit analysis, attempts might be made to directly assess the monetary value of various states of "aesthetics" and "social service." These judgments are usually somewhat artificial and may be difficult to make. These and other associated inaccuracies and difficulties may lead to the suppression of the intangible factors (such as "aesthetics") as decision elements, or at least to their being given too little weight in the decision. This is not to say that it is never appropriate to perform cost-benefit analysis or to try and evaluate monetary equivalent values for nonmonetary attributes. The choice of decision modeling approach should be based on the question of which one would provide the best insight and hence is likely to lead to the best decision and outcome. If nonmonetary attributes can easily and accurately be converted to monetary equivalent values, then cost-benefit analysis may be all that is required to analyze the decision.

In general this conversion of nonmonetary factors to monetary values is a form of *reduction in dimensionality* of the problem. The degree to which we formalize multiple attributes in a model should depend on how much insight the various approaches are expected to produce. If the decision maker is comfortable in assuming that he can reduce the dimensionality of a problem without losing potential model insight, then it should be done. A multiple attribute problem such as the government's housing/development decision, could be reduced to a single dimension of money, in which case it essentially becomes a cost-benefit analysis. The key question is whether the reduction in number of attributes to one, in a cost-benefit approach, supports the real decision process to the same extent as if the attributes are treated separately, then incorporated into a multiattribute utility function. Cost-benefit analysis is similar in approach to the utility framework in that both involve a reduction of various dimensions into a single measure; however, the utility framework is more comprehensively flexible in structure and usually is more powerful in insight. Whereas cost-benefit analysis requires the translation of nonmonetary elements into monetary equivalent measures, the multiattribute utility approach does not require such direct conversion. The utility approach requires assessments of various dimensions of value on utility scales, followed by a combination process on these scales.

---

## EXAMPLE 7–3

### Zinco Productions (E)

In Zinco Productions (D), Bob Schroer was faced with a decision regarding equipment purchase in which outcome values were measured in terms of money (*M*) and quality (*Q*) dimensions. To make a choice, Mr. Schroer had a number of options available:

1. He could take a holistic approach and evaluate options based on ($M$,$Q$) pairs without attempting to explicitly articulate $M$-$Q$ trade-offs or preference functions.
2. He could attempt to reduce the dimensionality of the problem from two dimensions of value to one by assessing values (in monetary terms) for various quality outcomes. The problem could then be treated as an expected monetary value problem or as unidimensional utility analysis. In this instance, this strategy may well be appropriate because increased quality does normally lead to certain monetary consequences, hence the $M$-$Q$ relationship should have the potential to be fairly readily identified.
3. He could assess the utility function over the two-dimensional space and perform an expected utility analysis. As part of this process, he would check whether it is appropriate to assume mutual utility independence. We note that option 2. above, which involves reduction of dimensionality, includes the implicit assumption of utility independence.

---

It is not possible to state that any one of the above approaches is generally superior to any other. In some problems, no analysis is needed because the preferred alternative is obvious in a holistic sense. This comment relates to a more general statement (made by Ronald Howard), referred to in Chapter 1, that decision analysis is *what you do when you don't know what to do*. Problems that are not complex, or that despite their complexity have an obviously preferred strategy, do not need the decision analysis/expected utility framework. Unfortunately for most decision makers (but perhaps fortunately for professional decision analysis consultants), many of today's business and public sector problems do not fall into this category.

If the preferred strategy is not obvious, then the holistic approach may be significantly aided by a model. In the multiattribute context, if the number of attributes is small and the nonmonetary attributes can readily be converted to their monetary equivalent values, then it may be useful to attempt to reduce the problem to a single dimension (money). In the Zinco Productions case this would require the direct elicitation of monetary values for various quality states or differences between those quality states.

If it is not a reasonably straightforward matter to convert nonmonetary outcomes to their monetary equivalents, then a multiattributed utility analysis is likely to be appropriate. In such cases, the decision maker should consider whether mutual utility independence can be reasonably assumed.[1] If so, then the additive utility function can sometimes be used, and if not, other more complex structural forms can be adopted. Although indepen-

---

[1] Independence of attributes refers to attributes being separate from each other, in terms of their contributions to the multiattribute utility measure.

dence of attributes does not imply that additivity exists, the additive functional form is often a good first-pass approach, which can later be modified or refined.

---

## EXAMPLE 7–4

### Job Selection

Judy Souter, an MBA student who is about to graduate, has interviewed with a number of large organizations. Since she is an excellent student, she has been offered four jobs. She approached her decision analysis professor for advice as to which job to accept. The professor suggested that a number of approaches were possible for her decision. He said that she could take a "no analysis" route and make a holistic choice. This process would involve considering each job offer in aggregate and going with her instincts and gut feelings. He asked whether she had a current strong preference for any of the jobs. Judy replied that one of the jobs did attract her more than the others, but she wasn't sure. Her professor asked her whether the difficulty in making a choice was principally a result of her uncertainty about the characteristic nature of the jobs or more a result of there not being a job that stood out from the rest. Judy replied that she had a lot of information about all four jobs and their related attributes. She stated that she didn't really feel uncertain about any of them. She went on to say that her difficulty was in committing herself to any of the jobs because each one was attractive in some way but unattractive in others. Her professor suggested that Judy should write down the dimensions of value that were important to her. He remarked that just by doing that, she might become clearer in her own mind about which job she preferred intuitively. If that didn't result in her establishing a clear preference, he invited her to call and see him again. Judy left his office and made a list of the factors that she generally felt were important. If you were in Judy's position what would your list of attributes be?

---

## Utility Function Structures

In the context of two attributes only, $X$ and $Y$, we define a utility function, $U(X,Y)$ so that numerical utilities can be specified for ranges $X_0 < X < X_1$ and $Y_0 < Y < Y_1$. The utility function $U(X,Y)$ represents the preference (desirability) pattern of the decision maker over a two-dimensional domain.

In Mr. Schroer's case (see the Zinco Productions (D and E) examples) it would be useful for him to know at least some of his preferences for quality and money. Of course we can already guess that, like most of us, he prefers more money to less money and higher quality to lower quality. However, his decision (in Example 7–1) will involve trade-offs across these dimensions, and he may be aided in making that decision if he carefully specifies his rate of trade-off. Is his rate of trade-off constant? Does it vary with values of quality and cost? If he can specify his utility function, $U$(quality, money) then he can use this utility function to gain insight about his decision problem.

In the case of a two-attribute $(X, Y)$ preference system, it is very useful to determine whether the utility for each attribute is independent of the value of the other attribute. If it can be determined that independence does exist, then the task of assessing utilities becomes considerably easier.

A two-attribute utility function can be represented as a three-dimensional graph. In general the utility function is shown as a surface (see Figure 7–1). The function could be directly assessed, through systematically evaluating utilities of $U(X, Y)$ and joining these points together on a graph (as was done in Chapter 6 for unidimensional utility).

Independence of utility between $X$ and $Y$ may be one way or reciprocal. One-way independence can occur if the utility of one variable is independent of the value of the other but the utility of the other is not independent of the first. The variable $X$ is *utility independent* of $Y$ if relative preferences over $X$ are not dependent on the value of $Y$.

If $X$ is independent of $Y$ and $Y$ is independent of $X$, then a condition of *reciprocal independence* (also known as mutual utility independence) occurs.

**FIGURE 7–1** A Two-Attribute Utility Function

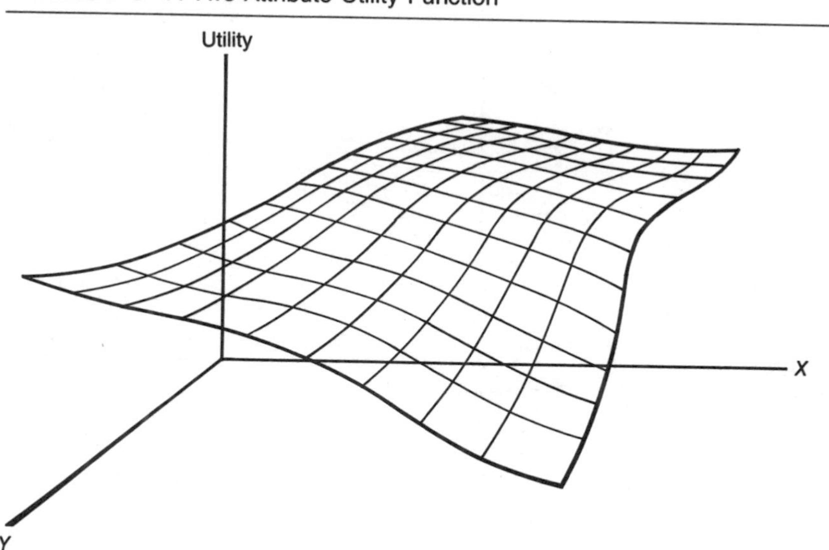

**FIGURE 7–2** A Two-Attribute Utility Function (where one attribute, *X*, is independent of another, *Y*)

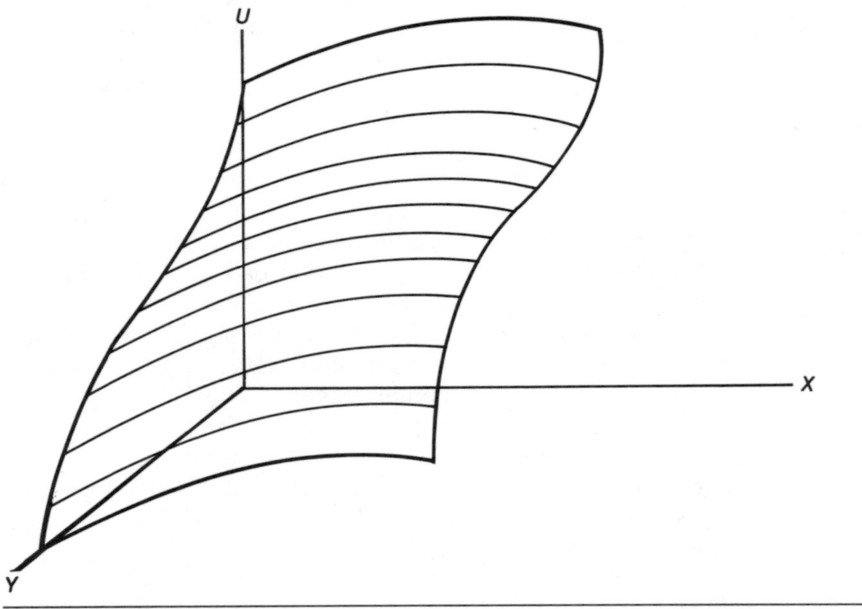


**FIGURE 7–3** *Y* Is Utility Independent of *X*

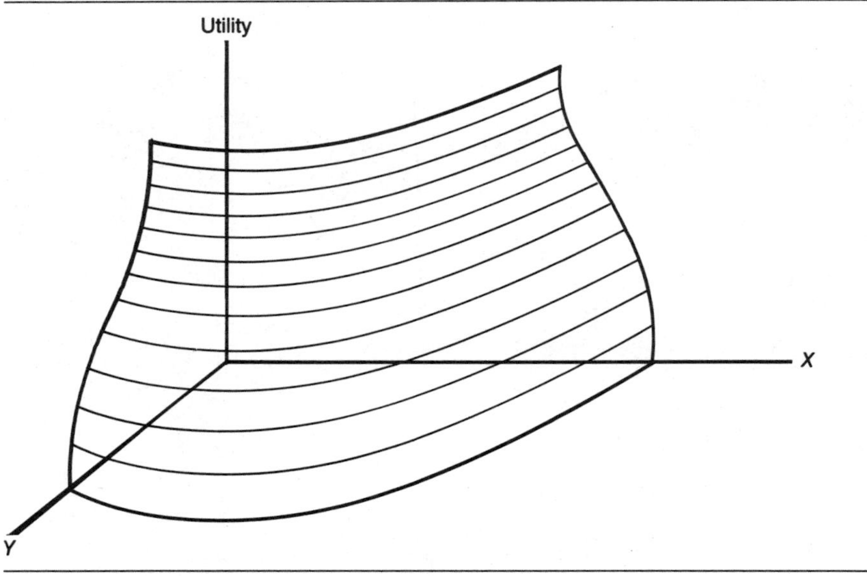

Independence can be tested by assessing a series of unidimensional utility functions. To test whether $X$ is independent of $Y$, we would establish a unidimensional utility function of $X$, known as $U(X, Y_i)$ for various values of $Y_i$. If the preference pattern over $X$ is invariant at different levels of $Y_i$, then $X$ can be said to be utility independent of $Y$. Graphically, if the condition holds that $X$ is utility independent of $Y$, then the general shape of the utility functions $X$ (at various levels of $Y$) would be the same.

Figure 7–2 shows a utility function where $X$ is utility independent of $Y$. Note that if various cuts were taken of this surface parallel to the $X$-$U$ plane, the resultant conditional utility functions of $X$ (given various $Y$) represent the same preference pattern.

Similarly if $Y$ is utility independent of $X$, Figure 7–3 shows that if various cuts were taken of the curve by a plane parallel to the $Y$-$U$ plane, the preference pattern of $U$ as a function of $Y$ is unique.

**FIGURE 7–4** Indifference Curves

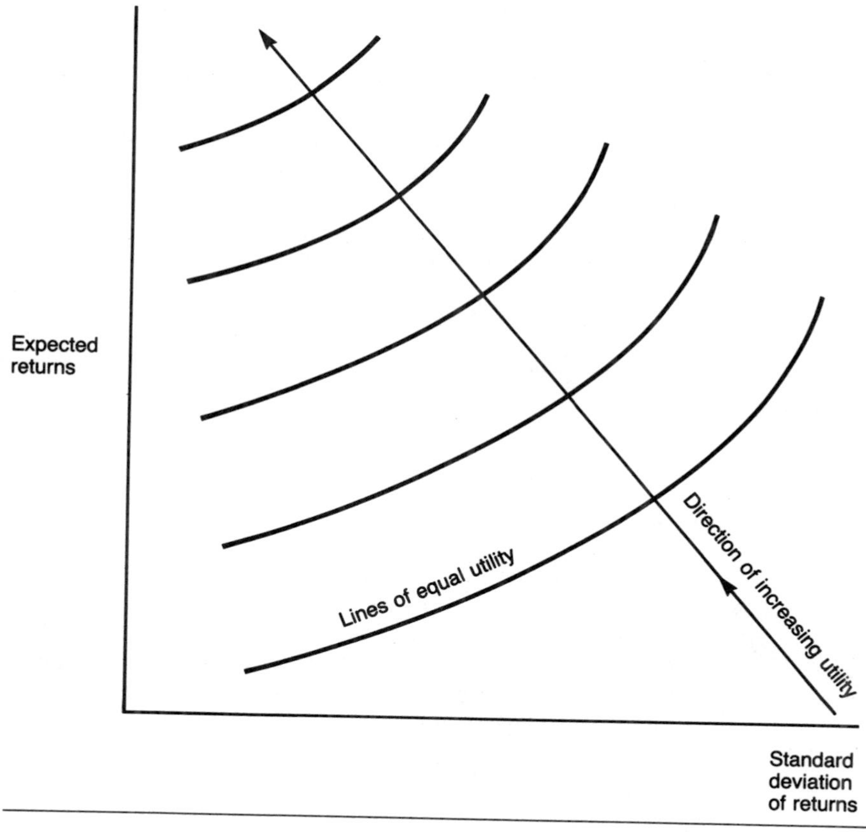

If projections of a two-attribute utility surface are made onto the $X$-$Y$ plane so that points having equal utility are joined together, then a series of curves, called *indifference curves*, can be drawn. Figure 7–4 shows a set of indifference curves for an investor who preferred higher expected returns on investment to lower, and lower standard deviations of returns to higher. The arrow on Figure 7–4 shows the general direction of increasing utility. The investor does not increase his utility by moving along each of the curves on Figure 7–4 because these lines join points of equal utility. However, movement from one curve to another implies a change in utility.

## Additive Utility Functions: Two Attributes

Reciprocal independence occurs if $X$ is utility independent of $Y$, and $Y$ is utility independent of $X$. An important special case of reciprocal independence is where the utility function if *additive*. Additive utility is defined as

$$U(X,Y) = k_1 U_1(X) + k_2 U_2(Y) \qquad [7\text{–}1]$$

where $k_1$ and $k_2$ are constants.

In Equation [7–1], we are expressing the idea that a two-attribute utility function may be *separable* into the weighted sum of two unidimensional utility functions. Equation [7–1] presumes reciprocal utility independence ($X$ is independent of $Y$, and $Y$ is independent of $X$) and additivity. If these assumptions hold, then the utility functions $U(X)$ and $U(Y)$ can be separately assessed and become independent inputs to the multiattributed utility function. If additionally we assume an additive structure, we can use Equation [7–1], and "rate and weight," where the values $k_1$ and $k_2$ are the relative measures of importance of the attributes.

---

## Example 7–5

### Acme Insurance

The president of the Acme Insurance Company was considering two alternative product pricing and advertising proposals. The various strategies had been devised by his marketing manager. Each strategy would result in a market share and rate of return on investment as shown in Table 7–1. Strategy 1 could lead to two possible outcomes, and strategy 2 could lead to three possible outcomes. Figure 7–5 shows his decision tree.

**TABLE 7–1** Acme Insurance Company Strategies

| *Strategy* | | *Market Share* | *Rate of Return* | *Probability* |
|---|---|---|---|---|
| 1 | Outcome 1 | 4 | 12 | 0.6 |
| | Outcome 2 | 6 | 6 | 0.4 |
| 2 | Outcome 3 | 5 | 8 | 0.3 |
| | Outcome 4 | 3 | 13 | 0.5 |
| | Outcome 5 | 4 | 8 | 0.2 |

**FIGURE 7–5** The Acme Insurance Decision Tree

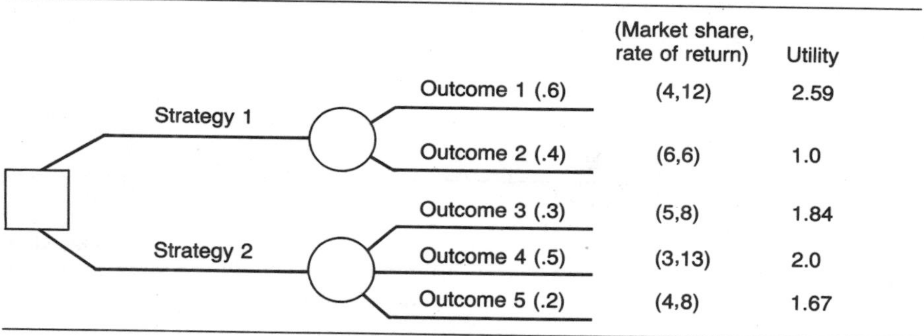


The president decided that his preference structure for "market share" and "rate of return" was such that the two attributes were mutually utility independent and additive. That is:

$$U(\text{market share, rate of return}) = k_1\, U(\text{market share}) + k_2\, U(\text{rate of return})$$

He believed that his preferences for various market share values were not affected by the value of rate of return and vice versa. He assessed his value (utility) functions as shown by Figure 7–6a and 7–6b.[2] Note that the upper and lower bounds of the domains of these utility functions are the highest and lowest values of "market share" and "rate of return."

The president had to assign weights to the attributes. He felt that "return on investment" was generally a more important attribute than "market share." He realized that the weights would be strongly related to the utility scales that were used and to the ratings on those scales. For example, if he set: $k_2 = 2k_1$ this implies that "rate of return" generally has twice the weighting of "market share." If his utility functions had been scaled differently, his weights would have to be adjusted to preserve this

[2] In technical terms there are differences between value functions and utility functions [see Keeney and Raiffa (1976)]. For our purposes, however, it is not necessary to distinguish between them because they both represent the preference pattern of the decision maker.

**FIGURE 7–6a** Utility for Market Share

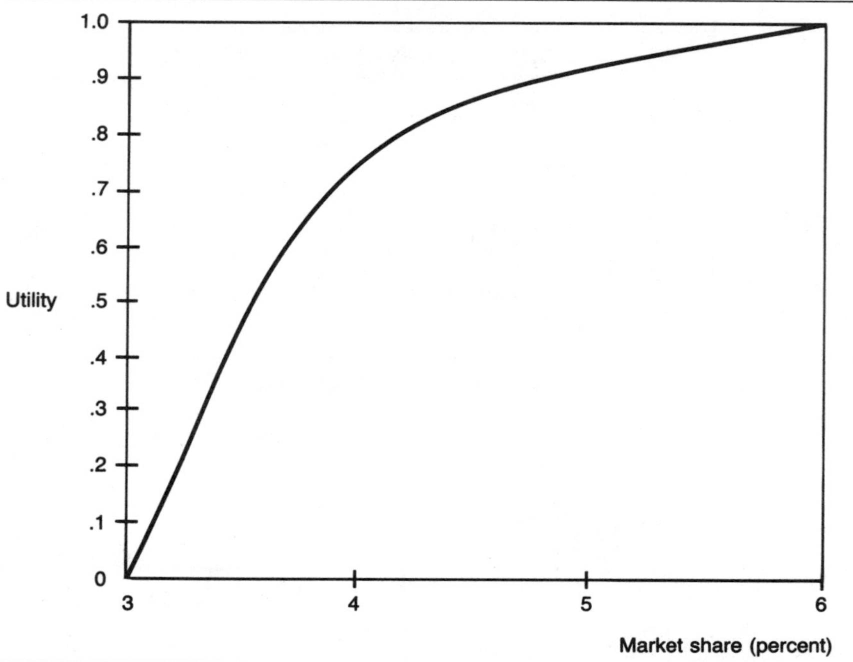


**FIGURE 7–6b** Utility for Rate of Return

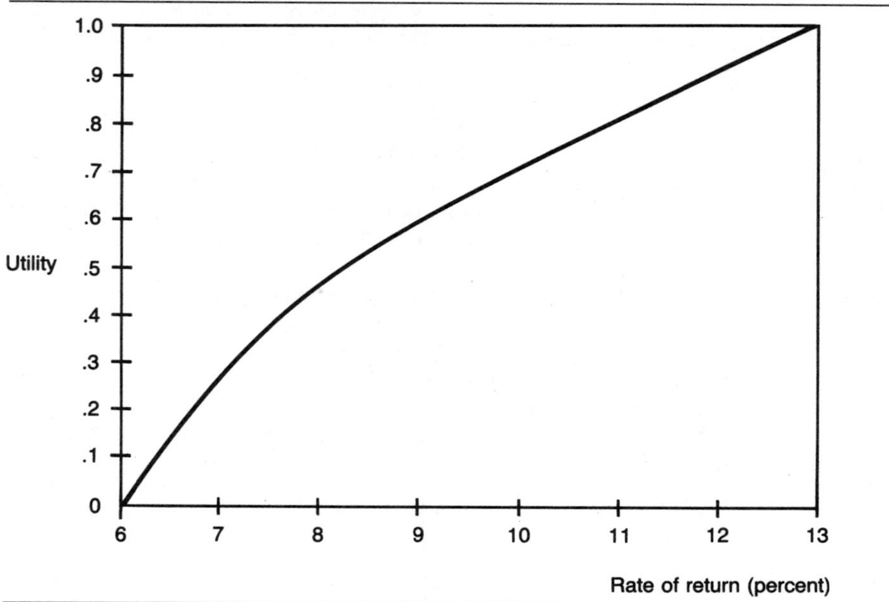

relativity. For example, if he had chosen to define his utility function for "rate of return" from a lower bound of 0% to an upper bound of 20% (instead of the current domain of 8%–13%) then the spread of utility values across the four alternative strategies would be reduced. Other things being equal, the effect would be to lower the relative importance of rate of return in the multiattributed utility function.

In general, the decision maker should not just set his attributes weights ($k$ values) by judging the general relativities in importance of the attributes. Attention must be given to the scales used in the individual unidimensional utility functions and to the spread of assessments on those scales.

Taking these things into account, the president set $k_2 = 2k_1$. We can then evaluate utilities for each strategy, by assuming that $k_1 = 1$ and $k_2 = 2$. The utilities can be read from Figure 7–6. These unidimensional utility functions are constructed using methods outlined in Chapter 6. The utilities of the outcomes are:

$$\text{Outcome 1: } U = 1 \times 0.75 + 2 \times 0.92 = 2.59$$
$$\text{Outcome 2: } U = 1 \times 1 + 2 \times 0 = 1$$
$$\text{Outcome 3: } U = 1 \times 0.92 + 2 \times 0.46 = 1.84$$
$$\text{Outcome 4: } U = 1 \times 0 + 2 \times 1 = 2$$
$$\text{Outcome 5: } U = 1 \times 0.75 + 2 \times 0.46 = 1.67$$

The expected utilities, as shown on Figure 7–5, are:

$$\text{Strategy 1: } EU = 0.6 \times 2.59 + 0.4 \times 1 = 1.954$$
$$\text{Strategy 2: } EU = 0.3 \times 1.84 + 0.5 \times 2 + 0.2 \times 1.67 = 1.886$$

The model points to strategy 1 being superior to strategy 2.

---

## Additive Utility: More than Two Attributes

The same concepts and principles apply for cases of more than two attributes. Those cases merely involve greater degrees of complexity and hence more complex assessment processes.

As the number of attributes in a decision problem grow, the advantages of assuming a simplifying utility function structural form grow rapidly. Consider first the two-attribute case detailed in the preceding section. The assessment of a utility function with a two-dimensional domain space is not exceedingly difficult. If a simplifying structure such as mutual independence plus additivity cannot be assumed, it is feasible to directly assess the complete bivariate function. However, as the number of attributes grows, the assessment task for assessing the whole utility space grows extremely rapidly. For example, with only six attributes, the direct assessment task of the whole utility space is a daunting prospect indeed. If the whole utility space is being evaluated, the size of the assessment task grows approximately as an exponential function of the number of attributes. On the other hand, if mutual utility independence is assumed, the utility function assessment task grows linearly with the number of attributes, since the individual utility functions are assessed separately and then combined.

Although the relative ease of assessment makes the additive function a very attractive one, it should not be used unless it is considered to be a reasonably close fit to the preference pattern characteristics. There are a large number of circumstances where the additive form actually is a good representation and can be used with confidence. However, for each application, readers are urged to carefully consider the implications of assuming additivity (or for that matter, any structural form) before going ahead with the analysis. If the basic additive form is a close approximation but improvements are required, it may be possible to extend the representation of Equation [7–1] by introducing extra terms in the following model

$$U(X,Y) = k_1U_1(X) + k_2U_2(Y) + k_3U_1(X) \times U_2(Y) \qquad [7\text{–}2]$$

The extra term allows for a form of interaction to be included in the representation. Many other forms of decomposition of $U(X,Y)$ are available and of course these can all be applied to utility functions having larger numbers of attributes than two.

The following example describes a process for using a simple additive decomposition in a case where there were seven attributes. It would be instructive for the reader to consider how much more complex the assessment task would be if the simple additive decomposition that is used could not have been assumed.

---

## Example 7–6

### A Purchasing Decision

Geoff Utile has decided to purchase a new car. He has narrowed his search down to three models that are similar in overall design and almost identical in cost. One of the cars is Japanese, one is American, and one is European. Geoff decided to carefully analyze the problem of which car was best for his purposes. He had test driven each one and read some reviews in motor magazines. He was having great difficulty making an intuitive choice and wanted to figure out just what was the basis of his decision problem. Geoff began by thinking carefully about the nature of his preferences. All three cars met his basic needs and were satisfactory on all of his decision criteria. He felt that at this level his preference function was additive, in that the various attributes were utility independent. He wanted to learn more about his preferences by systematically listing his attributes. They were comfort, general driveability, fuel economy, appearance, features, engineering quality, and power. Geoff realized that his desire for each car was a function of all of these attributes. In utility terms

**TABLE 7-2** Auto Purchase Assessments

| | *Car 1 (Japan)* | *Car 2 (United States)* | *Car 3 (Europe)* |
|---|---|---|---|
| Comfort | 6 | 9 | 7 |
| General driveability | 5 | 3 | 9 |
| Fuel economy | 9 | 6 | 7 |
| Appearance | 5 | 8 | 8 |
| Features | 6 | 7 | 5 |
| Engineering quality | 7 | 6 | 9 |
| Power | 3 | 8 | 5 |

$$U(\text{car}_i) = \text{function [comfort, general driveability, fuel economy, appearance, features, engineering quality, power]}$$

Geoff thought carefully about the nature of this function. He decided that within the domains of the attributes he had defined, it was reasonable to assume complete utility independence and additivity. He thought that over a wider domain this would not be the case. For example, if he were comparing a 4-cylinder small car with a large V-8 stationwagon, it would be unreasonable to consider the attributes as fully separable. In his current decision, he had narrowed the choice to three similar cars, and the assumption of additivity seemed valid to him within the domain of his attributes. Hence he assumed that

$$\begin{aligned} U(car_i) = {} & k_1U_1(\text{comfort}) + k_2U_2(\text{general driveability}) \\ & + k_3U_3(\text{fuel economy}) + k_4U_4(\text{appearance}) \\ & + k_5U_5(\text{engineering quality}) + k_6U_6(\text{power}) \\ & + k_7\,U_7(\text{features}) \end{aligned} \qquad [7\text{-}3]$$

In structuring the function this way, Geoff also considered whether he had defined a good set of attributes. A good set of attributes would have represented all the factors of importance to Geoff in a meaningful way and also not double counted any aspects. Attributes need to be separate from each other or close to it. For example, if two attributes such as "fuel economy" and "total running cost" were considered as separate attributes, their inclusion in the utility function might lead to overemphasizing the cost of gas, because they really are not separate. It is important to try to define a set of attributes that closely describe all important factors but do not substantially intersect in the factors they represent.

Geoff made the assessments shown in Table 7-2.

Geoff had made each of the assessments on a zero to 10 scale, where zero was a low score and 10 was a very high score. He did this as a manner of standardizing his evaluations for each attribute. Table 7-2 contains the utility assessments that are needed to evaluate Equation [7-3].

The values of $k_i$ ($i = 1$ to 7) in Equation [7-3] are the relative importance factors (attribute weights) for the utility function. Geoff compared various attributes in a pairwise manner and made the following statements:

1. Fuel economy is twice as important as power.
2. Comfort is as important as fuel economy.

3. Comfort is 1.5 times as important as engineering quality.
4. Appearance is as important as power.
5. Features are as important as engineering quality.
6. General driveability is 1.5 times as important as power.

In terms of the $k_i$ values in Equation [7-3] these statements translate to:

$$
\begin{aligned}
k_3 &= 2k_6 \\
k_1 &= k_3 \\
k_1 &= 1.5k_5 \\
k_4 &= k_6 \\
k_7 &= k_5 \\
k_2 &= 1.5k_6
\end{aligned}
$$

A solution set for these equations is:

$$
\begin{aligned}
k_1 &= 2 \\
k_2 &= 1.5 \\
k_3 &= 2 \\
k_4 &= 1 \\
k_5 &= 1.33 \\
k_6 &= 1 \\
k_7 &= 1.33
\end{aligned}
$$

Any other solution set would have values that are all the same positive multiple of those given above. Geoff had made enough comparisons to define this solution set but made a few more pairwise comparisons to check on his consistency and on the representativeness of these attribute weights.

As a result of these further comparisons, Geoff adjusted some of the weights to achieve the set:

$$
\begin{aligned}
k_1 &= 1.8 \\
k_2 &= 1.5 \\
k_3 &= 2.2 \\
k_4 &= 1 \\
k_5 &= 1.33 \\
k_6 &= 1 \\
k_7 &= 1.4
\end{aligned}
$$

He then used these weights and the data in Table 7-2 to calculate utilities using Equation [7-3].

$$
\begin{aligned}
U(\text{car } 1) &= 1.8\times6 + 1.5\times5 + 2.2\times9 + 1\times5 + 1.33\times7 + 1\times3 + 1.4\times6 \\
&= 63.83 \\
U(\text{car } 2) &= 1.8\times9 + 1.5\times3 + 2.2\times6 + 1\times8 + 1.33\times6 + 1\times8 + 1.4\times7 \\
&= 67.7 \\
U(\text{car } 3) &= 1.8\times7 + 1.5\times9 + 2.2\times7 + 1\times8 + 1.33\times9 + 1\times5 + 1.4\times5 \\
&= 73.5
\end{aligned}
$$

Although these differences are not very large they do reflect the stated preferences of the decision maker and the functional form that he chose. The difference between the first ranked car (car 3) and the second ranked car (car 2) is 5.8 utiles or about a 9% difference.

Geoff was able to review his assessments. He did not just accept the results and go out to buy car 3. He checked on exactly why the ranks came out as they did. For example, he had assessed car 3 as substantially better than car 2 in "general driveability" and "engineering quality," and a little better in "fuel economy." According to Geoff's rating and weighting system, this more than made up for car 2's superior "comfort," "features," and "power." He thought some more about various dimensions of value and ratings before making up his mind.

---

How did this analysis help Geoff? First, it provided a mechanism and structure that helped him to *systematically articulate his preferences*. Second, it gave him a method for *trading off across various attributes* he valued. Third, all of the diverse attributes were *translated to a common measure*, albeit an artificial one. Geoff was forced to quantify his feelings for such highly subjective attributes as appearance and comforts. He also had to express his preferences for more tangible factors such as fuel economy. Note that for any attribute, he was under no compulsion to linearly convert actual ratings (where they exist) to utilities. For example, there is no necessity for him to rate 30 miles per gallon as twice as good (on the zero to 10 utility scale) as 15 miles per gallon, or to rate 150 horsepower as 1.5 times as good as 100 horsepower. Similarly, it is rare to see a unidimensional utility function for monetary outcomes (such as wealth or net assets) that is linear, except over small domains. Linear utility on individual measures is a special case, as considered below.

## A Special Case: Linear Additivity in Scoring Rules

Scoring models are often used as devices for evaluating items such as graduate school admission applications, bank loan applications, and insurance policy risk levels. These scoring rules are not strictly utility models, however they do involve the same aim and process as multiobjective utility modeling: the formal structuring and aggregation of different dimensions of value to a single measure.

In some cases it may be reasonable to assume that not only are the attributes separable (mutually utility independent) and the function additive, but also that each unidimensional function is linear in the attribute being measured.

For example, in a graduate school admission decision process, various linear additive functions have been used to score applicants

$$\text{Applicant score} = k_1 \begin{pmatrix}\text{admission test}\\ \text{score}\end{pmatrix} + k_2 \begin{pmatrix}\text{grade point}\\ \text{average}\end{pmatrix} + k_3 \begin{pmatrix}\text{average referee}\\ \text{ranking}\end{pmatrix} \quad [7\text{–}4]$$

In this instance there is not only an additive decomposition of the score (which can be considered as a form of value or utility function), but it is also assumed that differences in attribute values should be reflected as linear differences in the aggregate score. For example, in Equation [7–4] it is implicitly assumed that a difference of 0.5 in grade point average has the same value regardless of the admission test score and the average referee ranking. This is the result of the independence and additivity assumptions. Indeed, the added assumption of linearity means that this 0.5 point difference is not only independent of the value of the other attributes but is also independent of the absolute value of the grade point average itself.

As with all other modeling approaches, we should always carefully verify whether the assumptions of a model fit the problem before applying that model. As an example, for those readers who are familiar with the Graduate Management Admission Test (GMAT), do you think it is reasonable to include it in a linear additive model? Does a point difference of 50 on the GMAT Total Score mean the same thing if that difference is between 450 and 500 or between 650 and 700? To answer that question, we would need to consider the form of the preference pattern of the decision maker. Figure 7–7 shows alternative possible forms. Figure 7–7a shows the assumed functional form of the linear additive model. If this were close to the actual preference pattern and the additivity property was also valid, then the linear additive model could be a very useful scoring model. However, if the actual preferences were nonlinear, such as in Figure 7–7b then, the use of a linear scoring model would be inappropriate. Figure 7–7b shows a preference function that is nonlinear, so that GMAT scores above $X$ are all quite highly valued, but GMAT scores below $X$ are generally much lower valued. The preference function drops rapidly for scores below $X$.

For variables that are not linearly related to value (utility), it is often possible to linearize (convert to a linear form) through redefinition of the variable or through using a mathematical transformation (such as taking logarithms). With these extensive options at the disposal of decision makers, the linear additive function has been found to be a very useful functional form in scoring rules, value, and utility functions. It is quite robust and applicable to a wide variety of decision problems.

The linear additive model is also one of the few multivariable functional forms that can be conveniently assessed on a revealed preference basis. It was suggested earlier in this volume that utility functions can generally be assessed by either observing past decisions and deducing preference patterns (revealed preference) or by having the decision maker directly or indirectly assess the function. In most cases, the revealed preference method is difficult to implement. However, if a linear additive form can be assumed and data is available, then linear regression procedures can be used to determine attribute weights. In the instance of graduate school admissions, data relating various independent variables (such as in Equation [7–4]) to performance in or after graduate school can be used to establish coeffi-

**FIGURE 7–7a** Linear Scoring Rule

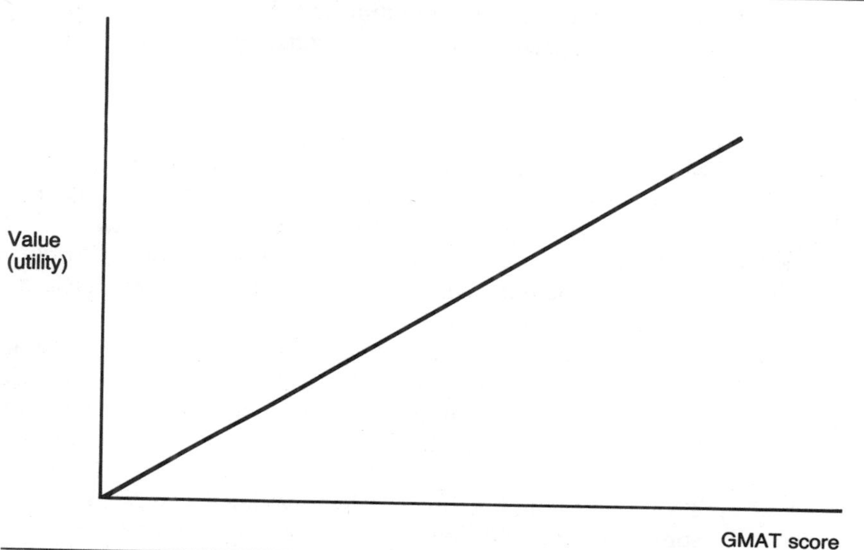


**FIGURE 7–7b** Nonlinear Scoring Rule

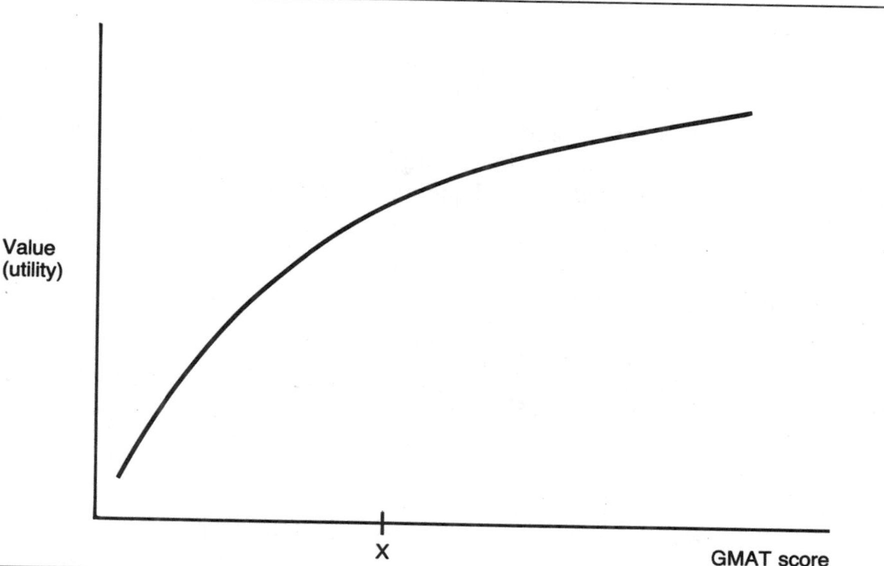

cients (weights) for each attribute. It is important to carefully consider the relevance of the variable set and the data set to the decision and not to fall prey to errors of extrapolating the decision rule or scoring mechanism to applications outside the general range and context of that data set.

### Other Utility Functional Forms

More complex utility function structures may be of a variety of forms. For most of these forms, many assessments are required. These can take the form of assessments on individual attributes or on sets of attributes. For assessing individual attributes in a total set of $k$ attributes, it is usual to specify particular levels $k-1$ of them and, given these conditions, assess utilities for the $k$th attribute.

Suppose for a two-attribute case that the decision maker wishes to establish five points on the utility scale for each attribute. If additivity can be assumed, then a total of six assessments need to be made. This is three assessments for each attribute (the end points are prespecified). If additivity cannot be assumed then each point on a five-by-five grid must be defined. Two points could be prespecified leaving 23 assessments to be made, unless some other simplifying structure can be assumed.

Now consider a more complex attribute system consisting of six attributes. The direct specification of the whole utility space is a task almost too horrendous to consider. Fortunately, in most complex problems we can either introduce a simplifying structure or avoid specifying the whole utility space by focusing mainly on those regions of the utility space relevant to the problem.

## OTHER MULTIATTRIBUTE METHODS

A number of other methods are available for aiding decision making in problems involving multiple attributes. These include lexicographic ordering, dominance and satisficing rules (as option screens), and conjoint measurement.

### Lexicographic Ordering

The lexicographic ordering procedure involves a ranking of attributes in order of importance. The alternative decision strategies are then compared on the most important attribute, and unless there is a tie for the highest value of this attribute, the alternative with the highest score is chosen. If there is a tie on the most important attribute, then all decision strategies except those involved in the tie are eliminated, and the remaining strategies are compared on the second most important attribute. This process continues until the tie is broken by considering further attributes of lower importance ranking.

The lexicographic procedure obviously is not as comprehensive as the expected utility rule. It does not model trade-offs that the decision maker may wish to make. It also implicitly assumes complete mutual utility independence. It may be useful in terms of providing decision-making insight in cases where one attribute is substantially more important than all others.

## Dominance and Satisficing

In multiattribute decision problems, the principle of dominance can be used to eliminate clearly inferior decision strategies. An alternative strategy dominates another if it is at least as good on all attributes and is also preferred on at least one attribute.

The dominance principle can easily be used to screen out alternatives, but may not lead to the selection of a single preferred strategy. Mean-variance dominance was examined in Chapter 5. Satisficing means specifying ranges for attributes, within which alternatives are acceptable. These are often minimum acceptable conditions and can be used as option screens.

---

## Example 7–7

### A Personnel Decision

A decision problem facing a personnel manager involved the selection of a computer programmer to manage a corporate computer system. He had interviewed six job applicants and rated them on a number of criteria that he considered to be important. Table 7–3 shows his ratings. Each attribute was considered on a scale of zero (worst) to 10 (best).

**TABLE 7–3** Attribute Ratings

| *Applicant* | *Qualifications* | *Technical* | *Enthusiasm* | *Integrity* | *Leadership Skills* |
|---|---|---|---|---|---|
| 1 | 0 | 6 | 9 | 9 | 5 |
| 2 | 4 | 7 | 3 | 8 | 8 |
| 3 | 9 | 8 | 5 | 7 | 3 |
| 4 | 4 | 8 | 7 | 9 | 8 |
| 5 | 8 | 4 | 6 | 2 | 9 |
| 6 | 5 | 3 | 4 | 7 | 6 |

Based on these ratings, the personnel manager decided to see if the principle of dominance could be used to screen out any applicants. He also decided that some of the attributes had minimum requirements as follows:

Qualifications: Minimum rating = 2
Technical ability: Minimum rating = 4
Integrity: Minimum rating = 5

Further, the personnel manager rated the attributes in order of importance as:

1. Technical ability.
2. Integrity.
3. Enthusiasm.
4. Qualifications.
5. Leadership skills.

What could be gained from a lexicographic ordering procedure? First, the dominance rule eliminates applicant 2 because applicant 4 is at least as good on all attributes and better on at least one. Are any other applicants dominated? The search for dominated alternatives involves a set of pairwise comparisons that could easily be programmed into a computer. However, if the number of alternatives is not large, a careful visual search of the data should successfully identify all dominated alternatives.

Second, the minimum acceptable levels that would satisfy the needs in the three specified attributes lead to the elimination of:

Applicant 1 (Qualifications too low)
Applicant 6 (Technical ability too low)
Applicant 5 (Integrity too low)

As a result of using dominance and satisficing rules, only applicants 3 and 4 remain on the "short" list. The personnel manager then applied his attribute rankings in the lexicographic procedure. The highest ranked (most important) attribute was "technical ability" for which applicants 3 and 4 were tied. The next ranked attribute was "integrity" on which applicant 4 was judged to be superior to applicant 3. Hence this process leads to the suggested selection of applicant 4.

How did the application of this set of rules help the decision maker? Dominance and satisficing really do make a lot of sense in terms of formalizing what most rational people would like to perceive as sensible decision behaviors. The assumptions of the lexicographic procedure (no attribute trade-offs, attribute independence) are somewhat limiting. These procedures are relatively easy to implement because they avoid the need to completely specify a multiattribute utility function. However, there are many complex decision problems where trade-offs across alternatives are appropriate and in fact may be the heart of the problem. In many such cases, dominance and satisficing principles do not eliminate all but one strategy. Hence these rules are seen to have definite but limited usefulness in multicriteria decision making, principally as option screening devices.

### Conjoint Measurement

The major focus in this chapter on multiattribute utility, and in the previous chapter (on unidimensional utility), was on utility assessment procedures that involved comparisons of hypothetical gambles or hypothetical trade-off situations. Conjoint measurement is a holistic method for identifying preference patterns. It does not generally require the specification of gambles or decomposition of multiattribute functions and assessments on hypothetical decision situations. Instead, it requires judgments of decision alternatives, and the utility function is deduced from those judgments. In this sense, conjoint measurement is a *revealed preference* procedure. Judgments on alternatives can be simple pairwise comparisons. The attractive feature of this method is that judgments are usually quite real to the decision maker. Disadvantages are that a functional form must be prespecified for the utility function and that the judgments may not produce the set of information to accurately determine the multiattribute utility function (Rothermell and Schilling 1986).

## APPLYING MULTIATTRIBUTE MODELS

Multiattribute utility approaches and decision analysis processes can be useful at several levels. First they provide a focal point or reference procedure for problem definition. A decision maker who is struggling with a complex problem may have difficulty because of the complexity of the set of objectives (attributes) that he is addressing. In such a case he can gain decision support by using the multiattribute utility process to help *structure* and *articulate* his preference set.

Second, the multiattribute utility process can be used as a framework for group decision making. Both in public and private sectors, many decisions involve participative groups. Within a group or committee, individuals may perceive that quite different criteria should be applied in making a choice. The multicriteria utility approach is useful because issues can be debated within a framework. The approach provides the ground rules by defining that: "There shall be a specified set of attributes." Based on this premise, the group can debate the definition of attributes using guidelines as outlined in this chapter. Hence the approach is a very useful and concise tool for *communication and debate*.

Third, decisions can involve many interest groups that may be in conflict with one another. It is useful to note that in such cases, these groups essentially are in conflict because they have different preferences. The modeling of these preference functions (using utility concepts) can create a better *understanding of the complexity* of the problem. Many decisions and management processes encompass multiple interest groups with conflicting views. These include labor-management negotiations, siting of public (e.g., jail) and private (e.g., nuclear power plant) facilities, a multitude of political issues and social welfare policies, etc. These decisions are complex, strategic in nature, and warrant the level of sophisticated analysis encompassed in a multiattribute utility analysis.

Finally, we note that a fourth benefit of such analyses is *the answer,* in the form of a recommended strategy. As stated in earlier chapters, the preferred alternative (as output by the modeling process) should be interpreted very much as a function of both the inputs and the model structure. Thus this best strategy can be strongly affected by the assumptions of the model. So long as we keep in mind that the whole process is designed to *support* our judgment in decision making and *not to replace* it, then we are unlikely simply to accept answers as produced by models. Indeed, as discussed in detail in Chapter 8, we can gain a lot of insight by observing the effect of changing the assumptions of a model on the answers.

When should multiattribute decision models be used? Given that some considerable effort is involved, it is obviously not worth doing a detailed analysis on a decision that is not of substantial importance. In general, the decision of whether or not to do a formal analysis is probably best made on a gut-feel, or intuitive basis. If the stakes are high, the complexity exists, and time permits, then such a modeling process is probably justified. The level of sophistication of the model should be appropriate to all of these variables, and of course must be such that the insights produced will potentially be effective in decision support. To conclude this section, we note that the relationship between model sophistication and quality of insights is normally not linear and often not even monotonically increasing. Simple models can often be nearly as useful as more sophisticated ones, and sometimes even more so!

## Multiattribute Decisions Involving Life and Death

A number of decisions made by public and private sector organizations involve health implications or life/death risks. The construction and operation of roads, bridges, power plants, and factories are examples of processes that can lead to injuries or deaths. On a personal basis, individual decision makers make choices about driving habits, jay walking, smoking, mountain climbing, and a host of other activities affecting the probability of serious injury or premature death.

From the point of view of formal decision making or policy setting by corporations and government, it is almost inconceivable to think that a variable such as "number of lives lost" could be treated as just another attribute of a decision. Yet decisions having life and death implications are made every day. Consider, for example, a government decision of whether or not to legislate the compulsory fitting of airbags to cars or compulsory use of seat belts. On an individual basis, consider the decision of whether to buckle up a seat belt. These decisions involve changing the likelihood of death for individuals and on a macroscale, changing the number of deaths and injuries due to highway accidents.

Two aspects of decision problems involving life and death make them particularly difficult to deal with. The first is that it is very difficult to get an organization to rationally consider trade-offs between possible lives lost and other measures such as money. In an ex-post (revealed preference) sense it may be possible to deduce such trade-off rates. For example, if a decision to not implement air bags in cars was made by a government, we could calculate (albeit very roughly) that the cost of the program, $\$X$, divided by the projected number of lives saved, $Y$, yields a figure (in dollars per life) that society was not prepared to pay. Of course such a calculation would be only a ballpark estimate because many other factors are involved. Nevertheless these types of decisions (which boil down to essentially trading off dollars for lives) are frequently made by government agencies and corporations.

A second difficult aspect of such decisions is that the events leading to losses of life are generally very unlikely. Difficulties associated with dealing with these low probabilities (rare events) have been discussed in Chapter 4.

Decisions involving life and death elements are very difficult to make and to rationally justify, yet they commonly occur. How can decision analysis procedures help?

Decision analysis and, in particular, the multiattribute utility approach can help such decision processes by providing a framework for problem structuring and logical analysis. Choices of strategy that may affect lives are never easy to make, and the decision analysis approach cannot in a sense make them any easier, *but it can ensure that such decisions are well considered*. For example, consider a government agency that is reviewing the status of child-proof packaging of medicines and other poisonous substances. If it recommends a higher degree of package security, there are implications both in terms of cost and lives lost. These attribute values can be forecast for a number of alternatives that the agency is considering. If a bivariate utility function can be established for these two variables, then an expected utility model can be applied. The very process of articulating such a utility function focuses attention on the relevant policy issue, that of the trade-off between lives lost and monetary consequences.

## EXAMPLE 7–8

### Choice of Technology at Baltimore Gas and Electric

Keeney, Lathrop, and Sicherman (1986) report on a utility company's choice of a power generation technology in a decision to add electric generating capacity. The overall objective of "selecting the best technology" was decomposed into the following elements:

Economic impact.
Management impact.
Environmental impact.
Socioeconomic impacts.
Health and safety.
Public attitudes.
Feasibility.

Some of these major objective categories directly became attributes in a multiattribute utility function. Others were further decomposed. For example, "economic impact" was decomposed into attributes, "customer cost" and "shareholder return." This useful decomposition reflects the different economic impacts of the technology choice on the two distinct groups. The "socioeconomic impacts" category ultimately led to six attributes in the utility function:

Water usage.
Transportation impact.
Community disruption.
Local employment.
Visual impact.
Local tax revenue.

The "health and safety" objective was operationalized as two attributes, namely, "mortality" and "morbidity." Of the 15 attributes in the final utility model, all components were modeled as additive with one additional multiplicative term. The multiplicative term recognized the dependency between customer cost and shareholder return.

---

This example is a classic case of multiattribute utility modeling shedding light on a problem. A different approach such as cost-benefit analysis would not specifically have brought out the issues and trade-offs between objectives that the decision really involved. It would have been very difficult, and perhaps rather arbitrary, to translate some of the nonmonetary attributes into cost-benefit terms. The multiattribute utility approach accounted for the complexity of multiple objectives in a powerful, insightful manner.

## SUMMARY

For many decision problems, the relevant objectives of the decision maker are complex and cannot be expressed in a single dimension. Multiattribute utility functions can be used to represent preferences over multiple dimensions and encompass those preferences in the solution of decision analysis models.

Many functional forms are possible. The additive form is often used, and even where it does not fit actual preferences exactly, it is often robust and may be useful as a decision process aid. For those who are not experienced decision analysts, the use of functional forms more complex than the additive structure is not recommended. The additive function is often a good enough approximation to make its use worthwhile. It is normally much better to use such an approach than to use a unidimensional function for problems that clearly involve multiple dimensions of value. The worst thing to do is to ignore important dimensions of value.

Related methods such as dominance, satisficing, and lexicographic ordering can be used to assist in the determination of decision strategies.

Revealed preference methods such as conjoint measurement do not require the articulation of the utility function but allow its deduction based on certain assumptions about functional form.

All of the methods of choice outlined in Chapters 5, 6, and 7 can be considered as forms of utility-based decision rules. For example, EMV assumes unidimensional utility and linear preference. In this sense we could consider the multiattribute utility criterion as the umbrella (or the root of a hierarchy of methods) from which other methods are derived. Most of these other methods involve specific assumptions about the form of the utility function or some of its properties.

Finally, there is no conclusive proof that better decisions are made by people who use formal decision-support methods such as decision analysis/expected utility. However the majority of people who learn about these procedures, and subsequently use them, claim to have enhanced their thinking processes and understanding of decisions and sources of complexity, and in many cases, claim to have successfully molded these thinking algorithms into their decision behavior.

## FURTHER READING

Keeney and Raiffa's (1976) volume presents technical issues and their explanation of many of the issues covered in this chapter. Additional references are to articles by Huber (1974), Bell (1979), Fishburn (1967), and Keeney (1972). Each of these articles deals with important aspects of assessing multiattribute utilities.

## REFERENCES

BELL, D. E. 1979. "Consistent Assessment Procedures Using Conditional Utility Functions." *Operations Research* 27, pp. 1054–1066.

FISHBURN, P. C. 1967. "Methods of Estimating Additive Utilities." *Management Science* 13, pp. 435–53.

GRANGER, C. H. 1964. "The Hierarchy of Objectives." *Harvard Business Review* 42 (May–June), pp. 63–74.

HUBER, G. P. 1974. "Methods for Quantifying Subjective Probabilities and Multiattribute Utilities." *Decision Sciences*, 5, pp. 430–458.

KEENEY, R. L. 1972. "An Illustrated Procedure for Assessing Multiattributed Utility Functions." *Sloan Management Review* 14, pp. 37–50.

KEENEY, R. L., J. F. LATHROP, and A. SICHERMAN. 1986. "An Analysis of Baltimore Gas and Electric Company's Technology Choice." *Operations Research* 34, no. 1 (January–February), pp. 18–39.

KEENEY, R. L., and H. RAIFFA. 1976. *Decisions with Multiple Objectives*. New York: John Wiley & Sons, pp. 41–55.

ROTHERMELL, M. A., and D. A. SCHILLING. 1986. "Conjoint Measurement in Multiple Objective Decision Making: A New Approach." *European Journal of Operational Research* 23, pp. 310–19.

## PROBLEMS

1. Can you envisage what the three-dimensional surface looks like that corresponds to the set of indifference curves of Figure 7–4? Try to draw a three-dimensional graph that could represent it, assuming that adjacent indifference curves on Figure 7–4 represent equal utility increments.
2. Under what general circumstances might it be reasonable to reduce the dimensionality of a multidimensional problem to a unidimensional utility representation? Describe a business/management example where it is reasonable to collapse a multidimensional problem into a unidimensional preference pattern. Describe an example where you would prefer not to reduce dimensionality.

3. How can the satisficing and dominance rules be used in decision problems with multiple attributes? Are they alternative or complementary approaches to utility?
4. For multiattribute utility problems, how can the decision maker check to see if two attributes are mutually utility independent?
5. Suppose that you are looking for a new job and have had a few offers. To assist your choice process, articulate your dimensions of value associated with your career:
   *a.* Begin by listing the features of a job that are important to you.
   *b.* Adjust your list of job attributes to about five (between three and seven) items.
   *c.* Does your list of attributes have the properties of being: complete, operational, decomposable, nonredundant, and of minimum size? Can your list be refined to improve on these dimensions?
   *d.* Do you have the correct level of detail and decomposition? Is each of your variables clearly defined? For example, if "location" is one of your attributes, do you mean location with respect to which part of the world or country, or which suburb of a city, or proximity to beaches or snowfields? Should you decompose your "location" attribute to allow it to be more clearly defined? Check each of your attributes.
   *e.* If you are satisfied that your list of attributes is well tuned to represent your dimensions of value, check for mutual utility independence by trying to articulate whether each attribute's unidimensional preference pattern would be affected by changes in values of the other attributes.
   *f.* If you went no further than this with the analysis (that is, you did not actually rate each job on each attribute), would the definition of your attributes have helped your decision process? Do you have a better understanding of your preference patterns as a result of this exercise? If so, in what way?
6. Refer to Table 7–2.
   *a.* Are any of the alternatives dominated?
   *b.* How would the decision process have been altered if the decision maker had specified satisficing (minimum) levels of 5 for both "power" and "driveability" attributes?
   *c.* Use a lexicographic ordering procedure to recommend a choice where "appearance" is the most important attribute and "fuel economy" is second most important.
7. Judy Souter (see Example 7–4) was about to choose a job after graduating with an MBA when she received another offer. She had previously structured her attributes as:

   Location (region of the country).

Benefits (first year).
Prospects (advancement).
Nature (of work).
Job satisfaction.

For each of the five attributes, she considered whether her unidimensional utility function was affected by the other four. Her conclusion was that if there was any utility dependence it was very minor. As a result of thinking through the issue of utility independence, Judy realized that two of the attributes, "nature (of work)" and "job satisfaction" were closely related. She felt that although they were not exactly the same thing, one led to the other. As a result, she combined them into a single attribute.

She also considered the attribute "travel." It was important to her that she not be out of town for too long although she did enjoy some limited travel for business purposes. After considering whether to include it as an attribute, Judy decided that "travel" could be collapsed into her new attribute "job nature and satisfaction." Her rankings are shown in Table 7–4.

The rankings reflected the reasons that Judy could not easily make a choice based on holistic judgments. The job with the best pay and prospects (job 3) did not rank high on "location" and "nature." In fact, none of the jobs was outstanding in all aspects.

*a*. Were any of the jobs dominated by any other?

*b*. Using an additive utility structure, Judy assessed relative importance factors for each attribute as:

$$\begin{aligned}&\text{Location: } k = 0.1\\&\text{Benefits: } k = 0.4\\&\text{Prospects: } k = 0.2\\&\text{Nature: } k = 0.3\end{aligned}$$

Calculate a utility score for each job.

*c*. As Judy was about to make a choice, she received a phone call from a small new company that had previously contacted her. She had not heard from them after her visit to their facility and

**TABLE 7–4** Judy's Job Rankings by Attributes*

| *Job* | *Location* | *Benefits* | *Prospects* | *Nature* |
|---|---|---|---|---|
| 1 | 4 | 3 | 6 | 9 |
| 2 | 6 | 2 | 5 | 6 |
| 3 | 4 | 9 | 8 | 5 |
| 4 | 7 | 8 | 4 | 2 |

* 0 = worst, 10 = best

had assumed that they were not interested in her. The company president apologized for not calling her sooner, stating that he had been going through a process of reorganization of his senior staff that had to be completed before a decision could be made on the position that Judy had applied for.

The president offered her a fairly low starting salary with a large yearly bonus conditional on sales goals being met for the product line that Judy would manage. Judy felt that as product manager she would have a good degree of control over those sales and that the goals were probably achievable. She thought the probability of getting the bonus each year was about 0.7.

She added a row to her table as follows:

| *Job* | *Location* | *Benefits* | *Prospects* | *Nature* |
|---|---|---|---|---|
| 5 | 6 | 8 with probability 0.7<br>3 with probability 0.3 | 6 | 7 |

She was risk averse and would have preferred simply to get a salary with no bonus element but the company president insisted on it.

Was it possible for Judy to incorporate her risk aversion into her multiattribute utility analysis? If so, how? Apply the additive model to the new job and compare it to the others.

8. The research and development manager of a large manufacturer was allocated an additional $250,000 in his budget over and above his expectations. This allocation allowed him to consider funding some projects that he had previously been unable to consider. Each project would require about $200,000. He ranked the candidate projects according to a set of criteria of importance as follows:

| *Project* | *Short-Term Returns (less than 3 years)* | *Long-Term Returns (greater than 3 years)* | *Technology Spinoffs* | *Market Share* | *Competitive Position* |
|---|---|---|---|---|---|
| 1 | 8 | 2 | 4 | 6 | 5 |
| 2 | 4 | 6 | 2 | 7 | 8 |
| 3 | 0 | 9 | 6 | 4 | 3 |
| 4 | 3 | 8 | 4 | 7 | 7 |
| 5 | 2 | 6 | 5 | 5 | 9 |
| 6 | 7 | 6 | 3 | 3 | 3 |

Some of the projects were process oriented, in that they would primarily result in reduced production costs. Others were product oriented and would result in an improved product and higher market share and competitiveness. The R&D manager also chose to discriminate between short-term returns and long-term returns on investment because the projects differed substantially in their nature and time horizon. Some were strictly developmental in nature (projects 1 and 6) whereas others involved substantial elements of research, albeit applied research in some cases. The manager wished to use an additive scoring system and assigned attribute weights as follows:

| | |
|---|---|
| Short-term returns | 0.25 |
| Long-term returns | 0.25 |
| Technology spinoffs | 0.05 |
| Market share | 0.25 |
| Competitive position | 0.20 |

*a*. Calculate the utilities of each project.

*b*. If the manager was able to release funds from other parts of his budget to allow him to undertake two of the six projects, which might be some likely candidate pairs?

*c*. What other considerations would enter into the decision process apart from the individual value (utility) of each project?

*d*. The projects were not all assured of success, even though success was presumed in the foregoing analysis. How could uncertainty be taken into account in the analysis?

9. A product designer was considering three alternative product designs. On each one he had ranked the attributes of importance: "price," "appeal," and "quality." He decided that these were all independent of each other and assessed a utility function

$$U = \text{Price} + 2\ \text{Appeal} + 0.7\ \text{Quality}$$

The designs were rated as:

| | *Price* | *Appeal* | *Quality* |
|---|---|---|---|
| Design 1 | 2 | 3 | 2 |
| Design 2 | 4 | 8 | 7 |
| Design 3 | 6 | 5 | 5 |

Rank the designs according to the model. How robust are the rankings to the rates and weights?

10. A decision maker was choosing a new machine for his factory. His utility function was assessed in terms of its production cost and capacity

$$U = \frac{\text{Capacity}^2}{4} - \text{Cost}$$

He had carefully scaled this function so that costs were in thousands of dollars and capacity was in units per minute. For his application he was uncertain about the future operating cost and capacity of the available machines as follows:

| | *Cost ($000)* | *Capacity (units/minute)* |
|---|---|---|
| Machine 1 | 40 with probability 0.5<br>50 with probability 0.5 | 10 with probability 0.7<br>12 with probability 0.3 |
| Machine 2 | 45 with probability 0.6<br>60 with probability 0.4 | 9 with probability 0.4<br>12.5 with probability 0.6 |

Assume that "cost" and "capacity" are statistically independent. Calculate the expected utility of each machine.

11. A large university was considering replacing its outdated computer system. The large mainframe system was now overloaded and often broke down, incurred large maintenance costs, and was unable to serve some faculty research needs. The computer center manager had collected information on a large number of available systems with the necessary capacity for the university system. After talking to the marketing people of a number of companies, the manager narrowed his search to five systems. He structured a set of attributes: Price, capacity, expansion potential, compatibility with present system, software, and service.

    These attributes seemed to be a good set, except that he decided to decompose capacity into two attributes: number of terminals that could be supported and processing speed. He contacted each of the supplier companies again, and after further discussion, made the following assessments on a scale of zero (worst) to 10 (best).

| | *System* | | | | |
|---|---|---|---|---|---|
| | *1* | *2* | *3* | *4* | *5* |
| Price | 8 | 6 | 4 | 8 | 5 |
| Capacity: Terminals | 4 | 5 | 7 | 8 | 4 |
| Speed | 4 | 7 | 5 | 4 | 7 |
| Expansion potential | 5 | 8 | 3 | 2 | 6 |
| Compatibility with present system | 9 | 4 | 6 | 8 | 5 |
| Software | 8 | 7 | 5 | 9 | 9 |
| Service | 10 | 6 | 8 | 9 | 6 |

All the systems met the manager's minimum criteria. These minima were on price and capacity only.

*a.* Are any of the systems dominated?

*b*. The manager had a committee with which he debated the importance of the various attributes. They eventually chose the following weights:

| | |
|---|---|
| Price | 0.3 |
| Capacity: | |
| Terminals | 0.2 |
| Speed | 0.15 |
| Expansion potential | 0.1 |
| Compatibility with present system | 0.05 |
| Software | 0.15 |
| Service | 0.05 |

Use a linear additive model to score each system.

*c*. The linear additive model implies an assumption of mutual utility independence between all possible pairs of attributes. Do you think this is a valid assumption? Discuss possible dependencies, and how in the light of these dependencies, the additive model provides insight about the decision.

12. One of the university computer committee members (problem 11, above) believed that there was uncertainty about the compatibility of three of the systems with the present system, as well as expansion potential and service. He assessed the following probabilities:

| | *Compatibility* | | *Expansion* | | *Service* | |
|---|---|---|---|---|---|---|
| *System* | *Score* | *Probability* | *Score* | *Probability* | *Score* | *Probability* |
| 1 | 8 | 0.4 | 4 | 0.5 | 10 | 1 |
| | 9 | 0.4 | 6 | 0.5 | | |
| | 10 | 0.2 | | | | |
| 3 | 4 | 0.3 | 2 | 0.2 | 7 | 0.2 |
| | 5 | 0.5 | 3 | 0.3 | 8 | 0.8 |
| | 6 | 0.2 | 4 | 0.4 | | |
| | | | 5 | 0.1 | | |
| 5 | 8 | 0.4 | 5 | 0.1 | 5 | 0.2 |
| | 9 | 0.6 | 6 | 0.6 | 6 | 0.5 |
| | | | 7 | 0.3 | 7 | 0.3 |

Systems 2 and 4 were deemed to have very little uncertainty about them. Determine the expected utility of each system.

13. The British and French governments have long been considering a tunnel for transporting cars and trains under the English Channel. Various designs and configurations are possible. Taking the position of either of these governments, structure a set of objectives you think would be relevant. Operationalize these into a set of well-

defined attributes for a multiattribute utility representation. Define the measurement scale for each attribute. (Hint: See Example 7–8 for guidance.)

14. A state government parks and environment department was considering selling a number of offshore oil leases to private oil companies. Structure a set of attributes for this decision, defining each one carefully.
15. The chief executive officer of a large company was considering moving his head office out of Manhattan, either to New Jersey or to another major city such as Chicago or Los Angeles where new markets were rapidly developing for his products. Structure a set of attributes for this decision. Define each one so that it could be measured.

CHAPTER EIGHT

# Sensitivity Analysis

## OUTLINE



## OBJECTIVES

After completing this chapter, you should be able to:

1. Discuss the nature of the sensitivity analysis process.
2. Use the notion of sensitivity analysis in all phases of decision analysis to enrich the analysis process.
3. Identify assumptions, both explicit and implicit, about problem identification, model structure, and evaluation.
4. Critically challenge various kinds of assumptions made in decision analysis and draw inferences about the robustness of solutions.
5. Conduct parametric sensitivity analyses, which are quantitative analyses relating the effect of altering model input values to model outputs.

## INTRODUCTION

This chapter describes a thinking style and process of sensitivity analysis. It suggests that sensitivity analysis should not be just a postoptimality step in decision analysis, but should be woven into the fabric of every step of the process.

Sensitivity analysis is an important part of decision analysis. A sensitivity analysis generally involves checking the effects of the model assumptions on the model solution. In Chapter 1, the stages of decision and management science modeling were described as model construction, model solution, and model interpretation. Inevitably, the decision analyst and decision maker must make a number of simplifying assumptions during the model construction phase. The model is then solved and assumptions are reviewed and analyzed as part of the model interpretation process. This description is of the simplest kind of decision analysis process (see Figure 8–1) where there is no recycling from one phase to another. In this simple process, sensitivity analysis is considered to be a single step in a decison analysis process composed of quite distinct phases.

Most real decision processes and useful decision analysis processes are more complex, more fuzzy than this simple interpretation. They involve moving from one phase of the analysis to another in many different patterns. Sensitivity analysis is a most useful tool when it is not relegated to the role of a postsolution step in decision analysis, but rather *embedded into every step of the decision analysis process*. Figure 8–2 shows a decision analysis process that includes this more useful, "embedded" concept of sensitivity analysis and a possible set of recycle arrows. The recycle arrows indicate that the decision analysis thinking algorithm may spark the decision maker to review any phase of the process at any time. Not all possible arrows are shown.

Figure 8–2 is a useful summary of this chapter. It shows the many aspects of sensitivity analysis. Table 8–1 sets out this same information in summary form and presents six forms of sensitivity analysis. It is certainly possible to classify differently from this interpretation, but as long as the philosophy of sensitivity analysis is correctly identified, such differences are only minor. To summarize, the suggested philosophy and process is one of *checking and questioning assumptions as you go,* so that the embedding of sensitivity analysis in decision analysis is part of an analytic process that can involve a number of recycle steps within the process. Good models tend to evolve from such structured cyclic processes.

The following sections of this chapter deal with each of these aspects of sensitivity in more detail. They consider issues of sensitivity to assumptions that are made at every step along the way in a decision analysis. The integrated sensitivity analysis process tends to productively increase the "learning as you go" phenomenon and may lead to a number of cyclic loops from one phase to another, as shown in Figure 8–2.

**FIGURE 8–1** The Basic Decision Analysis Process

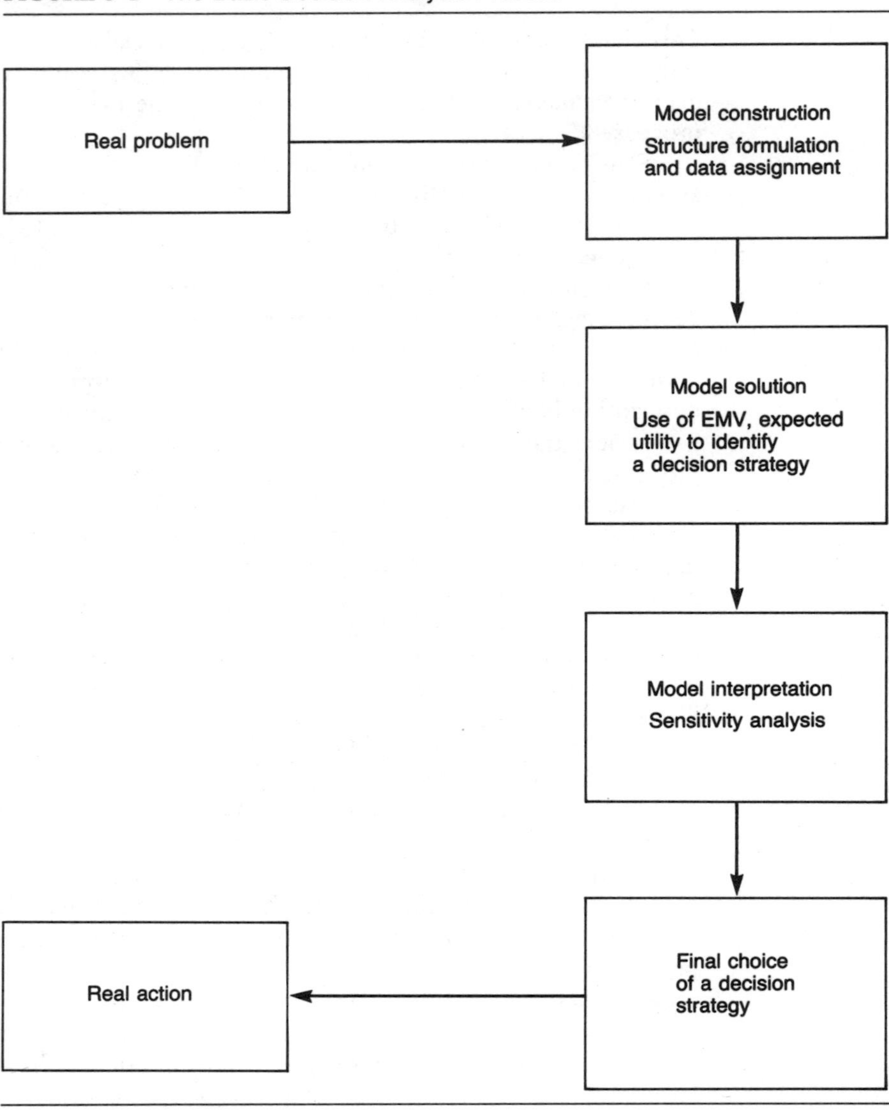


This *integrative view of sensitivity analysis* in decision analysis is in considerable contrast to the usual sensitivity analysis process described as part of the linear programming modeling process with which many readers will be familiar. In the linear programming context, the analytic process is well structured, and sensitivity analysis (also called postoptimality analysis) is normally limited to an examination of the effect of altering parameter values. Although this parametric sensitivity analysis is very powerful and

FIGURE 8–2 A Decision Analysis Process that Embeds Sensitivity Analysis Throughout

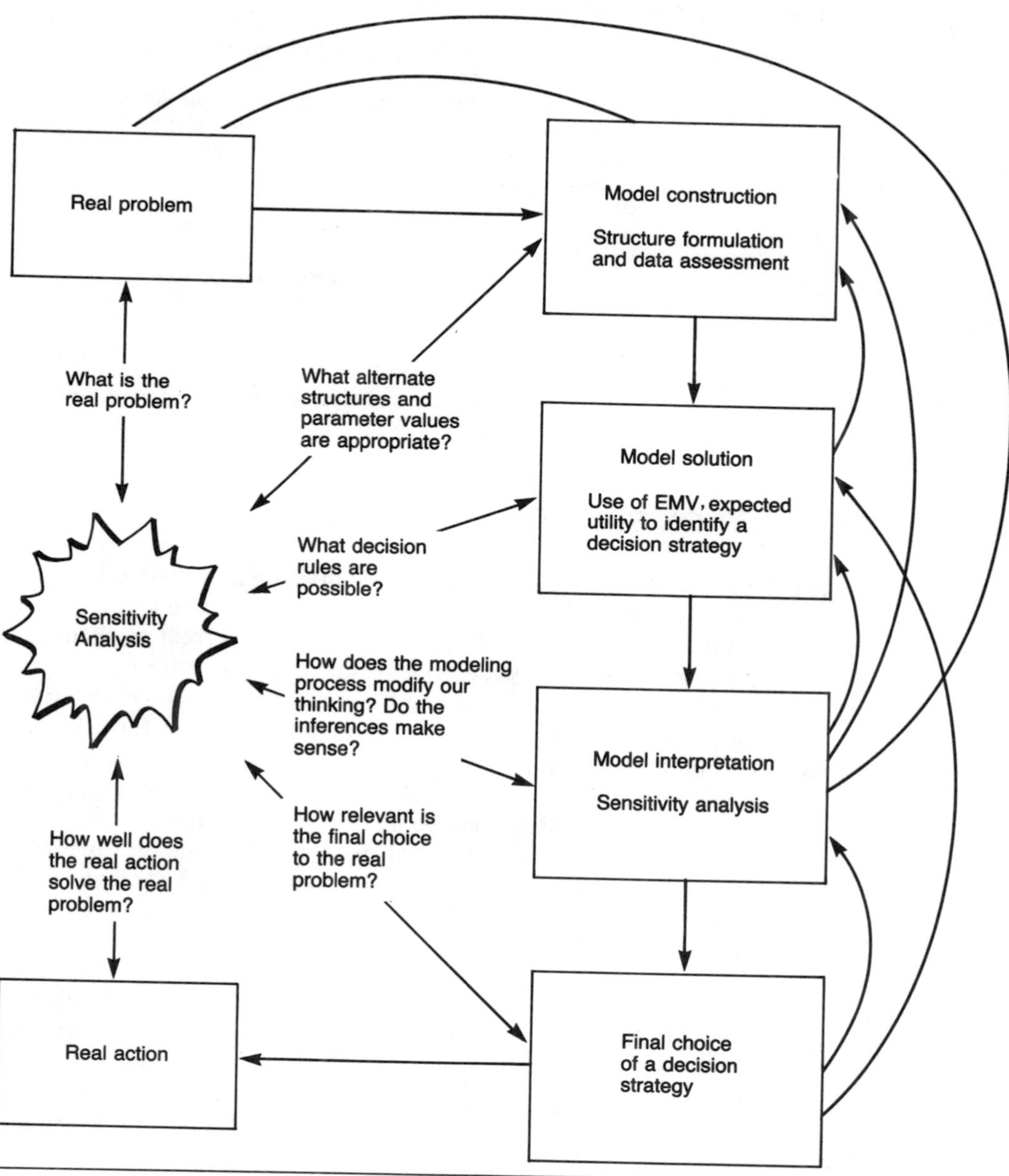

**TABLE 8–1** Types of Sensitivity Analysis

| *Decision Phase* | *Sensitivity Analysis Questions* |
|---|---|
| Real problem definition | What is the real problem and how do various definitions of it affect our decision behavior? |
| Model construction | What alternate modeling approaches and structures are possible? What is the effect of changes on the assumed values of parameters? |
| Model solution | What is the effect of changes in decision criteria? |
| Model interpretation | How does and how should the modeling process change our thinking about the problem? |
| Final choice | How relevant is the bottom line decision strategy (model output) to the real problem? |
| Real action | How well does the real action solve the real problem? |

produces useful insights, it reflects a narrow view of sensitivity analysis represented more by Figure 8–1 than by the richer process represented by Figure 8–2.

## PROBLEM IDENTIFICATION SENSITIVITY ANALYSIS

The first type of sensitivity analysis we should investigate is that of problem identification. We want to know what the *real problem* is, and identification is often not a trivial matter. Only if we can identify the correct problem can we then treat it properly with a good decision and some effective real action. There is normally very little to be gained from efficiently solving the wrong problem. This phenomenon is often called an "error of the third kind." Hence a decision maker who perceives a problem should not automatically assume that what he sees is the *real* problem. Our initial perceptions are not always correct. The observation may be merely of a symptom or may be of some peripheral element of the real problem. A good example of misidentification is when a production process is observed to have very high levels of work in process inventory. This inventory can be viewed as a problem in itself, or else as a possible symptom of an underlying production problem, such as a poorly balanced production line. Increasing inventory levels may have been the factory floor's response to dealing with a set of unreliable suppliers or unreliable processing equipment. The question is, when we noticed that inventories were high, were we observing the real problem or just a symptomatic response to some other real problem? In this problem context, the answer to this question often requires a great deal of investigation.

Before we consider another managerial example, consider the following analogy from the field of medicine. Mr. X is an air traffic controller who has two broken marriages behind him. He develops symptoms (including depression and stomach upsets) indicating that he has developing hypertension and a potential ulcer. The doctor finds that Mr. X has a lot of stress to deal with both in his work and personal environments (and he also needs a high income to pay his ex-wives). There are a number of elements in Mr. X's story: the need for money, the stress, the developing hypertension and potential ulcer, and the symptoms (including depression and stomach upsets). Which of these elements is the *real* problem, or is the problem the sum of all these elements? The answer to this question may shed light on which element should be treated. In decision analysis terms, the real problem must be defined before a real action can be chosen. Mr. X initially believed that the problem was the depression and stomach upsets. He wanted prescriptions for antidepressant and stomach treatment drugs. Alternatively, if the stress was the real problem should his treatment have been attending a stress management program? If his major source of stress was his money problem, could his financial problems be alleviated or managed? Were there any other contributing factors?

In searching for a clear definition of the real problem, we must scan the environment that surrounds the business or subsystem of the business experiencing difficulty. Any changes that we notice in the environment may present a clue or lead us to the real problem. Alternatively, comparison of key parameters with a similar organizational unit which is *not* having a problem may help.

Just as in a complex medical case, the question of what is the real problem can be very complex in a managerial context. Managers must very often search for *clarity of definition of a problem* in a murky sea of conflicting information and opinion. Ambiguity and the potential for misinterpreting data and circumstances abound!

Creativity in problem solving is a very important part of managerial decision processes. A number of problem-solving paradigms and processes have been documented (Evans 1986). In the context of problem identification sensitivity analysis, the creative process requires the *questioning of assumptions* about problem definition and the *imagination of alternative definitions*.

## EXAMPLE 8–1

### Identifying a Problem at XYZ Manufacturing Inc.

Mr. James Bigalo, the chief executive officer of XYZ Manufacturing Inc., knew he had a problem. His company had lost some market share and was not meeting his expectations in terms of contribution to profit. He was particularly upset by this low profit because it was sure to be a difficult issue at the annual general meeting of stockholders coming up in three months. He thought that if only he could get a handle on the problem immediately, he could solve it in time to either improve his financial performance or at least be able to promise a forthcoming improvement.

After pondering the situation all weekend, he arrived at his office on Monday morning determined to pinpoint the problem by focusing on nothing else for as long as necessary. Given the extent of his commitments, he intended to have a clear problem statement in mind by 5 P.M. that day.

He began by resisting the temptation to call a meeting of the 8 or 10 people (various vice presidents and others) who might usefully be able to debate the issues. He was not generally a meetings-oriented person and believed that a two-hour meeting of 10 executives (20 executive hours) was neither an efficient nor an effective process.

He wrote an initial description of the situation. He noted that for the first two quarters of his financial year, aftertax income was low. Third-quarter projections were not any better. Next, he noted that sales revenue was quite steady. His business analyst had provided him with data that indicated market growth. Since prices had been stable, a few quick calculations convinced him that he was losing market share. Even so, the reasonably constant revenue picture was not the element causing a poor bottom-line result. Mr. Bigalo noted that total costs were higher than last year and were also widely fluctuating even though the manufacturing operation was a level production system.[1]

Mr. Bigalo called his VP in charge of marketing who told him that their drive for higher quality was successful. The problem was that the manufacturing division couldn't produce a high-quality product at a reasonable cost. Moreover, the new quality requirement was causing increased rework in the factory, and delivery of finished goods was taking longer and becoming unreliable. The marketing manager complained of having difficulty holding on to existing clients, much less attracting new orders.

The VP with responsibility for overall financial control was Mr. Bigalo's next call. She pointed out that increased interest rates had led to higher costs that had been balanced by reduced working capital investments as a result of the XYZ program to reduce inventories. She also noted that the reduction in inventories had led to problems in the manufacturing system, such as component shortages and production stoppages.

Mr. Bigalo then called on Andrew Carr, who was in charge of the manufacturing function. The two were old friends and had risen through the ranks of the company together. Whereas Mr. Bigalo was an accountant by training, Andrew had begun his career as a mechanical engineer in the process engineering department.

Andrew claimed that the financial performance in the current year was a short-term phenomenon. He argued that while Mr. Bigalo did have a short-term financial performance problem, there was a much more important problem of a long-term strategic nature. That problem was that various senior executives wanted the manufacturing system to simultaneously perform well on a number of criteria, and it just couldn't be done. Andrew explained that there were many sorts of goals that he could strive for. He listed them as:

---

[1] Level production means that a constant production rate is maintained throughout a given time horizon.

1. Excellence in quality.
2. Low-cost production.
3. Short delivery lead times.
4. Fast response to orders.
5. Production of a range of models.
6. Production reliability.
7. Maximum capacity.

Andrew explained that some trade-offs had to be made and that he could not satisfy everybody. He suggested that the company had bravely decided to reduce inventory and that this experience had taught him a lot. In particular, it brought to light a number of other production problems that had previously been hidden, and it also demonstrated that the company did not have a clear and consistent statement of manufacturing strategy. He described the company environment as too volatile, where a drive for quality occurred one month and a cost-cutting exercise was undertaken the next.

By lunchtime, Mr. Bigalo was ready to call a meeting of his inner circle of three. They discussed the situation and decided that the short-term problem of financial performance was important, but secondary to the strategic problem of establishing and managing according to an effective, workable manufacturing strategy.[2]

Mr. Bigalo decided to investigate what he now saw as a two-part problem by:

1. Looking for ways to bolster the bottom line to a reasonable figure. He had a number of tools at his disposal including the alternatives of financial, marketing, or short-term production strategies.
2. Confronting the longer-term problem by identifying the basis on which XYZ chose to compete across its production mix.

He was considerably more interested in effectively solving the long-term problem than the short-term problem because he knew that the company could easily survive a poor year, particularly if a well-conceived future plan was developed.

Mr. Bigalo felt satisfied that he had been on a useful fishing expedition that day. He had become aware of a number of people's perceived problems and had integrated their opinions and data into a picture of the real problem. He felt ready to structure a model of the problem by listing alternative strategies and sources of uncertainty.

---

A number of general issues arise from the XYZ Manufacturing example. Mr. Bigalo was presented with a number of perceived views of a problem. Which one was the real problem? In general, how do you know for sure when you have identified the real problem? The answer is that you don't know for sure, but through the use of common sense and systematic process you can generally decrease the likelihood of making errors of the third kind. Sensitivity analysis with respect to *what is the real problem* involves a

---

[2] Readers who wish to investigate this topic further are referred to R. Hayes and S. Wheelwright (1984).

systematic search that normally may involve obtaining input from a number of people and analyzing the data.

We should also ask, as part of this process, what are the consequences of my real actions if I have indeed not identified the real problem? Suppose, for example, that Mr. Bigalo had accepted his marketing vice president's view of the problem and acted upon that view. Alternatively the VP of financial management had expressed a very different problem that would lead to a different set of potential actions. We can conclude that *sensitivity to errors of the third kind (solving the wrong problem) is usually high*. No matter how creative, elegant, or efficient a problem solution is, there is often little to be gained if that solution is not addressed to the correct problem. In the context of problems that are strategic in nature, the impact on the organization of solving the wrong problem may be very substantial. Hence, in decision analysis, it is most useful to begin asking "what if" and "why" questions from the very beginning of the process, at the problem identification stage.

## MODEL CONSTRUCTION SENSITIVITY ANALYSIS

There are many aspects of sensitivity analysis in the model construction phase of decision analysis. The first is to choose a model type, once a problem is defined to the satisfaction of the decision maker.

### Choice of Modeling Approach

The first type of model construction sensitivity analysis is: "What if I choose a different modeling approach?" As examples, consider the following situations:

**1.** A production manager has identified a quality control problem in his operating process. He chose initially to use a decision tree to model the situation. On further reflection, he realized that the relationships between variables were mostly linear, and the sources of uncertainty in his problem were not of great importance. He considered the effect of trying to formulate a linear program to represent his problem. What sorts of insights and what sorts of decision strategies would be produced by employing one approach rather than the other? Most experts would agree that different approaches would produce different sets of inferences about the problem. In other words, sensitivity to modeling approach is high.

**2.** An insurance company has outgrown its old head office building and is going to move up town to a new facility.[3] Their problem is what to do with

[3] This example is adapted from a case study entitled "Property Development in Caracas" in P. G. Moore, et al. (1976).

the old building. Options include sale, rental as office space, or redevelopment as either a hotel or apartment block. Uncertainties in terms of future rents and property values exist.

Two modeling approaches were suggested. The first was a decision analysis model incorporating a decision tree and the use of a unidimensional utility function. This approach involved the assessment of cash flows over a 20-year time horizon for each alternative and their discounting to net present values (NPV). The uncertainties in NPV would reflect the riskiness of each alternative and be accounted for in the expected utility calculations.

The second approach, to use the capital asset pricing model (CAPM), would enable the company to clearly consider the alternative uses of the building as an addition to a portfolio of assets. The two suggested modeling approaches were quite different in their assumptions and emphases. It is likely that the insights and suggested decision strategies would be different.

In general terms, we are never forced to choose a particular modeling approach. We should use our common sense in choosing the one which is likely to be the most valuable. If two or more approaches appear to be potentially useful, then a pertinent question is: What is the effect of using one rather than another?

If time and resources allow, two or more potentially useful modeling approaches could be used. The case for using multiple approaches in problem solving has been argued by two prominent decision analysts, Rex Brown and Dennis Lindley (1986). They have suggested that *plural analysis,* where several singular approaches are undertaken in parallel, is a ''central feature of intelligent everyday thinking.'' Brown and Lindley make a good case for deliberately using more than one modeling approach, preferably using approaches with dissimilar features. Of course, different approaches may produce different answers and inferences, leaving the decision maker with the job of reconciling these results. This may itself be a difficult process, however it brings into focus both a *clear distinction between problem and models and a recognition that inferences are normally dependent on model structure*.

The first kind of model structuring sensitivity analysis is asking: ''What if we choose another approach?'' Although the question forces the decision maker and analyst to confront some difficult issues, the resolution of those issues is usually very worthwhile.

## Model Design

A second type of model structuring sensitivity analysis is model design. Some model design issues in decision analysis are listed here.

**1.** Different sets of elements can be included in a decision tree representation. Of a variety of alternative actions and sources of uncertainty, which are to be included in the decision tree and which can reasonably be excluded? Further, what is the effect of these model design decisions?

**2.** Even for a given set of decision elements, their organization as a model and juxtaposition on a decision tree can be varied. These model design decisions generally have a substantial impact on model output.

**3.** The level of aggregation and detail can vary within a given model design. Should an uncertain quantity be represented as continuous or discrete? If it is discrete, should there be 3 or 5 or 10 levels of its value in the model? Should revenue be included as an aggregate measure, or should price and quantity be defined separately? Some of these sensitivity analysis issues were described in earlier chapters as fundamental questions in decision analysis and reflect the importance of structural sensitivity analysis.

Examples of sensitivity to model design matters abound. The importance of leaving out a relevant decision element cannot be overestimated. For example, in the Midwestern Utility problem (in Chapter 2 where the utility company was considering settling an issue with the county or going to court), if a counteroffer had not been assumed possible, a very different solution and set of inferences would have resulted. Another possibility that was not included in that decision tree model (Figure 2–7) was to go to court and consider a settlement process during the court process. On that same example, the decision tree could have been designed with the court outcome having a different number of outcomes from the three that are shown. Instead of having a set of outcomes as "win," "partial win," or "lose," a 5-outcome or 10-outcome design could have been used.

More generally, the different model designs that can be constructed for a problem can be envisaged in terms of concepts of vertical and lateral thinking. Vertical thinking can be described as "digging the same hole deeper. Lateral thinking is concerned with digging the hole somewhere else" (de Bono 1977). Figure 8–3 shows how these concepts relate to a decision tree representation format. Generally, lateral thinking is the process of creating more alternative actions and strategies whereas vertical thinking involves following through the consequences of a particular strategy.

**FIGURE 8–3** Lateral and Vertical Thinking Modes in Decision Tree Analysis

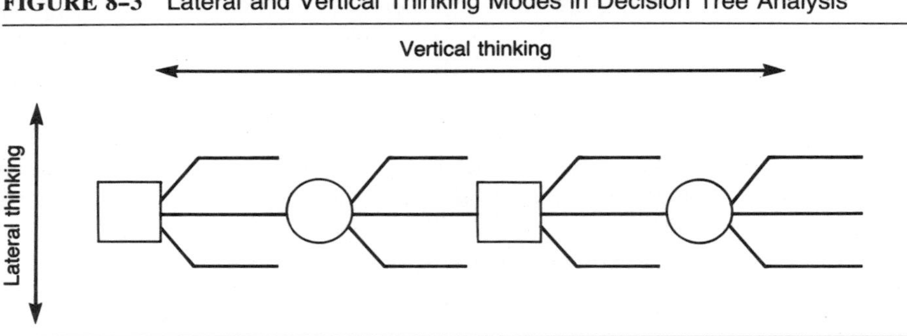

In summary, we note again that many of these sensitivity analysis issues have been mentioned as decision analysis design issues in previous chapters. Thus we see the integrated nature of the sensitivity analysis style of thinking in decision analysis.

## Parametric Sensitivity Analysis

Parametric sensitivity analysis involves the examination of the effect of changing numerical values in a decision model. These numerical values can be probabilities or payoffs, or utilities. We can perform break-even analyses whereby we identify the value of a parameter that makes two competing decision strategies equally desirable. Alternatively, we can observe the general degree of robustness of the ranking of decision strategies with respect to the assumed values of parameters. It is often useful to represent such analysis in graphical form.

---

## Example 8–2

### D&J Systems

D&J Systems is a successful mail-order business dealing in Christmas decorations, cards, stationery, and kitchen utensils. It had recently been approached by two producers of cosmetics who were looking for mail-order distributors. In considering whether to distribute cosmetics, the principal source of uncertainty facing D&J Systems was projected profit. This was really based on sales uncertainty since costs were generally known. Figure 8–4 shows the decision tree as it was structured by the owners of D&J Systems. Sales levels were shown as either high or low, with these terms representing different actual quantities on various branches. The decision makers were intuitively attracted to the option of distributing both brands of cosmetic, because they could then offer a complete range of products by complementing one brand with products from the other. Their initial analysis tended to support those intuitions. (See Figure 8–4.) However they were not confident about some of their quantitative assessments and wanted to check the robustness of the solution to these inputs. They had calculated their profit projections using sales and cost estimates discounted to present values. The subsidiary models through which present values had been determined had been set up using a computerized spreadsheet program.

They noted that the two best options were "brand A only" and "both brands," each with a low pricing strategy. The "both brands" option had the highest expected monetary value (EMV). The decision makers felt that they might have underestimated the probability of high sales if they chose to distribute "brand A only" with a low price strategy.

**FIGURE 8-4** D&J Systems Decision Tree

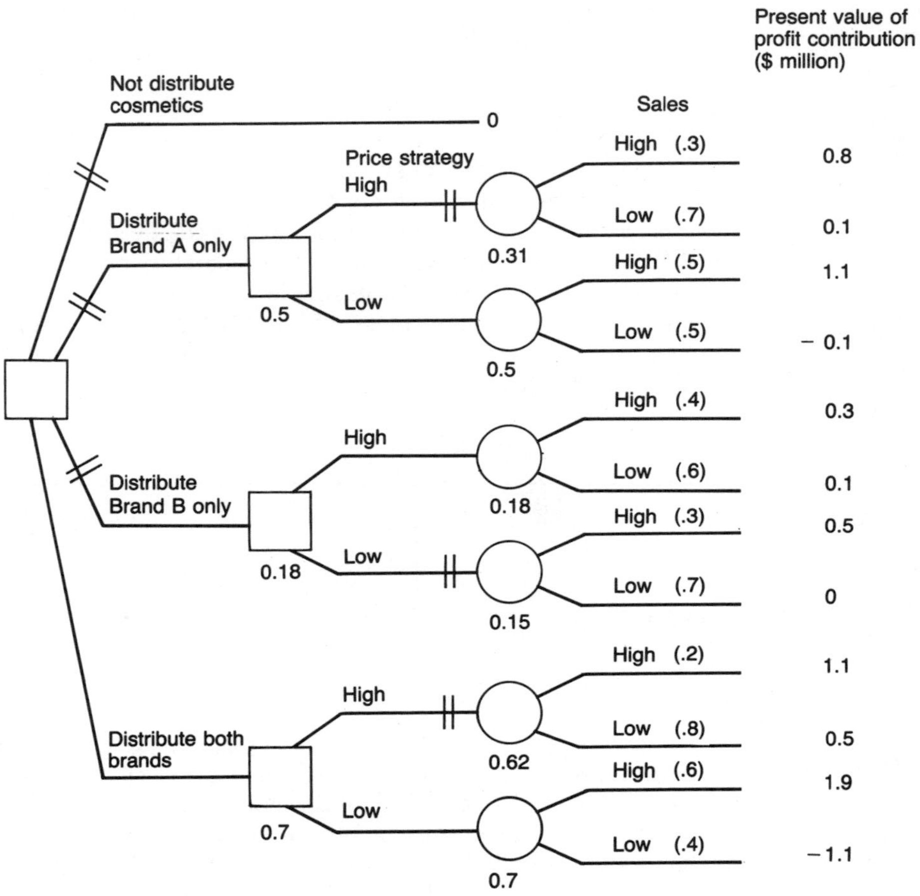

Sensitivity to the probability estimate can be studied by assuming some different values of this estimate and recalculating the EMV:

| *Probability of High Sales (brand A only, low price)* | *EMV ($ million)* |
|---|---|
| 0.5 | $0.5 \times 1.1 + 0.5 \times -0.1 = 0.5$ |
| 0.6 | $0.6 \times 1.1 + 0.4 \times -0.1 = 0.62$ |
| 0.7 | $0.7 \times 1.1 + 0.3 \times -0.1 = 0.74$ |
| 0.8 | $0.8 \times 1.1 + 0.2 \times -0.1 = 0.86$ |
| 0.9 | $0.9 \times 1.1 + 0.1 \times -0.1 = 0.98$ |

The EMV value increases linearly with the probability estimate. Since the EMV of the best alternative ("both brands, low price") was 0.7, it may be useful to determine the break-even point whereby the EMVs of this best branch and the "brand A only, low price" branch are equal. To do this most easily, we define the parameter in question (probability of high sales given a "brand A only, low price" strategy) as p and write an equation equating the EMVs of the two branches being compared:

$$p \times 1.1 + (1 - p) \times -0.1 = 0.7.$$

The solution is $p = 0.67$.

The decision makers believed that although their initial assessment of $p = 0.5$ may have been a little low, it was certainly not so low as to make 0.67 a reasonable possibility. With everything else being equal, they concluded that their possible underestimation of $p$ would not have, on its own, caused the EMV based rankings of strategies to be wrong.

---

Although useful insights can result from these "one-off" sensitivity analyses, they are subject to the assumption of everything else being equal. How can we test sensitivity when two or more assumed quantities are uncertain? When two or three parameters that interact in the model are to be the subject of sensitivity analysis, is it reasonable to simply do one-off sensitivity analysis? To this question we must generally answer no, because one-off sensitivity analysis typically does not capture complex interactions. To illustrate, consider the effect of changes in price ($P$) and quantity ($Q$) on revenue ($R$) in the formula:

$$R = P \times Q$$

Let us assume that base-case assumptions are $P_1 = 3$ and $Q_1 = 5$. What is the effect on revenue of increasing $P$ and $Q$ each by one unit? The new values of price and quantity are[4]

$$P_2 = P_1 + \Delta P = 4$$
$$Q_2 = Q_1 + \Delta Q = 6.$$

Revenue has changed from

$$R_1 = P_1 \times Q_1 = 3 \times 5 = 15$$

to

$$R_2 = P_2 \times Q_2 = 4 \times 6 = 24$$

That is

$$\Delta R = R_2 - \mathrm{R}_1 = 9$$

---

[4] The $\Delta$ notation indicates an incremental change in value.

We can say

$$\begin{aligned} \Delta R &= \Delta P \times Q + P \times \Delta Q + \Delta P \times \Delta Q \\ &= \quad 5 \quad + \quad 3 \quad + \quad 1 \\ &= \quad 9 \end{aligned} \qquad [8.1]$$

The important point in this example is that if we conducted sensitivity analyses on $P$ and $Q$ individually, we would pick up the $P \times \Delta Q$ and the $\Delta P \times Q$ terms, but would *not* account for the $\Delta P \times \Delta Q$ term!

One-off sensitivity analysis usually takes reasonable account of first-order effects. However, as illustrated above, the sum of the effects of individual changes may not equal the whole. The utility of one-off sensitivity analysis is very high when there is simple interaction between a number of uncertain parameters. When there are such interactions, one-off sensitivity analysis becomes a useful first pass at understanding sensitivity and should be followed up by a more detailed investigation.

A more detailed investigation can take on a few forms. The first form is to take a set of variables that are to be the subject of sensitivity analysis and *simultaneously* examine the effect of various changes on the dependent parameter. The second approach is to consider these parameters as uncertain quantities themselves and conduct a formal analysis by assessing probability distributions for them.

Let us consider how, for a relatively simple problem, we could simultaneously examine the sensitivity of a set of parameters. Returning to the D&J Systems decision problem (see Figure 8–4), consider the effect of changes in both the quantity and estimated probability of profit contribution for the "distribute brand A only, low price" branch. Suppose that the decision maker was uncertain about both probability ($p$) of high sales and level of profit ($P$), which were originally assumed as \$0.3 million and \$0.8 million respectively. It is relatively simple to calculate (probability, profit) pairs that would lead to EMV values for the "brand A only, low price" branch of \$0.7 million (that is, the same value as the optimal strategy profit).

For the "brand A only, low price" branch

$$\begin{aligned} EMV &= p \times P + (1 - p) \times (-0.1) \\ &= p\,(P + 0.1) - 0.1 \end{aligned}$$

Hence

$p \times (P + 0.1) - 0.1 = 0.7$ (at the break-even point where the EMVs of the two best strategies are equal).

$P = 0.8/p - 0.1$

An infinity of solutions exist to this equation, including:

| *p = Probability of High Sales* | *P = Profit of High Sales ($ million)* |
|---|---|
| 0.5 | 1.5 |
| 0.6 | 1.23 |
| 0.7 | 1.04 |
| 0.8 | 0.9 |
| 0.9 | 0.79 |

Figure 8–5 shows the relationship as a curve and also shows other similar curves. Given this high-quality information base, the decision maker can clearly see the nature of relationships between parameters and their combined effects on EMV. D&J Systems management was able to make an informed assessment of the likelihood that a "brand A only, low price" strategy would have a higher EMV than the base-case optimal strategy based on the sensitivity analysis.

Note that the calculations above assumed that $p$ and $P$ were changed from their base-case assumed values. A number of other relevant parameters were still assumed to be constant, such as the value of profits if low sales eventuated.

If a greater number of variables are included in the simultaneous sensitivity study, interpretations quickly become increasingly difficult to make because of our limits as humans to think in multiple dimensions and process such information effectively. If more complex analyses are required, we cannot generally use graphical methods of representation for more than three parameters at a time and tend to simplify and decompose our analyses to consider subproblems.

In summary, the type and design of a model and the assessed parameter values all have a strong impact on the power of a model to produce useful inferences. Sensitivity analysis not only fosters the questioning of assessments, but also allows the decision maker to *understand the relationships between model inputs and outputs*. Sensitivity analysis provides insight about which assumptions are critical to the analysis and resulting decision strategy. First, model construction sensitivity analysis can question the type and design of a model and result in the consideration of different structures. A second element is sensitivity to parameter estimates in which the effect of different quantitative inputs is measured. Last but not least, we reemphasize that sensitivity analysis should be part of decision analysis process thinking in "real time." This means that it should be an additional decision process consideration that is integrated into every step of the analysis. As such, sensitivity analysis can be much more useful than simple postoptimality analysis.

**FIGURE 8–5** Correlation of Probability ($p$) and Profit ($P$)

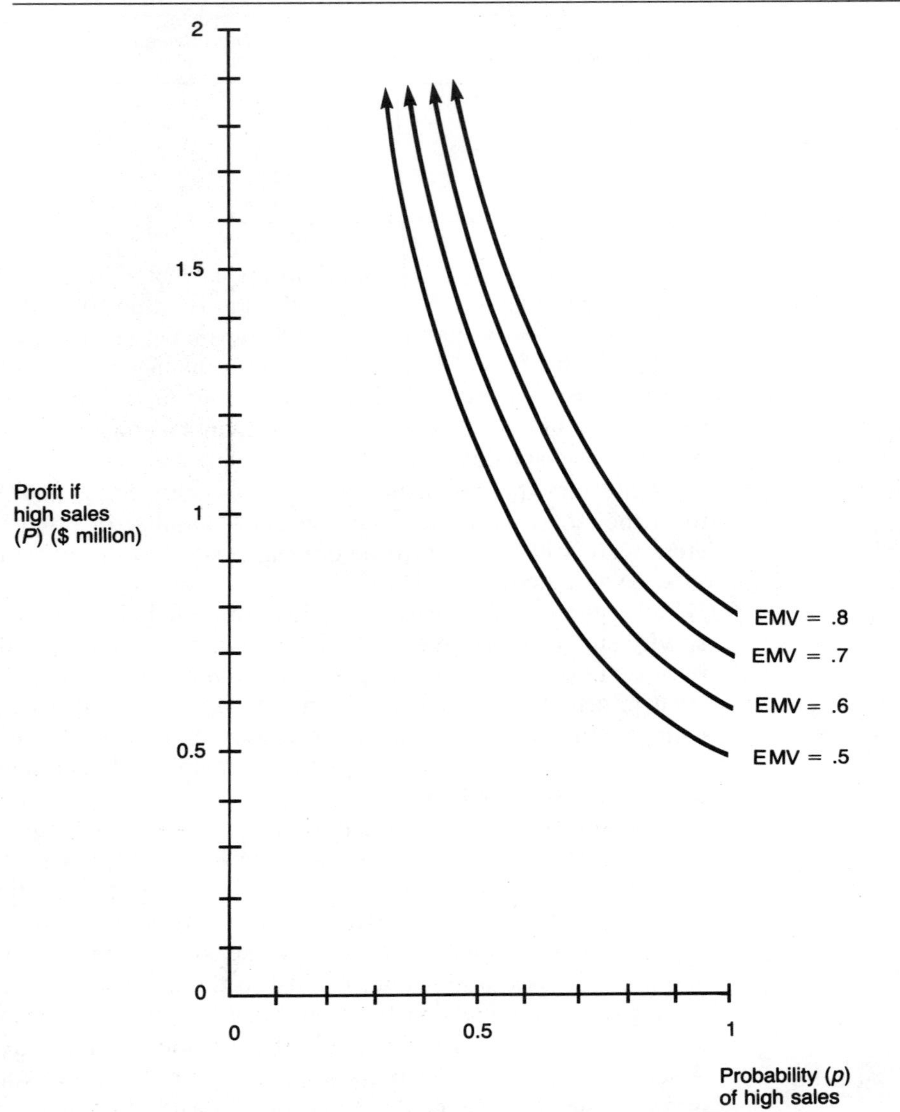

## MODEL SOLUTION SENSITIVITY ANALYSIS

The model solution phase consists of using a decision rule to identify the best strategy. Sensitivity analysis in this context can be used to examine the effect of particular decision rules on the model output. For example, what is the effect of using a unidimensional utility function rather than EMV? Let us deduce what the effects are in general and then study an example. If the utility function is generally concave (representing risk aversion), then, relative to the EMV solution, expected utilities will give lower values and rankings to risky strategies. The converse applies to convex (risk-preferring) utility function representations. These generalizations are useful but rather broad, and it is difficult to draw powerful inferences at a more detailed level on other than a case-by-case basis. For example, what would the general effect be of using a logarithmic utility function rather than an exponential? The logarithmic utility function represents decreasing risk aversion, and the exponential represents constant risk aversion. From our knowledge of these properties, we can make deductions about how the use of one or the other would affect the choice of a decision strategy.

While we can make useful general statements about purely risk-averse and purely risk-preferring utility representations, what about those functions having both concave and convex sections? As discussed in Chapter 6, there is a good deal of evidence to suggest that many decision makers have that sort of utility function. If so, how does the shape of the function affect the decision strategy? When the answer to this question cannot be deduced, the most useful procedure is to perform the numerical sensitivity test and observe the robustness (or lack of robustness) of the decision strategy with respect to these assumptions.

In an earlier chapter we explored the issue of sensitivity to assumed degree of risk aversion (Example 6–6, Solar Technics). The results of the sensitivity analysis were conveniently expressed as a graph (Figure 6–19) showing the expected utility (translated to a certainty equivalent value) for each decision strategy as a function of the degree of risk aversion. In that example, the sensitivity analysis allowed the company president to conclude that the solution was robust to substantial changes in the degree of risk aversion. We note that in Example 6–6, the best EMV strategy was *not* the best expected utility strategy.

The calculations involved in this kind of sensitivity analysis are repetitive in nature and can be performed using a calculator. Many of us find it easier to use a spreadsheet computer package to facilitate these sorts of calculations, or even to write a short program to solve this problem. The advantage of a spreadsheet format is that the results of the parametric or decision rule sensitivity analysis can be automatically graphed using the same software package. Although it is usually a simple matter to write a computer program in a language such as BASIC to do sensitivity analysis, it is not convenient to use BASIC for directly producing graphical forms of output.

For sensitivity analysis in decision analysis, computer packages such as ARBORIST are very useful aids. Once a decision tree is created as an ARBORIST file, it can easily be edited and reexamined with a modified structure or some different data. For parametric sensitivity analysis, ARBORIST recalculates expected values and displays and results in graphical form, using in-built sensitivity analysis functions.

## Multiple Criteria Utility Functions

Another useful form of sensitivity analysis occurs when modeling multiple attributes. In this context, it may be useful to question the effect of attribute definition, model structure, and assessment of coefficients and parameters. We can use sensitivity analysis to ask such questions as:

1. How good a representation do we have of the decision maker's preferences? Are there alternate ways of usefully defining the attributes, and how might these affect the solution?
2. Is the assumed structure of the utility function the only reasonable one? How might other structures drive the problem to a particular decision strategy?
3. How confident are we in the parameter assessments? How do different assessments affect the optimal decision strategy derived from the model?

The first category of questions relates to the criteria discussed in Chapter 7. There is often more than one way to define a set of attributes that are complete, operational, decomposable, nonredundant, and of minimum size. Given these multiple criteria, the process of designing a multiattribute utility function is in itself a difficult multicriteria problem. Trade-offs may be necessary.

For example, with other things being equal, a choice may be necessary between a set of attributes that are highly operational but not easily decomposable, and another set that are less easy to operationalize but easier to decompose. In sensitivity analysis terms, it becomes a useful exercise to investigate how different attribute definitions affect the decision problem and its solution.

The second category of questions above examines the effect of assuming particular multicriteria functional forms. Let us suppose for example, that a linear additive form is first assumed as in Examples 7–5 and 7–6. In each of these examples, what would the model output decision strategy be if a different form was used? In Example 7–5, it might be useful to consider the possibility of an extra term in the utility function as follows:

$$U\begin{pmatrix}\text{market} & \text{rate of} \\ \text{share,} & \text{return}\end{pmatrix} = k_1 U_1\begin{pmatrix}\text{market} \\ \text{share}\end{pmatrix} + k_2 U_2\begin{pmatrix}\text{rate of} \\ \text{return}\end{pmatrix} + k_3 U_1\begin{pmatrix}\text{market} \\ \text{share}\end{pmatrix} \times U_2\begin{pmatrix}\text{rate of} \\ \text{return}\end{pmatrix}$$

The third term models interactive effects. For example if high levels of market share and rate of return were individually preferred but for some reason the simultaneous occurrence of high levels or low levels of both was particularly abhorred or desired above and beyond that which the first two terms capture, then the third term may be a useful addition. The effect of adding such a term to the equation is a sensitivity analysis issue. How much better does the model become by adding such extra terms? Is the improved representation worth the extra model complexity and the added assessments that must be made?

---

## EXAMPLE 8–3

### Car Purchasing Revisited

Consider the car purchase decision (Example 7–6). While doing his basic analysis, Geoff decided that not all the attributes he had defined were perfectly independent of each other. Let us recall that "independence" in this context does not refer to probabilistic or statistical independence but rather *independence of preferences* in a set of attributes. In particular, Geoff decided that he would feel somewhat different about the general driveability of a car based on its comfort. He felt that if comfort was high, his feeling (that is, his preference) for general driveability would be generally better than if comfort was low. He saw that car 2 in Table 7–2 had a low score on "general driveability" but high "comfort." He wanted to increase the score for car 2 because of the synergy that he felt for these two attributes. He believed that a "comfort" score of nine (car 2) should lead him to appreciate "general driveability" by more than the raw score of three and its inclusion in the additive model could account for. Temporarily ignoring the various other attributes, Geoff felt that his preferences for comfort and general driveability were not captured by his individual preferences. In utility function terms:

$$U(\text{comfort, general driveability}) \neq U_1\,(\text{comfort}) + U_2\,(\text{general driveability})$$

Two main strategies are available. The first is to use a more complex model that includes a representation of dependence. However, Geoff did not want to proceed so formally, and chose instead to estimate a reasonable adjustment amount for "general driveability." He thought about adding a term to the utility function but thought that to do so would introduce a number of complexities he did not want to deal with. Instead he merely noted the fact that for car 2, the "comfort" rating was nine as against six and seven for cars 1 and 3. This higher comfort level caused him to revalue the "general driveability" from three to five. On following through his model, he noted that the appropriate attribute weight was 1.5, so the revaluation adjustment added three points to the car 2 total score. This brought the car 2 score closer to the car 3 score, but did not change the overall rankings.

Another sensitivity analysis question relates to the completeness and redundancy of the set of attributes. The decision maker should consider whether all the important attributes have been included exactly once. Missing out or double counting some dimension of value may significantly affect the model solution. For example, if the attribute "general driveability" had been completely omitted from the analysis, the rankings would be changed, and car 2 would be the highest ranked. It is often useful to check on whether the solution is sensitive to such changes.

For multiattribute utility functions the third category of model solution sensitivity analysis concerns the quantitative assessments. Again, looking at the assessments in Table 7-2 (Example 7-6), sensitivity analysis seeks to determine the effect of different assumptions and assessments on the results. In that example, we note the difference between the first- and second-ranked alternatives as 5.8 utiles. Since the attribute weights were all 2.2 or less, a single change would have to be of magnitude 3 on a 0 to 10 scale to change the rankings. An example of such a change is for "engineering quality" to be assessed as six instead of nine for car 3. Although single changes have to be quite large to change the car rankings, a combination of two or more feasible small changes could have the same effect. The situation with attribute weights is similar. For example, a change in attribute weight from 1.5 to 2 is a substantial change, yet relative scores would generally change by less than three utiles as a result of this alteration.

For the car purchase example, we can generally conclude that for most small single changes of numerical assessments, the rankings are robust. However, the difference in utility scores between the two best cars is only 5.8/73.5 = 8%, which does not represent an overwhelmingly dominant preference by any means. Any two or more small numerical changes or a structural or definitional change may have resulted in different rankings.

---

In summary, the solution stage of decision analysis requires the application of a decision rule. In many cases it is useful to examine the effect on the solution of choosing different decision rules. For multiple criteria models, the elements of model type, design (structure), and assessment determine the utiles and rankings of strategies. These model inputs should be closely examined to see how they affect the model outputs, checking the robustness of the results to alternate sets of assumptions.

## MODEL INTERPRETATION SENSITIVITY ANALYSIS

Many decision and management science books suggest that the model interpretation stage is where the analyst should perform sensitivity analysis. Put more strongly, some argue that the model interpretation stage *is* the sensitivity analysis! Using the framework of the embedded, integrated concept of sensitivity analysis developed in this chapter, the model interpretation phase is where the lessons learned from the modeling process are translated into relevant knowledge about the real problem. See Figure 8–2. Here we determine which of the inferences from the model can be applied to the real problem, and how.

Sensitivity analysis in the model interpretation stage is the point at which the modeling process should be reviewed in a critical manner. It is a point in the analysis at which we should say: *"What has the modeling process taught us that is relevant to the problem?"* As pointed out in earlier chapters, the things that we learn from modeling are certainly not limited to the bottom-line decision strategy the model identifies as optimal.

In this phase of the analysis we are interested in identifying the assumptions that may have limited the realism of the model. What alternative assumptions could have been made to allow us to improve the power of the model? Note the feedback loops on Figure 8–2, which indicate that we may choose to reformulate or modify the model at this stage, or any other.

At the model interpretation stage it is also useful to review the decision process more generally. It is often useful to try to envisage what course of real action would have been taken in the complete absence of a decision modeling (decision analysis) process. That holistic solution can be compared to the decision strategy suggested by the model.

Ultimately, the decision maker should ask the question: "What do I know now that I didn't know before?" Further, the decision maker should consciously make a choice about whether any further decision modeling is warranted.

---

### EXAMPLE 8–4

### Midwestern Utility Revisited

Consider the decision faced by Midwestern Utility described in Chapter 2. (Midwestern had to choose between going to court or settling beforehand.) Having drawn a decision tree and performed a decision tree analysis, it was useful for the decision makers to review their decision process and consider its value. If we compare their state of knowledge about the real problem before and after the analysis process, we observe the following:

1. Initially, there was a considerable fuzziness about what the problem was and what were the key decision elements.
2. A process of model structuring fostered the identification of the problem and its representation as a decision tree model. This process created structural clarity. The fog was beginning to clear.
3. It was useful to quantify parameters. These estimates helped to identify which strategies seemed feasible.
4. The process formally allowed for inputs from experts. These inputs were directly used as model inputs.
5. It was possible to experiment with different decision tree structures and numbers to check the robustness of the solution strategy.
6. The modeling process took a messy, unclear problem and provided the insight for the decision makers to make what they perceived to be a rational, informed decision.
7. Sensitivity analysis pervaded the whole analysis process. Alternative problem definitions were considered. Different model structures were created. More than one set of assessments were made. Model validity was questioned.

---

Throughout all these sensitivity analysis stages, the goal of generating insight to help solve the real problem was kept in mind. To conclude this section on model interpretation sensitivity analysis, we reemphasize that it is important to review the assumptions made throughout the analysis process because these assumptions have a strong influence on the power and usefulness of the insights that are generated. This sensitivity analysis, which occurs before a final choice is made, keeps us "humble" in the sense that it helps us to distinguish the complex real problem from the simple model. As a result, we are likely to be able to successfully refocus our thinking from the model back to the complexities of the real problem before committing to a real action.

## SENSITIVITY TO FINAL CHOICE

In making a final choice, we must revert from an analytic framework (that focuses on decomposition) to a holistic philosophy and mode of thinking. In this stage of the decision process, we must realistically consider the *real problem* (which should be well-defined by now) and some alternate *real actions*. The decision analysis process has not changed the real problem at all. The sources of uncertainty still exist, and the real uncertainty has not been lessened or increased as a result of the analysis process. However, the analysis process has improved our understanding of the problem, measurement of the uncertainty and of our own risk attitudes and preference functions. Using the insight that was generated by the modeling process we must make a real decision "under uncertainty." In this context, sensitivity analysis questions are:

1. How well does the final choice (of a decision strategy) solve the problem? Here we are concerned with real actions and the real problem, not models.
2. How do alternate real actions compare with each other? Do they have a similar effect on the problem, or are they significantly different?

At this stage, we must account for the real problem complexities that may not have been addressed by the model.

---

## EXAMPLE 8–5

### Eurocorp Auto Equipment

Eurocorp was a large company that manufactured a wide range of car accessories and parts in Europe, ranging from power steering and cruise-control equipment, to car batteries and alarms systems. A recent product development breakthrough was a cheap device for saving fuel in diesel engines by premixing a small amount of hot air with fuel in a chamber and injecting this (nonexplosive) fuel-air mixture into the cylinder (where it was mixed with more air and became explosive). The device could be added relatively easily to existing engines. Eurocorp's directors had decided to manufacture the product in the United States after a successful European market had developed and a test market in Baltimore proved promising.

After considering a number of locations and factory process designs, a short list of three was considered. The thinking within Eurocorp was that any of the three would be satisfactory but a best solution was desired. A team of Eurocorp people went on a tour of the sites to collect detailed data and negotiate on local taxes, land, construction, utility and labor costs, labor availability, degree of unionization, proximity to distribution centers, and a host of other factors relevant to the decision. A decision analysis model was used to incorporate uncertainty about various costs and sales volumes given certain location factors, distribution and price strategies, and facility designs.

When the analysis was completed, after a number of revisions and refinements, the time came for the chief executive officer of Eurocorp to commit the company to a strategy and allocate the necessary resources. The CEO considered the analysis carefully and then returned to his original problem definition. He looked at the real

**FIGURE 8–6** Possible Plant Locations for Eurocorp

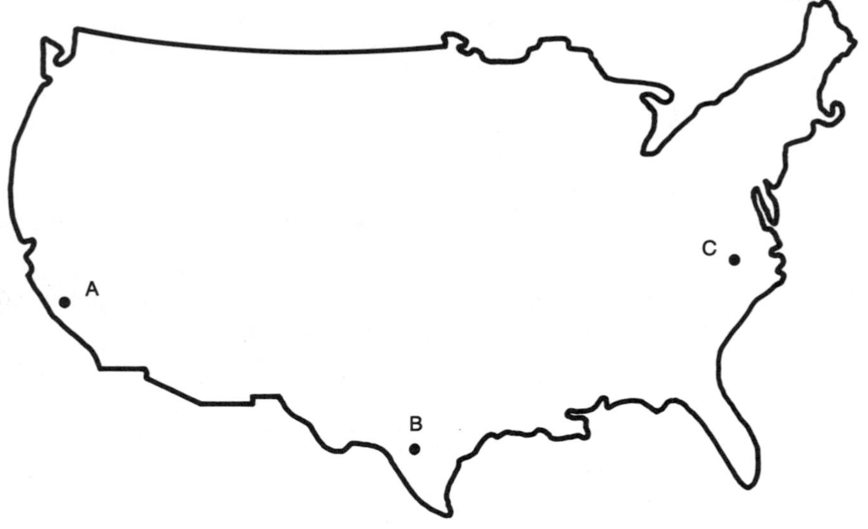


actions he had to choose between. He thought that the model did a very good job of determining which solution was best, and his analytical experts had carefully stated their assumptions of tax rates, inflation rates, prices, etc. However, they had considered the problem as limited to a single facility plan only, whereas the CEO was now thinking of a broader problem of locating one facility this year and a second and possibly third facility after about three years.

Whereas location B (see Figure 8–6) seemed to be most desirable if only one facility was to be built, this location was not clearly the best solution to the multiplant "dynamic" problem the CEO was considering. The chief executive decided to rethink the problem as a multiperiod, multifacility, capacity and production facility problem. He realized that the location and system design that was the optimal solution to the single-facility problem might not be a part of the best solution to the longer-term problem. The decision needed to incorporate the trade-offs between what was best in the short term and what would be optimal over a longer time horizon. When he suggested this to his analysts, they modified their model and suggested that a strategy of "location C now and location A in three years" was best. The chief executive noted that a relatively simple reformulation of the problem definition and context caused a substantially different recommended strategy. He then sat down with his assistants to review the problem again and make the difficult choice.

---

This example illustrates how the original problem definition and model construction phases shape the recommended decision strategy that comes from the model. The choice of a real action is critically dependent on the problem definition. During that choice phase, the relevance of various feasible real actions to the real problem should be investigated. In the Eurocorp example, a single-plant location decision was initially modeled, and the choice in this instance may well have proved to be unsatisfactory when a more realistic (potential multifacility) problem was considered. Referring to Figure 8–2, as part of the "final choice" phase, the decision maker may require the revision of a number of the previous steps. In practice, this happens quite frequently because it is at the final choice phase where major sums of money are committed.

In the Eurocorp example, a plant located at site B may be a very good solution for three to five years, but after that the company may be wishing that it had two plants (at sites A and C). The concept of regret (see Chapter 5) is a useful one in this context. Note that the key decision element that changed when the problem was reformulated was the time horizon.

## SENSITIVITY TO REAL ACTION

After the final choice of a decision strategy is made, the decision is implemented. Typically, a decision strategy is chosen without all the details being known in the sense that it is usually impossible to foresee all the consequences of a decision. As the decision strategy becomes known within an organization, there is often a need to modify it and to make a number of *supplementary decisions*. The process of *implementation* requires the decision maker to *monitor* and *control* the real action in the context of the problem. From these implementation experiences there is often much to be learned, both about the effectiveness of the chosen decision strategy and about the usefulness of the decision process.

Consider as an example, the economic management of a national economy. This is something that we are all able to observe on an ongoing basis. Governments use a number of instruments, including fiscal and monetary policy devices, to guide the course of an economy. In the context of this example we can bring to life the aspects of decision analysis implementation. Economies are continuously monitored. Hundreds of different statistics are compiled on daily, weekly, monthly, and yearly bases. The analysis of these statistics leads to decisions, policies, and actions. Suppose, for example, that a government makes a decision to tighten the primary money supply by a certain amount. Once the decision is implemented, careful monitoring provides information that may lead to subsequent money supply decisions, fine-tuning of the original action, or complementary actions in other spheres of the economy (for example, tax policy).

The fundamental implementation issue is one of sensitivity analysis: "How well does the chosen action solve the problem?" It is usual to make some initial observations about the effectiveness of a decision strategy and then ask "what if" questions about further developments. These developments may be either chance events that become resolved through time or subsequent events over which the decision maker has control. Note that at this point we are no longer considering the decision analysis from the analytic viewpoint but have chosen a strategy and are watching our progress in real time as we make our way through the decision tree. In most cases it is inevitable that we learn more about the problem as time passes, and it is useful to be thinking continually about "what if" issues (that is, sensitivity analysis) during the implementation phase. This monitoring may lead us to modify our thinking and possibly even change our decision strategy in midcourse in some cases.

**FIGURE 8-7** Managerial Decision Analysis

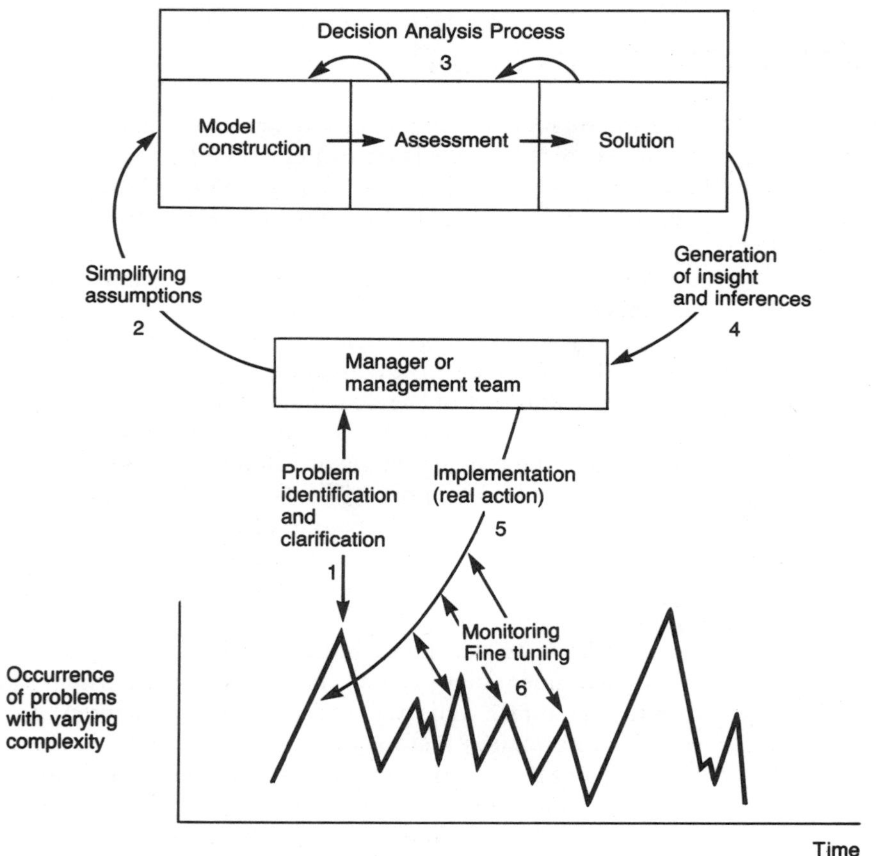

The process of implementing decisions in real time is quite different in nature from the planning perspective taken during the decision model construction and analysis phases. Figure 8–7 represents managerial processes which, in real time, deal with problems that occur on an ongoing basis. As problems are identified (continually through time), analyses are conducted, and decision strategies are chosen and implemented. Fine tuning of decision strategies occurs almost continuously through time also. This diagram illustrates how the manager of a system (such as an economy or a public or private organizational unit) interactively moves through problem identification, analysis, and implementation stages.

In Figure 8–7, stage 1 is the problem identification and clarification stage. This is followed by the setting up of the decision analysis (stage 2). Stage 3 is the decision analysis process itself, including a number of sensitivity analyses as previously described. Stage 4 is the generation of insights through the use of decision analysis. Stage 5 is the choice and initial implementation of a real action. Stage 6 is the monitoring and control of the problem, including subsequent fine tuning of decisions.

The manager monitors the system on a continuing basis and fine tunes his decision strategies accordingly. This *prescriptive* view of managerial activity relies heavily on a continuous questioning of decision strategy effectiveness and decision analysis assumptions. The emphasis that this view is prescriptive is to distinguish it from various descriptive views of managers and management processes. Our view is predicated on the assumption that management is a continual process of decision making. Within this framework, sensitivity to real action is the process of following decision strategies through, collecting information, and modifying those strategies where necessary.

## SUMMARY

Figure 8–2 summarizes the integrated approach that incorporates sensitivity analysis into virtually all aspects of decision analysis processes. This state of continuous sensitivity on the part of the decision maker to assumptions and assessments fosters an awareness of the dependence of model solutions on model inputs. It also provides clarity of distinction between the real problem and real action, on one hand, and the elements of the model, on the other.

Sensitivity analysis to model structuring assumptions can enhance the creativity process. Questioning the validity of assumptions naturally leads to lateral thinking about other possible assumptions. This may, in turn, lead to the discovery of a new way of defining the problem or of a new potential decision strategy or relevant source of uncertainty.

Sensitivity analysis with respect to the assessment of parameters gives the decision maker a feel for what are the important driving forces in a problem as well as knowledge about the robustness of various decision strategies.

A decision analysis process that involves a single pass through each phase and only a postoptimality sensitivity analysis is very unlikely to be as useful as an integrative process that involves almost continuous "what if" questioning and recycling from one phase to another. Hence a decision process, as shown in Figure 8–2 is generally likely to provide better decision support than a once-through process, as shown in Figure 8–1.

## FURTHER READING

Most textbooks on quantitative analysis in general and decision analysis in particular focus on only one form of sensitivity analysis. That is the parametric analysis that considers the effect of plugging in different numerical assessments on the model solution.

A broader approach has been suggested by Thomas and Samson (1986) in considering subjective aspects of decision analysis. This more flexible concept of decision analysis argues for a multiple set of passes through each phase of a complex decision analysis as follows (1986, p. 235):

> There is less concern about methodological issues such as probability and utility assessment. More attention is now given to aiding the decision maker in problem formulation, screening of alternative options, and in promoting effective dialogue about problem characteristics and policy issues. In other words, the important principle in modifying decision analysis should be that formulation and evaluation of ill-structured problems requires a creative mix of analytic inputs and continual debate. It must be recognized that it is almost impossible to undertake anything other than an exploratory and preliminary analysis at the first attempt. If so, this "first pass" analysis should be documented and subjected to critical comment and review by the policy-making group. In the course of this process, debate about the problem will become more focused around questioning of assumptions, generation of further alternatives and anticipation of future contingencies. . . .
>
> This modified decision analysis is an approach and a broad investigative research strategy rather than a technique, and is not necessarily performed in a series of sequential steps. Some steps may be excluded or handled in an informal manner. The order of the steps may be varied and, indeed, the relevance of the objective structure, problem assumptions and the importance of excluded factors may be continually reassessed. In particular, the philosophy of the modified decision analysis approach strongly emphasizes the point that the identification of new options is even more important and necessary than anchoring firmly on analysis and evaluation as goals of the analysis.

These views support a multipass process where assumptions are constantly challenged and the decision process is flexible in being able to contain a variety of cycles through various phases of it.

Keeney and Raiffa (1976) discuss some issues related to parametric sensitivity analysis in the context of both unidimensional and multidimensional utility functions. Hertz and Thomas (1983) present a sensitivity analysis and discuss and advantages of sensitivity analysis relative to the use of risk analysis procedures. They also mention a form of structural sensitivity whereby: "A preliminary sensitivity analysis is often used to screen and identify those input variables which need to be specified in probabilistic form." (Hertz and Thomas, 1983, p. 2.)

A number of articles have been written that develop mathematical methods for conducting parametric sensitivity analysis. For the technically oriented reader, articles that should be of interest include two published in *Decision Sciences* [Evans (1984) and Schneller and Sphicas (1985)] and two from the *Engineering Economist* [Beenhakker (1975) and Findlay (1975)]. These articles all focus on questioning the quantitative assessments and model structure aspects of sensitivity analysis.

The broader issues of sensitivity analysis have not been adequately focused on by many decision science researchers. The issues of sensitivity analysis in problem identification and the generation of alternative solutions require processes of creative thinking. Edward de Bono has written extensively in this field and popularized the concept of lateral thinking. Most social science, business school, and general libraries contain some of de Bono's works, and they are strongly recommended for the reader who wishes to learn more about processes of questioning assumptions and creative thinking. Reference to several of de Bono's reports are listed at the end of this chapter. Processes of creative thinking in problem definition are also referred to by Howard (1986) who discusses errors of the third kind, and by Evans (1986) in the context of decision sciences. Evans's discussion includes such concepts as brainstorming, deliberate provocation (to create new ideas), and lateral thinking. Finally, Schwenk and Thomas (1983) have investigated the role of decision aids in problem formulation processes, and Woolley and Pidd (1981) have considered a variety of problem structuring methodologies.

## REFERENCES

BEENHAKKER, H. L. 1975. "Sensitivity Analysis of the Present Value of a Project." *The Engineering Economist* 20, pp. 123–149.

BROWN, R. V., and D. LINDLEY. 1986. "Plural Analysis: Multiple Approaches to Quantitative Research." *Theory and Decision.*

*DE BONO, E. 1969. The Mechanism of Mind.* New York: Simon & Schuster.

———. 1977. Information Processing and New Ideas—Lateral and Vertical Thinking. In *Guide to Creative Action,* eds. S. J. Parnes; R. B. Noller; and A. M. Biondi. New York: Charles Scribner's Sons.

———. 1984. *Tactics: The Art and Science of Success.* Boston: Little Brown.

———. 1986. "Ideas about Thinking: Excerpts from Edward de Bono's *Letters to*

*Thinkers.*'' *Journal of Production and Innovation Management* 3, no. 1, pp. 57–62.

EVANS, J. R. 1984. ''Sensitivity Analysis in Decision Theory.'' *Decision Sciences* 15, no. 2 (Spring), pp. 239–47.

________. 1986. ''Creative Thinking and Innovative Education in the Decision Sciences.'' *Decision Sciences* 17, no. 2, pp. 250–62.

FINDLAY, M. C., III. 1975. ''A Sensitivity Analysis of IRR Leasing Models.'' *Engineering Economist* 20, no. 2, pp. 123–49.

HAYES, R., and S. WHEELWRIGHT. 1984. *Restoring Our Competitive Edge*. New York: John Wiley & Sons.

HERTZ, D.B., and H. THOMAS. 1983. *Risk Analysis and Its Applications*. New York: John Wiley & Sons.

HOWARD, R. A. 1986. *An Appreciation of Decision Analysis*. Paper presented at ORSA/TIMS meeting, April, Los Angeles.

MOORE, P. G., H. THOMAS, D. W. BUNN, and J. HAMPTON. 1976. *Case Studies in Decision Analysis*. New York: Penguin Books.

SCHNELLER, G. O., and G. SPHICAS. 1985. ''On Sensitivity Analysis in Decision Theory.'' *Decision Sciences* 16, pp. 399–409.

SCHWENK, C. R., and H. THOMAS. 1983. ''Formulating the Mess: The Role of Decision Aids in Problem Formulation.'' *Omega* 10, no. 2, pp. 1–14.

THOMAS, H., and D. A. SAMSON. 1986. ''Subjective Aspects of the Art of Decision Analysis: Exploring the Role of Decision Structuring, Decision Support, and Policy Dialogue.'' *Journal of the Operational Research Society* 37, no. 3, pp. 249–65.

WOOLLEY, R. N., and M. PIDD. 1981. ''Problem Structuring—A Literature Review.'' *Journal of the Operational Research Society* 32, pp. 197–206.

## PROBLEMS

1. What does sensitivity analysis generally mean? What is the object and subject of sensitivity analysis?
2. In operations research, sensitivity analysis is usually confined to postoptimality analysis. Explain this concept.
3. In decision analysis, the same postoptimality view of sensitivity analysis is possible as expressed in question 2, above. Compare this concept with the broader definition and process of sensitivity analysis discussed in this chapter.
4. What is an error of the third kind?
5. Can we be absolutely certain that we have correctly defined a decision problem? If so, how can we achieve this state of certainty? If not, how can we know when to stop refining our problem definition and begin formulating a decision model?

6. Compare the cyclic process of decision analysis (Figure 8–2), which incorporates sensitivity analysis into each step, with the more streamlined process (Figure 8–1). Which form of process is likely to be more flexible? Which is simpler? Which is faster to implement? Which is likely to be more effective in generating insights about complex problems?
7. What are the various types of sensitivity analysis as defined in this chapter? How can they enrich the decision analysis process?
8. Consider the problem facing Professor Ambivalent described in Chapter 3. He could have defined his problem a number of different ways. What were they? Is one definition better than another? Could different problem definitions have led to different decision strategies?
9. In the XYZ Manufacturing example (Example 8–1), it was possible to define a marketing, production, financial management, or a more general strategic problem. Give a brief description of each one. Is it possible for different people in the same organization to define a problem so differently? Which view of the problem is the most relevant one for the company?
10. In constructing a decision tree model, what general steps should be followed? Can different decision trees be used to model a problem?
11. How can a decision maker best ensure that the juxtaposition of decision elements in a decision tree is correct?
12. What is plural analysis?
13. How can the level of detail in a decision tree vary? If the decision maker in Example 8–2, D&J Systems, had wanted to include a more detailed description of the chance event nodes on the decision tree, how could it be done? Draw a decision tree with twice as many possible outcomes as in Figure 8–4.
14. D&J Systems owners were looking at a number of other possible business expansion options in addition to the cosmetics opportunity. If we redefine the problem to include a number of these, how can the decision analysis (Figure 8–4) be used in the broader context?
15. Consider Figure 8–4. Suppose that the profit contribution on the "distribute both brands, low price strategy, high sales" branch was only \$1.7 million instead of \$1.9 million. Would the optimal decision strategy change? What is the break-even point for this parameter that would lead to the two best strategies having the same EMV?
16. In the D&J Systems example, suppose that two parameters are allowed to change simultaneously. They are the probabilities on the bottom branches of Figure 8–4:

$$p = P(\text{high sales/both brands, high price})$$
$$q = P(\text{high sales/both brands, low price})$$

Form an equation in terms of $p$ and $q$ that defines the region in which the low price strategy has a higher EMV than the high price strategy. Plot this line on a $p$-$q$ graph and identify the regions on either side of the line.

17. Consider Figure 8–4. Use the methodology outlined in problem 16 to perform pair-wise comparisons of the three options (brand A only, brand B only, both brands) assuming a high price strategy.
18. Consider Figure 8–4. For the branch "both brands, high price strategy," let $x$ be the probability of high sales (base case .2) and $X$ be the profit contribution if sales are high (base case \$1.1 million) on this branch. Let both these parameters vary, and calculate a number of $(x,X)$ pairs so that the EMV of this branch is \$0.6, \$0.7, \$0.8, \$0.9, and \$1.0 million. Plot these lines on a graph showing $x$ on the vertical axis and $X$ on the horizontal axis.
19. Use ARBORIST to solve problem 15 above.
20. Can ARBORIST be used to solve problem 16 above? Is two-way simultaneous sensitivity analysis possible on ARBORIST, or does it need a series of one-way analyses?
21. Set up the D&J Systems decision tree (Figure 8–4) on ARBORIST. Use it to check the sensitivity of all the probability pairs (there are six altogether) to see which ones can affect the optimal decision strategy as identified on Figure 8–4.

## Case Study

### Digmout Mines Inc. (A)

The management of a foreign subsidiary of Digmout Mines mining company was facing a difficult decision. The company owned and operated a number of mines in the foreign country, and there was a good deal of industrial unrest in the industry that was rapidly spreading and escalating. The original source of the problem was a claim for more pay. The more militant union faction had gained a lot of support as a result of a mining accident that had resulted in a number of fatalities. Figure 8–8 shows the decision tree that the divisional CEO had constructed. Three major options were open to the company in his view. The miners were currently at work but were engaged in a work slowdown. Production rates averaged about 60% of normal volumes, and under these conditions the mines were losing money fast. Calculations had been made based on a three-month time horizon. It was assumed that everything would be settled one way or the other by that time. Profit contributions were estimated in

**FIGURE 8–8** An Industrial Relations Decision Problem (Digmout Mines Inc.)

| Decision | Outcome | Profit Contributions ($ million) |
|---|---|---|
| Give in | Cost high (.1) | 40 |
| | Cost medium (.3) | 70 |
| | Cost low (.6) | 80 |
| Arbitration | Cost high (.1) | 60 |
| | Cost medium (.6) | 70 |
| | Cost low (.3) | 80 |
| Negotiate hard | They give in (.1) | 80 |
| | Standoff (.4) | 55 |
| | They strike (.5) | 40 |

millions of dollars and placed at the ends of the decision tree branches. After a series of meetings with various experts, probabilities were also assigned to various possible chance outcomes.

If management gave in to the wage demands, full production would be immediately resumed, but the future cost of this action was uncertain because it was not clear as to how much "flow on" would occur to other mines and possibly other industries.

A second alternative was to agree with the union to engage in a process of arbitration, which would be an agreement to abide by the decision of a neutral third party. If this path were chosen, the outcome was highly uncertain. Digmout's divisional chief had assessed payoffs and probabilities based on a three-level structure of possible arbitration outcomes.

A third alternative was to follow Digmout's usual practice and negotiate hard with the union, possibly risking a long period of work slowdown and a possible strike.

Note that the profit contributions shown on the decision tree are over a six-month period and include substantial profits made in the previous quarter. The magnitude of difference between the best and worst outcome ($40 million) shows the magnitude of the decision.

## CASE QUESTIONS

1. Roll the decision tree back using the EMV criterion and rank the strategies according to their EMVs.
2. Construct risk profiles for each strategy. Calculate variances, and rank the strategies in terms of their riskiness.

3. The CEO of Digmout's foreign division had recently used a decision analysis consultant who had assessed the risk attitude of the division's top level executives. He telephoned the consultant and asked for a specification of a utility function which would be a representative one for the company. The consultant said that he thought an exponential function would be most appropriate, because he had observed approximately constant risk aversion in conducting his study. The consultant was reluctant to give a single figure for the function constant, but estimated the limits of a range which he said would contain the true value as:

   $$1 \times 10^{-7}\ \$^{-1} \text{ to a maximum of } 5 \times 10^{-7}\ \$^{-1}$$

   Calculate the expected utility and certainty equivalent values for each decision strategy for these values and others inside the range, and plot the certainty equivalent values for each decision strategy as a function of the degree of risk aversion. What was the optimal strategy as suggested by the expected utility rule? Are the rankings sensitive to the risk-aversion parameter? Is the expected utility solution identical to the EMV solution? (Hint: writing a short computer program can ease the burden of calculation in this exercise.)
4. The CEO was less than confident that the specified range was correct. He extended the range to $5 \times 10^{-8}$ to $8 \times 10^{-7}$. Replicate his results, and interpret them.
5. The CEO also wanted to check on what would have resulted if he had used a logarithmic utility function instead of an exponential. Apply a logarithmic function with risk aversion of $1.5 \times 10^{-7}$ and compare the rankings with those for an exponential with the same degree of risk aversion.
6. When the divisional CEO checked with the parent company head office before making a decision, the parent's CEO had a number of things to say. His first reaction was that the use of a divisional utility function was not a reasonable procedure. He argued that the division was wholly owned, hence, the parent company's utility function was the appropriate one. The parent company used an exponential function with risk aversion of $2 \times 10^{-7}\ \$^{-1}$. Did the use of the parent company's utility function lead to a different ranking?
7. The parent company's CEO also commented that the choice of a time horizon for the decision tree seemed critical. The assumptions of three months into the future and six months (three past, three future) on the cash flows were criticized as arbitrary and too short. Comment on whether the choice of a time horizon might be important. If the future time horizon were increased to 12 months, might the rankings of the strategies change? If so, why?

CHAPTER NINE

# Simulation in Decision Analysis

## OUTLINE



## OBJECTIVES

After completing this chapter, you should be able to:

1. Discuss the risk analysis process and note its contribution to decision analysis.
2. Distinguish between the expected value/rollback approach and the risk analysis (simulation) rollforward approach.
3. Describe the strengths and weaknesses of various approaches to investment analysis.
4. Apply the Monte Carlo method and use simulation in decision analysis problems.
5. Interpret the output of a risk analysis.
6. Merge the risk analysis/simulation process into a decision analysis/expected utility process where rollback is infeasible.

## INTRODUCTION

This chapter focuses on simulation procedures that are an effective way of analyzing uncertainty in complex decision problems. Some decision trees are so large, involving many thousands or even hundreds of thousands of end points, that the complete evaluation of the various strategies is difficult or impossible. Where such large and complex decision trees exist, we can effectively evaluate strategies by *sampling* branches from the tree and calculating probability distributions of important variables. This process, which involves *randomly choosing paths* through a large decision tree, is called *Monte Carlo simulation*. Like any sampling process, the result is usually not perfectly accurate, however, as sample size increases, accuracy increases and acceptably good answers are not difficult to achieve. This field of decision analysis, involving strategy evaluation where decision trees are large and where each strategy encompasses a large number of possible events, is also called *risk analysis*. Risk analysis is best conceptualized as a special case or part of decision analysis. It features powerful simulation methods for evaluating strategies in complex decision trees.

In this chapter we will define the process of risk analysis as a set of steps paralleling the stages of decision analysis (see Chapter 2). Further, we will provide a detailed examination of simulation procedures to allow the reader to set up sampling processes when decision trees become very large.

First, let us consider a brief example that illustrates how relatively simple problems can lead to huge decision trees. A financial controller was considering an investment in fixed assets with uncertain cash flow ramifications over 10 years. For each of these years, he assessed a probability distribution comprising five discrete outcome events. The total number of endpoints on a decision tree, for each strategy, is: $5 \times 5 \times 5 \times 5 \times 5 \times 5 \times 5 \times 5 \times 5 \times 5$. This number is $5^{10}$, or 9,765,625. This rather simple problem involving independent yearly cash flows over 10 years leads to a decision tree with almost 10 million endpoints (see Figure 9–1). The rollback procedure of decision analysis is infeasible!

The primary purpose of risk analysis, as a particular form or part of decision analysis, is to evaluate individual decision strategies on very large decision trees, usually through extensively sampling the branches from that tree.

Risk analysis can also be used as a comprehensive extension of the concept of parametric sensitivity analysis. Whereas sensitivity analysis often involves changing the value of one or sometimes two variables at a time from their base-case assumption, risk analysis methods allow the decision maker to represent all parameters about which there is uncertainty as random variables. Where a decison tree is structurally so large that rollback is infeasible, Monte Carlo methods are a powerful alternative. *The main contribution of risk analysis is in carefully analyzing the combined effects of multiple sources of uncertainty to produce an aggregate picture of total*

**FIGURE 9–1** An Investment Decision Tree with Uncertain Cash Flows

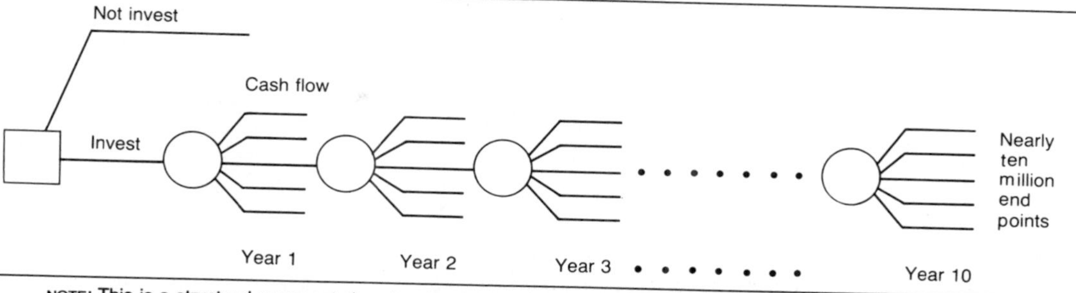


NOTE: This is a structural representation showing the model structure but not all the branches and nodes.

*uncertainty*. This picture is in the form of a probability distribution on some relevant decision variable. In decision analysis the rollback procedure can involve both decision and chance event nodes, whereas in risk analysis the primary analysis generally involves chance event nodes only and decisions based on such analyses are made separately.

## THE STAGES OF RISK ANALYSIS

Risk analyses are generally implemented according to the set of steps defined in Figure 9–2, many of which are identical to decision analysis steps. Note also that "feedback looping" between steps usually occurs. For example, after step 3 is completed, steps 1 or 2 may be revisited. The looping occurs because the decision maker learns more and more about the problem through the process of analysis. Indeed many experienced analysts claim that the value of risk analysis lies at least as much in what they learn from the process as from the numerical answers.

The steps are summarized in Figure 9–2, and their description follows.

### Step 1: Define the Problem

In this step the bounds of the problem must first be defined and alternative actions and sources of uncertainty identified. An example of a problem may be that a company's profits are not reaching expectations in a particular product line. From this broad definition, there follows a number of possibilities. First, either profits must be raised or expectations lowered or both. If profits are to be raised, should this be accomplished through raising revenue or lowering cost? More specifically, if costs are to be lowered should the emphasis be on reducing fixed costs or variable costs? Should the emphasis be on production, financing, or marketing costs? If marketing budgets are trimmed, how will revenue be affected?

**FIGURE 9–2** The Stages of a Risk Analysis

1. Problem Definition
Define possible actions, uncertainties, time horizon
2. Model Construction
Define variables
Choose level of detail
3. Input Variable Assessment
Define variable ranges, probability distributions
4. Calculation
Analytic or Monte Carlo methods
5. Model Output Interpretation
Compile and check results, question initial assumptions, perform sensitivity analysis
6. Decision Making
Using the output to aid in choice
Stochastic dominance, expected utility

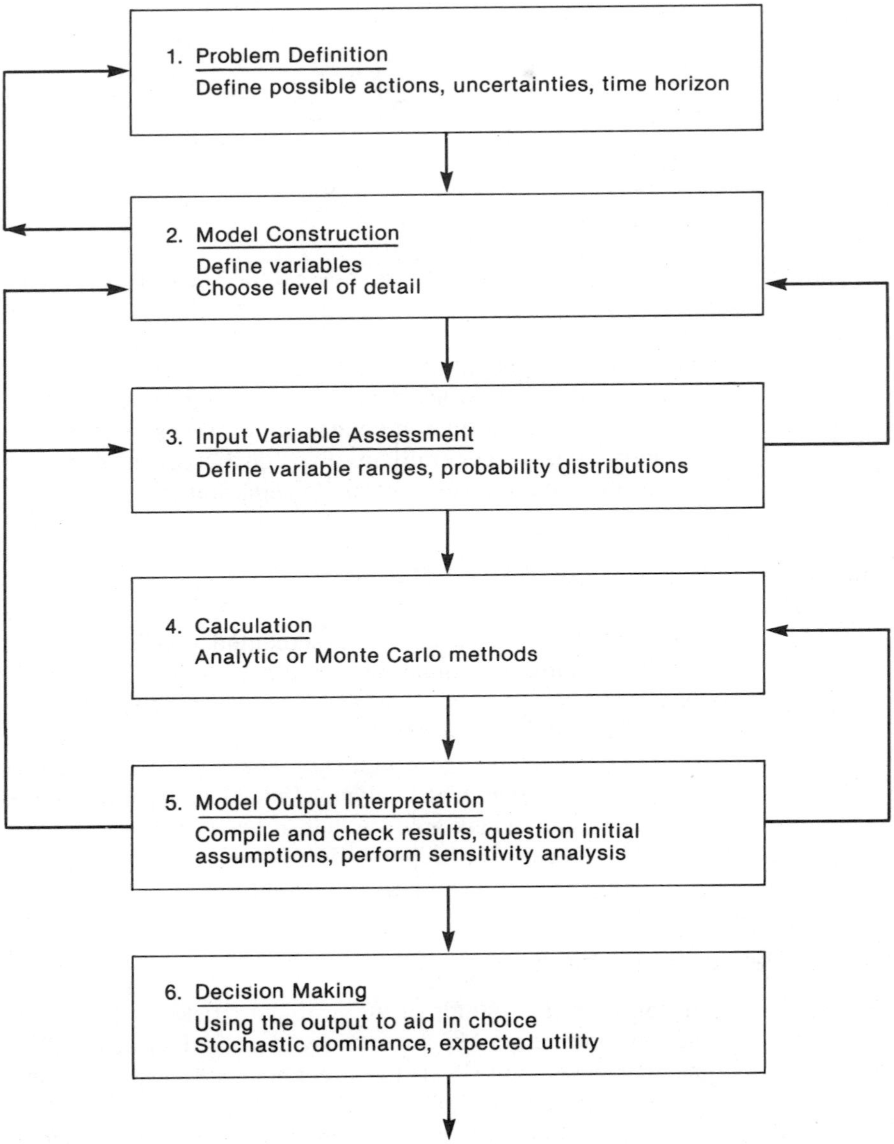

From the preceding series of questions, one very important issue in problem structuring is identified as the breadth or scope of the problem versus its degree of specificity. The broader the problem statement, the more difficult it is to focus on relevant details. Too narrow a problem statement may, however, result in a nice solution to a subproblem, that is, suboptimization.

It is very important to define the right problem and to view it from the correct perspective, neither too broadly nor too narrowly. Further, it is important to understand the ramifications of the alternatives both within the defined problem statement and also outside that definition. For example, if the problem is defined as: "The marketing budget is too large. How can we most effectively trim it by 15%?", the alternative actions must be evaluated both in terms of their effect on the marketing budget and on sales revenues, production costs, etc. A 15% reduction in advertising expenditure may reduce sales (and revenue) by 3%, and resulting lower volumes may cause per unit production costs to rise. These complex relationships and dependencies must be identified before they can be modeled.

The final element of importance in problem structuring is the time element. The time horizon of the problem should be defined. It should be no longer than necessary, yet long enough to include all the important effects of the problem and its alternative solutions.

## Step 2: Construct the Model

A risk analysis model is primarily an evaluation model that relates a set of input variables to an output variable. The output variable is usually a key variable that figures strongly in the objective function associated with the decision. The important feature of risk analysis models is that many of the input variables are uncertain quantities and are explicitly treated as such.

Many important choices must be made at the model-construction stage regarding the output variable and the set of input variables. The issue of problem scope and breadth (referred to in Step 1 above) translates into model construction choices about the *level of aggregation* of input variables. If pretax profit ($\pi$) is chosen as the output variable to be investigated, a simple model involving revenue ($R$) and total cost ($TC$) is

$$\pi = R - TC \qquad [9\text{–}1]$$

More detailed cuts can be taken of the input variable set by defining revenue in terms of the product price ($P$) and quantity ($Q$)

$$R = P \times Q \qquad [9\text{–}2]$$

Total cost can be subdivided into fixed costs ($FC$) and unit variable costs ($VC$)

$$TC = FC + Q \times VC$$

Alternative breakdowns are obviously possible, such as

$$TC = CF + CM + CP$$

where *CF, CM,* and *CP* are respectively the costs of financing, marketing, and production. Similarly each of these items can be further detailed, such as

$$CP = CL + CRM + CE + CPE$$

where *CL, CRM, CE,* and *CPE* are, respectively, the costs of labor, raw materials, energy, and plant and equipment.

Clearly, it is important to define the correct set of variables in the model, having neither too many variables nor too few. Too much detail results in unnecessary model complexity, and too little would limit the amount of insight to be gained. Experiments with different model structures are recommended.

## Step 3: Assess Input Variables

Probability distributions must be assessed for all input variables that are uncertain quantities. This assessment is usually done by either specifying a distribution form (such as the normal distribution, uniform, lognormal, exponential, or others) or by defining a discrete distribution or a set of fractiles, as outlined in Chapter 4.

If a distribution form is chosen, the decision maker must choose parameter values for it. For example, in the previous illustration, fixed costs may have been estimated as normally distributed with a mean of \$1 million and standard deviation of \$70,000.

Discrete distributions can be specified as a series of probabilistic statements. For example, raw materials might be specified as:

In the range \$ 60,000–\$ 90,000 with probability 0.3
In the range \$ 90,000–\$120,000 with probability 0.5
In the range \$120,000–\$150,000 with probability 0.2

In such cases, we often use either equal-width ranges (as above) or equiprobable ranges. However, exceptions to this rule of thumb do occur. For example, a decision maker may wish to specify three levels for quantity sold as high, medium, or low:

High quantity with probability 0.2
Medium quantity with probability 0.6
Low quantity with probability 0.2

Since quantity is really a continuous variable, this representation by three specific outcomes is an inexact one. Each point (high, medium, and low) is, however, implicitly representative of a range, hence, this practice is a reasonable and popular one. Indeed, since many people think in terms of high, medium, or low possibilities, this is often a very convenient form of assessment. In doing assessments, we should strive to accurately and unambiguously define variables and descriptive terms.

Different degrees of fineness can be used for discrete probability distributions. For most situations, three levels is a reasonable minimum number to adequately represent a distribution. Considerably more information can be contained if five levels are used rather than three, and in a few cases up to 10 levels may be justified, particularly if equiprobable ranges are used.

The assessment phase for a risk analysis is similar to that for decision analysis. The information base for a distribution may be purely subjective or may be partly or strongly influenced by some relative frequency or other information. The decision maker or analyst may call on experts to provide independent probabilistic inputs. In the previous profit illustration, marketing managers may be required to supply information on sales quantity. Similarly, production engineers might be called on to estimate production cost ranges and probabilities, and purchasing experts could supply probabilistic estimates of raw materials costs.

## Step 4: Calculate

It is in this step that risk analysis (simulation) and decision analysis involving a rollback procedure are most different. Once the model is specified and the probability distributions for the input variables of a risk analysis are assessed, the probability distribution of the output variables must be calculated using either analytical or numerical methods.

Analytical methods can be used where distribution functions are specified and where their combination is tractable. Unfortunately, only a limited number of cases lend themselves to analytical solution. As an example, consider again the simple model

$$\text{Profits} = \text{Revenue} - \text{Total costs}$$

$$\pi = R - TC$$

If $R$ and $TC$ are both normally distributed, then so is $\pi$. Moreover, if $R \sim N(\mu_R, \sigma_R^2)$ and $TC \sim N(\mu_{TC}, \sigma_{TC}^2)$ then $\pi \sim N(\mu_R - \mu_{TC}, \sigma_R^2 + \sigma_{TC}^2 - 2\sigma_{R.TC})$.[1] For cases where the model relationships are complex and mixes of distribution forms are used, analytical methods of combination become more difficult or indeed impossible to implement.

For these situations and cases where discrete distributions are used, numerical solution methods are employed. Two possible numerical approaches can be taken. The first involves calculation of the complete out-

---

[1] The notation $N(\mu_i, \sigma_i^2)$ refers to a normally distributed parameter with a mean of $\mu_i$ and variance of $\sigma_i^2$. $\sigma_{R.TC}$ is the covariance of $R$ and $TC$.

come space of the output distribution based on a complete enumeration of all combinations of input variables. This method is feasible for small problems but quickly grows in computational complexity and difficulty as model size increases.

The second method of numerical calculation (called Monte Carlo simulation) requires repeated random sampling from the input distributions and subsequent calculation of a set of sample values for the output distribution. As with all sampling situations, increases in sample size produce more and more accuracy in the closeness of the calculated output distribution to the true underlying distribution. Monte Carlo techniques are powerful and flexible. Their popularity is increasing, and their importance justifies their detailed discussion in a later section.

In simulation-styled risk analysis we *repetitively simulate* the rollforward of the decision tree, in contrast to rolling it back. After actually playing out the decision strategy many times for a large decision tree and keeping track of the results of each simulation trial, we build up a data bank of the simulation trial outcomes that becomes a useful probabilistic description of the consequences of a decision strategy. In the example represented by Figure 9–2, a complete rollback procedure is infeasible in practice, even using a computer, because the number of endpoints is so large. However if we simulate the process *so that for any simulation trial, the likelihood of a particular cash flow is equal to its assessed probability,* we can get a very good idea of the cash flow distribution with far less than a million trials. A few hundred trials, or a few thousand for the enthusiast, gives a good approximate answer. This number of trials can easily be performed on a personal computer, using a variety of software packages, or a relatively simple customized program.

## Step 5: Interpret the Model Output

In this phase of the analysis, the output distribution is carefully examined and the assumptions made about model structure and input variables are questioned. The decision maker wants to know how sensitive the output distribution is to changes in either the form of the model or the input probability distributions. Such changes are often examined by recalculating the risk analysis with different assumptions and assessments, and comparing the results with the base case.

## Step 6: Use the Risk Analysis in Decision Making

Decision problems involve making choices between alternatives, and *a single risk analysis may only be an evaluation of one alternative.* For a problem with many alternatives, more than one risk analysis might be needed. For example, in an investment analysis, each possible investment opportunity could be separately analyzed to produce separate distributions of some appropriate financial measure of value such as net present value (NPV) or internal rate of return (IRR). In Step 6, the final phase of a risk analysis, the output probability distributions are used to provide insights about the alternatives and to guide choice.

If a utility function has been formally assessed, expected utilities can be calculated and compared. Alternatively, the NPV or IRR distributions can be compared directly to see which produces a higher chance of reaching certain goals or a lower likelihood of loss. A third mode of analysis is stochastic dominance, which involves comparing complete probability distributions based on generally assumed preference properties such as risk aversion.

## MONTE CARLO SIMULATION

### Monte Carlo Sampling from Discrete Distributions

## EXAMPLE 9–1

### Profit Forecasting[2]

Consider a firm that has three unrelated product lines and needs to forecast its total net profit for the coming year. Uncertainty exists in the revenue and cost structures of each product; however, the three divisional managers have assessed their profit distributions as shown in Table 9–1. These profit distributions are assumed to be

**TABLE 9–1** Profit Distributions for Three Products in Example 9–1

| *Product 1* | | *Product 2* | | *Product 3* | |
|---|---|---|---|---|---|
| *Profit* | *Probability* | *Profit* | *Probability* | *Profit* | *Probability* |
| | | $800,000 | 0.1 | | |
| $ 75,000 | 0.2 | 850,000 | 0.3 | $500,000 | 0.5 |
| 125,000 | 0.5 | 900,000 | 0.5 | 550,000 | 0.5 |
| 175,000 | 0.3 | 950,000 | 0.1 | | $\Sigma = 1$ |
| | $\Sigma = 1$ | | $\Sigma = 1$ | | |

[2] This example could be solved without using Monte Carlo simulation. It is specifically included to illustrate the differences between the Monte Carlo approach and the process of completely enumerating all outcomes.

**TABLE 9-2** Evaluation of All Possible Outcomes for Example 9-1

| *Product 1* | *Product 2* | *Product 3* | *Total* | *Probability* |
|---|---|---|---|---|
| 75 | 800 | 500 | 1375 | 0.2 × 0.1 × 0.5 = 0.01 |
| 75 | 800 | 550 | 1425 | 0.2 × 0.1 × 0.5 = 0.01 |
| 75 | 850 | 500 | 1425 | 0.2 × 0.3 × 0.5 = 0.03 |
| 75 | 850 | 550 | 1475 | 0.2 × 0.3 × 0.5 = 0.03 |
| 75 | 900 | 500 | 1475 | 0.2 × 0.5 × 0.5 = 0.05 |
| 75 | 900 | 550 | 1525 | 0.2 × 0.5 × 0.5 = 0.05 |
| 75 | 950 | 500 | 1525 | 0.2 × 0.1 × 0.5 = 0.01 |
| 75 | 950 | 550 | 1575 | 0.2 × 0.1 × 0.5 = 0.01 |
| 125 | 800 | 500 | 1425 | 0.5 × 0.1 × 0.5 = 0.025 |
| 125 | 800 | 550 | 1475 | 0.5 × 0.1 × 0.5 = 0.025 |
| 125 | 850 | 500 | 1475 | 0.5 × 0.3 × 0.5 = 0.075 |
| 125 | 850 | 550 | 1525 | 0.5 × 0.3 × 0.5 = 0.075 |
| 125 | 900 | 500 | 1525 | 0.5 × 0.5 × 0.5 = 0.125 |
| 125 | 900 | 550 | 1575 | 0.5 × 0.5 × 0.5 = 0.125 |
| 125 | 950 | 500 | 1575 | 0.5 × 0.1 × 0.5 = 0.025 |
| 125 | 950 | 550 | 1625 | 0.5 × 0.1 × 0.5 = 0.025 |
| 175 | 800 | 500 | 1475 | 0.3 × 0.1 × 0.5 = 0.015 |
| 175 | 800 | 550 | 1525 | 0.3 × 0.1 × 0.5 = 0.015 |
| 175 | 850 | 500 | 1525 | 0.3 × 0.3 × 0.5 = 0.045 |
| 175 | 850 | 550 | 1575 | 0.3 × 0.3 × 0.5 = 0.045 |
| 175 | 900 | 500 | 1575 | 0.3 × 0.5 × 0.5 = 0.075 |
| 175 | 900 | 550 | 1625 | 0.3 × 0.5 × 0.5 = 0.075 |
| 175 | 950 | 500 | 1625 | 0.3 × 0.1 × 0.5 = 0.015 |
| 175 | 950 | 550 | 1675 | 0.3 × 0.1 × 0.5 = 0.015 |

independent of each other for illustrative purposes. Note that the assessments were made as various probabilities for profit values in equal increments (of $50,000).

The product 3 division manager decided to represent his uncertainty by assessing only two equally likely possibilities. This procedure is reasonable where the uncertainty is low (i.e., the distribution is narrow). More outcomes are generally needed when the uncertainty is high.

Since there are only 24 (3 × 4 × 2) possible outcomes for total profit, complete enumeration of all possibilities is feasible. In Table 9-2, each combination is considered, and the probabilities are calculated. The complete distribution is then shown in Table 9-3 as a risk profile. This output distribution is calculated by adding together the probabilities of each of the seven distinct profit outcomes.

**TABLE 9-3** Total Profit Distribution for Example 9-1

| *Profit (thousands)* | *Probability* |
|---|---|
| 1,375 | 0.01 |
| 1,425 | 0.065 |
| 1,475 | 0.195 |
| 1,525 | 0.32 |
| 1,575 | 0.28 |
| 1,625 | 0.115 |
| 1,675 | 0.015 |
| | $\Sigma = 1$ |

Let us now compare Monte Carlo results with those calculated above. The Monte Carlo procedure involves generating separate random numbers for each input variable and assigning corresponding values to the input variables for each trial. Random numbers are most easily generated as integers between 0 and 10 (or 0 and 100 if two-digit numbers are needed) or as decimals between zero and one. A random number is equally likely to have any value within a prescribed range. A table of random numbers is provided in the appendix of most statistics books, and most computer systems contain random number generators. For product 1, Table 9–4 shows single-digit random numbers and their corresponding trial profit values.

Similarly, for products 2 and 3 the relationships in Table 9–5 apply.

**TABLE 9–4** Assignment of Random Numbers to Profit Values (product 1)*

| *Random Numbers* | *Trial Profit Values (thousands of dollars)* |
|---|---|
| 0,1 | 75 |
| 2,3,4,5,6 | 125 |
| 7,8,9 | 175 |

* Note that the quantity of these equally likely randomly generated digits is in proportion to the assessed probabilities of the corresponding profit values. That is, two random numbers for profit = 75 (probability = 0.2), five random numbers for profit = 125 (probability = 0.5), and three random numbers for profit = 175 (probability = 0.3).

**TABLE 9–5** Assignment of Random Numbers to Products' 2 and 3 Profits

| *Product 2* | | *Product 3* | |
|---|---|---|---|
| *Random Numbers* | *Trial Profit (thousands of dollars)* | *Random Numbers* | *Trial Profit (thousands of dollars)* |
| 0 | 800 | | |
| 1,2,3 | 850 | 0,1,2,3,4 | 500 |
| 4,5,6,7,8 | 900 | 5,6,7,8,9 | 550 |
| 9 | 950 | | |

It does not matter which particular random numbers are assigned to which trial profit value, as long as the relative numbers of random numbers assigned to each value are proportional to the underlying probability of those profit values. For the sake of convenience, we usually assign integer random numbers as groups of consecutive numbers.

Random numbers, or more precisely "pseudorandom" numbers (almost random numbers), can be generated by computers. FORTRAN and BASIC compilers have random-number generators built in. So do some spreadsheet programs and many special purpose simulation packages. To solve the present example for the output distribution using Monte Carlo simulation, a relatively simple computer program was used to generate large quantities of random numbers and automatically assign corresponding values of profits for each input distribution according to the relationships shown in Tables 9–4 and 9–5. For each trial, the randomly generated profit values for each product are then used to calculate a trial value of total profit. *If many trials are run, the frequency count of trial values for total profit becomes a good estimate of the underlying profit distribution.*

Since we know the underlying distribution in this simple illustration, we can examine the relationship between number of trials and simulation accuracy. Table 9–6 shows the underlying probabilities and the frequency counts for repeated runs of various trial sizes. It is interesting to note the computer time used (using uncompiled BASIC on an IBM PC) for each run, as this gives an approximate feel for the cost of running a Monte Carlo simulation.

From these results we can certainly conclude that *accuracy improves markedly with increases in numbers of trials*. The probability estimates are derived by dividing the frequency counts shown in Table 9–6 by the total number of trials for that run. For cases of only 10 trials the resemblance of

**TABLE 9–6** Monte Carlo Results for the Total Profit Distribution*

| *Profit* | *1375* | *1425* | *1475* | *1525* | *1575* | *1625* | *1675* | *Approximate Computer Time per Run* |
|---|---|---|---|---|---|---|---|---|
| *True Probabilities* | *0.01* | *0.065* | *0.195* | *0.32* | *0.28* | *0.115* | *0.015* | |
| Number of trials | | | | | | | | |
| 10 | 0 | 0 | 1 | 2 | 4 | 3 | 0 | |
| 10 | 0 | 0 | 1 | 6 | 2 | 1 | 0 | < 1 second |
| 10 | 0 | 1 | 2 | 4 | 2 | 1 | 0 | |
| 100 | 0 | 4 | 24 | 28 | 34 | 9 | 1 | 1¼ seconds |
| 100 | 2 | 6 | 22 | 26 | 27 | 17 | 0 | |
| 100 | 1 | 5 | 15 | 34 | 28 | 15 | 2 | |
| 100 | 0 | 9 | 26 | 31 | 24 | 8 | 2 | |
| 1000 | 7 | 63 | 191 | 318 | 279 | 120 | 22 | 11 seconds |
| 1000 | 11 | 62 | 207 | 317 | 283 | 101 | 19 | |
| 1000 | 6 | 77 | 198 | 299 | 290 | 108 | 22 | |
| 10,000 | 97 | 659 | 1955 | 3228 | 2744 | 1151 | 166 | < 2 minutes |
| 10,000 | 104 | 646 | 1945 | 3208 | 2833 | 1106 | 158 | |
| 10,000 | 103 | 637 | 1945 | 3196 | 2803 | 1155 | 161 | |
| 100,000 | 1025 | 6393 | 19622 | 32028 | 28074 | 11276 | 1582 | < 16 minutes |

* In each row of this table, divide the various frequency counts by the total number of trials for that row, and compare the resultant likelihood estimates with the true, known probabilities at the top of the table.

the simulation distributions to the underlying "correct" distribution is poor. These ($n = 10$) distributions do however have central tendency (higher frequency counts in the center of the distribution than the tails) as does the true distribution, but there the resemblance ends. The simulation estimates are particularly poor in the low probability classes at the distribution tails. As expected if we simulate only 10 trials, it would be a surprise to get 1 or more trials in a category that has an underlying probability of 0.01 (i.e., 1/100).

As we increase the number of trials to 100, we observe a marked increase in accuracy, with the estimates being quite close in some of the higher probability classes and some trial results falling in the lower probability classes. This is, however, still a random sampling procedure, and estimation errors are still sizable in the distribution tails when 100 trials are used. For example, a profit of $1,375 has an underlying probability of 0.01. The estimates with 100 trials per run were 0, 0, 0.01, and 0.02, which, taken individually are generally not very accurate.

When 1,000 trials per run were used, the accuracy improved to the point of being acceptable for most decision making purposes. For most of the profit classes, the estimated probabilities round off to be correct for the first significant digit and in some cases also for the second digit.

When 10,000 trials were used, the accuracy was high, even in the distribution tails. In most cases, second and perhaps even third significant digits could be reliably estimated. Although better accuracy is generally achieved with more trials, the increase in trial size to 100,000 for this example is unnecessary for most purposes because the improvement in precision is quite small.

These trials were run on an IBM personal computer in BASIC. Many faster machines and languages exist. Even when running 10,000 trials, the computer time was low (about two minutes) and could have been reduced further had the program been compiled.

For many real problems, the model complexity does not allow us to calculate the underlying correct distribution. When we wish to run a simulation, it is sometimes difficult to judge how many trials to use. If it is suspected that some important outcomes have low probabilities, generally larger numbers of trials are needed. One way of telling whether you have used enough trials is to run three or more simulations for a given trial size and examine the stability of the estimates across runs. It is important to use a different random-number sequence for each run. This means reseeding the random number generator on a computer so that different sequences of random numbers are used in different simulation runs. If the estimates are generally close across different simulation runs, the trial size is probably sufficient. If wide variations in the estimates occur, then an increased trial size is probably justified. Ultimately, it is reasonable to combine the results from various sets of trials to obtain the best estimate.

## Monte Carlo Sampling from Continuous Distributions

For input distributions that are continuous in form, trial values are generated in a similar manner as for discrete variables. The cumulative distribution is defined as the integral of the probability density function, and random numbers are mapped across the cumulative function to produce trial values. Some examples follow.

**Sampling from the Uniform Distribution Function.** Consider the uniform distribution shown in Figure 9–3. The cumulative distribution can be used to map from random numbers on the vertical axis to input variable values on the horizontal axis. This procedure can be performed graphically as for the examples in Figure 9–3 or mathematically on a computer. The cumulative function for a uniformly distributed variable $X$, with lower limit $a$ and upper limit $b$ is given by

$$P(X \leq x) = \frac{x - a}{b - a}$$

Hence for a random number $y_i$ generated in the range between zero and one, the trial value for the input variable $X$ would be

$$X_i = a + (b - a)y_i$$

**Sampling from the Negative Exponential Distribution.** The negative exponential distribution has probability density function

$$f(x) = \lambda e^{-\lambda x}$$

where $\lambda$ is a distribution parameter. It is a useful distribution in queueing theory applications where it is used to approximate service time. It is also used to model insurance claim sizes in certain circumstances. The cumulative function $F(x)$ is found by integrating the density function and is given by

$$F(x) = 1 - e^{-\lambda x}$$

Hence for a random number $y_i$ the corresponding trial value of the input variable $X_i$ is given by

$$X_i = \frac{-1}{\lambda} \ln(1 - y_i)$$

**Sampling from the Normal Distribution.** The normal distribution is a commonly used function for representing uncertain quantities. It possesses the property of symmetry about its mean and is unimodal. Further, when many uncertain quantities are combined in certain ways, the resulting aggregate distribution may be approximately normal even if the individual distributions are not. The normal distribution can be used to approximate other distributions such as the binomial and Poisson under certain conditions.

**FIGURE 9–3** The Uniform Probability Distribution

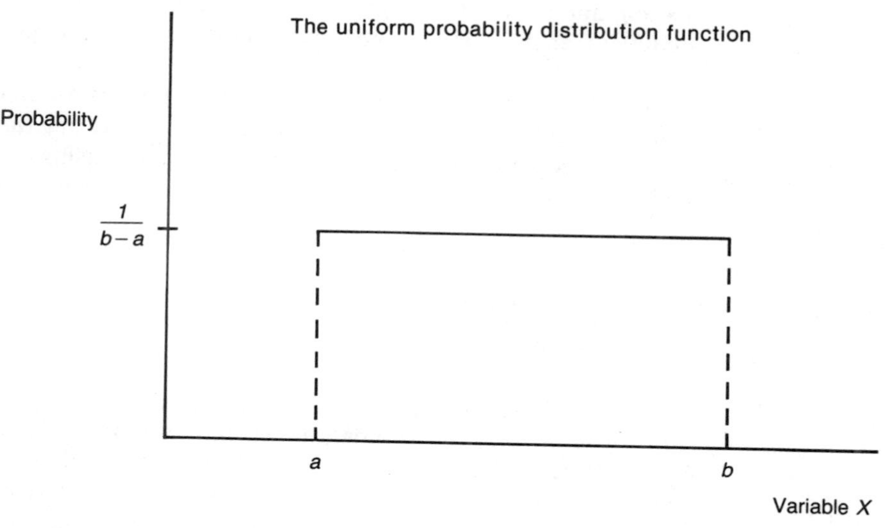


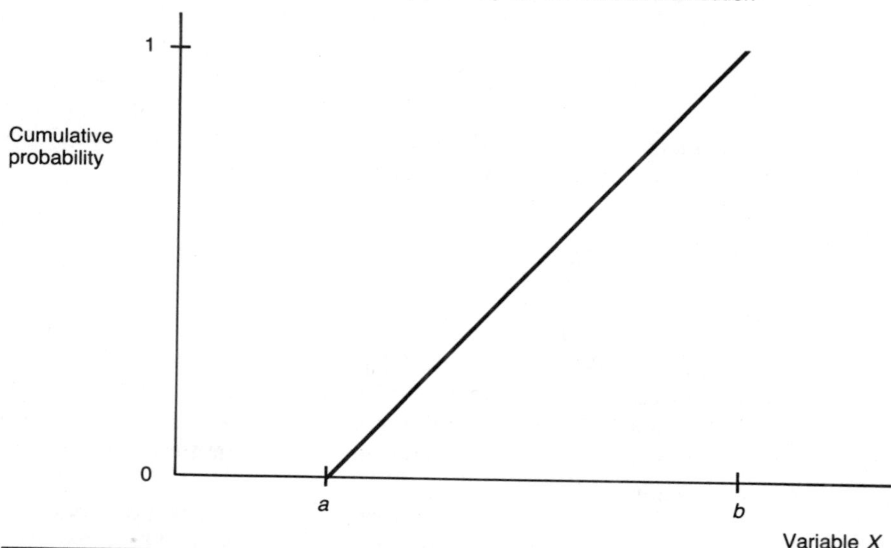


The probability density function of the normal distribution cannot readily be integrated to yield a cumulative distribution. To use the normal distribution in Monte Carlo simulation, we must either discretize it or find another technique. Discretizing (dividing it into some finite number of intervals) the distribution is a feasible method. This can be accomplished by chopping the distribution into equal-width intervals and assigning sets of random numbers to those intervals. The number of random numbers associated with each interval must be proportional to the probability of that interval.

For the normal distribution, another technique is possible. If we take the sum of 12 uniformly distributed random numbers as one random event, this sum is approximately normally distributed. When using computers for risk analysis, this method is the most accurate and simplest to employ.

## AN IMPORTANT RISK ANALYSIS APPLICATION: INVESTMENT ANALYSIS

Path-breaking developments in risk analysis are attributable to David Hertz (1965) who developed risk-analytic techniques in his 1965 *Harvard Business Review* article. This article was of such importance that the *Harvard Business Review* sold over 150,000 reprint copies and republished the article in 1979. The article developed a new methodology for analyzing investments and lead to the development of special purpose computer programs for conducting Monte Carlo simulations. We consider here the application of risk analysis to capital investment projects (originally considered by Hertz) and begin by examining alternative methods for accounting for risk.

In recent years a popular investment appraisal criterion has been net present value (NPV). For a series of cash flows over time ($CF_i$) the discounted net present value is given by

$$NPV = CF_0 + \frac{CF_1}{1 + r} + \cdots \frac{CF_i}{(1 + r)^i} + \cdots \frac{CF_n}{(1 + r)^n}$$

where $r$ is the appropriate discount rate per period and $n$ is the life of the project. We assume that $CF_0$ occurs immediately, and if we summarize the periodic cash flows to be annual, then $CF_1$ occurs 12 months from the present. The parameter $r$ becomes an annual discount rate (normally an opportunity cost of capital) and is assumed constant across periods in this simple model.

Note that the NPV formula itself does not contain probabilities or explicitly account for uncertainty in any way. There are, however, a number of ways in which uncertainty can be treated in this context.[3]

[3] The author wishes to acknowledge this classification of approaches as having been suggested by Howard Thomas (private communication).

## Approach 1: Ignore Uncertainty

One possible approach is to use best single-point estimates of cash flow ($CF_i$) values and ignore uncertainty. This approach would seem unreasonable in cases where uncertainty is moderate or large, but may be reasonable, for example, in evaluating fixed-return deposits in insured bank accounts (which are virtually risk free).

## Approach 2: Adjust Cash Flow Estimates

If uncertainty is known to exist and the decision maker is not risk neutral, a second possible approach is to adjust the cash flow point estimates from their best estimates. This adjustment of the numerators in the NPV formula would result in a decrease of inward cash flows for risk averters. For such conservative decision makers, lowering of inward cash flows is a form of using certainty equivalent values. If comparisons between various investments are to be made, the size of risk adjustments would be a function of the implicitly considered uncertainty in each one. To illustrate, in a comparison between blue-chip stocks and highly leveraged commodity futures, the risk averter would lower the inward cash flow estimates of the futures options more than those for the stocks to reflect his aversion to the extra uncertainty.

Approach 2 is superior to approach 1 in some circumstances, since from a normative viewpoint, accounting for uncertainty is generally better than ignoring it. However, the mechanism used to account for uncertainty in this approach is informal, and cash flows that are really uncertain quantities are still being replaced by fixed-point estimates (albeit risk adjusted ones).

## Approach 3: Mean Variance

A third possible approach is to estimate the expected (i.e., mean) NPV and variance of NPV by estimating these summary statistics for $CF_i$ values and combining them. The danger in this instance is that variance may not be an adequate measure of risk. This is especially true for asymmetrical distributions where skewness or truncation may be an important feature.

## Approach 4: Risk Adjustment of the Discount Rate

The denominators of the fractions in the NPV formula exist to allow time discounting of future cash flows. Discount rates are normally positive to reflect the fact that present values of future cash flows are lower than the nominal $CF_i$ values. It is feasible to use not only a time adjustment but a *time plus risk* adjustment. For example, if the time rate of discount is 12% per year, it is feasible to use discount rates in the range of 13–25% to account for the uncertainty of future cash flows.

For cash flow projections, the uncertainty generally increases as we forecast further ahead (although exceptions do exist). Certainly this is accounted for in risk-adjusted costs of capital because as the time subscript $n$ increases, the discount factor increases as $(1 + r)^n$. There is, however, little flexibility in this method, as it forces a particular risk-adjustment pattern unless individual adjustments are made for each value of $n$. Further, the process of translating beliefs about uncertainty of cash flows into appropriate risk-adjustment discount factors is indirect and imprecise.

### Approach 5: Treating Cash Flows as Uncertain Quantities

The risk analysis approach proposes that the uncertain cash flows be treated as such, with a probability distribution assessed for each one. Monte Carlo or analytic techniques can then be used to calculate a distribution for NPV. The other approaches do not produce this level of information as an output, but rather produce single-point estimates or at best a mean and variance of NPV. *The essence of risk analysis is that if a decision maker is uncertain about the value of a variable or set of variables, he should treat them as random variables, assess probability distributions for them, and use techniques to allow his uncertainty about input variables to be translated into uncertainty about output (decision) variables.*

---

## Example 9–2

## Analysis of a Machine Replacement Decision

We will examine the Monte Carlo approach in NPV calculations for a machine replacement decision in which two options were available. A well-known technology was available for a high initial cost ($0.9 million). This machine is certain to last 10 years and produce $350,000 of profit per year. The second option involves an innovative design and process which is not yet fully proven. The new machine costs $0.5 million and will provide profits of either $100,000, $300,000, or $500,000 per year with equal probability. Further uncertainty is associated with the life of this new machine which is expected to be anything from 6 to 15 years with equal probabilities. To begin with, the individual cash flows and life expectancy are all considered to be independent of each other. The company generally used a 15% cost of capital in NPV calculations.

The NPV of the well-known technology machine is

$$NPV = -900{,}000 + \sum_{i=1}^{10} \frac{350{,}000}{(1.15)^i}$$
$$= \$856{,}500$$

Because of the two sources of uncertainty (cash flows and machine life) for the new technology option, the number of possible outcomes is very large, and the complete set of possibilities cannot be easily calculated. Hence, Monte Carlo methods should be used. For each Monte Carlo trial, a random number is generated for machine life $t$ so that equally likely outcomes in the range 6 to 15 are generated. For each year of machine life, random numbers are again used to generate a cash flow for that year. NPV for each trial is then calculated as

$$NPV = -500{,}000 + \sum_{i=1}^{t} \frac{CF_i}{(1.15)^i}$$

Repeated runs of 100 trials (performed on a computer) yielded a stable output distribution. The ranked output data of NPV values from a typical run is shown in Table 9–7.

**TABLE 9–7** Monte Carlo Results for the New Technology NPV (thousands of dollars)*

| | | | |
|---|---|---|---|
| 52.3 | 827.1 | 1048.7 | 1240.3 |
| 145.6 | 829.0 | 1049.0 | 1251.9 |
| 227.9 | 837.1 | 1061.6 | 1269.5 |
| 352.6 | 846.4 | 1064.1 | 1270.1 |
| 414.1 | 848.9 | 1065.7 | 1273.6 |
| 415.0 | 855.5 | 1066.1 | 1291.1 |
| 487.9 | 875.9 | 1067.5 | 1301.3 |
| 491.8 | 876.1 | 1075.9 | 1303.0 |
| 506.4 | 883.0 | 1088.7 | 1316.2 |
| 544.3 | 902.4 | 1090.8 | 1328.2 |
| 648.7 | 913.4 | 1094.5 | 1357.9 |
| 650.5 | 915.5 | 1122.0 | 1367.0 |
| 655.0 | 916.2 | 1134.7 | 1371.6 |
| 687.1 | 916.8 | 1136.0 | 1372.3 |
| 698.4 | 932.3 | 1155.7 | 1374.5 |
| 710.7 | 932.9 | 1159.2 | 1374.7 |
| 726.6 | 945.0 | 1175.7 | 1399.6 |
| 726.7 | 947.5 | 1189.4 | 1402.9 |
| 734.7 | 949.9 | 1191.7 | 1444.6 |
| 761.6 | 966.0 | 1192.4 | 1455.3 |
| 784.5 | 981.5 | 1193.9 | 1494.2 |
| 794.4 | 996.4 | 1199.1 | 1523.4 |
| 816.0 | 1000.9 | 1204.3 | 1574.1 |
| 823.4 | 1006.4 | 1216.4 | 1625.8 |
| 825.5 | 1032.6 | 1222.0 | 1630.3 |

* The results have been ordered in this table from lowest to highest. The order in which the trial results are produced by the computer is, of course, random.

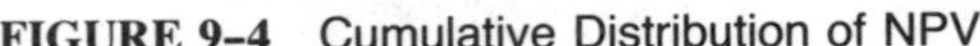

**FIGURE 9–4** Cumulative Distribution of NPV

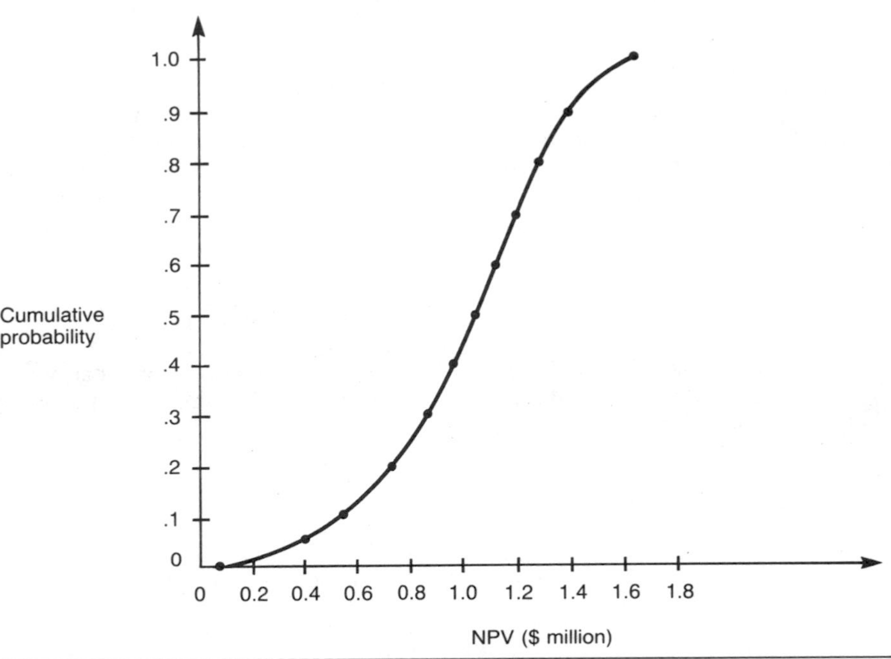


This data can be summarized in the form of a histogram or presented graphically. Figure 9–4 is a cumulative distribution of the output NPV distribution. Note that in 69 of the 100 trials the NPV of the new technology machine exceeded the NPV of the old technology machine.

The risk analysis provides a high quality of information upon which the decision maker can base his choice. Many probabilistic statements can be made from the results of the risk analysis. For example, there is a better than 50:50 chance that the NPV of the new technology will be more than $1 million. This chance is zero for the old technology. There is also an almost 1 in 10 chance of making less than $0.5 million with the new technology.

*The decision between the two types of machines must still be made by the manager. The risk analysis does not tell which option is best.* He must use his judgment and risk attitude to decide. The risk analysis does help by providing a very clear picture of possible cash flow patterns and NPV outcomes should he decide to take the risk with the new technology.

It is a simple matter to conduct sensitivity analysis in risk analysis. For example, one assumption which is often questioned is the discount rate used in the NPV formula. To examine the effect on NPV of the discount rate, the risk analysis was

**FIGURE 9–5** Net Present Value Sensitivity to Discount Rate

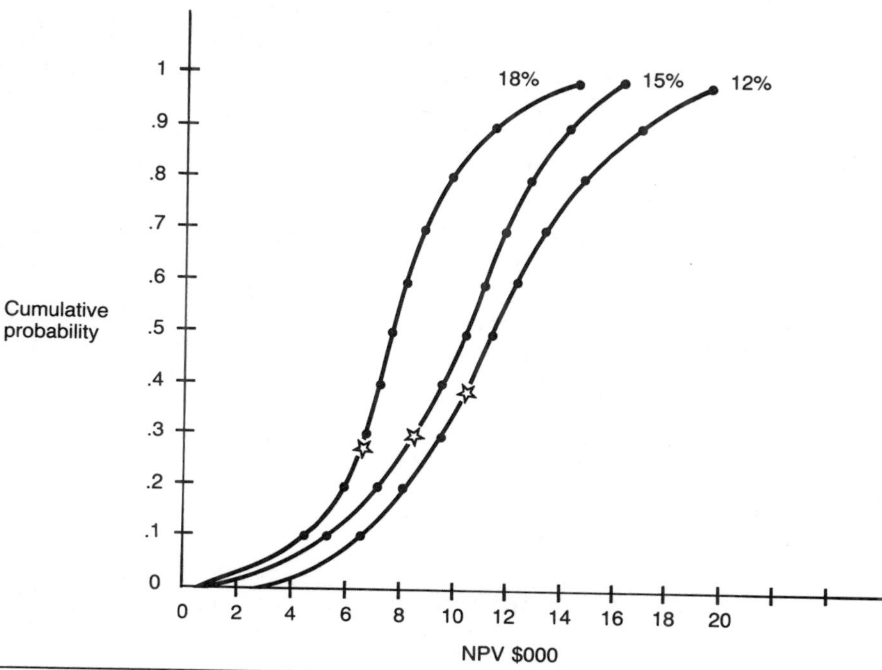


* NOTE: Asterisks indicate the net present values of the well-known technology.

performed again with rates of 12% and 18%. Figure 9–5 shows the results, and the asterisks on each distribution show the NPV of the well-known technology.

---

## Probabilistic Dependence

The preceding discussions and examples have generally assumed that probabilistic independence exists between the uncertain quantities in any risk analysis. In many real applications some dependencies exist, and so we must examine how to handle dependence in risk analysis. Consider, for example Equation [9–2], which equates revenue to the product of price and quantity. For most markets, price and quantity are not independent (i.e., the elasticity of demand is not zero). Indeed, price and quantity are often negatively correlated.

To account for dependence in Monte Carlo techniques, conditional distributions are usually specified. For truly independent variables, only unconditional distributions need to be specified.

Consider the treatment of discrete variables first. For the price-quantity example of Equation [9–2], assume that price can take on values $p_i$ for $i = 1$ to $n$, and quantity can take on values $q_j$ where $j = 1$ to $m$. If dependency exists then assessments must be made of $P(p_i)$ and $P(q_j/p_i)$ or $P(q_j)$ and $P(p_i/q_j)$. The total number of conditional assessments is then $m \times n$, hence, the assessment task can be much larger (and more tedious!) in cases where dependencies exist. If each variable is to be specified at five levels, 25 conditional assessments must be made. A very real incentive exists in practical terms, to reduce to only three levels per variable. The number of conditional assessments would then be cut from 25 to 9. A trade-off situation exists between number of assessments and fineness or accuracy of representation.

## EXAMPLE 9–3

### The Machine Replacement Decision Revisited

Let us revisit the NPV example and assume certain dependencies across time for the cash flows. Specifically, let us assume it was known that if the machine generated high cash flows in a particular year, there was a high likelihood of high cash flows the next year, and vice versa for low cash flows. Table 9–8 shows the general relationships for cash flows in year $n$ and cash flows in year $n + 1$.

The cash flow distributions for year $n + 1$ are conditional on the year $n$ cash flows. These distributions reflect the fact that if the machine performed well in a particular year, management felt it was more likely to work well rather than badly the next year, and vice versa for poor performance.

These relationships can be readily incorporated into the computer program, and Monte Carlo techniques can be used to determine output NPV distributions. Note that

**TABLE 9–8** Cash Flow Relationships (thousands of dollars)

| *Year n* | 100 | 300 | 500 |
|---|---|---|---|
| Year $n + 1$ | $p(100) = 0.8$<br>$p(300) = 0.15$<br>$p(500) = 0.05$ | $p(100) = 0.2$<br>$p(300) = 0.6$<br>$p(500) = 0.2$ | $p(100) = 0.05$<br>$p(300) = 0.15$<br>$p(500) = 0.8$ |

**FIGURE 9–6** Cumulative Distributions of Net Present Value with Dependent Cash Flows

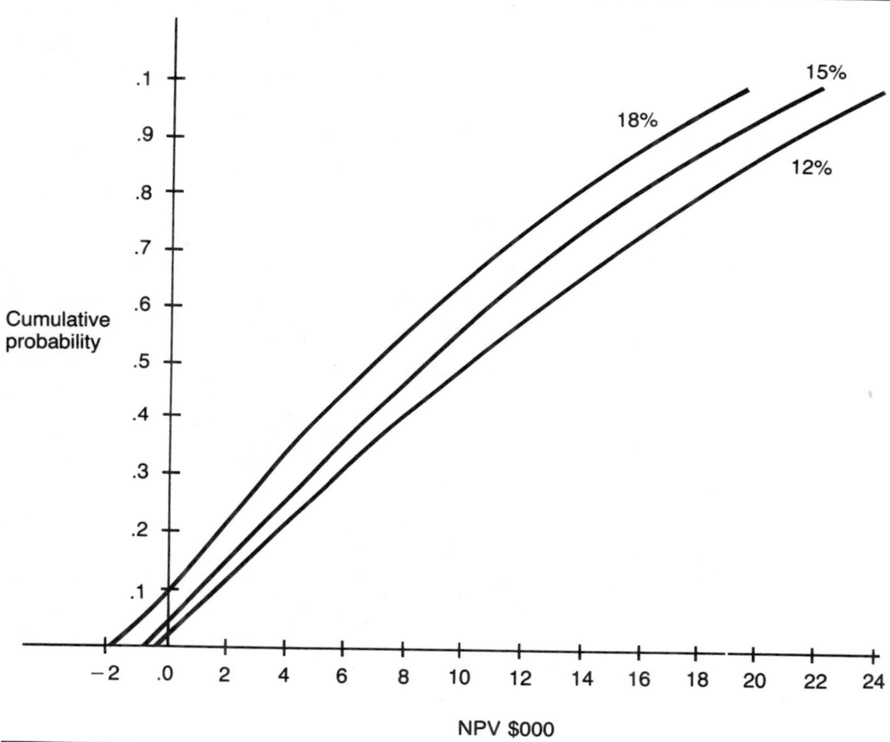


there is now for any trial a much increased likelihood for streams of high cash flows and streams of low cash flows across time. Hence, there is an expectation of considerably more frequent extreme values of NPV, both high and low, than when independence was assumed. In cases where independence of cash flows was assumed, many trials had a few high and a few low cash flows that tended to balance out and result in a moderate NPV. This effect of the "law of large numbers" is greatly decreased when the dependence relationships of Table 9–8 are assumed.

The output distributions for the "dependence" case are plotted in Figure 9–6. Comparison of Figure 9–5 with Figure 9–6 shows that the positive autocorrelation of cash flows through time produced just what was expected. A considerable increase in NPV distribution spread is observed when dependence is assumed as in Table 9–8. Note also that the cumulative distributions in Figure 9–6 have central sections that are almost straight lines (apart from minor random effects). The characteristic *S* shape (see Figures 9–4 and 9–5) that reflects the existence of a definite mode and a degree of central tendency is not present under the present dependency conditions because many trials had relatively consistently high or consistently low cash flows.

Continuous variables are more difficult to handle when dependence exists. In effect, unless certain compatible sets of continuous distributions are used, the easiest way of handling dependence is to discretize the variables. More complex forms of structure for representing dependencies between continuous variable do exist. These often involve multivariable correlations that are technically feasible to model but in practice can lead to serious assessment difficulties and biases.

---

## Computerized Monte Carlo Analysis

The process of generating random numbers and trial values is further described in this section. The flow diagrams for the NPV example described above are shown in Figures 9–7 and 9–8. Figure 9–7 shows the flow diagram when independence is assumed, and Figure 9–8 shows a slightly more complex diagram for the case where cash flows were sequentially dependent. Note that Figures 9–7 and 9–8 are not very complex flow diagrams. They show that the essence of the calculation process is the Monte Carlo sampling and the development of output formats.

Computers have made risk analysis into a feasible approach even for complex decision problems. The calculation phase is performed quickly and accurately (by the computer) once the program is set up, allowing us to perform a variety of sensitivity analyses at low cost. Computers also have made it feasible to run a large enough number of Monte Carlo trials to ensure that accuracy is high. For example in Figure 9–8, a program that did 100 trials took just seconds on an IBM PC using BASIC (a slow language).

For relatively simple problems, computer programs can easily be written by most management science practitioners. However, for more complex problems, simulation packages are available for off-the-shelf purchase. These include IFPS, GPSS, and other special purpose simulation languages, as well as many spreadsheet packages.

---

## Example 9–4

### Gas Exploration at Amsco

Bob Smith was the production director of Amsco, a medium-sized oil and gas producer. The company had a good deal of experience in the business of producing and selling gas but felt that their decision processes about individual wells were not

**FIGURE 9–7** NPV Example Flow Diagram Assuming Independent Cash Flows

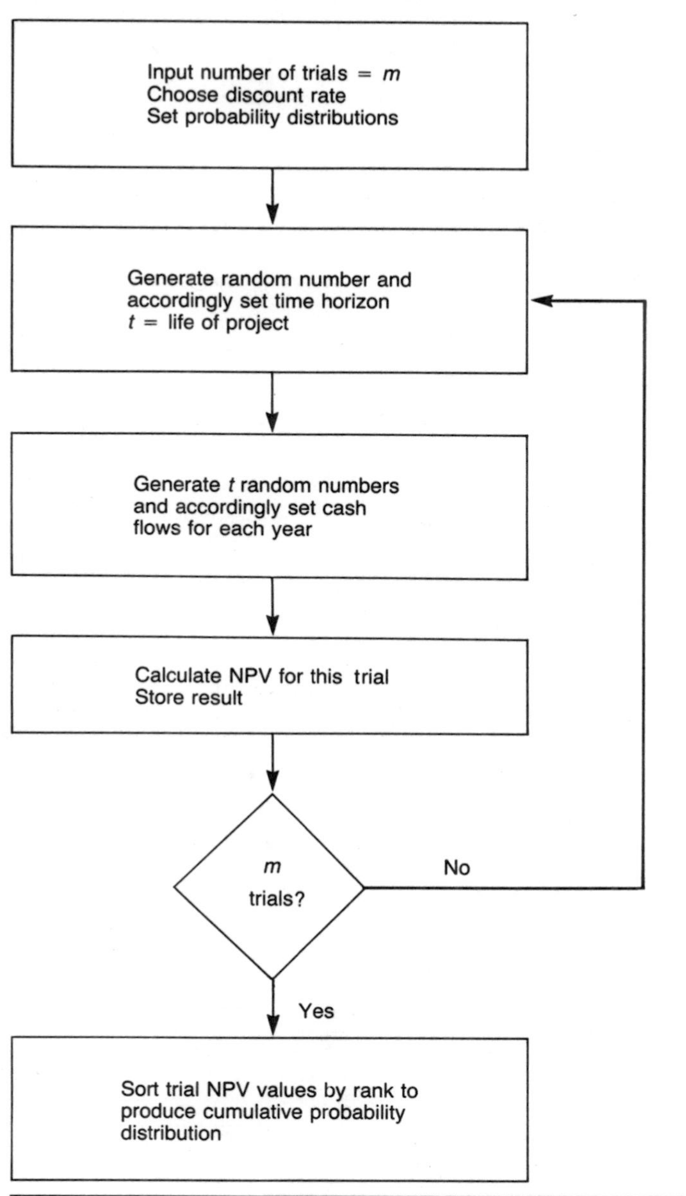

**FIGURE 9–8** NPV Example Assuming Dependent Cash Flows

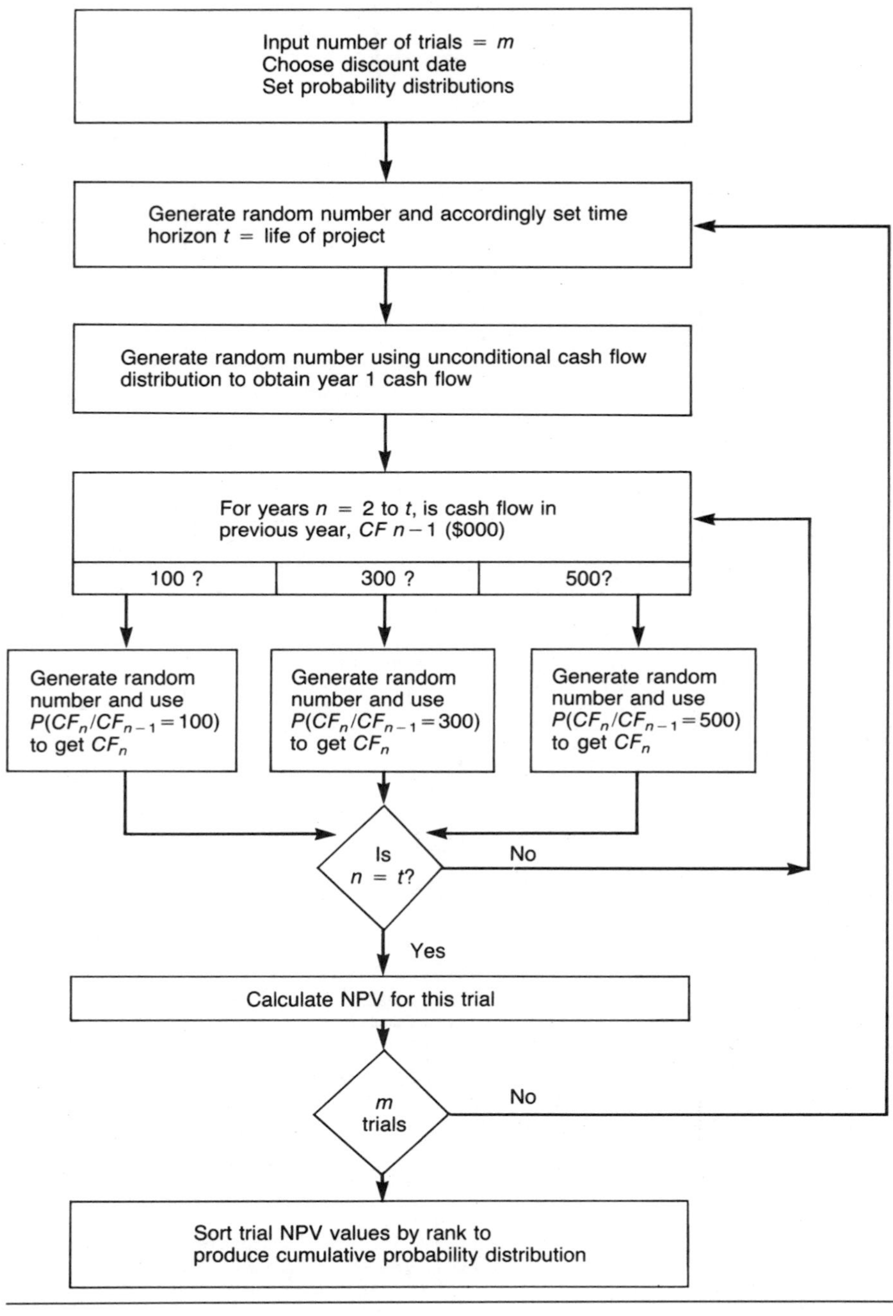

sophisticated enough to match the complexity of the decision. Most of the complexity in the decision process for a gas well was a result of uncertainty. There were a number of critical uncertain quantities which Mr. Smith knew affected the financial success or failure of a well:

1. Net pay thickness: a measure of the deposit thickness of gas available in the bed.
2. Recovery factor: the proportion of gas in the bed that can be recovered. It is affected by stratigraphic factors and cannot be very accurately estimated.
3. Investment cost, which is dependent upon exact depth of the bed and other geological factors. Experience has shown that investment costs are often affected by unforeseen factors as well.
4. Start-up time: the time between the date of investment and the date of the first revenue-producing gas flow. Start-up time can be affected by both technical and market uncertainties.

The company knew that each of these four uncertain quantities would have a significant impact on the ultimate profitability of the well. Mr. Smith knew that he could take one of a number of approaches to the problem. In the early days of the company's operation, uncertainty had essentially been ignored, and profits had been estimated using expected values.[4] More recently, decision tree methodologies had been used in other parts of the company for analyzing problems involving uncertainty. This approach seemed like a reasonable possibility to Mr. Smith, but he knew that with four sources of uncertainty his decision tree would resemble a bushy mess and perhaps defeat the primary purpose of the analysis (which was to cast insight on the problem). He wanted to do more than just roll back a decision tree. Mr. Smith wanted a better way to analyze his risk. He employed highly skilled, well-paid geological engineers who were able to give him probabilistic information about each of his uncertain quantities. He had heard that another oil and gas company was using risk analysis, and he decided to inquire about it at next week's industry association meeting.

Mr. Smith met with an old friend who worked for another oil and gas organization at the industry association meeting. His friend told Mr. Smith that risk analysis was indeed a useful approach and soon after sent him a book on the subject. Although the book gave him an initial grasp of the subject, Mr. Smith decided to hire a consultant to help him.

When the consultant arrived, Mr. Smith negotiated a shrewd deal with him. Since the consultant was highly confident of the usefulness of the risk analysis approach, Mr. Smith was able to convince him to demonstrate it on this problem for a nominal fee, and if it really did prove useful in aiding the drill/no-drill decision, then Mr. Smith contracted to pay the consultant a substantial sum to set up a computerized analysis system which would allow Mr. Smith to use it on all his future drill/no-drill decisions.

The consultant began work by asking Mr. Smith about the decision elements affecting profit, and Mr. Smith was able to produce the following formulae that the company had used before

---

[4] Expected value does not ignore uncertainty, but it is nevertheless a single-point estimate which measures central tendency and does not account for spread in a distribution.

$$NPV = -I + \sum_{i=i_1}^{i_2} \frac{(P \times Q \times F - C)_i}{(1 + r)^i}$$

$$Q = X \times Y \times \frac{A}{20} \times D$$

where

- $I$ = initial investment
- $P$ = price ($2.8/Mcf)
- $Q$ = quantity
- $F$ = royalty and taxes factor (.79)
- $C$ = operating cost ($4,000/month)
- $r$ = annual discount rate (16%)
- $X$ = pay thickness
- $Y$ = recovery factor
- $A$ = effective area of the deposit (800 acres)
- $D$ = density (880 Mcf/acre ft)[5]
- $i_1$ = time until revenue is generated by the well (years)
- $i_2$ = time until the well is shut down (years)

Mr. Smith explained that the investment ($I$) was almost exclusively made up front and did not need to be discounted because it was already a present value. The critical uncertain quantities were pay thickness ($X$), recovery factor ($Y$), investment ($I$), and the time to start up ($i_1$). It was assumed as a matter of standard practice that the well would produce 5% of its recoverable gas per year, and operate for 20 years, so Mr. Smith wanted to assume $i_2 - i_1 = 20$.

The consultant visited with a number of geologists and engineers in the company to collect further information about the decision process and the particular well in question. It turned out that the investment decision was a two-stage process involving an initial drilling operation down to the bed, at which point the pay thickness could be accurately determined. Costwise, this was the major part of the operation. Past experience had led to the adoption of a rule that if net pay thickness ($X$) was less than six feet, the well would be abandoned at that point. If net pay thickness equalled or exceeded six feet, a small further investment would be made to enable gas to be "pulled" and sold.

The consultant asked various experts in the company to supply probabilistic information about the uncertain quantities. Although the engineers and executives of the company had been making decisions under uncertainty for years, they were not used to explicitly expressing their uncertainty as probability statements, and the consultant had to train them using a subjective probability calibration exercise that he had developed. In the end, the inputs to the risk analysis were:

1. Net pay thickness ($X$), which was determined (from past experience and geological information) to be approximately normally distributed with mean $\mu_x = 8$ feet and standard deviation $\sigma_x = 2$ feet.
2. Recovery factor ($Y$), which was determined to be uniformly distributed between extremes of 0.5 and 0.95. History had shown that recovery factors had

[5] This factor measures how much gas product exists per unit volume.

no central tendency (i.e., were not modal) and that they were essentially equally likely to be anywhere in the specified range.

3. Investment cost ($I$), which was specified as the discrete distribution:

| *Investment Cost (I) (millions of dollars)* | *Probability* |
|---|---|
| 0.8 | 0.1 |
| 1.0 | 0.2 |
| 1.2 | 0.2 |
| 1.4 | 0.3 |
| 1.6 | 0.2 |

This investment cost reflected uncertain drilling costs and did not include the $300,000 that would be spent to connect the well to supply lines if the net pay thickness ($X$) was equal to or more than six feet.

4. The time to start up (given that $X \geq 6$ feet), which was also expressed as a discrete distribution:

| *Time from Investment to First Revenue ($i_1$)* | *Probability* |
|---|---|
| 2 years | 0.3 |
| 3 years | 0.6 |
| 4 years | 0.1 |

The consultant drew up a flow chart of the risk analysis program (see Figure 9–9) and then wrote a computer program to calculate the output distribution of NPV. He decided not to bother flying home to where he could have used his existing risk analysis software as he knew that the program would take less than an hour to write.

The cumulative distribution of NPV is shown in Figure 9–10. Note that the distribution shows that there is a 17% chance that no revenue will be produced because net pay thickness is less than 6 feet. This can be verified by simply noting that $\mu_x = 8$ feet and $\sigma_x = 2$ feet, hence for a normally distributed $X$ variable, $P(X < 6) = 0.16$. The small difference between the 17% obtained from the simulation and the 0.16 true value is due to random error in the simulation. The total probability of making a loss on this project (negative NPV) is 0.31. Although considerable risk is involved, the average NPV over all the trials is a healthy $311,000.

The consultant showed Mr. Smith how to interpret the output data and also how easy it was to conduct sensitivity analyses. Mr. Smith learned a great deal about the factors that *drive* the NPV and their interaction by checking the sensitivity of the NPV distribution to various input assumptions, such as gas price and discount rate. He also changed some of the input probabilities and ran the program under three different conditions to enable comparisons between NPV distributions. In Figure 9–10, the steps on the low NPV portion of the graph reflect that if net pay thickness is under six feet, the NPV is equal to the initial investment (which is described by a discrete distribution). The dashed line on this part of the graph is an approximation for a

**FIGURE 9–9** Flowsheet for the Gas Exploration Analysis

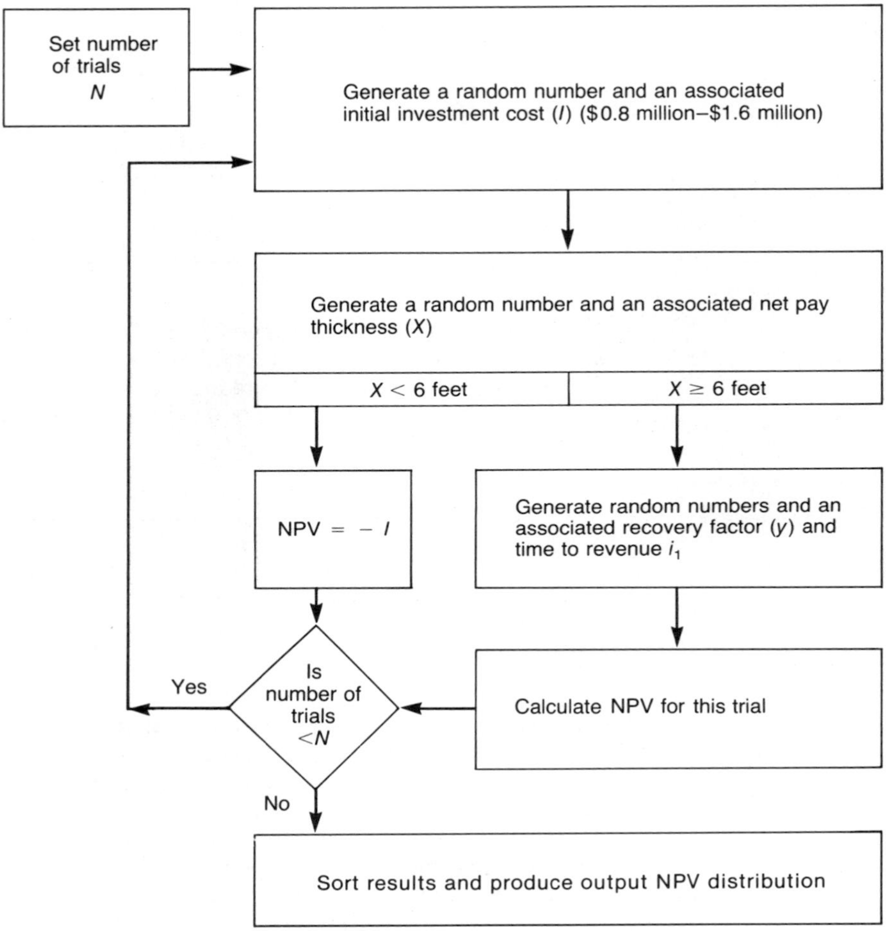

continuous distribution of $I$. Note also that the $S$ shape of the curve exists above NPV amounts of −$800,000. For lower NPV amounts there is a discontinuity because no revenue is generated for net pay thickness under six feet. Even if revenue is produced, losses (as high as $600,000) were possible. However, the probability of a positive NPV was about 0.7, and this included:

$$P(\text{NPV} > \$0.5 \text{ million}) = 0.5$$

$$P(\text{NPV} > \$1 \text{ million}) = 0.25$$

and a maximum NPV of over $2.2 million.

**FIGURE 9–10** Cumulative Probability Distribution for the Gas Exploration Example

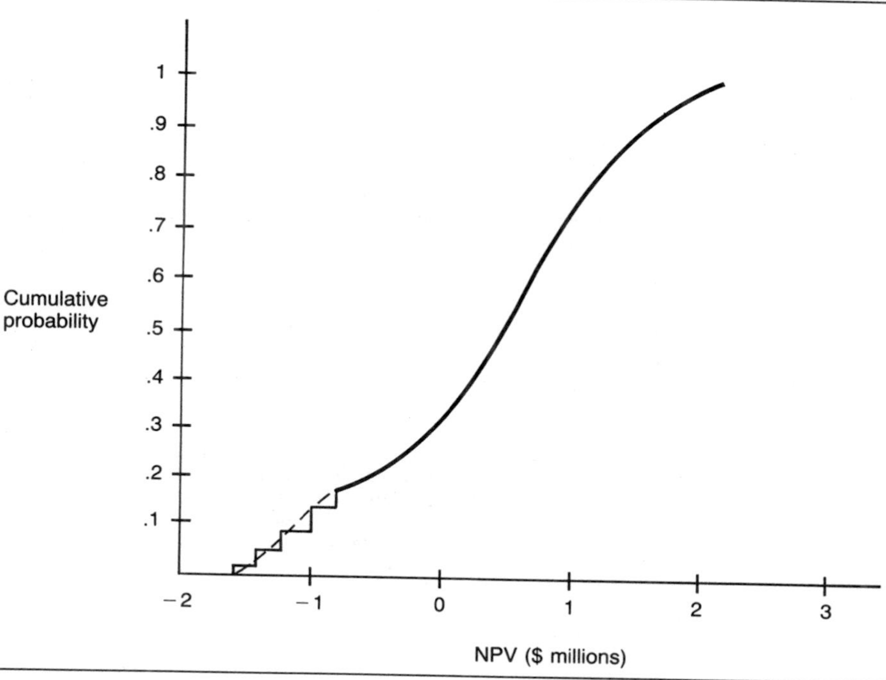


Mr. Smith was impressed by the analysis and stated that he now had a much better feel for the uncertainty involved in the decision. He asked the consultant whether he could analyze all his drill/no-drill decisions using such a method and, further, whether a comparison of cumulative distributions would help him make choices between drilling sites. At this point the consultant explained the principles of stochastic dominance to Mr. Smith and showed him how to use the risk analysis program for any drill/no-drill decisions.

Mr. Smith then said that he had one final question: This analysis seemed to be an excellent way of analyzing individual wells, but that his real job was to make drill/no-drill decisions repeatedly so that at any time the company had a good portfolio of wells. The consultant explained that the portfolio problem was a considerably more complex one, but that the risk analysis approach was still a useful one in this new context. Indeed, it was feasible to individually analyze each well and determine its NPV distribution and then to screen out those wells that were relatively unattractive. The wells that remained in the feasible set could then by analyzed in sets (or groups) so that Monte Carlo simulations would produce NPV distributions for groups of wells.

Mr. Smith replied that this would be a most useful decision support system, and he retained the consultant to modify his original program to calculate NPV distributions for groups of wells. Figure 9–11 shows a simplified flow diagram for that

**FIGURE 9–11** Risk Analysis for a Portfolio of Gas Wells

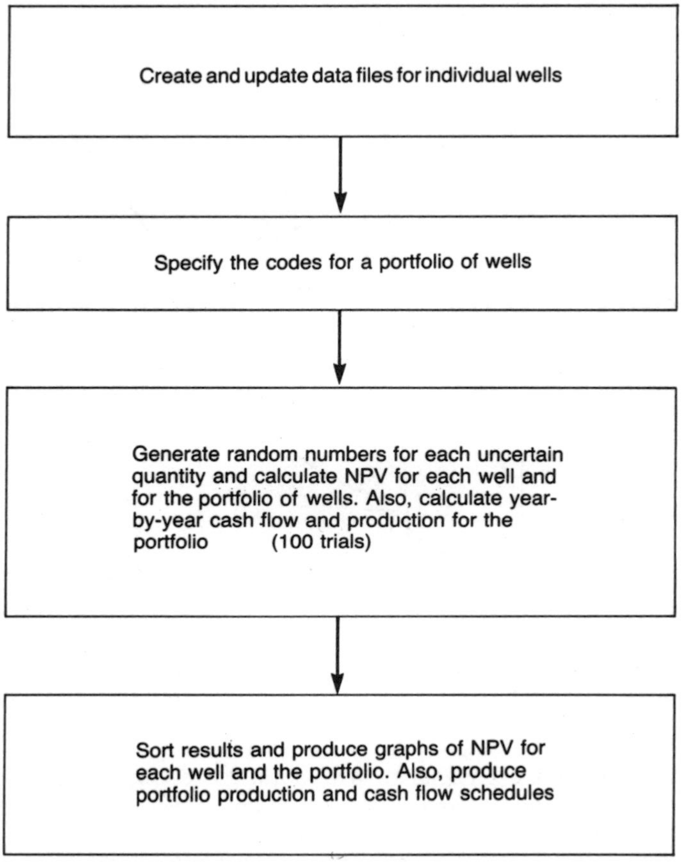

program. It was set up so that the input data for each well was stored in a data file and the user would simply specify a well number or code for each member of the portfolio.

Mr. Smith used the system to construct and compare portfolios of wells. He used certain constraints and guidelines to help him construct sets of sensible portfolios. For example, he had a set of demand forecasts for each of the next 10 years that acted as minimum production constraints. Hence, he had requirements to replace old wells with new production capacity.

Another useful mode of analysis which Mr. Smith performed was portfoliowide sensitivity analysis. He was able to make changes in variables (such as gas price) that affected some or all of the wells in any portfolio. Since different wells had different break-even points and different gas price sensitivities, he was able to determine not only the NPV distributions, but also the trade-offs between expected NPV and various risks.

After using the system for about three months, Mr. Smith reflected on how different his decision process was as a result of having this decision aid. He had just had the consultant come back and modify the system to treat gas price as an uncertain quantity rather than as fixed, to reflect his increasing uncertainty about future prices. Mr. Smith thought back to his past decisions on individual drill/no-drill choices and admitted that they were often made with a hope and a prayer. He felt much more confident about the quality of his decisions and decision processes now. On the consultant's last visit, Mr. Smith had remarked: "The actual riskiness of this business hasn't dropped in the past three months, in fact if anything, the expectation of deregulated gas prices has increased the feeling of uncertainty in the industry. From my perspective, this system has given me the ability to *understand the risks much better.* I still have a lot of tough decisions to make, but now I think I make many more good decisions than bad ones and that certainly is an improvement. We won't be able to effectively measure the resultant improved financial performance of the company for a few years, but I can confidently forecast that our stock price is going to be on the up and up."

## SUMMARY

The risk analysis approach and its associated techniques provide a powerful and flexible tool for managers to analyze complex problems with many sources of uncertainty. In some cases, analytical solutions can be derived, however Monte Carlo simulation techniques can more generally be used to solve risk analysis problems. The risk analysis process is an important part of the decision analysis process when decision trees become large and involves the stages of problem definition, model formulation, assessment, calculation, sensitivity analysis, and choice.

Monte Carlo techniques require the generation of random trials to establish an output distribution and can be performed by hand (for simple problems) or by computers. The results of a risk analysis are a probability distribution for a decision variable. The explicit treatment of uncertain quantities as such rather than as point estimates is the strength of the risk analysis approach.

If uncertain quantities are statistically related (dependent), conditional distributions should be assessed. The analyst or decision maker should carefully consider whether or not variables are related, and if so what is the nature of such relationships.

## FURTHER READING

A growing literature on risk analysis reflects its increasing importance both as an approach to decision making under uncertainty and as a set of techniques. Hertz and Thomas (1983 and 1984) have published two volumes which together provide an excellent coverage of the state of the art in risk analysis.

These volumes modify and amplify the early contribution of Hertz (1965), which is reprinted in the *Harvard Business Review* (1979).

Other early contributors of note were Hespos and Strassman (1965) and Hillier (1969). Hespos and Strassman proposed stochastic decision trees as a means of developing the properties of risk analysis in a decision tree format. Hillier developed the analytic approach to risk analysis.

Carter (1972) critically examined the strengths and limitations of risk analysis. Carter, Hayes (1975), and Hull (1977) address the issue of how to most effectively make use of risk analysis outputs.

Risk analysis has been applied to a wide variety of problems as evidenced by the case descriptions in the Hertz and Thomas volumes and the variety of sources in which studies involving risk analysis are to be found. One of the early applications of risk analysis was to oil and gas drilling decisions (Smith and Monkin, 1970). More recently, risk analysis has been proposed as an approach for strategic business planning. Strategic planning problems are typically complex, with a poorly defined structure, multiple conflicting objectives, and many possible sources of uncertainty. Wagner (1980) and Hertz and Thomas (1984) should be consulted in this domain.

## REFERENCES

CARTER, E. E. 1972. "What Are the Risks in Risk Analysis?" *Harvard Business Review,* July–August, pp. 72–82.

HAYES, R. H. 1975. "Incorporating Risk Aversion into Risk Analysis." *Engineering Economist* 20, Winter, pp. 99–121.

HERTZ, D. B. 1979. "Risk Analysis in Capital Investment." *Harvard Business Review.* Originally published in 1964. Reprinted in *Harvard Business Review,* September–October, pp. 169–81.

HERTZ, D. B., and H. THOMAS. 1983. *Risk Analysis and Its Applications.* New York: John Wiley & Sons.

________. 1984. *Practical Risk Analysis.* New York: John Wiley & Sons.

HESPOS, R. F., and P. A. STRASSMAN. 1965. "Stochastic Decision Trees for the Analysis of Investment Decisions." *Management Science* 11, no. 10, August, pp. B244–59.

HESS, S. W., and H. A. QUIGLEY. 1963. "Analysis of Risks in Investments Using the Monte Carlo Technique," *Chemical Engineering Progress* 42, p. 55.

HILLIER, F. S. 1969. *The Evaluation of Risky Interrelated Investments.* Amsterdam: North-Holland.

HULL, J. C. 1977. "The Input to and Output from Risk Simulation Models." *European Journal of Operational Research* 1, pp. 368–75.

SMITH, M. B., and B. MONKIN. 1970. "Probability Models for Petroleum Investment Decisions." *Journal of Petroleum Technology* 22, May, pp. 543–50.

WAGNER, G. R. 1980. "Strategic Thinking Supported by Risk Analysis." *Long Range Planning* 13, June, pp. 61–68.

## PROBLEMS

1. Discuss the advantages of the risk analysis process relative to other methods. Why do we use a Monte Carlo sampling procedure, which is inexact, when it is always theoretically possible to find exact answers?
2. How can dependence be handled in risk analysis?
3. Since in a random-number table, any digit is equally likely to appear in any position, how can random numbers be used to represent distributions that are not uniform [rectangular]?
4. How can the Monte Carlo process give decision makers better insight for making decisions under uncertainty than methods that use point estimates or summary statistics?
5. How is it possible to know how many Monte Carlo trials is enough in a particular risk analysis?
6. Toss a coin 10 times.
   *a*. Should you expect to get exactly five heads and five tails with probability one (assuming a fair coin)?
   *b*. Suppose you did not know the underlying probabilities of heads and tails outcomes. Would three tosses of the coin be enough to use as a basis for assessing these probabilities? Would five tosses be enough?
   *c*. Begin a process of tossing the coin, each time recording the result and using all the available information to estimate the probability of heads. What is the nature of the relationship between the number of tosses and the stability of the probability estimate in this process? Stop tossing the coin when the probability becomes close to, and stays near 0.5.
7. Use a random-number table to simulate 10 trials of the process of three coins being simultaneously tossed. How many random numbers do you need per trial? What probability distribution did you obtain with 10 trials, of the number of heads that appeared each time?
8. The Poisson distribution is a discrete distribution often used to represent random arrival processes. Its distribution formula is

$$P(X = x) = \frac{e^{-\lambda}\lambda^x}{x!}$$

   where $\lambda$ is a distribution parameter equal to the average number of arrivals.
   *a*. For the Poisson distribution with $\lambda = 3$, calculate the probabilities of 0, 1, 2, 3, 4, 5, 6, and more than 6 arrivals.
   *b*. Calculate the cumulative distribution.
   *c*. Use random numbers to simulate 10 trials from this random process.

*d.* Is the average of your 10 trials exactly equal to 3? If not, explain why.

9. The manager of a department store wishes to forecast Christmas season sales in the store's departments. His assistant has told him that in the past, sales are primarily related to the state of the economy. His assistant forecast four possibilities as follows:

| | *Probabilities* | *Sporting Goods Sales* |
|---|---|---|
| Economy very strong | 0.2 | $80,000 |
| Economy moderately strong | 0.3 | $75,000 |
| Economy weak | 0.4 | $65,000 |
| Economy depressed | 0.1 | $40,000 |

The sporting goods department manager said that in his experience, sales were also affected by the weather. He generally agreed with the above forecasts presuming good weather, but suggested that sales would be 20% lower if pre-Christmas weather was generally bad. He assessed a one in four chance of bad weather. The store manager related sales to net profits using the relationship:

$$\text{Net profit} = 0.28 \times \text{sales} - \$2{,}500$$

*a.* Calculate the exact probability distributions of sales and net profits.

*b.* Use random numbers to generate 10 trial values for the state of the economy and the weather. Use these trials to generate a distribution for net profit for the sports department. Compare the results with those of part *a* above.

10. An auto manufacturer is considering whether or not to continue exporting its sedan model to a foreign country or to invest in an assembly plant there.

If export is continued, cash flows to the company will be affected by many factors such as labor and material costs, finance costs, and exchange rates. The company forecasts that over the 10 years' planning horizon, annual aftertax profit contributions from exports would be:

$20 million with probability 0.2
$25 million with probability 0.4
$30 million with probability 0.2
$35 million with probability 0.2

A discount rate of 16% per annum was appropriate.

Recently, the company negotiated for very favorable tax incentives from the foreign government should it choose to build an assembly plant there. With an investment of $200 million from the company, the foreign government would supply the remaining necessary capital to build the plant. Further, the cheaper labor in the new plant and better tax conditions led to projected annual cash flows (after-tax) as follows:

$25 million with probability 0.1
$40 million with probability 0.25
$50 million with probability 0.5
$60 million with probability 0.15

For both alternatives, cash flows were independent across time.

*a*. Calculate the expected value of NPV for both alternatives. Which alternative has the higher degree of uncertainty in its cash flow?

*b*. Use risk analysis procedures to develop probabilistic estimates for each alternative. Run 10 Monte Carlo trials for each alternative, and plot the NPV cumulative distributions on the same graph. What do you conclude?

11. Raymond Flymouse, the president of Flymouse Inc., wished to analyze the economics of launching a new product. Two pricing strategies were possible if the launch was to go ahead. The product was a floating lawn mower which worked on a Hovercraft principle. The low-price strategy ($150 per unit) would produce a low profit per unit but higher sales volume than the high-price strategy ($220 per unit). Specifically, the following estimates were made for price and quantity:

| *Sales under Low-Price Strategy* | | *Sales under High-Price Strategy* | |
|---|---|---|---|
| 50,000 units with probability | 0.1 | 25,000 units with probability | 0.2 |
| 75,000 units with probability | 0.2 | 50,000 units with probability | 0.3 |
| 100,000 units with probability | 0.3 | 75,000 units with probability | 0.3 |
| 125,000 units with probability | 0.2 | 100,000 units with probability | 0.2 |
| 150,000 units with probability | 0.1 | | $\Sigma = 1$ |
| 175,000 units with probability | 0.1 | | |
| | $\Sigma = 1$ | | |

Fixed costs were assumed constant at $850,000 and total variable costs were assumed as $100 per unit.

Use Monte Carlo simulation (run 10 trials) to develop profit distributions for each alternative and develop a pricing strategy.

12. *a*. Write a computer program to solve the NPV problem (Example 9–2) described in the chapter. Plot the output distribution, and interpret the results in terms of the uncertainty of NPV. Assume independence of cash flows.

*b*. Use the given dependence relationships between cash flows to solve the NPV example. Conduct a sensitivity analysis of the discount rate.

13. *a*. Use the data in problem 11 to develop profit distributions by programming the simulation on a computer and running 100 trials. How does the result compare with that generated in problem 11 using only 10 trials?

    *b*. Referring to problem 11, after a preliminary analysis in which sales quantity was the primary source of uncertainty, Mr. Flymouse realized that he had been erroneously treating fixed and variable costs as constants. In fact, his fixed costs were not known constants, and after revising his production plans he decided that fixed costs were equally likely to be anywhere in the range of $800,000 to $1 million. He also noted that variable costs would be tied to sales quantity because of economies of scale that could be feasible in raw material procurement and labor efficiency. His initial estimate of variable cost ($100) was based on a total volume of 100,000 units. He revised this to be

    $$\text{Cost} = \$(120 - \text{Sales volume}/5{,}000)$$

    He also wished to account for the fact that this best estimate could be plus or minus 10%. His costs could then be represented by a uniform distribution between the bounds of $0.9 \times (120 - \text{volume}/5{,}000)$ and $1.1 \times (120 - \text{volume}/5{,}000)$. Mr. Flymouse wondered how his deeper thinking about the problem affected his profit distribution. Program a computer to solve this revised problem including the dependency relationship between cost and volume.

14. An investment manager was considering taking an equity position on behalf of his investment fund in a mineral exploration venture, which seemed promising but risky. There was a 50% chance that all monies invested would be lost in the cost of exploration and that no revenue would be forthcoming. There was a 50% chance that sufficient deposits would be found to make a commercially viable extraction process attractive. The deal proposed to the investment manager was a $5 million investment that would give his company 33% of the equity. There was to be no debt involved in the venture until initial exploration had been done. The investment manager was faced with a proposition that involved a 50% chance of losing $5 million and a 50% chance of uncertain revenues that could be quite high. The initial returns to investment could accrue after two years, should the project be successful. In each of years 2 through 15, cash flows of either $0.8 million, $1 million, or $1.2 million would result with probabilities of 0.2, 0.5, and 0.3 respectively. The $5 million investment would be immediate.

    *a*. Assuming the cash flows to be independent, determine the expected net present value of the proposition, and use Monte Carlo simulation to construct a risk profile. The appropriate cost of capital (discount rate) was 12.5%.

*b*. In refining his thinking about this investment and the analysis involved, the fund manager further investigated the length of time over which positive cash flow returns could be expected. This was an uncertain factor itself, and he thought that the returns were equally likely to be over any time horizon from 10 to 20 years, starting in year 2. Include this uncertain factor in your risk analysis.

*c*. He refined his analysis again by noting that cash flows in a particular year were likely to be correlated with cash flows in the year before, and the year after. He assessed factors to take this into account. Specifically, if cash flows in any year were $0.8 million or $1.2 million, the probabilities of cash flows in the next year being $1.2 million or $0.8 million, respectively, were zero. The probabilities of cash flows moving up or down by $200,000 however, were not zero. If cash flows in any year were $0.8 million, the probability was 0.2 that in the following year they would be $1 million, and similarly if cash flows in a given year were $1.2 million. If cash flows in a given year were $1 million, the probability of them being $1 million in the next year was 0.7, with higher and lower values in the next year being equally likely. Include this factor in your risk analysis and produce an expected value estimate and a risk profile for this venture. Assume initial cash flows as given by the originally assessed probabilities. Run 5 trials by hand and use a computer simulation to run 100 trials.

15. The owner of a chain of automotive repair businesses was examining his projected revenues over the next two years. He owned a total of 20 facilities which he categorized as large, medium, or small. He had 10 large, 6 medium, and 4 small facilities. The large facilities each had projected cash inflows over the time horizon of $1 million, $800,000, or $700,000 with respective probabilities of 0.6, 0.2, and 0.2 each. The medium-sized facilities each had projected cash inflows over the time horizon of $400,000, $300,000, and $200,000 with respective probabilities of 0.5, 0.3, and 0.2. The small facilities each had net cash inflows of $200,000, $150,000, and $100,000 with probabilities 0.6, 0.3, and 0.1 respectively.

*a*. Calculate the total expected net cash inflow, and determine an aggregate risk profile for the 20 installations. Is a Monte Carlo approach the only feasible one?

*b*. An assumption made in the owner's initial analysis was that no economic downturn would occur. He wished to review this assumption, and to do so, he wanted to include a multiplicative factor in his analysis should a downturn occur. He decided that a major downturn or a minor downturn or no downturn might occur with probabilities 0.2, 0.3, and 0.5, respectively. A downturn would differentially affect the net cash inflows of his businesses depending upon their size. A major downturn would decrease, from the base-case assumptions, the net cash inflow of his large businesses by a factor of 1.5, of his medium-sized businesses by a factor of 1.7, and his small businesses by a factor of 2. A minor downturn would decrease his large, medium, and small business net cash inflows by factors of 1.25, 1.4, and 1.6, respectively. Include this factor in your risk analysis, and recalculate expected net cash inflows and a risk profile.

16. The owner of a large brewing company who also owned a baseball team and a substantial part of a National Football League team was interested in diversifying into the professional ice hockey business. It had always been a favorite sport of hers, and the opportunity had just arisen to purchase a major share of a good, but not top-ranking, hockey organization. After investigating the potential monetary costs and benefits involved in owning the major share in this organization, assessments were made of the possible cash returns. Top-ranking teams in the league were generally found to be profitable, whereas medium teams were found to be slightly unprofitable, and low-ranking teams were more unprofitable. This was primarily because top-ranking teams attracted larger crowds, were featured on national television more often, and could attract high-quality players at lower prices. The required investment was $18 million, which included the purchase cost and the cost of building the team in the first year into a top-ranking team. The annual cash returns of top-ranking teams were $3 million. Middle-ranked teams usually lost about a half million dollars per season, and low-ranked teams usually lost about $1 million. The investment was being considered for a 10-year period only, after which it would be sold. It's value at the end of that period was projected at $30 million if the team was a top-ranking one, only half as much if it was a middle-ranking team, and a quarter as much it if was a low-ranking team.

    A transition matrix showing the probabilities of a team in year $n$ being of a certain standard in year $n + 1$ is shown below. This matrix wasdevised based on historical data and an analysis of the managerial talent and resources that would be applied. If purchased, the team will be a top-ranking team in year 1. The opportunity cost of capital for the investor was 15%.

*Transition Matrix*

| | | *Year n + 1* | | |
|---|---|---|---|---|
| | | *Low Rank* | *Middle Rank* | *Top Rank* |
| Year *n* | Top rank | 0.1 | 0.4 | 0.5 |
| | Middle rank | 0.3 | 0.4 | 0.3 |
| | Low rank | 0.5 | 0.4 | 0.1 |

Use Monte Carlo analysis to construct a risk profile for the investment.

## Case Study

### RW Industries

Robert Wilson, founder and president of RW Industries had an important decision to make. His company manufactured souvenir items that were marketed mainly through large universities. His main items in terms of total sales were place mats, coffee cups, and beer glasses. In each case he bought the mats, cups, and glasses and applied the appropriate university insignia or logo, in his factory. Last year his sales had been over $600,000 and resulted in $120,000 in retained earnings.

His decision concerned a proposed agreement to make calendars. These calendars would be marketed through the same channels as his other products (university bookstores and other merchants), and he had already negotiated contract conditions with three major universities. The calendars would show scenes of the various campuses and mark the various dates that were important to students and staff.

Before he signed and sealed his contracts, Mr. Wilson decided to review the economics of these deals once again. His revenue would be $3.80 per unit (retail price was to be $5.95), and each of the three universities had guaranteed his minimum annual sales of 2,500, 4,000, and 6,000 units. They had each also suggested further orders if demand was high. Each contract was for five years. Mr. Wilson estimated that in the first year, sales at each university had a 50:50 chance of being high enough to require more calendars. He also thought that these likelihoods were independent across the three universities. He had already agreed with his distributors that further orders, should they occur, would be in multiples of 1,000 units. He thought it highly likely (0.9 probability) that if any further orders accrued, they would be 1,000 units for each university. If 2,000 additional units were ordered by any of the three universities, he decided that he would be very pleasantly surprised. He assigned a 0.1 probability to this occurrence.

In order to produce the calendars, he would have to buy some machinery and incur other fixed costs, which he originally estimated as totaling $115,000. However, he was unsure about this initial cost and represented his uncertainty as being normally distributed with a mean of $115,000 and standard deviation of $15,000. His variable costs were to be $1.10 per unit, but he was not confident of this figure and chose a normal distribution with a mean of $1.10 and standard deviation of 10 cents to reflect his uncertainty.

His cost of capital was to be 15% per annum.

At the end of five years, he knew there was a chance that he would renegotiate for new contracts but decided to assume such possibilities away and examine the cash flow picture over a five-year horizon only. The machinery he bought would have a salvage value anywhere between $10,000 and $20,000 at the end of the five-year period.

Mr. Wilson thought that the possibilities of reorders, which were 0.5 for each university in year 1, would increase because of repeat purchases in subsequent years. He made the following assessments:

| *Year* | *Probability of Reorders* |
|---|---|
| 1 | 0.5 |
| 2 | 0.55 |
| 3 | 0.6 |
| 4 | 0.65 |
| 5 | 0.65 |

Although he realized that there was probably some further dependence between reorder possibility and reorder size, he decided to assume independence of reorder size across time because each year's calendar was to have a different layout and different photographs.

## CASE QUESTIONS

1. Calculate the expected NPV of Mr. Wilson's venture.
2. Identify the major sources of uncertainty. Run a Monte Carlo simulation with 100 trials (on a computer) to produce a distribution of NPV.
3. Use the NPV distribution to note:
   *a.* The range of the distribution.
   *b.* The probability of NPV being negative.
   *c.* The interquartile range.
   Since this decision had to be made in March for September production (for next year's calendars), it seemed reasonable to assume that cash flows would all occur at the end of the year (apart from the initial investment, which was immediate).
4. In order to help Mr. Wilson come to a quick decision, his son John (who had recently finished an MBA) helped him get a feeling for his attitude toward risk. John asked his father to give his certainty equivalent values of two gambles as follows:

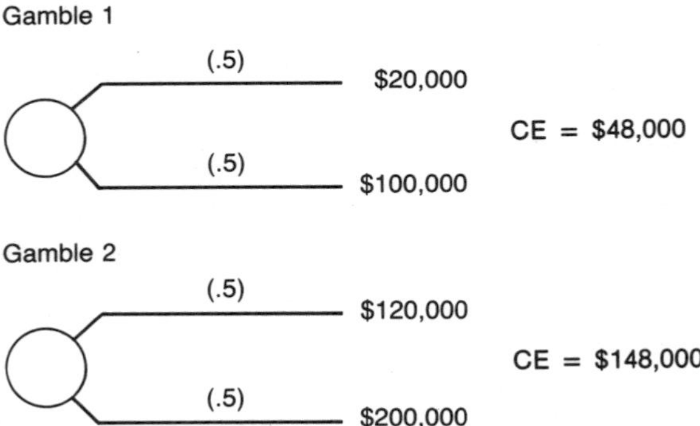

John knew that his father was constantly risk averse because gamble 2 was just the same in form as gamble 1 with the cash flows being $100,000 higher and his father gave certainty equivalents which were $12,000 less than the mean in both cases.

5. Fit an exponential utility function to Mr. Wilson's gambles, of form

$$U(\$X) = -e^{-kX}$$

and calculate $k$. Use this utility function to evaluate the expected utility of the NPV distribution and compare it with that of another venture with a known constant present value of $25,000.

## CASE STUDY

### Northern Insurance Brokers (NIB)[1]

Northern Insurance Brokers is a firm of insurance agents who act as worldwide consultants and insurance/reinsurance brokers. They have offices in five capital cities of states in Australia.

In August 1978, Leonard Tyne of NIB began an investigation of the insurance package held by one of NIB's clients which was one of Australia's major internal airlines. He was particularly concerned with his client's aircraft hull insurance. Losses resulting in insurance claims could be classified into one of two types:

1. Partial damage to a hull resulting in relatively small claims.
2. Complete losses where the hull insurance would pay for a replacement aircraft.

The current insurance cover held by the airline for hull damage was a policy whereby the annual premium paid was equal to 150 percent of the actual losses incurred within that year, subject to an annual minimum of 40 cents per $100 insured and an annual maximum of $2.10 per $100 insured.

The group of underwriters who held the hull insurance approached Mr. Tyne with a suggestion of a modified hull insurance policy. They suggested that the modified policy conditions would be more suitable both to the insurer and the insured, and they asked Mr. Tyne to put the suggestion to the airline. The modified policy would have a premium set equal to losses, with a minimum of 60 cents per $100 insured and a maximum premium of $1.30 per $100 insured.

Mr. Tyne suggested that the client should view the opportunity as a chance to arrange for a modified type of insurance that might well work out to be significantly cheaper. Alan Jones, who was considered the airlines' statistical expert, was commissioned to study and investigate the possibility.

---

[1] This case was developed by D. A. Samson and Howard Thomas at the Australian Graduate School of Management.

He began by gathering necessary data. A reasonably large amount of data was available in claims resulting in partial hull damage. Partial hull damage usually occurred during take-off and landing, and experience allowed Mr. Jones to predict that partial hull damage resulted in insurance claims of between $150,000 and $300,000 per year. On the question of total hull destruction Mr. Jones was less confident of being able to assess the risk because of the very small amount of data available on Australian cases.

He knew that most serious accidents and failures occurred near airports and that taking off and landing were the most dangerous parts of flying. He needed to estimate the risk of a crash occurring and therefore decided to begin with a point estimate figure based on combined European and American data of past years. The probability of an aircraft crashing in a one-year period was found to be 0.005, and he decided to use this figure in his initial calculations.

Data on fleet size and value were also collected:

Fleet Size and Value Data

| | | *Book Value* | | *Insured Value* | |
|---|---|---|---|---|---|
| *Aircraft* | *Number* | *Plane* | *Fleet* | *Plane* | *Fleet* |
| 727/200 | 8 | $5.5m | $44.0m | $5.7m | $45.6m |
| 727/100 | 2 | 4.9m | 9.8m | 5.0m | 10.0m |
| DC9 | 12 | 3.6m | 43.2m | 3.8m | 45.6m |
| Fokker Friendship | 12 | 1.2m | 14.4m | 1.3m | 15.6m |
| Twin Otter | 6 | 0.6m | 3.6m | 0.65m | 3.9m |
| Total | 40 | | $111.4m | | $120.7m |

## CASE QUESTION

Use Monte Carlo methods to develop a loss distribution for the fleet. Evaluate the cost and benefits of each insurance program.

CHAPTER TEN

# Revision of Probabilities

## OUTLINE



## OBJECTIVES

After completing this chapter, you should be able to:

1. Describe the procedure for, and usefulness of, the probability revision process.
2. Combine prior probability distributions with conditional likelihood probabilities for both discrete and continuous probability distributions.
3. Understand how a decision maker can incorporate new information, such as expert opinions, into a decision analysis.
4. Model decision problems that include choices about gathering various forms of new probabilistic information.

## INTRODUCTION

This chapter focuses on the probability revision process, and makes use of a statistical rule, called Bayes Theorem, which is a mechanism for updating probability distributions in order to incorporate additional evidence or information about an uncertain quantity.

In some decision analyses, probabilistic information can be obtained about an uncertain quantity from more than one source. It is useful to be able to accurately combine our existing beliefs about an uncertain quantity when additional information becomes available.

This feature of decision analysis is important because, as managers, we are often in a position of needing to choose whether to obtain more information about an uncertain quantity, for example in the form of market surveys, polls, and expert opinions on a variety of important items. In operations management, we must choose whether or not, and if so, how much quality acceptance sampling to do when we are uncertain about the quality of delivered raw materials. In financial management we may be uncertain about the state of some accounting measures, such as average accounts receivable, and may wish to sample a number of accounts to improve our knowledge state, in order to make better informed policy decisions.

Subjective probability assessments that are made about uncertain future events reflect the decision maker's degree of belief about the likelihood of those events. In those decision situations where it is possible to modify one or more probability assessments on the basis of new information, Bayes Theorem can be used to calculate the updated probabilities that are necessary inputs for the decision tree.

Bayes Theorem involves three major elements. The first is the *prior probability distribution,* which is an input to the Bayes Theorem formula. This distribution represents the information at hand before the additional information becomes available. To illustrate, consider the example of a company that is deciding on whether to launch a new product. The company is about to conduct a market survey. It has *prior* information about market share that can be expressed as a prior probability distribution.

When the additional information becomes available, it can be combined with the prior probability distribution. The additional information may be a market survey result or an expert opinion and must be interpreted in terms of the parameter expressed in the prior probability distribution. This data is called the *likelihood information*. It is imperative that we recognize that the likelihood data is a set of *conditional probabilities* representing the likelihood of the observation (for example, a particular market survey result) *given* the assumed value of the parameter in question. In a market survey context, the market survey result (expressed as market share) must be interpreted in terms of the previously assumed possible values of market share. The *likelihood* probabilities are the probabilities of obtaining the particular market survey result given the various assumed market share

**FIGURE 10–1** The Probability Revision Process

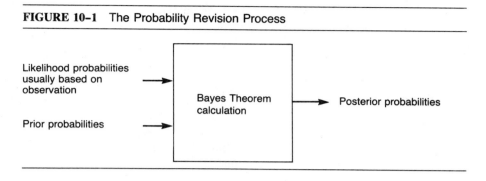

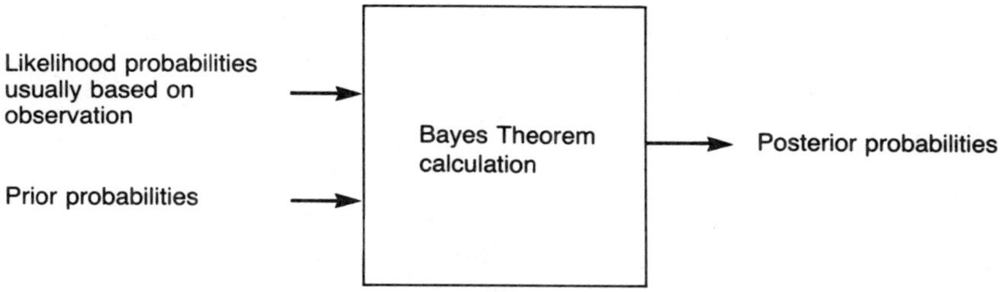

values. It is worth reemphasizing that likelihood values are *conditional* probabilities.

The Bayes Theorem formula is used to calculate composite probabilities that merge the prior probability distribution and the conditional likelihoods. These composite probabilities are called the *posterior probability distribution* (see Figure 10–1). Posterior probabilities are also conditional probabilities.

This chapter develops and illustrates the use of Bayes Theorem for revising probabilities in managerial decision contexts. The reader should begin by becoming familiar with the concepts involved, and then acquire the skills to manipulate Bayes Theorem. We will begin with a brief consideration of the technical (statistical) aspects of Bayes Theorem. Second, we will illustrate these concepts with a number of examples that explore the way in which multiple sources of information can be combined. Finally, this chapter outlines a number of managerial decision contexts in which Bayes Theorem can play a useful role. The Bayes Theorem methodology for probability revision, which is thoroughly developed in this chapter, is then used extensively in Chapter 11 to examine the value of information in decision analysis.

## BAYES THEOREM

Bayes Theorem can be expressed as a simple formula relating various conditional and unconditional probability values to each other. The use of Bayes Theorem in managerial decision analyses comes from its ability to derive and combine probabilistic information from separate sources into a useful form.

Let us develop Bayes Theorem from some simple probability concepts. Consider two random variables (uncertain quantities) called $X$ and $Y$. To illustrate, $X$ might be national market share (NM) and $Y$ might be market share as indicated by a local survey (SI) of potential customers.

Consider the probability of particular results such as $X$ taking on a particular value "$x$" (for example, 3%) and $Y$ taking on a particular value

"$y$" (for example, 4%). In general the probability of both these occurrences ($X = x$ and $Y = y$) is[1]

$$P(X = x \text{ and } Y = y) = P(X = x/Y = y) \times P(Y = y) \qquad [10\text{–}1]$$

For our example

$$P\begin{pmatrix}\text{NM} \\ = 3\%\end{pmatrix} \text{ and } \begin{pmatrix}\text{SI} \\ = 4\%\end{pmatrix} = P\begin{pmatrix}\text{NM} \\ = 3\% \text{ given } \text{SI} \\ = 4\%\end{pmatrix} \times P\begin{pmatrix}\text{SI} \\ = 4\%\end{pmatrix}$$

Equation [10–1] states that the probability of $X$ being $x$ and $Y$ being $y$ is the product of the conditional probability of $X$ being $x$ given that $Y$ takes on value $y$, multiplied by the unconditional value that $Y$ has taken on value $y$ (in the first place).

Similarly, we can switch the positions of $X$ and $Y$ parameters in Equation [10–1] and equally truly express the probability of $X$ being $x$ and $Y$ being $y$ as

$$P(X = x \text{ and } Y = y) = P(Y = y/X = x) \times P(X = x) \qquad [10\text{–}2]$$

For our example:

$$P\begin{pmatrix}\text{NM} \\ = 3\%\end{pmatrix} \text{ and } \begin{pmatrix}\text{SI} \\ = 4\%\end{pmatrix} = P\begin{pmatrix}\text{SI} \\ = 4\% \text{ given } \text{NM} \\ = 3\%\end{pmatrix} \times P\begin{pmatrix}\text{NM} \\ = 3\%\end{pmatrix}$$

We can equate these two expressions [10–1] and [10–2] for the joint probability of $X = x$ and $Y = y$ and write

$$P(X = x/Y = y) \times P(Y = y) = P(Y = y/X = x) \times P(X = x) \qquad [10\text{–}3]$$

Equation [10–3] equates the right-hand sides of Equations [10–1] and [10–2].

Bayes Theorem can be written as a simple rearrangement of Equation [10–3]

$$P(X = x/Y = y) = \frac{P(Y = y/X = x) \times P(X = x)}{P(Y = y)} \qquad [10\text{–}4]$$

For our example

$$P\begin{pmatrix}\text{NM} \\ = 3\% \text{ given } \text{SI} \\ = 4\%\end{pmatrix} = \frac{P\begin{pmatrix}\text{SI} \\ = 4\% \text{ given } \text{NM} \\ = 3\%\end{pmatrix} \times P\begin{pmatrix}\text{NM} \\ = 3\%\end{pmatrix}}{P\begin{pmatrix}\text{SI} \\ = 4\%\end{pmatrix}}$$

Bayes Theorem is useful because it allows us to calculate probabilities that have the *reverse direction of conditionality* from the probabilities we know. Referring to Equation [10–4] if we know the *unconditional* probabilities of $X = x$ and $Y = y$ and also the conditional probabilities of ($Y = y$ given $X = x$), we can use the formula to calculate the conditional probabilities of ($X = x$

---

[1] Note that the slash (/) in the equation represents a state of conditional probability.

given $Y = y$). *The reason that Bayes Theorem is useful in decision analysis is that we often need probabilistic information in a different form from the way it naturally occurs*. We use the term *naturally occurs* somewhat loosely here, to mean the way we can most easily assess or collect data on conditional probabilities.

We can illustrate the meaning of priors, likelihoods, and posterior probabilities with an important managerial example. In Chapter 8, Example 8–1, we introduced James Bigalo, chief executive with a problem, but he was having difficulty defining its nature. Let us assume that there were only two possible events, $E_1$ and $E_2$

$E_1$ = "It's a marketing problem"
$E_2$ = "It's a production problem"

Before consulting any of his colleagues, Mr. Bigalo could have assigned probabilities to the events $E_1$ and $E_2$. These would be Mr. Bigalo's prior probability beliefs. He then consults a first colleague who expresses an opinion about whether it's $E_1$ or $E_2$. Mr. Bigalo can then say: "Suppose it *really is* $E_1$." Given that assumption, what are the likelihoods that the colleague would have been correct (and stated $E_1$ as the problem) or incorrect? Conversely, Mr. Bigalo could calibrate his colleague's ability to identify the problem correctly if it was really $E_2$. These conditional probabilities are Mr. Bigalo's conditional likelihoods and represent *his* beliefs about his colleague's ability to correctly identify the problem. He might base these beliefs primarily on the track record of his colleague's past predictions in similar situations. If Mr. Bigalo then wants to revise his prior (unconditional) probabilities about whether the problem is really $E_1$ and $E_2$, he can use the calibrations of his colleague and the colleague's prediction itself to come to a set of posterior probabilities. Bayes Theorem is merely the mechanism for accurately performing the probability revision process.

If Mr. Bigalo then asks another colleague for a view about the problem, his posterior probabilities from the first iteration become his prior probabilities for the second probability revision process. To quantify this illustration, assume the prior probabilities are

$$P(E_1) = 0.8$$
$$P(E_2) = 0.2$$

The first colleague that Mr. Bigalo consults says that the problem is $E_1$. Mr. Bigalo believes that this colleague is pretty astute and would have a 90% chance of being right. Hence

$$P\text{ (Colleague says } E_1/\text{It is } E_1) = 0.9$$

On the other hand, Mr. Bigalo feels that even if the problem is really $E_2$, this colleague would still have a 30% chance of predicting that the problem is $E_1$. Hence

$$P\text{ (Colleague says } E_1/\text{It is } E_1) = 0.3$$

Bayes Theorem gives us

$$P\ (\text{It is } E_1/\text{Colleague says } E_1) = \frac{P(\text{Colleague says } E_1/\text{It is } E_1) \times P(\text{It is } E_1)}{P(\text{Colleague says } E_1)}$$

The denominator of the right-hand side of this equation is given by

$$\begin{aligned} P(\text{Colleague says } E_1) &= P(\text{Colleague says } E_1/\text{It is } E_1) \times P(\text{It is } E_1) \\ &\quad + P(\text{Colleague says } E_1/\text{It is } E_2) \times P(\text{It is } E_2) \\ &= 0.9 \times 0.8 + 0.3 \times 0.2 \\ &= 0.78 \end{aligned}$$

Hence

$$\begin{aligned} P(\text{It is } E_1/\text{Colleague says } E_1) &= \frac{0.9 \times 0.8}{0.78} \\ &= 0.923 \end{aligned}$$

Bayes Theorem indicates that Mr. Bigalo should revise his probability that the problem actually is $E_1$, from 0.8 to 0.923, and his probability that it is $E_2$ should drop from 0.2 to

$$1 - 0.923 = 0.077.$$

Note that the extent to which his prior beliefs were revised by his colleague's view were directly related to the degree of likelihood that he assigned to his colleague's *reliability* in being correct about the problem. Bayes Theorem is an important topic in decision analysis because it is a means for accurately expressing and combining various sources of probabilistic information.

## Table Format for Using Bayes Theorem

A convenient way to use Bayes Theorem is to systematically express the appropriate components of Bayes Theorem in a table format. Table 10–1 shows this format.

The table format for using Bayes Theorem is often more convenient than the formula because the table format requires the information to be systematically displayed and manipulated. Each row of the table represents one application of the Bayes Formula. Whereas one application of the formula calculates one posterior probability, the table format allows the whole posterior distribution for a particular observation outcome to be calculated at once. The table format and the formula require exactly the same calculations to be performed and lead to the same results.

Equation [10–4] and Table 10–1 relate directly to each other. In Equation [10–4], the posterior probabilities are calculated and expressed as the left-hand side. Hence in terms of the terminology of Table 10–1, the "event" variable is $X$ where $X$ can take on various $x$ values $X = x_i$ for $i = 1$ to $n$. The "observation" in Table 10–1 is a particular observation of $Y = y$. In these

**TABLE 10-1** A Bayesian Revision Calculation Procedure

| *Event* | *Prior Probabilities* | *Likelihoods* | *Joint Probabilities* | *Posterior* |
|---|---|---|---|---|
| $\text{Event}_1$ | $P(\text{Event}_1)$ | $P(\text{Observation/Event}_1)$ | $P(\text{Event}_1) \times P(\text{Observation/Event}_1)$ | $P(\text{Event}_1) \times P(\text{Observation/Event}_1)/P(\text{Observation})$ |
| $\text{Event}_2$ | $P(\text{Event}_2)$ | $P(\text{Observation/Event}_2)$ | $P(\text{Event}_2) \times P(\text{Observation/Event}_2)$ | $P(\text{Event}_2) \times P(\text{Observation/Event}_2)/P(\text{Observation})$ |
| ⋮ | ⋮ | ⋮ | ⋮ | ⋮ |
| $\text{Event}_n$ | $P(\text{Event}_n)$ | $P(\text{Observation/Event}_n)$ | $P(\text{Event}_n) \times P(\text{Observation/Event}_n)$ | $P(\text{Event}_n) \times P(\text{Observation/Event}_n)/P(\text{Observation})$ |
| | $\Sigma = 1$ | | $\Sigma = P(\text{Observation})$ | $\Sigma = 1$ |

terms, the posterior probabilities in Table 10–1 are the same as the right-hand side expression of Equation [10–4].

The Bayesian revision process and its application via the table format can be summarized in a series of steps:

**Step 1.** What is the event or variable of interest? Define how this event has relevance to the decision problem. Define the specific levels that the variable of interest can take on. (See column 1 of Table 10–1.)

**Step 2.** Assess the prior probability distribution. Since the prior probabilities *are* a distribution, these probabilities must sum to a value of one (see column 2 of Table 10–1). Techniques for assessing probabilities are detailed in Chapter 4.

**Step 3.** Define the possible observations that could be made. For each observation relevant to the decision problem, assess or calculate the conditional probability of its occurrence given various event states as defined in column 1. These likelihood probabilities go into column 3 of Table 10–1. A single table refers to only one particular observation. Note that the likelihood probabilities are not a probability distribution, hence, they need not sum to one.

**Step 4.** The rest of the procedure can be accomplished with a calculator. The joint probabilities are calculated by multiplying, row by row, the prior and likelihood probabilities. After the joint probabilities are calculated, sum them and write the sum at the bottom of column 4. This sum is

$$\sum_{i=1}^{n} P(\text{Event } i) \times P(\text{Observation/Event } i)$$

This sum equals the unconditional probability, $P$(Observation). This probability is often useful in the decision analysis.

**Step 5.** The posterior probabilities (column 5) are calculated by dividing each joint probability value by the sum of the joint probabilities. The posterior probabilities are a distribution and should sum to be one. In some instances, rounding off of these numbers may be necessary to achieve this. Note that the ratios between the posterior probabilities are the same as those between the joint probabilities from which they are derived. The posterior probabilities are calculated by normalizing the joint probabilities. Dividing the joint probabilities by their sum ensures that the posterior probabilities sum to one.

In summary, Bayes Theorem allows us to calculate probabilities with a reversed direction of conditionality (see Figure 10–2) from those that are known. The conditional probability information that we originally have is often of the opposite direction of conditionality to what is required as an input to the decision tree. *In other words, we may know or be able to estimate $P(Y = y/X = x)$ but want to know $P(X = x/Y = y)$!* Bayes Theorem is the mechanism by which we can calculate one from the other.

**FIGURE 10–2** Input and Output Information for Bayes Theorem

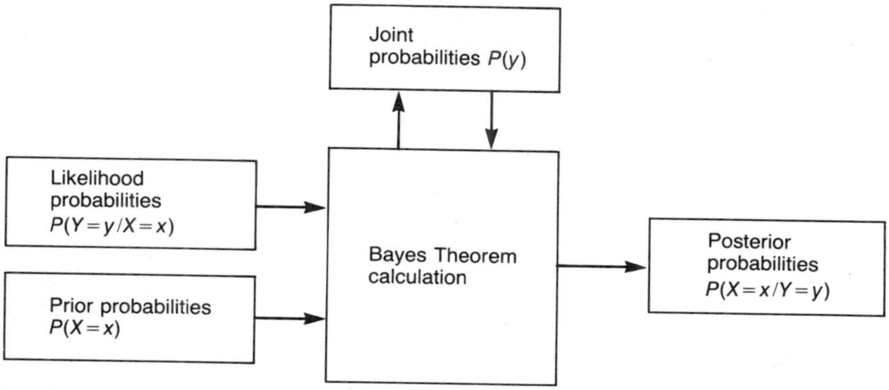

## Example 10–1

### Advance Electronics (A)

Advance Electronics produced electronic control devices (ECD) which were used for very fast computers, known as supercomputers. The production process for a new model of chip was rather unreliable and could be counted upon to occasionally produce a bad batch of ECDs. The production manager had observed that good and bad batches appeared to occur at random. About 20% of all batches had proved to be bad in the past. If the production system was working well, the yield was 95% (that is, 95 out of 100 ECDs would pass a functional quality test). If the production system was "off spec," the yield dropped to 25%. The production equipment could not be observed to go off spec because nothing obvious happened that could be sensed. However, if it was known immediately afterward that a bad batch had been produced, the system could be shut down and retuned, which was costly but necessary.

A test was available that could determine whether individual ECDs were working properly or not, but it was expensive for the company to test each unit. The company's major customers had agreed to accept all batches with yields of 90% or better and send back (at considerable expense to the company) all other batches.

The production manager of the ECD process wanted to know what he would learn by functionally testing one ECD in each batch.

Let us define what we *know* and what we *want to know* in this problem. The important event is whether a particular batch is "good" (having 95% yield) or "bad" (having 25% yield).

**TABLE 10–2** Bayesian Revision Given a Sample Result of "Good"

| *Event* | *Prior Probability* | *Likelihood* | *Joint* | *Posterior* |
|---|---|---|---|---|
| Batch is good | 0.8 | 0.95 | 0.76 | $\frac{0.76}{0.81} = 0.94$ |
| Batch is bad | 0.2 | 0.25 | 0.05 | $\frac{0.05}{0.81} = 0.06$ |
| | | | $\Sigma = 0.81$ | $\Sigma = 1$ |

We have unconditional probabilities based mainly on historical data

$$P(\text{Good}) = 0.8$$
$$P(\text{Bad}) = 0.2$$

This is the prior probability information.

If we sample a single ECD from the batch, what information do we get? We *know* the conditional probabilities of getting a good or a bad ECD given that the batch is good or bad. They come from the yield data.

We *know*

$$P(\text{Sample ECD is good/Batch is good}) = 0.95$$
$$P(\text{Sample ECD is bad/Batch is good}) = \underline{0.05}$$
$$\Sigma = 1$$

Also

$$P(\text{Sample ECD is good/Batch is bad}) = 0.25$$
$$P(\text{Sample ECD is bad/Batch is bad}) = \underline{0.75}$$
$$\Sigma = 1$$

These probabilities, above, are the (conditional) likelihoods.

We *want to know*

$P$(Batch is good/Sample ECD is good)
$P$(Batch is bad/Sample ECD is good)
$P$(Batch is good/Sample ECD is bad)
$P$(Batch is bad/Sample ECD is bad)

These are the posterior probabilities.

Note that the direction of conditionality is opposite in what we *know* and what we *want to know.*

To calculate the results using Bayes Theorem we can use the table format as described earlier in this chapter. A separate table must be made for each different observation. Table 10–2 shows calculations for a sample ECD being good.

---

Let's review the probability revision process. First, note that the Bayesian probability revision process transforms the prior probabilities into posterior probabilities by weighting them in proportion to the sample likelihoods. We are considering the probabilities of uncertain events, *P*(Batch is good) and *P*(Batch is bad). To begin with we have only *prior* information about these events. We want to know how various sample observations will affect our probabilities (translate them into posteriors). Bayes Theorem gives us the exact answers.

We should note that the Bayesian process recognizes that certain sample results were more or less likely, given the presumption of one or other event. These are indeed the likelihoods. Then, of course, we also want to know what the likelihoods of the various events are, given the sample result. These are the conditional posterior probabilities which we calculate.

In the Advance Electronics example, the table format for a sample result of "bad" is shown by Table 10–3.

If the sample result is assumed to be a bad ECD, the likelihood probabilities are the complements of those in the previous table. Reemphasizing, the likelihoods express the probability of the sample observation given the event state. The posterior probabilities are the probabilities of the event given the sample observation. Note that the probabilities in Tables 10–2 and 10–3 are generally rounded to two significant figures.

Now we can compare the posterior probabilities with the prior beliefs for the good and the bad sample in the Advance Electronics example. The sample, even though it was only a sample size of one, had a substantial impact on the probabilities. From Table 10–2 (where a sample result of "good" was assumed) the prior probabilities of a good or bad batch were 0.8 and 0.2 respectively, and the corresponding posteriors were 0.94 and 0.06. The probability of the batch being bad has been reduced by a factor of more than three on the basis of a sample of size one.

The impact of the sample is also large in the case (Table 10–3) where the sample is assumed "bad." The probabilities change (that is, the posterior probabilities are different from the prior probabilities) by a factor of nearly four. A sample result of bad gives a strong indication (probability = 0.79) that the batch is bad. The odds were originally four to one (0.8/0.2) that the batch was good, but a likelihood sample result of "bad" was 15 times more likely if the batch was bad, hence the adjustment (from prior to posterior probabilities) by a factor of 15 is made by the Bayes Theorem process.

**TABLE 10–3** Bayesian Revision Given a Sample Result of "Bad"

| *Event* | *Prior* | *Likelihood* | *Joint* | *Posterior* |
|---|---|---|---|---|
| Batch is good | 0.8 | 0.05 | 0.04 | $\frac{0.04}{0.19} = 0.21$ |
| Batch is bad | 0.2 | 0.75 | 0.15 | $\frac{0.15}{0.19} = 0.79$ |
| | | | $\Sigma = 0.19$ | $\Sigma = 1$ |

## Using Posterior Probabilities in Decision Trees

Let us use the Advance Electronics (A) example to explore how the prior, joint and posterior probabilities relate to a decison analysis. In that example the production manager pays a penalty for shipping a bad batch. It is useful for him to sample because from Tables 10–2 and 10–3 we know that the sample (even though it is only of one component) improves his resolution of whether the batch is good or bad. On the other hand, the act of conducting a sample costs money. Let's begin with the base case of no sample. If no sample is taken and the batch is shipped, since no extra information comes to hand as a result of sampling, the relevant probabilities are the priors. See the bottom branch of node $D_1$ of Figure 10–3. If he chooses not to sample, the production manager must live with the probability of 0.2 of shipping a bad batch.

The top branch (from node $D_1$) represents a decision to sample. The immediate outcome from sampling is a sample result. The probabilities of a sample result being good or bad are 0.81 and 0.19. These probabilities sum to one as they form the unconditional probability distribution of the sample result. They were calculated as the sums of the joint probabilities in Tables 10–2 and 10–3 respectively.

**FIGURE 10–3** Decision Tree for Advance Electronics (A)

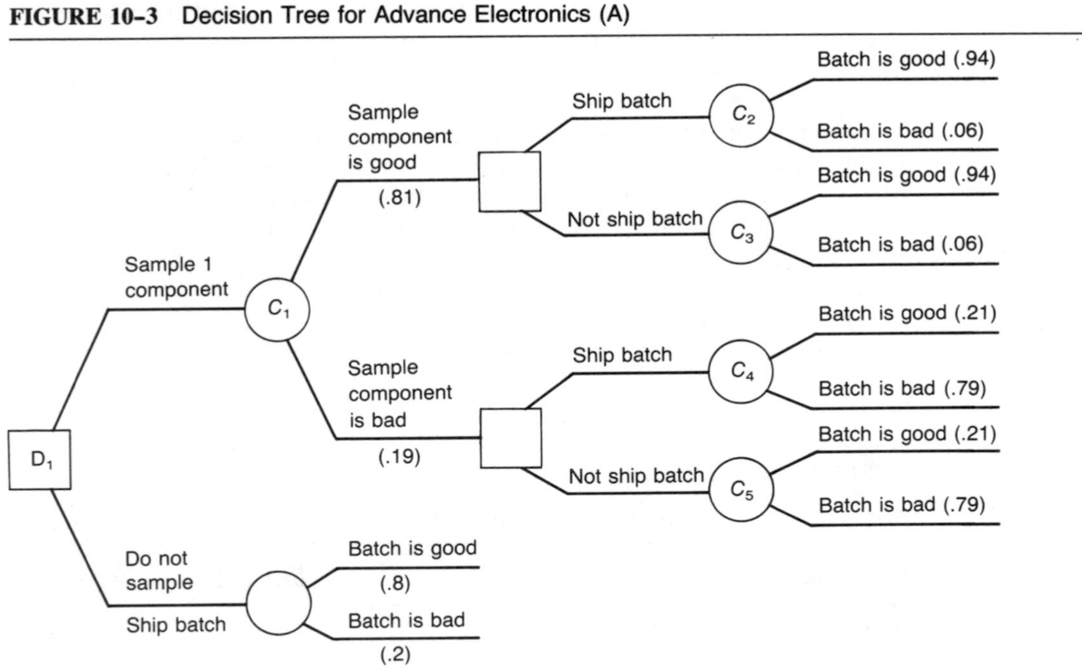

The probabilities of the uncertain sample result (node $C_1$ on Figure 10–3) are given by the *unconditional probabilities,* calculated as part of the Bayes revision process. The *conditional probabilities* of the batch being good or bad, *given* that the sample outcome of one component is good or bad, are the posteriors. Figure 10–3 shows the various posterior probabilities as calculated in Tables 10–2 and 10–3 in their appropriate places on the decision tree.

It is not possible to suggest a decision strategy for Advance Electronics because the costs and revenues of sampling and shipping/not shipping a good or bad batch have not been given. However, we can note that where the sample outcome is known before the ship/not ship decision is made, the probability of shipping a bad batch is 0.0486 (0.81 × 0.06) and the probability of not shipping a good batch is 0.0399 (0.19 × 0.21), presuming that the indication of the sample outcome is followed. The sample information provides the decision maker with an opportunity to improve his resolution, particularly in identifying batches that are likely to be bad.

To conclude this section, we note that when information from observation (such as samples) is available, the decision of whether to sample can be incorporated into the decision tree. Bayesian revision allows for the complete set of probabilities that are needed for this analysis to be calculated. Observations generally (but not always) improve the resolution of the decision maker by providing information *(likelihood probabilities)* that can be used in combination with *prior* beliefs to provide posterior probabilities.

## SOME IMPORTANT SPECIAL CASES

Some special cases warrant illustration and interpretation.

**Case 1: Uniform Prior Probabilities.** Table 10–4 shows a case where the prior probabilities are equal. When prior probabilities are equal, posterior probabilities become proportional to the conditional likelihood probabilities.

**TABLE 10–4** Uniform Prior Probabilities

| *Event* | *Prior Probabilities* | *Likelihoods* | *Joint Probabilities* | *Posterior Probability* |
|---|---|---|---|---|
| $E_1$ | 0.5 | 0.7 | 0.35 | $\frac{0.35}{0.55} = 0.636$ |
| $E_2$ | 0.5 | 0.4 | 0.20 | $\frac{0.20}{0.55} = 0.364$ |
| | | | $\Sigma = 0.55$ | |

**Case 2: Extreme Prior Probabilities.** When the prior probabilities indicate certainty, that is, they are all zero or one, then likelihoods have no effect on determining the posterior probabilities. (See Table 10–5.)

When the prior probabilities are extreme, the posterior probabilities are identical to them. This simply means that if a decision maker is absolutely certain about an event's outcome, observations are unnecessary and indeed have no effect. Indeed, if this state of prior certainty exists, it makes little sense to treat the event variable as a random variable.

**Case 3: Uniform Likelihood Probabilities.** Table 10–6 shows a case where the likelihood probabilities are the same for a set of events. In such instances, the sample observation was equally likely to occur whether the event state was $E_1$ or $E_2$, hence, the occurrence of this sample leads to posterior probabilities that are identical to the priors.

**Case 4: Extreme Likelihoods.** Table 10–7 shows a Bayes revision calculation for two events when the likelihoods are extreme. In such a case the observation has led to likelihoods that express certainty that $E_1$ does not occur and $E_2$ does occur. This is reflected in the Bayes revision and the resultant posterior probabilities.

**TABLE 10–5** Extreme Prior Probabilities

| *Event* | *Prior Probabilities* | *Likelihoods* | *Joint Probabilities* | *Posterior Probability* |
|---|---|---|---|---|
| $E_1$ | 1 | 0.7 | 0.7 | 1 |
| $E_2$ | 0 | 0.3 | 0 | 0 |
| | | | $\Sigma = 0.7$ | |

**TABLE 10–6** Uniform Likelihood Probabilities

| *Event* | *Prior Probabilities* | *Likelihoods* | *Joint Probabilities* | *Posterior Probability* |
|---|---|---|---|---|
| $E_1$ | 0.7 | 0.7 | 0.49 | $\frac{0.49}{0.7} = 0.7$ |
| $E_2$ | 0.3 | 0.7 | 0.21 | $\frac{0.21}{0.7} = 0.3$ |
| | | | $\Sigma = 0.7$ | $\Sigma = 1$ |

**TABLE 10-7** Extreme Likelihoods

| *Event* | *Prior Probabilities* | *Likelihoods* | *Joint Probabilities* | *Posterior Probability* |
|---|---|---|---|---|
| $E_1$ | 0.9 | 0 | 0 | 0 |
| $E_2$ | 0.1 | 1 | 0.1 | 1 |
| | | | $\Sigma = 0.1$ | $\Sigma = 1$ |

## BAYES THEOREM AS A COMBINATION OF PROBABILITY RATIOS

For all sets of probabilities that are not extreme, where the prior and likelihood probabilities are neither uniform nor extreme, both the prior and likelihood information influence the resultant posterior probabilities. The relative extent to which each of these inputs influences the resultant posterior depends on their values, both absolutely and relatively to each other. For example, if the prior information for events $E_1$ and $E_2$ leads to assessment of probabilities of 0.4 and 0.6 respectively, and the likelihood probabilities are 0.5 and 0.01, then the posterior probabilities will be much more strongly influenced by the likelihood information and will resemble it closely. This similarity is because the likelihood data is extreme and the prior probabilities were not. The likelihood information was described as extreme because the observation was 50 times (0.5/0.01) more likely given one event ($E_1$) than the other. On the other hand, the prior probabilities are different by a factor of only 1.5 (0.6/0.4).

To gain a fuller understanding of how and why Bayes Theorem combines information sources, we can more formally examine the interaction of prior and likelihood probabilities. Let us define, for a variable or event having only two possible outcomes, $E_1$ and $E_2$

$$\text{Prior ratio} = \frac{\text{Probability of event } E_1}{\text{Probability of event } E_2}$$

$$\text{Likelihood ratio} = \frac{\text{Likelihood of observation given event } E_1}{\text{Likelihood of observation given event } E_2}$$

The posterior ratio is the product of these ratios defined above. We define the posterior ratio as

$$\text{Posterior ratio} = \frac{\text{Probability of event } E_1 \text{ given the observation}}{\text{Probability of event } E_2 \text{ given the observation}}$$

and note the important relationship

$$\text{Posterior ratio} = \text{Prior ratio} \times \text{Likelihood ratio}$$

**TABLE 10–8** Bayesian Revision with a Prior Ratio of 3:1 and Likelihood Ratio of 2:1

| *Event* | *Prior Probabilities* | *Likelihoods* | *Joint Probabilities* | *Posterior Probability* |
|---|---|---|---|---|
| $E_1$ | 0.75 $\left(\frac{3}{4}\right)$ | 0.67 $\left(\frac{2}{3}\right)$ | 0.5 $\left(\frac{1}{2}\right)$ | 0.857 $\left(\frac{6}{7}\right)$ |
| $E_2$ | 0.25 $\left(\frac{1}{4}\right)$ | 0.33 $\left(\frac{1}{3}\right)$ | 0.0833 $\left(\frac{1}{12}\right)$ | 0.143 $\left(\frac{1}{7}\right)$ |
| | | | $\Sigma = 0.5833 \left(\frac{7}{12}\right)$ | $\Sigma = 1$ |

Note that the likelihood probabilities generally need not sum to one even though they do in this example.

For example, if our prior beliefs are that $E_1$ is three times as likely as $E_2$, and an observation is made or expected that would be twice as likely if event state $E_1$ occurs rather than $E_2$, then the posterior probabilities must be in a ratio of

$$\frac{3}{1} \times \frac{2}{1} = \frac{6}{1}$$

Table 10–8 shows the Bayes calculation in decimals and fractions.

## REPEATED OBSERVATIONS

Where more than one observation occurs, there are two main ways of applying Bayes Theorem. Both lead to the same final result. The first procedure is to treat the observations separately and reapply Bayes Theorem for each, with the posterior probabilities of the $i^{th}$ probability revision becoming the prior probabilities for the $i + 1^{th}$. Figure 10–4a illustrates this process. The second method involves the calculation of joint likelihood probabilities for all observations and their incorporation into a single Bayes calculation procedure. (See Figure 10–4b.)

## EXAMPLE 10–2

### Advance Electronics (B)

The production manager of Advance Electronics wanted to know what the probabilities would be if he were to sample not one, but two ECDs in a particular batch. We

**FIGURE 10–4** Two Methods for Accounting for Repeated Observations

a. Method of serial calculation

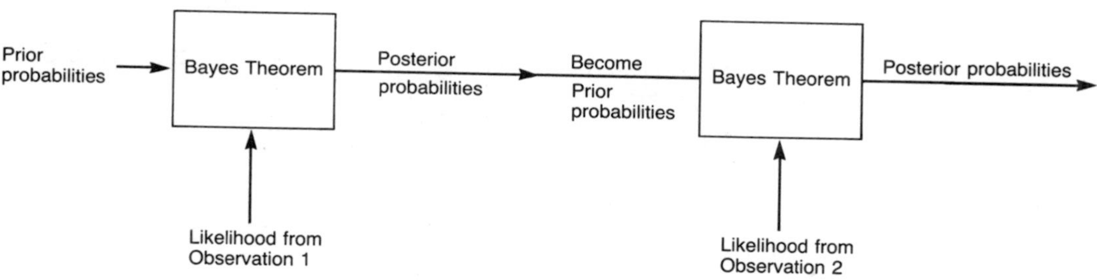


b. Method of combined likelihoods

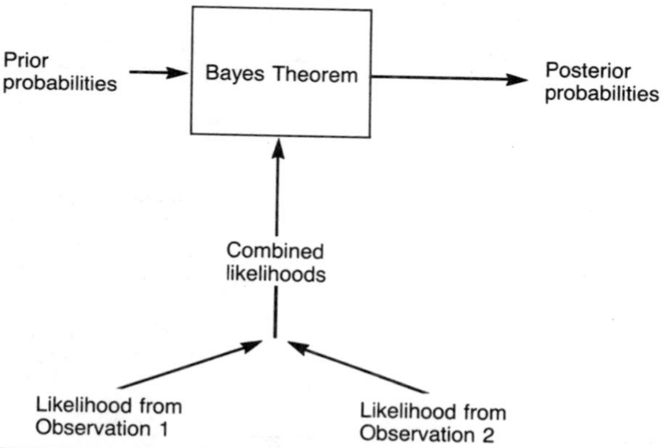


presume here that the sampling is one ECD at a time with replacement of sampled items in between samples.[2]

Figure 10–5 shows the additional branch on the decision tree. Let us now calculate the probabilities required for the various branches of Figure 10–5.

The probabilities associated with the sample outcome of two good ECDs can be evaluated by using the posterior probabilities for the sample of one from Table 10–2 where the sample result was "good." These posterior probabilities become prior probabilities for the second ECD sample observation. See Table 10–9.

---

[2] Sampling with replacement from a batch of items means that each sampled item is replaced in the batch before another is sampled. Assuming this process makes the calculations simpler. We will examine the difference between sampling with replacement and sampling without replacement in a later section of this chapter.

**FIGURE 10–5** Advance Electronics (B) Decision Tree Branch for a Sample of Two ECDs

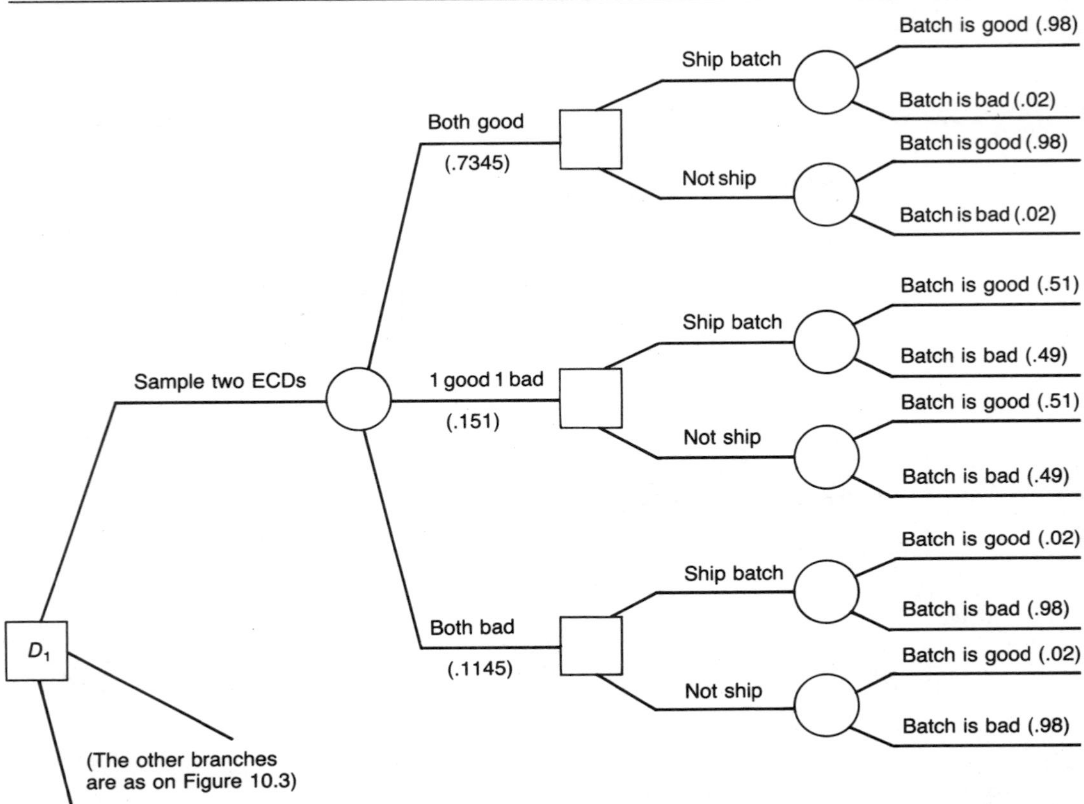


Note that in cases where a decision is made to not ship the batch, the uncertainty about whether the batch is good or bad is probably not important, and this final chance event node could be omitted from those branches.

Similarly, the probabilities of two samples being of bad ECDs can be shown as in Table 10–10, which uses the posterior probabilities from Table 10–3 as priors for the second observation. If the first sampled ECD is good, the probabilities associated with the second being bad are shown in Table 10–11. Also, if the first sampled ECD is bad and the second is good, the probabilities are shown in Table 10–12.

**TABLE 10–9** Second Sample "Good" Bayesian Revision

| *Event* | *Prior Probability* | *Likelihoods* | *Joint Probability* | *Posterior Probability* |
|---|---|---|---|---|
| Batch is good | 0.94 | 0.95 | 0.893 | 0.98 |
| Batch is bad | 0.06 | 0.25 | 0.015 | 0.02 |
| | | | $\Sigma = 0.908$ | |

**TABLE 10–10** Second Sample "Bad" Bayesian Revision

| Event | Prior Probability | Likelihoods | Joint Probability | Posterior Probability |
|---|---|---|---|---|
| Batch is good | 0.21 | 0.05 | 0.0105 | 0.02 |
| Batch is bad | 0.79 | 0.75 | 0.5925 | 0.98 |
| | | | $\Sigma$ = 0.6030 | |

**TABLE 10–11** Second ECD "Bad" after First ECD "Good"

| Event | Prior Probability | Likelihoods | Joint Probability | Posterior Probability |
|---|---|---|---|---|
| Batch is good | 0.94 | 0.05 | 0.047 | 0.51 |
| Batch is bad | 0.06 | 0.75 | 0.045 | 0.49 |
| | | | $\Sigma$ = 0.092 | |

**TABLE 10–12** Second ECD "Good" after First ECD "Bad"

| Event | Prior Probability | Likelihoods | Joint Probability | Posterior Probability |
|---|---|---|---|---|
| Batch is good | 0.21 | 0.95 | 0.1995 | 0.51 |
| Batch is bad | 0.79 | 0.25 | 0.1975 | 0.49 |
| | | | $\Sigma$ = 0.397 | |

Note that the posterior probabilities in Tables 10–11 and 10–12 are identical as would be expected. A combined result of "one good, one bad" must be equally likely in either order.

---

When the calculations are made serially for repeated observations, the unconditional probabilities of sample results are not immediately obvious as the sums of the joint probability columns. They must be determined through multiplying probabilities from a number of tables. When sample sizes are anything but very small, the serial calculations in which Bayes Theorem is applied repeatedly become very tedious.

The method of combining observation data to calculate combined sample likelihoods is generally easier because only one Bayes calculation is needed. Let us calculate the conditional likelihoods for the Advance Electronics (B) example. For a random sample of two ECDs (assuming replacement between samples) the likelihood probabilities are given below for a *good batch*

$$
\begin{aligned}
P(\text{Both good}) &= 0.95 \times 0.95 &&= 0.9025 \\
P(\text{One good, one bad}) &= 2 \times 0.95 \times 0.05 &&= 0.095 \\
P(\text{Both bad}) &= 0.05 \times 0.05 &&= \underline{0.0025} \\
& && \Sigma = 1
\end{aligned}
$$

Note that the factor 2 in the (one good, one bad) calculation signifies the two permutations in this binomial process.

Similarly, if the batch is bad, the likelihoods are

$$
\begin{aligned}
P(\text{Two good}) &= 0.25 \times 0.25 &&= 0.0625 \\
P(\text{One bad, one good}) &= 2 \times 0.25 \times 0.75 &&= 0.375 \\
P(\text{Two bad}) &= 0.75 \times 0.75 &&= \underline{0.5625} \\
& && \Sigma = 1
\end{aligned}
$$

The Bayes revisions for these three possible combined observations are shown in Tables 10–13, 10–14, and 10–15.

**TABLE 10–13** Combined Result of "Two Good" ECDs

| *Event* | *Prior Probability* | *Likelihoods* | *Joint Probability* | *Posterior Probability* |
|---|---|---|---|---|
| Batch is good | 0.8 | 0.9025 | 0.722 | 0.98 |
| Batch is bad | 0.2 | 0.0625 | 0.0125 | 0.02 |
| | | | $\Sigma$ = 0.7345 | |

**TABLE 10–14** Combined Result of "One Good, One Bad"

| *Event* | *Prior Probability* | *Likelihoods* | *Joint Probability* | *Posterior Probability* |
|---|---|---|---|---|
| Batch is good | 0.8 | 0.095 | 0.076 | 0.51 |
| Batch is bad | 0.2 | 0.375 | 0.075 | 0.49 |
| | | | $\Sigma$ = 0.151 | |

**TABLE 10–15** Combined Result of "Two Bad" ECDs

| *Event* | *Prior Probability* | *Likelihoods* | *Joint Probability* | *Posterior Probability* |
|---|---|---|---|---|
| Batch is good | 0.8 | 0.0025 | 0.002 | 0.02 |
| Batch is bad | 0.2 | 0.5625 | 0.1125 | 0.98 |
| | | | $\Sigma$ = 0.1145 | |

Apart from rounding errors, the posterior probabilities in Tables 10–13, 10–14, and 10–15 can be observed to be in accordance with those of corresponding samples in the serial calculations procedures (see Tables 10–9, 10–10, 10–11, 10–12). Also, the calculations in Tables 10–13, 10–14 and 10–15 produced unconditional probabilities for the sample results that can be placed directly onto the decision tree (see Figure 10–5).

To conclude this section, we note that in general, joint likelihood probabilities from repeated or multiple observations can be calculated and are appropriately weighted by the Bayesian revision process. We also note that likelihoods tend to be higher when a sample result is representative of an event (or close to it) and tend to be lower when a sample result is not representative of an event. The way that Bayes Theorem combines probabilistic information sources makes a great deal of common sense, and in keeping with the decision analysis philosophy of formalized common sense, Bayes Theorem allows us to exactly weigh subjective prior and observed sample information. Bayes Theorem automatically gives the correct amount of weighting to the separate information sources (prior and conditional likelihood).

## THEORETICAL PROBABILITY DISTRIBUTION LIKELIHOODS

A number of discrete probability distributions can be used to assist in calculating likelihood probabilities. In the previous section of this chapter it was pointed out that sample sizes that are other than small cannot be easily analyzed if the trials are considered one at a time. Often, probability distributions can be used to describe likelihood distributions in sampling situations. Let us examine a few of the more commonly observed distributions, the binomial, hypergeometric, Poisson, and normal.

### Binomial Process Likelihoods

The binomial distribution can be used to describe processes with only two possible outcome states (often called success and failure) where repeated samples have the same probabilities of achieving these two states. This property is known as the stationarity property.

---

## EXAMPLE 10–3

### Advance Electronics (C)

Advance Electronics produced batches of 100 ECD units. A decision was being made about the possibility of sampling some number of ECD units from each batch. The condition of these sample units would be used as an indication of the yield of the batch. The production manager at Advance Electronics reported on his investigations to his boss, the vice president of manufacturing. The VP suggested that if samples of one and two ECD units provided useful information, larger samples should be even better. The VP was of the opinion that the cost of sampling was not all that high and that the production manager consider a sample size of four.

The production manager decided to do the Bayes revision calculations to see whether larger samples would provide better resolution regarding whether a particular batch was good or bad.

He began by presuming that sampling would be with replacement. The stationarity property is therefore obeyed, and the binomial distribution can be used to describe the conditional probabilities of various sample results. If the batch is good, the probability of success is 0.95 for each trial, and if the batch is bad, the probability of success is 0.25. Success is defined as a single sampled ECD proving to be good when tested.

The likelihood probabilities are given by the binomial probability distribution

$$P\begin{pmatrix} r \text{ successes from } n \text{ trials} \\ \text{given probability of success } p \end{pmatrix} = \frac{n!}{(n-r)! \times r!} \times p^r \times (1-p)^{n-r}$$

For the cases of the batch being good, $p = 0.95$, and the likelihood distribution is

$$P(n = 4, r = 0) = \frac{4!}{0!4!}(0.95)^0(0.05)^4 = 6.2 \times 10^{-6}$$

$$P(n = 4, r = 1) = \frac{4!}{1!3!}(0.95)^1(0.05)^3 = 0.000475$$

$$P(n = 4, r = 2) = \frac{4!}{2!2!}(0.95)^2(0.05)^2 = 0.01354$$

$$P(n = 4, r = 3) = \frac{4!}{3!1!}(0.95)^3(0.05)^1 = 0.17147$$

$$P(n = 4, r = 4) = \frac{4!}{4!0!}(0.95)^4(0.05)^0 = 0.8145$$

For the event "batch is bad," $p = 0.25$, and the likelihood probabilities are

$$P(n = 4, r = 0) = \frac{4!}{0!4!}(0.25)^0(0.75)^4 = 0.316$$

$$P(n = 4, r = 1) = \frac{4!}{1!3!}(0.25)^1(0.75)^3 = 0.422$$

$$P(n = 4, r = 2) = \frac{4!}{2!2!}(0.25)^2(0.75)^2 = 0.211$$

$$P(n = 4, r = 3) = \frac{4!}{3!1!}(0.25)^3(0.75)^1 = 0.047$$

$$P(n = 4, r = 4) = \frac{4!}{4!0!}(0.25)^4(0.75)^0 = 0.004$$

These likelihood probabilities are inputs to the Bayesian revision calculations as shown in Table 10–16 through to Table 10–20.

From Table 10–16 we can see that a sample of four yielding zero good ECD units is extremely unlikely ($6.2 \times 10^{-6}$) given that the batch is good. As a result, the posterior probabilities indicate that should such a sample result occur, the probability of the batch being good (i.e., having the property $p = 0.95$) is very small (0.000078). Such a sample result ($n = 4$, $r = 0$) would lead to the overwhelming conclusion that the batch is bad.

From Table 10–17 we can conclude that a sample of size $n = 4$ leading to a result of $r = 1$ (one good ECD) also is strong evidence that the batch is bad. Such a sample result should lead us to revise our prior odds from 4 to 1 that the batch is good (0.8/0.2) to posterior odds of over 220 to 1 (0.99552/0.00448) that the batch is bad.

**TABLE 10–16** Bayesian Revision ($n = 4$, $r = 0$)

| *Event* | *Prior Probability* | *Likelihoods* | *Joint Probability* | *Posterior Probability* |
|---|---|---|---|---|
| Batch is good | 0.8 | $6.2 \times 10^{-6}$ | $4.96 \times 10^{-6}$ | 0.000078 |
| Batch is bad | 0.2 | 0.316 | 0.0632 | 0.999922 |
| | | | $\Sigma = 0.063205$ | |

**TABLE 10–17** Bayesian Revision ($n = 4$, $r = 1$)

| *Event* | *Prior Probability* | *Likelihoods* | *Joint Probability* | *Posterior Probability* |
|---|---|---|---|---|
| Batch is good | 0.8 | 0.000475 | 0.00038 | 0.00448 |
| Batch is bad | 0.2 | 0.422 | 0.0844 | 0.99552 |
| | | | $\Sigma = 0.08478$ | |

**TABLE 10–18** Bayesian Revision ($n = 4, r = 2$)

| *Event* | *Prior Probability* | *Likelihoods* | *Joint Probability* | *Posterior Probability* |
|---|---|---|---|---|
| Batch is good | 0.8 | 0.01354 | 0.01083 | 0.204 |
| Batch is bad | 0.2 | 0.211 | 0.0422 | 0.796 |
| | | | $\Sigma = 0.05303$ | |

If two good and two bad ECD units are found in a sample of four, there is still substantial evidence that the batch is more likely to be bad (by a likelihood ratio factor of 0.211/0.01354 = 15.6). The prior ratio of 1:4 is combined with this likelihood ratio to produce a posterior ratio of close to 4:1 that the batch is bad (see Table 10–18).

---

Another very interesting aspect of the use of information in decision making can be deduced from these examples. It specifically concerns the effect of *sample size* on the likelihood probabilities and as a result, on the posterior probabilities. From classical statistics, we know that in general, larger sample sizes produce better estimates of population mean values. There is generally less uncertainty about a sample mean for a larger sample than for a smaller one. The relationship is given by

$$\text{Standard error of sample mean} = \frac{\text{Population standard deviation}}{(\text{Sample size } n)^{1/2}}$$

From this we can infer that when sample sizes are larger, there is generally less uncertainty associated with the sample mean. Although the Bayesian and classical viewpoints of sampling are quite different, the Bayesian revision process automatically accounts for the relationship between sample size and standard error in a precise manner.[3] The result is that even for cases where the sample mean is the same, the likelihood probabilities are such that the effect of sample size is taken into account as part of the process!

To illustrate this point, let us look back and compare the data in Tables 10–14 and 10–18. In the case of Table 10–14 the observation was $n = 2$, $r = 1$, that is, a sample of two yielding one good and one bad ECD. In Table 10–18 the observation was $n = 4$, $r = 2$. In both cases the sample means were 50% good ECDs (and, of course, 50% bad). Is a sample result of $n = 2, r = 1$ identical to a result of $n = 4, r = 2$? The answer to this question is certainly a *no,* and the differences are illustrated by Tables 10–14 and

---

[3] See Chapter 11 for a more detailed discussion of this issue.

10–18. There is considerably more information in the larger sample as reflected in the difference between the likelihood ratios. In this example the likelihood ratio is given by

$$\text{Likelihood ratio} = \frac{\text{Probability of the sample result given that the batch is good}}{\text{Probability of the sample result given that the batch is bad}}$$

For the small ($n = 2$, $r = 1$) sample, this ratio was 0.24 (from Table 10–14). For the large ($n = 4$, $r = 2$) sample this ratio was 0.064. The inverses of these ratios are 4:1 and 15.6:1 respectively. Given that the prior probabilities were the same for both samples, the larger sample (with its more extreme likelihood ratio) led to posterior probabilities that were considerably more different from the prior probabilities than did the smaller sample. The larger sample had more influence on the posterior probabilities than did the smaller sample, even though the two samples had the same sample mean.

In general, we can conclude that in Bayesian statistics, more weight is generally given to larger samples than to smaller samples because larger samples generally provide more reliable sample means. Perhaps the most fascinating thing about Bayes Theorem is its precision in adjusting these prior probabilities by the exactly correct amount. Sample size is automatically integrated into the Bayes Theorem calculation algorithm through its effect on the likelihoods. In summary, larger samples contain more information as reflected in the likelihoods and the resulting posterior probabilities.

Tables 10–19 and 10–20 show the rest of the Bayes calculation for a sample of size $n = 4$.

**TABLE 10–19** Bayes Revision ($n = 4$, $r = 3$)

| *Event* | *Prior Probability* | *Likelihoods* | *Joint Probability* | *Posterior Probability* |
|---|---|---|---|---|
| Batch is good | 0.8 | 0.17147 | 0.1372 | 0.9346 |
| Batch is bad | 0.2 | 0.047 | 0.0096 | 0.0654 |
| | | | $\Sigma = 0.1468$ | |

**TABLE 10–20** Bayes Revision ($n = 4$, $r = 4$)

| *Event* | *Prior Probability* | *Likelihoods* | *Joint Probability* | *Posterior Probability* |
|---|---|---|---|---|
| Batch is good | 0.8 | 0.8145 | 0.6516 | 0.9988 |
| Batch is bad | 0.2 | 0.004 | 0.0008 | 0.0012 |
| | | | $\Sigma = 0.6524$ | |

The Bayes calculations show us how we should revise our prior beliefs as a result of sample observations. In effect, for a sample size of four, we should strongly suspect that a batch is good if the sample contains either three or four good ECD units. Otherwise, with varying degrees of confidence depending on whether the sample result was $r = 0, 1,$ or $2$, it is more likely that the batch is bad.

A comparison of Tables 10–2, 10–9, and 10–20 can be used to further illustrate the effect of sample size. These tables start with the same prior beliefs about whether the batch is good or bad. They show calculations of posterior probabilities for samples of one, two, and four ECD units respectively, when all sampled units were good. All three tables refer to identical observed sample means of 100%. As sample size increases, we can see the evidence that the batch is likely to be good become stronger and stronger.

## Hypergeometric Process Likelihoods

The hypergeometric probability distribution describes uncertain events such as sampling without replacement. Many quality control sampling processes, where produced or delivered batches or materials, components, or products are involved, are actually hypergeometric rather than binomial. However, the binomial distribution is often a very good approximation (even when sampling is without replacement), as long as the process does not stray too far from being stationary (that is, having the same probability of success across trials).

In the Advance Electronics example, for batches of 100 ECDs, the probability of success changes as each ECD is sampled unless it is replaced. For example, in a good batch (containing 95 good and 5 bad ECDs) if the first ECD sampled is good, the probability of the next being good is no longer 95/100, but rather 94/99. These fractions are indeed very similar, but the same does not apply if we consider two consecutive sample trials of bad ECD units. In that instance the probability of picking bad ECD units changes from 5/100 to 4/99 if sampling is without replacement. These fractions are quite different in value. As more bad ECD units are picked, their likelihood of being picked changes from 5/100 to 4/99, 3/98, 2/97, 1/96, 0/95. This is certainly not a stationary sampling process. Hence, we must be careful when assuming that the binomial distribution is a reasonable approximation in situations of sampling without replacement. Strictly speaking, the hypergeometric likelihood process should be used, unless the binomial is a good approximation. Alternatively, in some instances the population and sample sizes may be large enough to make a normal distribution approximation reasonable.

While on the subject of accuracy of approximations, we should keep in mind the purpose for which we do the Bayes calculations. The ultimate aim is to provide probabilistic data as part of a decision analysis model that is used to support a decision-making process. The reader should think about the degree of precision that is generally appropriate for a probability number on a decision tree. Although we have, for the purposes of accuracy, shown probabilities with three or even four significant digits in some of the above tables, is this degree of accuracy necessary for decision-making processes? Is it likely that a decision or inference would change given the knowledge that a probability is 0.1483, or is it sensible to round this number to 0.15? The number of significant digits used should be consistent with the accuracy of the information.

The most reasonable conclusion about accuracy in calculation and approximation is that for each decision context, common sense should prevail. When sample sizes are small relative to population sizes, the binomial distribution usually produces results that are very close to those of the hypergeometric.

To illustrate, we calculate the hypergeometric probabilities for some of the Advance Electronics likelihoods. The hypergeometric distribution is given by[4]

$$P(R = r) = \frac{\binom{k}{r}\binom{N-k}{n-r}}{\binom{N}{n}}$$

$$P(R = r) = \frac{\dfrac{k!}{(k-r)!r!}\;\dfrac{(N-k)!}{(N-k-n+r)!(n-r)!}}{\dfrac{N!}{(N-n)!\,n!}}$$

where

$N$ = Population (batch size)
$k$ = Number of successes in the batch
$n$ = Sample size
$r$ = Number of successes in the sample

---

[4] In this context, the symbol "!" means "factorial" and is defined as:

$$n! = n \times (n-1) \times (n-2) \times \ldots \times 3 \times 2 \times 1$$

Also, we define $0! = 1$.

For the case of

$$N = 100$$
$$k = 95 \text{ (the good batch)}$$
$$n = 4$$
$$r = 3$$

the hypergeometric calculation is

$$\frac{\dfrac{95!}{92! \times 3!} \quad \dfrac{5!}{4! \times 1!}}{\dfrac{100!}{96! \times 4!}} = 0.1765$$

The binomial approximation was quite close to this, being 0.1715. Another example was for $n = 4$ and $r = 0$. In this case four defectives were to be picked from a total of five in the batch. Do you expect the binomial approximation to be accurate in this instance? The hypergeometric probability calculation is

$$N = 100$$
$$r = 0$$
$$n = 4$$
$$k = 95$$

$$P(r = 0) = \frac{\dfrac{95!}{92!\ 0!} \quad \dfrac{5!}{4!\ 1!}}{\dfrac{100!}{96!\ \ 4!}} = 1.27 \times 10^{-6}$$

This probability is considerably smaller (about a factor of 5) than the binomial approximation of $6.2 \times 10^{-6}$ because the binomial process assumes stationarity. In the case of all the sampled ECD units being bad, the successive trial probabilities are 5/100, 4/99, 3/98, and 2/97. The binomial assumes trial probabilities for bad ECD units that are all 5/100.

## Poisson Process Likelihoods

The Poisson distribution can be used to describe the probability of events where random, independent events occur from a large population. Random arrival processes such as telephone calls to a switchboard, arrivals at a service center, equipment breakdowns, and quality defects may be distributed according to the Poisson distribution under certain conditions. For a likelihood observation to be a Poisson generated process, the assumptions of the Poisson distribution must be applicable, and the decision-related event must be defined by the Poisson parameter (which is the average arrival rate).

## EXAMPLE 10–4

### Advance Electronics (D)

The process by which ECDs are produced requires the use of a delicate machine which sprays a very thin coating of metal alloy onto a plastic surface. For no apparent reason, this machine randomly went out of adjustment about once a week. A new machine was bought to replace this one, and the equipment salesman had guaranteed that the new machine would go out of adjustment very rarely. The production manager at Advance Electronics was uncertain about what "very rarely" meant. He defined four possible states of events as:

State 1: Average rate of maladjustment = 1/month.
State 2: Average rate of maladjustment = 2/month.
State 3: Average rate of maladjustment = 3/month.
State 4: Average rate of maladjustment = 4/month.

He assigned probabilities of 0.4, 0.3, 0.2, and 0.1 to these states respectively. He made a note of his prior beliefs. By assigning a nonzero probability to the 4/month event, he was admitting that he thought there was at least some chance that the new machine would be as bad as the old machine.

After operating the machine for a month, the production manager was pleased to note that it did not go out of adjustment even once. He used Bayes Theorem to update his probabilities assuming that the breakdown process was random and followed a stable (constant average breakdown rate) Poisson process.

The likelihoods were

$$P\begin{pmatrix}\text{No breakdown in} & / & \text{Breakdown rate} \\ \text{month 1} & & = 1/\text{month}\end{pmatrix} = 0.368$$

$$P\begin{pmatrix}\text{No breakdown in} & / & \text{Breakdown rate} \\ \text{month 1} & & = 2/\text{month}\end{pmatrix} = 0.135$$

$$P\begin{pmatrix}\text{No breakdown in} & / & \text{Breakdown rate} \\ \text{month 1} & & = 3/\text{month}\end{pmatrix} = 0.050$$

$$P\begin{pmatrix}\text{No breakdown in} & / & \text{Breakdown rate} \\ \text{month 1} & & = 4/\text{month}\end{pmatrix} = 0.018$$

These probabilities can be calculated using the Poisson distribution formula[5]

$$P(X = x) = \frac{e^{-\lambda} \times \lambda^{x}}{x!}$$

[5] In this Poisson distribution formula, $e$ is the exponential constant, $x$ is the event variable, and $\lambda$ is the assumed average breakdown rate.

**TABLE 10-21** "Out of Adjustment" Rate Probability Revision

| *Event (Breakdown Rate)* | *Prior Probability* | *Likelihood* | *Joint Probability* | *Posterior Probability* |
|---|---|---|---|---|
| 1/month | 0.4 | 0.368 | 0.1472 | 0.7379 |
| 2/month | 0.3 | 0.135 | 0.0405 | 0.2030 |
| 3/month | 0.2 | 0.050 | 0.01 | 0.0501 |
| 4/month | 0.1 | 0.018 | 0.0018 | 0.0090 |
| | | | $\Sigma = 0.1995$ | |

The Bayes revision process for this example is given in Table 10-21.

The evidence of no adjustment problems in the first month lead to a revision of probabilities so that the probability of the breakdown rate being 1 per month is increased and all the rest are decreased.

---

There are a number of other probability distributions that can be used to describe random processes. These are described in detail in more technically oriented books on statistics and statistical decision theory, and reference is given to them at the end of this chapter. Before studying some managerial problems that require the use of Bayes Theorem, we shall consider some probability distributions that have special properties in relation to Bayes Theorem.

## CONJUGATE FAMILIES OF DISTRIBUTIONS

There are some families of distributions that have special properties. Specifically, for certain prior probability distribution forms and likelihood distribution forms, it is known that the posterior probability distribution has the same distribution form as the prior. Further, formulae can be derived that relate the parameters of the prior, likelihood, and posterior distributions. These formulae make the posterior distribution easy to identify. We will not derive these formulae here, but merely present some results and give references to sources where the details may be found.

### Normal Prior Distribution and Normal Likelihood Process

Perhaps the best known conjugate family of distributions is the normal prior, normal likelihood combination which leads to a normally distributed posterior distribution.[6] The formulae that relate the parameters for a random variable $X$ are

$$\frac{1}{\sigma^2_{\text{Posterior}}} = \frac{1}{\sigma^2_{\text{Prior}}} + \frac{1}{\sigma^2_{\text{Likelihood}}}$$

$$\overline{X}_{\text{Posterior}} = \frac{\dfrac{1}{\sigma^2_{\text{Prior}}}\overline{X}_{\text{Prior}} + \dfrac{1}{\sigma^2_{\text{Likelihood}}}\overline{X}_{\text{Likelihood}}}{\dfrac{1}{\sigma^2_{\text{Prior}}} + \dfrac{1}{\sigma^2_{\text{Likelihood}}}}\,,$$

where

$\overline{X}$ signifies mean value and
$\sigma^2$ signifies variance.

## EXAMPLE 10–5

### Currant Cost Accounting Inc.

Angela Currant operated a highly specialized accounting and auditing consulting company. She and her staff assisted clients in cases where companies had accounting problems requiring special skills that public accountants normally didn't have. In one instance, she was called in to help estimate the mean size of a company's weekly materials and energy costs. The costs fluctuated depending on a number of factors, such as total production volume, product mix changes, and quality specifications. The best previous estimates available were that mean materials and energy costs (per $100 of sales) were normally distributed with a mean of $25 and a standard deviation of $5. Ms. Currant asked the client company's cost accountant to carefully compile data for 36 successive weeks on materials and energy costs (per $100 sales). The sample of 36 weeks of observations was found to be approximately normally distributed with a mean of $32.50 and a standard deviation of $10. (This sample provides the likelihood information.)

[6] A *normal prior* refers to a normally distributed prior distribution. A *normal likelihood* is a conditional likelihood that for a given event value is normally distributed. A *normal posterior* refers to a normally distributed (conditional) posterior distribution.

For the sample mean, the standard deviation (known as standard error of the mean) is given by $10 \div \sqrt{36} = 1.667$.[7] Ms. Currant then calculated that the parameters of the posterior distribution, which was also normally distributed, were

$$\frac{1}{\sigma^2_{Posterior}} = \frac{1}{5^2} + \frac{1}{(1.667)^2}$$
$$\sigma^2_{Posterior} = 2.5$$
$$\sigma_{Posterior} = 1.58$$
$$\overline{X}_{Posterior} = \frac{\frac{1}{(5)^2}25 + \frac{1}{(1.667)^2}32.5}{\frac{1}{(5)^2} + \frac{1}{(1.667)^2}}$$
$$= 31.75$$

---

Note that the posterior mean falls between the prior mean and the likelihood sample (observed) mean. Note also that the posterior mean is much closer to the likelihood mean than to the prior mean. This is because the posterior mean is a weighted average of prior and likelihood means and the weights are the inverses of the variances. Since the prior distribution had a higher variance, the likelihood distribution (being "tighter") had more influence on the posterior mean. These concepts can be very effectively illustrated graphically. Figures 10–6, 10–7, and 10–8 show the effect of three different likelihood distributions on a particular prior distribution. Let us presume prior statistics of:

$$\overline{X}_{Prior} = 20$$
$$\sigma^2_{Prior} = 25 \text{ (hence } \sigma_{Prior} = 5)$$

in the cases of Figures 10–6, 10–7, and 10–8. These figures show the effect of different likelihood probabilities (caused by different observations) with the same prior distribution.

Figure 10–6 shows the probability distributions for the likelihood being normal with parameters $X = 32.5$, standard error (se) = 1-2/3. The posterior in this case has parameters as calculated above, namely $X_{posterior} = 31.75$ and $\sigma_{posterior} = 1.58$.

From Figure 10–6 we can see that the likelihood distribution was weighted more than the prior distribution in the process of determining the posterior distribution. Let us contrast this example with the following one that incorporates a larger standard error of the sample (likelihood) mean.

---

[7] The standard error of a mean equals the population standard deviation divided by the square root of the sample size.

**FIGURE 10–6** Likelihood Distribution 1

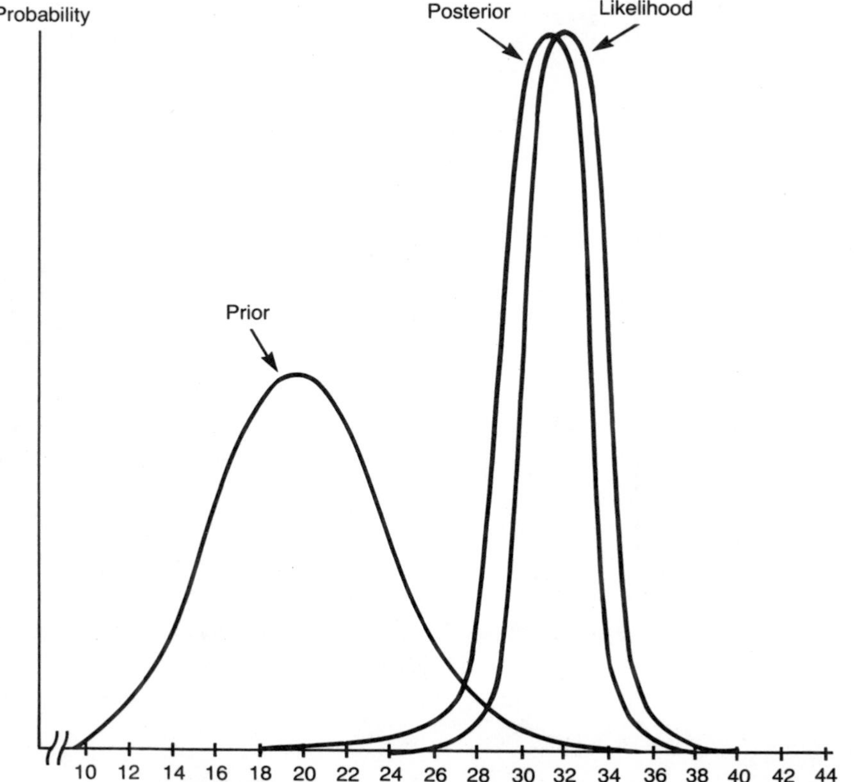


NOTE: In this chapter $N(X,Y)$ denotes a normally distributed parameter with mean = $X$ and standard deviation = $Y$. Also, prior distribution = $N(20,5)$, likelihood distribution = $N(32.5,1.67)$, and posterior distribution = $N(31.75,1.58)$.

Figure 10–7 plots a likelihood distribution with $\overline{X}_{\text{likelihood}} = 32.5$ and $se_{\text{likelihood}} = 5$. In this case the posterior mean and variance are given by

$$\frac{1}{\sigma^2_{\text{Posterior}}} = \frac{1}{25} + \frac{1}{25}$$

$$\sigma^2_{\text{Posterior}} = 12.5$$

$$\sigma_{\text{Posterior}} = 3.53$$

$$\overline{X} = \frac{\frac{1}{25}(20) + \frac{1}{25}(32.5)}{\frac{1}{25} + \frac{1}{25}}$$

$$= 26.25$$

**FIGURE 10–7** Likelihood Distribution 2

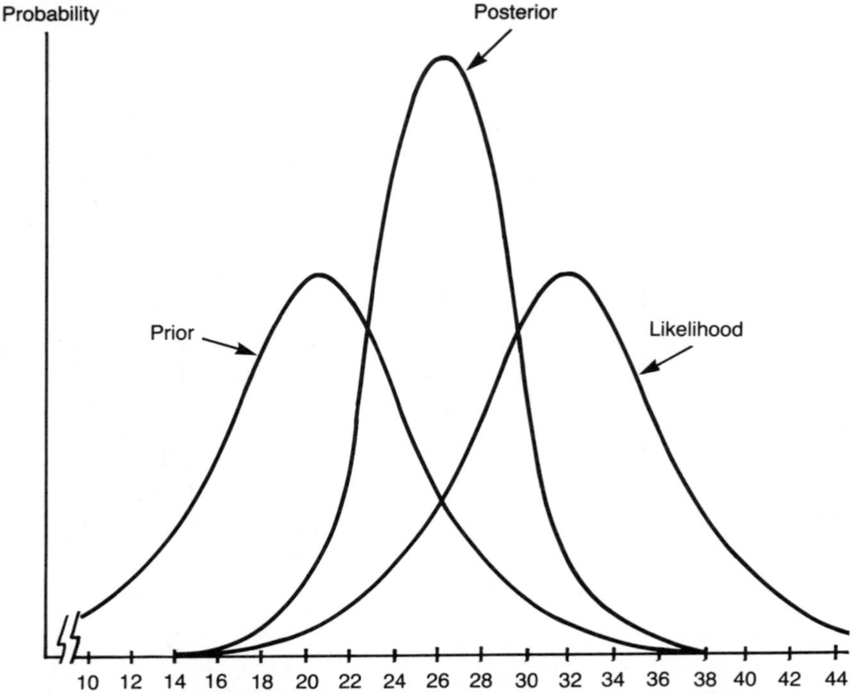

NOTE: In this chapter $N(X,Y)$ denotes a normally distributed parameter with mean = $X$ and standard deviation = $Y$. Also, prior distribution is $N$ (20,5), likelihood distribution is $N$(32.5,5), and posterior distribution is $N$(26.25,3.53).

In Figure 10–7 both the prior and likelihood distributions have the same standard deviation. Hence, the posterior distribution has a mean that is exactly halfway between the prior and likelihood means.

Note that the posterior distribution in Figure 10–7 has significantly less spread about the mean than either the prior or the likelihood distribution. We can interpret this by considering what information the likelihood distribution has added to the prior state of knowledge. When only the prior information was available, we thought that the uncertain quantity was equally likely to be above or below a value of 20. As a result of the likelihood observation, we now know a lot more than this. For example, we now believe that the uncertain quantity is quite unlikely to have a value of less than 20. In this sense, the likelihood observation has added information about the uncertain quantity, and hence, the variance of the posterior is less than that of the prior distribution than we began with. Let us consider again the equation

$$\frac{1}{\sigma^2_{\text{Posterior}}} = \frac{1}{\sigma^2_{\text{Prior}}} + \frac{1}{\sigma^2_{\text{Likelihood}}}$$

Rearranging

$$\sigma^2_{\text{Posterior}} = \frac{1}{\dfrac{1}{\sigma^2_{\text{Prior}}} + \dfrac{1}{\sigma^2_{\text{Likelihood}}}}$$

$$= \frac{\sigma^2_{\text{Prior}} \times \sigma^2_{\text{Likelihood}}}{\sigma^2_{\text{Likelihood}} + \sigma^2_{\text{Prior}}}$$

The nature of this relationship is that given $\sigma^2_{\text{Prior}}$ and $\sigma^2_{\text{Likelihood}}$ are always strictly greater than zero, we will always achieve the results

$$\sigma^2_{\text{Posterior}} < \sigma^2_{\text{Prior}}$$

and

$$\sigma^2_{\text{Posterior}} < \sigma^2_{\text{Likelihood}}$$

Figure 10–8 shows a likelihood distribution that is normally distributed with parameters *N*(32.5, 10). This likelihood has a higher standard deviation than the previous examples (reflecting a smaller sample size).

**FIGURE 10–8** Likelihood Distribution 3

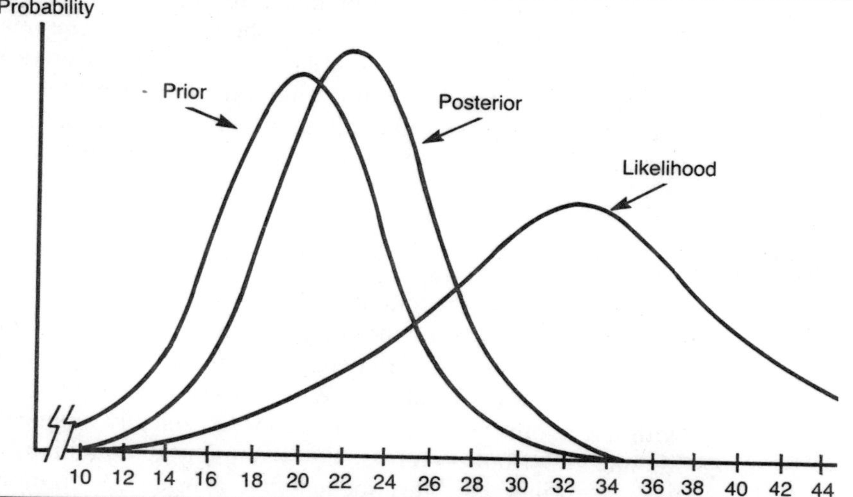


NOTE: In this chapter *N*(*X*,*Y*) denotes a normally distributed parameter with mean = *X* and standard deviation = *Y*. Also, prior distribution is *N*(20,5), likelihood distribution is *N*(32.5,10), and posterior distribution is *N*(22.5,4.47).

We can calculate the posterior distribution parameters as

$$\frac{1}{\sigma^2_{\text{Posterior}}} = \frac{1}{25} + \frac{1}{100}$$

$$\sigma^2_{\text{Posterior}} = 20$$

$$\sigma_{\text{Posterior}} = 4.472$$

$$\bar{X}_{\text{Posterior}} = \frac{\frac{1}{(25)}\,20 + \frac{1}{(100)}\,32.5}{\frac{1}{25} + \frac{1}{100}}$$

$$= 22.5$$

From Figure 10–8, the larger variance (relative to Figure 10–7) of the likelihood distribution (meaning that the likelihood observation was less precise) leads to a posterior that is influenced more by the prior. The posterior distribution has a mean quite close to that of the prior and a variance that is only slightly reduced from that of the prior. In this case the observation that led to the likelihood distribution did not add much information to the prior state of knowledge, relative to previous examples.

For the normal distribution conjugate family the variance of the posterior distribution is a function of other variances only (that is, variances of both the prior and likelihood). On the other hand, the mean of the posterior distribution is a function of four parameters, namely the means and variances of both the prior and the likelihood. Indeed the posterior mean is a weighted average of the prior mean and the likelihood mean. In this function, the weights are the inverses of the variances. The relationship between the likelihood and posterior variances for a given prior variance is shown by Figure 10–9. A similar relationship exists between the posterior and prior variances (for a given likelihood variance). The posterior variance asymptotically approaches the prior variance as the likelihood variance increases.

## Other Conjugate Families

A number of other conjugate families of distributions exist. Raiffa and Schlaifer (1961) give further details of a number of these and show how the posterior distribution parameters can be calculated from those of the prior and likelihood distributions. Whereas the normal distribution is conjugate with itself, other distributions are more typically conjugate with other than identical distribution forms. For example, the beta distribution is conjugate with the binomial. This means that a prior distribution that has a beta functional form will lead to posterior distribution that is also of beta functional form if the likelihood process is described by the binomial distribution.

**FIGURE 10–9** Relationship between Likelihood Distribution Variance and Posterior Distribution Variance for a Given Prior Distribution

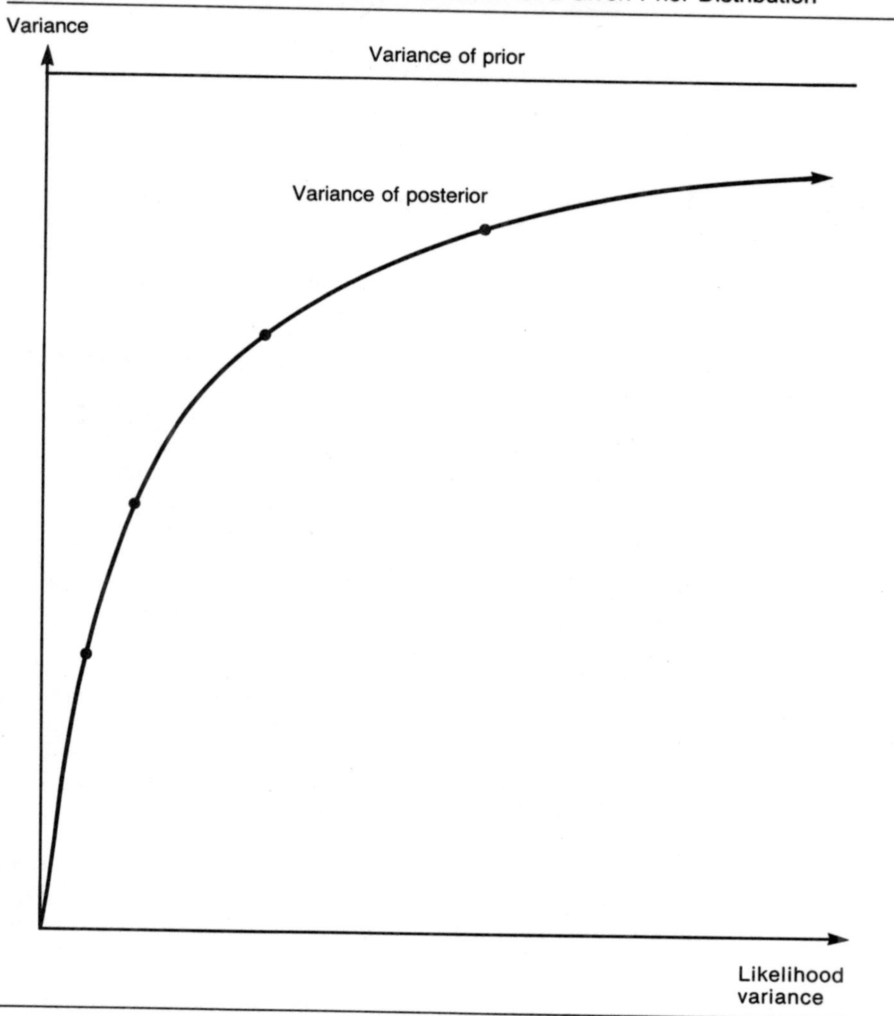


Similarly, the gamma distribution is conjugate with a Poisson likelihood function.

## SOME ILLUSTRATIVE APPLICATIONS OF BAYES THEOREM

A number of decision problems have led to decision analysis models that required the use of Bayes Theorem. We describe a selection of these below.

## EXAMPLE 10–6

### Reschem Services (A)

Reschem is a medium-sized chemical analysis and research company. Its bread and butter income came from a large number of contracts in which it supplied analytical services to a multitude of industrial companies. Most of these companies were not large and found it more economical to use Reschem than to establish their own analytical laboratory. Reschem also did some business with lawyers by providing expert testimony on matters involving materials and chemical analysis.

Reschem employed a total of 550 people, including about 70 senior researchers, 200 research officers, and 100 other laboratory staff. The other people managed or indirectly supported the laboratory personnel and functions.

In the past, a small proportion of Reschem's operating budget had always been allocated to chemical research projects that did not directly produce revenue for the company. These projects were undertaken as longer-term investment, and they also served to satisfy the creative urges of Reschem's best people. There had lately been a good deal of talk within the company about one of these projects, a possible new development in rocket fuel technology. Reschem's CEO, Dr. Rod Davies, was considering a substantial investment in this project. It had previously been funded at a low level.

One of Reschem's senior researchers had found a way to form a new compound using a special catalyst. The compound's molecular structure was a closely guarded secret. It had been given the coded name of RF 90. It consisted of carbon, nitrogen, sulphur, and hydrogen, and naturally existed in two forms, known as alpha and beta. The alpha form was not useful, but the beta form seemed to be very useful as a rocket fuel potentially superior to those currently used in the NASA and military programs. Dr. Davies knew that if he could demonstrate potential success, he would attract a large amount of government backing and ultimately a substantial royalty on fuel manufacturing processes. The problem he faced was that so far, it had not been possible, even in carefully controlled laboratory conditions, to manufacture beta fuel without a substantial amount of alpha fuel. Dr. Davies looked at the preliminary work and assessed the likelihood of successfully being able to separate the alpha and beta forms of the RF 90 compound. The attempted separation would require an extremely expensive piece of equipment which would have to be designed and built specially for this purpose. Dr. Davies was not optimistic about being able to separate the two forms and assessed a probability of success of 0.15. This number was not all that low relative to the probability of success for other research projects given the radical nature of the project.

Before making a final decision to fund or not fund the project's next step, Dr. Davies decided to get expert opinions. He contacted a colleague at the University of Texas and another at NASA who were generally considered to be very knowledgeable in this field. Dr. Davies thought that each of these experts would probably have an 80% likelihood of correctly judging the outcome of the research process. Each of the experts agreed to assess the project and make a firm prediction about whether the separation would work or not. Each also quoted a fee as compensation for the substantial amount of time required in their investigations. They agreed to sign contracts that guaranteed the complete secrecy of the project.

Dr. Davies wondered about how this expert information might help his decision and whether it was worth the rather large consulting fee.[8] He translated the assessments of reliability of the consultants to probability statements. For each expert:

$$P(\text{Success is predicted/Success would occur}) = 0.8$$
$$P(\text{Failure is predicted/Success would occur}) = 0.2$$

$$P(\text{Success is predicted/Failure would occur}) = 0.2$$
$$P(\text{Failure is predicted/Failure would occur}) = 0.8$$

Dr. Davies considered getting either one or both assessments. The Bayes revisions of his prior probabilities for one expert are shown by Tables 10–22 and 10–23.

Tables 10–22 and 10–23 show how the Bayes revision of probabilities occurs given that only one outside expert is consulted. Dr. Davies thought that given the 80% reliability of the experts and the costs and benefits, he would go ahead with the project if he used only one expert who suggested that it would work.

Tables 10–24, 10–25, and 10–26 show the Bayes revisions for observations involving two experts.

Dr. Davies realized from these calculations that he would be able to go ahead with the project quite confidently if both experts predicted success. Of course he had

**TABLE 10–22** Bayes Revision Assuming One Expert Predicts Success

| *Event* | *Prior Probability* | *Likelihood* | *Joint Probability* | *Posterior Probability* |
|---|---|---|---|---|
| Success | 0.15 | 0.8 | 0.12 | 0.41 |
| Failure | 0.85 | 0.2 | 0.17 | 0.59 |
| | | | $\Sigma = 0.29$ | $\Sigma = 1$ |

**TABLE 10–23** Bayes Revision Assuming One Expert Predicts Failure

| *Event* | *Prior Probability* | *Likelihood* | *Joint Probability* | *Posterior Probability* |
|---|---|---|---|---|
| Success | 0.15 | 0.2 | 0.03 | 0.04 |
| Failure | 0.85 | 0.8 | 0.68 | 0.96 |
| | | | $\Sigma = 0.71$ | $\Sigma = 1$ |

[8] Dr. Davies would like to have been able to weigh the cost of obtaining the expert information against the benefits the information would produce. To do this, he would need to include these elements on a decision tree.

**TABLE 10–24** Bayes Revision Where Both Experts Predict Success

| *Event* | *Prior Probability* | *Likelihood* | *Joint Probability* | *Posterior Probability* |
|---|---|---|---|---|
| Success | 0.15 | $0.8 \times 0.8 = 0.64$ | 0.096 | 0.74 |
| Failure | 0.85 | $0.2 \times 0.2 = 0.04$ | 0.034 | 0.26 |
| | | | $\Sigma = 0.13$ | $\Sigma = 1$ |

**TABLE 10–25** Bayes Revision Where One Expert Predicts Success and One Predicts Failure

| *Event* | *Prior Probability* | *Likelihood* | *Joint Probability* | *Posterior Probability* |
|---|---|---|---|---|
| Success | 0.15 | $2 \times 0.8 \times 0.2 = 0.32$ | 0.048 | 0.15 |
| Failure | 0.85 | $2 \times 0.8 \times 0.2 = 0.32$ | 0.272 | 0.85 |
| | | | $\Sigma = 0.32$ | $\Sigma = 1$ |

**TABLE 10–26** Bayes Revision Where Both Experts Predict Failure

| *Event* | *Prior Probability* | *Likelihood* | *Joint Probability* | *Posterior Probability* |
|---|---|---|---|---|
| Success | 0.15 | $0.2 \times 0.2 = 0.04$ | 0.006 | 0.01 |
| Failure | 0.85 | $0.8 \times 0.8 = 0.64$ | 0.544 | 0.99 |
| | | | $\Sigma = 0.55$ | $\Sigma = 1$ |

assumed that their judgments would be fully independent of each other. He had also decided that the best strategy was to go ahead if no expert information were collected. Hence, if the experts' opinions were split, he would go ahead with the project. He decided to set all the probabilities down on a decision tree, which had a first decision node of whether to consult with zero, one, or two experts, and a second node of whether to go ahead with the project. Figure 10–10 shows Dr. Davies' decision tree. From it, he was able to conclude that the hiring of experts did help him partially to resolve (that is, to reduce) the effective uncertainty he faced. If he did not consult any experts, he had an 85% chance of making a poor investment. If he consulted only one expert, this chance was reduced to $0.29 \times 0.59 = 0.17$, and the additional risk of not funding a project that would have been successful is added (probability $= 0.71 \times 0.04 = 0.0287$). His chances of making a correct decision thus improved substantially if he consulted one expert and accepted that expert's recommendation. His resolution got even better in the case of two experts. He had decided to go ahead with the project if either or both of the two experts recommended it. Hence the probability of funding a failure is $0.32 \times 0.85 + 0.13 \times 0.26 = 0.35$. His probability of not funding a

**FIGURE 10–10** Dr. Davies' Decision Tree for the RF 90 Compound

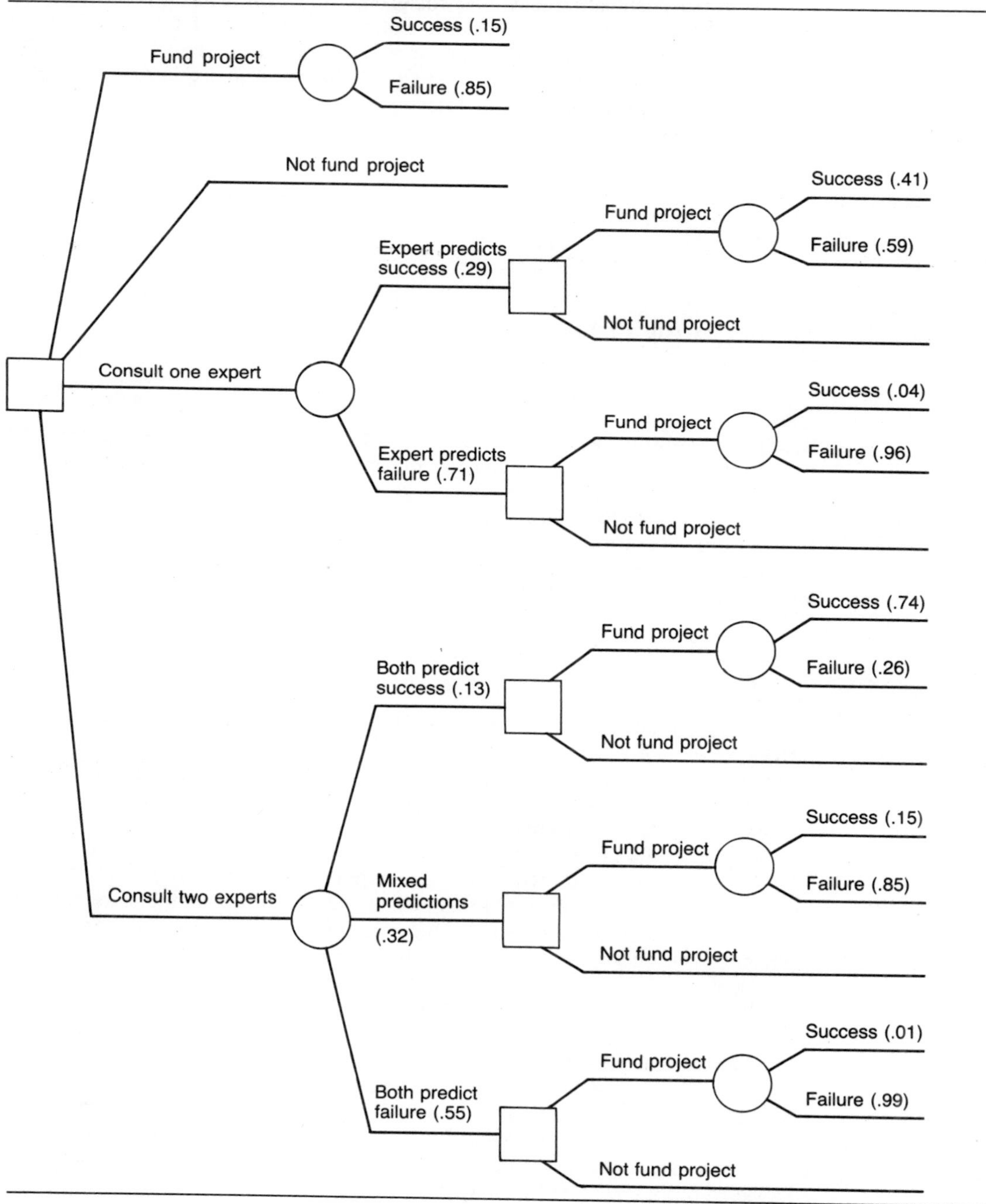

success became 0.55 × 0.01 = 0.0055. He weighed these various probabilities along with the potential benefits and costs. The Bayesian revision processes had allowed him to do a *preposterior analysis,* that is to consider in detail the ramifications of obtaining likelihood observation, before committing to a decision about them. Dr. Davies was pleased to have been able to analyze the decision problem so thoroughly and went off to consult some of his Reschem colleagues so that he might get their feedback and do some sensitivity analysis on his assumptions.

---

## Example 10–7

### Farmer Brown (A)

Bob Brown is a farmer who has harvested 150,000 bushels of soybeans. He must sell his crop during the next week to pay off a number of his creditors. He is in a quandary as to whether or not to sell it today (Monday) or to wait until next Monday. He believes that the price per bushel may vary by plus or minus two cents between today and next Monday, or else stay the same. He considered the price movements over the past few weeks and the current and forecast weather, then assessed the following probabilities for price movements over the next week

$$P(\text{Price rise of two cents}) = 0.4$$
$$P(\text{Price stable}) = 0.4$$
$$P(\text{Price fall of two cents}) = 0.2$$

Farmer Brown had recently received a letter from a company that claimed to be successful in forecasting daily and weekly price movements in agricultural commodities. In the letter the company offered an "instant, over-the-phone price forecasting service." The farmer telephoned and was told that he could have his first forecast for free with no obligation whatsoever. When he asked what the success rate of the forecasts was, he was transferred to the company's soybean expert who told him that all previous forecasts and results had been kept on a computer. The forecaster said that for some reason, over a large number of weekly forecasts, the company was much better at forecasting price rises than declines. Farmer Brown said that he had summarized his price expectations into three possible scenarios: no price change or a movement in either direction of two cents per bushel. The forecaster consulted his computer and said: "For week-ahead wheat forecasts, I can tell you the following. Over weeks when the price has risen two cents, we were able to forecast price rises 65% of the time. In other words, given a random sample of 100 weeks when the price rose two cents, we forecast a price rise 65 times. When prices are stable, we forecast rises 25% of the time, and when prices actually fall by two cents, we forecast price rises 10% of the time." The farmer asked for corresponding figures for forecasts of no price change and price declines. He used the success rate data to write out a set of conditional probabilities for the company

*P*(Price rise forecast/Actual rise of two cents) = 0.65
*P*(Price rise forecast/Actual price stable) = 0.25
*P*(Price rise forecast/Actual fall of two cents) = 0.1
*P*(Price stable forecast/Actual rise of two cents) = 0.3
*P*(Price stable forecast/Actual price stable) = 0.4
*P*(Price stable forecast/Actual fall of two cents) = 0.2
*P*(Price fall forecast/Actual rise of two cents) = 0.05
*P*(Price fall forecast/Actual price stable) = 0.35
*P*(Price fall forecast/Actual fall of two cents) = 0.7

The forecaster asked the farmer what he thought the likelihoods were of various price movements over the next week, and the farmer told him what his prior probabilities were. Together they calculated a set of revised (posterior) probabilities to see how the farmer's prior beliefs would be revised by a prediction from the forecaster. In these calculations a forecast of price rise, price stable, or price fall would be considered to have a reliability based on the past history of the forecaster. Tables 10–27, 10–28, and 10–29 show the Bayes calculations.

Mr. Brown then considered the results to see whether having the forecast before making the decision would help him make a better decision. He asked his wife to help him. Mrs. Brown had a master's degree in applied statistics and an MBA. She had been a successful Wall Street analyst before she and Farmer Brown (as she called him) decided to go back to the land. After looking at the calculations, Mrs. Brown concluded that the success rate of the forecasts was far from perfect, but the forecast would certainly reduce the uncertainty about prices that Farmer Brown had expressed

**TABLE 10–27** Bayes Revision if a Price Rise Is Forecast

| *Event* | *Prior Probability* | *Likelihood* | *Joint Probability* | *Posterior Probability* |
|---|---|---|---|---|
| Price rise (two cents) | 0.4 | 0.65 | 0.26 | 0.69 |
| Price stable | 0.4 | 0.25 | 0.1 | 0.26 |
| Price fall (two cents) | 0.2 | 0.1 | 0.02 | 0.05 |
| | | | $\Sigma = 0.38$ | $\Sigma = 1$ |

**TABLE 10–28** Bayes Revision if a Stable Price Is Forecast

| *Event* | *Prior Probability* | *Likelihood* | *Joint Probability* | *Posterior Probability* |
|---|---|---|---|---|
| Price rise (two cents) | 0.4 | 0.3 | 0.12 | 0.375 |
| Price stable | 0.4 | 0.4 | 0.16 | 0.5 |
| Price fall (two cents) | 0.2 | 0.2 | 0.04 | 0.125 |
| | | | $\Sigma = 0.32$ | $\Sigma = 1$ |

**TABLE 10–29** Bayes Revision if a Price Fall Is Forecast

| *Event* | *Prior Probability* | *Likelihood* | *Joint Probability* | *Posterior Probability* |
|---|---|---|---|---|
| Price rise (two cents) | 0.4 | 0.05 | 0.02 | 0.06 |
| Price stable | 0.4 | 0.35 | 0.14 | 0.47 |
| Price fall (two cents) | 0.2 | 0.7 | 0.14 | 0.47 |
| | | | $\Sigma = 0.3$ | $\Sigma = 1$ |

in his prior distribution. She told Farmer Brown that the forecasts would help his decision process because:

1. Without a forecast, his strategy is to wait and sell next week. This carried with it a 20% chance of a price fall that was the downside of this strategy.
2. With a forecast, the best strategy appeared to be wait and sell next week if a price rise or stable price was forecast. If a price fall was forecast, the best thing to do was to sell now. The probabilities of making an error in terms of picking a strategy that would be regretted were all less than the 0.2 chance of making an error if a forecast was not used. Specifically, the probabilities of choosing the wrong strategy were different for each forecast and are given by

$$P(\text{Wrong strategy/Forecast of price rise}) = 0.05$$
$$P(\text{Wrong strategy/Forecast of price stable}) = 0.125$$
$$P(\text{Wrong strategy/Forecast of price fall}) = 0.06$$

Mrs. Brown concluded that the forecaster's information was valuable because his success rates were good and because the chances were moved more in favor of a good decision if the forecaster's information was used.

Mrs. Brown suggested that Farmer Brown get the forecast and use it to help make a decision. Further, she suggested that they should find out the cost of using the forecasting service and consider using it in the future. Farmer Brown replied that he would certainly call the company back and get the free forecast. He suggested that they should see how the free forecast turned out before considering paying for future forecasts. Mrs. Brown replied that while that strategy seemed reasonable at first, she was concerned that the first forecast might be wrong as a matter of chance and that this random event of one trial might stop them from using a generally good information source. She explained: "They are not claiming 100% success with their predictions. However, they certainly do better than someone who was picking price movements with a dartboard (at random). If the first forecast turns out to be wrong, there is no reason to believe that the next few wouldn't be correct."

Farmer Brown telephoned the forecaster and was given his free forecast. He arranged to be sent a copy of the company's newsletter and some information on prices for further forecasts. He also drew a decision tree with Mrs. Brown's help which helped to clarify his options. (See Figure 10–11.) On the decision tree, Farmer Brown placed the posterior and other probabilities that he had calculated.

**FIGURE 10–11** Farmer Brown's Decision Tree

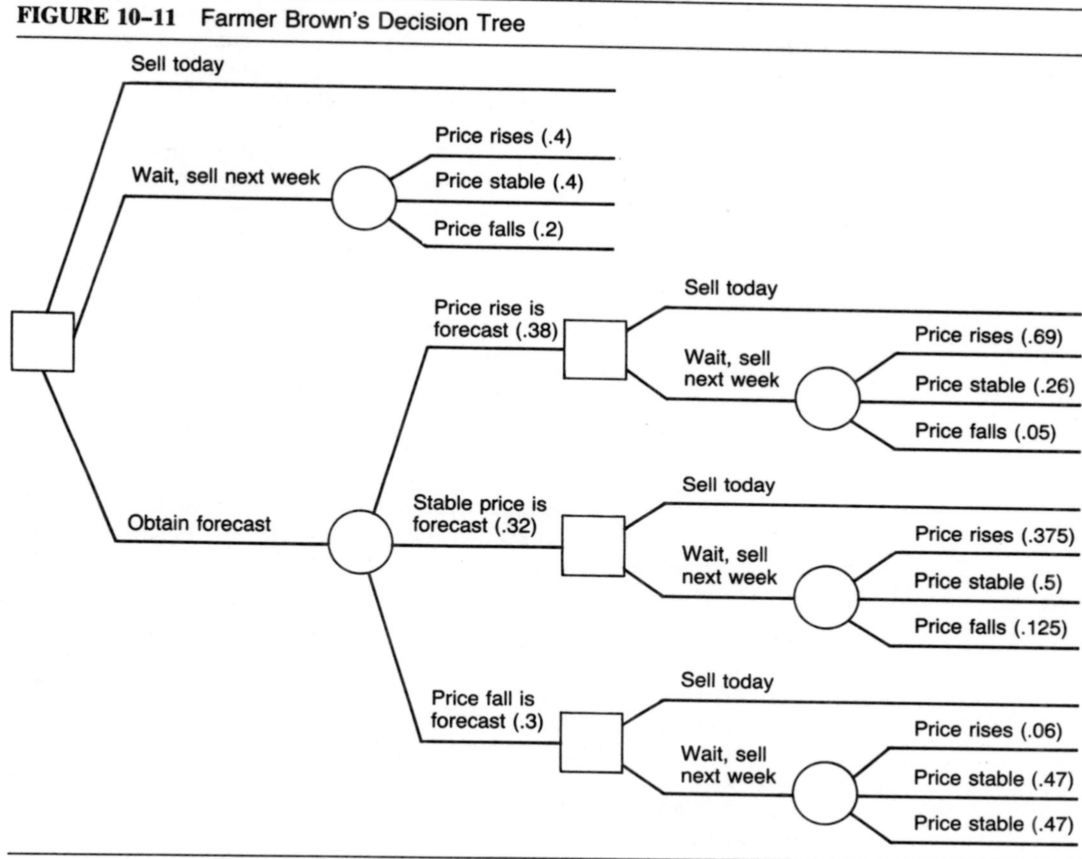


## EXAMPLE 10–8

### Pilot Plants at Chemoil Pharmaceuticals

Chemoil was a large, well-diversified company with a broad product mix across the energy (oil and gas), chemical (plastics, chlorine, ammonia, soaps, detergents, propellents), and pharmaceuticals industries. Its divisions had small research budgets, but they generally had a large process development focus. The company had a history of successfully taking new products and new processes for existing products from the drawing board or laboratory stage to the commercial process stage. Jim Case, the new director of operations at one of Chemoil's divisions, was interested in increasing Chemoil's process development effectiveness. He studied a number of the company's case histories of both successful process and product developments as well as failures. He noted that some of the processes had been scaled up directly from laboratory to commercial-scale facilities and some involved the intermediate step of building and operating a pilot plant. Jim interviewed a number of people in the company and concluded that there did not seem to have been any substantial rhyme or reason associated with the decision to build or not build a pilot plant. It was almost never obvious with new processes whether a pilot plant was desirable or not. In retrospect however, project and plant managers had strong feelings about the plant scale-up process. He heard such comments as:

1. "The pilot plant was a waste of time and money. The process would have worked just as well without it."
2. "Imagine if we had gone ahead without a pilot plant. We never would have found out about that corrosion problem and might all be dead now."
3. "By investing $150,000 in the construction and operation of a pilot plant we learned enough to lower construction costs by over $1 million."
4. "The process is simple, straightforward, and quite similar to one or two others that already exist. We were right in going straight from the laboratory to the full-scale unit."

These comments referred to different projects and highlighted the fact that every project was different. Across its various divisions, Chemoil spent over $30 million each year on pilot-scale projects. Most of these cost between $50,000 and $3 million. As a divisional operations director, Jim wanted to see a consistent set of policies and a decision framework applied to such decisions. He formulated the problem as shown by Figure 10–12.

Jim realized that the decision of whether or not to build a pilot plant is greatly dependent upon the value of the information that the pilot plant is expected to provide

**FIGURE 10–12** Chemoil Pilot Plant Problem

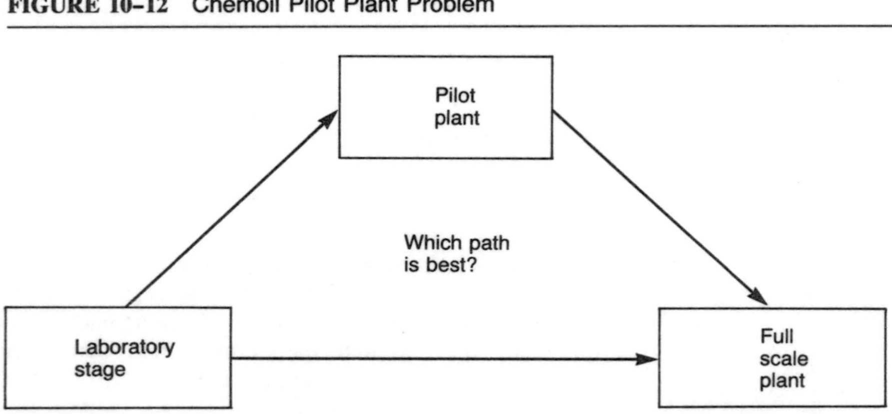

**FIGURE 10–13** Pilot Plant Decision Tree

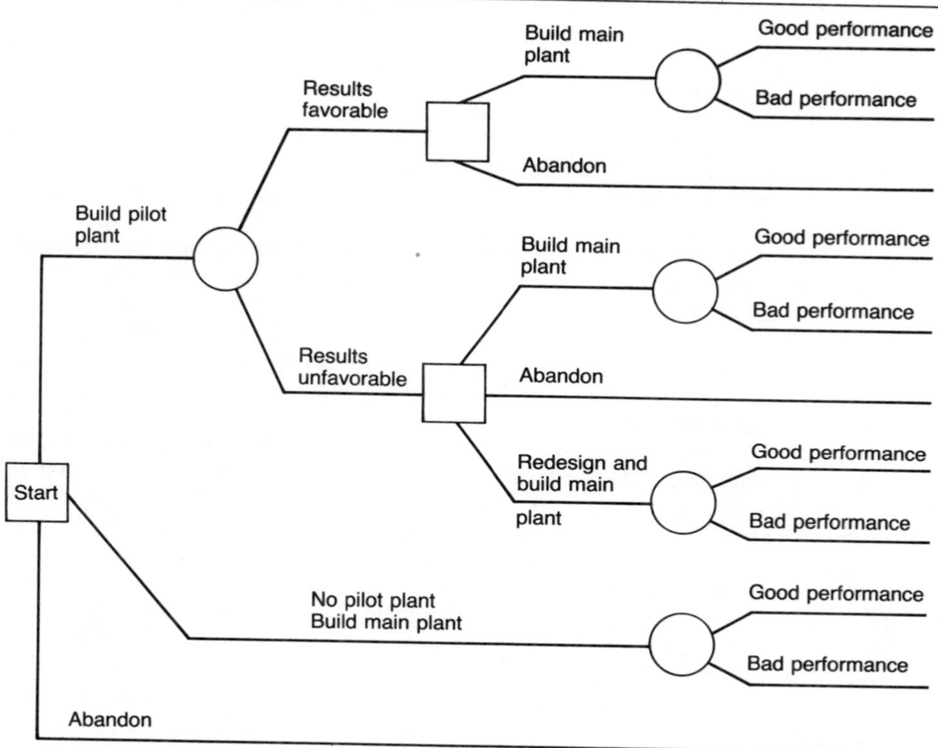


because in nearly all cases the only valuable product of a pilot plant is information (whether direct or indirect). Direct information may relate to technical factors such as chemical reaction rates, heat and mass transfer rates, yields, operating conditions, possible corrosion problems, power requirements, chemical processing-stage efficiencies. In some cases the actual products of a pilot plant may be used as a test product or as a raw material in the next processing stage, and in this case the aim is still to obtain information—indirect information on factors such as quality and suitability.

Jim decided that the focus on information and the inherent uncertainty in the process made it suitable for modeling using decision analysis. As a result he chose to analyze the decision for a pilot plant that was shortly going to be made by his division using a decision tree. He wanted to see what insights he could generate by using this framework.

The decision tree for one particular situation is shown in Figure 10–13. Initially, consideration of the problem resulted in the definition of a large number of options and sources of uncertainty. The decision tree that was drawn was then so complex as to be virtually unworkable, thus defeating the purpose of its construction (which was to allow a logical rational viewing of the main elements of the situation). It was therefore necessary to prune the tree, laying bare the major issues and discarding those which were less important.

The option shown in Figure 10–13 as "build pilot plant" would in reality lead to a large number of possible outcomes. However, for the purposes of analysis it was reduced to just two outcomes in the model.

A similar situation was evident for the "build plant" options where the results of the ensuing chance event node could in reality lead to a much greater number of states than the two shown in Figure 10–13. However, it was decided that two states were enough to represent the uncertainty in an initial analysis.

The assessment of uncertainties was carried out by a team comprising engineers and marketing people who were able to make the overall assessment of the unconditional probability of good performance of the full-scale process as 0.9. In assessing the probability of success of the pilot study it was realized that the information that could be obtained from the pilot plant was far from perfect, meaning that it was possible that favorable results at the pilot stage could lead to a plant that would perform poorly. On the other hand, it was realized that even if the pilot plant did not perform well, the main plant might work, particularly if faults could be rectified and the main plant redesigned. The recognition of this uncertainty resulted in a set of assessments of the reliability of the pilot plant as shown in Table 10–30. The conditional probability statements in Table 10–30 represent assessments in the form of "pilot plant performance given full-scale performance." Assessments were made in this form so that past experience could be drawn upon. Table 10–30 should be read horizontally, that is, if the main plant reaches a state of "good performance" there was assessed a 0.95 probability that the pilot plant would have yielded favorable results and a 0.05 probability of unfavorable pilot plant results.

Bayes Theorem was then used to calculate the conditional and unconditional probabilities for insertion on the decision tree. It was also decided that if the pilot plant results were unfavorable and the plant was redesigned and possibly retested, the probability of good performance would be 0.8.

Jim realized that each path on a decision tree must lead to an eventual outcome state with a corresponding value associated with that state. The monetary values of each outcome state were assessed taking into account:

1. Pilot plant cost.
2. Reduced cost of the full-scale plant due to the pilot study.
3. Cost of time delay due to the pilot study.

**TABLE 10–30** Outcome Probabilities

| | *Pilot Plant* | | |
|---|---|---|---|
| *Full-Scale Plant* | *Favorable* | *Unfavorable* | *Totals* |
| Good performance | 0.95 | 0.05 | 1.0 |
| Poor performance | 0.15 | 0.85 | 1.0 |

4. Plant cost.
5. Cost and benefits of redesign.
6. Plant performance.
7. Sales and operating costs.

It was decided to consider these monetary amounts in terms of the present value of future cash flows and initially to use a decision criterion of expected monetary value (EMV). Aspects of possible aversion to risk were neglected at that stage. Jim noted that the EMV criterion looks at the probability-weighted averages of the values of possible outcomes and leads to a decision that chooses the set of paths with the highest possible EMV, without placing direct value on the inherent riskiness of decision strategies. The actual values of the assessments for the present case are shown in Table 10–31 and Figure 10–14. Once the monetary values of outcomes and the probability distributions of chance events are known, the decision criterion is used to determine the best strategy.

Application of the EMV criterion to the decision tree shown in Figure 10–14 leads to an optimal strategy of "no pilot plant, build main plant." This option has an EMV of $19.3 million, which is higher than the next best option of $19.07 million (by only 1.2%). Jim knew that the decision analysis approach advocates that in all cases (and particularly in cases such as this when competing options are only marginally different in value) he should examine the sensitivity of the solution to the input estimates and assumptions.

In testing the sensitivity of the solution, it was felt that the critical inputs to the analysis were

1. The estimated overall probability of plant success.
2. The value of HP and RHP.

**TABLE 10–31** Assessment of Monetary Outcomes

| Item | Description | Value |
|---|---|---|
| HP (high profit) | Present value of all profits assuming technical and marketing success | $22 million |
| LP (low profit) | Present value of all profits assuming technical failure and, hence, marketing difficulties | −$5 million |
| PPC (pilot plant cost) | Current estimate of pilot plant construction and operating cost | $1 million |
| DC (delay cost) | Present value of cost of delay caused by the pilot study | $0.4 million |
| PPB (pilot plant benefit) | Present value of benefits and savings in construction costs of main plant as a result of pilot plant experience | $0.25 million |
| RC (redesign cost) | Present value of cost of redesigning plant if pilot plant operation is unsuccessful | $0.3 million |
| RHP (redesign high profit) | Present value of profits if pilot plant fails and redesign is forced | $16.45 million |
| RLP (redesign low profit) | Present value of profit if redesigned plant is unsuccessful in technical or marketing aspect | −$5.3 million |

NOTE: Figures shown are in present value terms and include all cash flows (present and future).

**FIGURE 10–14** Pilot Plant Decision Tree

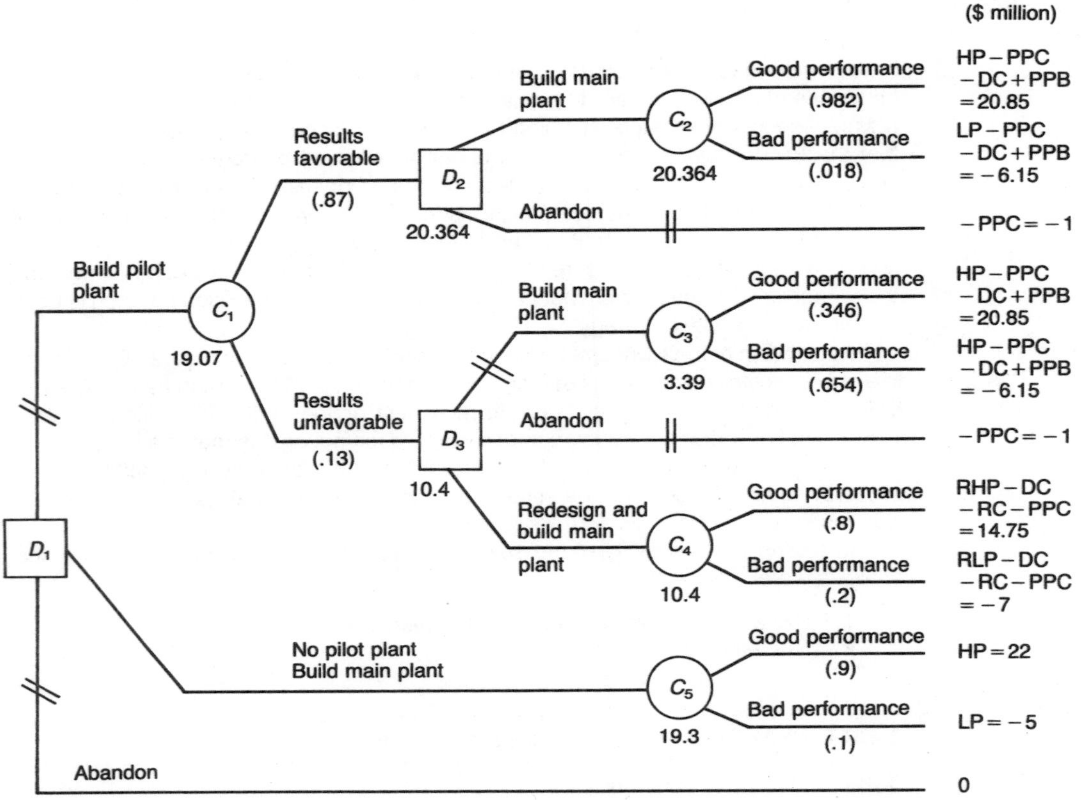

($ million)

Build pilot plant
$C_1$
19.07
Results favorable
(.87)
$D_2$
20.364
Build main plant
$C_2$
20.364
Good performance
(.982)
HP − PPC − DC + PPB = 20.85
Bad performance
(.018)
LP − PPC − DC + PPB = −6.15
Abandon
− PPC = −1
Results unfavorable
(.13)
$D_3$
10.4
Build main plant
$C_3$
3.39
Good performance
(.346)
HP − PPC − DC + PPB = 20.85
Bad performance
(.654)
HP − PPC − DC + PPB = −6.15
Abandon
− PPC = −1
Redesign and build main plant
$C_4$
10.4
Good performance
(.8)
RHP − DC − RC − PPC = 14.75
Bad performance
(.2)
RLP − DC − RC − PPC = −7
$D_1$
No pilot plant Build main plant
$C_5$
19.3
Good performance
(.9)
HP = 22
Bad performance
(.1)
LP = −5
Abandon
0

In retrospect it was felt that the estimated probability of plant success of 0.9 might have been a little high, so the problem was reworked assuming that this estimate was 0.8. This change affected the conditional probabilities as shown in Figure 10–15. It was found that when the probability estimate of 0.8 was used, the pilot plant option at decision node $D_1$ had a higher EMV (17.84) than the alternative (16.6). See Figure 10–15.

The critical value of this probability estimate at which the two main options had equivalent expected monetary values was 0.886. This factor was therefore considered as one to which the solution was highly sensitive.

A second input Jim examined was the estimates of HP and RHP. The values of LP and RLP were considered fairly accurate since they represented low sales and were composed mainly of cost estimates. The HP and RHP figures included a sales estimate, and it was felt that differences in present value of plus or minus $1 million were conceivable. The EMV criterion was reapplied with the appropriate changes

**FIGURE 10–15** Revised Pilot Plant Decision Tree

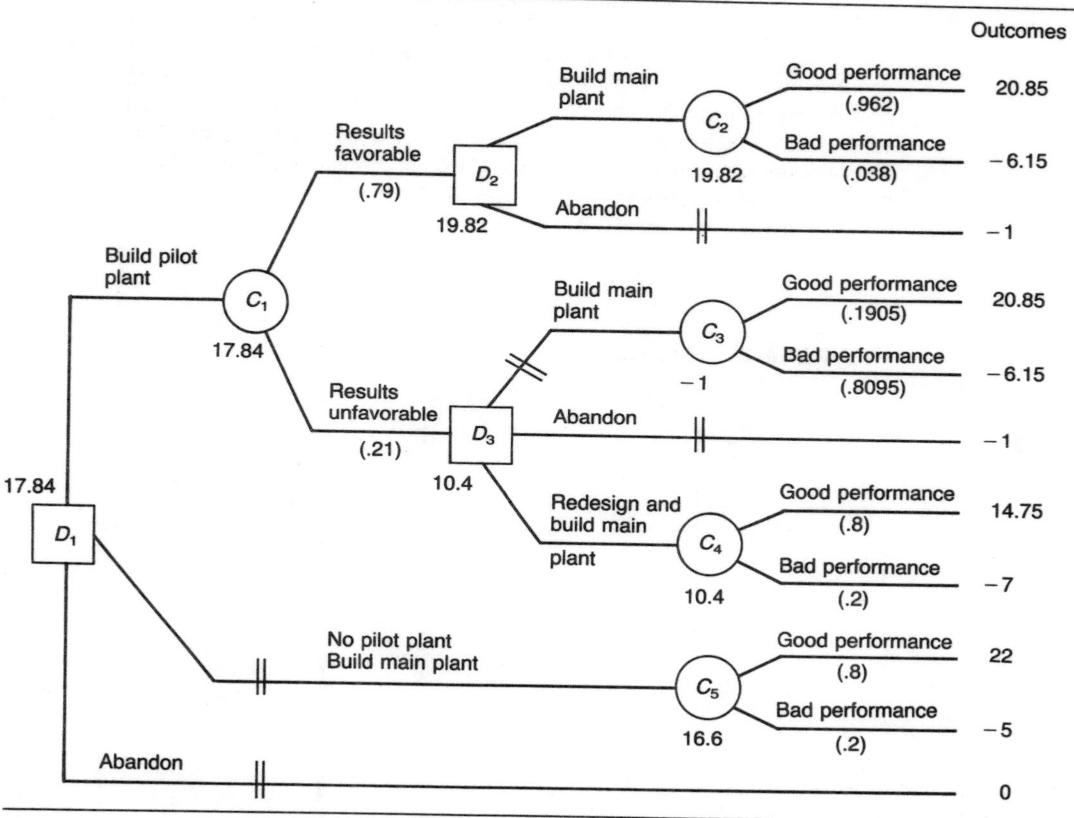


made (Table 10–32), and it was concluded that the solution was not highly sensitive to these factors.

Jim did not consider the rollback procedure leading to the solution in Figure 10–14 as a final solution to the problem, but as a basis upon which to gain inference and consider intangibles and other modifying factors.

**TABLE 10–32** Reassessment of Monetary Outcomes

| *High Profit* | *Redesign High Profit* | *Expected Monetary Value (pilot plant)* | *Expected Monetary Value (no pilot plant)* |
|---|---|---|---|
| 22.0 | 16.0 | 19.0 | 19.3 |
| 23.0 | 17.0 | 20.0 | 20.2 |
| 21.0 | 15.0 | 18.1 | 18.4 |

Referring to Figure 10–14, Jim pointed out to his colleagues that it was important to realize that the EMV figures of nodes $C_1$ and $C_5$ were not monetary amounts but weighted averages. He noted that the 19.07 figure at $C_1$ is representative of four possible outcomes, and these outcomes, along with their associated probabilities of occurrence were plotted on a risk profile (Figure 10–16). Consideration of the risk profile and comparison with the risk profile of the main competing option (Figure 10–17) may lead to a different decision than that which assumed that EMV maximization was an appropriate decision rule. The risk profiles show that the probability of making a loss is much smaller if the pilot plant is built. Jim noted that a decision maker who was averse to risks of this magnitude might well decide to play it safe and opt for

**FIGURE 10–16** Risk Profile for "Build Pilot Plant" Option

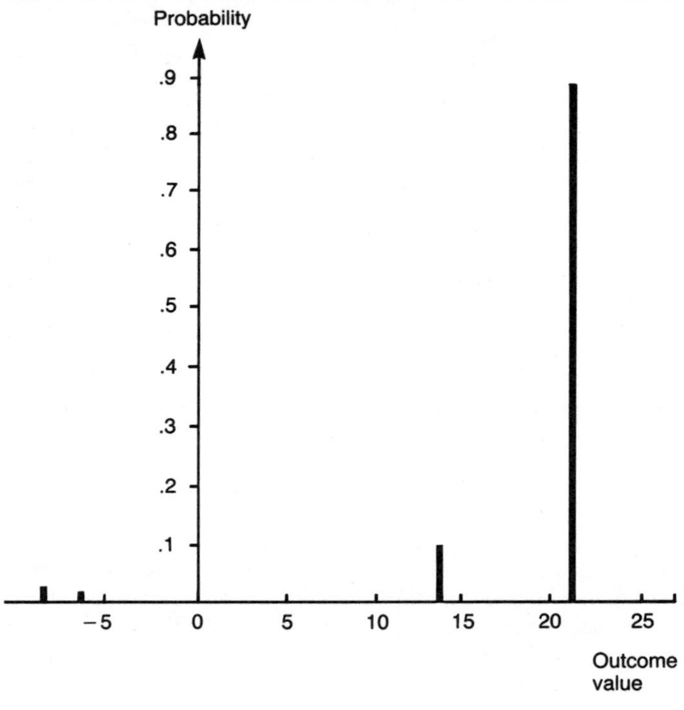


| Value | Probability |
|---|---|
| 20.85 | .87 × .982 = .854 |
| −6.15 | .87 × .018 = .016 |
| 14.75 | .13 × .8 = .104 |
| −7 | .13 × .2 = .026 |

**FIGURE 10–17** Risk Profile for "No Pilot Plant" Option

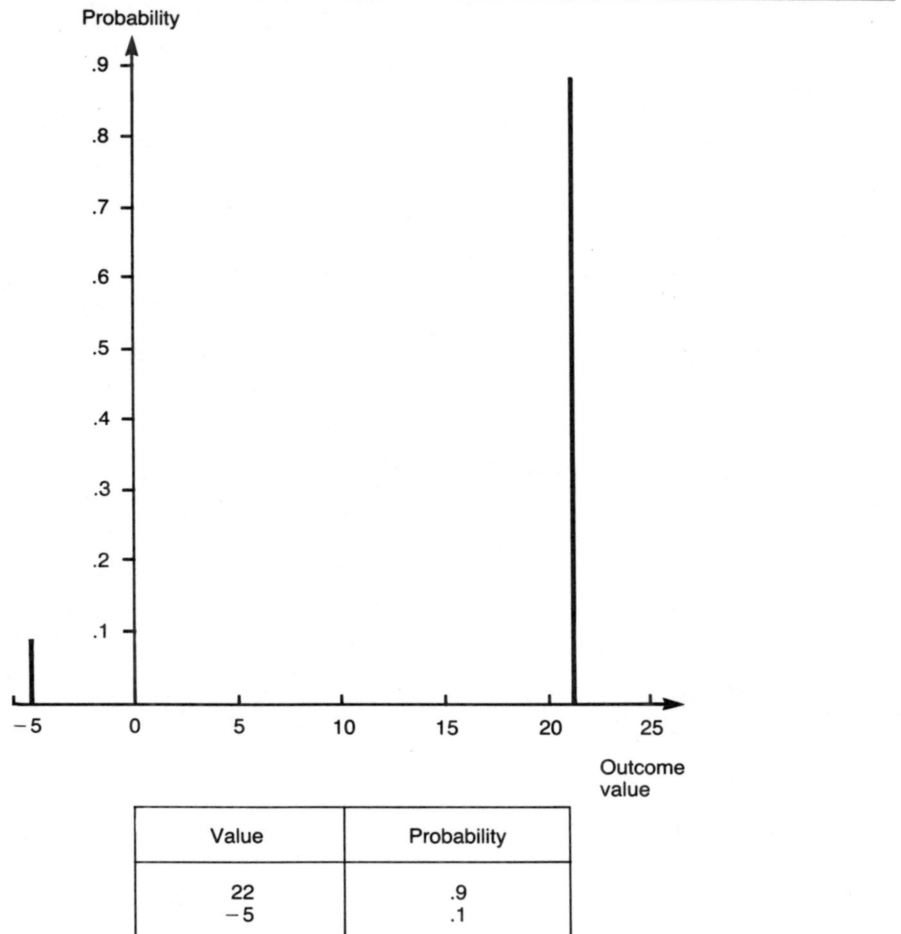


| Value | Probability |
|---|---|
| 22 | .9 |
| −5 | .1 |

the pilot plant even though, based on averages (EMV), it is not the best option. Indeed, a highly risk-averse decision maker might in fact decide to abandon the project completely at the $D_1$ node rather than face even a small probability of loss.

Jim used the Bayes formula to calculate the posterior probabilities for this problem. The Bayes Theorem calculations were as follows

$A_1$ = Event of major plant good performance
$A_2$ = Event of major plant poor performance
$B_1$ = Event of pilot plant results favorable
$B_2$ = Event of pilot plant results unfavorable

Then for $B_1$ and $B_2$

$$P(A_j/B) = \frac{P(A_j)\ P(B/A_j)}{\sum_{i=1}^{2} P(A_i)\ P(B/A_i)}$$

$$P(A_1/B_1) = \frac{0.9 \times 0.95}{0.9 \times 0.95 + 0.1 \times 0.15}$$

$$= 0.982$$

$P(A_2/B_1)$ is the complement of $P(A_1/B_1)$

$$P(A_2/B_1) = 0.018$$

$$P(A_1/B_2) = \frac{0.9 \times 0.05}{0.9 \times 0.05 + 0.1 \times 0.85}$$

$$= 0.346$$

$P(A_2/B_2)$ is the complement of $P(A_1/B_2)$.

$$P(A_2/B_2) = 0.654$$

The unconditional probabilities were

$$P(B_1) = P(B_1/A_1)P(A_1) + P(B_1/A_2)\ P(A_2)$$

$$= 0.87$$

Hence

$$P(B_2) = 0.13$$

---

## Example 10–9

### IBDA[9]

IBDA (The Institute of Bayesian Decision Analysts) was an organization aimed to foster research and the dissemination of information about Bayesian statistics. The society had 10,000 members and produced three journals. The main journal was the *Journal of Bayesian Decision Theory* (*JBDT*) and was circulated to all members. The

[9] This is a fictitious organization. However the issue described in this example is adapted from a real problem.

**TABLE 10–33** Bayes Revision Process

| *Event* | *Prior Probability* | *Likelihood* | *Joint Probability* | *Posterior Probability* |
|---|---|---|---|---|
| $P = 0.05$ | 0.6 | 0.0028 | 0.00168 | 0.089 |
| $P = 0.10$ | 0.3 | 0.0988 | 0.00889 | 0.469 |
| $P = 0.15$ | 0.1 | 0.0838 | 0.00838 | 0.442 |
| | | | $\Sigma = .01895$ | $\Sigma = 1$ |

two other journals were the *Journal of Applied Bayesian Statistics* (*JABS*) and the *Bayesian Statistical Quarterly* (*BSQ*). All members received *JBDT* at no cost and had the option of purchasing either or both of the others. In recent years, a number of the members had been lobbying for an alteration to this system that would allow a choice of any one of the three journals to be supplied to any member at no cost. The president of IBDA wanted to get an assessment of how widespread this preference was before deciding on whether to go through a formal voting procedure with all his 10,000 members. In his opinion, only a relatively small proportion of the members wanted such a change. He assessed his prior probabilities as

$$P(\text{Proportion who wanted the change} = 0.05) = 0.6$$
$$P(\text{Proportion who wanted the change} = 0.10) = 0.3$$
$$P(\text{Proportion who wanted the change} = 0.15) = 0.1$$

On the day before an IBDA council meeting he instructed his secretary to call 100 randomly selected members and find out whether they would vote for or against the change. She reported back that 12 out of the 100 members were in favor of the change. This result was more than the president expected, and he revised his probabilities by using the binomial distribution to calculate the conditional likelihoods.

The likelihood probabilities were

$$P(n = 100, r = 12 \text{ sample result}/p = 0.05) = 0.0028$$
$$P(n = 100, r = 12 \text{ sample result}/p = 0.10) = 0.0988$$
$$P(n = 100, r = 12 \text{ sample result}/p = 0.15) = 0.0838$$

These likelihood probabilities can be calculated using the binomial distribution formula or can be found in the tables presented as an appendix to most business statistics textbooks.

The Bayes revision process is shown by Table 10–33.

The survey served to modify the president's beliefs about the proportion of members who were in favor of the change. The probability revision process had merged the president's prior subjective assessments with some sample evidence. Since the sample result was higher than the mean of the prior distribution, his views about the proportion of members who wanted the change were accordingly revised. He reconsidered the decision that he would recommend at the next day's meeting of the IBDA council.

## SUMMARY

Multiple sources of information can be effectively used in decision analysis through combining them to form a posterior probability distribution. The Bayesian revision process combines unconditional prior probabilities with the conditional probabilities of some observation (which is usually described in terms of the prior distribution random variable). The resulting posterior probability distribution has the opposite direction of conditionality from that of the likelihood probabilities. Bayes Theorem is not limited to accounting for one observed event, but can be used repeatedly to update beliefs about an uncertain quantity. In such repeated applications, the posterior probability distribution of the last iteration becomes the prior distribution for the next.

In some instances where particular (conjugate) combinations of probability distributions are used, it is not necessary to calculate a set of revised probabilities. For conjugate families of distributions, the parameters of the posterior distribution can be directly determined as a function of the parameters of the prior and likelihood distributions.

Bayes Theorem can be applied in a wide variety of situations. These applications all relate to the use of additional information in decision making. Examples include the use of survey results as an input to decision processes and the use of "expert" predictions where the expert is known to be an imperfect forecaster.

As will be seen in the next chapter, the usefulness of Bayes Theorem in decision analysis is mostly in determining the value of information. It provides a method for explicitly including the information-gathering phase of a decision (which is usually not costless) into the decision analysis.

## FURTHER READING

The statistical result which constitutes Bayes Theorem was first published (by Thomas Bayes) over 200 years ago. Only relatively recently has Bayes Theorem found a useful place in modern decision analysis.

Two excellent treatments of the subject are given by Robert Winkler (1972) and Howard Raiffa (1968). For the reader who wishes to explore this aspect of decision analysis further, Winkler's book is a very good next step. Another useful volume is by Holloway (1979).

A more technical treatment was published by Raiffa and Schlaifer (1961). This volume is suited to the more mathematically oriented reader who wishes to explore statistical aspects of combining probabilistic information from multiple sources.

## REFERENCES

HOLLOWAY, C. 1979. *Decision Making Under Uncertainty*. New York: Prentice-Hall.

RAIFFA, H. 1968. *Decision Analysis*. Reading, Mass.: Addison-Wesley Publishing.

RAIFFA, H., and R. SCHLAIFER. 1961. *Applied Statistical Decision Theory*. Boston: Harvard University, Division of Research.

WINKLER, R. L. 1972. *Introduction to Bayesian Inference and Decision*. New York: Holt, Rinehart & Winston.

## PROBLEMS

1. Explain the concepts of prior probability, conditional likelihood, and posterior probability.
2. What does Bayes Theorem do? Can it be used for discrete and continuous random variables?
3. Is Bayes Theorem a necessary step in all decision analysis problems? If not, how can the decision maker or decision analyst know when it is appropriate to use Bayes Theorem?
4. With reference to conditional probabilities, explain the concept of direction of conditionality.
5. Invent a simple example where a decision maker needs to reverse the direction of conditionality in a decision analysis. In doing so define the prior, conditional likelihood, and posterior parameters.
6. When we consider systems of various kinds, we are often interested in estimating the system reliability. Explain how prior beliefs about reliability could be expressed as a probability distribution. If a system is observed, how can the observation be translated into a set of conditional likelihood probabilities?
7. Following from problem 6, how can a prior view of reliability be updated to take the observation into account?
8. What is a preposterior analysis?
9. What is the correct interpretation of extreme conditional likelihood probabilities (that is, probabilities that are zero or one)? In such a case, why do the prior probabilities have no impact on the posterior probabilities?
10. What is the information content in a uniform prior distribution? Suppose that a decison hinges critically on the value of a parameter that can take on any of five values. If the prior probabilities are all assessed as equal and a relevant observation is made, what would

be the relationship between the conditional likelihood probabilities and the posterior distribution?

11. Referring to problem 10, would the impact of the observation on the posterior distribution be changed if the prior probabilities were not equal? If so, how would the influence of the observation change as the prior probabilities generally become more unequal?

12. A company that manufactures pumps buys various components from a variety of suppliers. One of the key components for a particular model is the pump impeller, which is made by a subcontractor. In a shipment of 100 of these impellers, it is very time-consuming and expensive to measure the angles of the blades on all of the pieces, but it is feasible to test a small number. For those impellers that do not have the blades correctly placed, the pump efficiency will be low when functional tests are made. Past experience with batches of these components indicates that batches are either very good (having 5 defectives) or very bad (having 20 defectives). The production manager of the pump company assumed that this phenomenon had to do with which person in the supplier company prepared the batch. Assuming that batches have either 5 or 20 defectives, how could samples be used to shed light on the likelihood of a batch being a good or bad one?

    In the past, 90% of batches had been good (5 defectives only). Use Bayes Theorem to calculate posterior probabilities for various observation outcomes if sample size is 1, 2, 5, or 10.

13. Referring to problem 12, redo the Bayes calculations assuming prior probabilities of 0.6 and 0.4, rather than 0.9 and 0.1. Compare the results of problems 12 and 13, and demonstrate how the effect of the observation is a function of the value of the prior probabilities. Discuss these issues in terms of the prior ratio, likelihood ratio, and posterior ratio concepts.

14. Robert Paysley owns a tax consulting business. He is at a government auction of smoke and fire damaged equipment and is considering bidding on a set of three personal computers. He has been able to visually inspect the computers but was not allowed access to any other information. He feels that the computers will be an excellent buy so long as the central processing units (CPUs) are OK. This model of computer suits his purposes exactly. But Robert is worried about whether the central processing units will require expensive repair.

    The auction manager has offered to tell him whether the computers are OK or not. However, the auction manager expects to be paid an amount per computer for the information because it would cost money to test each machine.

After inspecting the machines again, Robert sat down and quantified his uncertainty as follows:

| *Number of Computers with Damaged CPUs* | *Probability* |
|---|---|
| 0 | 0.5 |
| 1 | 0.1 |
| 2 | 0.1 |
| 3 | 0.3 |

He felt that since all the machines had been exposed to about the same amount of fire/smoke hazard, it was most likely that either all or none were damaged.

Since he would pay a fixed amount for information for each computer, Robert had to decide whether to buy the information on zero, one, two, or three computers. He could instruct the auctioneer on how many to test. The computers could be sold only as a set, not individually.

Draw a decision tree representing this problem, and use Bayes Theorem to calculate the probabilities associated with the various branches of the tree.

15. Refer to Example 10–1, Advance Electronics (A). Recalculate the posterior probabilities for this example using prior probabilities of

$$P(\text{Good}) = 0.6$$
$$P(\text{Bad}) = 0.4$$

16. Refer to Example 10–2, Advance Electronics (B). Use the same prior probabilities as in problem 15 above to calculate the posterior probabilities associated with samples of two ECD units. Demonstrate that the serial calculations (treating each sampled ECD as a separate observation) lead to the same results as the procedure using a combined calculation process.
17. Assume that in Example 10–3, Advance Electronics (C), sampling was performed without replacement. Use the hypergeometric distribution to calculate likelihood probabilities, and compare these with those obtained using the binomial likelihood process.
18. A survey specialist wishes to examine the effect of sample size on the posterior probability distribution associated with a local election. She considered two events: The candidate of interest would poll 20% or else 30%. She initially assigned equal probabilities to these events.

Calculate the posterior probabilities associated with samples of size 5, 10, 20, 50, and 100 so that in each sample, the poll (sample mean) results in 40% indicating they would vote for the candidate of interest. Plot a graph of sample size versus posterior probability ratio.

19. Recalculate the posterior probabilities for problem 18 above using different prior probabilities, namely

$$P(\text{Candidate polls } 20\%) = 0.7$$
$$P(\text{Candidate polls } 30\%) = 0.3$$

and

$$P(\text{Candidate polls } 20\%) = 0.4$$
$$P(\text{Candidate polls } 30\%) = 0.6$$

Plot the points on the same graph and observe the relationship between the influence of the various prior and the various likelihood probabilities on the posterior distribution.

20. A government agency which handled public aid programs was looking at ways in which it could more efficiently manage its accounts receivable in the area of third-party medical and dental payments. These payments were in the category of "medical" in that the government paid bills on behalf of public aid recipients. In cases where it was later discovered that insurance coverage existed, accounts receivable were created and invoices were sent out.

The system was just being overhauled and computerized. It currently existed as a set of approximately 15,000 files. To get a feel for the volume of money involved, the agency director did two things. First, he asked the section manager to estimate the amount of accounts receivable. The second initiative was a quick and dirty survey of 20 accounts.

The section manager suggested that the population mean was $25 and that the standard deviation was $5. These figures applied to single consultations only. He suggested that there was symmetry across the mean and that the distribution form was normal.

The survey results also showed a normal distribution form, with a sample mean of $35 and a sample standard deviation of $7. The agency director was unhappy with the discrepancy between the prior estimate and the survey result, thinking that neither was particularly reliable.

He asked for a second survey to be done, of 500 accounts. It resulted in a sample mean of $33.50 and a sample standard deviation of $6.

*a*. Uses Bayes Theorem to integrate the information from the section manager and the first survey.

*b*. Use the posterior distribution of (part *a*) as the prior distribution in a second application of Bayes Theorem. The second survey is the likelihood observation, in this instance.

*c*. Plot all the distributions on the same graph.
*d*. For the two surveys estimate a combined sample mean and standard deviation, and reapply Bayes Theorem using the original prior estimates. Is the posterior distribution identical to that of part (*b*)?

21. In Example 10–7, Farmer Brown wanted to test the sensitivity of the posterior probabilities he calculated to the input priors. In particular he decided that two things might be useful:
    *a*. He revised his prior probabilities because he felt that his original estimates might have been too optimistic. The new prior probabilities are:

$$\begin{aligned} P(\text{Price rise of two cents}) &= 0.3 \\ P(\text{Price stable}) &= 0.3 \\ P(\text{Price fall of two cents}) &= 0.4 \end{aligned}$$

    Calculate the new posterior probabilities.
    *b*. He decided to delete from his considerations the possibility that prices would be stable. He then assigned probabilities of 0.4 and 0.6 respectively for price rise and fall likelihoods.

    Redraw his decision tree for this modified problem, and use Bayes Theorem to calculate the relevant probabilities.

## CASE STUDY

### Printem Inc

Printem Inc, a Californian publishing company, was considering signing a young author to a contract for a book on Bayesian statistics. The author was negotiating an advance with the company based on arguments about sales. The company's editor had said he thought that of the top 100 universities in the country, no more than five would adopt the book as a text. He thought that at least two universities would adopt, but he had no idea about whether the number of adopters would be two, three, four, or five and that these events were equally likely.

The author argued that the number of adopters might be substantially higher. He had sent a copy of his outline and a few chapters to the textbook decision makers of 10 randomly sampled universities from the top 100. One of these 10 had indicated they would adopt. As a result, the author argued that 10% of universities would be adopters and suggested that the evidence was overwhelming. Since the advance normally paid was a function of the expected number of adopters, a heated debate followed.

**1.** The editor was prepared to revise his prior beliefs based on the sample evidence. Use Bayes Theorem to take into account the sample information, and calculate posterior probabilities.

**2.** The author said to the editor that the percent of adopters in the sample was 10% and that there was no reason to expect any different a result from the whole population. The author argued that by defining a prior probability distribution as he had, the editor had unfairly assumed that no more than five adoptions could possibly occur. The author argued that the prior should extend to at least recognize that 10 adoptions were possible.

Recalculate the posterior probabilities assuming that in the prior distribution the number of adopters was equally likely to be any integer number in the range 2–10. What is the effect of assuming a different prior distribution on the mean of the posterior distribution?

**3.** The editor argued that the sample of 10 was probably a lucky one for the author. He reasoned that there probably were only two or three actual adopters, and that by luck, one of them had been included in the sample of 10. The editor refused to change his opinion, saying that if two or three other surveys were taken, the result would probably be no adopters out of 10. The author claimed that the editor's arguments were totally unreasonable and could not be statistically justified.

## CASE QUESTION

Discuss these points of view. Was one argument reasonable and the other one not?

## CASE STUDY

### Bangpay Insurance Company

Sheila Hayes had founded an insurance company as a subsidiary of a larger financial services organization. She had a great deal of autonomy in managing her operation as long as her insurance business was growing. The senior executives of her company had suggested that she not aim at making any underwriting profit, but concentrate on competitive pricing, breaking even on premiums, claims and expenses, and concentrating on growth. The growth generated substantial funds for investment by the parent as working capital in other ventures.

In an effort to charge competitive prices, Sheila had analyzed the process of what factors were related to the incidence of policyholders making claims, particularly in auto insurance, which was by far her biggest product line. She had access to industry data about how factors such as age, location, driver sex, occupation, and car type were related to the probability of that policy having one or more claims in a given policy year. For example, based on historical evidence, a young male driver with a class X car (a sports car) who lived in territory Y had a 0.20 probability of having one or more claims per year.

Sheila believed that within a policy category there were a variety of types of drivers. She felt that since the 0.20 was based on relative frequency data, it was purely a statistical average. She decided that rather than charge all such drivers the same rate, she would presume that some of those drivers were less likely to have claims than others. She expressed her belief about the variance about this mean as a probability distribution:

| *Expected Probability of Claims for a Particular Policy Type* | *Prior Probability* |
|---|---|
| 0.15 | 0.3 |
| 0.20 | 0.4 |
| 0.25 | 0.3 |

Sheila felt that she should experience rate these policyholders. After one year of insurance, the probabilities of claims for each policy should be revised to account for the policyholders' claims experience. She did not, however, know how to integrate her prior beliefs with observed evidence.

## CASE QUESTIONS

1. Use Bayes Theorem to provide posterior probabilities for Sheila. Assume that claims are generated according to a Poisson process. Calculate how Sheila should revise her prior beliefs for observed cases of no claims, one claim, and two claims in the first year.
2. What would the posterior distribution be for a policyholder who has no claims in five years?
3. What would the posterior distribution be for a policyholder who has one claim in 10 years?
4. After two years, two policyholders with the same prior probabilities have each had one claim, one of them in the first year, and the other in the second. Demonstrate using serial calculation that after two years, these two policyholders who started with the same priors (given above), had the same overall history, and hence, have the same posterior distribution.

CHAPTER ELEVEN

# The Value of Information

## OUTLINE



## OBJECTIVES

After completing this chapter, you should be able to:

1. Incorporate decision alternatives about information collection into decision tree models.
2. Calculate the expected value of perfect information (EVPI) and interpret it in a variety of decision situations.
3. Calculate the expected value of imperfect information (EVII) and interpret it in a variety of decision situations.
4. Discuss the classical and Bayesian approaches to sampling.
5. Understand the factors that affect EVPI and EVII in decision analysis.
6. Describe the economics of sampling in terms of cost, benefit, and sample size.
7. Discuss the more complex issues about formally analyzing information collection, including sequential decisions and the incorporation of the expected utility rule into decisions involving information collection.

# INTRODUCTION

Information is very important to managers in their decision-making processes. Useful information for making managerial decisions can take many forms, for example, knowledge about a managerial problem, quantitative data describing parameters, or knowledge about a process, such as how to conduct a decision analysis. Just as a book can provide information about decision analysis, managers can change their states of knowledge about decision problems by gathering information.

This chapter is concerned with decisions about gathering information. In this context, the main purpose for gathering information is to improve the decision maker's overall prospects by altering the risk profile. The information generally reduces or resolves that uncertainty. Better decision strategies can often be achieved when uncertainty is reduced. Information about an uncertain quantity can be *perfect,* and lead to the complete resolution of uncertainty, or *imperfect,* in which case uncertainty may be partially resolved.

Information can provide decision makers with the ability to improve their *decision status* or position, through reducing the uncertainty they face *before* committing to a decision strategy. In this context, the information has value to the decision maker if it improves the value of, or leads to a better decision strategy. Further, it is possible to explicitly incorporate decisions to collect information into decision analysis models. A decision maker can include branches on a decision tree that include options of collecting information. For example, Figures 10–10 and 10–11 in the preceding chapter are examples of decision trees requiring initial choices about collecting information. These choices must be made before the major decision can be made.

Let us consider the value of perfect information. Perfect information is completely reliable. In a forecasting sense, perfect information foretells the future with complete accuracy. In real contexts there are very few situations where information about future events is absolutely perfect, however the concept is extremely useful because it provides an upper bound in value for imperfect information.

In decision analysis we can calculate the value of perfect and imperfect information. For imperfect information, Bayes Theorem (see Chapter 10) is usually required as a calculation procedure. Imperfect information may change a decision maker's beliefs about the likelihood of certain events, but it does not completely eliminate the uncertainty. In contrast, perfect information eliminates the source of uncertainty to which it refers, by transforming it into certainty.

In a broader managerial context, information plays a vital role in organizations. When information is organized into a useful form, we use the term *information system.* Further, an information system that describes some aspect of an organization's performance or characteristics is called a management information system (MIS). As a field of study in its own right, MIS has been increasingly acknowledged as an important aspect of an organization's design and operation. An increasing body of research evidence shows that the way in which organizations use information can be of strategic importance. Many publications exist in this field including Ein-Dor and Segev (1981), Ackoff (1967), Dearden (1972), and McKenney and McFarlan (1982).

In this chapter, and indeed in decision analysis generally, the focus is to consider the decision maker as an individual (Howard, 1980). In this sense, we are using decision analysis to evaluate particular sets of information with respect to how they influence particular decisions. We are not concerned here with the broader value of information systems to organizations, although decision trees have been used to analyze problems of choosing an organizational structure (Duncan, 1979), and establishing the value of information systems (Schell, 1986).

Once the benefit from having a particular set of information is known, it can be compared with the assessed cost, and can lead to a decision about information collection that is integrated with a decision strategy about a managerial problem. Decisions about whether to collect information before choosing a decision strategy can be very effectively analyzed using decision analysis.

## INFORMATION ABOUT UNCERTAIN QUANTITIES

Information can change the degree of uncertainty a decision maker faces. The addition of information usually reduces a decision maker's state of uncertainty. It is however, not clear that this is always the case. For example, if you believe that a new product has an 85% chance of succeeding and a survey is generally negative, resulting in a revision of your success probability to 0.5, has your uncertainty been reduced? In this instance we are considering information in an ex-post (after the fact) manner. In decision analysis, when we are weighing up the costs and benefits of collecting information in an ex-ante (before the fact) sense, information cannot reduce the EMV of the optimal decision strategy for any decision tree. Here, we assume the cost of obtaining the information is separately accounted for. At worst, information may not change the optimal decision strategy at all, in which case the information has no expected value. *Information may have value as measured by the difference in expected value between the new, optimal decision strategy (with the information) relative to the EMV of the old, optimal decision strategy (without the information).* In decision analysis we can calculate the value of information and then compare it to the cost of obtaining that information.

Suppose that you are highly uncertain about a parameter $P$. Your probability distribution is $f(P)$. There are many ways of measuring uncertainty when it is reflected as a probability distribution, such as range, interquartile score, and variance. Regardless of how we measure uncertainty, information has value if it changes the uncertainty we face so as to improve the overall prospects associated with the optimal decision. It is important to note that *information can only have value if it affects a decision strategy.* The value of information is calculated as an *expectation* (expected value). The expected value is positive when the information raises overall prospects by changing the uncertainty (risk profile) that a decision maker faces and by changing the optimal strategy. Further, information can have value to a risk-neutral or even risk-seeking decision maker. If an EMV decision rule is to be applied on a decision tree, branches that incorporate additional information may (but do not necessarily) lead to improved decision strategies. Hence, the concept of information value need not be linked to that of risk aversion, even though information is usually gathered to reduce the decision maker's uncertainty. *A decision maker who is not risk averse may still be able to make a better decision if uncertainty is reduced or resolved before he commits to an action, rather than after.* Suppose, for example, that you are a risk-neutral decision maker, considering whether to sell your 10,000 IBM shares today or to wait until next Monday. If reliable information were available about price movements between today and Monday, you might be able to use it to make a better decision. Remember that in this instance you are risk neutral, and the fact that the information may have value is not caused by your risk aversion. Now, if the information caused you to change your decision from "sell today" to "wait," or vice-versa, then it has value. If the information does not make you change your decision strategy, but confirms your choice as the best one, then it has no value in decision analytic terms, even though you may now be more confident that your original strategy is correct.

Let us briefly revisit the Advance Electronics (A) example, from Chapter 10, to illustrate these points. In Figure 10–3 the decision maker begins with a decision to sample or not to sample one ECD unit from a batch. The monetary cost of sampling can be placed on the end points of appropriate branches, or simply subtracted from the expected value at node $C_1$ on Figure 10–3. The benefit of sampling one ECD comes from the improvement of prospects, if there is one. To determine this benefit, we need to estimate the relevant cash flows for the various end points of the decision tree and use the rollback procedure to determine an optimal strategy. The *value of the information* in terms of overall prospects *is a function of both the probabilities and payoffs on the tree*. Figure 11–1 shows the Advance Electronics (A) decision tree, with a set of assessed cash flow payoffs on it. When the rollback procedure is applied to Figure 11–1, the optimal decision strategy is "do not sample."

The cost of sampling is assessed at \$100 on Figure 11–1. Investigation of the "sample 1 component" branch shows that regardless of the sample result, the best thing to do is to ship the batch, mainly because the penalty for shipping a bad batch in this instance is not very high, only \$500. Hence,

**FIGURE 11-1** Decision Tree for Advance Electronics (A)

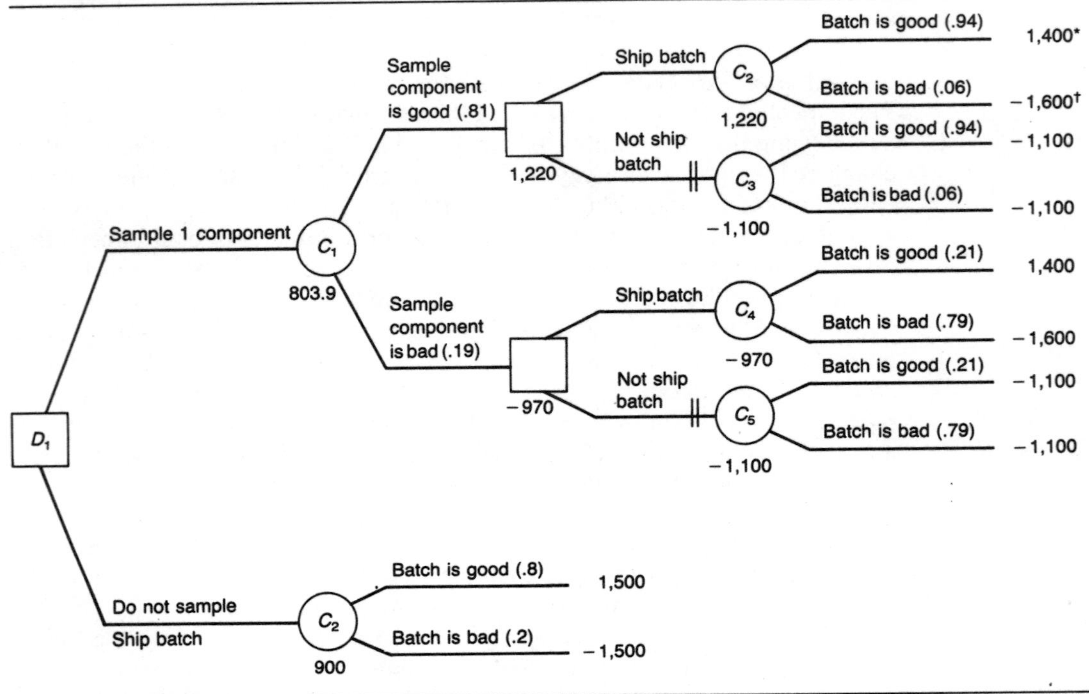


Cash Flow Data:

ECD unit costs $10 to produce.
ECD unit price is $25.
Cost of testing one unit is $100.
Cost of shipping a bad batch is $500 above and beyond the cost of producing it, which is $10 × 100 units = $1,000.

* This cash flow of $1,400 is the $2,500 revenue, less $1,000 production cost, less $100 sample/test cost.

† This cash flow is the production cost, $1,000, the sample test cost, $100, and the bad batch penalty, $500.

the sample information is worthless because it produces no real improvement in prospects (and the sample result does not influence choice!). The rollback reflects the $100 cost of sampling in the difference between the "sample one component" and "do not sample" branches. The calculated EMV of $803.90 at node $C_1$ is such because of the rounding errors inherent in the probabilities. A more accurate calculation (without using rounded probabilities) would have led to this figure being exactly $800. Apart from rounding errors the $100 difference between the expected value at nodes $C_1$ and $C_2$ reflects purely the cost of the valueless sample.

It is very interesting to note what the result would be if the penalty for shipping a bad batch were so high as to make the sample information valuable. In Figure 11–2, all cash flows are the same as for Figure 11–1 except the bad batch penalty is increased from \$500 to \$5,000! How might this change affect the value of the sample information? Any sample result that clearly indicates a high probability of a bad batch is likely to have some value in this instance. When the rollback procedure is applied to Figure 11–2, the optimal strategy is identified as "Sample one component, and ship the batch if the sampled component is good. Do not ship the batch if the sampled component is bad!" Under the new condition of a high bad batch penalty (\$5,000), the inference produced by the sample, albeit imperfect information, has value. Can we evaluate the expected value of the sample information from Figure 11–2? First, note that this value is positive because the sample result affects the ship/don't ship action. Information, in this decision analytic context, cannot have negative value. The difference in expected value between the "sample" and "not sample" branches in Figure

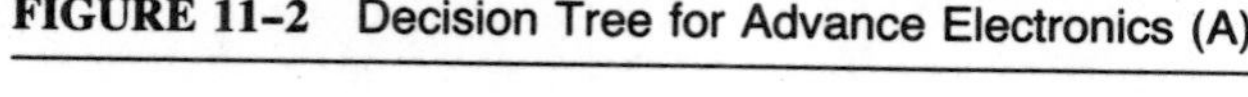

**FIGURE 11–2** Decision Tree for Advance Electronics (A)

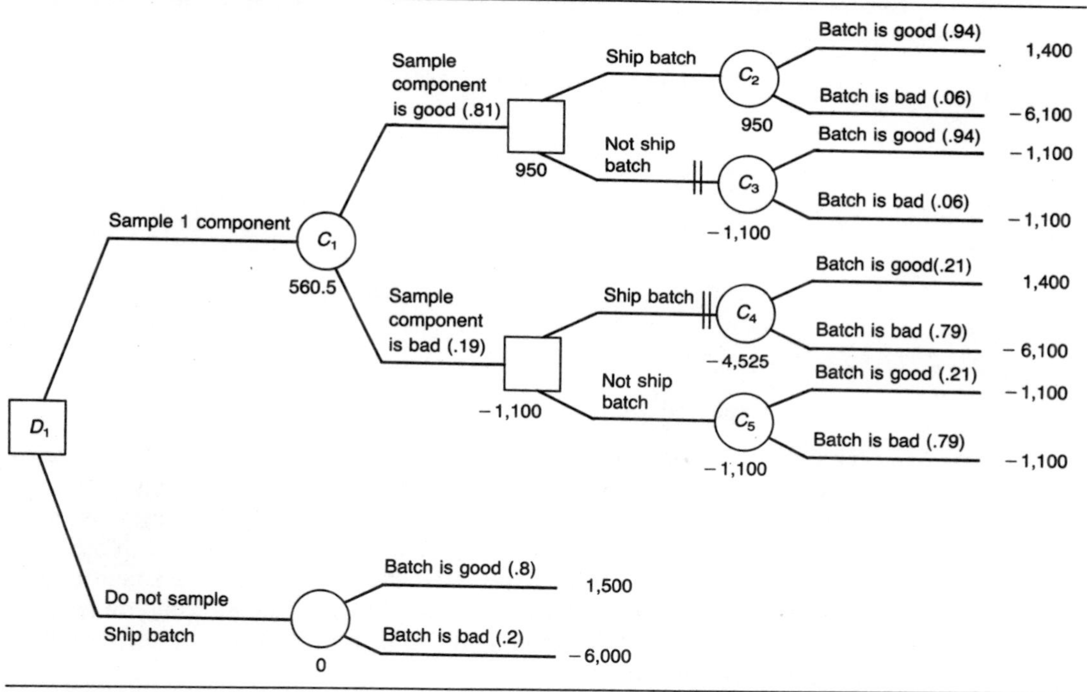


Cash Flow Data:

ECD unit costs \$10 to produce.
ECD unit price is \$25.
Cost of testing is \$100.
Cost of shipping bad batch is \$5,000 above and beyond cost of producing (\$1,000) it.

11–2 is \$560.50. Since the cost of sampling is already included on the "sample" branch, the intrinsic expected value of the sample information, gross of the cost of sampling is \$560.50 + \$100 = \$660.50. To note how the sample improves the overall prospects, let us compare the risk profiles of the two main strategies in Figure 11–2.

For the "sample" branch, we have nonblocked-off routes on the decision tree that lead to the following payoffs.

| *Cost in Dollars* | *Probability* |
|---|---|
| 1,400 | 0.81 × 0.94 = 0.7614 |
| −6,100 | 0.81 × 0.06 = 0.0486 |
| −1,100 | 0.19 |

The associated expected value is given by

$$\text{Expected value} = 1{,}400 \times 0.7614 - 6{,}100 \times 0.0486 - 1{,}100 \times 0.19 = \$560.50$$

For the "not sample" branch the risk profile is:

| *Cost in Dollars* | *Probability* |
|---|---|
| 1,500 | 0.8 |
| −6,000 | 0.2 |

The expected value for this strategy is

$$\text{Expected value} = 1{,}500 \times 0.8 - 6{,}000 \times 0.2 = 0$$

The overall prospects are generally improved by the sample information. Although the sample information leads to a decision strategy in which the probability of a loss has risen slightly, the probability of a large loss has declined greatly, and the expected value is substantially increased. Note that this illustration made use of the expected value rule, implying risk neutrality, and the positive value of information was not due to the information reducing the uncertainty a risk averter must face, but because it improved the available overall prospects.

In this example, the decision maker makes no expected profit if he ships batches without sampling. Under that strategy, every fifth batch, on average, would lead to a large loss, offsetting the profits of the four good batches.

In this instance, expected value is a particularly good decision rule for a decision model, because playing the averages is a powerful and sensible strategy over a long run of many batches.

## THE EXPECTED VALUE OF PERFECT INFORMATION (EVPI)

In the majority of managerial decisions, sources of uncertainty exist that are not resolved until after the decision maker commits to a decision strategy. Indeed, if all the uncertainty were resolved before the decision maker chooses an action, the decision would be made under certainty and not under uncertainty.

Consider a very simple decision tree with only one decision node and one source of uncertainty (Figure 11–3). If the decision maker can obtain perfect information about the source of uncertainty, Figure 11–3 should be transposed to Figure 11–4. In Figure 11–4, the uncertainty is resolved before the choice between strategy A and strategy B is made.

**FIGURE 11–3** Decision Must Be Made in the Light of Uncertainty

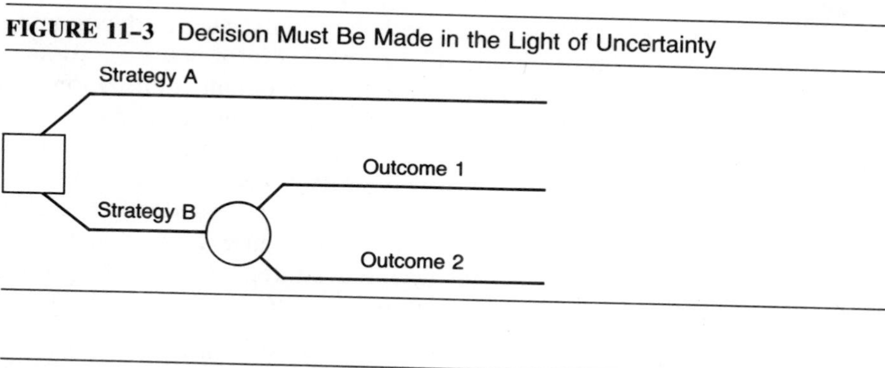


**FIGURE 11–4** Perfect Information Is Available about Outcomes before the Decision Is Made

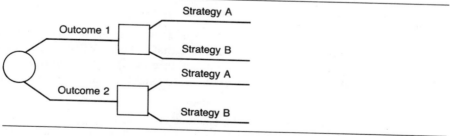

Strategy A
Outcome 1
Strategy B
Strategy A
Outcome 2
Strategy B

The critical question is: "How much better off are we by being in the Figure 11–4 position than the Figure 11–3 position?" The answer to this question must be: "to the extent of the value of the perfect information." The value of the information about the uncertain quantity is equal to the advantage we gain from knowing the outcome before a choice is made (Figure 11–4) relative to having to make a choice and then observe the resolution of the chance outcome (Figure 11–3). Before we quantify this measure of advantage, consider the following important points:

1. Perfect information about a source of uncertainty can only have an *expected* value, not a certain value. This is because before the fact, we cannot know whether the information is "outcome 1 will definitely occur" or "outcome 2 will definitely occur." We can only assign probabilities to these events. The events themselves may have different values. Hence, we quantify the advantage of foresight as an *expected value of perfect information* (EVPI).
2. A lower bound on the expected value of perfect information is zero, since we can never become worse off by finding out the value of an uncertain quantity. If, however, the information about an uncertain quantity does not change our decision strategy, what was the expected value of that information? Zero, of course. Positive EVPIs are associated with decision strategies that would be altered by the presence or absence of that information.
3. The choice of whether to obtain information usually requires an additional decision node on the decision tree, or at least an additional branch emanating from a decision node. In the case of Figure 11–3 we must choose a strategy and experience an outcome. It may be that one of the strategies is better suited to one of the outcomes than the other. In that case, Figure 11–4 is likely to lead to a better outcome because the strategy is chosen given perfect hindsight about the uncertain quantity.

The expected value of perfect information is defined as[1]:

EVPI = Expected value of the optimal strategy *with* perfect information − Expected value of the optimal strategy *without* the perfect information

As with most elements of decision analysis, this definition makes a good deal of common sense. Note that unless EVPI is zero, the optimal strategy with perfect information is a different one than the optimal strategy without that information. In essence, to calculate the EVPI, we subtract the EMV of

[1] The order of subtraction is dependent on whether costs or profits are being used. The important point is that EVPI values can never be negative. If costs are being used the order of subtraction in this EVPI formula should be reversed.

the best strategy on the decision tree from the EMV of the decision tree branch which incorporates perfect information. Some examples will help to illustrate this concept.

## EXAMPLE 11–1

### A Risky Investment

You are offered a chance to speculate on a risky investment involving a gamble of $5,000. You may get a $10,000 return if the venture is successful, or you may lose all your money. The outcome depends on whether a corporate takeover attempt is successful or not, and you have the opportunity to buy a small parcel of stock options for $5,000 which will either become worthless or become worth $15,000 in which case you would net a $10,000 profit. See Figure 11–5. You assess a 50:50 chance of success. Now suppose that someone offered to tell you what the outcome of the venture would be *before* you had to decide whether or not to invest. Your decision tree would be transformed to Figure 11–6, assuming you believed the information to be perfectly reliable.

Whereas the optimal strategy for an EMVer without the information is to gamble (EMV = +$2,500), the optimal strategy with perfect foresight about the venture outcome will depend on that outcome. The optimal strategy can be stated as:

If "Failure" then don't invest ($0)
If "Success" then invest ($10,000)

Note that the optimal strategy is now different from the optimal strategy (without perfect information) and that the payoffs are different also.

**FIGURE 11–5** A Risky Investment Example

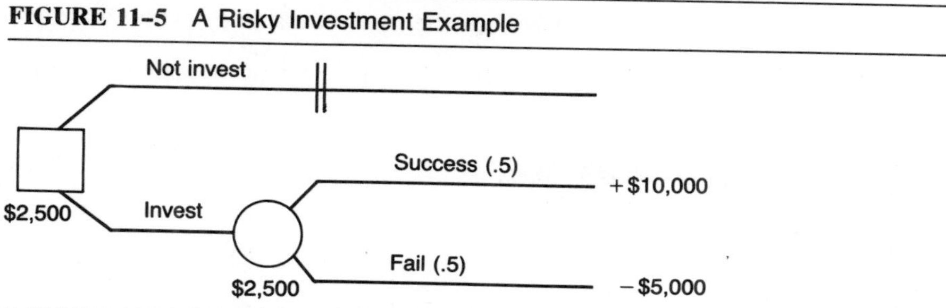


NOTE: You may invest $5,000 in stock options, which will either be lost or will triple in value, yielding a net return of $10,000 cash flow.

**FIGURE 11–6** The Risk Investment Example Given Perfect Foresight about the Outcome

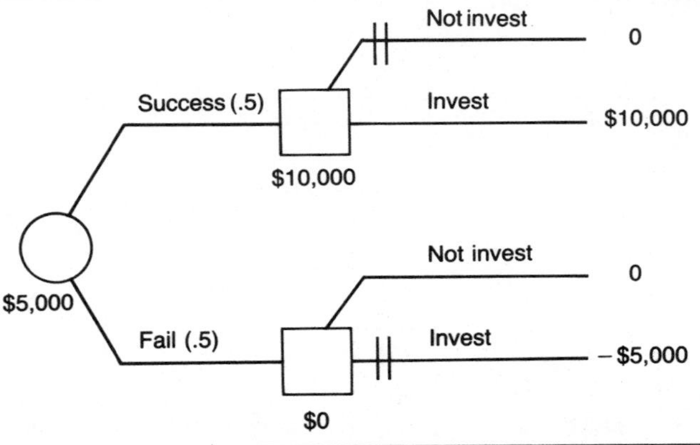


Let us compare the situations of having the perfect information (PI) with that of not having it. If we do not have PI:

$$\text{EMV without PI} = 0.5\,(\$10{,}000) + 0.5\,(-\$5{,}000) = \$2{,}500$$

Before we get the perfect information, we assign probabilities about what it will be. The probabilities that we use should be the same as the prior probabilities of each outcome. In this example we assume that if we get perfect information, it will have a 0.5 chance of indicating a "success" outcome and a 0.5 chance of indicating "failure." If it's "success" the best strategy is to "invest" and gain $10,000 for sure. If it's "failure," the best strategy is "Not invest" and experience a zero payoff.

Hence the EMV of the optimal strategy with PI is:

$$\text{EMV with PI} = 0.5\,(\$10{,}000) + 0.5\,(0) = \$5{,}000$$

The EVPI is $5,000 less the $2,500 that was the EMV of the optimal strategy without PI:

$$\text{EVPI} = \$2{,}500$$

It can be shown that EVPI is equal to the EOL (expected opportunity loss) of the optimal strategy without perfect information. EOL values can be

**TABLE 11-1** Payoffs for Example 11-1

| | *Succeed* | *Fail* |
|---|---|---|
| Invest | 10,000 | −5,000 |
| Don't invest | 0 | 0 |

**TABLE 11-2** Regret (Opportunity Loss) Values for Example 11-1

| | *Success* | *Failure* | *Expected Opportunity Loss* |
|---|---|---|---|
| Invest | 0 | 5,000 | $0.5 \times 0 + 0.5 \times 5{,}000 = 2{,}500$ |
| Don't invest | 10,000 | 0 | $0.5 \times 10{,}000 + 0.5 \times 0 = 5{,}000$ |

calculated from a regret table. Table 11-1 is a payoff table, and Table 11-2 shows the associated regret values.

From Table 11-2 the EOL of the optimal act ("invest") is $2,500 equalling the calculated EVPI.

**FIGURE 11-7** Risky Investment Example Including the Decision to Obtain Perfect Information

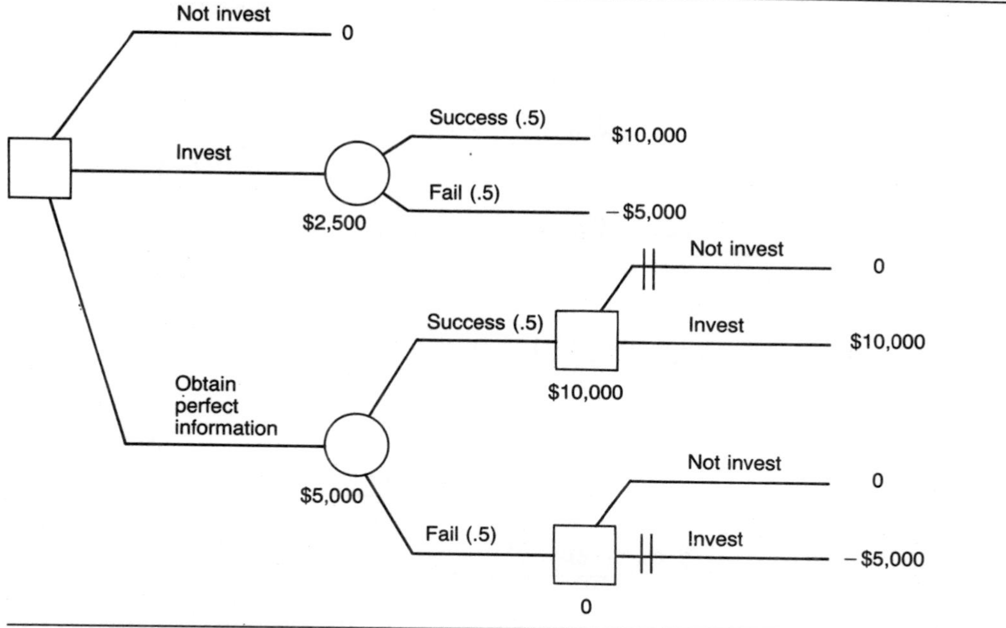


NOTE: The cost of obtaining the information is not included in this analysis.

The useful feature of decision analysis in this context is that it provides the capability for us to include the decision to gather information as a formal part of the analysis. See Figure 11–7. In this simple example we have presumed that the perfect information is supplied at no cost. Obviously, *if* the cost of obtaining it were greater than $2,500, it would not be worthwhile.

---

## EXAMPLE 11–2

### Hunk Diamond Revisited

Example 2–4 described the decision facing Dr. William Hunk. He was uncertain about whether his $800,000 diamond would be stolen, and assigned a value of 0.05 to that probability. He was considering taking out an insurance contract that would cover loss due to theft at a premium cost of $75,000. How much would perfect information about the uncertain event be worth? Figure 11–8 shows the appropriate decision tree. If PI

**FIGURE 11–8** The Hunk Diamond Decision Tree

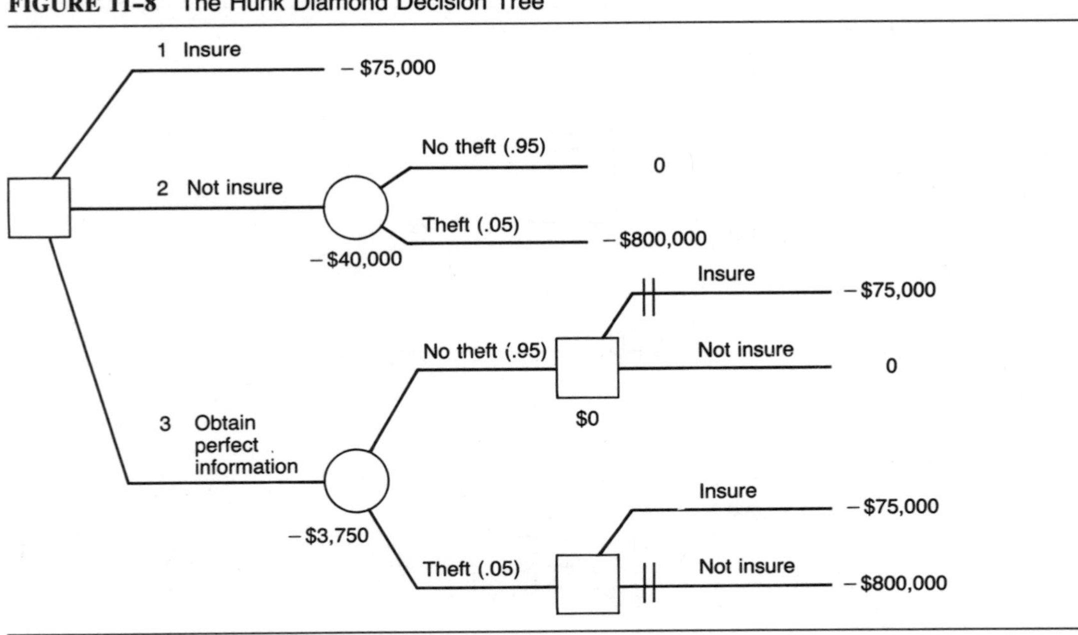

**TABLE 11–3** Dr. Hunk's Payoff Table

| | *Theft* | *No Theft* |
|---|---|---|
| Not insure | −800,000 | 0 |
| Insure | −75,000 | −75,000 |

**TABLE 11–4** Regret Table for Dr. Hunk

| | *Theft* | *No Theft* | *Expected Opportunity Loss* |
|---|---|---|---|
| Not insure | −725,000 | 0 | 36,250 |
| Insure | 0 | 75,000 | 37,500 |

is not available, the EMV of the optimal act (not insure) is −\$40,000. If PI is available, the EMV of the PI branch is −\$3,750, an improvement of \$36,250. With foresight about whether or not the theft would occur, Dr. Hunk would not insure if he knew for sure that there would be no theft ($p$ = 0.95) and would insure if he knew that the theft would occur ($p$ = 0.05).

Dr. Hunk's payoff table is shown as Table 11–3.

We can again show that the EVPI is equal to the EOL of the optimal act. The associated regret table is shown as Table 11–4, and the EMV of the optimal act without PI is \$36,250.

---

Let us emphasize that we are not yet accounting for possible risk aversion but merely using expected values. We reemphasize that the expected value of perfect information lies not in the attitudinal preference for certainty rather than uncertainty of the decision maker in the sense of risk aversion, but in the fact that foresight about outcomes allows for more informed decision strategies that can lead to better outcomes. However, it is worth thinking about whether a risk averter would generally place higher or lower value on perfect information than a risk-neutral decision maker. Would a risk averter pay a premium above and beyond EVPI? We shall examine this question in a later section of this chapter.

## EXAMPLE 11-3

# Orange Computers Inc. (A)

Orange Computers Inc. was a small company set up by a technical specialist who had previously worked for a large computer company. He invested $50,000 of his own money and attracted $100,000 from a group of venture capitalists to develop a new type of computer screen display. If successful, the manufacturing rights would be sold. Figure 11-9 shows the decision tree facing the company's founders. They knew that the technology was basically proven but were unsure about what the manufacturing cost of the screen would be. They were also uncertain about the quality of the screen's visual resolution. Depending upon both these factors, the manufacturing rights could vary in value from virtually nothing to over a million dollars. The payoffs on Figure 11-9 are discounted cash flows associated with the project including both revenues and costs. The project was undertaken because the chances of making a loss were about one third $(0.4 \times 0.8) = 0.32$, and the EMV was positive.

Can we separately evaluate perfect information about cost and quality? First, suppose that PI was available on cost only and that quality was still unknown. We assume that development cost and quality are statistically independent. Figure 11-10 shows the decision tree. Compare branch 3 with branch 2. Branch 3 has a higher EMV because having prior knowledge of cost only would cause the EMVer to not invest if cost was known to be high. Note also that on branch 3, if cost is known to be high, the decision maker would not invest and thus have no chance of securing the $300,000 discounted cash flow (should quality turn out to be high).

Now consider PI about quality. Branch 4 shows that no matter whether quality is known to be high or low (before the fact), the decision to invest would still be made, assuming that an EMV rule is used. Hence, branch 4 has the same EMV as branch 2.

**FIGURE 11-9** Orange Computers Inc. Decision Tree

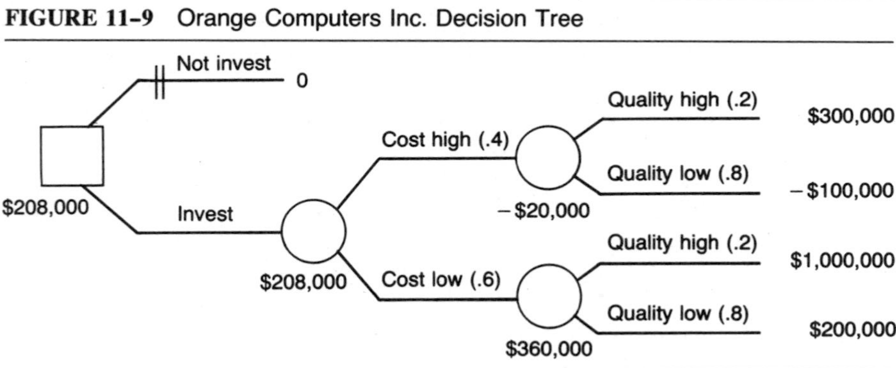

FIGURE 11–10 Orange Computers Inc. Decision Tree, Including Information Branches

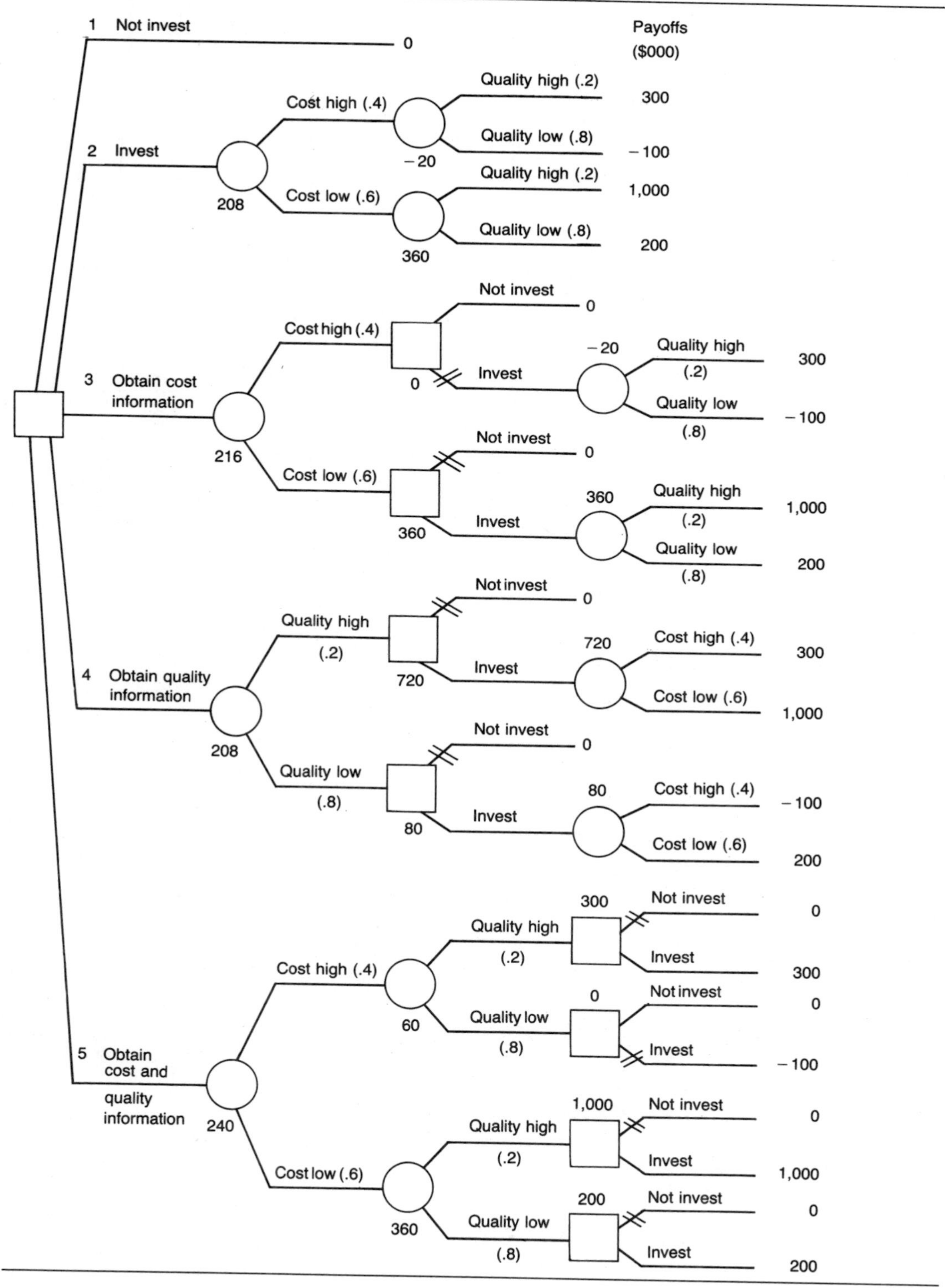

$$\begin{aligned} \text{EVPI (Cost)} &= \$216{,}000 - \$208{,}000 \\ &= \$8{,}000 \\ \text{EVPI (Quality)} &= \$0 \end{aligned}$$

Based on this illustration, can we forecast the EVPI associated with perfect foresight about both quality and cost? Can we assume that

$$\begin{aligned} \text{EVPI (Cost and Quality)} &= \text{EVPI (Cost)} + \text{EVPI (Quality)} \\ &= \$8{,}000 \end{aligned}$$

Branch 5 on Figure 11–10 shows that the EMV of the optimal strategy if both "cost" and "quality" are known in advance is $240,000. We have demonstrated that the *equality presumed above is incorrect and the individual EVPIs are not additive.* Comparisons of the outcome possibilities demonstrate this:

No PI:

$$\begin{aligned} 0.08 \times 300{,}000 &= 24{,}000 \\ 0.32 \times -100{,}000 &= -32{,}000 \\ 0.12 \times 1{,}000{,}000 &= 120{,}000 \\ 0.48 \times 200{,}000 &= \underline{96{,}000} \\ & \phantom{=} 208{,}000 \end{aligned}$$

Cost PI:

$$\begin{aligned} 0.4 \times 0 &= 0 \\ 0.12 \times 1{,}000{,}000 &= 120{,}000 \\ 0.48 \times 200{,}000 &= \underline{96{,}000} \\ & \phantom{=} 216{,}000 \end{aligned}$$

Quality PI:

$$\begin{aligned} 0.08 \times 300{,}000 &= 24{,}000 \\ 0.12 \times 1{,}000{,}000 &= 120{,}000 \\ 0.32 \times -100{,}000 &= -32{,}000 \\ 0.48 \times 200{,}000 &= \underline{96{,}000} \\ & \phantom{=} 208{,}000 \end{aligned}$$

Cost and quality PI:

$$\begin{aligned} 0.08 \times 300{,}000 &= 24{,}000 \\ 0.32 \times 0 &= 0 \\ 0.12 \times 100{,}000 &= 120{,}000 \\ 0.48 \times 200{,}000 &= \underline{96{,}000} \\ & \phantom{=} 240{,}000 \end{aligned}$$

A review of the nonblocked-off routes on Figure 11–10 will show that having cost information in advance brings a little advantage (EVPI = 8,000), having quality information in advance brings no advantage (EVPI = 0), and having both cost and quality information in advance brings a *substantial* advantage (EVPI = $240,000 – $208,000 = $32,000).

In general, it is not reasonable to assume that the *simultaneous* EVPI about two or more uncertain quantities is equal to the sum of the individual EVPIs. Although it has been demonstrated (Merkhofer, 1977) that in some instances EVPIs are close to being additive (as a first-order approximation), the above example demonstrates that it may be a dangerous practice to assume that approximate additivity applies in general. Although this nonadditivity may be counterintuitive to some readers, there is a very good reason for it. In essence, we should not expect a measure such as EVPI to possess a property of additivity across sources of uncertainty because of the maximization concept embedded in the EVPI function. EVPI is the difference between two expected values, one which encompasses the perfect information and one which does not. Under certain conditions, EVPIs are additive, but these should be considered as special cases. In most decision analysis applications, even if there are multiple sources of uncertainty, it is useful to calculate the EVPI for each source of uncertainty separately. When a number of different sources of uncertainty exist, the determination of a sequential strategy of which information to obtain becomes an interesting decision problem in its own right.

In practical terms, there are some cases where perfect predictive information is actually available. Although market surveys produce sample information (which is imperfect), it is sometimes possible to obtain perfect information about a whole population through census or referendum procedures that include every member of the population. In managerial decisions where the action of a supplier, customer, or competitor is an uncertain factor, it may be possible to purchase perfect information. Even if perfect information is not available, *imperfect information* may be available, and *the calculation of EVPI gives an upper-bound value for imperfect information*.

## THE EXPECTED VALUE OF IMPERFECT INFORMATION (EVII)

In considering imperfect information, the concept of reliability is important. Whereas perfect information is 100% reliable, imperfect information may have a reliability of anything between but not equal to zero and 100%. In this sense reliability is defined as the probability with which forecasts turn out to be correct. To illustrate, let's consider the pleasant scenario of having 10,000 shares of IBM stock to sell, either today or next Monday. Suppose that someone offers you an IBM stock price forecast. Your first thought may be to consider how reliable the forecast is likely to be. A 100% reliable forecast implies that the information is perfect. In other words, the indicated price forecast is absolutely guaranteed to be correct. If a forecaster is known to be 90% reliable, we can interpret this as meaning that on 90% of occasions his forecast will be correct, and he will steer you wrong on 10% of occasions.

Although it is convenient to interpret reliability in this relative frequency manner, it is just as reasonable to consider reliability as a degree of belief about the next forecast. Note also that we are considering a notion of overall reliability here. It is quite possible that a forecaster may be more reliable in forecasting price rises than price falls, or vice versa. This was the case in the Farmer Brown example in Chapter 10.

In terms of the expected value of information, what is the worst reliability that a forecaster can have? Is it a zero reliability forecaster? Assume that payoff functions are linear, and to keep things simple, assume only two possible outcome states, namely, prices rise and prices fall. Indeed, in a world of only two outcomes, a forecaster with zero reliability (who steers you wrong every time) is just as good as a forecaster with 100% reliability, as long as the zero reliability can be recognized. If you know that a forecaster *always* gets it wrong, then this is a perfect (that is, perfectly awful) prediction, and such information is just as valuable as a perfectly correct prediction.

If the forecaster's reliability is known, the worst kind of forecast is the one that doesn't help at all. In a two-outcome event space, with linear payoff/losses, a 50% reliable forecaster would generally be the worst forecaster to have.

Imperfect information can range in value from a minimum of zero to an upper bound of EVPI (which may itself be zero). In the case of stock price forecasting, a 50% reliable forecaster, who gets it right exactly as often as wrong, provides no useful information. A forecast with reliability $p$% has the same value as a forecast with reliability $(100 - p)$% provided that the reliability is known. Hence, in the field of imperfect information there are many degrees of imperfection, ranging from "awful" at the worst to "almost perfect" at the best. Perfect information is simply the extreme case of the best possible limiting instance of imperfect information.

The expected value of imperfect information (EVII) can be more difficult to calculate than EVPI. Perfect information provides complete certainty about an uncertain quantity, but imperfect information serves to change the degree and nature of uncertainty without eliminating it.

Imperfect information provides forecasts and indications about uncertain quantities, but these forecasts are not absolutely reliable. Examples of imperfect information sources are market sample surveys and political election polls. Experienced marketing managers and politicians know that surveys and polls are not usually 100% accurate. In production systems management, many measurement, inspection, and quality tests are also not completely reliable, thus the information they provide is imperfect. In financial management, professional brokers and advisors usually have a lot of advice to give clients about future stock prices, interest rates, exchange rates, and other uncertain quantities. These sources of information and forecasts can also be described as imperfect, because they sometimes turn out to be true, and sometimes false.

The important notion is that we can use the language of probability to describe the reliability of an information source or accuracy of a forecast. We can use Bayes Theorem to incorporate an imperfect forecast with our prior beliefs (see Chapter 10). It is then possible to *formally incorporate the decision of whether to obtain the imperfect information into the decision analysis*.

## EXAMPLE 11–4

### Industrial Espionage: Orange Computers Inc. (B)

The management of Orange Computers Inc. (described in Example 11–3) was very interested in knowing whether a particular competitor had developed a new technology to the point whereby it could be incorporated into certain products. If the technology was developed, the competitor's products would soon become superior to a product Orange had developed and wished to launch. Figure 11–11 shows the decision tree facing the company. At a meeting of Orange executives, it was recognized that this uncertain factor was a key to the success or failure of this product. Bob Kitchener, who had founded the company some years before, was not happy about

**FIGURE 11–11** Orange Computers Inc. Decision Tree

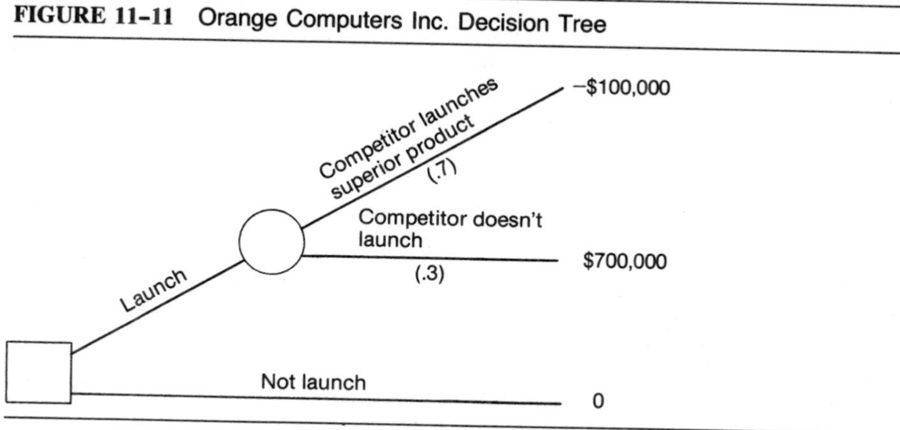

making a launch/no launch decision in the face of such a high degree of uncertainty. He said: "How can we get some information about whether they have got their new technology to work or not? Surely we can do better than assuming a probability of 0.7."

"There are a few ways we can go about it," said his assistant, Bill Bartz. "As you know, we have used one of their ex-employees before to assist us in making assessments. Sarah Short, remember? She has been correct in many of her past assessments of how the company would behave. I think she would probably have an 85% chance of getting it right if we asked her to forecast their behavior on this one."

"Let's incorporate that possibility into our decision tree," said Bob. "She'll probably want about $5,000 for supplying her expert opinion. I wonder if it's worth it, because even after we get her view, there will still be some uncertainty. You know, I am sure that for $50,000 we could hire someone inside their company to tell us for

**FIGURE 11–12** Orange Computers Inc. Decision Tree Including Two Options for Obtaining Information

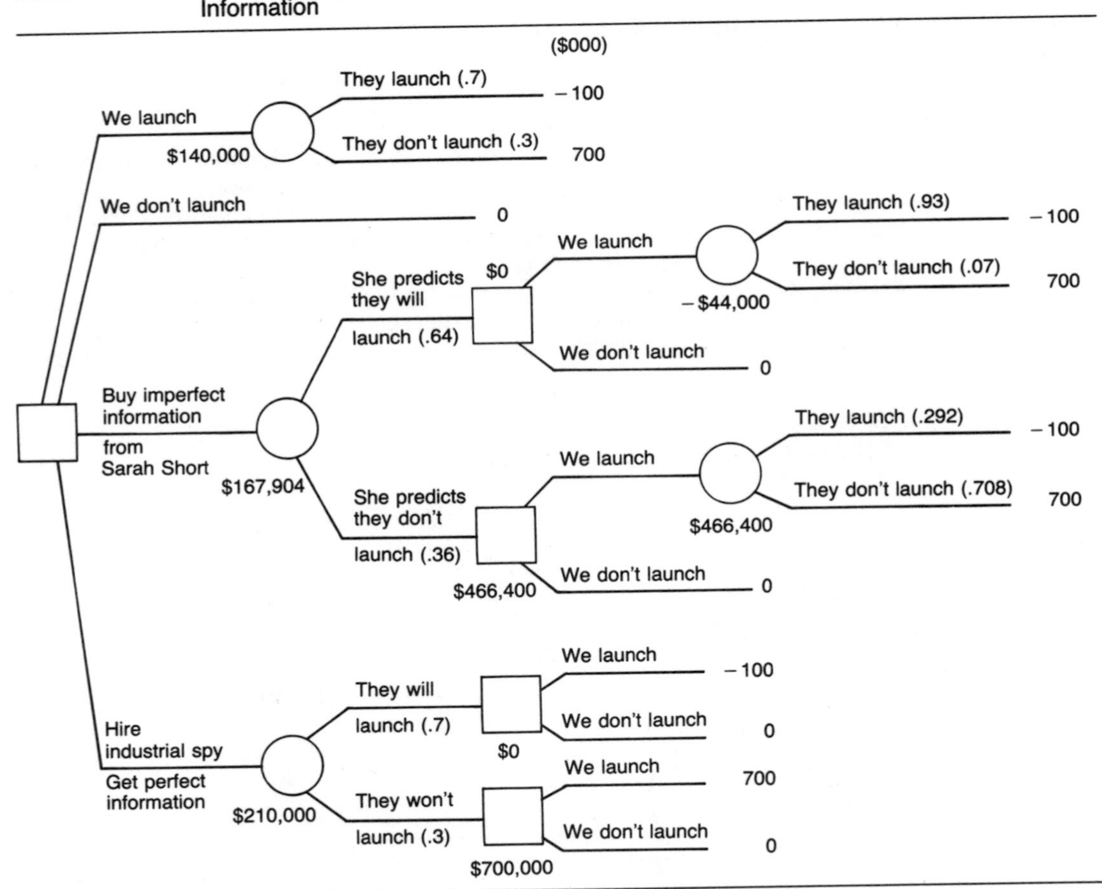

**TABLE 11-5** Bayes Calculation if Sarah Short Says "They Won't Launch"

| *Event* | *Prior* | *Likelihood* | *Joint* | *Posterior* |
|---|---|---|---|---|
| They launch | 0.7 | 0.15 | 0.105 | 0.292 |
| They don't launch | 0.3 | 0.85 | 0.255 | 0.708 |
| | | | $\Sigma = 0.36$ | $\Sigma = 1$ |

**TABLE 11-6** Bayes Calculation if Sarah Short Says "They Will Launch"

| *Event* | *Prior* | *Likelihood* | *Joint* | *Posterior* |
|---|---|---|---|---|
| They launch | 0.7 | 0.85 | 0.595 | 0.93 |
| They don't launch | 0.3 | 0.15 | 0.045 | 0.07 |
| | | | $\Sigma = 0.64$ | $\Sigma = 1$ |

sure! In fact for $50,000 we could hire an industrial spy to find out their true intentions! Bill, figure out exactly what is best and get back to me quickly, would you?"

Bill added two extra branches on to the existing decision tree. (See Figure 11-12.) He also translated some information into probabilistic form:[2]

$P$(SS predicts launch/They do launch) = 0.85
$P$(SS predicts no launch/They do launch) = 0.15
$P$(SS predicts launch/They don't launch) = 0.15
$P$(SS predicts no launch/They don't launch) = 0.85

Tables 11-5 and 11-6 show Bill's calculation of posterior probabilities for this problem.

---

The EMV calculations on Figure 11-12 do not include the costs of collecting the information. These costs ($5,000 if Sarah Short is used and $50,000 for an industrial spy) could have been included in the decision tree analysis by subtracting the appropriate amounts from appropriate cash flows. The net contributions to profit after accounting for information costs are:

Branch 1: We launch EMV = $140,000
Branch 2: We don't launch EMV = $0

[2] Bill assumed that Sarah Short (SS) not only had an overall 85% chance of getting it right but that her chances of getting it right were equal for both outcomes. Of course, alternative assumptions are possible.

Branch 3: Consult Sarah Short EMV = \$167,904 − \$5,000
= \$162,904

Branch 4: Buy perfect information EMV = \$210,000 − \$50,000
= \$160,000

The best option is to buy the imperfect information. The perfect information is more reliable and inherently more valuable, but in this instance, the increase in EMV associated with the perfect information does not justify the substantial extra cost of the perfect information. Had the perfect information been cheaper to obtain, or the reliability of Sarah Short been a little less than 85%, the best option would have been to purchase the perfect information. Note that for this example:

EVPI = \$210,000 − \$140,000 = \$70,000
EVII = \$167,904 − \$140,000 = \$27,904

---

## EXAMPLE 11–5

### Reschem Services (B)

Figure 10–10 shows Dr. Davies' decision tree regarding the RF 90 compound decision at Reschem. Dr. Davies wanted formally to evaluate the worth of collecting opinions from one or two experts about the success or failure of the project. The cost of funding the project was \$500,000, and the revenue if successful would be \$6 million. Each expert was expected to charge a \$125,000 fee for their extensive time input and tests that they would carry out.

From Figure 11–13, the rollback details of the decision tree show:

Branch 1: Fund project: Expected profit = \$475,000
Branch 2: Not fund project: Expected profit = \$0
Branch 3: Consult one expert: Expected profit = \$627,850 − \$125,000
= \$502,850
Branch 4: Consult two experts: Expected profit = \$712,300 − \$250,000
= \$462,300

We can see that the optimal strategy is to consult one expert. Note the interesting outcome that although two independent experts were available with identical characteristics (cost and information reliability) one was a good investment but a second was not. This is the result of the fairly complex interplay of all the factors, including prior probabilities, likelihood probabilities, costs, and payoffs. In a sense we can interpret this result as a form of decreasing economy of scale to information amount. Ignoring the cost of the experts, a first expert increases the EMV by over \$150,000 by

**FIGURE 11–13** Dr. Davies' Decision Tree for the RF 90 Compound

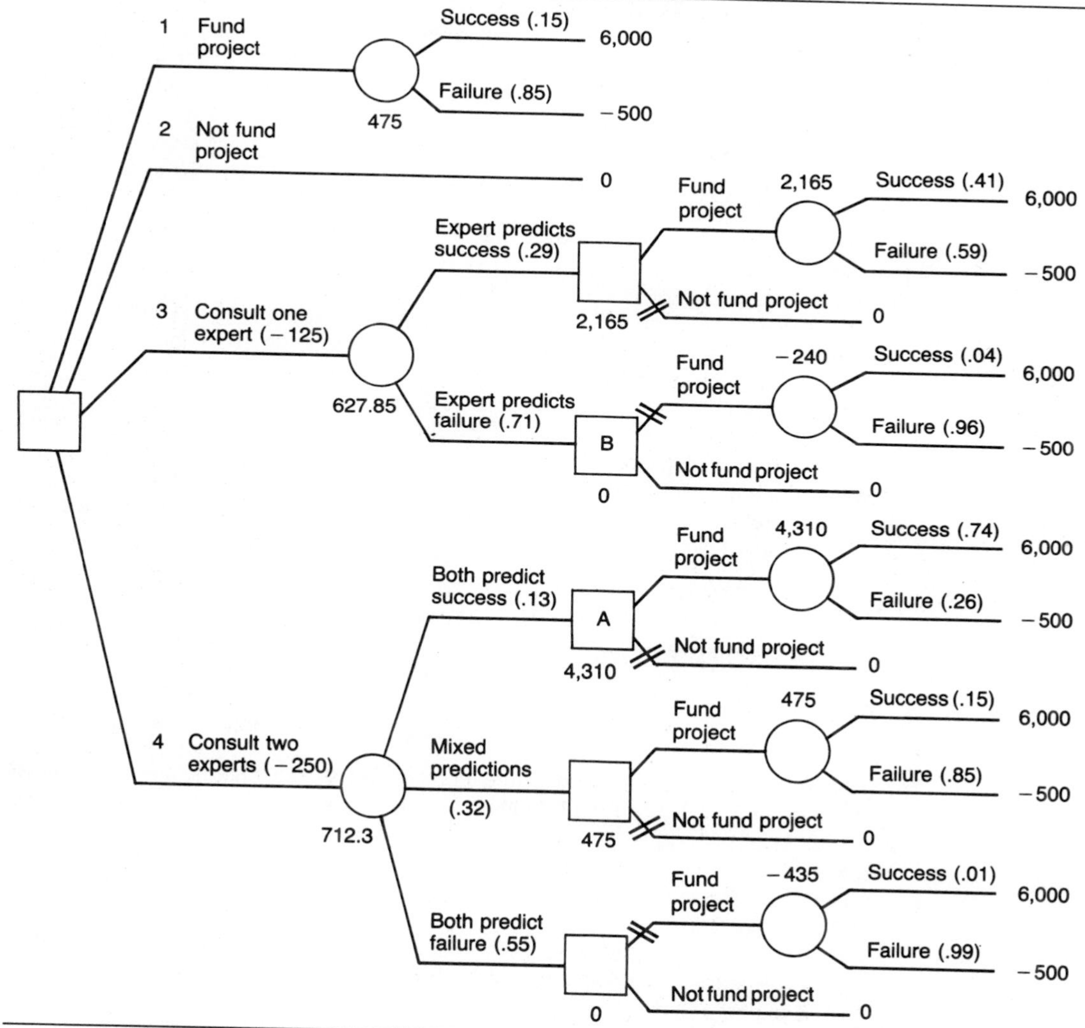

NOTE: Payoffs and expected values are in thousands of dollars.

changing the probabilities on which Dr. Davies would act more in his favor. Things improve even more with the second expert. The two experts improve on the initial EMV by $237,300 ($712,300 − $475,000). This improvement, however, is only about $85,000 more than the EMV with one expert and does not justify the cost of the second expert.

In this example two major forces are acting with respect to the effect of expert information. The first is that because Dr. Davies would be able to have a much better set of probabilities to base his decision on given one expert, there is less room for improvement if a second expert is called in. With one expert the probability of achieving success, given that the project is funded, moves from 0.15 to 0.41, and the probability of funding a failure moves from 0.85 to 0.59. Also, if one expert predicts failure, the probability of actual failure moves from 0.85 (prior) to 0.96, leaving relatively little uncertainty for the second expert to resolve!

A second important factor is that if a second expert is considered as a marginal addition to the first, Dr. Davies has a 0.32 chance of being left in the awkward position of mixed predictions. In that case, because the experts are equally reliable, he is in the same position (node *A*, Figure 11–13) as if he had consulted no experts, except that he has wasted \$250,000 on expert's fees.

We should note that in decision trees such as Figure 11–13, essentially every element of the analysis plays a role in determining the result and should be considered as a possible candidate for sensitivity analysis. For example, consider the assumed \$6 million profit if the project is successful. Is the solution sensitive to this element alone? Surely if this figure were extremely large, say \$100 million, the project would be worth funding even if one or two experts predicted failure. If so, it would be interesting to know where the break-even point is. To do this, we can simply equate the EMV expressions for competing alternatives. Let $R$ be the profit from success. Let us begin by assuming that the expert information is free.

$$\begin{aligned}\text{EMV (Fund)} &= 0.15R - \$500{,}000 \times 0.85\\ &= 0.15R - \$425{,}000\\ \text{EMV (Consult one expert)} &= 0.29 \times (0.41R - 0.59 \times \$500{,}000) + 0.71 \times (0.04R\\ &\quad - 0.96 \times \$500{,}000)\\ &= 0.15R - 425{,}000 \text{ (apart from rounding errors)}\end{aligned}$$

This only applies if \$$R$ is less than \$12 million

Note that $R$ = \$12 million is the point which would reverse the decision at decision node *B* in Figure 11–13. Indeed, free expert opinions add no value if they do not result in an altering of the decision strategy. If $R$ is greater than \$12 million, even free expert information with the reliability described would be worthless.

However, the information is not free, hence the break-even point must be less than \$12 million.

To find the exact break-even point, we can write an expression for the EMV of branch 3 of Figure 11–13, assuming \$6 million < \$$R$ < \$12 million and *including* the \$125,000 expert's fee:

$$\begin{aligned}\text{EMV (Branch 3)} &= 0.29\,(0.41R - 0.59 \times 500{,}000) + 0.71 \times 0 - 125{,}000\\ &= 0.12R - \$210{,}550\end{aligned}$$

The EMV of branch 1 was $0.15R$ – \$425,000. We equate these expressions to find the break-even value of $R$

$$0.12\,R - \$210{,}550 = 0.15R - \$425{,}000$$

The solution is

$$R = \frac{214{,}450}{0.03} = \$7.15 \text{ million}$$

**TABLE 11-7** Regret Table for Dr. Davies

| | *Success* | *Failure* | *Expected Opportunity Loss* |
|---|---|---|---|
| Fund project | 0 | 0.5 million | 0.15 × 0 + 0.85 × \$0.5 million |
| Not fund project | \$6 million | 0 | 0.15 × \$6 million |

The result of this investigation has shown that if the profit from success is underestimated by a little over \$1 million, it is not even worth getting one expert. The expert's fee is such that even though his information would cause a decision strategy change of $R$ in the range, \$7.15 million to \$12 million, the expert information is not worth obtaining.

Note that a complete sensitivity analysis would also include comparisons of branch 4 (Figure 11-13) with branches 1 and 3.

Finally, what would be the value of perfect information to Dr. Davies? A regret table (Table 11-7) can be used to determine EVPI.

$$\begin{aligned} \text{EVPI} &= \text{EOL of the optimal act} \\ &= 0.15 \times 0 + 0.85 \times \$0.5 \text{ million} \\ &= \$425{,}000 \end{aligned}$$

Less formally, we could have noted that without the perfect information we would fund the project. Perfect information would only help if it indicated failure, in which case we could, given this perfect foresight, save \$500,000. Since the prior probability of failure is assessed as 0.85, so must the probability of such an indication by the perfect predictor. Hence the perfect information has an expected value of 0.85 × \$0.5 million = \$0.425 million. In general, it is very instructive to determine EVPIs by thinking the problem through, as we have done in this paragraph, rather than mechanically determining the EOL of the optimal act.

## Example 11-6

### Farmer Brown Revisited

Figure 11-14 shows a decision tree representation of the problem that Farmer Brown faced in Example 10-7. He had 150,000 bushels of soybeans to sell today or keep for a week. He believed that the price might rise by two cents per bushel, fall by two cents per bushel, or stay stable. His possible gain or loss totalled \$3,000. Appropriate payoffs are shown in Figure 11-14 relative to the base case of "sell today."

Rollback of the decision tree leads to EMVs of \$600 for "wait, sell next week" and \$969.60 for "obtain forecast." Hence the EVII is \$369.60. Of course this is the expected gain from using the forecast without taking into account any costs.

**FIGURE 11-14** Farmer Brown's Decision Tree

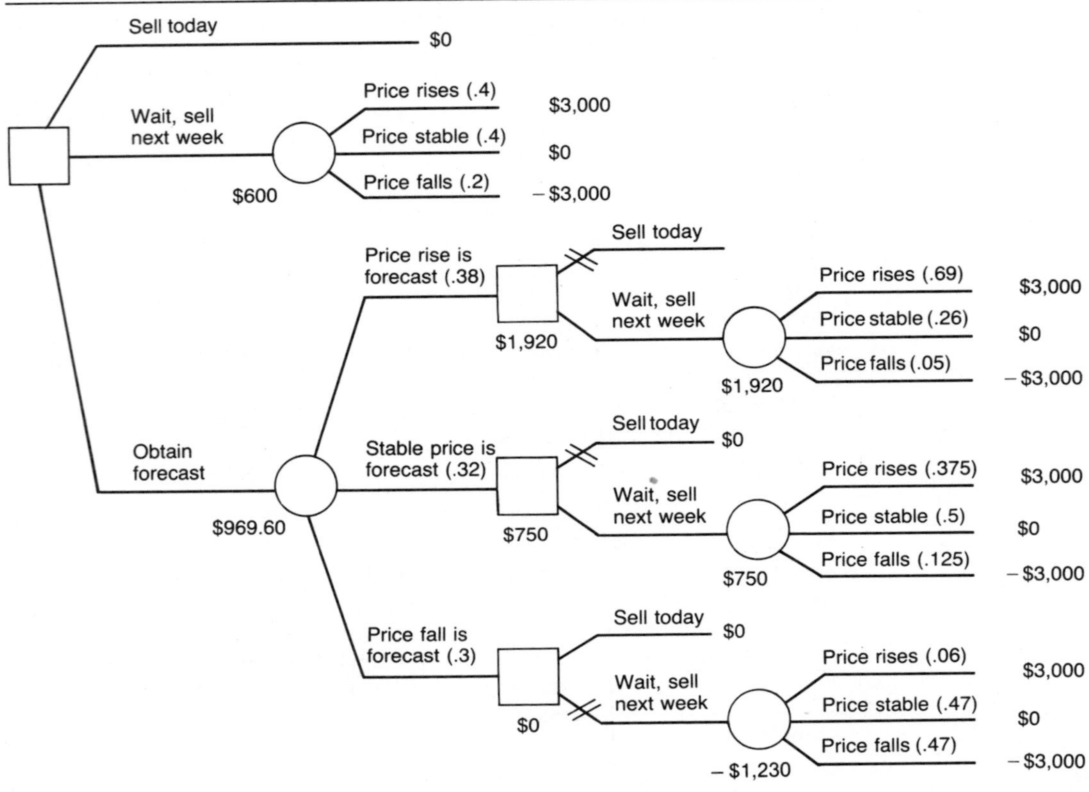


The EVPI can be calculated as the EOL of the optimal strategy from Table 11-8. From Table 11-8 the EOL of the optimal strategy is $600, and by definition this amount is the EVPI. Let us now determine the EVPI in a more intuitive manner. The best strategy given no extra information is "wait, sell next week." Perfect information would not help if it indicated a price rise or price stability. It would help if it indicated a

**TABLE 11-8** Farmer Brown's Regret Table

| | *Price Rise* | *Price Stable* | *Price Fall* | *Expected Opportunity Loss* |
|---|---|---|---|---|
| Sell Today | 3,000 | 0 | 0 | 1,200 |
| Next week | 0 | 0 | 3,000 | 600 |

price fall because it would lead to a strategy change. The likelihood of a "price fall" indication is the prior probability, 0.2, and the gain is \$3,000. Hence

$$\begin{aligned} \text{EVPI} &= 0.2 \times \$3{,}000 \\ &= \$600 \end{aligned}$$

---

## USING EVII AND EVPI IN DECISION ANALYSIS

Where it is worthwhile formalizing the decision to collect information and expected values can be reasonably used to represent preferences, EVII and EVPI are very useful concepts in decision analysis.

For Farmer Brown, the first forecast was free, but since subsequent forecasts come at a price, he may wish to weigh carefully not only his decisions about the timing of his crop sales, but also the procurement of professional forecasts. The decision analysis framework, and particularly EVII, provides a comprehensive aid to allow him to integrate the information procurement and crop sale decisions. The method is rational and totally precise. Its level of decision support is limited only by what is assumed away in constructing the decision model and by the accuracy of data. If, for example, the professional forecaster were to overstate his forecasting performance, Farmer Brown would be entering an incorrect data set into the decision analysis and could end up with a misleading result.

As with all modeling procedures, we must take care with accuracy of input data. Just how much care we need to take depends on the sensitivity of the solution to the various inputs. Sensitivity can be determined for any parameter and is a very useful part of decision analysis.

There may be other things that were not encompassed in the EVPI or EVII calculations. Certainly one of the important ones is attitude toward risk. If Farmer Brown were risk averse, the advantage from reduction of uncertainty would exist to an extent over and above that which is represented by EVII and EVPI. Other structural assumptions, such as the assumption that only three outcomes are possible in Farmer Brown's case, affect EVPI.

We should note that in using the term *reduction of uncertainty* we are not referring to changing the unconditional probabilities of success or failure of an event. For example in the Reschem decision (Example 11–5), the acquisition of perfect or imperfect information *does not* change the underlying probability of success or failure of the project, given that it is attempted. The information does change, however, the probabilities that the decision maker faces when he must commit to an action. In Figure 11–13, if no expert is consulted, Dr. Davies would fund the project (branch 1) with only a 0.15 chance of success. If he consults one expert, and follows the expert's recommendation, he would only fund the project if success is recommended. In that case his conditional chance of success is 0.41. Since the information is imperfect, there is a negative aspect, which is the small chance ($0.71 \times 0.04 = 0.0284$) that he would have chosen to not fund the project, and that it would have been a success if he had funded it. Overall, however, the ex-ante probability of project success is of course unchanged.

In the Farmer Brown example, the market price behavior of soybeans will not be affected by his decision to sell/wait or to collect information. The probabilities that he faces, however, being conditional if he buys information, do change from the unconditional priors that he faces if he does not obtain a forecast.

To summarize, the uncertain prospects that a decision maker faces can be altered with the use of imperfect information, but uncertainty is not eliminated if the information is imperfect, and the decision maker must still play a game against nature. Both the costs and benefits of information can be explicitly accounted for. Perfect information however, transforms uncertainty into perfect certainty.

## THE EXPECTED UTILITY OF INFORMATION

When the decision maker is risk averse or risk seeking, the value of information is normally different from EVPI or EVII unless these values are all zero. This is because the information changes the risk profile of the decision problem as well as the expected value. EVPI and EVII only account for changes in expected value, whereas expected utilities account for the decision maker's preference in a much more comprehensive sense. EMV (representing risk neutrality) is a special (linear) case of expected utility.

To determine whether information should or should not be collected by risk-averse or risk-seeking decision makers, the costs and benefits of the information should all be included on the decision tree. The expected utility decision criterion can then be applied in the usual way. This procedure simply includes the decision to collect information as part of the decision analysis, and allows it to be included in the process of determining the optimal strategy.

To do this, a useful general method is to assume a trial value for the cost of the information and include this trial value on the decision tree. The expected utility criterion is then applied. Through a process of trial and error, various information costs are assumed until the expected utility of the "information collection" branch equals the expected utility of the "no information" branch. In the special case of an exponential utility function, this method is unnecessary because this function has the property of constant risk aversion.

## EXAMPLE 11–7

### Reschem Services (C)

In the Reschem example, Dr. Davies was considering the option of consulting one or two experts before making a project funding decision. In Figure 11–13, the expected value of imperfect information was found to be $152,850 for one expert. For the purposes of simplicity and clarity we will omit the option of consulting two experts in the present discussion.

Dr. Davies noted the high degree of uncertainty associated with this project and wanted to account formally for his risk preference function. He went through a utility assessment process and fitted an exponential curve to his preference data set. The best-fitting curve was

$$U(X) = -e^{-10^{-8}X}$$

where $X$ represents monetary values.

His next step was to roll back the decision tree using the expected utility criterion. His first attempt included the previously assumed consultant fee of $125,000. Note that in Figure 11–15 this fee is been represented as $C$.

Let us compare some key data that arise from the first trial expected utility analysis (Figure 11–15). Note in passing that in Figure 11–15 up to seven significant digits were preserved throughout the calculation to ensure accuracy of the data. This degree of precision is often not necessary and in fact is sometimes nonsensical. In this instance it facilitates a very accurate illustration of the certainty equivalent concept of information value.

We can draw a number of inferences about the interplay of the risk aversion and the uncertainty resolution that occurs when using the imperfect expert prediction. The EVII for this example is $152,850. We assumed a trial cost of information of $125,000, and Figure 11–15 shows that the "consult one expert" option is still the most attractive. The certainty equivalent value of this branch, $483,488, is better than that for the next best branch by

$$\$483{,}488 - \$448{,}430 = \$35{,}018$$

Hence, as a next trial we should use a higher cost of information. Since the difference between the certainty equivalent values was close to $35,000, a good next trial cost figure is $125,000 + $35,000, that is, $160,000.

When comparing the expected values with the certainty equivalent values, we note that the differences are not the same for the various branches as shown in Table 11–9.

The "EMV − certainty equivalent" values in Table 11–9 can be interpreted as risk premium values. Since the uncertainty is reduced by consulting the expert, so is the risk premium.

**FIGURE 11–15** Dr. Davies' Revised Decision Tree

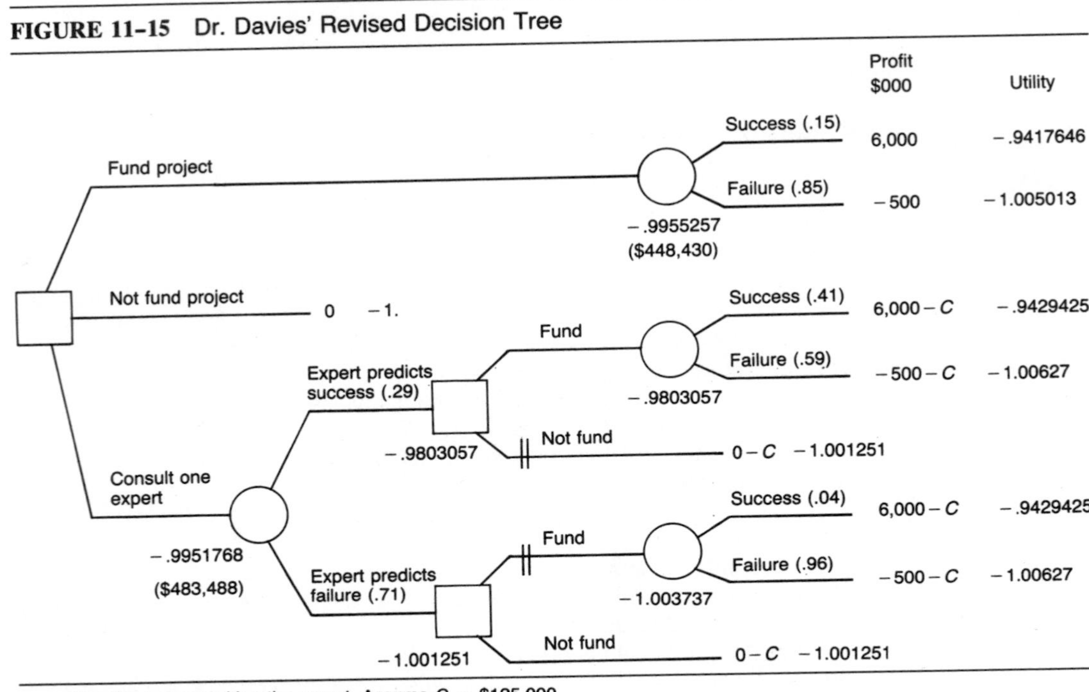


$C$ = Cost of consulting the expert. Assume $C$ = $125,000

The rollback of the decision tree with a new trial cost of $160,000 shows that the expected utility values of the "fund project" and "consult one expert" branches were almost exactly equal. The accuracy is to six decimal places. The second guess was not just lucky to be so accurate but had to be correct because the adjustment of $35,000 was made from the difference between the certainty equivalent values of the first trial. This would not be the case for utility functions other than the exponential (see Figure 11–16).

The property of constant risk aversion characterizing the exponential utility function ensured that only two trials were necessary. For other utility functions that

**TABLE 11–9** Data from the Reschem Decision Analysis

| *Branch* | *EMV* | *Certainty Equivalent* | *EMV Minus Certainty Equivalent* |
|---|---|---|---|
| Fund project | 475,000 | 448,430 | 26,570 |
| Not fund project | 0 | 0 | 0 |
| Consult one expert | 502,850 | 483,488 | 19,362 |

**FIGURE 11–16** Dr. Davies' Revised Decision Tree

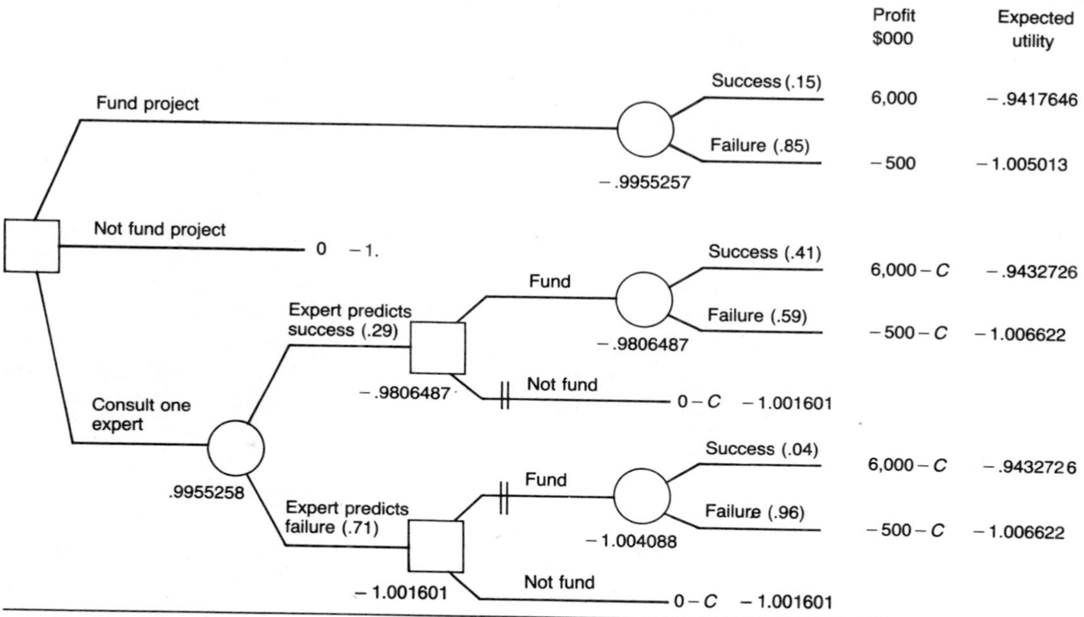

Profit $000
Expected utility
Fund project
Success (.15)
6,000
−.9417646
Failure (.85)
−500
−1.005013
−.9955257
Not fund project
0 −1.
Success (.41)
6,000 − $C$
−.9432726
Fund
Expert predicts success (.29)
Failure (.59)
−500 − $C$
−1.006622
−.9806487
−.9806487
Not fund
0 − $C$ −1.001601
Consult one expert
Success (.04)
6,000 − $C$
−.9432726
Fund
.9955258
Expert predicts failure (.71)
Failure (.96)
−500 − $C$
−1.006622
−1.004088
Not fund
−1.001601
0 − $C$ −1.001601

$C$ = Cost of consulting the expert. $C$ = $160,000.

may not have this property, more than two trials would probably be necessary to converge on a solution.

---

To summarize, the Reschem Services (C) example demonstrated that for risk-averse decision makers, imperfect information that reduces uncertainty is worth more than EVII. The certainty equivalent value of imperfect information (CEVII) was $160,000 whereas the EVII was $152,850. As the degree of risk aversion increases, CEVII would increase. For the same example we can calculate the certainty equivalent value of perfect information (CEVPI). The expected utility with perfect information would be

$$-e^{-10^{-8} \times (6 \times 10^{6} - c)} \times 0.15 + -e^{-10^{-8} \times (0 - c)} \times 0.85$$

With $C$ = $428,940, the value of this expression is −0.9955257. This is the same expected utility as for the "fund project" option. Thus, if perfect information were available, it would have a CEVPI of $428,940 to the decision maker, having the utility function as specified. EVPI for this example was $425,000. CEVPI was greater than EVPI, but not by very much because the assumed degree of risk aversion was very low. As the risk-aversion parameter increases, so does the expression (CEVPI − EVPI).

For comparison purposes, if the risk-aversion parameter $k$ is increased from $1 \times 10^{-8}$ to $5 \times 10^{-8}$, the certainty equivalent, CEVPI, becomes $442,820. This change represents an increase in risk premium from $3,940 to $17,820.

Let us recap by noting that information can be evaluated when a decision maker's attitude toward risk is not neutral. In such cases it is appropriate to measure the value of information in certainty equivalent terms facilitating comparisons between CEVII and EVII, and between CEVPI and EVPI. Information generally would have more value for risk-averse decision makers than for risk-neutral decision makers (unless it is valueless), and CEVPI and CEVII generally increase with higher degrees of risk aversion.

## CLASSICAL AND BAYESIAN APPROACHES TO SAMPLING

Two main schools of thought exist in the field of statistics, particularly in reference to using sample information to determine parameter values. These approaches are the classical and the more modern Bayesian approach.

The Bayesian approach is an integrated part of modern decision analysis as described in this chapter and the preceding one. It aims to use all relevant information in parameter assessment, including subjective prior beliefs as well as sample information where it is feasible to obtain such data. The Bayesian approach aims to be concerned with economic factors (costs and benefits) associated with information collection and analysis.

The classical approach tends to focus on the use of relative frequency data from samples or surveys, and to exclude the use of subjective probabilities. The classical statistician, unlike the Bayesian, does not generally make probabilistic statements about parameters or events but attempts to objectively report on the results of surveys or experiments.[3] This is typically done in one of two ways. The first is to calculate a point estimate and standard error. The second is to calculate a confidence interval. Outlines of these classical methods of statistics are given in most introductory texts on business statistics, of which Newbould's (1984) is a good example. Classical statisticians generally do not recognize the validity of the Bayesian process of combining subjective prior and observation likelihood information

---

[3] For a detailed description and history of these views of statistics see H. Raiffa (1968), Chapter 10.

sources. To many Bayesians it is not immediately obvious how a confidence interval can be used in a decision analysis. Whereas probabilities can clearly be combined with payoffs or utilities, it is not evident that a confidence interval or a point estimate and standard error can be similarly integrated into decision analysis.

In contrast with the classical view, Bayesians "believe that Bayes Theorem is the necessary keystone of the whole edifice of statistical inference." (Allais 1984, p. 68.)

The relationship between decision making and the classical versus Bayesian approaches is examined in more detail by Bierman, Bonini, and Hausman (1986). They point out that classical statistics may not produce as useful insights as Bayesian statistics. Many students in business and economics have difficulty in seeing any direct link between a confidence interval and a business decision. For example, the usual choice of a 0.95 or 0.99 confidence interval is by convention but is really an arbitrary one. For the purposes of decision making, the expression of probabilistic statements in a Bayesian manner is a more direct set of inferences than a confidence interval. This is likely to be so, even if a subjectively assessed prior is not admitted and a uniform prior distribution is used. As a separate issue, it appears unreasonable in decision making not to make use of every source of information that can be economically justified.[4] If a marketing manager is considering conducting a market survey for a new product launch, shouldn't his own views, providing they are properly calibrated as probability statements, be incorporated with the results of a survey? Bayesian statisticians say yes, classicists say no. Bunn has written:

> Now, the fact that Bayesian inference allows us to express probability distributions upon hypotheses, as well as events, is a distinguishing feature from the more traditional frequentist approach to statistical inference. In non-Bayesian inference, a hypothesis is a statement about nature and, being true or false, has no uncertainty attached to it. The Bayesian approach looks at the perspective of the decision maker and seeks to use probability theory to encode his uncertainties. (D. Bunn 1982, p. 100.)

## COMPARING THE COSTS AND BENEFITS OF INFORMATION

The formal inclusion in decision models of alternatives to either obtain or not obtain information is only worthwhile if that information has *both* substantial benefits and costs. First, if the benefits of collecting information are high but the costs are minimal, of course the information should be

---

[4] The reader should realize that these views are those of a self-confessed Bayesian. You may wish to give a classical statistician equal time.

**FIGURE 11–17** Relationship between the Cost and Benefit of Information

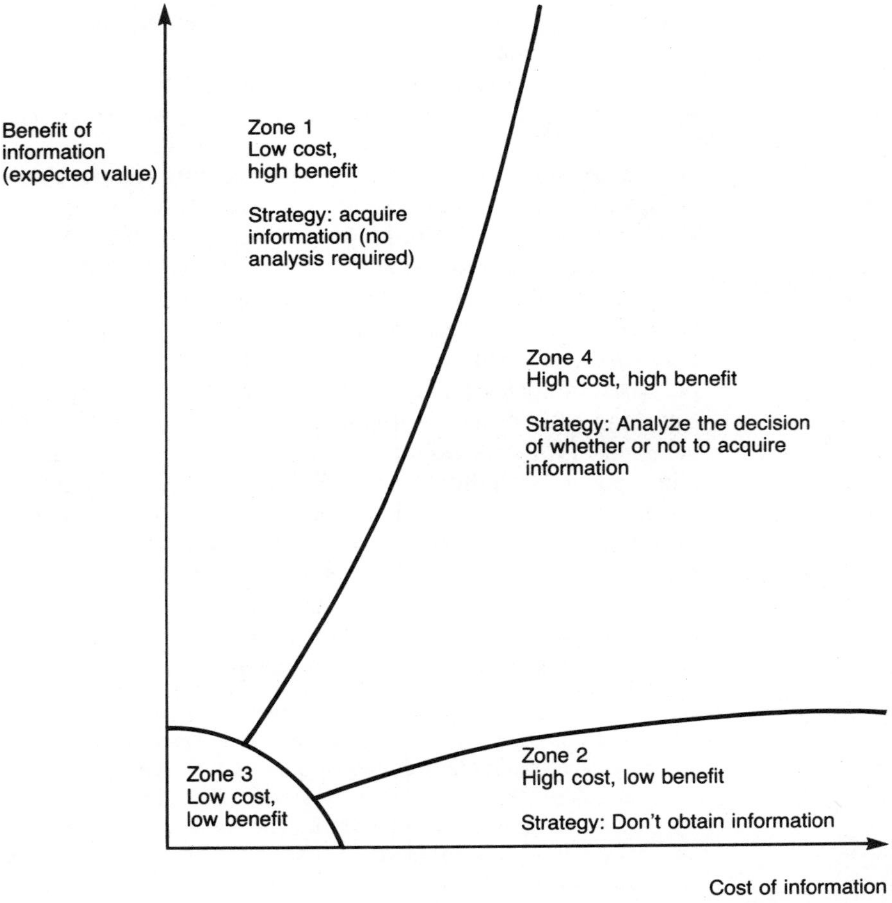

obtained, and there is no need to conduct a formal analysis that includes this issue. In the Reschem example, if Dr. Davies were able to obtain the experts' opinions for $1, they should certainly have been obtained without much consideration. See zone 1 on Figure 11–17.

Second, if the benefit of a set of information is known to be low relative to the high cost, it may not be necessary to support the decision to acquire information with formal analysis. In the Reschem example, if the expert information had cost $10 million, it would obviously not have been worthwhile. See zone 2 on Figure 11–17.

Third, if both the benefits and costs of information are very low, there will be little effect on the major decision, whether information is gathered or not. In the Reschem example context, if $1 could have bought an opinion that had a very poor reliability, this option could be easily discarded. In Figure 11–17 this point would be very close to the origin.

In all three instances above it would be obvious to the decision maker what to do. There is no need in those cases to formalize common sense. The fourth possibility, when costs and benefits are high, occurs when formal analysis can help the decision process. That is because it is not intuitively obvious in zone 4 (Figure 11–17) as to whether the information should be gathered. In zone 4, decision analysis is very useful because as stated earlier in this book and elsewhere, it is "what you do when you don't know what to do." (R. A. Howard 1980, p. 5.) For Dr. Davies in the Reschem example, the expert information helped him by increasing his chances of making a correct funding decision. The reliability and, hence, the benefit of the information was substantial. the decision to consult one or more experts required careful analysis because the cost was also substantial.

## Cost, Benefit, and Sample Size in Surveys

In the preceding section, the relationship between information cost and benefit was examined. In the context of market surveys or samples of items, it is often important to decide upon the sample size.

Sample size is not the only design parameter of a survey, but it is rarely unimportant. As sample size increases, so does the EVII of the survey information. When the sample size becomes equal to the population size, the information becomes perfect. Figure 11–18 details the general relationship between sample size and information benefit. The marginal expected benefit (measured as EVII) decreases as sample size increases.

Figure 11–18 also shows a cost function. The cost function assumes a fixed cost associated with organizing the survey and a constant variable cost. The EVII asymptotically approaches the EVPI as sample size increases. This occurs as the weight of evidence in the likelihood probabilities increases relative to the weighting of the prior distribution.

Figure 11–18 also plots the expected net gain from sampling (ENGS), where for any sample size:

$$ENGS = EVII - \text{Cost}$$

The optimal decision in an expected value sense is to choose the sample size which has a maximum value of ENGS. This is shown as point *A* in Figure 11–18.

**FIGURE 11–18** Relationship between Cost, EVII, and Sample Size

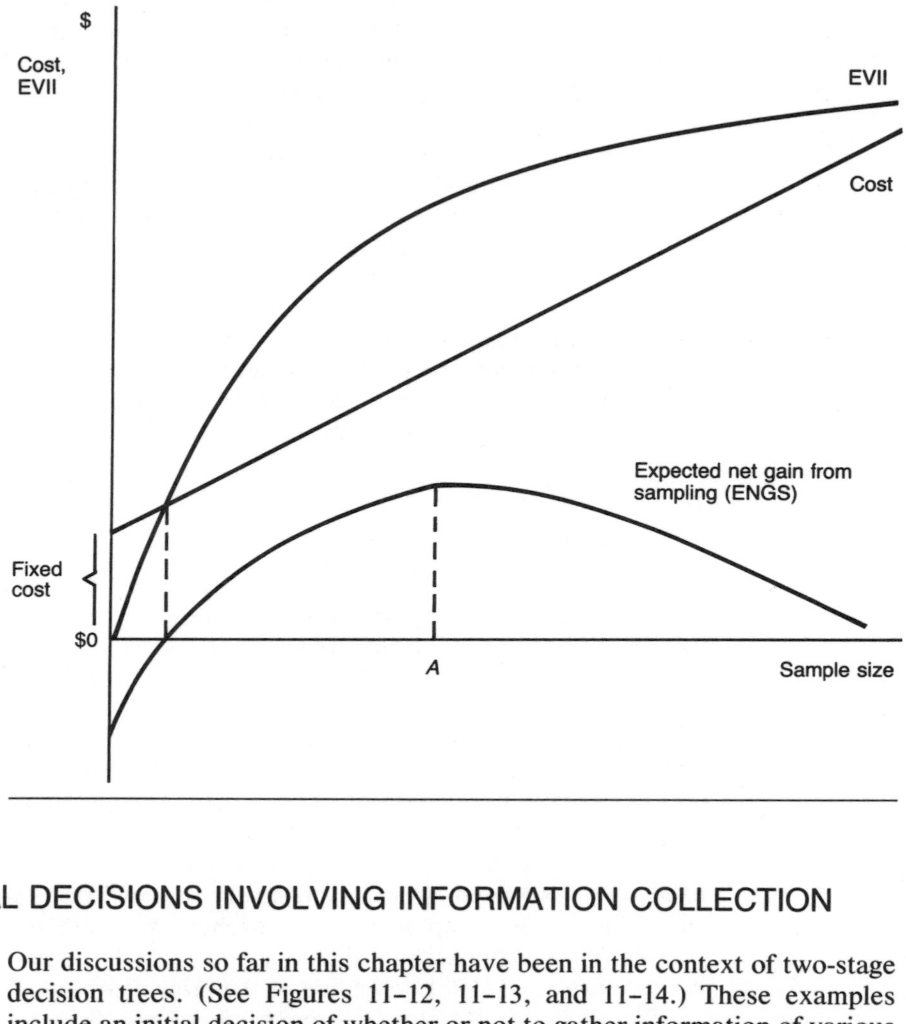

## SEQUENTIAL DECISIONS INVOLVING INFORMATION COLLECTION

Our discussions so far in this chapter have been in the context of two-stage decision trees. (See Figures 11–12, 11–13, and 11–14.) These examples include an initial decision of whether or not to gather information of various types, and a subsequent major decision related to the main problem. In many actual situations, we are not limited to only one opportunity of obtaining information. We can obtain some information, and given that knowledge, then choose to obtain more or not.

In the case of imperfect information, we could obtain some information and then decide, based on the observed result, about whether to obtain more information before making a choice concerning the main problem. Figure 11–19 shows the sequential nature of this process as a generic decision tree structure. In Figure 11–19, an initial decision must be made to gather information or not. This generally refers to imperfect information because perfect information would completely resolve the uncertainty. If no information is gathered at node 1, then a choice must be made about the main problem. If information is acquired, then observation outcomes become known at node 2. These may be survey results, expert opinions, or predictions. Given each of these outcomes, a decision can then be made to either acquire further information or make a choice about the main problem. At

**FIGURE 11–19** A Sequential Process of Imperfect Information Acquisition

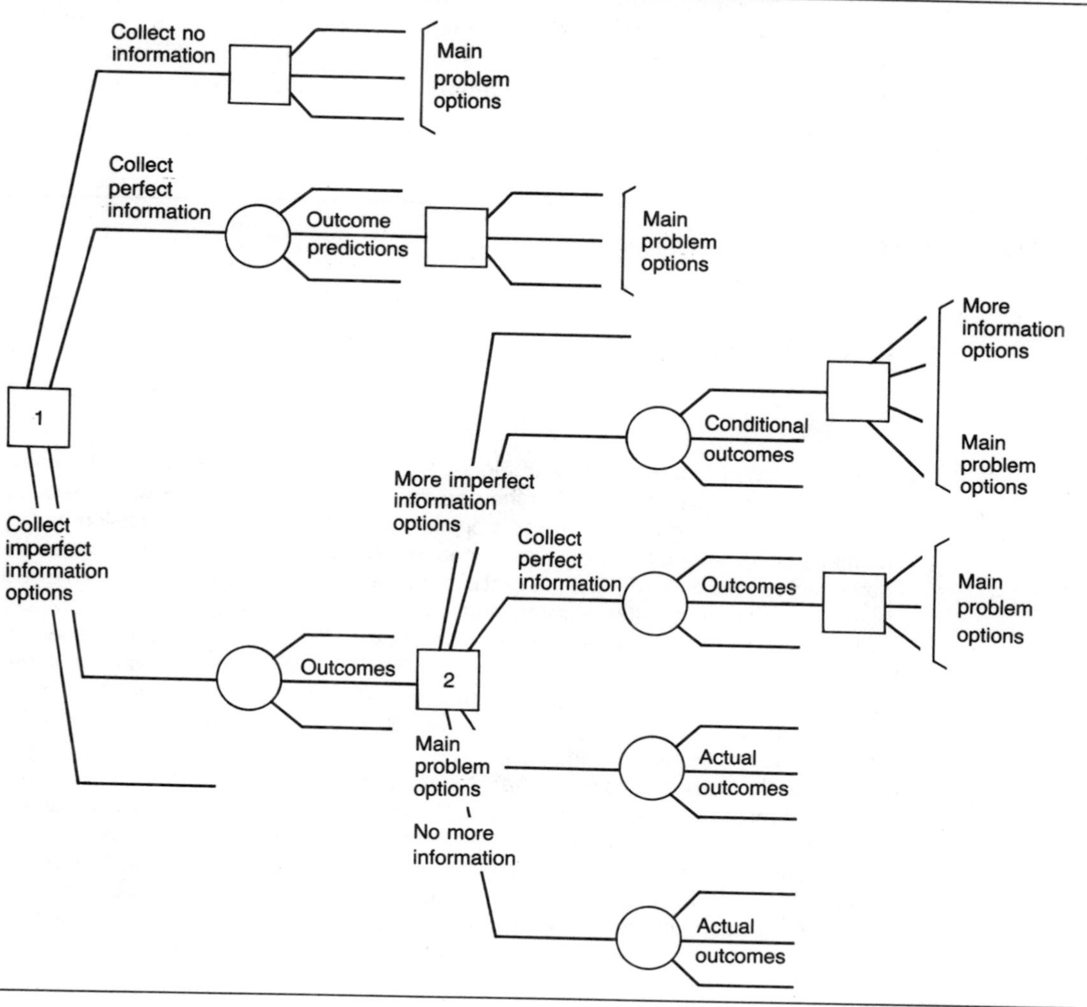

any decision node, even if one or more imperfect information sources have been tapped, it may be feasible to collect perfect information.

It is feasible to have a large number of sequential samples of imperfect information. It is possible to conduct a series of market surveys, consult a large number of experts, or sequentially perform a number of tests in a quality acceptance sampling procedure. The number of branches on a decision tree grows rapidly as the number of stages increases. Even though large and complex decision trees may result, it is feasible to formally analyze multiple observation, sequential information acquisition decision processes. As is discussed in Chapter 15, computerized decision analysis packages, such as ARBORIST, are ideally suited for problems with large decision trees involving repeated sequences of branches.

So far in this discussion of sequential decisions we have considered decision problems involving a single source of uncertainty. In fact, it may be sensible to collect information sequentially when more than one source of uncertainty exists.

## Example 11-8

### Reschem Services (D)

A comparison of Figure 11-20 with Figure 11-13 shows that in Figure 11-20 a new option exists on branch 3. That is the decision alternative to consult with a second expert after receiving the first expert's opinion. (Previously, an initial decision had to be made about whether to consult zero, one, or two experts, and no other information-gathering options existed.) The present conception on branch 3, Figure 11-20 has the potential to provide a better decision strategy (higher EMV) than any previous branch. The decision maker has more flexibility on this branch than on any other with regard to acquiring information.[5] Indeed, branch 3 in Figure 11-20 dominates branch 4 because branch 3 includes all branch 4 options and some other opportunities. Let us calculate the probabilities required for branch 3. Tables 11-10 and 11-11 show the probabilities for the first expert.

When Dr. Davies considers what strategy to employ at nodes *A* and *B* in Figure 11-20, he must use the posterior probabilities from the first Bayes calculation as his priors for the next revisions. Tables 11-12 through 11-15 show the outcomes.

Figure 11-20 shows these probabilities on the appropriate branches. The results show that for this example, knowledge of the first expert's prediction would lead Dr. Davies to not consult the second expert regardless of the first expert's prediction.

[5] For a definition of flexibility in this context, see Merkhofer (1977).

**FIGURE 11–20** Dr. Davies' Decision Tree (including possible sequential information acquisition)

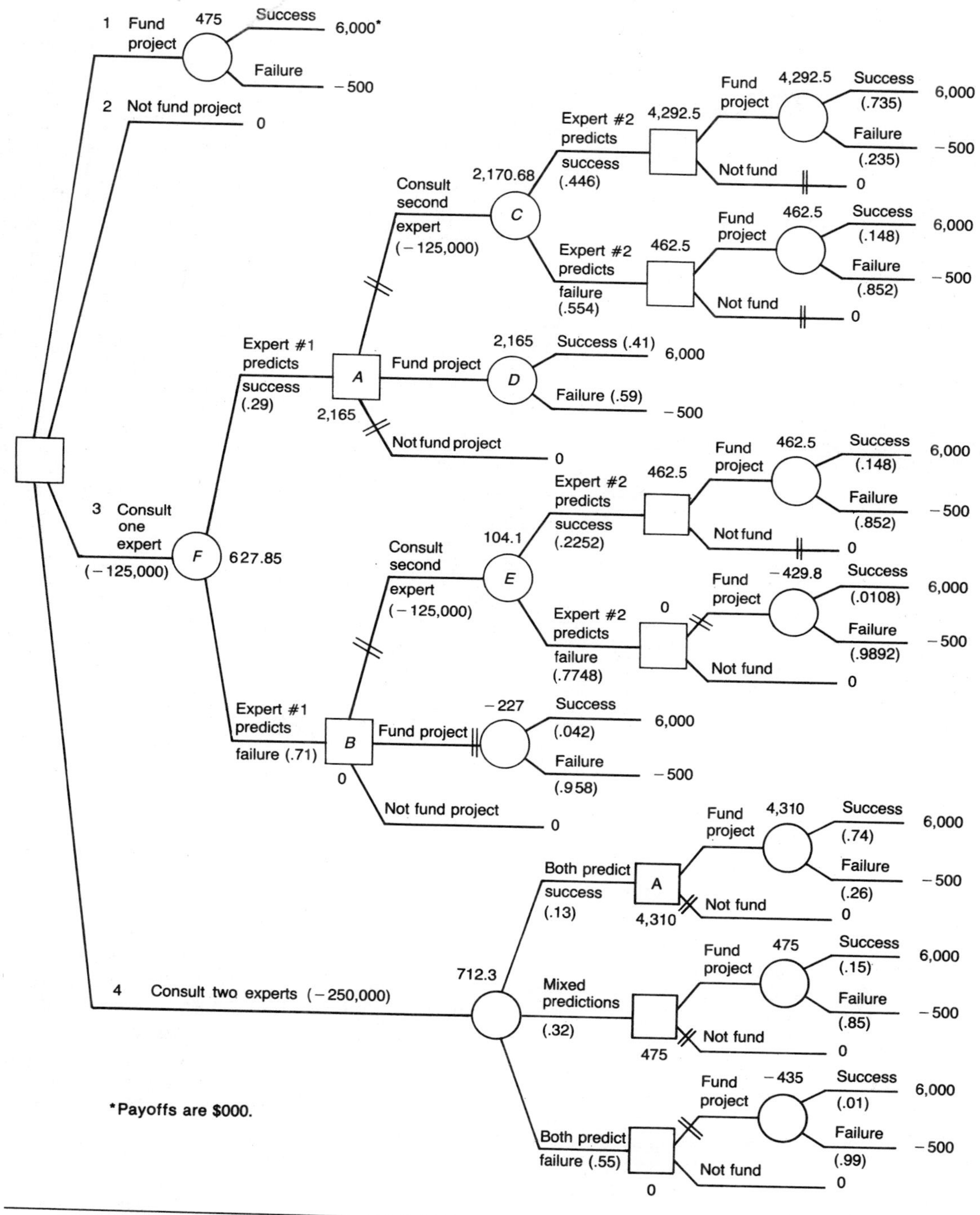


*Payoffs are $000.

**TABLE 11-10** First Expert Bayes Revision (success predicted)

| Event | Prior | Likelihood | Joint | Posterior |
|---|---|---|---|---|
| Success | 0.15 | 0.8 | 0.12 | 0.41 |
| Fail | 0.85 | 0.2 | 0.17 | 0.59 |
| | | | Σ = 0.29 | |

**TABLE 11-11** First Expert Bayes Revision (failure predicted)

| Event | Prior | Liklihood | Joint | Posterior |
|---|---|---|---|---|
| Success | 0.15 | 0.2 | 0.03 | 0.042 |
| Failure | 0.85 | 0.8 | 0.68 | 0.958 |
| | | | Σ = 0.71 | |

**TABLE 11-12** Second Expert Predicts Success Given First Expert Predicted Success

| Event | Prior | Likelihood | Joint | Posterior |
|---|---|---|---|---|
| Success | 0.41 | 0.8 | 0.328 | 0.735 |
| Failure | 0.59 | 0.2 | 0.118 | 0.265 |
| | | | Σ = 0.446 | |

Note that in Figure 11-20 the second expert's fees are assumed to be incurred at the branches joining nodes *A* to *C* and also *B* to *E*.

It is very possible that in other cases there would be an advantage, in terms of prospects, to be gained from sequential information gathering. For example, let us suppose that the experts in this case charge fees of only $100,000, thanks to some sharp negotiating on Dr. Davies part. Under these new conditions, the best strategy from node *B* is to consult the second expert because the net EMV is $104,100 − $100,000 = $4,100. At branch *A*, however, the second expert would not be consulted. Hence the complete decision strategy for branch 3, Figure 11-20 would be: "Consult one expert. If he predicts success, fund the project. If he predicts failure, consult the second expert. If the second expert predicts success, fund the project. If the second expert predicts failure, don't fund the project."

Note that in this decision strategy, the second action is a function of the first expert's prediction. This strategy could not be encapsulated by branches that do not consider sequential information gathering but only provide one opportunity to collect

**TABLE 11–13** Second Expert Predicts Failure Given First Expert Predicted Success

| *Event* | *Prior* | *Likelihood* | *Joint* | *Posterior* |
|---|---|---|---|---|
| Success | 0.41 | 0.2 | 0.082 | 0.148 |
| Failure | 0.59 | 0.8 | 0.472 | 0.852 |
| | | | Σ = 0.554 | |

**TABLE 11–14** Second Expert Predicts Failure Given First Expert Predicted Failure

| *Event* | *Prior* | *Likelihood* | *Joint* | *Posterior* |
|---|---|---|---|---|
| Success | 0.042 | 0.8 | 0.0336 | 0.148 |
| Failure | 0.958 | 0.2 | 0.1916 | 0.852 |
| | | | Σ = 0.2252 | |

**TABLE 11–15** Second Expert Predicts Success Given First Expert Predicted Failure

| *Event* | *Prior* | *Likelihood* | *Joint* | *Posterior* |
|---|---|---|---|---|
| Success | 0.042 | 0.2 | 0.0084 | 0.0108 |
| Failure | 0.958 | 0.8 | 0.7764 | 0.9892 |
| | | | Σ = 0.7748 | |

information. To follow this through, let us demonstrate that the flexibility provided by sequential sampling in this example results in a higher EMV than in a nonsequential process. From Figure 11–13, if the consultant's fees were only $100,000 the EMVs are:

Branch 3: Consult one expert: EMV = $527,850
Branch 4: Consult two experts: EMV = $512,300

From the "sequential" branch of Figure 11–20, the EMV would be determined by countinuing the rollback procedure as follows:

Node *B:* EMV = $4,100
Node *A:* EMV = $2,165
Node *F:* EMV = $630,761
Subtract expert 1 Fee
Yields branch 3 EMV = $530,761

Hence the optimal strategy would have been to consult one expert only at first, and to then consult the second if the first predicted failure.

If two imperfect information sources were available that were not identical in their reliabilities (likelihood probabilities) and costs, then two sequential branches would be required, namely:

1. Expert 1, then possibly expert 2.
2. Expert 2, then possibly expert 1.

These two branches need not generally have the same EMV, unless the opinions were indistinguishable.

Sequential information gathering provides more flexibility than situations where only a single decision is being made to gather information. If there is no fixed cost incurred each time information is gathered and the variable cost is constant for each observation, a sequential information-gathering strategy must be at least as good as a two-stage decision tree strategy where only one information gathering step occurs.

In the context of a market survey or in quality testing, if there were no fixed cost and merely a constant cost per item sampled, it is sensible to conduct a number of small samples and frequently review the economics of gathering further data. In this way, a decision maker is less likely to gather more data than is necessary to swing the major decision. Of course in real decision problems, there are fixed costs, and economies of scale to sample size may occur. It would not be practical, for example, to evaluate a "stopping rule" using decision analysis after every call in a telephone survey. The preposterior analysis would become an enormous task! However, if the plan involves telephoning 5,000 people to get a market survey estimate, it may be worth stopping after every 50 or every 100 calls to examine the results. At these points, the results may indicate that the market share posterior distribution is such that further calling is not warranted, and the major decision can be made.

In a case like that of Dr. Davies where expert opinions cost $100,000 or more per throw, the sequential preposterior analysis may identify a (sequential) strategy that is more profitable than can be obtained with a single information-gathering step.

## SUMMARY

Information is a central element in decision making. For many decision analyses we go through a process which begins with problem identification and model structuring. To gain inference from a model we need to supply it with specific information. In decision analysis the main data requirements are probabilities, payoffs, and utilities. In many real problems the possibility exists for experimentation and the resultant generation of information pertaining to a parameter or event in a decision problem. The cost of conducting the experiment may be large, and hence, the decision to experiment may itself warrant a decision analysis. Fortunately, the decision to experiment may be integrated into the major decision analysis about the problem so that the value of the information can be determined. This can be a very powerful tool for the manager.

Methods are available for evaluating the benefit of obtaining information from experiments of all kinds. Bayes Theorem provides for the incorporation of the likelihood information into the decision analysis so that inferences from observations can be accurately combined with prior beliefs. The expected value of information can be specifically determined and compared with the cost. Hence, when a decision is being made about gathering information that might assist in a complex decision analysis, this (information collection) step can itself be formally supported by including it in the decision analysis model.

Where EMV is an appropriate decision rule, EVPI and EVII can be determined. If expected utility is being used, CEVPI and CEVII can be calculated. No matter which rule is used, a preposterior analysis can be constructed to formally assist in decisions regarding sample design, pilot plant construction, purchase of forecasts, gathering expert opinions, and other forms of experiment or observation.

Since information is normally gathered at some cost, it is sensible, unless that cost is very small, to evaluate the net benefits to be derived from the information. In a managerial context this can only be done in terms of how that information affects decision strategies. Classical statistics cannot address the integration of information gathering with the economics of a decision. Bayesian statistics in decision analysis provide a powerful model for doing so.

## FURTHER READING

A number of sources are available for those who wish to read more in this field. Winkler (1972) covers most of the important technical issues and is a very good starting point. Raiffa (1968) has also written about the value of information in decision analysis.

Bierman, Bonini, and Hausman (1981) have considered information on uncertain quantities which are continuous in nature in a similar manner to Winkler. In particular, they discuss decision making with the normal distribution.

Finally, Raiffa and Schlaifer (1961) give a mathematically oriented treatise on the technical issues as does La Valle (1978). Holloway (1979) gives some further managerial examples of the value of information.

## REFERENCES

ACKOFF, R. L. 1967. "Management Misinformation Systems." *Management Science* 14, no. 4, December, pp. 147–56.

ALLAIS, M. 1984. "Foundations of Utility and Probability." In *Progress in Utility and Risk Theory,* eds. O. Hagen and F. Wenstop. New York: D. Reidel Publishing.

BIERMAN, H.; C. P. BONINI and W. H. HAUSMAN. 1986. *Quantitative Analysis for Business Decisions*. Homewood, Ill., Richard D. Irwin.

BUNN, D. 1982. *Analysis for Optimal Decisions*. New York: John Wiley & Sons.

DEARDEN, J. 1972. "MIS is a Mirage." *Harvard Business Review* 50, no.1, January-February, pp. 90–99.

DUNCAN, R. B. 1979. "What Is the Right Organizational Structure? Decision Tree Analysis Provides the Answer." *Organizational Dynamics* 7, no. 3, Winter, pp. 58–80.

EIN-DOR, P., and E. SEGEV. 1981. *A Paradigm for Management Information Systems*. New York: Praeger Publishers.

HOLLOWAY, C. A. 1979. *Decision Making under Uncertainty*. Englewood Cliffs, N.J.: Prentice-Hall.

HOWARD, R. 1980. "An Assessment of Decision Analysis." *Operations Research* 28, pp. 4–27.

LA VALLE, I. 1978. *Fundamentals of Decision Analysis*. New York: Holt, Rinehart & Winston.

MCKENNEY, J. L., and F. W. MCFARLAN. 1982. "The Information Archipeligo—Maps and Bridges." *Harvard Business Review,* September, pp. 109–19.

MERKHOFER, M. W. 1977. "The Value of Information Given Decision Flexibility." *Management Science* 23, no. 7, March, pp. 716–27.

NEWBOULD, P. 1984. *Statistics for Business and Economics*. Englewood Cliffs, N.J.: Prentice-Hall.

RAIFFA, H. 1968. *Decision Analysis*. New York: Addison-Wesley Publishing, Chapter 10.

RAIFFA, H., and R. L. SCHLAIFER. 1961. *Applied Statistical Decision Theory*. Cambridge, Mass.: Harvard University Press.

SCHELL, G. P. "Establishing the Value of Information Systems." *Interfaces* 16, no. 3, May-June, pp. 82–89.

WINKLER, R. L. 1972. *Introduction to Bayesian Inference and Decision*. New York: Holt, Rinehart & Winston.

## PROBLEMS

1. What factors would you intuitively consider when deciding on whether or not to gather information?
2. Suppose that you are a marketing manager, and there is a substantial amount of uncertainty about the potential market share for your new product. How would you make an intuitive choice about a market survey, test market, or other information-gathering device?

3. Referring to problem 1, how can decision analysis generally help in the information-gathering decision?
4. Referring to problem 2, how could decision analysis be used to assist in this problem?
5. Define the expected value of perfect information, both formally, and in terms of its meaning in a single-state decision problem with a decision variable $D_i$, $i = 1 \ldots m$ and a random variable $r_j$, $j = 1 \ldots n$. Associated payoffs are $P_{ij}$.
6. Define the expected value of perfect information in your own words, using no symbols.
7. Can EVPI ever be negative? Can it be zero?
8. If a decision analysis model incorporates two or more sources of uncertainty, does perfect information about both of them have the same expected value as the individual EVPIs? Explain your answer.
9. What is the expected value of imperfect information, EVII?
10. What does imperfect information mean in the following contexts:
    *a.* A market survey.
    *b.* An expert prediction about the potential for a new product or technology.
    *c.* An election poll.
    *d.* A forecast of future inflation rates.
11. How would the Bayesian and classical approaches differ in the context of a market survey? For this class of problem, describe each method of analysis separately, and highlight the similarities and differences.
12. Information can be gathered in a number of steps. Consider the case of an oil wildcatter who is investigating a large, previously unexplored region. He has two main sources of information:
    *a.* Seismic data (relatively inexpensive).
    *b.* Exploratory drill data (expensive).

    How could he use decision analysis to support his intuitive decision process? Seismic and exploratory drill data can be gathered at a number of points in the region.
13. Western Mineral Company was interested in a joint venture proposition with a company that had the exploration and mining rights to a parcel of land in South America. The venture had the potential of huge profits if certain minerals were discovered. Western's chief executive officer knew that other companies would be bidding for the joint venture and wondered how much he should offer the South American company. In the first instance he considered offering $40 million for a 40% share in the venture. It was known that the local company would keep a 60% interest. He had called a consultant, who specialized in dealing with South American companies and

governments. For a fee, the consultant had offered to go on a study tour of the particular country of interest to investigate whether a bid of $40 million would be successful. The consultant stated that he would come back and give his expert opinion, but would not accept any liability if his prediction turned out to be wrong. The consultant argued that his opinion was very useful because he had a great deal of experience in this sort of activity and had a success rate (in terms of his predictions coming true) of 80%.

Western's CEO reconsidered the situation. The consultant would only provide an 80% reliable indication and would require a $50,000 fee plus an estimated $10,000 in expenses. The CEO had little idea of the likelihood of a $40 million bid being successful and assessed a prior probability of 0.4. Success would lead to an expected revenue for Western of $60 million in present value terms.

Initially, the decision problem was framed as being a fixed price bid ($40 million).

*a.* Draw a decision tree modeling the decision problem Western faces, and calculate EVII. What is the best decision strategy?

*b.* Suppose that the consultant's reliability was not actually 80%. Calculate EVII values assuming that this reliability is 50%, 70%, 90%, and 100%, and draw a graph of EVII versus reliability.

14. The CEO of Western Mineral Company was reconsidering the bidding problem introduced in problem 13 (above). He decided to consider offering a higher bid price than $40 million. He would only be able to submit one bid. He estimated that if he increased his bid from $40 million, the likelihood of it being accepted was a linear function as follows:

| *Bid Price* | *Likelihood of Success* |
|---|---|
| $45 million | 0.55 |
| $50 million | 0.7 |
| $55 million | 0.85 |
| $60 million | 1 |

He felt that a bid of $60 million would lead to no gain in expected value terms, since the price of the bid would then equal the expected gain.

He telephoned the consultant and renegotiated with him at great length. The consultant refused to promise to predict an exact "minimum successful bid price" but did agree to forecast which of the prices ($40, $45, $50, $55, or $60 million) would be the lowest successful bid. The CEO called in an executive vice president who had recently attended a decision analysis program and asked for her help in structuring a representative decision tree.

*a.* Draw a decision tree encapsulating the various bid price options and the possibilities of a forecast being obtained, which might or might not prove to be correct. Assume an 80% reliable forecast.

*b.* What is the EVII?

*c.* What is the best decision strategy?

15. Western Mineral Company's CEO was considering making a \$40 million bid for a joint mineral venture. If successful the expected profit was \$20 million. See problem 13 above. The expected revenue of \$60 million was in fact an uncertain quantity, and the CEO's executive vice president pointed out that it might be useful to consider this in their analysis. They assessed revenues of \$30 million, \$60 million, and \$90 million as being equally likely.

    *a.* Draw a decision tree which initially involves the option of a single bid price only (\$40 million) that may or may not be successful. The probability of the bid being successful is 0.4.

    *b.* Calculate the EVPI for this source of uncertainty. That is, what is the maximum price that should be paid for perfect information about whether the \$40 million bid would succeed?

    *c.* The uncertainty about revenue depended on the nature, quantity, and quality of minerals in the deposit. Calculate EVPI for this source of uncertainty.

    *d.* Calculate the simultaneous EVPI associated with perfect information about both the bid being successful or failing and the revenue outcome.

16. Western Mineral Company's CEO decided that he might gain more insight from a decision model that included his attitude toward risk because he felt very uneasy about the high degree of uncertainty associated with the bidding decision. He assessed his utility function and found that an exponential utility function form fitted closely with a parameter: $1.2 \times 10^{-8}$.

    Use this function and parameter to redo problems 13, 14, and 15, replacing EVPI with CEVPI and EVII with CEVII.

17. Dr. Hunk (see Example 11–2) had his diamond valued by a leading jewelry company. They assured him that its market value was \$1.3 million. He contacted the insurance company to ask for a quote on the insurance premium. The underwriter quoted him a new premium of \$100,000. Calculate the EVPI for his decision.

18. The president of Orange Computers Inc. (see Example 11–3) was reconsidering his decision. In light of the recent high growth in the industry, he decided that if the cost turned out to be low and the

quality high, profit would be substantially higher than $1 million. Recalculate the EVPIs associated with cost and quality separately, assuming that payoffs on the "low cost, high quality" branch may be 1.25, 1.5, 1.75, and $2 million. Assume that all other elements are as originally assessed. Plot the relationship of these EVPI values against the low cost, high quality payoff.

19. Refer to problem 18. For the Orange Computers Inc (A) example, calculate the EVPI of jointly knowing cost and quality, for low cost, high quality payoffs of 1.25, 1.5, 1.75, and $2.0 million. Plot this EVPI information on the same graph as used in problem 18.
20. Calculate the EVPIs of cost and quality in the Orange Computers Inc (A) example as the probabilities of cost and quality being high vary from zero to one. Plot the graphs showing each EVPI as a function of each probability. Use probability increments of 0.1.
21. In the Orange Computers Inc (B) example, Bob decided that in this instance Sarah Short's opinion was not 85% reliable. Conduct a sensitivity analysis, and show EVII on a graph as a function of her reliability in the range of 0.6 to 0.9.
22. In the Orange Computers Inc (B) example, the best decision strategy was to consult Sarah Short, assuming an EMV rule is appropriate. How much less reliable would she have to be (in terms of a reduction from 85%) to no longer be included in the optimal strategy, other things being equal?
23. In the Reschem Services (B) example, what would the EVPI be if Dr. Davies' prior probability for project success had been 0.2 rather than 0.15. Compare your answer with the EVPI of $425,000 (when the success probability is 0.15), and explain why it is different.
24. In the Reschem Services (C) example, Dr. Davies wanted to see how robust the optimal decision strategy was to the assumed degree of risk aversion. Redo the analysis with risk-aversion parameters 20%, 50%, and 100% higher than those originally assumed.
25. In Figure 11–1, EVII was zero, and the sample information was valueless. In Figure 11–2, the bad batch penalty was $5,000, and EVII was not zero.
    *a.* Calculate EVII for a number of values of the bad batch penalty as the penalty varies in the range, $500 to $5,000.
    *b.* Plot a graph of EVII on the vertical axis and bad batch penalty on the horizontal axis, assuming all other factors as in Figure 11–1.
    *c.* Formulate an algebraic equation for EVII as a function of bad batch penalty that describes this relationship.
    *d.* What is the smallest value of the bad batch penalty that leads to a positive EVII?

# Case Study

## Sunbelt Software Services (A)

Jim Morrison, senior vice president of Sunbelt Software Services (SSS), was a professional manager who had been a senior marketing manager in a large computer company for over two decades before he started out on his own. SSS was a company employing a number of software engineers who developed a variety of products ranging from computer games to commercial mini and mainframe special purpose languages. The company had been started by three computer programmers who spent about five years developing and selling programs before they hired Jim. They hired Jim because as one of them said: "We have spent five years having fun, developed some fine products, and in doing so have also made a lot of money for some other people. It's time we got organized and planned our product development, financing, and particularly our marketing in an integrated manner."

Jim was focusing his attention at the moment on a development that had recently been made by one of the company's computer whizzes. The product could, if further developed, allow basically incompatible computers to communicate efficiently. A major problem in large multidivisional companies, as well as government agencies was that a variety of brands and types of computers were usually acquired, and direct communication between systems was often difficult or impossible. It was desirable in these organizations to be able to perform data base matches or merges of various types but was often very difficult. The new development was a very fast and flexible language base. The project was formally called ML (Meta Language), and the consensus view was that with about three years of work, there was a good chance of it being a real winner for SSS. Jim wanted to concentrate that work into a twelve-month period. His cost of capital was 15%.

Jim was responsible for deciding whether SSS should commit such a large share of their resources to the project. He needed to estimate the profitability of the project and sat down to think about price, sales volume, and development cost. He thought that he could get about $500,000 for the rights if he sold out to a large computer company right now.

Alternatively, if the company committed about $250,000 in development costs, a salable product would surely result.

The major source of uncertainty was sales volume. Jim didn't know how many sales would occur, particularly since the company had not developed or marketed this class of product before.

First Jim investigated the total market size. He estimated that the totality of customers was about 400, including 50 state government agencies, 50 major city administration offices, 200 corporations, and some universities and other institutions. Jim considered doing a survey of some of these potential customers. He thought first about calling a number of MIS (management information systems) executives and conducting a quick and dirty survey, or doing a series of marketing presentations in person. He decided to start with the survey. Jim telephoned people in 30 large organizations, who seemed likely customers. He got a mixed reaction: Some people were enthusiastic, while others said that they didn't have a problem that his product would address. Based on the data he collected, he did two things. First, he revised his total market to 300. Second, he assessed values for a variable he called "percent penetration." Given the set of 300 potential customers, the percent penetration variable represented the number of sales that would eventuate.

Since percent penetration was a key source of uncertainty, he assessed a probability distribution for it. To do this, he worked with the assumed price of $20,000 per customer for the system. His distribution was:

| *Percent Penetration (assumes price = $20,000 market size = 300)* | *Probability* |
|---|---|
| 0.1 | 0.2 |
| 0.2 | 0.2 |
| 0.3 | 0.3 |
| 0.4 | 0.2 |
| 0.5 | 0.1 |

Jim realized that he was very uncertain about how many sales he could achieve. This uncertainty was expressed in the probability distribution, which had a low degree of central tendency and a large range. In fact, he admitted to his colleagues that his uncertainty covered a factor of five (0.5/0.1) in terms of market penetration. He thought they would achieve anything from a minimum of 30 to a maximum of 150 sales.

Jim thought that it would be useful to do a more formal market test. He proposed to Jane Davidson, the product developer, that the two of them visit a few organizations and present their product concept in detail. To do this, some further work would be needed on the software, and Jane estimated the cost at $20,000. It was thought that about half of this cost would be a saving later on, if the product was fully developed. It would also cost an average of $3,000 for each presentation in travel and other associated costs for the two of them. Even with these costs, Jim suggested that they do five such presentations over a representative set of potential customers. He expected two main benefits from their survey. The first was information on market penetration that could be used to update his prior beliefs. The second was information on customer needs to drive the software design process.

## CASE QUESTION

How can the information that is collected be expected to lead to a better decision?

## Case Study

### Sunbelt Software Services (B)

After Jim Morrison and Jane Davidson had made five presentations of their new product to customers, they returned to the office to consider their findings. Two of the five potential customers had said they would buy the product as soon as it was available. A third had said that it was useful but priced too high, and that he would buy it for $10,000 but not $20,000.

Jim said that it was obvious that more sales could be achieved if the price was dropped. However, he insisted on a price of $20,000, adding that prices could be lowered later. Jim still had an offer of purchase for the product for $500,000 cash open to him. Indeed, the offeror contacted him regularly, and Jim thought he could negotiate the sale price up to $700,000, particularly if he used the information about the two customers he had identified.

## CASE QUESTION

How can decision analysis procedures be used to support this decision?

# CHAPTER TWELVE

# Implementation of Decision Analysis

## OUTLINE



## OBJECTIVES

After completing this chapter, you should be able to:

1. Describe some past implementations of decision analysis.
2. Discuss the strengths and weaknesses of decision analysis in a variety of implementation contexts.
3. Understand the power of decision analysis as a decision aid and its flexibility in terms of the variety of decision contexts described in the chapter.
4. Outline a set of implementation guidelines to improve the effectiveness of decision analysis.
5. Use these guidelines yourself, when implementing decision analysis.

## INTRODUCTION

The implementation of decision analysis is the *application of a set of formalized common sense methods to solve real problems*. We can conceive of implementation in a number of managerial contexts.

The first is the use of decision analysis to solve a single problem. This in itself can be a substantial task if the problem is complex, even if there is only one decision maker.

The second is the solving of a complex decision problem when a number of people participate in the decision-making process. In this second context, we must often consider a more complex decision-making process. In strategic decision problems and major public decisions, extra dimensions of complexity, such as multiple attributes, may add to the problem. Although decision analysis does not directly address the complexities for decision-maker groups, it can be used effectively as a medium of communication between participants in a group decision-making process. In this context the decision analysis structure provides a means for focusing the debate about a problem.

The third context is when decision analysis is used as a philosophy and decision-making aid for a series of decisions. In this context, decision analysis is often used to support the formulation and implementation of long-term corporate strategies. Ultimately, we can conceive of organizational designs specifically formed to facilitate managerial decision making. In such organizations, the decision analysis philosophy could be effectively embedded into an organization's culture.

In this chapter we will review and examine a number of published cases in which decision analysis was used to address managerial problems.

Finally, some implementation guidelines will be discussed. These highlight the strengths and limitations of decision analysis, with particular emphasis on how it can be implemented to best advantage.

## SYNOPSIS OF SOME DECISION ANALYSIS APPLICATIONS

### Case 1: Mexico City Airport[1]

The problem involving the Mexico City airport was characterized by a number of elements of complexity. The first was the political nature of the decision. Two previous studies had been done on behalf of the Mexican government, and these had resulted in very different recommendations. The

---

[1] The main analysts in this case were Ralph Keeney, Richard de Neufville, and Howard Raiffa. The case was reported by de Neufville and Keeney (1972), Keeney (1973) and Keeney and Raiffa (1976). Readers who wish to get a more in-depth account of this analysis are directed to those sources.

studies were done by different government departments. The third study (using decision analysis) had to contend with the political situation surrounding the first two studies.

The problem was complex because it could be defined in a number of different ways. It also involved a number of dimensions of value, a long (undefined) time horizon, and a large set of alternatives, as well as various sources of uncertainty. It required a total of 50 work-days of the consultants' time.

The problem was one that has faced many large cities. A major international airport, built over 30 years before, was near built-up areas and was operating at close to its maximum capacity. Growth in the demand for air travel had prompted the previous two studies. The decision analysis consultants were asked to consider airport development in relation to location, operating policy, and the timing of different airport developments. Keeney and Raiffa point out that the initial problem definition was not the same as the ultimate problem that they worked on! The consultants said:

> During the short three-month period (the summer of 1971) in which we were associated with the airport problem, it took on many forms. Much of the time was used in defining the problem, but it seemed to be more than this. There wasn't a single problem, but many interrelated problems: What is the best manner to provide acceptable air service for Mexico City? How can one contribute to a reconciliation of differences of judgment, "facts," and opinion of independent government agencies concerned with airport development, in order to improve quality of information available to the decision makers? What strategies for developing the airport facilities are best in light of the financial and political realities facing the government? The focus of the analysis shifted as the Secretaria de Obras Publicas became more sensitized to issues we felt might be important, as we became more familiar with the total environment in which this analysis was situated, and as segments of the study felt to be important were completed. (Keeney and Raiffa 1976, p. 347.)

The consultants produced two main models. The first was a static model. This model involved some limiting assumptions, and hence, was amenable to detailed analysis. The second modeling approach was to construct a dynamic model in which a number of elements which had previously been assumed as constant were allowed to change.

During the initial period of the analysis, the problem definition changed from a relatively narrow review of the past studies and alternatives to a broader problem statement: "How should the airport facilities of Mexico City be developed to assure adequate service for the region during the period from now to the year 2000?"

The problem was structured to involve the two main locations, Texcoco Airport (in Mexico City) and Zumpango. Air traffic was classified into four categories, namely, international, domestic, general, and military aviation. Over the defined time horizon, it was assumed that any of these categories of traffic could be moved from one site to another only at "windows" in time spaced 10 years apart. Even with these restrictions of four aircraft types and three periods where real action could be taken, there were a large number of possible strategies. Indeed, Keeney and Raiffa (1976, p. 443) report that 100 alternatives were evaluated.

The objectives were defined in terms of project cost, capacity provided, airport access time, system safety, social disruption, and noise pollution. These six criteria were defined in specific measurable terms. For example, access time was measured in minutes of travel time to airports weighted by numbers of travellers from each zone of the city.

For uncertain quantities such as "the extent of noise pollution," probability distributions were assessed. Information was gathered on factors such as access time.

A multiattribute utility function was assessed. Sensitivity analysis in terms of calculation of expected utilities was possible through the use of a computer program which the consultants set up. This program allowed the user to supply changes to base-case inputs and observe the expected utility outputs. This sensitivity analysis allowed for different utility function forms as well as parameter values. A short list of the best strategies was developed. All of the best 10 alternatives involved moving commercial air traffic to Zumpango, but major differences between these strategies existed with respect to the timing of moves and the actions that should be taken with military and general aviation.

A less abstract dynamic model was constructed that assumed an initial decision could be made in the year of the analysis (1971) followed by further decisions after about five years (depending on local political events).

The objectives incorporated into the dynamic model were much broader than those in the static model. They were: effectiveness, political consequences, externalities, and flexibility. Effectiveness summarized the six objectives of the static model. Political consequences were described as those affecting the president. Flexibility concerned the breadth of range of options that would be available in the future. Externalities covered budget consequences, support and infrastructure decisions, national prestige, and other factors.

Sources of uncertainty were defined in terms of events that could occur between the first decision stage (1971) and the second (1975). These included safety events, demand changes, technology changes, and social or political changes.

The next step in the analysis was to specifically define five alternatives for more detailed scrutiny. All of these involved some commitment to the new airport site, but not a major and rapid move that would quickly phase out the old site.

The analysis changed the policy of the relevant government department that had previously been in favor of a full-blown rapid development of the new site. Keeney and Raiffa claim that the decision analysis increased the "awareness of the relative influence of the different attributes and of the dynamic issues'' (Keeney and Raiffa 1976, p. 472). This is rather a modest statement, since in fact the decision analysis provided a great deal of insight about both the problem and its various possible solutions. The problem was complex in many ways, including uncertainty, conflicting objectives, a long time horizon and an overriding political environment of decision making. The decision analysis formalized common sense approach provided a legitimate, logical, and sound basis for decision making. It also provided a basis for communication and a substantial inference base regarding the alternative strategies. The analysts did not strongly recommend any single decision strategy. This responsibility was left to the decision maker, in this case, the president of Mexico. However, a sound decision analysis provides the underpinnings for a sound decision.

Perhaps the ultimate test of an analysis is to ask what would have been an alternative analysis/decision process, had decision analysis not been used. Many other cities have made similar decisions without using decision analysis. We believe that although some of these other cases many have had less complexity and more intuitively obvious solutions, others were also rather messy (like Mexico) and could have benefited from the *clarity* that the decision analysis process can provide. The case in Sydney, Australia, is an example, where a very long public investigation (a Royal Commission) was held and a great deal of money was spent on cost-benefit and other analyses. Although a decision was finally made in that instance, a study of the long process indicates that a decision analysis, conducted early in the piece, could have led to an effective early decision and a possible large cost saving.

This line of argument is, in a sense, hypothetical, for it is impossible, when a decision is implemented, to accurately measure the effectiveness of the analysis process in terms of the outcomes relative to ''what could have been.'' Remember also that sometimes, good decision strategies based on sound analysis lead to bad outcomes as a matter of chance, and vice versa. However, we must believe that while chance may play a substantial part, we do have some control over our fate in both corporate and public management systems (and as individuals). Thus the motivation for sound decision analysis and effective strategies is strong.

## Case 2: Fire Protection in Airports

David Shpilberg and Richard de Neufville (1975) have documented an interesting analysis regarding how to manage the possibility of fires in airports. They describe the problem as follows (1975, p. 134):

> Within certain legal and financial limitations, a planner has two basic choices in planning fire protection. First, there is the degree to which one invests in physical protection systems, such as sprinklers, fire stations, hydrants, and the like. Second, there is the choice of insurance coverage: full coverage, self-insurance, or something in between. All together, a large number of alternative protection strategies exist for any property.

The major source of uncertainty is of course the extent of fire damage, which may be zero in any given airport-year, or minor, or in extreme cases, catastrophic.

The analysts limited their decision tree to include only two levels of fire protection equipment and eight levels of insurance deductible. They considered the occurrence of a loss due to fire, and the extent of this loss should it occur, as separate sources of uncertainty. They used decision analysis to incorporate decisions about fire equipment purchase and insurance purchase and policy design in the light of uncertainty (of loss).

An interesting aspect of this case is the use of subsidiary models. Ten years of fire loss data was gathered for 21 airports, and a probability distribution was fitted to this data. These probability distributions were assessed separately for airports of various sizes, both with and without fixed fire protection.

A simplifying assumption was made in the analysis, namely that one fire at most can occur per airport per year. Given that the probability of loss due to a fire in a large airport is a little higher than one in four, this could be an assumption worth modifying in a more sophisticated decision analysis. The main source of these fires is from fuel spills and stored cargo.

To aid in a choice of a decision strategy, a decision tree model was constructed with decision nodes for the fire equipment decision and the deductible, and chance event nodes for loss occurrence and size of loss. Given only two strategies for equipment and eight deductible alternatives, along with the loss frequency and severity possibilities, the decision tree had about 100 endpoints.

In considering a risk management decision such as the airport fire decision, what sort of decision rule is appropriate for rollback of the decision tree? The one which we often may think of first is EMV; however, when large losses are possible, EMV does not usually represent our risk attitude. Most of us are not risk neutral when it comes to insurable risks. Also, there are only a very few kinds of insurance worth buying on an expected value basis because many insurance companies base their premiums on an "expected value plus loadings" basis.[2] Since an important element in this decision is the decision maker's nonneutral risk attitude, unidimensional utility functions need to be assessed.

It is important to realize that the insurance company that quotes a price may not be using the same claims distribution as the buyer. The analysis presented by Shpilberg and de Neufville was a single-stage decision and

---

[2] This is a somewhat simplified view. To make overall profits, insurance companies can make small underwriting losses in times when they are offset by substantial investment gains. Prices must also take into account the prevailing market conditions. Some insurers strive to set prices to generate premium income to fund investments, whereas others insist on breaking even or making profits on their underwriting activities. Also, prices in this industry move in a cyclical manner, and the time between premium collection and claim payout is very different across insurance accounts.

presumed a particular type of insurance. Further insights may be gained by considering not only yearly insurance coverage (with an assumed maximum of one claim) but rather a variety of insurance types. Ignoring the many types of fire protection facilities that could be used in combination with insurances, there are a variety of insurances that can be purchased. For example, evenbased insurance specifically covers a prespecified number of loss events. Given that it is available, a sequential decision problem exists because event-based insurance can be bought at any time. There is also the possibility of buying any number of event coverages at the starting point and of making a series of subsequent purchase decisions. If this insurance purchase problem includes the possibility of deductibles where the insured is responsible for a fixed amount of the loss, or coinsurance where the insured carries a prespecified percentage liability of the loss, a large number of strategies are possible.

Figure 12–1 shows the sort of structural decision tree described by Shpilberg and de Neufville. In contrast, Figure 12–2 is a more complex structure, requiring more data, but yielding insights over a broader range of alternatives. Fortunately, in implementing decision analysis we do not have to choose between decision tree models and suggest that one is right and all others are wrong. Indeed, Figures 12–1 and 12–2 complement each other in terms of the inferences they yield. Figure 12–1 provides a detailed static analysis that could be used to flesh out the relationships between insurance cost, deductible, and equipment cost/benefit. Figure 12–2 builds on this insight, providing a broader spectrum of decision strategies. It should be noted that insurance often becomes substantially more expensive after significant loss events.

Shpilberg and de Neufville concluded that decision analysis can help to structure complex problems so as to provide a better understanding of tradeoffs. Although they did not provide an analysis, their model structure could have been further developed to include possible nonmonetary consequences such as personal injury and death. They suggest the use of multiattribute utility analysis. It is likely that this more complex model would more realistically model both the airport operators and the public interest since

**FIGURE 12–1** Static Decision Model

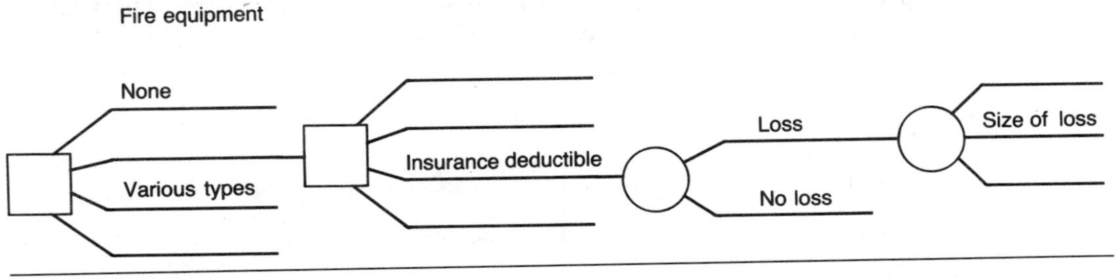

**FIGURE 12–2** Dynamic Decision Model

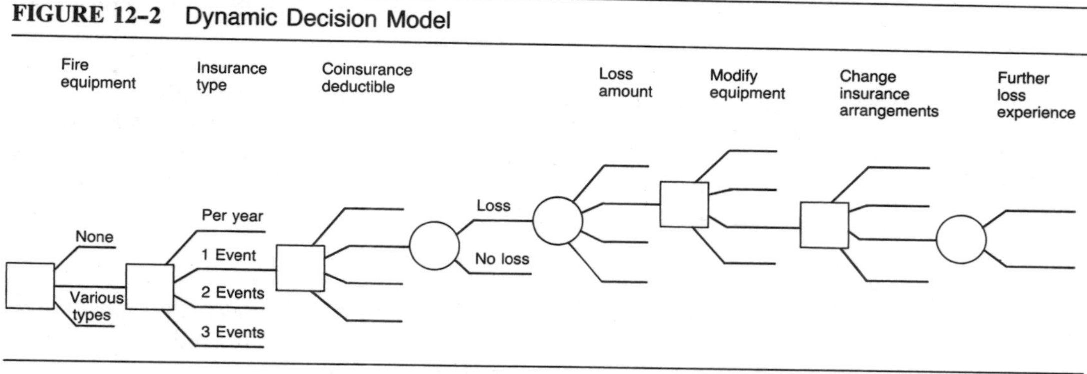


major fires could result in major losses to both life and property. Given current trends in our court systems to value lost lives in millions of dollars, the inclusion of this factor is important. It is possible that the use of a multiattribute function

$$\text{Utility} = u(\text{lives lost, injuries, property damage})$$

would point to a different decision strategy than the unidimensional function which considered only property damage. An alternative approach to formalizing a multiattribute utility function is to convert lives lost and injuries into monetary equivalents and use the unidimensional approach as an approximate method.

The problem which was analyzed in this case study involved a number of complexities. Two independent kinds of strategies (equipment and insurance) could be combined in a variety of ways. Loss frequency and severity were uncertain. Losses of both property and people would be possible in a fire. The decision analysis provided a procedure both for structuring the problem and also for decomposing it. Once the separate elements of preference (utility), loss distributions, equipment possibilities, and insurance alternatives and prices are investigated, the model acts as a synthesis device for putting it all together and observing the results. As usual, sensitivity would produce some powerful insights: not just sensitivity to the changing of quantifiable parameters but to changes in model structure as well.

## Case 3: Decision Analysis in a Capital Investment Problem

Hax and Wiig (1976) detail how decision analysis was used to address a capital investment problem. Their article is a very useful reference for students of decison analysis because it outlines a number of important elements in the context of generally applying decision analysis to capital investment problems. They describe a problem that had a few sources of uncertainty and a number of decision options. Hax and Wiig refer to the important decision elements of time, uncertainty, risk attitudes, and trade-offs across decision criteria.

An additional important element is the strategic context of the investment. The four elements listed above generally refer to the individual capital investment decisions as if they were made in isolation. Although it is not necessary for this to be so, many decision analyses of investment decisions do a very good job of considering the decision in isolation but a very poor job of relating the decision alternatives and payoffs to the other activities of the firm. We will return to discuss this issue further after reviewing the investment decision presented by Hax and Wiig.

The investment problem was for a mining company that needed to increase its reserves of ore. The government was soliciting bids for two large parcels of land that contained ore deposits. The mining company had the options of bidding alone or with a partner. They also were able to bid sequentially for the land parcels, with the outcome of the first being known before the second bid had to be submitted. They only required one of the land parcels. A partnership strategy would lower both the amount of risk and return.

As well as the bidding strategy, the company had production decisions to make regarding whether to produce alone or with a partner. Hax and Wiig (1976, p. 22) further describe the situation:

> If the bidding were successful, the government property would be developed. If the bid were to be won with a partner, the partnership should be extended to the exploitation phase. If the bidding were unsuccessful, a partnership would be required since the deposits currently owned by the firm were not enough to allow a large-scale exploitation.

They assumed away decisions regarding plant capacity, facility design, and process technology that would introduce even more complexity into the decision.

The decision tree representing this problem involves an initial decision node of bid alone or bid with partner, each of which can be matched to any bid price. See Figure 12–3. This diagram is a structural representation only and does not show all the nodes and branches. Figure 12–3 does show how events will develop, in that land parcel 1 must be bid on initially, and if it is lost, land parcel 2 will be bid on. Many sources of uncertainty exist. New facilities such as mines, manufacturing facilities, and hospitals have long lives, hence, long-term forecasts are an important aspect of the consideration of their feasibility. Future operating costs and prices can be treated as uncertain quantities. Although operating costs can sometimes be forecast with reasonable accuracy, prices are often highly variable over long terms. For example, world mineral and agricultural prices fell substantially during the mid-1980s. Who would have predicted during the oil crisis of the mid-1970s, when alternate energy supplies were so exhaustively researched, that the price of crude oil would be less than $10 per barrel in 1986? Remember

**FIGURE 12–3** A Capital Investment Decision Tree*

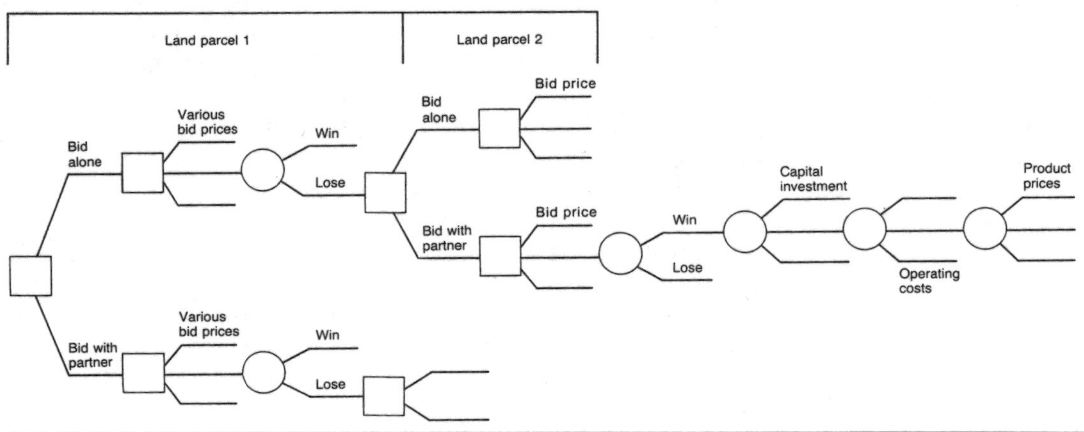


* Not all branches are shown on this structural representation.

Adapted from A. C. Hax and K. M. Wiig, "The Use of Decision Analysis in Capital Investment Problems, *Sloan Management Review*, Winter 1976, pp. 19–48.

that prices in 1974 were over $30 per barrel and that ten 1986 dollars are equivalent to less than four 1974 dollars. Despite the difficulty associated with predicting the future, these long-term uncertain elements need to be forecast. We can begin with a simple, deterministic model, in which we use point estimates. However, since one of the important things we wish to measure is how much uncertainty is associated with the project, probability distributions should be assessed for important uncertain quantities. The standard techniques for subjectively assessing probability distributions are discussed in Chapter 4.

The payoffs on the ends of the decision trees should normally be present values. These payoffs take into account all cash flows and appropriately convert them through discounting procedures to equivalent present values, usually as of the time of the analysis or of the investment. Many theories exist with respect to the calculation of discount rates for converting future and past cash flows into present values. Some decision makers estimate the opportunity cost of capital. Others consider their preference pattern across time for funds. Whether you consider alternative sources or uses of capital funds, we suggest that risk discounting should not be used. The uncertainties are accounted for explicitly in the probability distributions and should not be encapsulated in a risk-adjusted discount rate. This issue is discussed in Chapter 9 in the context of simulation modeling.

Figure 12–3 shows a decision tree that grows quite a large number of branches. The first very important point to note is that the decision analysis approach can formally encapsulate techniques such as NPV (net present value) and IRR (internal rate of return) as measures, using them as payoffs on branch endpoints. Our view is that methods that use risk-adjusted discount rates in NPV calculations do not yield comparably powerful insights for the decision maker. For example, the capital asset pricing theory (CAPM) provides a complex set of assumptions and a formula for determining a risk-adjusted cost of capital that can be used in NPV calculations. Its applicability seems limited to specific cases that closely fit the assumed probability distribution forms. Where NPVs are calculated with purely time relations and no risk adjusting, these values can usefully be input into decision analysis models such as Figure 12–3.

Where a decision tree of manageable size can be used to represent a problem, the first thing to do once all the data inputs are obtained is an expected value rollback. From Chapter 4 we know that the expected value rule is a very useful one, but it has a number of limitations. It can be used to screen out the worst alternatives. For example, a decision tree with approximately the complexity of Figure 12–3 may have 50 or more identifiable strategies. These can be reduced to a short list of the 10 or so that are substantially higher in expected value than the others.

As has been pointed out in a number of earlier chapters, it is then useful to "look behind" the expected values and plot risk profiles, which are probability distributions of the payoff measure (NPV or IRR). From these distributions we can often identify some strategies which are stochastically dominated (see Chapter 5) by others.

Given the expected value and risk profile information, the decision maker may often be able to make a choice, or at least use this information about the model to look again at the real-world problem in a more informed way. Further, at this stage it is common for managers to reflect on the analytic model and conduct some sensitivity analysis. See Chapter 8 for a detailed discussion.

If the decision tree is so large as to make using the expected value rule impractical, simulation can be used, which is a process of sampling from the branches. It is not difficult at all to conceive of decision trees, which pertain to capital investment problems, that are very large. Consider, for example, a problem with three decision variables and three sources of uncertainty. If each of these elements is represented by a node with five branches the number of endpoints on the structure is $5 \times 5 \times 5 \times 5 \times 5 \times 5 = 5^6 = 15{,}625$! Attempting an expected value rollback of a decison tree with over 15,000 endpoints would be tedious and time-consuming for a computer, and out of the question for a human being. Appropriate simulation procedures for such models are considered in detail in Chapter 9, and the role of computers in decision analysis is further considered in Chapters 14 and 15.

If decision makers need help in understanding or articulating their preferences in solving a capital investment problem, utility theory is a powerful prescriptive device. In the first instance it can be used to synthesize risk and return to a single measure. The riskiness expressed in probability distributions of NPV can be evaluated by a unidimensional utility function.

A second important use of utility theory is in situations where multiple objectives exist. For capital investment decisions, cash flows associated with the project may not be the only relevant dimension of value. Hax and Wiig suggest that in the land parcel case, both profit and market share were of value to the decision maker. From this we can imply that decision makers would not choose the option with maximum profit unless it also had maximum market share. They may be prepared to trade off some direct monetary profit for increases in market share. The methods outlined in Chapter 7 suggest how such trade-offs can be supported by utility models.

Finally, we return to the point mentioned earlier, of the evaluation of decisions in isolation versus consideration as part of a portfolio of investment projects. Figure 12–3 represents an investment in isolation of the other activities that the company is engaged in. Hax and Wiig's original analysis went a little further than this, because they noted that the availability of funds for this project was dependent upon another project within the company. They described a situation in which the degree of success of the other venture would force the company into a partnership to raise the money to develop the site and produce the refined ore product.

More generally, although a budget constraint may affect a project in a portfolio sense, this is only part of the picture. Sets of projects may or may not fit together well as a portfolio for a number of reasons. One is the timing of cash flows. Where projects are likely to have large cash inflows or outflows it may be useful to have matching sources and uses of funds within other projects. This is often not critical because of the buffer systems available. Money can be lent or borrowed from money markets to offset temporary surpluses or shortages. A more important factor is the degree of balance and risk spreading or diversification that can be achieved by having a portfolio of projects. Decision makers should consider how well a proposed project complements the existing set of investments and cash flow patterns. What sources of risk does it have in common with those in the existing portfolio? Although some criticisms were made earlier of the capital asset pricing model, we note that it can be used to yield considerable insight about how an individual project's value varies in relation to a common portfolio of projects, and ultimately to the value of an economy.

Figure 12–4 shows a process for evaluating individual projects in isolation. This view of a project allows for the detailed investigation of the project characteristics. However, once this is done, it is important to take a step back from the detail and look more broadly at the context of how the investment interacts with the set of others in the company. See Figure 12–5. For the strategic decision maker, the first (decision in isolation) analysis requires a purposeful "blindering" process, akin to putting a telephoto lens on a camera. It provides a zoom and a narrow focusing, yielding specific

**FIGURE 12–4** Decision Analysis Process for an Investment Considered in Isolation

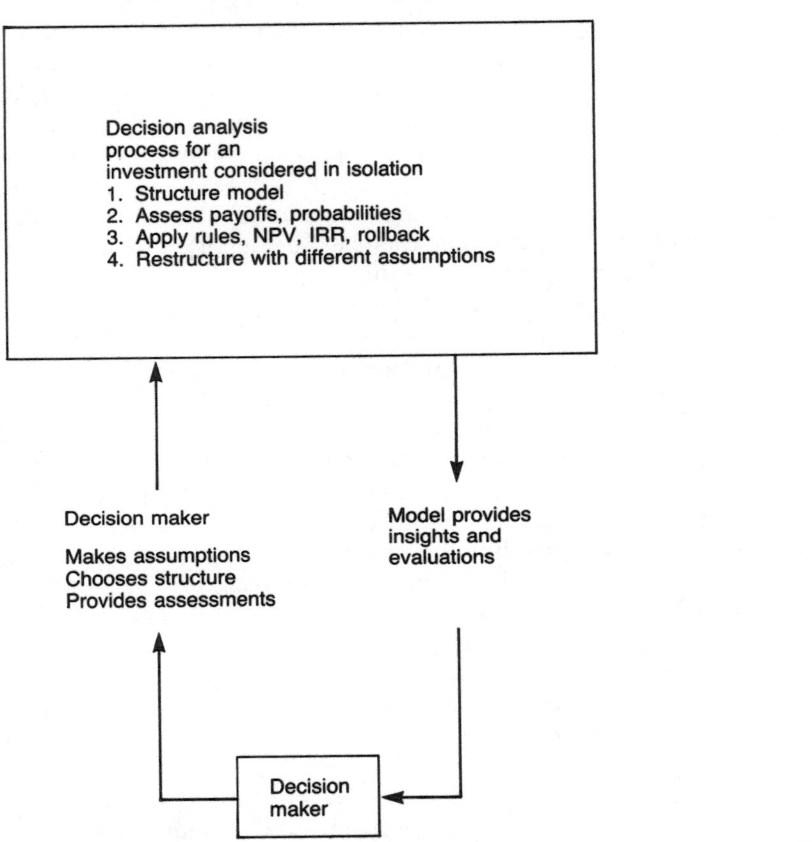


detail. The second analysis requires removing the blinders and viewing the broad spectrum of investments through a "wide angle lens."

In terms of the expected utility model that represents a strategy, we can write the condition for a decision strategy as:

$$\text{For project K: } EU(\text{Project K}) = \max_{\substack{\text{all } j \text{ in} \\ \text{project K}}} \left[ \sum_{\substack{\text{all } i \text{ for} \\ \text{a given } j \\ \text{in project K}}} [p_{ij} \times U(P_{ij})] \right]$$

where

$p_{ij}$ are the probabilities of outcome $i$ given strategy $j$
$P_{ij}$ is the payoff of outcome $i$ given strategy $j$

**FIGURE 12–5** Broader Investment Appraisal (including a detailed analysis of the new project in isolation and an investigation of its fit with the existing portfolio)

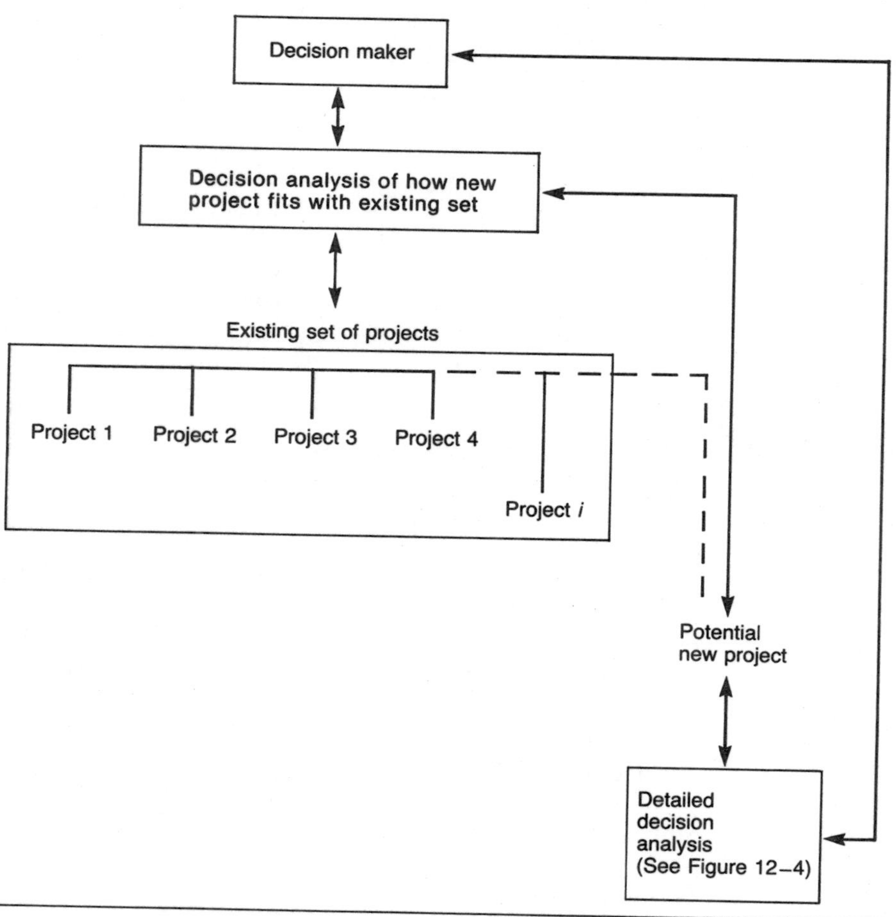


This is the kind of model which could be applied to Figure 12–3, in the determination of an optimal decision strategy.

The broader context involves a maximization of expected utility with respect to choosing the optimal *set* of investments, including their individual decision strategies. Hence the utility function can be the connecting link containing the preference information from the broader context that can be applied to individual new investments. Within the expected utility framework, apart from the case of constant risk aversion, decision strategies for new projects are affected by the value of others.

We wish to choose a Set $X$ where

$$X = \{X_1 \ldots X_k \ldots X_n\}$$

such that $X$ has the highest expected utility of all possible sets.

For a company with a given (existing) set of projects $X$, the analysis of a new project $X_{\text{new}}$ should involve evaluating the expression:

$$\begin{matrix}\text{Expected} \\ \text{utility}\end{matrix} (X + X_{\text{new}}) - \begin{matrix}\text{Expected} \\ \text{utility}\end{matrix} (X)$$

This expression may be approximated by the expected utility of $X_{\text{new}}$ in some instances, however, we suggest that, at the least, a qualitative consideration be made of the portfolio effects of a new project, and where appropriate, covariances of returns be assessed and integrated into a portfolio context analysis. This topic is discussed further in Chapter 9 in the context of risk analysis and in Chapter 14 in the case of strategic decision making in an insurance company.

## Case 4: An Oil Exploration Problem

J. Hosseini (1986) reported on a decision analysis implementation where the decision concerned whether or not to drill for oil in one of two possible locations. (This type of problem was one of the first classes of problem to be reported as a decision analysis application [Grayson 1966].) Hosseini describes the process of drilling for oil in a number of steps that can be modeled as a sequential set of decisions. The first process is investigation of possible sites (gathering geological information). Then, if preliminary indications are positive, a drilling permit must be obtained and the exact site must be chosen and developed.

The commitment to drill an exploratory hole in a new area, or a development well in an existing field, is not a single-stage decision process but one in which "go/no go" decisions can occur in a few stages. From each hole, samples of rock are retrieved and examined for structure, composition, and porosity. An optional drill-stem test measures two additional parameters of interest, fluid pressure, and oil/water ratio. The next major go/no go decision concerns the completion of the hole by introducing a steel pipe. Hosseini notes that this step can be as expensive as drilling the hole.

There are many sources of uncertainty in this process, both geological/technical and economic. The geological uncertainties relate to the existence and extent of recoverable oil and include consideration of geological structure, pressure, and rock composition. The sequential decision process involves a number of information collection steps. Uncertain economic factors relate to costs and revenues, specifically oil prices, capital, and operating costs. Hosseini also notes the existence of uncertainty about future changes in tax structures as impinging on these decisions.

In the particular instance cited by Hosseini, a decision had to be made between two sites. At one of these sites, some information was already available from previous holes drilled in the vicinity. The other site involved a more complex series of information-gathering steps. Figure 12–6 is a simplified representation of this type of problem.

Payoffs are determined as net present values (discounted net cash flows). Hosseini, acting as a decision analysis consultant, used an expected utility analysis for the relatively small operator who was his client. For a large operator, who might have many hundreds of wells, it may be reasonable to use an expected value criterion for the decision regarding each individual well. The law of large numbers is acting in such instances, meaning that over a large number of oil wells some will be winners and some losers, and the aggregate payoff will be close to the sum of the expected values.

Just as in the mining investment example (Case 3, earlier in this chapter), the decision can be initially analyzed as if it were in isolation, and then

**FIGURE 12–6** An Oil Exploration Decision

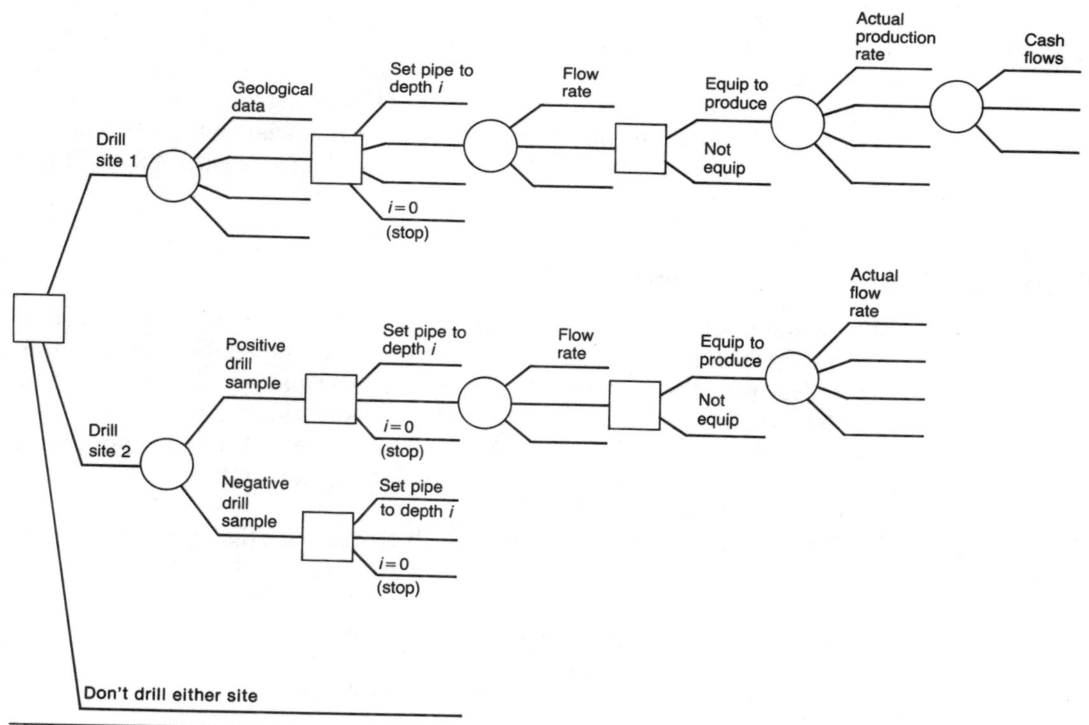

considered in the broader context of the company's strategy. It may, for example, be necessary to drill a hole for oil and gas even though the expected NPV is not favorable because of capacity requirements. A company that produces oil and gas for sale to a large customer such as the city of Chicago may have long-term contractual obligations that constrain its capacity strategy. In such circumstances, a well that does not have very desirable potential performance characteristics may have to be developed to help satisfy the market supply constraint. There are two ways of viewing this situation: The first is that the "decision in isolation" context provides limited first-pass insight, and a broader context must be subsequently considered. The second is that the effects of not meeting the contractual obligations, which may include financial penalties, should be included as cash flows in the analysis. No matter which approach is taken, the broad strategic aspects of major investment decisions should be adequately addressed, over and above the detailed appraisal of the particular project.

For the particular application of the oil drilling decision reported by Hosseini, the consultant reported that the decision analysis approach was very useful, practical, and usable, with the information derived from the analysis proving invaluable in capital allocation decisions. Further, it was reported that without decision analysis, it was almost impossible to make a choice based on consistent logical and analytical procedures. The other side of the coin, and perhaps the more important side, was how the client felt about the analysis. In this instance the client declared: "Decision tree analysis provided us with a systematic way of planning these decisions and a clearer insight into the numerous and varied financial outcomes that are possible given the choice of any one alternative" (Hosseini 1986, p. 78).

## Case 5: Decision Analysis in China

Pollock and Chen (1986) have written about a public policy decision faced by the government of Shanghai, China. The decision involved devising a strategy to deal with the high pollution levels of the Huangpu River.

This problem is an interesting one in itself, and a description of it follows. Pollock and Chen found that there were substantial differences between Chinese cultures and decision-making styles, and our Western style of decision analysis.

The problem involved a series of goals to decrease the water pollution in a specified section of the river. These goals were:

By 1984, restore the 1980 level of water quality.
By 1990, restore the 1963 level of water quality.
By 2000, restore the 1957 level of water quality.

Actions being considered included:

1. Expanding waste water removal systems that by-pass the river and take water straight to the Yangtze River and East China Sea. Waste water treatment facilities would be required.
2. Constructing household treatment plants in the city.
3. Tapping upstream (clean) water for use in the city.
4. Constructing canals to allow the use of Yangtze River water.

Pollock and Chen list the decision criteria as:

1. Cost of investment and system operation.
2. Health effects.
3. Industrial production.
4. Land use for plants, canals, etc.
5. Commercial fishing output.
6. Flood control capability.

The analysts found that the Chinese culture, which provided the context for this decision, included a decision-making style that was very different from the Western, decision analytic system. The differences permeated all aspects of the decision process, and we are forced to conclude that the decision analysis philosophy is unlikely to be acceptable in Eastern government systems.

The process of generating alternatives, screening out the poor and dominated options, and scrutinizing the feasible set in detail was not acceptable in this case. Instead, Pollock and Chen report on a process that seems incomplete and unclear according to our Western precepts. The Western analysts report on avoidance of confrontation and conflict and a reluctance to recognize the existence of competing alternatives. Option screening was also avoided.

The decision analysis approach is intended to explicitly recognize uncertainty, measure it, and take account of it when choosing a strategy. Pollock and Chen report on a decision-making style and process that operates in a planned society and economy, planned to the extent that uncertainty is assumed away. Uncertainty about cost, technology, effectiveness of actions in reducing pollution, implementation timing, benefits, and other elements were ignored.

The decision analysis approach separates decision nodes, where control is available to the decision maker, from chance events. It recognizes the "good decision, bad outcome" possibility. Pollock and Chen report that the cultural style ignores uncertainty and treats a bad outcome as meaning that a bad decision was made.

The assessment of preferences is difficult in Western organizations, simply because of the difficulty that many decision makers have of eliciting trade-offs, both between risk and return and across dimensions of value. However the experiences of many decision analysts have taught us that preference functions generally can be effectively represented as utility functions. Pollock and Chen concluded that in China, the development of a utility representation is nearly impossible. Pollock and Chen note that decision analysis is *reductionist*, *empirical*, *quantitative*, *and democratic*. How then can it be a useful decision support process for a culture and style that it does not properly fit?

This case provided some useful specific insights into a decision-making culture that is very different to that of the Western world. Further, it provides us with a very useful insight: that even a formalized common sense approach like decision analysis may not fit acceptably within all organizations. In terms of implementation, there are a number of American and European organizations that have particular and peculiar decision-making styles that may not be suited to decision analysis or perhaps any other form of formal analysis.

Although its popularity as an analytical decision support process is increasing, many organizations are not used to explicitly accounting for uncertainty, brainstorming for alternative actions, and expressing preferences "out loud." As a result, managers who are being introduced to decision analysis for the first time often need to be generally informed about it, and shown how it can be used to enhance their abilities and support their decision-making processes.

## Case 6: Decision Analysis Forecasting Models

Ulvila (1985) has reported in general how decision analysis can be used as a framework for forecasting. His process is applied to a problem faced by a division of Honeywell Inc. Ulvila points out that the distinctive feature of the decision analysis framework which makes it suitable for long-term forecasting is its ability to combine subjective assessments with data. Statistical extrapolation methods do not normally incorporate judgment in this way and are limited to assuming steady state: that is, that the underlying forces driving the time series will not change.

With respect to implementation, Ulvila (1985, p. 378) states:

> The approach taken was to build a composite forecast for the division by combining decision tree analyses of individual products. During the project, Honeywell's planners and managers worked closely with decision analysis consultants and, by the time that the initial project ended, Honeywell had acquired the skills needed to carry out the analyses in-house. This type of analysis is now a regular part of Honeywell's project evaluation, planning, and forecasting activity.

The problem was modeled in two phases. Separate decision trees were first used to develop forecasts for each product. Subsequently, a decision tree was used to examine various combinations of products.

The main decision tree for each single product modeled the likelihood of various projects being funded from outside sources through various stages of development. For the defence division of Honeywell, the outside source was the Department of Defense. The stages were defined as "advanced design," "full-scale engineering development," "low-rate initial product," and "full-scale production." Figure 12–7 shows an example of such a decision tree. The tree shows that the development process is multistage in nature and can be represented by a series of chance event nodes that represent the possiblility of the project continuing at each of these stages. Note that the decision maker may actually have some control over this, hence, an argument can be made for having decision nodes as well, to represent these stages.

The decision tree (Figure 12–7) incorporates the decision (by Honeywell) to proceed at each stage, given Department of Defense funding, into the chance event node. In other words, it was assumed that Honeywell would proceed at each stage, given funding. The final chance event at the end of each branch represents the uncertain quantity associated with financial performance of each project. The single-product decision tree was supported by a series of subsidiary trees that for each outcome set, modeled uncertain revenues, costs, profits, and measures of financial performance, such as net present value and internal rate of return. The inference produced by these subsidiary models can be included in summary form on the single-product decision tree.

Given that this form of analysis is carried out over a set of potential products, the problem of choosing an optimal subset of products to develop can also be effectively modeled using decision analysis. Figure 12–8 shows the interdependence between products $X$ and $Y$. Probabilities and payoffs need to account for technological commonality, customers needs, foreign sales, marketing, and investment commonalities. In Figure 12–8, no decision nodes are shown, even though choices are obviously available for the decision maker. This has the effect of keeping the complexity of the decision tree to a reasonable level while allowing a good degree of detail to be encapsulated in it. Decision nodes could, of course, be included where appropriate.

Ulvila has clearly demonstrated that decision analysis can be effectively used to model the portfolio effects of various project sets. The flexibility of the modeling method allows it to be used to set strategy initially, and then be used as a model for sequential action-uncertainty sets. For example, a set of three potential products ($A$, $B$, $C$) may require an initial strategy decision to develop a subset from the alternative actions:

$$A, B, C, A + B, A + C, B + C, A + B + C$$

**FIGURE 12–7** Single-Product Decision Tree

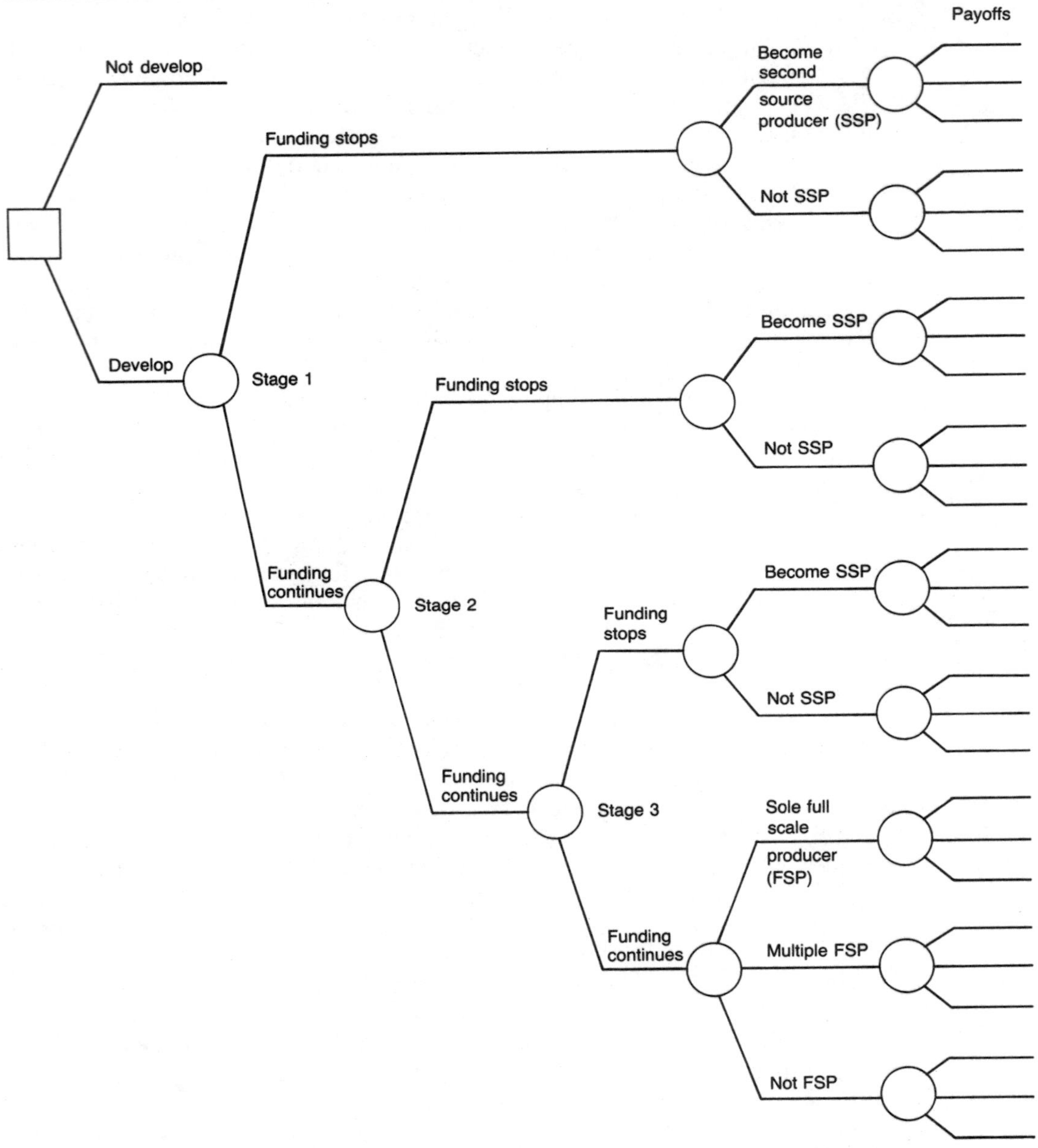


Note that the stages (1, 2, 3) represent critical steps in the development process, such as detailed design, engineering development and prototypes testing.

Decision tree adapted from J. W. Ulvila, "Decision Trees for Forecasting," *Journal of Forecasting* 4, no. 4, 1985, p. 379.

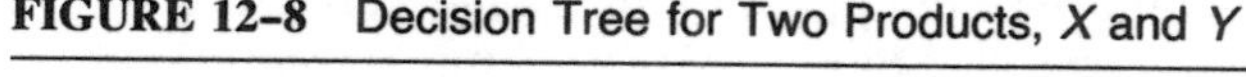


**FIGURE 12–8** Decision Tree for Two Products, *X* and *Y*

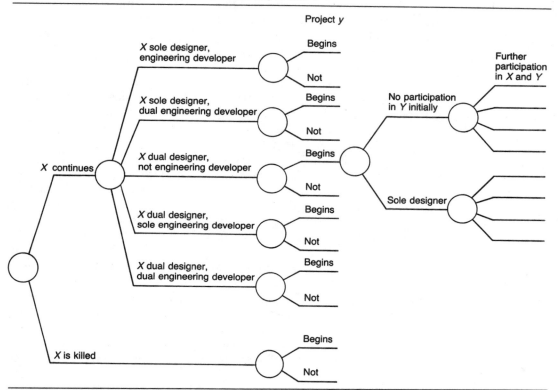

Decision tree adapted from J. W. Ulvila, "Decision Trees for Forecasting," *Journal of Forecasting* 4, no. 4, 1985, pp. 377–86.

Given the initial choice from these seven alternatives, a series of subsequent possibilities exist regarding funding and development of these products through various developmental stages. The full development of event trees for each strategy (decision trees comprising chance event nodes only) provides insight about possible financial futures. Ulvila demonstrates that two useful techniques can be employed to produce output data, as described in earlier chapters of this book. The first is rollback which provides expected value information. The second is "rollforward," which is the calculation of risk profile data. Ulvila points out that the decision tree approach produces probabilistic forecasts and also identifies points at which decisions can be made that affect sales and profits. This feature is not formally encompassed by traditional forecasting procedures.

Ulvila also makes a more general point about decision tree models that merits attention. He notes that in multistage decision analyses, decision nodes subsequent to the first require the choice of an action based on a rule such as EMV when the tree is rolled back. This procedure assumes that the initial model structure holds true in real time until that node is reached. In particular, it assumes that when subsequent decisions need to be made, only the information to the left of the decision node would be known, and only the prespecified actions will be available.

The dynamic nature of sequential decision processes often leads to new strategies becoming possible that are not envisaged during the initial analysis. In addition it is often possible to gather other information to that which was envisaged during the initial analysis. The result is that by the time a subsequent decision node is actually reached in the real-time unfolding of the problem, the assumed structure of the decision tree may no longer be a good representation. This time lag does not lessen the usefulness of decision analysis since we must do our best to account for possible futures when we initially construct a model, and recognize, of course, that we don't have perfect information in terms of the future. This imperfection means not only that we cannot predict the value of an uncertain quantity, but that we may be using a decision tree that will prove to be an imperfect structural representation. For example, initially, we may simply omit an important action alternative that comes to mind later.

We must, therefore, be prepared to restructure models as we learn more about the problem. Ulvila suggests that in some cases, this structural uncertainty and other modeling assumptions should lead us to represent action points on decision trees as chance event nodes rather than decision nodes. Through this method, details of uncertain quantities can be incorporated into probabilities of taking certain actions. In other words, instead of asking ourselves, "Would I choose action *A* or *B* if I were to arrive at this point on a decision tree?" we can ask, "What are the chances that I would choose action *A* rather than action *B* if I were to arrive at this point on a decision tree?" If a decision tree does not explicitly model all relevant sources of uncertainty, they can be included by modeling subsequent acts as events.

Ulvila points out that it is not necessary to treat the decision maker's actions as decision nodes. If there is uncertainty as to how to proceed, actions can be modeled using a chance event node. This conceptual development adds flexibility to the decision analysis method. To generalize the point even further, a decision node can be considered as a "special case" of a chance event node, whereby on a decision node we are prepared to assign probabilities of zero or one. If we are quite certain that events would proceed in a certain way at a node (presumably because we can exercise full control over them and are certain of how we would proceed), we can assign probabilities of zero and one and call the node a decision node. Otherwise, where the probabilities of branches emanating from a node are not all zero or one, it must be considered as a chance event.

## GENERAL IMPLEMENTATION ISSUES

This section contains a discussion of some general implementation issues and some guidelines to help the reader effectively use decision analysis in solving managerial problems. The implementation of decision analysis involves a variety of issues. Experienced decision analysts have learned that certain ways of applying decision analysis work better than others. Previously detailed reports by Howard, Keeney, Ulvila and Brown, and Moore and Thomas provide implementation limits and guidelines. Each of these decision analysts provides insight on implementing decision analysis, based on an intimate knowledge of the field and a good deal of experience.

Howard (1980, p. 22) suggests that:

> We must realize, however, that one of the arts of the decision analyst is the art of knowing how much and what kind of decision analysis to do. The degree of analysis can range from making simple lists to constructing giant interactive computer models. To be effective decision analysis must be "appropriate:" the extent of the analysis must be suitable to the means and ends of the decision maker. Thus simple problems of little consequence should receive very modest analysis, and complicated problems of great importance should be extensively studied. The question of whether the analysis was appropriate to the decision maker and his problem is one that should always be raised in judging effectiveness.

Howard's comment about analysis being appropriate is a very important one, no matter what kind of analysis is referred to. The level and nature of the analysis must fit the problem context. The Mexico City airport case required a substantial amount of time (fifty workdays of consultant time) because it was a high-stakes problem of considerable complexity.

In implementation terms, Howard's point about appropriateness can be related to another important guideline. Not only must the analysis be appropriate, it is also very important for all but the most trivial of decision analyses, that the decision maker be kept continually involved in the analysis process. Indeed, keeping the decision maker closely involved is usually the best way to ensure that the analysis is appropriate! This close involvement of the decision maker has a number of benefits. First, it lowers the chance of the analysts going off on an unrealistic tangent or wild goose chase of an analysis. They are less likely to make unreasonable assumptions if they stay close to the person who must actually deal with the decision problem. Second, we have emphasized a number of times in this book that the decision maker can learn much from the analysis process itself, and of course, this is only possible if the analyst and decision maker work closely as a team. Third, the decision analysis process is more likely to be a single-pass "draw the tree, crank the numbers, write the report" process if the analyst does it in isolation. This process form, as discussed in Chapter 8, is usually not very useful relative to the fuzzier process involving many passes through various phases of the analysis and sensitivity analysis-styled questioning of each step as the analysis proceeds.

The point of the exercise is to bring together the problem expertise (the decision maker) with the decision analysis process expertise (the consultant). It has generally been found that a much more effective solution occurs when this relationship involves frequent communication throughout the process. In addition, the decision maker is much more likely to accept the analysis and its results if he fully understands the process, and understanding can best occur when the decision maker has been an integral part of it. Decision analysis is not meant to be a black box, but rather the opposite (a transparent box), and as such should make continual use of the decision maker's familiarity with the problem.

Howard (1986) uses the word *transparent* in a different context. He suggests that decision analysis should be regarded as a vehicle for transforming opaque decision problems into transparent ones. In a similar vein, the analysis process itself should be transparent to the decision maker rather than opaque. The philosophy of decision analysis itself, as well as the insights that result from its application, is more likely to be accepted by managers who have been given a general appreciation of it.

Keeney makes a number of useful points about the art of successfully conducting a decision analysis and of implementing the resulting decision. First, we note his comments on checking consistency:

> It has been my experience that invariably there are inconsistencies in the initial assessments. In fact, this is one of the main reasons for the procedure, because once inconsistencies are identified, decision makers can alter their responses to reach consistency and better reflect their basic values. Furthermore, decision makers usually feel better after having straightened out their value structure in their own mind. Thus, it is essential to ask questions in different ways and to carefully reiterate through aspects of the assessment procedure until a consistent representation of the decision maker's values is achieved. (Keeney 1982, p. 816.)

Keeney (1982, p. 819) also lends his strong support to the previously expressed view that the analyst and the owner of the decision problem must be a team:

> Decision analysts obtain clearly articulated (often quantitative) information about the problem structure, possible impact, parameters for a model, and value judgments. In addition to the complexity of the problem substance, obtaining such information can be difficult because:
>
> 1. The information may be sensitive.
> 2. The natural procedures to process the information in one's mind often result in biased judgments.
> 3. The respondent may have vested interest in misrepresenting information.
>
> The decision analyst should be aware of any of these three possibilities.

In a recent article, Fischhoff (1980) draws an analogy between decision analysis and psychotherapy. Decision analysts try to formalize the thinking and feelings that the decision maker wishes to use on the problem. By clarifying and even quantifying the process, these thoughts and feelings are potentially opened for review by others (e.g., bosses, regulators, courts). In any assessment process, one should take the time and use any available devices to establish a rapport with the respondent and to make him or her feel comfortable. I always point out that the reason for the analysis is that the problems are too difficult to informally analyze consistently. Hence, a major purpose of these processes is to identify inconsistencies in the unassisted thinking of the respondent. It is critical to assure these individuals that they will have a first right to adequately review your work. Furthermore, they should have the option of changing their responses. This helps to ensure that no misrepresentation of their judgments occurs. What this boils down to is the need to build trust between the decision analyst and all respondents working on a decision problem. The establishment of this trust is the responsibility of the decision analyst.

Moore and Thomas (1976, p. 225) give some useful guidelines on getting started in using decision analysis. These include a number of points that are highlighted in the previous case studies and discussion of this chapter, but are worthy of reemphasis. They include the following:

1. Ensure that everyone concerned understands the process and philosophy. Education can relatively easily transform the black box into a transparent one.
2. Correctly define the problem. On this point, Keeney notes that problems are only rarely correctly defined at the beginning of the analysis. Hence the need exists for a process that involves much recycling. (Refer back to Figure 8–2.)
3. Try a number of model structures. As has been pointed out earlier, there is not a correct model in any absolute sense, however there are relatively good and relatively bad ones. Keeney points out that a pitfall of decision analysis can occur when people assume it solves the problem. It cannot solve the problem because it is ultimately a mere modeling procedure. As such it involves assumptions and abstractions, and usually addresses only part of the problem. Regarding this guideline of "try different model structures," we note that better models can be defined as those that produce more useful inferences. Hence, it is important at all stages to keep the goal in mind: *better decision making*. To this purpose, it is often useful to define the objectives of solving the problem early in the process, to ensure that the process is itself goal directed.
4. Moore and Thomas suggest that training in the concepts of probability should precede the assessment phase. Evidence has shown that training improves calibration.
5. Use all available information, and provide the decision maker with it when asking for probability assessments. Of course, as outlined in

Chapter 11, information that is not at hand can sometimes be obtained, and generally should be obtained when its value exceeds its cost.

6. Moore and Thomas (1976, p. 225) suggest that those getting started in the use of decision analysis should "stick to EMV as the decision criterion on the first analysis." Howard (1986) has indicated that the use of the expected utility rule is not necessary for the majority of decision analyses. This reflects both the power and usefulness of the EMV rule and the nature of the problems that confront managers that are addressable through decision analysis. Many problems that managers (especially private sector managers) must solve are unidimensional (that is, they concern money only) and can be addressed using EMV. However the really important problems, which can be classed as strategic and demand more attention that others, are usually the more complex, fuzzy, ill-structured messes that may require multiple criteria utility analysis to represent conflicting objectives. We reemphasize that the analysis must be appropriate in its design and depth to the nature of the problem.

## SUMMARY

Decision analysis is both an art and a science. No matter how well it is developed as a philosophy and decision-supporting framework, its usefulness is a very strong function of how well it is implemented. To summarize, good implementation practice really is a matter of common sense. We draw on implementation guidelines given by Joshi (1980) in the broader context of management science to provide a set of rules applicable to decision analysis. First, Joshi suggests that the analyst must identify and communicate with the decision maker: "Get the decision maker involved—make it his problem, his model, his solution" (Joshi 1980, p. 516).

The second important point is to choose the correct problem. Joshi cites the case of a new office building. Many complaints were received about the waiting time for elevators in the lobby. The complaints stopped after a TV was installed nearby. What was the problem, and was it properly solved? Alternative solutions involved changing the elevator control systems or installing another elevator. Either would have been considerably more costly than the TV set.

Joshi's next point is to use the right data. In decision analysis we can extend this to mean not only being careful about gathering data and assessments from experts, but also to do so with a consideration of the expected cost and benefit of the information.

Joshi recommends an explicit statement of assumptions. This certainly does make the process of doing sensitivity analysis a clearer task. (See

Chapter 8.) It also assists in the process of recognizing that the model addresses only a part of the problem.

Another guideline is to use the simplest model possible that addresses the problem. Indeed, a generally useful strategy is to start simple and sequentially build up only the complexity that is necessary.

Finally, when presenting an analysis and results, it is important to let the decision maker choose the real action to solve his real problem. By all means present him with a short list of alternative decision strategies and their evaluation analysis, but try to remain separate from the final choice. Let the decision maker use the insights produced by the decision analysis, and switch from the decomposition thinking mode back to the holistic, intuitive mode before choosing an action plan.

## FURTHER READING

Readers who wish more detail on any of the implementation cases summarized in this chapter should, of course, refer to the original sources as cited. Apart from the cases described in this chapter and elsewhere in this book, there are many other interesting applications that have been published, both in books and journals.

Two interesting books are by Howard and Matheson (1983) and editors Kaufman and Thomas (1977). Of the many journals that publish research articles in decision and management sciences, those which quite regularly contain decision analysis applications are *Interfaces, Decision Sciences*, and the *European Journal of Operational Research*. Interesting articles have also appeared in general management journals, notably the *Harvard Business Review* and the *Sloan Management Review*. Readers who wish to read further on decision analysis applications and implementation will find that looking through past issues of these journals can be most interesting, particularly in the cases of *Interfaces* and *Decision Sciences*. Conference proceedings of the American Institute of Decision Sciences, renamed the Decision Science Institute, also contain a variety of insightful application papers.

## REFERENCES

DE NEUFVILLE, R., and R. L. KEENEY. 1972. "Use of Decision Analysis in Airport Development for Mexico City. In *Analysis of Public Systems*, eds. A. W. DRAKE; R. L. KEENEY, and P. M. MORSE. Cambridge, Mass.: MIT Press.

FISCHOFF, B. 1980. "Clinical Decision Analysis." *Operations Research* 28, pp. 28-43.

GRAYSON, C. J. 1960. *Decisions Under Uncertainty, Drilling Decisions by Oil and Gas Operators*. Division of Research, Harvard Business School.

Hax, A. C., and K. M. Wiig. 1976. "The Use of Decision Analysis in Capital Investment Problems." *Sloan Management Review* Winter, pp. 19–48.

Hosseini, J. 1986. Decision Analysis and Its Application in the Choice Between Two Wildcat Oil Ventures." *Interfaces* 16, no. 2 (March-April), pp. 75–78.

Howard, R. A. 1980. "An Assessment of Decision Analysis." *Operations Research* 28, pp. 4–27.

Howard, R. A., and J. E. Matheson. 1983. *The Principles and Applications of Decision Analysis*. Menlo Park, Calif.: Strategic Decisions Group.

Howard, R. A. 1986. "An Appreciation of Decision Analysis." Paper presented at the TIMS/ORSA meeting, Los Angeles.

Joshi, M. V. 1980. *Management Science*. Belmont, Calif.: Duxbury Press.

Kaufman, G. J., and H. Thomas, eds. 1977. *Modern Decision Analysis*. New York.: Penguin Books.

Keeney, R. L. 1973. "A Decision Analysis with Multiple Objectives: The Mexico City Airport." *Bell Journal of Economics and Management Science* 4, pp. 101–17.

________. 1982. "Decision Analysis: An Overview." *Operations Research* 30, no. 5, p. 803.

Keeney, R. L., and H. Raiffa. 1976. *Decisions with Multiple Objectives*. New York: John Wiley & Sons.

Moore, P. G., and H. Thomas. 1976. *The Anatomy of Decisions*. New York: Penguin Books.

Pollock, S. M., and K. Chen. 1986. "Strive to Conquer the Black Stink: Decision Analysis in the People's Republic of China." *Interfaces* 16, no. 2, pp. 31–37.

Shpilberg, D., and R. de Neufville. 1975. "Use of Decision Analysis for Optimizing Choices of Fire Protection and Insurance: An Airport Study." *Journal of Risk and Insurance*, March, pp. 133–49.

Ulvila, J. W. 1985. "Decision Trees for Forecasting." *Journal of Forecasting* 4, no. 4, pp. 377–86.

Ulvila, J. W., and R. V. Brown. 1982. "Decision Analysis Comes of Age." *Harvard Business Review*, September-October, pp. 130–41.

## PROBLEMS

1. Describe the strengths and weaknesses of decision analysis. What are its pitfalls.
2. Debate the issue: "Decision analysis, even when it is poorly implemented, must be better than no analysis."
3. What is the point of doing a decision analysis for a problem that is basically political in nature? Consider the Mexico City airport decision, and comment on how a decision analysis can support a decision such as this.

4. Experienced decision analysts often suggest trying a few model structures. How can we tell which one is correct?
5. In both the Mexico City airport and Fire Protection cases described in this chapter, static and dynamic models were constructed. For each case, explain how these models complemented each other.
6. Why is it useful sometimes to consider an investment decision in isolation and also separately model and evaluate it as part of a portfolio?
7. Can decision analysis be used to model a variety of investment decisions, or is it limited to oil exploration and mining ventures? Is it an alternative procedure to the popular payback, net present value (NPV), and rate of return techniques? If so, how could we choose the most appropriate one? If not, what might be the relationship between decision analysis and these other measures?
8. You have been called in (as a management consultant) to help a company decide on whether a new machine (costing $5 million) should be purchased for its production process. Describe a process that you could go through to identify the alternatives and sources of uncertainty, followed by an evaluation of various strategies.
9. List a set of guidelines that you would prescribe as generally important for decision analysis implementation.
10. Describe two different organizations with which you are familiar, one which would facilitate the use of decision analysis and one which would not. Compare and contrast them.
11. As a new MBA graduate faced with a complex problem, what would you attempt to do in using decision analysis for the first time within an organization? Would you focus on using a decision tree as a model of the problem? Would you introduce unidimensional or multidimensional expected utility?
12. This is a role-playing exercise to be done by two people. One person should assume the role of a decision analysis consultant or a person who has taken a substantive course in decision analysis. The second person should assume the role of an experienced manager who has been successful in making a series of important decisions on behalf of his organization using seat-of-the-pants intuitive methods. A complex problem faces the company in which the stakes are very high, and the decision analysis consultant has been called in to give an outside opinion and provide expertise to the committee of senior executives who must deal with the problem. The manager has, in the past, preferred not to formalize his decision processes and is not well versed in analytic methods. Begin the process by having the manager describe the strategic problem that involves an organizational restructuring and a new direction for the business. The manager should invent a particular scenario for this. The decision analysis expert has the task of formalizing the common

sense approach, and introducing decision analytic methods to the process.

13. Consider Figure 12–2 which has three decision nodes followed by two chance event nodes, followed by two further decision nodes and a final chance event node. If this decision tree were to be drawn out in full to show all branches and nodes, it would be very large. How can such a decision tree be managed and used as a decision aid to model a problem effectively and produce insight for the decision maker? How much larger would a decision tree be that covered three or four or five years of operation, rather than Figure 12–2 which covers a two-year time horizon.
14. To what extent is decision analysis *culture specific*? Given that one of the cases in this chapter suggests that decision analysis is unlikely to be acceptable in China, can we conclude that decision analysis generally is more suited to some cultures rather than others? Applying this line of reasoning to corporate cultures, would you expect decision analysis to be more effective and better accepted in some corporations than others, due to the variety of inherent corporate cultures that exists?

---

## Case Study

### Mirassou Vineyards (A)[1]

In 1966, serious questions were being raised in the Mirassou family about what action should be taken regarding the vineyard's planting strategy, particularly in view of the recently proposed UpRight Harvester mechanical grape picker. The company was in the middle of establishing its own brand label wines in the market and shifting production from the rapidly developing and crowded San Jose area to more remote growing areas. Was the UpRight Harvester just another complication at this time in Mirassou's development, or was this the ideal moment to innovate new planting, growing, and harvesting methods?

---

[1] Mirrasou Vineyards (A) 9-673-105



This case was prepared by Daryl D. Wyckoff as the basis for class discussion rather than to illustrate either effective or ineffective handling of an administrative situation. Reprinted by permission of the Harvard Business School.

## Background of the California Wine Industry

In the mid-1960s, the California wine industry experienced an unprecedented boom; the popularity of wine in the United States soared. Per capita wine consumption per adult approached 2.5 gallons, and was expected to reach 3.4 gallons by 1980.[2] This growing demand, an expanding "drinking-age" population, and a growing disposable income among young Americans were all favorable trends.

At that time, the California wine industry accounted for approximately 74% of all wines consumed in the United States, compared to approximately 12% that was imported. The balance came from other states, including New York.

Wines are generally classified into three categories: table, dessert, and sparkling. Table and sparkling wines are legally classified as those containing not more than 14% alcohol, while dessert wines are those containing more than 14% alcohol.

Table wines are further divided into *varietal* and *generic* wines. Varietal table wines are named for the principal grapes used in their production (i.e., Cabernet Sauvignon, Zinfandel, Barbera, Chenin Blanc, and others). To bear a varietal name, by federal law, a wine must derive at least 51% of its volume from the grape for which it is named and have the aroma and flavor of that grape. Generic wines are typically named for various wine-producing districts in Europe because they possess the general characteristic of wines from those areas (i.e., Burgundy, Chablis, Bordeaux [or claret], or others).

Table wines are characteristically lighter and drier (not sweet) to the taste than dessert or sparkling wines, mostly due to the higher acidity and lower sugar content of the grapes from which they are made. Dessert wines, and the subcategory called appetizer wines, have a stronger and sweeter taste because of higher sugar content and, in some cases, the addition of fruit flavoring. Sparkling wines can be either sweet or dry, but are characterized by the effervescent nature resulting from carbonation.

It was estimated that shipments of table wine to United States markets would rise from 78.6 million gallons in 1966 to approximately 374.0 million gallons in 1980.[3] Dessert wines would fall from 103.5 million gallons in 1966 to approximately 53.6 million gallons in 1980, while sparkling wines would jump from 9 million gallons to 63.7 million gallons in the same period.

## Geographic Considerations

Certain grapes are closely identified with particular growing regions, according to John W. Larsen of Wells Fargo Bank, N.A.

The basic criterion for classification of the growing regions is a warm to temperate climate from April 1 through October 31. The California coastal region—especially the North Coast—is the coolest area where grapes are grown; its climate and soil conditions result in the longer maturing, low-yield grapes that go into fine wines. The soil and hotter climate of the Central Valley and southern California produce higher yield, faster maturing grapes for raisin, table, and standard wine usage.

---

[2] This description draws heavily from studies made by G. Michael Oberst and John W. Larsen, Wells Fargo Bank, N.A., San Francisco, California.

[3] G. Michael Oberst, Wells Fargo Bank, N.A.

Grapes for the sweet dessert wines are also generally found in central and southern California.

Some grapes do best in particular regions. For example, the Cabernet Sauvignon, Pinot Noir, and Pinot Chardonnay grapes can be grown most successfully in parts of the North Coast. Likewise, Malvasia Bianca and Tinta Madeira, used for making dessert wines, do their best in the warmer areas. There are, of course, many exceptions to these generalities. Due to the limited acreage available and generally lower fertility in coastal regions, an attempt has been made over the years to develop grapes that have all the wine-making characteristics of a coastal varietal, but which will grow in the Valley and other hotter areas. An outstanding example of this is the Ruby Cabernet developed by the University of California at Davis. This grape is a cross between the Carignane and the Cabernet Sauvignon and it does well in hot regions.

In addition to the fact that growing region has a distinct bearing on the most suitable type of grape to plant, it affects price as well. Zinfandel is a grape that does relatively well in all of California's growing regions. For example, Zinfandels grown in the San Joaquin Valley brought $135 per ton, while those grown in the North Coast brought $325 per ton. The difference relates to sugar-acid balance and other measures of quality. Connoisseurs feel that a Zinfandel produced in the cooler area is notably superior in taste and aging characteristics. The market value notes this difference.

The unique thing about the North Coast, which distinguishes it from any other wine-producing area in the United States, is the fact that it can produce wines, properly aged, that have the same characteristics as the finer wines produced in Bordeaux and other areas of France. Even to the experienced palate, the taste difference between the two is barely noticeable. The climate and soil of a growing region clearly have a bearing on suitable varietals as well as on price. The grower should be knowledgeable about the characteristics and limitations of the region under consideration.

## Summary of the Wine Making Process

The annual grape harvest usually begins in September and ends in late October. Following the harvest the grapes are crushed in a stainless steel crush stemmer. The free running juice is drained off, and the remaining pomace (skins, etc.) is gently pressed for additional juice. The juice is then pumped into stainless steel fermentation tanks. The pomace is discarded in making white wines. For red wines, it is pumped into the fermentation tank with the juice to provide some of the body and color of the wines.

To control the heat generated by the natural fermentation process, and to protect the delicacy and flavor of the wine, the juice is fermented under controlled temperature conditions. Red wines are allowed to ferment at a higher temperature than white wines to assist in the extraction of color from the skins that float to the top of the tank and form a "cap."

The fermented wine, either red or white, is then transferred between tanks several times so that the natural protein and other solid matter settles. It is then rough filtered and stored in tanks.

White wines which benefit from wood aging are often stored in 60-gallon French or American oak barrels; others are left in stainless steel tanks. Red wines are typically aged and stored in wood barrels. Once the wine maker tastes the wine and determines whether it has matured, it is bottled and corked for additional aging in glass, with wine breathing a very small amount of air through the cork. Following the initial aging, the wine is ready for sale.

From crush to shipment of bottled wine, white wines typically require one to two years, while red wines require an additonal one to three years. Even at that point, many consumers buy these "young wines" to be laid down for additional bottle aging.

## Five Generations of Wine Making

The members of the Mirassou family are very proud of their long tradition of wine making in California. In 1848, Louis Pellier came to California from France in what proved to be an unfruitful search for gold. After a brief time, he turned to planting grape vines and soon sent for fine cuttings from his native Bordeaux, France. The vines thrived, and in 1854 Louis's brother, Pierre, returned to France for more vines. On the long journey back to California, the ship was becalmed and the fresh water supply was exhausted. The resourceful Pierre Pellier made a deal with the ship's captain to buy his cargo of potatoes. Pierre inserted the cuttings in the moist potatoes he had slit open, thus saving the vines. Descendants of these vines still grow in the family vineyards. Henrietta Pellier, Pierre's daughter, married Pierre Mirassou, who was to become head of the family vineyards. Pierre Mirassou, Jr., eventually assumed control of the vineyard and was responsible for keeping the property and vines healthy during prohibition when many California vineyards and wineries were closed.

Pierre Mirassou's grandsons, Norbert and Edmund, continued to operate the vineyard, even in the face of the "encroachment of civilization" in the rapidly growing San Jose and Santa Clara county areas. Their business was traditionally involved in bulk production of high grade wines. The wine was produced at the winery in San Jose (at the lower end of the San Francisco Bay) and shipped in casks or barrels or rail tank cars to other wineries which processed it for distribution under their own labels.

The fifth generation (Edmund's sons: Daniel, Peter, and James—along with Norbert's son, Steve, and son-in-law, Don Alexander) decided that the Mirassou family should take a higher profile. In 1966, the members of the fifth generation launched a satellite business of bottling and retailing fine wines[4] under the Mirassou family label.

Mirassou Sales, the name taken by the fifth generation's venture, was a major break with family tradition. Mirassou Sales, if successful, was most likely to be a competitor with the other wineries that bought most of the production of Mirassou Vineyards, the operation of the fourth generation. The Mirassous were warned by several executives in the wine industry that such a venture was almost certainly doomed to failure because of the tremendous costs associated with promoting and establishing their own market.

---

[4] Wines were generally grouped as to retail price: up to $1.50 per bottle were "standard"; $1.50 to $3.00 per bottle were "premium"; over $3.00 per bottle were "fine."

**FIGURE A** Location of Vineyards

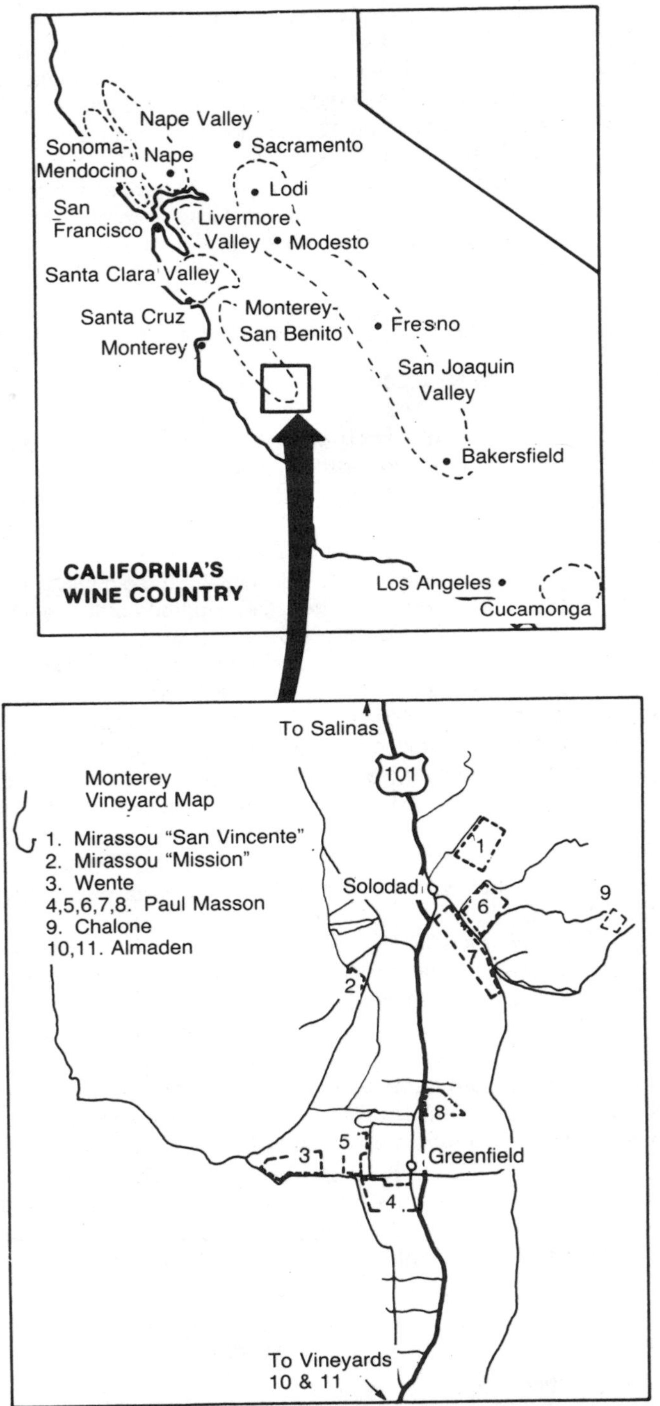


SOURCE: Reprinted by permission from *Time*; copyright Time, Inc.

In 1966, the first bottles of wine under the Mirassou label were sold at locations other than the vineyard. In that year, only 3% of the Mirassou production was devoted to this venture.

## "Subdivisionitis"

The Mirassous began to suffer from what E. A. Mirassou called "subdivisionitis." The expansion of housing developments and higher taxes in the increasingly populated areas in the San Francisco Bay area made opportunity costs on land so high that several vineyards began to search for new growing areas. In the early 1960s, Mirassou began planting in the Monterey area of central California, a distance of approximately 100 miles from its San Jose winery (see *Figure A* and *Exhibit 1*). In 1966, during this period of transition, the Mirassou family was approached with a novel proposition—a proposal for a mechanized grape harvester that was being developed by the UpRight Harvester Company.

## Economics of Grape and Wine Production

One of the most important aspects of developing a vineyard is the long period from the time of planting vines until full production is reached. During the first two years, production is zero. The yield of the vine slowly increases from the third through the fifth years; however, vines have a productive life of 35 to 40 years once they are established.

In addition to the costs of owning land (such as taxes, interest payments if financed, and opportunity losses) the costs of developing a vineyard are largely associated with culture and harvesting costs. Cultural costs are those associated with establishing and tending the vineyard. The typical cultural costs for a large acreage vineyard development have been studied in detail by the Wells Fargo Bank of California (see *Exhibit 2*).

The cost of land depends on the location and often is not related to the suitability of the land for growing grapes. More typically, land prices are set by alternative land uses.

**EXHIBIT 1** Acreage under Cultivation

| | *Santa Clara County* | | | *Monterey County* | | |
|---|---|---|---|---|---|---|
| *Year* | *Uncultivated* | *Planted Developing** | *Producing* | *Uncultivated* | *Planted Developing** | *Producing* |
| 1960 | 0 | 0 | 300 | 0 | 0 | 0 |
| 1961 | 0 | 0 | 300 | 300 | 0 | 0 |
| 1962 | 0 | 0 | 300 | 640 | 300 | 0 |
| 1963 | 0 | 0 | 300 | 640 | 300 | 0 |
| 1964 | 0 | 0 | 300 | 640 | 300 | 0 |
| 1965 | 0 | 0 | 300 | 640 | 300 | 0 |
| 1966 | 0 | 0 | 300 | 640 | 0 | 300 |

* Approximately three years are required before grape production, and five years are required to develop a fully producing vine after it is planted.

**EXHIBIT 2** Typical Cultural and Harvest Costs and Yields per Acre

| | Year | | | | |
|---|---|---|---|---|---|
| | *1* | *2* | *3* | *4* | *5 on* |
| *Cultural Costs* | | | | | |
| Management | $ 50 | $ 50 | $ 50 | $ 50 | $ 50 |
| String, wire, twine | 0 | 30 | 2 | 2 | 2 |
| Train vines | 0 | 55 | 12 | 12 | 12 |
| Prune and tie | 0 | 5 | 25 | 25 | 25 |
| Control of small animals, deer, birds | 8 | 2 | 10 | 10 | 10 |
| Water and labor | 18 | 20 | 12 | 12 | 12 |
| Miscellaneous labor | 5 | 8 | 15 | 15 | 15 |
| Repairs | 15 | 15 | 15 | 15 | 15 |
| County taxes | 20 | 21 | 21 | 21 | 21 |
| Tillage | 15 | 12 | 12 | 12 | 12 |
| Fertilizer and labor | 0 | 12 | 14 | 14 | 14 |
| Pest and disease control | 7 | 8 | 17 | 17 | 17 |
| Survey and planting | 20 | 2 | 0 | 0 | 0 |
| Rootings preparation | 20 | 2 | 0 | 0 | 0 |
| Scatter and drive stakes | 0 | 30 | 0 | 0 | 0 |
| Stakes | 0 | 200 | 0 | 0 | 0 |
| Land preparation | 200 | 0 | 0 | 0 | 0 |
| Pipeline work | 110 | 0 | 0 | 0 | 0 |
| Total cost per acre | $488 | $472 | $205 | $205 | $205 |
| *Harvesting Costs* | | | | | |
| Labor (hand) | 0 | 0 | 66 | 124 | 195 |
| Total cost per acre | $488 | $472 | $271 | $329 | $400 |
| *Typical Tonnage per Acre** | | | | | |
| Barbera grapes (approx. $95 per ton revenue)† | 0 | 0 | 4 | 7 | 10 |
| Chenin Blanc grapes (approx. $100 per ton revenue)† | 0 | 0 | 5 | 10 | 12 |
| Ruby Cabernet grapes (approx. $110 per ton revenue)† | 0 | 0 | 4 | 8 | 10 |

* Yield based on hand picking and normal cultural practices

† Prices subject to considerable fluctuation depending on popularity of wines produced from the grape

SOURCE: Wells Fargo Bank, N.A.

**EXHIBIT 3** Typical Trade Markup on a Case of Wine (Chenin Blanc)

| | *Case of 12 Fifths* |
|---|---|
| Juice | $ 0.72 |
| Winery expenses | 11.53 |
| Profit to winery (target) | 1.50 |
| Cost to primary distributor | 13.75 |
| Markup of primary distributor | 2.75 |
| Cost to wholesaler | 16.50 |
| Markup of wholesaler | 5.50 |
| Cost to retailer | 22.00 |
| Markup of retailer | 11.00 |
| Retail price | $33.00 |

Approximately 180 gallons of wine are produced from a ton of grapes. Of these 180 gallons, approximately 150 gallons are free-run juice of top quality. The remainder is pressed juice which is sold or used for lesser quality wines or is further fermented for stock for distilled spirits (i.e., brandy). The price buildup for a typical wine is shown in *Exhibit 3*.

Mirassou Vineyards has traditionally sold wine in bulk to other wineries for blending purposes and to supplement limited production at prices lower than that typically received from primary distributors. Mirassou Sales (the Mirassou fifth generation's venture) serves as the primary distributor.

## The UpRight Harvester

The potential of mechanically picking wine grapes has intrigued producers for many years. The level of interest in mechanical picking has been closely correlated with the increased militancy of the farm laborers, particularly under the organizational efforts of Caesar Chavez. Many growers became increasingly convinced that a time would come when it would be impossible to depend on any substantial pool of unskilled itinerant laborers to work as harvesters during the vintage season. It was described by one grower as "the type of work which most people don't want to do anyway, particularly in the hot, dry, and dusty California valleys where grapes grow best. It is not very romantic work, crawling on your knees under the vines." This situation was also reflected in the increased pay demanded by pickers. From 1956 to 1966, the pay per box of grapes increased from $0.15 to $0.38. This resulted in a harvesting cost of approximately $18 per ton of grapes. Additionally, some growers were experiencing lower yields of grapes picked per acre because of the unwillingness of workers to pick fruit that was difficult to reach.

The first effort to pick grapes mechanically was developed in the 1950s. It was called a "sickle-bar cutter" and opened and closed like scissors. It was to cut off long stems of carefully trained grapevine branches. Unfortunately, it was found that it was difficult to train the branches in the necessary configuration, and the device was never commercially successful.

The next mechanical picking method that was attempted in the early 1960s involved suction. It was hoped that ripe grapes could be sucked off the vine with a vacuum hose. In theory, the ripe grapes would separate from the stems without the leaves. Several different attempts in the United States and Germany demonstrated that it was possible to pick substantially more grapes than were picked from the vines by workers. There was also the problem, however, of sucking many of the leaves off the vines as well. Even the most successful of these devices that could separate the grapes and leaves tended to ingest some leaf particles. The chlorophyll from these particles gave the resulting wine a taste like alfalfa. The inability of the developers to correct this situation led to abandonment of the project by the mid-1960s. Some very disgruntled growers lost valuable vines to these lusty experimental machines.

Viticulturists doing research at the University of California proposed a new growing method using a wire trellis (see *Figure B*). Their idea was that the fruit-bearing vines should hang upon horizontally spaced wires separated three feet apart. Wallace Johnson—an inventor, engineer, and small grape grower—set out to develop a new approach to mechanical grape picking in conjunction with the trellis-growing method.

**FIGURE B** Trellised Grape Vines

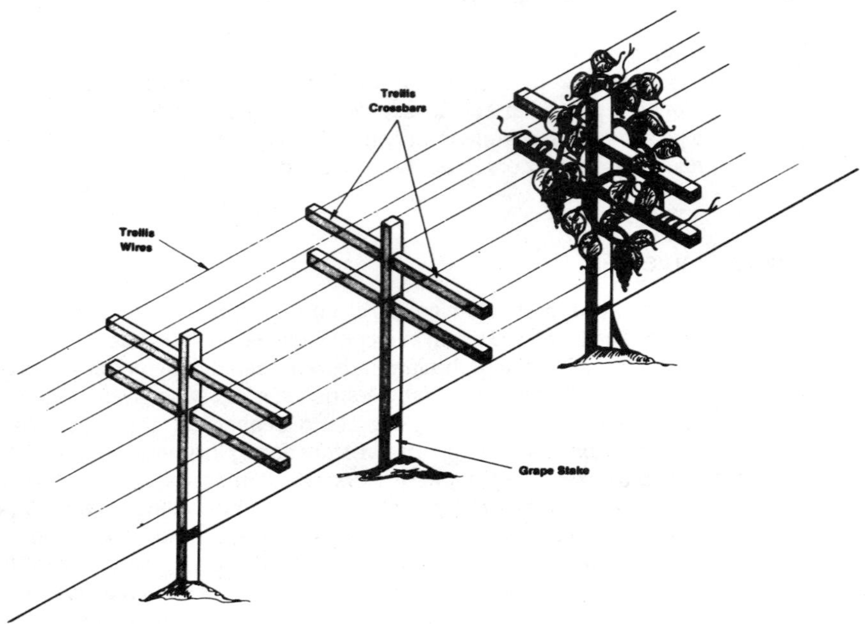


Schematic of trellised vines

The device, which he named the UpRight Harvester, straddled the rows of vines (see *Figure C*). A series of finger-like batons mounted within the harvester would strike the wires. As the harvester progressed along the row, the vertical impact of the batons upward on the wires would gently dislodge the ripe grapes from the stems. These grapes would then fall on catching conveyors.

One man drove the harvester straddling the row of vines. The falling grapes were then caught and carried by the catching conveyors into conventional field boxes. As a field box was filled it was dropped at the end of a row, and an additional field box would be attached. This entire operation could be handled by one man, but with two men it was a relatively easy task.

Johnson approached the members of the Mirassou family in 1966 with a proposal for testing the UpRight Harvester in their fields. For several reasons he had been frustrated by earlier attempts at securing a meaningful test. First, most growers were well aware of the failures of other mechanical harvesters. Second, mature producing grape vines were valuable assets that were easily damaged. Growers were concerned about stories of other devices that sucked all the leaves off the vines or made random hacks at the vines with large sickles. Third, even if the grapes could be picked, would the results be suitable for production of superior wine?

**FIGURE B** *(concluded)*

View of conventional, untrellised vines

Perhaps the most difficult problem in getting any larger grower to go along with the scheme was the planting requirement. It was necessary for the grower to plant the vines in a unique pattern to allow enough room for the machine to drive down the rows astraddle the vines and to produce the correct shaking motion of the branches. This essentially halved the number of vines per acre. It was also unclear if the machine would actually be able to pick all varieties of grapes equally well. The structure of the vine and the actual connection of the grape to the stem were different for different varieties.

Based on Johnson's estimates, the $42,000 machine could pick an acre of grapes in approximately one hour. Since the UpRight Harvester would only remove the ripe grapes on each pass, however, it would be necessary to make two passes over a field during the period that the grapes matured. The harvest that resulted from the new method would be considerably more thorough. Johnson estimated that the harvested fruit might increase 25% to 35%. He also pointed out that only ripe fruit would be harvested, whereas hand pickers tended to pick any fruit, mature or not, since filled field boxes were the basis of pay.

The penalty of the increased space between vines was perhaps not as great as it might first appear. Based on the work of researchers at the University of California at

**FIGURE C** UpRight Mechanical Grape Harvester

A closeup view showing harvester shaking vines and collecting grapes. Conveyors and V-shaped grape catchers can be seen at the base of the vines.

Davis, there was some evidence that such spacing might increase the yield by as much as 50% per vine, when combined with a suggested pruning method.

## Proposed Field Experiments

It was proposed to the Mirassou family members that their new vineyards be planted and developed in accord with the planting requirements that would accommodate the UpRight Harvester. If they were not prepared to take this step immediately, however, they might consider an alternative of preparing a limited test of the machine before such a major step. If a field was planted in one configuration, it could not be changed to the other without completely replanting because of the planting pattern.

Specifically, the plan being considered was to postpone any additional vineyard development until the demonstration could be made. The demonstration would require planting five rows each of 10 varieties of grapes to accommodate the harvester. This would represent the equivalent of a total of 20 acres.

**FIGURE C** *(concluded)*

View of harvester straddling trellised vines in field.

This plan had the advantage of minimizing the risk to Mirassou of the cost of the vines' destruction in these fields, and the opportunity loss associated with a two-year delay in developing the new fields. The possible gain was the opportunity to have the first newly planted vineyards that could be mechanically picked.

In attempting to make the decision, the Mirassou family was faced with the question of what the cost of the experiments would be to them and what the potential rewards would be if they proved successful. How would they measure the success of the experiment? And given this measure, at what level of success would they go ahead to fully adopt the new growing technology?

CHAPTER THIRTEEN

# Behavioral Aspects of Decision Analysis

## OUTLINE



## OBJECTIVES

After completing this chapter, you should be able to:

1. Discuss the concept of biases and inconsistencies in human decision processes.
2. Debate the issue of prescriptive versus description notions within the concept of decision analysis.
3. Outline some criticisms of decision analysis.
4. Outline some of the commonly observed biases in subjective probability assessment.
5. Describe the difficulties that can be associated with assessing utility functions.

## INTRODUCTION

This chapter is an examination of the behavioral aspects of decision analysis, including the psychological aspects of the way that people actually make decisions. When people are not aided by analysis and logic systems, their decision processes often suffer from inconsistencies in logic and biases in the subjective assessment of data. It is very important for students and practitioners of decision analysis to be aware of these biases and inconsistencies! An understanding of these issues can provide decision analysts and decision makers with the means to reduce the biases and effects of capricious decision behavior. This chapter focuses on documenting a number of commonly observed biases and inconsistencies that have been observed in various research studies. In interpreting and distilling these research results, our emphasis is mainly on the behavioral aspects of the assessment phase of decision analysis. This includes both the assessment of probabilities and utilities. In each of these tasks, a number of commonly observed biases exist that may cause the data that managers supply as inputs to decision models to be poor in quality, unless corrective actions are taken.

Two main conclusions can be drawn from the strong evidence, much of which is summarized in this chapter, that unaided decision processes are often poor in quality. The first point is that given our low levels of natural ability in making decisions under uncertainty and coping with complexity, the need for rational, logical frameworks such as decision analysis is strong. Second, *within* the structural framework of decision analysis, we should ensure that the inputs to such models are of high quality, with biases minimized, so that the inferences and insights produced are effective and useful.

Decision analysis has been extensively described in earlier chapters as a paradigm to suggest how decisions should be made. It is both a decision-making framework and a set of procedures and techniques. In this sense its primary focus is *prescriptive,* since its intent is to *aid* decision makers and *support* decision processes. It is *not normative* since it does not present an ideal theory in the classical sense. Further, it is *not descriptive,* since it generally does not seek to explain real decision processes.

In stating that an approach is prescriptive in nature, it is not sufficient merely to state its axioms and demonstrate its power. We must critically examine the implementation record of decision analysis. This will provide a feel for its general usefulness and also highlight its specific strengths and weaknesses.

To enhance our understanding of decision making under uncertainty, we must examine how people *do* make decisions and compare this evidence with how people *should* make decisions (as prescribed by decision analysis). The results of such comparisons provide fascinating insights on what aspects of decision-making processes can best be supported by decision analysis.

Behavioral decision theory is concerned with describing and understanding how decisions are made in practice and how decision-aiding approaches can contribute toward improving both process and results. Two major sources of information are available:

*a.* Case study reports which are descriptions of applications. Usually these report on successful applications although they may highlight difficulties that were encountered on the way.

*b.* Concentrated studies of particular aspects of decision making. These studies are often termed *laboratory* studies because in many instances they report on situations where subjects are placed in hypothetical situations and asked to make decisions or assessments. Both sources of information are valuable, however laboratory studies are somewhat more useful for our purposes of showing up implementation weaknesses and difficulties.

To summarize, even though decision analysis is a prescriptive model, it is extremely important for the practitioner to understand its empirical validity in detail. Hence, we must study the kinds of biases and unexplained elements that occur in real decision processes. Like most worthwhile things, decision analysis has some difficulties, however an understanding of these difficulties leads to the knowledge of how to use decision analysis most effectively.

The assessment difficulties do not diminish the power of decision analysis supported decisions relative to unaided decision processes. The difficulties are not in the logic and structure of the decision analysis framework itself, but in the inability of human decision makers to behave consistently in dealing with it. Indeed, the human biases are probably better dealt with within the logical framework of decision analysis than in an unstructured environment. As Coyle (1972, p. 83) has written, in the context of defining decision analysis, it is "the art of giving bad answers to questions to which otherwise worse answers would be given."

## THE PITFALLS AND LIMITATIONS OF DECISION ANALYSIS

The decision analysis approach has been widely studied, and as a result has been both praised and criticized. The strengths of decision analysis are generally its ability to structurally represent complex problems, provide clarity about those problems, and explicitly account for uncertainty (through subjective probability) and preferences (through utility) in an integrative manner. The criticisms have focused on many aspects, including:

*a.* The assumption of an individual decision maker which is considered unrealistic in many organizational settings.

*b*. Difficulties and biases in obtaining meaningful subjective probabilities.

*c*. Apparent violations of the expected utility axioms by decision makers.

It is very important for potential practitioners to have a good understanding of each of these issues, hence, each one is treated in detail below.

## THE ASSUMPTION OF A SINGLE DECISION MAKER

Although decision analysis, in its axioms, does not explicitly assume an individual decision maker, it does assume alternative generation, quantification, comparison transitivity, and substitution. (See the axioms in the appendix to Chapter 6.) These axioms do appear to be sensible and plausible when applied to individual decision makers in the sense that most of us would generally like to abide by them! When decisions are made by groups of individuals, it is possible for conflicts to exist among group members that can make the decision analysis paradigm more difficult to implement.

Group decision making is widespread in our society: in government, private sector, and even family decision making. Members of a group may disagree on many aspects of a decision, including which set of alternatives and chance events are appropriate and which probabilities and whose preference structure should be used.

*The decision analysis paradigm does not address the issue of how group conflicts regarding any decision element can be resolved.* Decision analysis assumes that structure, probabilities, and preferences can be supplied by the decision maker, whether the decision maker is an individual or a group.

Indeed, none of the well-known decision science and management science approaches deal effectively with group decision making. For example, linear programming requires the definition of variables, objective function coefficients, and constraints, and certainly does not address the issue of whether these model inputs were made by an individual or a committee.

Although decision analysis does not explicitly provide mechanisms for resolving group conflicts, practical experience has demonstrated to many decision analysts that it *actually is* a valuable decision-aiding approach in group decision-making situations. If the members of a group can agree to use decision analysis, it can become a *forum for communication*. Many group discussions naturally become sidetracked, unfocused, and unstructured, and if it is considered desirable, a committee chairman can use decision analysis to introduce a degree of structure to the process. It is often useful, when two or more people are in disagreement over problem structure, to have each of them draw a decision tree and discuss the differences between the trees. Once a consensus or an "agreement to disagree" is achieved, discussion can be focused around one or more structures regarding probabilities and consequence payoffs. The decision analysis approach can assist in achieving clarity about the real issues of contention.

It is possible that group members really disagree about a quantitative measure such as a probability. This fact can be identified and debated through the use of the decision analysis approach. The Delphi technique may be useful here. It involves the elicitation of opinions and judgments from individual group members (while they are kept physically apart) followed by an information exchange and another round of information elicitation. This cyclic process of information elicitation and information sharing can continue for as many cycles as is judged to be productive. Delphi methods are believed to improve forecasting accuracy and are regularly used in the private sector for forecasting and decision-making purposes.[1]

With respect to preferences and preference function structures, decision analysis does not offer a formal mechanism for aggregating (or averaging in some manner) the utility functions of individuals in a group. For example, if a decision is to be made between a very risky and a less risky option, what can be done if significant differences exist between group members? The answer to this question depends upon whose utility function is appropriate. For example, let us consider two situations:

*a.* Where two partners each own half of a business.
*b.* A large organization (government or corporate).

In case *a,* if the utility functions are quite close (perhaps small differences in degree of risk aversion exists) a natural strategy would be to compromise and form a group or corporate utility function, which is some average of the two individual functions. Figure 13–1 shows such a possible average. On the other hand, if the risk attitudes of the partners are so different that their utility functions are far apart, neither may be happy with a compromise. In such a case, the question is whether this partnership can flourish if decisions under uncertainty play an important role in it. Of the two partners shown in Figure 13–2, one would often be wishing to take risks even if the odds were not in his favor, and the other partner is highly risk averse. If their innate risk attitudes are so far apart, then neither decision analysis or any other decision aid will help them to see eye to eye with respect to risk.

In case *b* where the managers or elected officials of an organization must make decisions under uncertainty, they may all have different personal preferences and risk attitudes. Managers theoretically make decisions on behalf of the corporate owners, and elected officials and government employees theoretically make decisions on behalf of electors. Consequently, it

[1] See B. M. Bass, (1983).

**FIGURE 13–1** Averaging Two Utility Functions

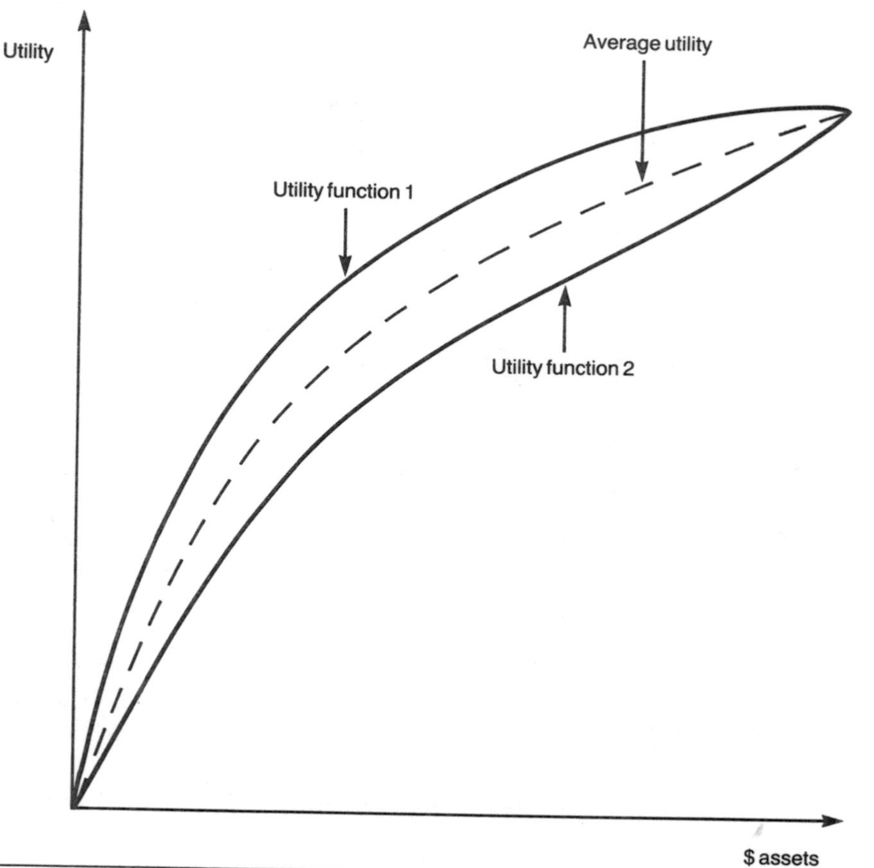


can be argued that the appropriate preference function is that of owners or electors. For very good practical reasons, corporate owners employ professional managers, and constituents elect government representatives. Although management and ownership may be separate, the members of a corporate committee should make decisions using the preference function of the owners.[2]

Of course, many practical reasons cause approximations to be made in this process. For publicly owned companies, it is impossible to continuously

[2] Note the prescriptive notion, "should."

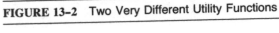

**FIGURE 13–2** Two Very Different Utility Functions

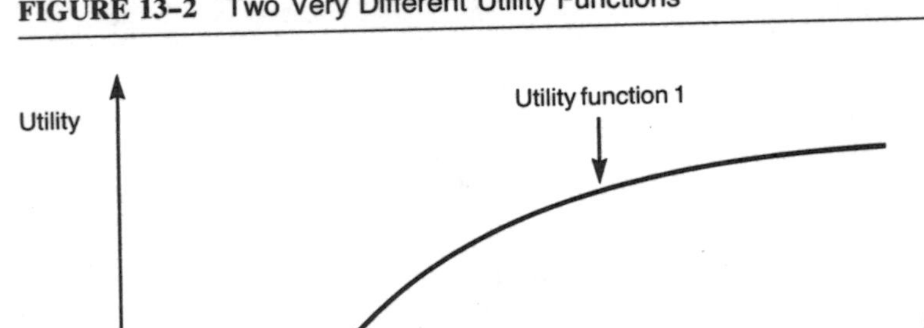

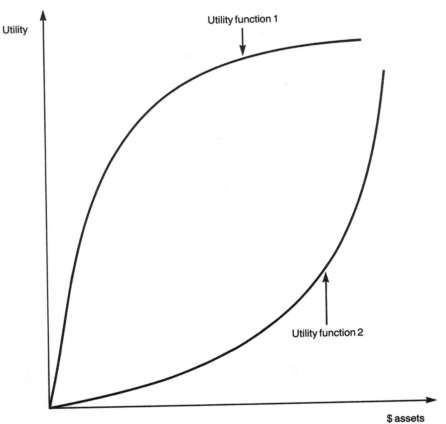


collect and aggregate the preference functions of the constantly changing set of owners. Owners can express their preferences at annual stockholders meetings and through processes of trading their stock.

Howard (1980) refutes the criticism of decision analysis, with respect to its inability to model group decision processes. He claims that the group decision-making issue has no room in decision analysis because all decisions are essentially individual ones. He argues convincingly that group decisions are sets of individual decisions where the individuals are acting under an agreement (for example, principal-agent).

# BIASES IN PROBABILITY ASSESSMENT

When decision makers confront uncertain quantities relevant to their decision, it is often useful for them to subjectively assess a set of probabilities to represent that uncertainty. Unfortunately, most of us do not naturally assess probabilities very accurately, that is, we are poorly calibrated. Training exercises can help us to become better calibrated, however only a few of us have the opportunity to be trained. It is important for decision analysts and decision makers to understand the nature of natural in-built biases that human information processors possess in order to help understand both our own biases and those of other people.

Many decisions involve decision makers in information collection processes. For example, a company president may ask his vice president of marketing to assess a probability distribution for the market share of a proposed new product. Similarly, the president may ask the production division for a probability distribution of product development and production costs. Indeed, one of the strengths of decision analysis is its ability to incorporate information from multiple sources into the model. Information about uncertainty needs to be communicated and used in models, hence we need both an *accurate language* (probability) and a *high quality of probability assessment skills*.

## The Need to Quantify

When two or more people are discussing the likelihood of an event, they may use words or numerical probabilities to describe their uncertainty. It has been found that in this context, *words* can mean very different things to different people. Evidence of this comes from a study conducted by Moore and Thomas (1975) who asked 250 executives to rank 10 expressions in decreasing order of likelihood. The expressions were: probable, hoped, expected, quite certain, possible, doubtful, unlikely, not unreasonable that, not certain, likely.

Table 13–1 shows the resulting average rankings obtained as well as the range. Expressions were ranked from 1 (highest likelihood) to 10 (lowest likelihood).

Note that the *range* of ranks for most of the expressions was high. A further experiment with a subset of the executives showed that they were not even individually consistent over time with the same expressions!

In other experiments, subjects have been asked to assign numerical probabilities to similar expressions, and large variances were observed (for most expressions) across subjects. The conclusion is that *words are clearly a very imprecise mechanism for communication about uncertain quantities.* Many *word* expressions of uncertainty mean different things to different

**TABLE 13-1** Ranking of Expressions*

| *Expression* | *Average Rank* | *Range of Ranks* |
|---|---|---|
| Quite certain | 1.1 | 1–3 |
| Expected | 2.95 | 1–6 |
| Likely | 3.85 | 2–7 |
| Probable | 4.25 | 2–9 |
| Not unreasonable that | 4.65 | 3–7 |
| Possible | 6.10 | 3–9 |
| Hoped | 7.15 | 3–10 |
| Not certain | 7.80 | 3–10 |
| Doubtful | 8.60 | 7–10 |
| Unlikely | 8.75 | 3–10 |

* Ranking of 1 = highest likelihood; ranking of 10 = lowest likelihood.

people. Most analysts would agree that there is much less ambiguity in a number (such as a probability of 0.9) than in an expression (such as "likely"). The probability can be interpreted as a relative frequency (that is, 9 times out of 10 in the long run), or as a degree of belief. *The number scale is naturally ordered whereas the word scale is not.* Numbers can be used in objective functions or decision criteria (such as EMV or expected utility) whereas words generally cannot.

Given these strong justifications for quantifying our subjective beliefs about the likelihoods of an uncertain quantity, it is important that we understand natural heuristics and possible biases that can be present both in ourselves and in the people with whom we communicate. As stated earlier, knowledge and training can help to reduce biases somewhat (but certainly cannot generally eliminate them entirely). The following descriptions of biases draw from the excellent research studies of Amos Tversky and Daniel Kahneman (1974).

## Bias 1: Representativeness

Representativeness is a heuristic that many people use when relating two events. For example, consider the following statement: John is a highly extroverted person, wears outlandish clothes, has long hair, uses drugs, and has been divorced three times. Now consider the possibility that John is: (*a*) an accountant; (*b*) a rock star.

The first type of representativeness is *insensitive to prior probabilities of outcomes*. One important and often ignored effect is the *base-rate probability*. Since there are many more accountants than rock stars in most environments, we should take this into account when assessing the probabilities that John is an accountant or a rock star. We generally tend to place too much emphasis on the description of John and its relationship to the stereotypes of accountants and rock stars, and be insensitive to the prior probabilities. There are probably considerably more accountants that fit the description of John then there are rock stars! Was that adequately reflected in your probabilities?

It is important for decision makers to use all sources of relevant information in assessing probabilities. In this example, before John was described to us we could have used prior probabilities to assess the likelihood that he was an accountant or a rock star. After the description of John is given, we should think in terms of "given that John is a rock star or accountant, what is the likelihood of such a description?" Bayes Theorem can then be used to calculate posterior probabilities that properly account for both sources of information.

Tversky and Kahneman found that subjects *properly* used prior probabilities when no description was given. However, after a description was given, most subjects ignored the prior probabilities and relied heavily on the representativeness heuristic.

A second type of representativeness is *insensitivity to sample size*. One form of this phenomenon is often observed as the inability of decision makers to estimate with accuracy the uncertainty associated with a sample mean. For example, judgments of the likelihood that an average height of a sample of men exceeds six feet were not affected by the stated sample size, even when that sample size varied over a large range. People generally do not intuitively account for the fact that large samples have sample means that are generally better estimates of the population mean than is the case for small samples. A random sample of two men has a much larger chance of the sample mean of their height being over six feet than for a random sample of 100 men. Moreover, studies conducted by Tversky and Kahneman showed that insensitivity to sample size occurs also in judgments of posterior probability.

A third type of representativeness is *misconception of chance*. People expect that even in small numbers of trials of a random process, the result is representative of the underlying process. This "law of small numbers" has been found to persist even in people who are trained in statistical methods.

Two examples of misconceptions of chance are the gambler's fallacy and the sequence likelihood examples. The gambler's fallacy is the viewing of random events as having a "correcting" effect. After observing a run of many heads outcomes on a coin toss sequence, the gambler's fallacy would lead to the reasoning that tails should be bet on because it must be coming next to even things up. In actual fact, short-term deviations, such as a run of heads, are not corrected but are merely diluted in the long run. Indeed after observing a long run of heads, a Bayesian might wish to revise his prior probability that the coin was fair and increase his assessment of the probability of heads.

Decision makers have also been found to be conservative in assessing the impact of evidence. Given a set of prior probabilities, intuitively judged posterior probabilities are usually less extreme than are the correct values (found using Bayes Theorem).

The fourth type of representativeness described by Tversky and Kahneman is *insensitivity to predictability*. Predictability is simply the degree to which some event is predictable, and experiments have shown that different predictability levels do not affect judgment (although they should). One experiment presented subjects with descriptions of the performance of a student teacher and asked them to evaluate the quality of that teaching lesson. Other subjects were given the same information and asked to predict the standing of the teacher five years later. Although the subjects were probably aware of the difference in predictability of these two quantities, their predictions were the same.

The fifth type of representativeness suggested by Tversky and Kahneman is *the illusion of validity*. People generally overestimate or are insensitive to differences in the validity of the relationship between an input to and an output from the judgment process. For example, people predict occupations (such as John the rock star) based on descriptions, even if those descriptions are old and unreliable. When there is more than one input, redundancy or correlation between inputs increases subjective confidence, but, according to statistical theory decreases accuracy.

The sixth type of representativeness is *misconceptions of regression*. It has been found that people do not understand nor sufficiently account for the effect known as "regression towards the mean." People generally have the illusion that outcome variables should be as extreme as input variables. Tversky and Kahneman describe a situation where flight trainees usually followed a very smooth landing (for which they were praised) by a poorer landing. Harsh criticism after a poor landing was followed by a better landing. Can we conclude that harsh criticism produces improvements while praise for high achievement is destructive? Indeed, psychologists argue strongly against this, and we can explain such sequences by noting the effect of *regression towards the mean*. It is a statistical phenomenon poorly understood by many. Simply put, in any set of repeated independent observations of an uncertain quantity or process, extreme observations are likely to be followed by less extreme observations.

## Bias 2: Availability

People tend to judge probabilities for events based on the *retrievability of past outcomes* involving that event. Availability biases arise when occurrences of an event are used to assess probabilities.

Familiarity tends to affect judgment. In reading lists of well-known personalities to subjects, Tversky and Kahneman reported that the judgments that were made on the relative numbers of names of men and women were affected by the relative fame of the groups of men and women. They also claim that salience affects judgments, so that for example, the observation of a burning house would have a greater effect on judgment than merely reading about it.

The second availability bias is due to *search set effectiveness*. People often judge likelihoods of events based on the relative availability of contexts which contain them.

The third availability bias is *imaginability*. Frequency of occurrence or probability are often linked to imaginability, where the relative availability of scenarios that can be generated affects the judgment of a likelihood. The judgment about the probability of an event is likely to be a function of how easily it can be imagined.

The fourth availability bias is that of *illusory correlation*. The perception of occurrence frequency for a pair of events is often seen as a function of the strength of the bond between them.

Availability is a frequently used heuristic for estimating likelihoods, and it can lead to serious biases. It generally involves placing too much emphasis on sample instances that can easily be retrieved.

### Bias 3: Anchoring and Adjustment

A strong effect observed in judgment processes is that of anchoring on a reference value and adjusting around it. When asked to make a set of probabilistic estimates about an uncertain quantity, most people use a natural heuristic of picking a point estimate that is some measure of central tendency (e.g., the mode, median, or mean) and developing their probabilistic estimates by adjusting around that anchor. Unfortunately, such adjustment processes are usually *underadjustment,* and often severely bias the assessments and produce distributions that are too narrow. It is natural when asked to assess an uncertain quantity, such as the circumference of the earth to begin with a point estimate anchor. If you were asked to assess a probability distribution for the circumference of the earth, how would you begin? Most of us choose an anchor and then (under) adjust.

## DISCUSSION OF THE IMPACT OF BIASES IN DECISION ANALYSIS

Heuristics are commonly used in judging probabilities even though they often lead to well-known biases. Many studies have shown that these biases occur consistently across subjects and across events. Training normally has the effect of temporarily reducing (but not eliminating) these biases. Consider the data shown in Table 13–2. A large study was conducted in which 2,600 probability distributions were assessed as five-point cumulative distributions. Assessors judged the 0.01, 0.25, 0.50, 0.75, and 0.99 fractiles for a variety of uncertain quantities.

**TABLE 13–2** Data for 2,600 Assessed Distributions

| | *Category* | | | | | |
|---|---|---|---|---|---|---|
| | *1* | *2* | *3* | *4* | *5* | *6* |
| Iteration 1 | 0.11 | 0.14 | 0.19 | 0.14 | 0.13 | 0.29 |
| Iteration 2 | 0.05 | 0.15 | 0.29 | 0.27 | 0.15 | 0.09 |
| IDEAL | 0.01 | 0.24 | 0.25 | 0.25 | 0.24 | 0.01 |

SOURCE: D. A. Samson and H. Thomas, "Assessing Probability Distributions by the Fractile Method: Evidence from Managers," *Omega* 14, no. 5, 1986, pp. 401–407.

In each case the subjects (some of whom were executives and some were graduate students) assessed the 0.01 and 0.99 fractiles first and then the median, followed by the quartile values. This is a standard assessment procedure. See Chapter 4.

Each distribution was classified into one of six categories depending upon which range (i.e., between which pair of assessed fractiles) the true value appeared in.

For example, if a true value for an uncertain quantity was less than the assessed 0.01 fractile, it was assigned to category 1. The full set of category assignations is as in Figure 13–3.

How many assessments would we expect to be in category 1 (that is, true value less than the 0.01 fractile)? The assessors were instructed to set the 0.01 fractiles so that there was, by definition, only a 0.01 probability of this occurrence. If they had been perfectly calibrated, the observed number of category 1 results would have been 26 (that is, 1% of 2,600). In fact, the observed percentage of category 1 distributions was 11%! Even larger discrepancies occurred for category 6. Subjects were obviously *overconfident* and had the 0.01 and 0.99 fractiles placed much too close together. Comparison of the observed and ideal values in Table 13–2 also shows that on

**FIGURE 13–3** Relationship between Position of True Value Relative to Fractiles and Categorization (1–6) of Answer

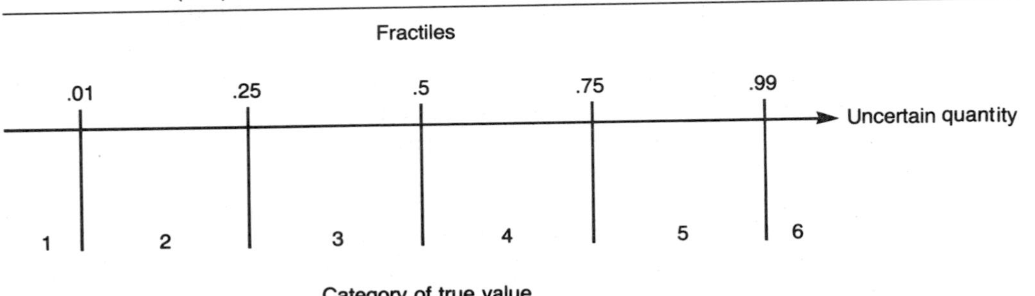

average, the quartile fractiles (0.25 and 0.75) were too close together. Subjects often underwent thinking processes of anchoring on a point estimate and then insufficiently adjusted around that anchor.

Separate results are shown in Table 13–2 for iteration 1 and iteration 2. Iteration 1 was performed by each subject on a set of 10 uncertain quantities. The subjects were then presented with their results and told of their overconfidence bias. Some further assessments were made. Note that the effect of this training was to significantly reduce the biases, however the iteration 2 results are far from ideal.

From this and other studies, it can be concluded that people generally have difficulty measuring and assessing uncertainty. Indeed, Howard (1980) has likened our poor ability as decision makers to handle uncertainty as a blind spot, being similar to our inability as humans to sense radioactivity!

In concluding this section, we note that there are many documented biases and heuristics in common use in probability assessment. These are principally representativeness, availability, anchoring, and adjustment (which leads to observed overconfidence). Many other biases have been observed, and even more severe problems exist for very high or very low probabilities. On average, low probabilities are overestimated and high probabilities are underestimated. Very high or very low probabilities pose even more basic challenges to our understanding of uncertainty. It is difficult to conceive of a probability of $10^{-8}$ (i.e., 0.00000001), which has been assessed as the probability of a nuclear power plant meltdown in a particular facility per year. It is difficult to assess these probabilities, and even more difficult to make good decisions when such serious consequences have such extreme probabilities.

Decision makers and students of decision making need to be aware of these biases and difficulties so that they can understand and hopefully improve the quality of their assessments and decisions. Further, *when dealing with others, it is important for us to realize that their judgments may be subject to some of the same biases as are commonly observed in experimental studies.* For example, a person who has just won three jackpots in quick succession on a Las Vegas poker machine is likely to give a higher estimate of $p$(jackpot) than if she had not won any. The jackpot probability is however an objective known value, and we would be observing a form of availability in such an assessment.

## BIASES IN UTILITY FUNCTION ASSESSMENT

In this section, we distill and present a growing body of evidence that shows that utility theory has problems to be overcome before it can be described as descriptively valid. Although utility theory has been widely used and strongly praised by many, recent evidence has illuminated some serious sensitivities and deficiencies in the empirical validity of this theory. We confine ourselves to an examination of unidimensional utility functions. These same biases and possibly others can also enter into multiattributed utility functions.

The sensitivities of utility theory are primarily to the method used to establish the utility function. Empirical studies have shown that the same person can establish many distinct utility functions, depending on how the function is constructed. Indeed, it is alarming that various methods which, from a prescriptive sense should produce the same utility function, can lead to different preference curves. One resultant issue worthy of debate is whether there is a deficiency in the theory itself (that is, whether it fails to account for something important to decision makers) or whether people are so inconsistent or irrational that they cannot conform to what is really a rational theory of behavior under uncertainty even when they want to. A third view of the empirical evidence is to retreat to what could be called an ivory-tower position of stating that the theory is normatively appealing (which it certainly is) and that empirical validity does not matter.

Although the evidence is not yet all in and decision analysis is in a process of continual development, a reasonable attitude would seem to be that utility theory does have its problems of empirical validity, but that even in its present (imperfect) form, it *still has a great deal of insight to offer to the decision maker*. It has been described by one prominent researcher as "the major paradigm in decision making since the Second World War (Schoemaker 1982, p. 529). If we were to discard it, what alternative approaches exist for modeling individual decisions under uncertainty? This question is extremely important, for there are no other serious contenders that the critics of decision analysis and expected utility can offer as replacements.

Given the shortcomings of utility theory as a descriptive tool, how can we use it to solve decision problems and make decisions? The answer to this important question is that decision analysis (including utility theory aspects) is not meant to directly solve decision problems but instead (through a modeling process) to provide *insight* about them. Even with the problems of assessing utility functions, it is certainly possible to learn a great deal about a decision through the application of these methods.

It is very important to understand the limitations and associated problems of expected utility to put its value as a practical (insight producing) tool into perspective. In the following sections we examine a number of biases and sensitivities that have been documented by empirical researchers.

## Biases Associated with Utility Function Construction

There are many ways to construct utility functions. The principles of how to construct a unidimensional utility function are discussed in Chapter 6. Most of the methods involved comparisons between a simple gamble and a certainty equivalent. The decision maker is normally presented with a gamble having a probability $p$ of outcome $x$, probability $(1 - p)$ of outcome $y$, and a certain value $c$. Given a set $(x,y,p,c)$ it is possible to specify sets of any three of these parameters and ask the decision maker for judgments about the fourth. A number of methods are available (Farquhar, 1984), and all of them should theoretically result in the same (that is, a unique) utility function. Recent research studies have shown that many other factors affect the judgments leading to the formation of a utility function. In practice, utility functions have been found to be anything but unique, rather they are highly sensitive to the assessment context.

Hershey, Kunreuther, and Schoemaker (1982) documented five important sources of bias that affect utility functions. The first effect was that certainty equivalent methods generally yield a higher degree of risk seeking than probability equivalence methods. Certainty equivalent methods involve the specification of $(x, y, p)$ and a judgment on $c$, whereas probability equivalent methods require a judgment on $p$ for a specified $x$, $y$, and $c$. Theoretically, these methods should yield the same utility function, but in practice they do not. The second effect was that the probabilities and payoffs used in the hypothetical gambles had an effect on the utility function. The third effect was that combining gain and loss domains (respectively, positive and negative values for some reference point for $x$, $y$, and $c$) leads to a different utility function than separate examinations of gains and of losses. The fourth effect was that it mattered whether a risk was being assumed or transferred away. The fifth bias was that the descriptive context of the hypothetical decisions affected the utility function (counter to the theory). Many other effects exist and the more important ones are listed below.[3]

*a.* Probability preferences or skewness preferences.
*b.* Variance preferences.
*c.* Utility of gambling.
*d.* Dependence between probability and utility.
*e.* Range effect.
*f.* "Chaining" errors.
*g.* Resistance to the sure thing principle.
*h.* Intransitivities.
*i.* Availability heuristic.
*j.* Cognitive overload.

Many sources of error exist, and it can be difficult to isolate them even in experimental settings. As a result, a number of things become clear for the practitioner. *The first is that utility functions have much to offer in terms of their ability to model attitudes towards risk, however the behavioral limitations associated with their assessment suggest that we should not place*

[3] Krzysztofowicz and Duckstein (1980).

*absolute faith in their prescription*. To put it more strongly, utility functions should be used (just like the other elements of decision analysis) to provide decision support and insight and not to replace the judgment and choice processes in any real decision.

A second recommendation is that *more than one method be used for utility assessment*. For example, if the certainty equivalent method (requiring judgment on $c$) was primarily used to establish a function, use the probability equivalence method (requiring judgments on $p$) or the value equivalence method (requiring judgments on $x$) to check for consistency and to revise the function.

A third guideline for practitioners is to *use gamble situations that are most similar to those in the decision problem being modeled*. Since differences in context affect the utility function, it makes good sense to use closely related contexts in the gamble and the decision. Unfortunately, we cannot confidently assume that utility functions established in one particular context are generally applicable to others (as the theory would suggest).

## Specific Examples of Errors

In this section we review some specific experimental results obtained by Kahneman and Tversky (1979, p. 265):

In one experiment, subjects had to choose between $A$ and $B$ where:

$A$ = 2,500 with probability 0.33
2,400 with probability 0.66
0 with probability 0.01

$B$ = 2,400 with certainty

The subjects also had to choose between $C$ and $D$ where:

$C$ = 2,500 with probability 0.33
0 with probability 0.67

$D$ = 2,400 with probability 0.34
0 with probability 0.66

Note that the expected utilities of the comparisons between $A \sim B$ and $C \sim D$ are identical. For the $A \sim B$ comparison we write

$$0.33\ U(2{,}500) + 0.66\ U(2{,}400) + 0.01\ U(0) \sim U(2{,}400)$$

which reduces to

$$0.33\ U(2{,}500) + 0.01\ U(0) \sim 0.34\ U(2{,}400) \qquad [13\text{–}1]$$

For the $C \sim D$ comparison we can write the expected utilities as

$$0.33\ U(2{,}500) + 0.67\ U(0) \sim 0.34\ U(2{,}400) + 0.66\ U(0)$$

which reduces to

$$0.33\ U(2{,}500) + 0.01\ U(0) \sim 0.34\ U(2{,}400) \qquad [13\text{–}2]$$

The equivalence of expressions, Equations [13–1] and [13–2], above implies that the $A \sim B$ and $C \sim D$ comparisons were identical in expected utility terms. Choices of $A$ (over $B$) and $C$ (over $D$) or alternatively, $B$ and $D$, are consistent with the theory, whereas choices of $A$ and $D$, or $B$ and $C$, are not. In the experimental study, 82% of subjects chose $B$, and 83% chose $C$, *including 61% who chose B and C!* Most people violated expected utility theory. These people exhibited a form of the *certainty effect* (or more generally, the probability effect). They overweighted certain outcomes (probability = 1) relative to uncertain outcomes. In decision analyses, it is prescribed that decomposition allows for probabilities and utilities to be separately assessed and then later combined using an expectation rule. This experiment shows that people confound probability and utility in their judgment processes. The use of different sets of probability values leads to very different utility curves.

Kahneman and Tversky also found that the certainty effect is *reflected* from gains to losses. For positive cash flows, there was a risk-averse preference for sure gains over larger gains that are merely probable. For negative cash flows, they observed risk-seeking preference for a loss that is merely probable over a smaller loss that is certain. We conclude that the overweighting of certainty produces risk aversion for gains and risk seeking for losses.

Kahneman and Tversky also demonstrated the *isolation effect,* which shows that different decompositions of a gamble can produce different choices. For example consider their overall gamble:

$$\begin{Bmatrix} 2{,}000 \text{ with probability } 0.5 \\ 1{,}000 \text{ with probability } 0.5 \end{Bmatrix} \quad \text{or} \quad \{1{,}500 \text{ with certainty}\}$$

This comparison was decomposed by Kahneman and Tversky into the following two scenarios:

1. In addition to whatever you own, you have been given 1,000. In addition, you are now asked to choose between

$$A = \begin{Bmatrix} 1{,}000 \text{ with probability } 0.5 \\ 0 \text{ with probability } 0.5 \end{Bmatrix} \quad \text{and } B = 500 \text{ with certainty}$$

2. In addition to whatever you own, you have been given 2,000. You are now asked to choose between

$$C = \begin{Bmatrix} -1{,}000 \text{ with probability } 0.5 \\ 0 \text{ with probability } 0.5 \end{Bmatrix} \text{ and } D = (-500) \text{ with certainty}$$

Note that if the bonus is integrated into the choices, scenarios 1 and 2 above are identical. The choices made by most subjects violated the axioms of expected utility (84% of subjects chose $B$ over $A$ and 69% chose $C$ over $D$).

These and other evidences led Kahneman and Tversky to the formulation of another theory (called prospect theory) in which decision makers are presumed to edit their prospects and then make choices based on their value as gains and losses rather than final asset states. In the editing phase of prospect theory, decision makers undergo a series of operations:

*a.* *Coding,* where outcomes are perceived as gains or losses relative to some reference point.
*b.* *Combination,* an algebraic simplification such as adding together of probabilities for equivalent outcomes.
*c.* *Segregation* of certain and uncertain components of a prospect.
*d.* *Cancellation* of components common to sets of prospects.
*e.* *Simplification* involving rounding of numbers (probabilities or payoffs). Note that very low probabilities can be rounded to zero under this operation.
*f.* *Dominance* where dominated alternatives are eliminated.

The evaluation phase of prospect theory comprises the use of a value function (rather than a utility function) and a decision weights function rather than a probability set. These new functions are designed so as to be descriptively valid, so that prospect theory improves upon the poor empirical validity of utility theory. Although prospect theory is relatively new and its usefulness is still being debated, it does represent a major step in thinking about behavioral decision theory. It does not have the very appealing prescriptive design of utility theory but does account for some common behavioral norms. Whereas utility theory effectively *prescribes* behavior, prospect theory *describes* behavior. Prospect theory has many imperfections even in a descriptive sense. For example, rounding of low probabilities to zero is only valid in a descriptive sense when the unlikely event is not extreme in value of consequences. For example, nuclear power plant meltdowns have extremely low estimated probabilities, but the seriousness of the event itself causes the meltdown possibility to have a major impact on design and operation decisions. Hence the definition of how low a probability must be before it can be ignored is value dependent. In other circumstances, a probability of 0.1 might be considered low enough to be rounded to zero.

Schoemaker (1982) has proposed that the failure of utility theory as a descriptive model is a result of "inadequate recognition of various psychological principles of judgment and choice." Humans have a tendency to cognitively simplify tasks, and Schoemaker suggests that decisions are made on decomposed options through relative comparisons. He also notes that real decision strategies vary with differences in task complexity. It has been argued that decision makers often *satisfice* rather than optimize, and it can be further argued that more satisficing and less optimizing should be expected as decision tasks become cognitively more complex. Satisficing can alternatively be considered as a form of optimizing, when a broader set of decision elements are considered (such as decision analysis cost and time).

A further descriptive shortcoming of expected utility is its portfolio context. The domain of a utility function is theoretically some final net asset state (although certain simplifications allow consideration of prospects). Hence, decisions should, according to the theory, be evaluated according to their effect on final assets. However, for all but the most important personal and financial decisions, people generally may make choices in isolation of each other.

## SUMMARY

To summarize, decision analysis (and particularly expected utility theory) has *many difficulties as a descriptive model, but these have not weakened its appeal as a prescriptive approach*. The deviations, inconsistencies, and errors made by human decision makers clearly cannot be well reflected in a theory that prescribes exhaustive search for full information (where economical and relevant), perfect calibration and adherence to the laws of probability, and optimization (i.e., expected utility maximization). Humans do not generally search exhaustively, nor are they perfectly calibrated as probability assessors, and they do not always optimize on decision problems. It is useful, however, to postulate an approach that appears intuitively to be one which would produce high-quality decisions if used properly. It also may be useful to strive toward such goals as perfect calibration, optimization, etc. at least for important decision problems. From a prescriptive point of view, decision analysis has provided a high-quality process from which we can measure and understand biases, deviations, behavioral shortcomings, and errors.

It is reasonable to expect that training and educated practice procedures may reduce some biases some of the time, but it is unreasonable to expect that anybody can be completely unbiased. Heuristics and biases such as availability, representativeness, overconfidence, anchoring, and adjustment are deeply ingrained cognitive processes.

Much effort is being devoted to modifying utility theory to improve its descriptive validity. Modifications may one day come in the form of a sudden breakthrough, although it seems likely that a theory with improved descriptive validity will either sacrifice prescriptive appeal or be more complex than expected utility in its present form. For example, some proposed modifications involve utility functions with more than one dimension of value. For example, Bell (1982) has suggested a function in which value is specified both for outcome (payoffs) and for decision regret. This extra degree of freedom allows for explanation of some of the inconsistent behavior described above.

In conclusion, we reiterate that our natural, human inability to behave in accordance with the axioms of decision analysis can be interpreted in two major ways: First that the theory is descriptively deficient, and second, that the motivation for using it as a prescriptive approach is very strong. If enough people had excellent natural decision-making abilities, even when problems are very complex, then there would be no need for decision analysis, or for this book! For better or worse, people's intuitive decision processes are so inconsistent and biased that formalized decision support is highly valuable.

## FURTHER READING

Behavioral decision theory is a rich and complex area of study in decision analysis. The brief descriptions given here cannot do full justice to the importance and complexity of the subject but are aimed rather at giving an introduction and an overview of the subject.

The interested reader should choose to pursue relevant issues further by referring to the articles referenced in this chapter. In addition, four major works by Hogarth (1980), Slovic, et al. (1977), Einhorn and Hogarth (1981), Pitz and Sachs (1984) also require inclusion in any reading list on this subject. Using these as a set of first readings, the detailed references given in each study will serve as a second generation of readings and allow interested readers to probe the fascinating subject areas of behavioral aspects of decision analysis.

## REFERENCES

BASS, B. M. 1983. *Organizational Decision Making*. Homewood, Ill.: Richard D. Irwin, p. 160.

BELL, D. 1982. "Regret in Decision Making under Uncertainty." *Operations Research* 30, no. 5, September–October, pp. 961–81.

COYLE, R. G. 1972. *Decision Analysis*. London: Thomas Nelson and Sons.

EINHORN, H. T., and R. M. HOGARTH. 1981. "Behavioral Decision Theory: Process of Judgment and Choice." *Annual Review of Psychology*, p. 32.

FARQUHAR, P. H. 1984. "Utility Assessment Methods." *Management Science* 30, no. 11, November, pp. 1283–1300.

HERSHEY, J. C.; H. C. KUNREUTHER; and P. J. H. SCHOEMAKER. "Sources of Bias in Assessment Procedures for Utility Functions." *Management Science* 28, no. 8 August, pp. 936–54.

HOGARTH, R. M. 1980. *Judgment and Choice: The Psychology of Decision*. Chichester, England, Wiley.

HOWARD, R. A. 1980. "An Assessment of Decision Analysis." *Operations Research* 28, no. 1, January, pp. 4–27.

KAHNEMAN, D., and A. TVERSKY. 1979. "Prospect Theory: An Analysis of Decision under Risk." *Econometrica* 42, no. 2, pp. 263–91.

KRZYSZTOFOWICZ, R., and L. DUCKSTEIN. 1980. "Assessment Errors in Multiattribute Utility Functions." *Organizational Behavior and Human Performance* 23, pp. 376–48.

MOORE, P. G., and H. THOMAS. 1975. "Measuring Uncertainty." *Omega, The International Journal of Management Science* 3, no. 6, pp. 657–72.

PITZ, G. F., and N. J. SACHS. 1984. "Judgment and Decision: Theory and Application." *Annual Review of Psychology* 35, pp. 139–63.

SAMSON, D. A., and H. THOMAS. 1986. "Assessing Probability Distributions by the Fractile Method: Evidence from Managers," *Omega, The International Journal of Management Science* 14, no. 5, pp. 401–7.

SCHOEMAKER, P. J. H. 1982. "The Expected Utility Model: Its Variants, Purposes, Evidence, and Limitations." *Journal of Economic Literature* 20, June, pp. 529–63.

SLOVIC, P.; B. FISCHHOFF; and S. LICHTENSTEIN. 1977. "Behavioral Decision Theory." *Annual Review of Psychology* 28, 1–39.

TVERSKY, A., and D. KAHNEMAN. 1974. "Judgment under Uncertainty: Heuristics and Biases." *Science* 185, pp. 1124–31.

## PROBLEMS

1. Why is it useful for decision makers to understand commonly observed biases and inconsistencies? Is it not reasonable to merely accept decision analysis as a prescriptive approach and attribute biases to human weaknesses?
2. How can an approach such as decision analysis be useful in any practical settings when the probability and utility assessment procedures are sensitive to method and context? Is it a case of "analysis paralysis" and if not, what is to be gained from a decision analysis?
3. If a person expresses a set of intransitive preferences to you, what should you do? Suppose you were conducting a decision analysis, and the president of your company judged a set of hypothetical situations resulting in intransitivity. What could be done about it?
4. In searching for a new job, a young decision analyst decided that three equally important attributes entered into the decision, namely

   $A_1$ = The proportion of his time which would be spent doing decision analysis

   $A_2$ = The degree to which his prospective boss and close colleagues appeared to behave consistently with the axioms of decision analysis

   $A_3$ = The expected utility associated with all his future (uncertain) cash flows as a result of this decision.

   He had been offered jobs with three major management consulting organizations (to preserve confidentiality we will call them *A*, *B*, and *C*) and ranked each job on each attribute as follows:

| | *Job 1* | *Job 2* | *Job 3* |
|---|---|---|---|
| Attribute 1 | A | B | C |
| Attribute 2 | B | C | A |
| Attribute 3 | C | A | B |

At first he decided to simply choose the option that did best on the most attributes, but that rule resulted in a three-way tie. He then decided to use a more sophisticated rule and rank the jobs by making pair-wise comparisons only.

Compare each pair of jobs, and for each comparison declare the "winner" to be the one which does best on the most attributes. What are the pair-wise results, and can this procedure lead to a reasonable choice? If not, suggest another suitable solution method for this choice problem.

5. Table 13–3 shows a number of expressions that can be used to describe likelihood.
   *a.* Next to each expression write down a probability which in your interpretation best corresponds to that expression.
   *b.* Next, find three other people, read each expression to each of them, and record their associated probabilities.
   *c.* Look at the range of probabilities for each expression. What can you conclude about the precision of using words and expressions to communicate about likelihoods?
6. This exercise is aimed at giving you practice at making subjective probability assessments.
   *a.* Use the five-point fractile method (described in Chapter 4) to assess cumulative probability distributions for the 10 uncertain

**TABLE 13–3** Likelihoods

| *Expression* | *Your Probability* | *Person 1* | *Person 2* | *Person 3* |
|---|---|---|---|---|
| 1. Usually | | | | |
| 2. Almost never | | | | |
| 3. Frequently | | | | |
| 4. Sometimes | | | | |
| 5. Likely | | | | |
| 6. Possible | | | | |
| 7. Doubtful | | | | |
| 8. Probable | | | | |
| 9. Maybe | | | | |
| 10. Quite likely | | | | |
| 11. Uncertain | | | | |
| 12. Unlikely | | | | |
| 13. Good chance that | | | | |
| 14. Almost impossible | | | | |
| 15. Improbable | | | | |

quantities shown below. Remember to follow the standard procedure of assessing the extremes (0.01 and 0.99 fractiles) first, followed in turn by the median (0.5 fractile), and the quartiles (0.25 and 0.75 fractile). Do not research these uncertain quantities to increase your knowledge about them. Use your existing knowledge, and reflect your uncertainty in the distribution. The uncertain quantities are:

1. The latitude of Helsinki.
2. The average distance to the moon.
3. The number of bytes on a 5¼″ double-sided, double-density floppy disk.
4. The shortest distance by road from Chicago to New Orleans.
5. The population of Champaign, Illinois.
6. The age of the oldest living tree.
7. The depth below sea level of the deepest trench on earth.
8. The weight of one gallon of water.
9. The population of Australia.
10. The probability of getting a flush (all cards of the same suit) in a poker deal.

*b.* Now that you have made the assessments, go back over each of your thought processes and consider heuristics you used and possible biases that may have occurred. Did you use representativeness, availability, or anchoring and adjustment?

7. In this exercise you will plot your utility function (using hypothetical gambles) in three different ways and compare each utility function to check if they are sensitive to the assessment method. For each assessment you are in the position of choice between receiving an uncertain amount between \$0 and \$100,000 or a certain amount.

METHOD 1

Assess your certainty equivalent ($CE_1$) for a 50:50 gamble between receiving \$0 and \$100,000:

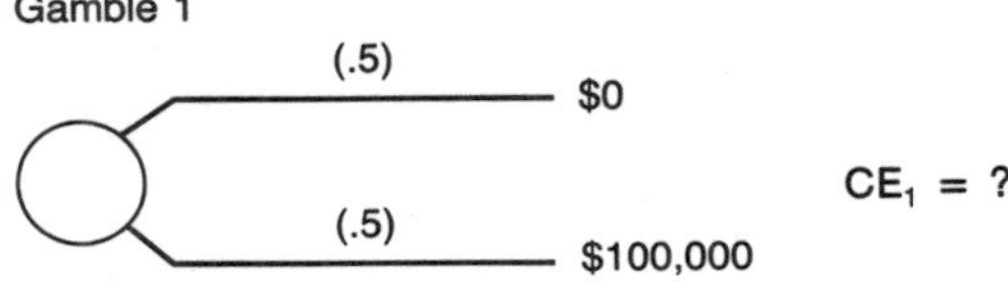


Now use the assessed value of $CE_1$ to assess $CE_2$ and $CE_3$ as follows:

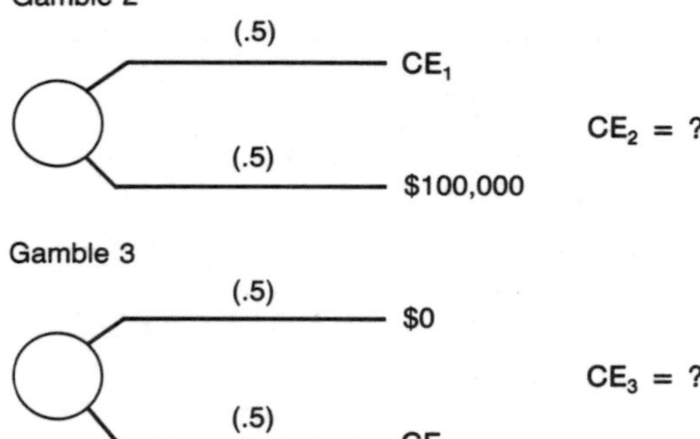


We can define

$$U(\$0) = 0$$

and

$$U(\$100{,}000) = 1$$

From gamble 1

$$U\,(CE_1) = .5\,(0) + .5\,(1)$$

From gamble 2

$$U\,(CE_2) = .5\,(.5) + .5\,(1) = .75$$

From gamble 3

$$U\,(CE_3) = .5\,(0) + .5\,(.5) = .25$$

Construct a graph with utility (zero to one) on the vertical axis and money ($0 to $100,000) on the horizontal axis. Plot the five points. Note that this method involved "chaining" of results from one gamble to another.

## METHOD 2

In this method we will judge similar gambles to method 1 except that we will use probabilities of 0.8 (for the higher amount) and 0.2 (for the lower amount).

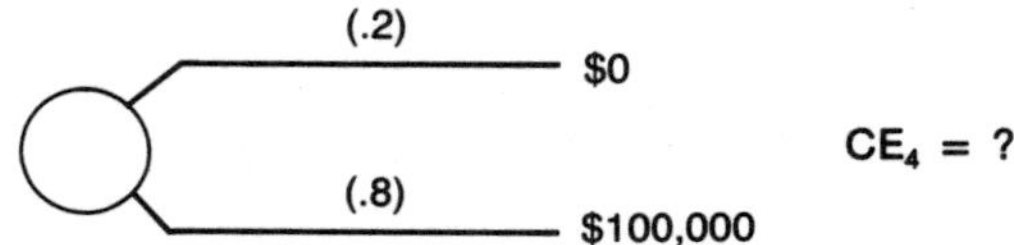

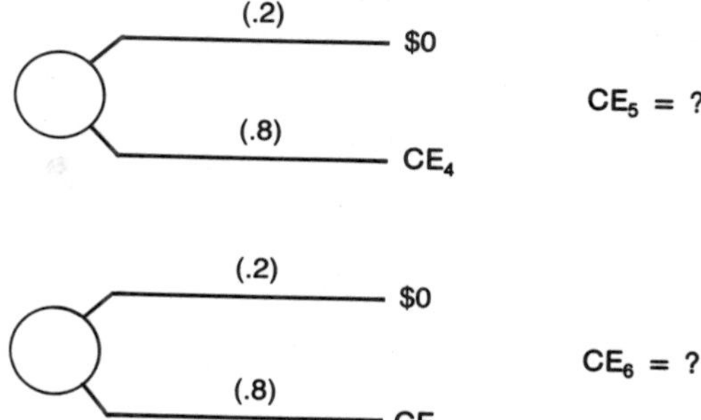


Through similar reasoning to that of method 1, we find that

$$U\ (CE_4) = .8$$
$$U\ (CE_5) = .64$$
$$U\ (CE_6) = .512$$

and

$$U\ (\$0) = 0,\ U\ (\$100{,}000) = 1 \text{ as before.}$$

Plot the new points on the same graph as for method 1. Is there any significant difference?

## METHOD 3

In this case we will vary the probabilities across gambles and keep the $0 and $100,000 payoff values across all gambles.

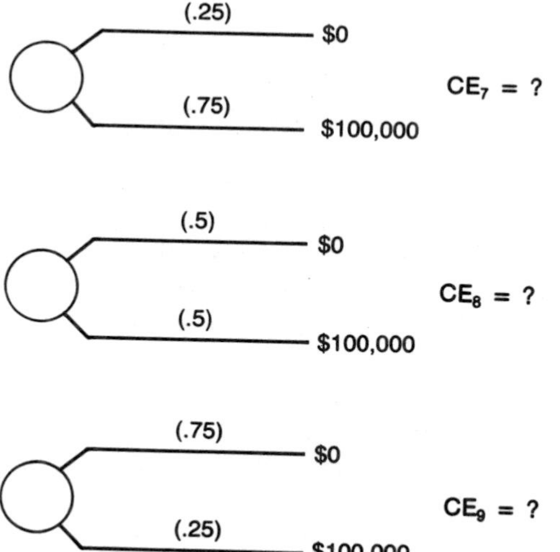

We have

$$U\ (CE_7) = 0.75$$
$$U\ (CE_8) = 0.5$$
$$U\ (CE_9) = 0.25$$

Plot your third graph and draw conclusions about how the different assessment methods affected the location and shape of your utility function.

8. *a.* Make intuitive judgments about each of the following individual choice problems.

   Problem 1
   A: A two-week vacation in Australia with certainty.
   B: A 50% chance of a four-week vacation in Australia, New Zealand, and Hawaii.

   Problem 2
   C: 1% chance of a four-week vacation in Australia, New Zealand, and Hawaii.
   D: A 2% chance of a two-week vacation in Australia.

   Problem 3
   E: Winning $10,000 with probability 0.01.
   F: Winning $5,000 with probability 0.02.

   Problem 4
   G: Winning $5,000 with probability 0.98.
   H: Winning $10,000 with probability 0.49.

   After you have made your judgments for each problem, write the expected utility expression for each. Were you consistent across the related problem pairs? Previous studies have found a large proportion of people who express preferences that are not consistent with utility theory. If you were inconsistent with the theory for one or both of the problem pairs, go back and review your choices, and see if you want to change one or more of them.

   *b.* Ask three other people to make choices on the above problems. The chances are good that one or more of them will violate the expected utility axioms. If they do violate the axioms, explain their deviance to them and note their reactions.

9. A man named John is randomly sampled from the population.
   *a.* What are your beliefs about the probability that John is an accountant or a rock star, *given no other information,* except that he is one of the two?
   *b.* *Given* the description of John earlier in this chapter (John is highly extroverted, wears outlandish clothes, has long hair, uses drugs, and has been divorced three times) assess proba-

bilities that John is a rock star or an accountant (again, given that he is one of the two).

*c.* *Given* that John is an accountant, what is the likelihood of his fitting the description above?

*d.* *Given* that John is a rock star, what is the likelihood of his fitting the description above?

*e.* Define the probabilities that you assessed as prior, likelihood, and posterior probabilities. Combine the prior and likelihood probabilities using Bayes Theorem and determine whether the calculated values of the posteriors are the same as those that you assessed. Did you exhibit a commonly observed bias?

*f.* Try this exercise on five other people, and report your results.

10. Decision analysis is a prescriptive framework and philosophy for individual decision making. Given that many decisions must be made by committees or other forms or coalitions of interest groups, how widespread and how relevant can decision analysis be?
11. List and describe the various biases that have been commonly observed to exist in subjective probability assessment processes.
12. What are the factors that have lead researchers to conclude that utility functions are context dependent and sensitive to the method of assessment that is used?

CHAPTER FOURTEEN

# Decision Support Systems

## OUTLINE



## OBJECTIVES

After completing this chapter, you should be able to:

1. Define what a decision support system is.
2. Outline the contribution computers can make in supporting decision processes.
3. Discuss the contribution decision support systems can make in different decision contexts such as strategic and tactical situations.
4. Define and describe expert systems concepts.
5. Define and describe artificial intelligence concepts.

## INTRODUCTION

*Decision support system,* DSS, has become a popular field of study and research over the past decade. With the explosion in microcomputer sales in business, the term *DSS* has been widely used, and sometimes misused, to describe a variety of software products and systems. An introductory study of decision support systems is relevant to the study of managerial decision analysis, because as managerial problems, organizations, and systems become increasingly complex, the analytic processes used by managers increasingly make use of computerized aid. Many decision analysis models can be enhanced by the use of computers. The most promising field of computer support for managerial decision making is DSS. In decision analysis, even if a DSS is not used to aid in the main decision model, it may well be useful to use DSS in subsidiary models that support the main model.

This chapter aims to provide basic information on decision support systems. It comprises a general definition and description of a DSS, and a consideration of a DSS design based on a decision analytic model. The fields of expert systems and artificial intelligence are also briefly reviewed.

There is a good deal of *commonality of purpose between the decision analysis paradigm and a DSS*. Both aim to aid decision-making processes so as to lead to better decisions. They are different, however, in their form and approach. Further, DSSs provide the opportunity for decision and management science models to be integrated with management information systems to enhance the potential for modeling managerial problems. Hence, there is a good deal to be learned from the field of DSS that can be of great use to decision and management scientists.

We will begin this chapter by introducing the concept of DSS. We will also provide a definition of expert systems and artificial intelligence as they relate to managerial decision making. Following that, a number of DSS applications are documented to give an appreciation of the strengths and limitations of such systems.

## WHAT IS A DECISION SUPPORT SYSTEM?

The words *decision support system* are easy to interpret as a system, that is, a set of interconnected elements, which aids or supports the act of decision making. This preceding interpretation is a very general one. More specifically:

1. "DSS is an interactive, computer-based system which supports managers in making unstructured decisions—decisions which no procedure or structured approach has ever defined" (Sprague and Watson 1979, p. 61).

2. "Decision Support Systems (DSS) are interactive computer-based aids designed to assist managers in complex tasks requiring human judgment. The aim of such systems is to support and improve a decision process" (Hackathorn and Keen 1981, p. 21).
3. "DSS aims at providing access to information systems and analytic models directly to managers and challenges the assumption that computers are mainly valuable for data processing operations or the creation of standardized information systems. . . . DSS also points toward a synthesis of the Management Information Systems field and Management Science" (Keen 1980, p. 33).
4. "DSS is about using any technologies—intellectual, analytic, financial and computer—to help improve creativity in decisions that really matter" (Keen 1985, p. 3).

DSSs have evolved into software systems comprising a user-friendly interface and language, and a model or set of models that draw upon a data base. Let us briefly compare and contrast DSS with management information systems (MIS) and electronic data processing (EDP). Three decades or so ago, electronic computer use was first applied in organizations. Their focus was on *data*, and they were developed and became recognized as *efficient* means for processing data. The efficiency and automation of data and transaction processing, which is characteristic of EDP systems, applies to the operational activities of the administrative functions of organizations.

Subsequent to the successful efficiency gains achieved through EDP, it was found that a very useful benefit associated with having EDP was that data could be organized into structured data bases to facilitate inquiry, data summary, and report generation, mainly by middle managers. These management information systems (MIS) provided the beginning of a focus on information for many organizations, both as a resource/asset and ultimately as a component of competitive strategy. MIS usefully involves the organization of *data* into organized sets of *information,* as well as the use of that information by managers.

DSS has taken on a different philosophy and focus to MIS. Managers, as decision makers, can often use MIS to gather the necessary information for making choices. DSS allows the manager to model decision problems and, usually within the same software system, access the necessary data as with MIS. To reemphasize, *DSS aims to integrate the decision science/management science field with the MIS field. A DSS normally contains some modeling characteristics.*

Whereas an MIS is not directly driven by managers wishing to solve problems, a DSS is. An MIS may produce weekly or monthly reports that summarize organizational measures of performance, and some can answer ad hoc inquiries about data sets. A DSS is controlled entirely by the user, who may have a variety of decision support needs. Hence a DSS needs to be flexible and able to provide timely responses to requests for decision aid. Like decision analysis, DSS is not designed to address the decision support needs of managers at a particular level in an organization. Indeed, just as with decision analysis, DSS can enhance communication between managers who are at different levels, in different divisions, and who perform different functions in organizations.

## DSS Components

A DSS normally comprises a data base, a model base, and a user interface software system. The data base most useful for decision support systems may itself be a complex structure comprising internal (organizational measures) and external (market/environment) data. In a corporation, the typical data base of accounting and financial measures may need to be substantially supplemented with internal data about production, personnel, marketing, and other measures, and external data about competitors, customers, market conditions, suppliers, and economies. A DSS data base needs to be flexible, easily accessible, and rich enough to satisfy the requirements of the system's models and users.

The model base is the subsystem which normally is of most interest to decision analysts. Within a DSS, a model or set of models is normally available for development and use. These models may take a variety of forms, including statistical, operations research/management science, decision analytic, simulation, and others. Apart from these classes of models, which also have a life outside the realm of DSS, specifically computer-oriented properties such as expert systems and artificial intelligence logics can also be incorporated within DSS.

From the perspective of decision and management science models, a DSS represents an opportunity, through computerization, to enhance their usability. With respect to decision analysis in particular, computerized decision tree packages do exist. These general purpose packages could be described as "shells" because specific decision tree models are created using them as software frameworks. Some of these packages are reviewed in detail in Chapter 15.

Our interest in DSS and its relationship to decision analysis is partly in the context of the decision analysis paradigm and method as the heart of a specific DSS.

We can consider DSS technology elements in terms of specific DSS, DSS generators, and DSS tools (Sprague, 1983). A specific DSS is a system designed to support the making of a decision or series of decisions. A DSS generator is a system through which one or more specific DSSs can be created. DSS tools are the basic hardware and software elements required to build a DSS.

The important functional components of a DSS are the model subsystem and data base. The medium through which the user and these functional elements interact is called the interface. The effectiveness of a DSS can be substantially enhanced or limited by the quality of the communication interface between the user and the computer. The idea of DSS is that users need not be computer specialists but can be the managers themselves. To enhance usability, input and output should preferably be in a natural language or close to it, and not in a computer language. A useful input/output structure is the hierarchical menu system. In this mode, users are prompted by multiple layers of menu screens and can move around within the system functions, get help, control the programs, enter commands, and access data and models via easy-to-use screens specifically designed to enhance the system's friendliness. This type of structure represents a powerful and convenient alternative to learning a command language.

## DSS AND DECISION MAKING

Different kinds of support systems are useful for different types of decisions. We begin this section by classifying decisions according to their degree of structure and domain, then examine the role of DSSs in these various decision contexts.

Simon (1960) has noted that decisions vary in the degree to which they are structured. Highly structured decisions are generally routine, repetitive, and hence, programmable. Unstructured decisions are unique and complex. Let us consider this dimension of "degree of structure" in the context of a mortgage department of a bank. For any mortgage or lending decision, a bank follows a decision process, usually including an interview, certification of documents, a credit check, and an inspection of the asset (in the case of a mortgage). Individual mortgage decision processes are routine and repetitive. They are performed by people who are acting in accordance with sets of rules or guidelines. This is a structured, programmable decision process.

Within the same mortgage/lending function of a bank, somebody must design the mortgage selection process rules and choose the form of the mortgage contract and interest rates the bank will offer. This process is much less routine and repetitive than the individual mortgage decision process. It involves elements of decision strategy that affect the whole of the operation and must account for various sources and uses of funds, risks, legal constraints, and competitive and environmental factors. The process of strategy formulation at this level is relatively unstructured. This decision process is difficult to prespecify and is nonprogrammed.

Programmed decisions can be effectively supported using rules and procedures which may or may not be computerized, depending on relative *efficiency* and *economy*. Nonprogrammed decisions may be supported by computerized systems, DSSs, where the emphasis is on decision-making *effectiveness*. For example, consider a company that builds and operates warehouses. In a warehouse, computer-aided inventory systems may be evaluated in terms of straightforward cost efficiency and quality of service dimensions.

Now consider a situation in which a trucking company has proposed to merge with the warehouse company. This decision process, to merge or not to merge, is not just a matter of cost efficiency or quality, but a more fundamental question of business strategy, competitive effectiveness, management structure, ownership, and financial structure. The merger decision is more complex and more difficult to program than the equipment purchase decision described above.

A number of different views of decision types and categories are possible. G. A. Gorry and M. S. Scott Morton (1971) categorized managerial decisions according to whether they were structured or unstructured (from Anthony, 1985) as:

1. Operational performance.
2. Operational control.
3. Management control.
4. Strategic planning.

Table 14–1 shows some examples within this framework.

DSSs are said to be most useful for *semistructured* decisions when semistructured decisions are partially programmable. *This raises the fundamental question surrounding DSS: To what extent, for which decisions, and in what manner can our human (carbon-based) brains be aided by computer (silicon-based) brains in decisions processes?* The first 13 chapters of this

**TABLE 14–1** Different Types of Decisions and Degree of Decision Structure

| | *Operational Performance* | *Operational Control* | *Management Control* | *Strategic Planning* |
|---|---|---|---|---|
| Structured | Payroll production | Accounts receivable | Budget analysis | Tanker fleet mix |
| Semistructured | Dispatching | Production scheduling | Forecasts | Site location |
| Unstructured | Solving a crime | Cash management | Budget preparation | Product planning |

Adapted from G. A. Gorry and M. S. Scott Morton, "A Framework for Management Information Systems," *Sloan Management Review* 13 (Fall 1971), pp. 55–70, and E. D. Carlson, "An Approach for Designing Decision Support Systems" in *Decision Support Systems,* W. C. House, ed. (New York: Petrocelli Books, 1983.)

book presented decision analysis and arguments for augmenting our natural decision-making abilities and processes with this framework of formalized common sense. In a similar manner we can examine the concept and the field of DSS. Basically, computers are very effective data processors, in terms of following organized sets of rules, instructions, and logics. In certain vertical thinking modes involving structured data processing, computers can clearly outperform human brains. On the other hand, computers are not yet able to outperform us on all thinking modes: They lack imagination, intuitive and lateral thinking potential, and impulsive creativity as we know it. *The strength of a DSS is the integration of man and machine, the synergistic coupling of human problem-solving potential with computerized analytic models and data processing/memory*. It is not so much in highly structured decision problems that potential gains in decision-making effectiveness exist. Computers have been providing gains in efficiency here for a few decades. It is in the arena of semistructured and unstructured problems that computers can potentially aid managers in new and powerful ways, in making more effective decisions.

The ability of computers to apply rules of optimization, simulation, evaluation, and analysis to data sets with speed and accuracy makes them valuable as decision support systems. Further, computers can help people overcome some of the limitations inherent in their unaided decision behavior, including forgetfulness and capriciousness, through providing a variety of memory aids and rational modeling approaches.

Ultimately, we must consider the ability of the DSS to capture human expertise and be artificially intelligent. The fields of expert systems (ES) and artificial intelligence (AI) are relevant to a study of DSSs because they represent the frontier of our achievements in computerized decision support. We will return to review these fields after considering a detailed case example of a DSS design.

## THE DESIGN OF A DSS FOR STRATEGIC PLANNING SUPPORT

Decision support systems have been used to help solve increasingly unstructured problems. A particular unstructured problem that virtually all organizations face is that of strategic planning. Thomas (1984) has discussed the role of decision analysis in the strategic management process. He describes strategic decision making associated with "a low level of initial structure, long time horizons, distinct political complications, wide-ranging effects within the organization, and a high sensitivity to environmental changes" (Thomas 1984, p. 140).

Strategic problems have commonly been characterized as wicked, messy, and ill-structured. They also are unique and typically involve uncertainty and multiple conflicting objectives.

## EXAMPLE 14–1

### Strategic Planning at XYZ Insurance Company[1]

Let us examine how an insurance company used a DSS to improve its strategic management process. To aid the long-term strategic planning process, the chief executive of XYZ Insurance created, over two decades ago, a policy and planning department, at the heart of which was a substantial computer program. This program, often called "the corporate model" was not directly accessible to the strategic managers themselves. Indeed, the chief executive and other decision makers were often presented with structured proposals, already evaluated in feasibility studies, to approve or disapprove. The problem and policy formulation processes became somewhat remote for many executives, and they were relegated to the position of making choices between future scenarios, projects, and initiatives which, in the main, were structured by others.

The computer program itself was written in a language that none of the senior managers understood. Computer specialists developed and ran it. The program was user-unfriendly, mainframe based, and inflexible in its range of use.

As a corporate model it was capable of forecasting macroeconomic trends and extrapolating time series data of the company's cash flow, sales volume, and other financial performance variables. A recent modification gave it the capability of producing balance sheets and income statements.

In a review of the policy and planning department's activities, one of the company's directors, Hal Johnston, noted the strong separation of the strategy formulation process undertaken by that department, although the decisions were ultimately made by the board. He called in a decision-making expert to work in a consulting role and investigate this aspect of the organization. Hal and the consultant, working as a team, noted that even within the policy and planning department, the computer program was perceived of as a mysterious black box. Very few people understood how it worked. The company's executives had very mixed feelings about it. They wanted to have a clearer understanding of it and a more direct control over its use.

The consultant realized that a decision-support system could provide the required user-friendliness, and that decision analysis could provide a useful modeling logic. He modeled the strategic planning problem with a computerized decision system as shown by Figure 14–1. The computer program which constituted this DSS was designed and implemented on a personal computer and was therefore available to a number of people. Program input and output processes were directed through a series of menus and were easy to understand and use. The system was flexible and

[1] Adapted from D. A. Samson, "Expected Utility Strategic Decision Models for General Insurers," *Astin Bulletin* 16, S45–S58 (Special Issue, April 1986).

FIGURE 14–1 A Strategic Decision Support System for XYZ Insurance

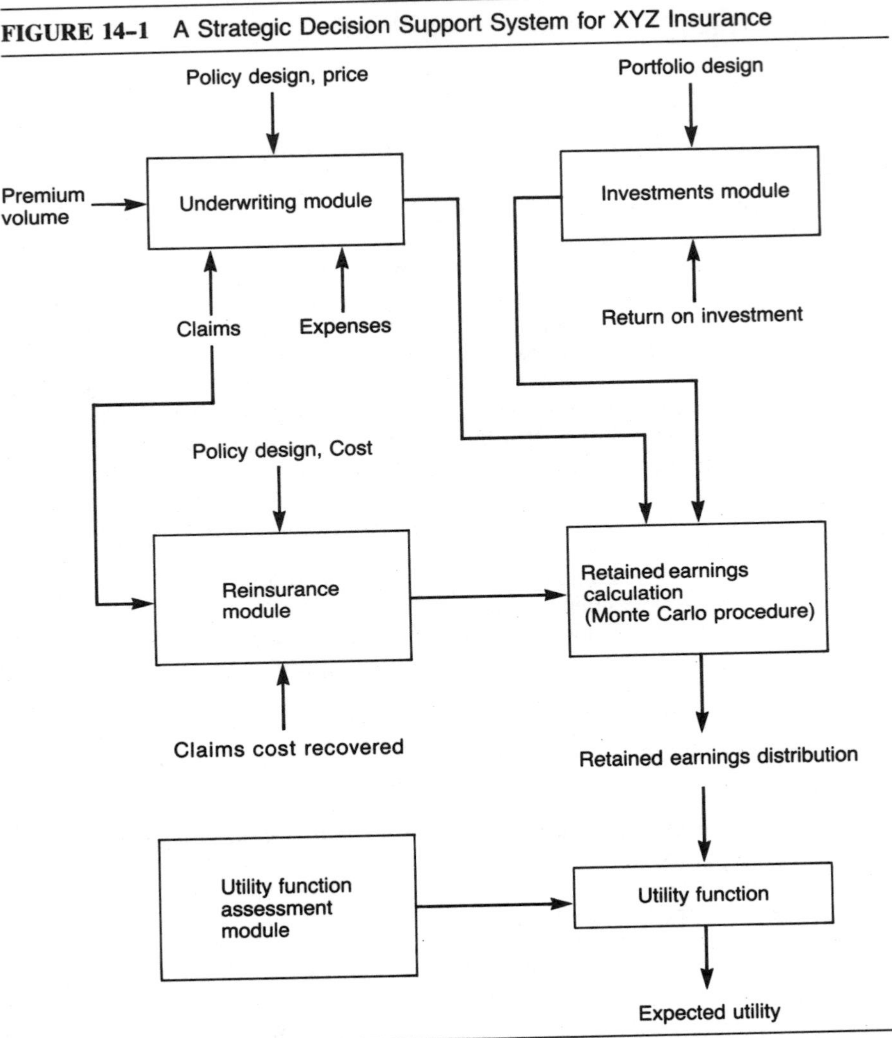


could be used for conventional policy formulation and evaluation processes or for ad hoc inquiries.

Hal noted that there were generally three modes in which strategic issues were considered within the company:

**1.** *Generalized Strategic Planning*. In this mode, directors and other senior executives and managers quite regularly conducted meetings and held discussions about the future of the organization. These managerial processes occurred without necessarily being prompted by specific events inside or outside the company.

**2.** *Consideration of Specific Issues.* Sometimes these were conceived as potential actions by managers within the company, and sometimes they were reactive to changes occurring in the marketplace or other parts of the environment. An example of a specific strategic issue within XYZ which came from an internally generated idea was the potential to gain a substantial tax advantage from rearranging some of the company's reinsurances and investments in a particular manner. A senior manager within the company had been *active* in thinking creatively about how the company could enhance its competitiveness. She had intuitively thought of how a tax advantage could be gained but needed to carefully examine all of the strategic and operational ramifications of this opportunity. The mechanism for doing so was the DSS (Figure 14–1).

A second type of specific issue is more *reactive* than the previous example. Underwriting profits in some personal lines of insurance were falling in the industry as claims and expenses consumed more and more of premium income. XYZ needed to consider what strategy to follow in a tightening market and how to react to its changing environment. Many actions were possible. For example, XYZ could have reexamined its product mix and perhaps dropped some of its less profitable products. The company could have chosen any of a number of pricing strategies. Claims adjustment efforts could have been altered, affecting both claims and expenses. Office and information-processing technologies could have been altered to affect claims and expense cost structures.

These individual strategies mentioned above could, of course, be taken in various combinations. They would, as strategies which were directly part of the underwriting module, have secondary effects on reinsurance and investment strategies. The DSS provided the framework for managers to think about the relationships between strategic variables and gain insight about the value of specific strategy sets.

**3.** *Sensitivity Analysis and Fine Tuning.* Once a strategy had been implemented, a series of subsequent follow-up decisions were often needed. These fine tuning decisions could be modeled on the DSS. The DSS was also very useful as a means for conducting a variety of sensitivity analyses.

Managers at the top of the organization were, for the first time, able to access a corporate model and *experiment with the company's future* in this manner. It was relatively easy to input a particular strategy set, evaluate it (using the expected utility rule), modify that strategy set to learn about the company and its environment as a system, and to identify which were good strategies. The DSS provided a thinking algorithm for considering the effects of individual strategies and strategy sets for the firm as a whole.

The DSS also became a forum for communication between managers in the company. Managers from different functional areas and divisions, and at different levels, often discussed various issues and decisions while sitting around a computer with the DSS running. For this to happen, the DSS had to be both powerful in its ability to generate inferences and user friendly.

One important issue in designing a DSS such as the XYZ strategic management system, is how much model structure to incorporate into the system. In the context of this example, a *minimum amount of structure* was seen as simply providing the balance-sheetlike relationships between the variables in Figure 14–1. Such a passive DSS would then allow the user to input a series of variable values (for decision variables) and probability distributions (for uncertain quantities). It would then run a series of Monte Carlo simulations and calculate output variable values, probabilities, and expected utility values. It was possible to directly or indirectly (via the user) link data base elements and subsidiary models (such as claims forecasting models) to the central DSS. More structure than in this first-pass, basic system design could be introduced. As with decision analysis models, designs with various levels of detail could be chosen.

---

More generally, another form of structure is in the systems and models themselves. How much flexibility does the user have to act as a model builder, or is the model to be completely specified and rigid as part of the system with the user specifying only some parameter values? At one end of this spectrum, the user can be the model builder starting from scratch, in which case the system is really a DSS generator or shell. Such a system contains little or no model structure specific to the particular problem or problem class. The shell provides no intelligence about the problem but is merely a good software system through which a specific DSS can be created. Although such systems provide little intelligence, they do provide a great deal of flexibility.

At the other end of the spectrum is the highly structured DSS. Many relationships between variables are built into the fabric of the DSS and may or may not be addressable by the user. If the structure was cleverly conceived, it may be very useful; however, lack of flexibility may be frustrating to some users.

In both extreme cases, those of no structure and of highly structured instances, there are quite severe limitations. For semistructured and unstructured problems (such as strategic business planning at XYZ) a compromise is often useful. A basic structure such as in Figure 14–1 was used in the XYZ case. This was supplemented by a series of rules of logic and relationships which could be called upon as options. For example, consider a situation where a manager observes a trend in a particular market segment toward lower insurance prices. Some managers might prefer to intuitively formulate some response strategies and simulate their effects using the DSS. For those managers, the basic structure model was available for use on a trial-and-error iterative basis. For other managers, it was preferred to allow the computer to suggest possible responses or at least directions of response in terms of the direction of change of parameter values. To enable this, various rules and logics had to be built in. This can be considered as a beginning of an *expert system* or *artificial intelligence* characteristic. These fields are considered more generally in the next section of this chapter.

As the ultimate in formal structure, it is possible in theory to "close the loop" in the DSS by including a search routine algorithm to find the globally

**FIGURE 14–2** Strategy Set for a Given Set of Inputs

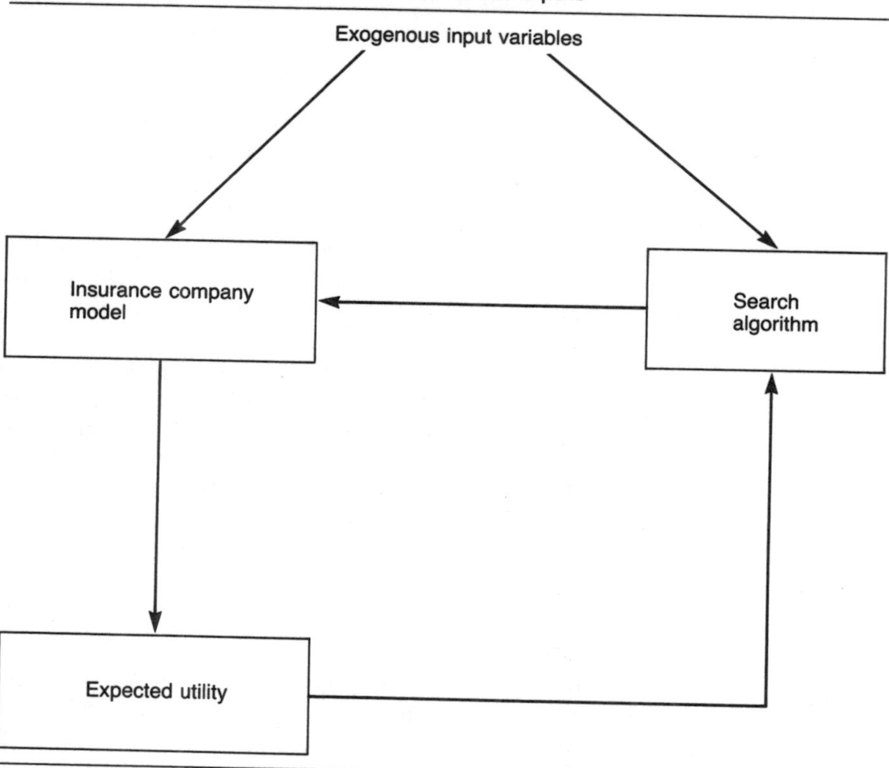


optimal strategy set (maximum expected utility) for a given set of inputs. This very high degree of structure is depicted in Figure 14–2. For complex problems such as the XYZ strategic management process, such automated procedures are likely to be inappropriate because they do not accommodate the major benefit of a computerized decision support system—that is, the *combination of human imagination, creativity, and intelligence with computer-based power in the form of rational modeling logic, memory, and data processing capacity.*

## EXPERT SYSTEMS AND ARTIFICIAL INTELLIGENCE

In recent years, new developments have occurred in computerized decision support which have been labelled *expert systems* and *artificial intelligence.* These fields have been defined in various ways, sometimes as subsets of each other or as very similar or as totally distinct. The following definitions are representative of most views, and taken together, give an effective description of each field.

## Expert Systems

**1.** "An expert system is a knowledge base of information which can perform as an 'expert': given sufficient data, it can make valid, reasoned deductions that can aid the user in making decisions." (O'Keefe 1985, p. 125.)

**2.** "Expert systems are computer software systems that use knowledge (rules about the behavior of elements of a particular subject domain), facts, and inference (reasoning) techniques to solve problems that normally require the abilities of human experts. The goals of expert systems include substituting for an unavailable human expert, assimilating the knowledge of multiple human experts, and training new experts." (Oxman 1985, p. 36.)

**3.** "Expert systems are programs or sets of programs designed to multiply the value of real experts by putting their knowledge at the fingertips of non-experts." (Lampert 1985, p. 139.)

**4.** "An expert system is a problem-solving program that achieves good performance in a specialized problem domain that generally requires specialized knowledge and skill. The systems process the knowledge of experts and attempt to mimic their thinking, skill, and intuition." (Ford 1985, p. 21.)

**5.** "An expert system for managers . . . is defined here as a system that captures the specialized knowledge that managers bring to bear on the decision making tasks they perform, and it uses this knowledge to diagnose potential or actual problems, make recommendations, and offer explanations of its diagnoses and recommendations" (Blanning 1984, p. 311.)

## Artificial Intelligence

**1.** Helferich (1984, p. 123) has written that: "The Handbook of Artificial Intelligence (Arron Barr and Edward Feigenbaum, editors) describes AI as "the part of computer science concerned with designing intelligent computer systems, that is, systems that exhibit the characteristics we associate with intelligence in human behavior—understanding language, learning, reasoning, solving problems, and so on."

**2.** "The AI branch of expert, or knowledge-based, systems can be seen as an extension of decision-support systems, with the greatest immediate and potential relevance for planning professionals." (Briggs 1985, p. 36.)

**3.** "Artificial intelligence (AI) can be defined as the subfield of computer science concerned with the use of computers in tasks which are normally considered to require knowledge, perception, reasoning, learning, understanding, and similar cognitive abilities." (Kerckhoffs et al. 1986, p. ix.)

**4.** "Artificial intelligence is a branch of computer science and engineering which derives many of its concepts from cognitive psychology." (Meador 1985, p. 601.)

## PUTTING IT TOGETHER: DSS, ES, AND AI

From the definitions and descriptions above it is clear that a particular DSS may or may not incorporate AI features. The second definition of AI (above) is a good categorization. AI concepts and features may be built into a DSS, essentially transforming it into an expert system.

Whereas a DSS is normally passive and may provide decision support through models and inferences from models about problems, expert systems (incorporating AI features) can be active and make deductions and recommendations founded on rules and logic.

**FIGURE 14–3** DSS Relationships

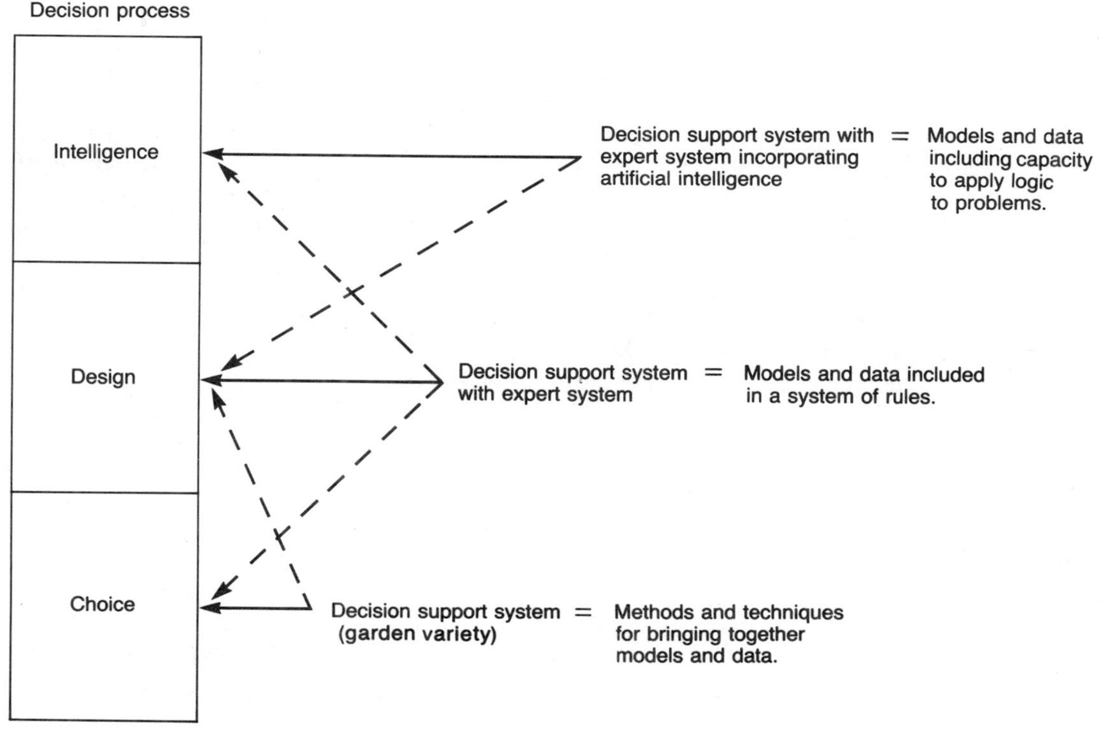

We can decompose managerial decision processes into phases of intelligence, design, and choice.[2] Previous decision-aiding philosophies, such as operations research, were mainly able to support the choice phase. Decision analysis provides design aids and a mechanism for more effectively using intelligence. (Earlier in this book we described decision analysis as a thinking algorithm.) In the case of DSS, where such systems merely use operations research techniques in a user-friendly manner, they primarily address the choice phase. However, when human expertise is encapsulated, DSS supports the design phase, and AI techniques also provide computer-based aid in the intelligence phase. Figure 14–3 shows these relationships, and the dotted lines on Figure 14–3 show that the boundaries and relationships are not fully sharp and clear, but that there is some overlap.

## APPLICATIONS: DESCRIPTIONS OF SOME DSS AND ES

A substantial and rapidly growing number of decision support systems and expert systems have been developed and implemented. It is an interesting exercise to examine a representative sample of these to understand how they can enhance managerial decision processes.

### XCON: VAX Production at Digital Equipment Corporation

Briggs (1985) reports on XCON, an AI/ES that allows Digital Equipment to efficiently and effectively configure its VAX computer product. Such expert systems operate with the expertise encapsulated as a series of rules, many of which are styled as "if . . . then . . . else." Briggs reports that XCON has 4,500 rules and has successfully processed over 100,000 orders, some of which include nearly 10,000 components. Weighed against the obvious advantages of having an automatic system for translating customer needs into a complex computer system configuration is the development cost of that system. We note that XCON consumed a number of *years* in its development, as do many other substantial DSSs and ESs. Given that the cost of developing a sophisticated DSS or ES may run into six or seven figures and cannot be guaranteed to be effective, the decision to develop a specific DSS or ES is itself a complex decision problem.

### MYCIN: Diagnosis and Treatment of Infectious Diseases

Bonczek et al. (1980) describe MYCIN, a computer program which accepts information about a medical patient, requests more information, such as test data, and suggests possible diagnoses and treatments. MYCIN allows for

---

[2] This decomposition is due to Simon (1960).

input and output to be English-like. It also is capable of explaining its deductions and diagnoses.

This system contains knowledge about diseases and symptoms and a rule-based inference process that draws upon the knowledge base. This design, including an inference "engine" and knowledge base, is proving to be a successful one in a number of systems. During a consultation with MYCIN, a patient-specific data base is established which is operated on by the rule system. Note that the knowledge base is one which can be modified as new knowledge is produced by medical researchers. Second, the knowledge base can be very large. In such systems, knowledge bases are limited only by computer memory or software limitations and can far exceed human retention/memory limits.

## STRATPORT: DSS for Strategic Planning

Larreche and Srinivasan (1983) have compiled a sophisticated program for supporting strategic planning and analysis processes.

STRATPORT contains a mathematical model and a user interface. It provides decision support for both strategy evaluation and strategy formulation with respect to resource allocation and management of funds. It typically involves the analysis of strategies which might be put in place over a two- to five-year period, and which may have effects lasting from 5 to 15 years. It provides a framework through which different resource allocation policies can be examined as portfolios.

Within STRATPORT, the organization is considered as a series of business units. Within each business unit, a framework is provided for analyzing potential profitability. Variables such as market share, market size, industry production, price, costs, and working capital are included in the analysis. Major output variables are profit and net cash flow. STRATPORT allows for sensitivity analysis to be performed and is flexible. For example, different costs of capital can be used in different business units.

The structure of the model is a set of functions relating the primary variables to each other. This modeling infrastructure includes:

1. A market function relating established market share to marketing investment.
2. A market maintenance function relating continued market share to marketing expenditure.
3. A capacity-investment function relating capacity changes to expenditure or resources reclaimed.
4. A working capital function which relates working capital requirements to various revenue levels.
5. A cost function, which uses an adaption of the Boston Consulting Group concept of cost being a function of total cumulative production volume.

6. A price-quantity relationship, relating price to cumulative production.

The system has sufficient structure to allow optimization to be feasible so that resource allocation decisions are suggested which achieve maximum net present value over the portfolio of business units. Larreche and Srinivasan point out that STRATPORT's strengths are its ability to combine managerial judgment with empirical data, and allowing the computer to handle the complexity of the optimization and mathematical analysis, yet providing powerful, understandable results and insights. Of course, just as a decision analysis model does not address all aspects of such a complex problem, neither does any DSS such as STRATPORT. For this reason, the creators of STRATPORT point out that it is important to understand its structure, scope, and limitations. For example, personnel, manufacturing, financial policy, and R&D policies are not explicitly included and, hence, must be considered externally to the system.

### AIS: Artificially Intelligent Statistician

Remus and Kottemann (1986) classify decisions as *primary,* that is actually making decisions, or *secondary,* that is, deciding how to decide. Secondary decisions are also known as meta-decisions or predecisions. Remus and Kottemann point out that in statistical analysis, packages such as SPSS focus on primary decisions by providing a set of analytic techniques. Artifically intelligent decision support is provided in their system by assisting the decision maker to determine what data sets are appropriate to the problem and which statistical techniques are appropriate in analyzing it. These are secondary decisions. These aspects are left entirely to the decision maker by conventional statistical packages. The AIS system also contains expertise and supports processes of handling more difficult statistical issues, such as multicolinearity, outliers, and transformations, which are normally left entirely to the user. They demonstrate how decision support systems and particularly AI procedures can aid both primary and secondary decision processes. Such a DSS is fundamentally different from packages such as SPSS, which rely on a substantial knowledge of statistics being held by the user. The extra component of AIS, not contained in SPSS is an expert system which embodies that knowledge of statistics. The aim is not to completely replace the need for a knowledge of statistics by human users, but to support and enhance it.

## SUMMARY

Decision support systems, which may or may not include AI/ES concepts, provide for powerful computer assistance and support of managerial decision making. They can provide substantial support in analyzing problems by integrating the analytical, logical, data processing, and memory capabilities of computers with the creativity of human decision makers.

In implementing DSSs it is important to have the support of top management in an organization and to involve the ultimate DSS users in the DSS design. King (1978, p. 263) notes that it is important to "incorporate implementation considerations into every step of problem-solving or systems design processes. . . . it is far better to develop an improved system which is implemented, than to develop one which is theoretically optimal, but which is not implemented."

For complex, semistructured and unstructured problems, decision analysis models become large and can benefit from being computer based. The XYZ Insurance example is an instance of a decision analysis which would have been too complex to implement without a computer. Given that computers can be used to enhance some decision analyses, the DSS design comprising a data base, model system, and user-friendly interface has much to commend it. The future of decision support would appear to be in the intelligent use of DSS, ES, and AI concepts, particularly when these systems are designed around powerful modeling paradigms such as decision analysis. These computer-based decision aids are already good at tackling structured problems, and substantial progress is being made in using them to support decision making in the context of semistructured problems. Apart from the direct benefits that can be derived from these systems, their use on relatively routine problems liberates managers to concentrate their human energy on the more complex and difficult unstructured problems that they face.

## FURTHER READING

Approximately 25 references have been given in the body of this chapter. Additional useful readings are by Holsapple and Whinston (1987), Bonczek, Holsapple, and Whinston (1981), Leigh and Doherty (1986), and Waterman (1986). Taken together they give an excellent coverage of the field of computerized decision support. Further treatment of the specific use of computers and complementary computer-based procedures in decision analysis is the subject of the next chapter of this book.

## REFERENCES

ANTHONY, R. N. 1985. *Planning and Control Systems: A Framework for Analysis*. Boston: GSBA, Harvard University.

BLANNING, R. W. 1984. "Management Applications of Expert Systems." *Information and Management* 7, pp. 311–16.

BONCZEK, R. H.; C. W. HOLSAPPLE; and A. B. WHINSTON. 1980. "Future Directions for Developing Decision Support Systems." *Decision Sciences* 11, no. 4, October, pp. 616–31.

________. 1981. *Foundations of Decision Support Systems*. New York: Academic Press.

BRIGGS, W. 1985. "Software Tools for Planning: DSS and AI/Expert Systems." *Planning Review* 13, no. 5, pp. 36–43.

CARLSON, E. D. 1983. "An Approach for Designing Decision Support Systems" in *Decision Support Systems,* W. C. House ed. New York: Petrocelli Books.

DIEBOLD, J. 1986. "Information Technology As a Competitive Weapon, *International Journal of Technology Management* 1, no. 1/2, pp. 85–99.

FORD, F. N. 1985. "Decision Support Systems and Expert Systems: A Comparison." *Information and Management* 8, pp. 21–26.

GORRY, G. A., and M. S. SCOTT MORTON. 1971. "A Framework for Management Information Systems." *Sloan Management Review* 13, Fall, pp. 55–70.

HACKATHORN, R. D., and P. G. W. KEEN. 1981. "Organizational Strategies for Personal Computing in Decision Support Systems." *MIS Quarterly* 5, no. 3, September, pp. 21–27.

HELFERICH, O. K. 1984. "Computers That Mimic Human Thought: Artificial Intelligence for Materials and Logistics Management." *Journal of Business Logistics* 5, no. 2, pp. 123–27.

HOLSAPPLE, C. W., and A. B. WHINSTON. 1987. *Business Expert Systems*. Homewood, Ill.: Richard D. Irwin.

KEEN, P. G. W. 1980. "Decision Support Systems: Translating Analytic Techniques into Useful Tools." *Sloan Management Review* 21, no. 3, Spring, pp. 33–44.

________. 1985. "A Walk Through Decision Support." *Computerworld* 19, no. 2, January 14, pp. 3–16.

KEENEY, R. L. 1982. "Decision Analysis: An Overview." *Operations Research* 30, no. 5, pp. 803–38.

KERCKHOFFS, E. J. H.; G. C. VANSTEENKISTE; and B. P. ZEIGLER. 1986. "AI Applied to Simulation." *Simulation Series* 18, no. 1, p. ix, San Diego: Society for Computer Simulation.

KING, W. 1978. "Developing Useful Management Decision Support Systems." *Management Decision* 16, no. 4, pp. 262–73.

LAMPERT, A. 1985. "Expert Systems Get Down to Business." *Computer Decisions* 17, no. 1, pp. 138–44.

LARRECHE, J. C., and V. SRINIVASAN. 1983. "STRATPORT: A Decision Support System for Strategic Planning" in *Decision Support Systems,* W. G. House, ed. New York: Petrocelli Books. Originally published in the *Journal of Marketing*.

LEIGH, W. E., and M. E. DOHERTY. 1986. *Decision Support and Expert Systems*. Cincinnati: South-Western Publishing Company.

MEADOR, C. L. 1985. "Architectural Forms and Functions for Future Decision Support Systems." Proceedings of the Eighteenth Annual Hawaii International Conference on System Sciences, pp. 601–7.

MINTZBERG, H.; D. RAISINGHANI; and A. THEORET. 1976. "The Structure of Unstructured Decision Processes." *Administrative Science Quarterly* 21, June, pp. 246–75.

O'KEEFE, R. M. 1985. "Expert Systems and Operational Research—Mutual Benefits." *Journal of Operational Research Society* 36, no. 2, pp. 125–29.

OXMAN, S. W. 1985. "Expert Systems Represent Ultimate Goal of Strategic Decision Making." *Data Management* 23, no. 5, April, pp. 36–38.

REMUS, W., and J. KOTTEMANN. 1986. "Toward Intelligent Decision Support Systems: A Proposal for an Artificially Intelligent Statistician." Paper presented at TIMS International Conference, Australia, to appear in MIS Quarterly.

SIMON, H. A. 1960. *The New Science of Management Decisions*. New York: Harper & Row.

SPRAGUE, R. H., and H. J. WATSON. 1979. "Bit by Bit: Toward Decision Support Systems." *California Management Review* 22, no. 1, pp. 60–68.

SPRAGUE, R. H. 1983. "A Framework for the Development of Decision Support Systems" in *Decision Support Systems,* W. C. House, ed. New York: Petrocelli Books.

THOMAS, H. 1984. "Strategic Decision Analysis: Applied Decision Analysis and Its Role in the Strategic Management Process." *Strategic Management Journal* 5, 139–56.

WATERMAN, D. A. 1986. *A Guide to Expert Systems*. Reading, Mass.: Addison-Wesley Publishing.

## PROBLEMS

1. What are the components of a decision support system?
2. How can a decision support system help managers to become more effective. Suggest some examples of management situations in the following contexts in which decision support systems could be used to increase the effectiveness of decision making.
   *a*. An unstructured decision process.
   *b*. A semistructured decision process.
   *c*. A structured decision process.
   *How* can decision support systems contribute in each of these contexts?
3. Can decision support systems replace managers? Give reasons for your answer.
4. What are the meanings of the terms: data base, model base, and user interface? Why is a user interface important?
5. Can computers think laterally? What are the definitions of expert systems and artificial intelligence in this context?
6. How much time would have been necessary, in your opinion, to create and make usable the decision support system described in the XYZ Insurance Company example, above? Would the same

system have been usable for a variety of insurance companies or would each one require customization, and if so how much?

7. In the XYZ Insurance example, how much detail should be built in to the system with respect to the structure of the program, and how much should be left to the insurance company managers?
8. In the XYZ Insurance example, what are the major benefits of having a decision support system that would justify its cost?
9. Are the concepts of expert systems and artificial intelligence really useful as decision aids? Are they little more than effective ways to implement decision science and management science models on computers?
10. Is ARBORIST a DSS? Does it contain ES or AI features? Justify your answer in terms of the definitions of these systems.
11. Is ARBORIST user friendly? What are the important dimensions or criteria by which user-friendliness of a system can be measured?

# CHAPTER FIFTEEN

# Complementary Decision Analysis Aids

## OUTLINE



## OBJECTIVES

After completing this chapter, you should be able to:

1. Discuss the strengths and weaknesses of decision analysis software, particularly ARBORIST and SUPERTREE.
2. Use ARBORIST as a decision tree model.
3. Discuss the role of spreadsheets in decision analysis.
4. Note the contribution that influence diagrams can make in decision analysis.
5. Compare decision trees and influence diagrams as modes of representation.
6. Discuss the analytic hierarchy process.
7. Debate the degree to which computers can contribute to the analysis of managerial decisions.
8. Describe the directions in which decision analysis software is developing and discuss the ways in which decision analysis can be more effectively implemented through the use of various complementary decision analysis aids.

## INTRODUCTION

This chapter focuses on using complementary aids and methods to enhance the implementation of decision analysis, and includes a discussion of some associated, relatively new procedures including some decision analysis software packages, influence diagrams, and the analytic hierarchy process.[1] In particular we will focus on the use of computers to enhance the implementation of decision analysis. In doing so, we note that decision analysis has been used effectively in solving managerial problems for over two decades, generally without the benefit of these computerized aids and other processes. Their development, however, increases the potential for more widespread support of managerial decision processes through analysis.

The relatively recent development of these complementary decision aids has arisen hand-in-hand with the proliferation of personal computers and the development of decision support systems. At the very least, they provide a mechanization and automation of decision tree and analytic procedures, releasing managers from being caught up in performing mechanical tasks, so that they can focus on the problem, the model, and its solution. Further, they are potentially able to capture modeling expertise and become valuable tools in supporting decision analysis and other similar processes. As such tools become increasingly powerful and, at the same time, user friendly, they will lead to higher incidences of the use of decision analysis and allow users to be more effective in using it to support managerial decision processes.

This chapter begins with a review of state-of-the-art decision analysis software. One of these software packages, ARBORIST, is supplied with this book. The documentation is provided as an appendix to this chapter. We then examine spreadsheet software as a decision analysis tool. The following section is an introduction to influence diagrams, a potentially powerful new decision analysis concept. Finally, we review the analytic hierarchy process, which is a method, somewhat similar to multiattribute utility methods, for analyzing decision problems that incorporate multiple criteria.

## DECISION (TREE) ANALYSIS SOFTWARE

A substantial and growing number of software packages are currently available that allow for computerized solution of management science and decision analysis models. For those who wish to try a *multipurpose* package that is reasonably user friendly and cheap, Erikson and Hall's package,

---

[1] Decision analysis software packages have existed for about two decades, one of the first and best being Schlaifer's MANECON system. This system, described in R. O. Schlaifer, 1971 *Computer Programs for Elementary Decision Analysis* (Boston: Harvard University Press, 1971), includes programs that fit utility functions and facilitate the assessment of probabilities.

*Computer Models for Management Science* (Addison-Wesley) is a useful starting point for solving small problems.[2] Many of these general-purpose packages include programs for solving decision trees, which usually do little more than perform Bayes Theorem calculations and decision tree rollback.

There are, however, two packages that are specifically focused on decision trees/decision analysis only, which merit detailed review. They are the best available decision (tree) analysis support systems commercially available. In the light of the detailed discussion of decision analysis in this book, it is relevant to critically review and analyze this state-of-the-art software, to determine both their strengths and limitations in terms of decision analysis support.

## ARBORIST[3]

ARBORIST is a decision analysis software package. It consists of computer programs that allow the user to construct a decision tree, display it on a computer screen and print it, roll back the tree, and conduct sensitivity analysis.

ARBORIST can be used on an IBM or TI personal computer. Appropriate graphics adaptors and memory capabilities are necessary.

ARBORIST is a decision tree shell, in the sense that the user is able to feed information about any decision tree into the computer and automate part of the decision analysis process. It has a very useful graphic display of decision trees, probability distributions, and sensitivity graphs. It allows the user to simultaneously view a portion of the tree in detail and still retain a macroview of the whole decision tree on another section of the screen. ARBORIST allows the user to incorporate formulae into the outcome values on a tree, and to import data and formulae from Lotus 1-2-3.[4]

ARBORIST requires an investment of time for the user to become familiar with its structure before it can be effectively used. This is a characteristic of virtually all powerful software systems. The return on that investment of time is that the mechanics of decision tree analysis are performed by the computer, including rolling back the tree, conducting sensitivity analysis, and calculating risk profiles. For very simple, small decision trees, ARBORIST is not needed. For larger and more complex decision trees, ARBORIST can be a very useful aid.

Another very useful feature of ARBORIST is its ability to manipulate subtrees. Where there is repetition of sets of nodes and branches on a decision tree, ARBORIST allows for these to be copied from one section of

---

[2] W. J. Erickson and O. P. Hall, *Computer Models for Management Science* (Reading, Mass.: Addison-Wesley Publishing, 1980).

[3] ARBORIST is a product of Texas Instruments. See the ARBORIST documentation appended to this chapter.

[4] Lotus 1-2-3 is a product of the Lotus Development Corporation.

a tree to others, making the tree-building process very efficient, relative to doing it by hand.

ARBORIST is not for the decision analysis novice. You must understand the basics of decision tree analysis prior to using ARBORIST. *Since it is a decision tree shell, ARBORIST cannot on its own create a decision tree for any particular problem.* This knowledge must be provided by the user. However for medium-sized and larger trees in particular, ARBORIST allows the analyst efficiently to do with a computer what may take many sheets of paper and a significant amount of time with a calculator. The in-built decision tree mechanics are of course error free, and the program checks that probabilities on branches emanating from a chance node sum to one. It is menu driven, requiring no knowledge of any computer language or programming skills. The documentation is good, and the package has been designed so that the user only rarely needs to refer to it, after an initial learning period.

In summary, this program contains a user-friendly system for creating, graphically representing, and thoroughly analyzing decision trees. It can be used to very good advantage with large decision trees and is particularly effective when repeated analyses are required as with sensitivity analysis.

## SUPERTREE[5]

SUPERTREE is a decision tree software package that allows the user to construct a decision tree and analyze it. A related product, SENSITIVITY, allows the user to investigate in detail the relationships between elements of a decision analysis.[6] These programs form a powerful combination, capable of evaluating large decision trees. On an IBM PC, decision trees with thousands of nodes can be manipulated. Apart from being a decision tree shell, SUPERTREE is able to calculate expected utilities and certainty equivalent values, using the exponential utility function, in which the user specifies the degree of risk aversion. It can also be used to calculate the expected value of imperfect and perfect information. It has a reasonably good graphical display of decision trees, however the user-friendliness of the data input (decision tree building) process is constrained. Unlike ARBORIST, one does not build a decision tree on SUPERTREE by directly graphing it. To build a tree, the user must number the nodes and specify predecessor and following nodes in response to prompts. This is rather like most PERT/CPM software packages where one cannot fully experience the process of graphically creating the diagram on the screen in real time. Instead, the user enters the numerical and descriptive decision tree data on a

---

[5] SUPERTREE is a product of SDG Decision Systems, Menlo Park, California.

[6] SENSITIVITY is a product of SDG Decision Systems, Menlo Park, California.

node-by-node basis and, when this is finished, SUPERTREE constructs and displays the tree.

Apart from this limitation, this package is a powerful one, having many features and the capability to interface a number of spreadsheets, including Lotus 1-2-3, Symphony, Multiplan, FSC-EPS, and IFPS.

SUPERTREE is able to provide plots of histograms or cumulative probability distributions and also evaluate sensitivity to changes in parameters, probabilities, or payoffs, and attitude toward risk. Like ARBORIST, it is menu driven and does not require knowledge of a computer language.

## DISCUSSION OF DECISION TREE SOFTWARE

An evaluation of decision tree software and a comparison of various available packages involves a variety of elements. Indeed, the decision to purchase a package or to use an available package can be considered as multiattributed and at least a little bit complex. We provide here a summary of the comparative strengths and weaknesses of ARBORIST and SUPERTREE. The reader is strongly encouraged to experience the various factors firsthand by using the ARBORIST package supplied with this volume!

The differences between ARBORIST and SUPERTREE are mainly that ARBORIST is a substantially better graphic decision tree aid, while SUPERTREE is more powerful and contains more features, such as allowing the use of exponential utility. In terms of using decision tree analysis as a decision process aid and generating insight for the user about the nature of a problem through constructing a decision tree, ARBORIST is superior. SUPERTREE is more powerful and boasts more analytic features related to the analysis of a decision tree.

It is useful to consider both these packages together, as the best available decision analysis software packages, to determine how computers can aid professional decision analysts and students of decision analysis. Each package allows the user to build a decision tree; however, for small decision trees of about three nodes or less, it is usually quicker and easier to perform the construction and calculation manually rather than to use the computer. The computer packages come into their own for medium sized (5–30 nodes) and large decision trees. Large decision trees become impossible to work by hand but can be capably manipulated by these packages. ARBORIST, suitably configured on a personal computer can handle approximately 1,000 nodes, and SUPERTREE can handle approximately 8,000 nodes.[7] The packages allow sets of nodes, which may appear in many places on a tree, to be efficiently reproduced. This repetition of series of nodes at various points

---

[7] The version of ARBORIST supplied with this volume is limited to 30 nodes.

on a middle-sized to large tree is an extremely valuable feature. Whereas without such packages, decision trees with 20 or more nodes are very tedious to analyze, they become relatively easy to manage with the aid of a computer. And of course, once a tree is built, sensitivity analysis, or any changes at all can be performed easily, and the tree can be reevaluated in seconds using this software.

A related advantage is with respect to those situations when a decision analyst chooses not to completely evaluate a decision tree but to sample from it using Monte Carlo simulation techniques. In Chapter 9 the details of Monte Carlo procedures were given, and it was suggested that when decision trees become large, complete analysis by hand becomes infeasible. One must then resort to Monte Carlo sampling. Given that packages like ARBORIST and SUPERTREE can handle large numbers of nodes effectively, the complete evaluation of large decision trees becomes easier, and the point at which the user resorts to Monte Carlo simulation is shifted to larger and larger trees as better software becomes available.

The user must have a good working knowledge of decision analysis to use either ARBORIST or SUPERTREE. The programs do not provide instruction about using decision trees or information about decision analysis in general. They *do* provide good shell systems within which decision trees can be effectively created by a knowledgeable analyst.

As previously mentioned, the programs do not provide a shell for multiattribute utility modeling but are generally limited to decision tree analysis only. This limitation prevents them from being complete decision analysis packages, because there is more to decision analysis than building decision trees. However, they are likely to be the forerunners of more sophisticated packages that will provide the process expertise currently lacking. In future versions of decision analysis packages, it is likely that expert system procedures (see Chapter 14) will be able to integrate decision analysis counselling and expertise with the existing decision tree mechanics. *For example, the human biases that are commonly observable and have been described in Chapter 13 could be documented in a knowledge base and used to aid in probability and utility assessment subroutines.* There is great scope for further development, and a sound basis for computer-aided decision analysis already is in existence. ARBORIST in particular contains advanced graphics features which make decision tree analysis on computers a very powerful analytical device.

## SPREADSHEET MODELING AND DECISION ANALYSIS

Jones (1986) has written that in the setting up of a decision tree and in its evaluation and sensitivity analysis, spreadsheets can be usefully employed to aid the analyst. He points out that decision tree construction is a dynamic process requiring many revisions, and that without computer aid, this process requires much time-consuming redrafting. Jones demonstrated that a spreadsheet program can be used to construct and display a decision tree, to manipulate and revise it, and to calculate the expected values and optimal strategy. He gives detailed demonstrations of how to use a spreadsheet to perform sensitivity analysis, both one-way (where a single parameter changes) and two-way (where two parameters change simultaneously). Spreadsheets have high-quality, powerful graphics features that can be employed to display sensitivity analysis outputs.

The disadvantages of the spreadsheet approach are the tediousness of setting up a tree and the supporting mechanisms in a spreadsheet. It is feasible, of course, to design and store a spreadsheet *macro,* which is a spreadsheet program, from which to generate trees for specific problems. The use of a macro is highly unlikely to be superior to a program such as ARBORIST, which is a focused decision tree shell already containing all the infrastructure to build and analyze decision trees.

In another article, Jones (1985) shows how a spreadsheet may be used to analyze a legal decision. The decision tree in this instance was constructed and graphically displayed on the spreadsheet, and formulae were used to connect variables affecting payoffs. Although the spreadsheet was effective in correctly performing the analysis and providing computerized aid, there is a great deal of effort required to automate the decision tree analysis process in this manner.

Although spreadsheets are not the best computer tool for setting up and solving decision trees, they can be extremely useful for analyzing *subsidiary models* that contribute to the decision analysis. Decision trees often require quantitative inputs that can be derived or calculated using spreadsheet-based models. Examples of subsidiary models are cash flow models and forecasting models. Sets of formulae can often be used to aggregate various cash flows such as components of revenue and cost, and spreadsheets can be used to perform time discounting to calculate net present value (NPV) and internal rate of return (IRR) values. Spreadsheets are efficient means for performing these types of calculations. In the forecasting context, it is often useful to apply formula-based forecasting models, in extrapolating time series data, to calculate a predicted value for a parameter. These parameter values, cash flows, and other forecasts, are often very important inputs to decision tree models. *The outputs of spreadsheet models can be useful inputs to decision tree models*. This has been recognized by the designers of ARBORIST and SUPERTREE, who have incorporated spreadsheet interfaces into these systems.

Bodily (1986) notes the increasing power and general usefulness of spreadsheets for managerial decision making. He demonstrates how a spreadsheet can be used to draw decision trees but suggests that this process is cumbersome. Although the use of spreadsheets for directly performing decision analyses is limited, Bodily makes the important point that the general modeling capabilities of spreadsheets are bringing the manager and the management science specialist closer together.

In summary, spreadsheets certainly can be used to set up and solve decision trees. There seems, however, to be little or no advantage in using them if a program like ARBORIST is available. The major disadvantage of general purpose spreadsheets is the time required to set up a decision tree. The spreadsheet approach is feasible, and in many instances, superior to manual methods, however the average manager cannot expect to duplicate the power and flexibility of ARBORIST or SUPERTREE for decision analysis use with a spreadsheet. The main contribution of spreadsheets is a vehicle for creating subsidiary models.

## INFLUENCE DIAGRAMS

Influence diagrams are different in form from decision trees but are similar in their purpose. Like decision trees, they are graphical (diagrammatic) representations of decision situations. However, they have a somewhat different design and set of construction rules. Influence diagrams have three kinds of nodes:

1. Decision nodes, shown as squares.
2. Chance event nodes, shown as circles.
3. Value nodes, shown as rounded rectangles.

These nodes are connected by arcs which, strictly speaking, are of two types:

1. Arcs going into value and chance event nodes are conditional and show probabilistic dependence between decision elements.
2. Arcs going into decision nodes represent the chronological order of events.

This distinction between different arc types is similar to that which implicitly occurs on decision trees and need not be formally considered when influence diagrams are constructed.

Influence diagrams are a fairly new development in decision analysis. They were generally not mentioned in decision analysis books published prior to 1980. However, considered as a decision aid, they are a powerful pictorial device for decision model structuring and are being increasingly used to complement (and in some cases replace) decision tree representations.

Influence diagrams are usually more compact forms of representation than decision trees. They tend to be most useful (relative to decision trees) when the decision trees contain repetitive patterns of branches. As mentioned above, they are still in the early days of development and application,

**FIGURE 15–1** Decision Tree (sources of uncertainty: demand, cost, and quality)

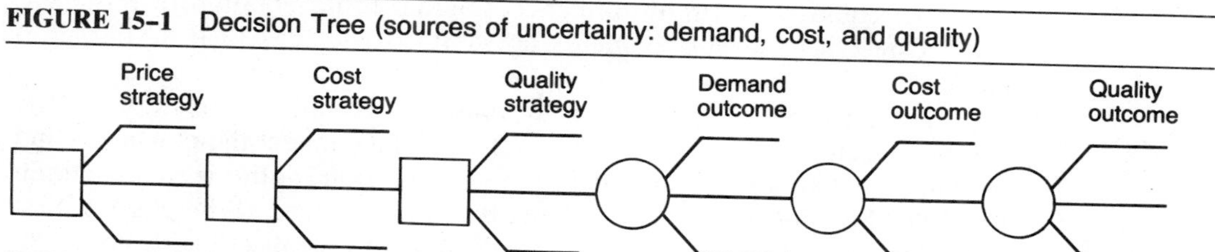


however there is great potential for increasing the power of decision analysis through their use.

Figure 15–1 represents a decision tree where the decision maker is assumed to have control over price, cost, and quality. The sources of uncertainty are demand, cost, and quality. Note that it is quite feasible to have a quality strategy and a cost strategy and still be uncertain about the outcomes of these variables. The decision tree (Figure 15–1) is a structural one and does not show all the branches, or all the consequences (or payoffs) of each outcome, but these could easily be included on the end of each final outcome or as they occur on the various branches.

**FIGURE 15–2** Influence Diagram Nodes for Decision Tree 15–1

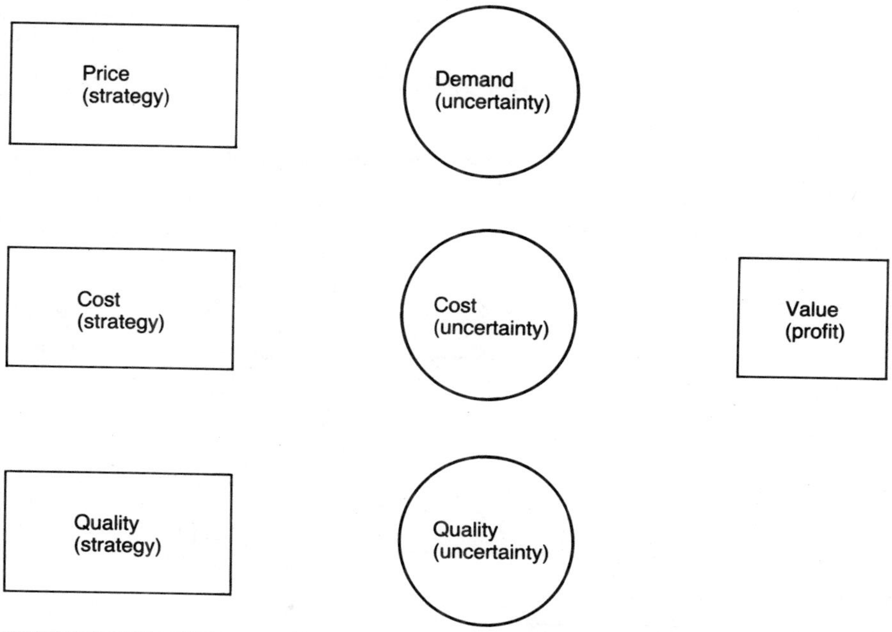

Price (strategy)

Demand (uncertainty)

Cost (strategy)

Cost (uncertainty)

Value (profit)

Quality (strategy)

Quality (uncertainty)

How could we form an influence diagram representation of this decision? Once the decision elements are defined and classified as decision, chance, or value nodes, they must be connected together via arcs.

Two approaches seem generally feasible. The first is to draw all the nodes on a sheet of paper (Figure 15–2) and then connect them. The second is to put the diagram together in a section-by-section synthesis first and then to make the appropriate connections between sections. Whereas the first approach seems reasonable for relatively small problems (10 nodes or less), the second approach seems reasonable for more complex problems.

Figure 15–2 shows the elements of the problem. A second step in constructing this influence diagram is to join the nodes. Figure 15–3 shows a set of arcs.

Confining our discussion to *quality of insight* about the problem produced by decision trees and influence diagrams as structuring aids, was there more to be learned from Figure 15–1 or from Figures 15–2 and 15–3? Certainly the influence diagrams showed the relationship between cost and quality strategies and outcomes in a more systematic manner than the decision tree. Further, the influence diagram specifically shows that demand is influenced by price and quality and not directly by cost. There may be an indirect effect of cost strategy on demand, via quality. This is not clearly shown by the decision tree. In general, the influence diagram represents

**FIGURE 15–3** Influence Diagram (arcs joining nodes)

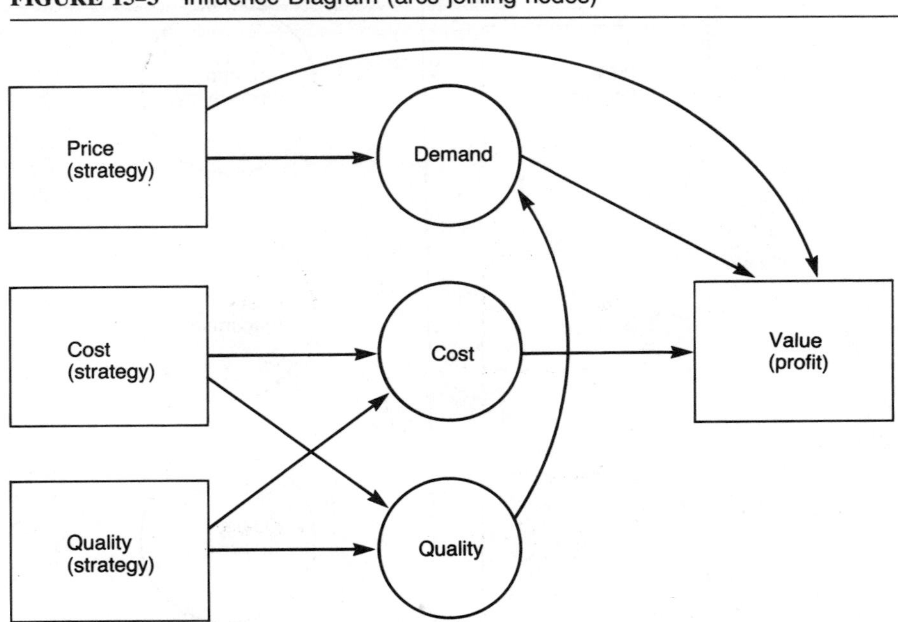

*influences* more directly than the decision tree does and is a very powerful representation for this purpose. However, the decision tree specifically displays the alternative strategies in detail, and the influence diagram does not.

Influence diagrams and decision trees should not be seen as competing or as alternative aids, but as *complementary* in nature. Each one has something useful to contribute to a decision analysis that the other lacks.

A lot of interest has been shown regarding the potential of influence diagrams as complementary aids to decision trees or even as diagrammatic forms that can be used instead of a decision tree. Shachter (1986) has developed an algorithm for evaluating influence diagrams and computerized it in an interactive computer program for influence diagram analysis. The analysis required to evaluate such diagrams directly can be a little complex, however influence diagrams play a useful role as thinking aids in the decision model formulation stage. Before, during, or after constructing a decision tree, it is often useful to try to construct an influence diagram. The purpose of this exercise is to gain inference about the nature and direction of influence of the various decision elements on each other.

Diffenbach (1982) takes a similar although somewhat broader approach to influence diagrams. Diffenbach argued that influence diagrams are qualitative tools only and must be supplemented by other quantitative analysis. Although they do provide qualitative insights about problems, more recent works by Howard, Matheson, Shachter, and others have developed influence diagrams into quantitative representations that are similar in analytic and representational power to decision trees.

An important general point is that both in decision trees and influence diagram representations, there is not a single correct model or picture rendering all others wrong and valueless. Indeed, a number of different representations may all contribute to an understanding of the real problem. We must keep in perspective the fact that the aim of decision modeling is to take real action to solve real problems. For example, a manager who felt that cost and quality strategies were highly integrated might prefer Figure 15–4 to Figure 15–3.

Influence diagrams can incorporate quantitative assessments of payoffs and probabilities and may be used to analyze and evaluate alternative strategies. In that sense they can be used to do everything that can be done with decision trees. However, for many purposes it is still more convenient to use decision trees. The role of influence diagrams is presented here as, at least, a very useful model structuring device.

To summarize, influence diagrams are a potentially powerful decision aid. They are likely to play a major role in the future development of decision analysis. It is possible that future decision analysis software packages will contain both decision tree and influence diagram capabilities, with the power to construct one from the other in an interactive process with the user.

**FIGURE 15-4** An Alternative Influence Diagram Representation

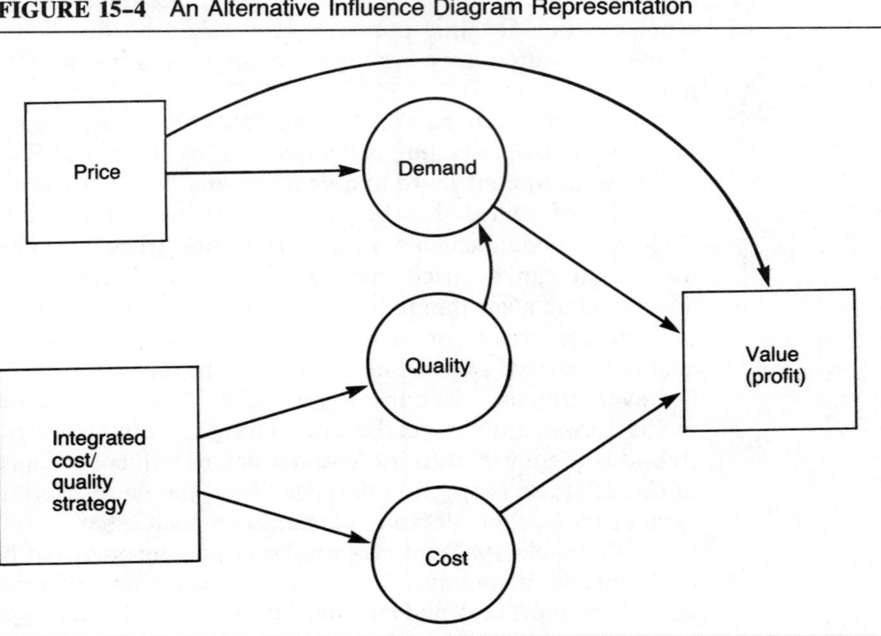


## THE ANALYTIC HIERARCHY PROCESS (AHP)

The analytic hierarchy process (AHP) is included in this book as a complementary aid to decision analysis, because it provides a framework for analyzing complex multiobjective decisions. It has much in common with the multiattribute utility approach outlined in Chapter 7 and some substantial differences. It has been developed into a user-friendly software package, EXPERT CHOICE.[8]

Saaty (1980 and 1986) has been the principal developer of the AHP. He points out (1986, p. 855) that it has been widely used, including applications in "a plan to allocate energy to industries; designing a transport system for the Sudan; planning the future of a corporation and measuring the impact of environmental factors on its development; design of future scenarios for higher education in the United States; the candidacy and election processes; setting priorities for the top scientific institute in a developing country and the faculty promotion and tenure problem."

AHP is based on what Saaty describes as three principles in problem solving:

---

[8] EXPERT CHOICE is a product of Decision Support Software, Inc., McLean, Va.

1. Decomposition, already described in detail in earlier chapters, meaning a description of objectives, alternative actions, and uncertainties. In the AHP, a hierarchy of structural elements is constructed that contains and relates a goal (that is, a single focus) to various criteria and to alternative actions.
2. Comparative judgments, which relate the importance criteria to the primary goal. This is similar to the attribute weighting process in multiattribute utility theory.
3. Synthesis of priorities, which calculates overall priorities for criteria and subcriteria according to the comparative judgments of importance that are made by the decision maker.

It is useful to compare the AHP to the methods described in Chapter 7. As mentioned earlier, the AHP can be implemented using a very well-designed software package, called EXPERT CHOICE. In fact, AHP can be applied with or without this computerized aid; however, the software provides a very good environment for doing the analysis and making the necessary judgments. The existence of this software is a major advantage for AHP in terms of the feasibility of implementation.

The analytic hierarchy process calls for a structure to be established of criteria and subcriteria, followed by a set of pairwise comparisons on the relative importance of those criteria. These pairwise comparisons made by the decision maker may, and usually do, contain inconsistencies. By asking for more than the minimum number of judgments to establish a set of weights, the AHP method uses a technique (known as *principal eigenvectors*) to establish a solution set of importance priorities. The decison maker also is informed of the degree of consistency of his or her judgments. By *consistency,* we mean the degree to which various sets of importance relativities can be reconciled into a single set of weights. For example, if a decision maker states that element *A* is strongly preferred to element *B,* and element *B* is strongly preferred to element *C,* then suggests that *C* is strongly preferred to element *A,* the consistency score would be poor. In decision analysis terms, such orderings would be considered to violate the axiom of transitivity. Saaty claims that transitivity and consistency are not requirements of AHP, and it is a matter of personal preference as to whether this is an advantage or diasdvantage for the user.

Belton (1986) suggests that the AHP is, in many applications, identical to a simple additive weighted value (utility) approach. In a critical analysis of the AHP, Dyer and Wendell (1985) point out that "the introduction of a new alternative may reverse the rankings of the previous alternatives. . . . This result is important because it implies that the rankings produced by the AHP are arbitrary."

Despite such criticisms the AHP approach is becoming quite popular. This may be because just as with decision analysis in general, the benefit of the approach comes from the problem-related insight generated by going through the process, as much as or more than by the bottom-line answer, or model solution. Belton (1986) reports on experiments in which the AHP and multiattribute value (utility) methods produced substantially different rankings and suggested strategies. Despite the differences and difficulties of each procedure, Belton notes that *both share the great strength of encouraging careful thought about a decision in a structured manner*. She points to the usefulness of what decision analysis, and these methods in particular, bring to a problem: that is, *a formalization of our intuitive, common-sense treatment of problem elements, including objectives and alternatives*.

In summary, the AHP has much to commend it. It can be conceptualized as a particular form and operationalization of multiattribute utility theory, although whether this is strictly the case is debatable. As such, its structure provides the advantage of ease of implementation and a measurement of consistency of preferences. Related disadvantages are those that result from the structural assumptions, namely, potential biases associated with ratio scale judgments and the tolerance of intransitivity of judgments and irrationality (Saaty, 1986, p. 841).

The software for implementing AHP is well worth using (demonstration versions are available at nominal costs) to give the student or practitioner of decision analysis a concept of how AHP works and how a computer can be used to effectively support an elicitation process.

## SUMMARY

Decision analysis software is commercially available to aid decision tree construction and analysis. This software, particularly ARBORIST and SUPERTREE, is of high quality and can greatly enhance decision analysis processes.

Influence diagrams are rapidly being developed as an alternative to decision trees as a mode of decision model representation. In some senses they are more concise than decision trees; however, decision trees have been used successfully for many years and are unlikely to be replaced as the main structural device of decision analysis practitioners in the near future. Again, good software is being developed, for example, at Stanford University, to enhance the implementation of influence diagrams as decision support mechanisms.

The analytic hierarchy process is similar to multiple criteria utility analysis and can indeed be considered as a special form of it. Good software (EXPERT CHOICE) is available to assist analysts in using AHP.

In general, we note that decision analysis has had very effective but not very widespread use throughout the 1960s and 1970s and early 1980s in managerial decision processes. The complementary aids, and particularly the advent of the merging of computer technology and decision analysis, create a new potential for the use of decision analysis on a more widespread basis and on a broader set of problems.

## FURTHER READING

Because of the relative newness of many of these complementary methods and aids, there have been relatively few applications of some of them which have been reported in generally available literatures. However, apart from those sources cited earlier in this text, there are some useful references available that the interested reader should follow up.

On the topic of the analytic hierarchy process, Wind and Saaty's paper (1980) examines applications of this method in the field of marketing. Another interesting paper by Saaty, Vargas, and Barzilay (1982) documents a very interesting application of the AHP to the Iran hostage rescue problem.

Influence diagrams are a new and potentially useful field of decision analysis. The interested reader should follow up with Howard and Matheson's (1981) paper and the book by Bodily (1985).

## REFERENCES

BELTON, V. 1986. "A Comparison of the Analytic Hierarchy Process and a Simple Multi-Attribute Value Function." *European Journal of Operational Research* 26, pp. 7–21.

BODILY, S. E. 1986. "Spreadsheet Modeling as a Stepping Stone." *Interfaces* 16, no. 5, September–October, pp. 34–52.

———. 1985. *Modern Decision Making*. New York: McGraw-Hill.

DIFFENBACH, J. 1982. "Influence Diagrams for Complex Strategic Issues." *Strategic Management Journal* 3, pp. 133–46.

DYER, J. S., and R. E. WENDELL. *A Critique of the Analytic Hierarchy Process*. University of Texas, Working Paper 84/85-4-24.

ERIKSON, W. J., and O. P. HALL. *Computer Models for Management Science*. Reading, Mass: Addison-Wesley Publishing, 1980.

HENRION, M. 1985. "Software for Decision Analysis." *OR/MS Today* 12, no. 5, pp. 24–28.

HOWARD, R. A., and J. E. MATHESON, 1984. "Influence Diagrams" in *The Principles and Applications of Decision Analysis,* Volume II. Menlo Park, Calif.: Strategic Decision Group.

JONES, E. 1985. "Risk Analysis with 1-2-3." *Lotus* (Magazine), July, pp. 65–67.

JONES, J. M. 1986. "Decision Analysis Using Spreadsheets." *European Journal of Operational Research* 26, pp. 385–400.

SAATY, T. L. 1980. *The Analytic Hierarchy Process*. New York: McGraw-Hill.

———. 1986. "Axiomatic Foundations of the Analytic Hierarchy Process." *Management Science* 32, no. 7, pp. 841–55.

SAATY, T. L.; L. G. VARGAS; and A. BARZILAY. 1982. "High Level Decisions: A Lesson from the Iran Hostage Rescue Operation." *Decision Sciences* 13, pp. 185–206.

SHACHTER, R. D. 1986. "Evaluating Influence Diagrams." *Operations Research* 34, 6, Nov-Dec, pp. 871–82.

WIND, Y., and T. L. SAATY. 1980. "Marketing Applications of the Analytic Hierarchy Process." *Management Science* 26, no. 7, pp. 641–58.

## PROBLEMS

1. Under what conditions would a decision analyst be better off using a software package like ARBORIST or SUPERTREE, rather than manually setting up and solving a decision tree?
2. What are the major differences between ARBORIST and SUPERTREE?
3. How user friendly is ARBORIST?
4. How can spreadsheets be used within decision analysis? Are they as powerful as the special purpose decision analysis packages, and are they as flexible?
5. How do influence diagrams contribute to decision analysis? In what ways can they complement decision trees?
6. What does the analytic hierarchy process do, and how can it complement decision analysis? What are its strengths and weaknesses?
7. Draw an influence diagram to represent the Mid-Western Utility case study (Chapter 2).
8. Draw an influence diagram to represent the Digmout Mines case (Chapter 8).
9. Draw an influence diagram to represent the James Jones Art Auction (A) case (Chapter 5).
10. Draw an influence diagram to represent the Universal Airlines case (Chapter 2).
11. Review the problem facing Professor and Mrs. Ambivalent (Chapter 3). Could the use of influence diagrams have helped in their decision model structuring process. Draw an influence diagram for them.

# Decision Tree Software

**User's Guide**

Material extracted from *Arborist Decision Tree Software User's Guide* with permission of the publisher.

Arborist Decision Tree Software User's Guide
TI Part No. 2249721-0001
Original Issue: February 1985
Revision A: May 1985
Revision B: May 1987



Your suggestions and comments about the accompanying Texas Instruments publication are welcomed. Please use the documentation questionnaire provided in the back of this manual to send us your comments.



Texas Instruments Incorporated
ATTN: Data Systems Group, M/S 2151
P.O. Box 2909
Austin, Texas 78769-2909

## PREFACE

Arborist™ Decision Tree software is a general purpose tool for decision analysis. It features a unique graphic user interface for decision tree construction, modification, and analysis. Arborist Decision Tree software is not complicated to use, and it is not restricted to one area of decision problem analysis. The software makes it convenient and effective to analyze many problems that previously were not cost effective to analyze.

This book is intended for use by those who have a good working knowledge of decision tree analysis techniques. This book is meant to help the reader learn how to use the Arborist Decision Tree software. It includes:

- Installation and start-up information.
- General information about the user interface, concepts, and terminology.
- A tutorial to familiarize the user with decision tree construction methods.
- A chapter about types of modeling (Arborist versus Lotus® 1-2-3®) with descriptions of some common operators and functions.
- A chapter detailing the available commands.
- Three appendixes that discuss error and recovery procedures, special graphic-printing procedures, and custom printer configurations, respectively.

The purpose of this book is not to provide comprehensive instruction in problem analysis and modeling using decision trees.

**TIPC Related Documentation**

The following document contains additional information related to the use of Arborist on a TIPC:

| Title | Part Number |
|---|---|
| *MS™-DOS Operating System*, Volumes 1 and 2 (Version 2.1) | 2243310-0001 |

**IBM PC Related Documentation**

The following document contains additional information related to the use of Arborist on an IBM PC or an IBM PC/XT™.

| Title | Part Number |
|---|---|
| *Disk Operating System* reference manual, Version 2.10 | 6024120 |

# CONTENTS

# CHAPTER 1: GETTING STARTED ON A TIPC

## System Requirements and Options

**System Requirements**

The Arborist software requires the following minimum system configuration:

- TIPC with:
  - 512K bytes of random access memory (RAM). Additional memory up to a total of 640K bytes allows you to build larger trees.
  - One double-sided diskette drive.
  - Three-plane graphics option.
- MS-DOS 2.1 or greater
- Associated documentation for the TIPC and for MS-DOS

**Recommended Options**

These system options are recommended for enhanced operation of the Arborist software. The options are not required for installation and full operation of the Arborist software.

- Color monitor
- Hard (Winchester) disk drive
- Texas Instruments Model 850 or 855 Printer

## TIPC Diskette Installation and Start-Up

### Installing Arborist on a Diskette

**NOTE:** You must have two diskette drives to perform this installation. Once the software has been installed, you can run it on a system that has only one diskette drive.

1. Format two diskettes and label them Arborist Master Diskette and Arborist Work Diskette (see the *MS-DOS Operating System* manual for details).

2. Insert the Arborist Installation Diskette in drive A.

3. Change the default drive to A.

4. Insert the Arborist Master Diskette into drive B.

5. Type INSTALL and press the **RETURN** key.

   This begins a series of copy operations. When prompted, insert the Arborist Work Diskette in drive B, and press any key to continue. Installation is complete when the following message is displayed:

   ```
   Rem Arborist Installation Complete
   ```

6. Store your Arborist Installation Diskette in a safe place.

## Starting Arborist From a Diskette

When you start Arborist, the Master Diskette must be in drive A. After start-up, use the Work Diskette (created in the preceding procedure) for normal work.

1. Insert the Arborist Master Diskette in drive A. If you have two disk drives, insert your Arborist Work Diskette in drive B.

2. Type `A:` and press **RETURN**.

3. Type `ARBORIST` and press **RETURN**.

   Arborist begins loading when the message `Loading Arborist` is displayed. Soon the following message is displayed:

   ```
   Please insert Arborist Work Diskette in drive B:
   Press any key to continue
   ```

4. If you have two disk drives, verify that the Arborist Work Diskette is in drive B and press any key to continue.

   If you have only one disk drive, replace the Arborist Master Diskette with the Arborist Work Diskette when the prompt appears. Press any key to continue. Then press any key when the following prompt appears:

   ```
   Insert diskette for drive B:
   Strike any key when ready...
   ```

5. Wait for the following message to be displayed:

   ```
   Copyright (C) 1985, Texas Instruments -- Press any
   key to continue.
   ```

6. Press any key to continue.

---

**NOTE:** During a normal start-up, the Arborist screen appears at this point in the procedure, and the remaining steps are not required. If this is not an initial start-up, you can now skip to Chapter 3.

The first time you start Arborist, however, a menu of monitor types (color versus monochrome) appears.

---

7. Specify the type of monitor (color or monochrome) by using the cursor-control (**Arrow**) keys to position the highlight on your monitor type and pressing **RETURN.**

   After you have selected the monitor type, a menu of printer types is displayed.

8. Specify the type of printer you are using by positioning the highlight over your printer type and pressing **RETURN**.

---

**NOTE:** You can use the Configuration command to add or change printers after the initial start-up procedure. See Chapter 6 for details.

---

If you select the custom printer option, refer to Appendix B, Custom Printer Configuration, for information on the configuration procedure.

9. Position the highlight over `Exit Menu` and press **RETURN** to select it.

If you selected a preconfigured printer type (anything other than the custom printer option) and your printer is capable of printing in compressed mode, the following message is displayed:

```
Use compressed mode to print the tree? (Y/N)
```

If your printer is not capable of printing in compressed mode, no message appears, and you can skip to step 11.

10. Press the **Y** key to turn on compressed printing or the **N** key for uncompressed printing.

    The compression-mode setting that you now select for your printer remains set until you change it. You can change this setting at any time using the Configuration command. See Chapter 6 for details.

11. You are now ready to learn about Arborist windows, decision tree display characteristics, the user interface, and some fundamental terms and concepts. Skip the rest of this chapter—as well as Chapter 2—and go to Chapter 3, Using Arborist Decision Tree Software.

## TIPC Hard Disk Installation and Start-Up

### Installing Arborist on a Hard Disk

1. Insert the Arborist Installation Diskette into drive A.

2. Type `E:` and press the **RETURN** key (to change the default drive to E).

3. Type A:WSETUP2 and press **RETURN**. This begins a series of copy operations.

4. Installation is complete when the message `Rem Arborist Installation Complete` is displayed.

**Starting Arborist From a Hard Disk**

1. Type E: and press **RETURN**.

2. Type ARBORIST and press **RETURN**.

3. Wait for the following message to be displayed:

```
Copyright (C) 1985, Texas Instruments -- Press any
key to continue.
```

4. Press any key to continue.

---

**NOTE:** During a normal start-up, the Arborist screen appears at this point in the procedure, and the remaining steps are not required. If this is not an initial start-up, you can now skip to Chapter 3.

The first time you start Arborist, however, a menu of monitor types (color versus monochrome) appears.

---

5. Specify the type of monitor by using the **Arrow** keys to position the highlight on your monitor type and pressing **RETURN.**

   After you have selected the monitor type, a menu of printer types is displayed.

6. Specify the type of printer you are using by positioning the highlight over the printer type and pressing **RETURN**.

---

**NOTE:** You can use the Configuration command to add or change printers after the initial start-up procedure. See Chapter 6 for details.

---

   If you select the custom printer option, refer to Appendix B, Custom Printer Configuration, for information on the configuration procedure.

7. Position the highlight over `Exit Menu` and press **RETURN** to select it.

   If you selected a preconfigured printer type (anything other than the custom printer option) and your printer is capable of printing in compressed mode, the following message is displayed:

   ```
   Use compressed mode to print the tree? (Y/N)
   ```

   If your printer is not capable of printing in compressed mode, no message appears, and you can skip to step 9.

8. Press the **Y** key to turn on compressed printing or the **N** key for uncompressed printing.

   The compression-mode setting that you now select for your printer remains set until you change it. You can change this setting at any time using the Configuration command. See Chapter 6 for details.

9. You are now ready to learn about Arborist windows, decision tree display characteristics, the user interface, and some fundamental terms and concepts. Skip the next chapter and go to Chapter 3, Using Arborist Decision Tree Software.

# CHAPTER 2: GETTING STARTED ON AN IBM PC

## System Requirements and Options

**System Requirements**

The Arborist software requires the following minimum system configuration:

- IBM Personal Computer with:
  - 512K bytes of random access memory (RAM). Additional memory up to a total of 640K bytes allows you to build larger trees.
  - One (double-sided) diskette drive.
  - Color Graphics Adapter (CGA) or Enhanced Graphics Adapter (EGA).
- PC-DOS 2.10 or greater
- Associated documentation for the IBM Personal Computer and for PC-DOS

**Recommended Options**

These system options are recommended for enhanced operation of the Arborist software. The options are not required for installation and full operation of the Arborist software.

- Color monitor
- Hard disk drive
- Printer

## IBM Diskette Installation and Start-Up

### Installing Arborist on a Diskette

**NOTE:** You must have two diskette drives to perform this installation. Once the software has been installed, you can run it on a system that has only one diskette drive.

1. Format two diskettes and label them Arborist Master Diskette and Arborist Work Diskette (see the *MS-DOS Operating System* manual for details).

2. Insert the Arborist Installation Diskette in drive A.

3. Change the default drive to A.

4. Insert the Arborist Master Diskette into drive B.

5. Type INSTALL and press the **RETURN** key.

   This begins a series of copy operations. When prompted, insert the Arborist Work Diskette in drive B, and press any key to continue. Installation is complete when the following message is displayed:

   ```
   Rem Arborist Installation Complete is displayed.
   ```

6. Store your Arborist Installation Diskette in a safe place.

### Starting Arborist From a Diskette

When you start Arborist, the Master Diskette must be in drive A. After start-up, use the Work Diskette (created in the preceding procedure) for normal work.

1. Insert the Arborist Master Diskette in drive A. If you have two disk drives, insert your Arborist Work Diskette in drive B.

2. Type `A:` and press **RETURN**.

3. Type `ARBORIST` and press **RETURN**.

   Soon the following message is displayed:

   ```
   Please insert Arborist Work Diskette in drive B:
   Press any key to continue
   ```

4. If you have two disk drives, verify that the Arborist Work Diskette is in drive B and press any key to continue.

   If you have only one disk drive, replace the Arborist Master Diskette with the Arborist Work Diskette when the prompt appears. Press any key to continue. Then press any key when the following prompt appears:

   ```
   Insert diskette for drive B:
   Strike any key when ready...
   ```

---

**NOTE:** During a normal start-up, the Arborist screen appears at this point in the procedure, and the remaining steps are not required. If this is not an initial start-up, you can now skip to Chapter 3.

The first time you start Arborist, however, a menu of color and monochrome display modes (including graphics adapter types) appears.

---

5. Specify the type of monitor/graphics adapter you are using by typing the number displayed beside your graphics adapter type. When prompted for verification, press the **Y** key if you have selected the type correctly. Press the **N** key to make another selection.

6. Wait for the following message to be displayed:

   ```
   Copyright (C) 1985, Texas Instruments -- Press any
   key to continue.
   ```

7. Press any key to continue.

   A menu of printer types is displayed.

8. Specify the type of printer you are using by using the cursor-control (**Arrow**) keys to position the highlight on your printer type and pressing **RETURN**.

   ---

   **NOTE:** You can use the Configuration command to add or change printers after the initial start-up procedure. See Chapter 6 for details.

   ---

   If you select the custom printer option, refer to Appendix B, Custom Printer Configuration, for information on the configuration procedure.

9. Position the highlight over `Exit Menu` and press **RETURN** to select it.

   If you selected a preconfigured printer type (anything other than the custom printer option) and your printer is capable of printing in compressed mode, the following message is displayed:

```
Use compressed mode to print the tree? (Y/N)
```

If your printer is not capable of printing in compressed mode, no message appears, and you can skip to step 11.

10. Press the **Y** key to turn on compressed printing or the **N** key for uncompressed printing.

    The compression-mode setting that you now select for your printer remains set until you change it. You can change this setting at any time using the Configuration command. See Chapter 7 for details.

11. You are now ready to learn about Arborist windows, decision tree display characteristics, the user interface, and some fundamental terms and concepts. Unless you need specific instructions on changing graphics adapter types (see the last section in this chapter), you can skip the rest of this chapter and go to Chapter 3, Using Arborist Decision Tree Software.

## IBM PC Hard Disk Installation and Start-Up

### Installing Arborist on a Hard Disk

1. Insert the Arborist Installation Diskette into drive A.

2. Type `C:` and press the **RETURN** key (to change the default drive to C).

3. Type `A:WSETUP2` and press **RETURN**. This begins a series of copy operations.

4. Installation is complete when the message `Rem Arborist Installation Complete` is displayed.

### Starting Arborist From a Hard Disk

1. Type `C:` and press **RETURN**.

2. Type `ARBORIST` and press **RETURN**.

---

**NOTE:** During a normal start-up, the Arborist screen appears at this point in the procedure, and the remaining steps are not required. If this is not an initial start-up, you can now skip to Chapter 3.

The first time you start Arborist, however, a menu of color and monochrome display modes (including graphics adapter types) appears.

---

3. Specify the type of monitor/graphics adapter you are using by typing the number displayed beside your graphics adapter type. When prompted for verification, press the **Y** key if you have selected the type correctly. Press the **N** key to make another selection.

4. Wait for the following message to be displayed:

   ```
   Copyright (C) 1985, Texas Instruments -- Press any
   key to continue.
   ```

5. Press any key to continue.

   A menu of printer types is displayed.

6. Specify the type of printer you are using by positioning the highlight over the printer type and pressing **RETURN**.

---

**NOTE:** You can use the Configuration command to add or change printers after the initial start-up procedure. See Chapter 6 for details.

---

If you select the custom printer option, refer to Appendix B, Custom Printer Configuration, for information on the configuration procedure.

7. Position the highlight over `Exit Menu` and press **RETURN** to select it.

   If you selected a preconfigured printer type (anything other than the custom printer option) and your printer is capable of printing in compressed mode, the following message is displayed:

   ```
   Use compressed mode to print the tree? (Y/N)
   ```

   If your printer is not capable of printing in compressed mode, no message appears, and you can skip to step 9.

8. Press the **Y** key to turn on compressed printing or the **N** key for uncompressed printing.

   The compression-mode setting that you now select for your printer remains set until you change it. You can change this setting at any time using the Configuration command. See Chapter 6 for details.

9. You are now ready to learn about Arborist windows, decision tree display characteristics, the user interface, and some fundamental terms and concepts. Unless you need specific instruc-

tions on changing graphics adapter types (see the last section in this chapter), you can skip the rest of this chapter and go to Chapter 3, Using Arborist Decision Tree Software.

## Changing the Graphics Adapter Type

You are asked to specify your type of graphics adapter and monitor the first time you run Arborist on an IBM PC. The following graphics adapters are supported for use with Arborist:

- IBM Color Graphics Adapter (CGA)
- IBM Enhanced Graphics Adapter (EGA)
- All other graphics adapters that are fully compatible with either the CGA or the EGA

The graphics adapter type is written to a file so that you will not need to specify it again. However, if you change the type of graphics adapter or monitor, follow these instructions to respecify the type of graphics adapter for Arborist:

1. Change the drive and directory to the drive and directory where Arborist resides. For diskette users, this is the drive containing your Arborist Work Diskette. (Make sure the Arborist Work Diskette is not write-protected.) For hard-disk users, this is directory \ARB2 on drive C.

2. At the PC-DOS prompt, type CLRMODE and press **RETURN**.

The next time you run Arborist, you are prompted to select the graphics adapter type.

# CHAPTER 3: USING ARBORIST DECISION TREE SOFTWARE

## Screen Windows

### Arborist Windows

The Arborist screen is divided into four functional windows. Each window displays a particular type of information. This makes it easier to find information.

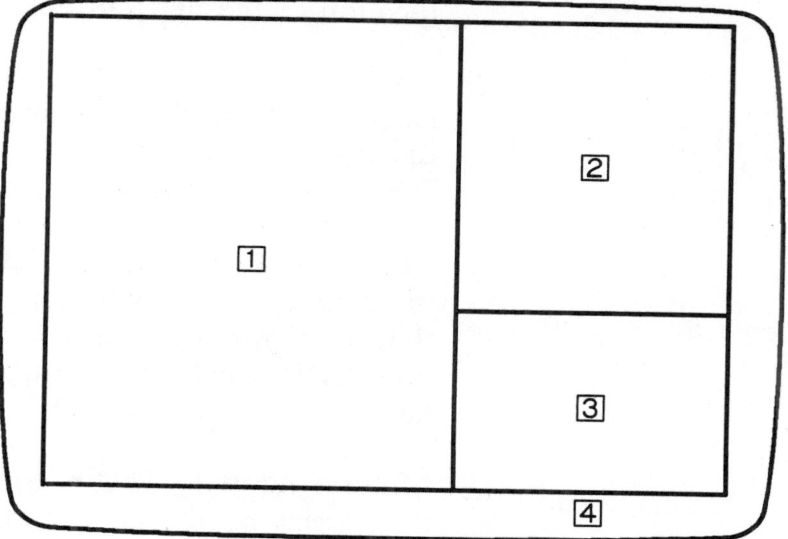


1 Focus window — This window is reserved for the main display of the tree; it focuses on a specific, detailed part of the tree. The Focus window shows both the tree structure and its associated textual information. The Focus window also displays sensitivity analysis and probability distribution graphs, which you will learn about later in this manual.

When you view a tree in the Focus window, the display consists of the *focus node* (which is always the node at the center of the display), the node at the *preceding level*, the nodes at the *following level*, and other nodes at the same level as the focus node.

One of the displayed nodes—the *current node*—is the node highlighted when you use the cursor control (**Arrow**) keys to move through the tree. When you move to the preceding or beyond the following level, the tree automatically scrolls in the window to adjust to the relative location of the new current node.

[2] Macro View window — This window is allocated for the macro display of the tree. It displays a larger portion of the tree than the Focus window, and it does not display textual node information. As you move through the tree in the Focus window, the current node in the Macro View window moves to echo that of the Focus window. The Macro View window also displays help information, selection lists, and the probability wheel.

[3] Menu window — This window is reserved for the display of all menus and the editing and display of textual node information.

[4] Message window — This window displays short messages. The items displayed in this window are as follows:

- One-line error messages
- Current command descriptions
- Status information
- Procedural prompts

**Attention Bars**

Attention bars are small bars appearing in the corners of windows. Arborist uses two types of attention bars.

The first type is a status bar. An example of a status bar is the `Active` indicator that appears at the right end of the Message window when a decision tree is being loaded from disk.

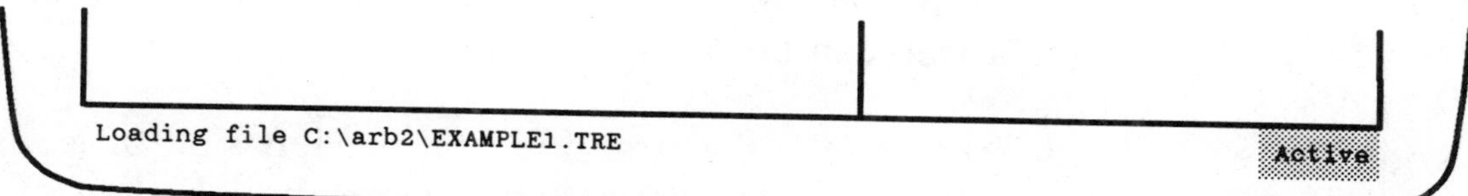


The second type is an information bar, which conveys information about the current operation, as when `Select` appears to indicate the window in which a Browse command is operational or when `Note` appears to indicate an error condition. Information bars also prompt you—as shown in the following message.

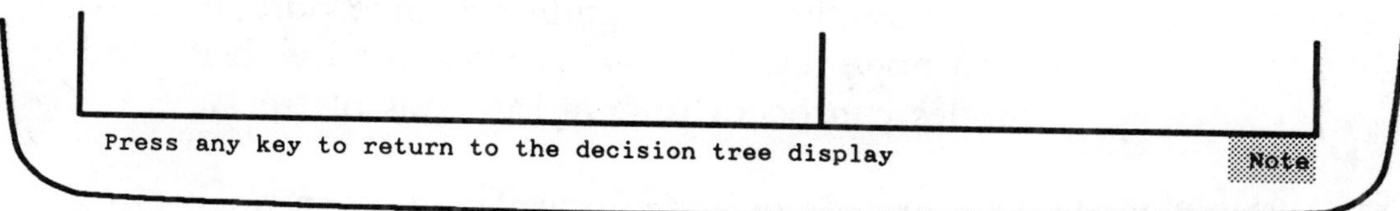


## Decision Tree Display Characteristics and Concepts

**Branch** — A *branch* is displayed as a solid line. Branches connect *nodes*, which represent points along the path of a tree at which some decision must be made or some uncertain (chance) event can occur.

**Decision Node** ■ — A *decision node* is displayed as a solid square and is associated with the branch that leads into it from the left. Conceptually, a decision node is a node at which one of several alternatives is taken. Any interior node of a tree can be a decision node.

**Chance Node**

●

A *chance node* is displayed as a solid circle and is associated with the branch that leads into it from the left. Conceptually, a chance node is a node at which one outcome of a chance event occurs. The outcomes are mutually exclusive. Any interior node of a tree can be a chance node.

**Root Node**

A *root node* is the first node on the left side of a tree. It is denoted by a branch from the left that is connected to either a decision node or a chance node.

**End Node**

---

An *end node* is displayed as a line segment. Visually, the line that represents an end node is a branch that has no token on its right side. Conceptually, an end node is a point in the decision tree that represents the final consequence of a series of decision alternatives and/or chance outcomes. An end node has some value associated with it. End nodes can occur only at the ends of trees.

**Undefined Node**

An *undefined node* is displayed as an open circle inside an open square and is associated with the branch that leads into it from the left. Undefined nodes can occur only as temporary end nodes.

**Annotations**

RATES RISE
(0.4)BAL*(RAT →

*Annotations* (sometimes called annotating information) are displayed in the Focus window as text above and below branches in a tree, as well as at the bottom left corner of the Focus window. Depending on the node type, Arborist supports four types of annotations that you can associate with nodes and branches: descriptions, probabilities, values, and formulas.

- *Descriptions* appear above branches and are often used to name the nodes that follow them.

You use descriptions to create logical labels for branches and nodes as you develop a decision tree structure.

- *Probabilities*—if applicable—appear enclosed in parentheses at the left underside of branches and are used to represent the percentage of probability that a given outcome will occur. The sum of the probabilities of all branches (outcomes) emanating to the right of a chance node must be 1. Probabilities appear only on branches that emanate from chance nodes.

- *Values* appear beneath branches (to the right of probabilities) and are used to assign some value to an end (or undefined) node. This value can be a number, an expression, or a decision variable (these terms are discussed further in Chapters 4 and 5).

- *Formulas* appear at the bottom left corner of the Focus window for a node that is the current node. When you move to another node, the formula(s) disappears and is replaced by either the formula(s) of the new current node or nothing if the new current node has no formulas. Formulas allow you to assign values to decision variables.

Finally, annotations sometimes display a *text overflow arrow*, which is a right-pointing arrow character that appears to the right of annotations on the tree display in the Focus window. The text overflow arrow indicates that the item to which it is appended is too long to be completely displayed on the screen.

To view the item in its entirety, you invoke the Change Values command and then select the item you wish to see by highlighting the appropriate item in the Annotate Node menu (that is, `Description`, `Probability`, `Value`, or `Formulas`). The complete item is displayed on the bottom two lines of the Menu window.

## How the Arborist Screen Appears on Your System

**Mapping Table**

Decision trees and their annotations are displayed in a graphic format. Depending on the type of graphics adapter and monitor your system has, the color, intensity, or token usage indicates the significance of the information. Refer to the table on the following page for the color, intensity, and token mapping for the various configurations.

**Interpreting the Table**

For example, if you are using an IBM-compatible monochrome system with an EGA installed, Arborist uses high intensity and two tokens to display the decision tree and its annotating information:

- High intensity is the normal display color of the tree.
- An asterisk inside the node indicates the current position in the tree (the current node). If the current node is a decision node or a chance node, the asterisk is inside the square or circle. If the current node is an end node, the asterisk is displayed to the right of the branch line.
- A dotted line indicates the best alternative(s) at all decision nodes after the tree has been evaluated. (When you evaluate a tree, the Arborist software traverses every possible path to its con-

**Color, Intensity, and Token Mapping Table**

| Configuration | Normal Tree | Current Node | Best Alternative |
|---|---|---|---|
| IBM EGA monochrome | High intensity | Asterisk | Dotted line |
| TI monochrome | | | |
| Focus window | Low intensity | High intensity | High intensity[1] |
| Macro View window | Low intensity | High intensity | Medium intensity |
| Compaq™ | | | |
| Focus window | Medium intensity | High intensity | High intensity[1] |
| Macro View window | Medium intensity | High intensity | Low intensity |
| TI color | Light blue | Yellow | Green[2] |
| IBM EGA color | Light blue | Yellow | Green[2] |
| IBM CGA color | Light blue | White | Magenta[2] |

**NOTES:**

Compaq is a trademark of Compaq Computer Corporation.

[1] Annotations—rather than nodes or branches—along the path are high intensity.

[2] Used for annotations in Focus window; for branches in Macro View window.

clusion in search of a best alternative. You will learn about tree evaluation in Chapter 4 when you use the Expected Value command). The dotted line indicates which decision alternative(s) have the best value at each decision node.

**Tutorial Screens** The screens printed in this manual are based on the display characteristics of the Arborist software for the IBM EGA monochrome monitor.

## User Interface

### Introduction

Arborist provides a graphics interface that allows you to interact directly with a graphic display of a decision tree.

When building the decision tree, you determine the type of node and number of branches desired, and Arborist handles the drawing and positioning of the tree for you. To view or modify an existing decision tree structure, you simply point at the desired position in the tree structure. Arborist automatically handles the shifting of the tree display.

### Pointing and Selecting In a Tree

Much of your input to Arborist is provided when you point at a specific location in the decision tree.

Pointing is accomplished by use of the cursor control (**Arrow**) keys. Use the **Up Arrow** or **Down Arrow** keys to move up or down one node in the tree. Use the **Left Arrow** or **Right Arrow** keys to move left or right one node. When moving around in the tree, you may hear a beep. The beep indicates that you have reached the last node in the indicated direction.

Special tree pointing mechanisms are available. When the Focus window is active, you can press the **HOME** key to make the focus node become the current node quickly, and you can press **SHIFT-HOME** (**CTRL-** on IBM-compatible keyboards) to make the root node become the current node.

---

**NOTE:** To use two keys that are written with a hyphen between them, press and hold the first key, press the second key, then release both keys.

---

When the Macro View window is active, you can press the **HOME** key to point to the node in the Macro View window that corresponds to the current node in the suspended Focus window. The **SHIFT-HOME** (**CTRL-** on IBM) key sequence points to the root node in the Macro View window.

After you have pointed to a location in the tree in the Focus window, you *select* it by pressing **RETURN**.

### Selecting Commands

You select commands in two ways. The easiest way is to press the character key corresponding to the first letter in the command menu item. For example, to select the Load command from the Input/Output menu, you press the **L** key. When you select a command this way, it is invoked immediately.

You can also use the **Arrow** keys to position the highlight over the desired command or menu item. Use the **Up Arrow** or **Down Arrow** keys to move up or down one item on a menu. Use the **Left Arrow** or **Right Arrow** keys to alternate between columns on a menu. As you move through the menu, the Message window displays a brief description of the highlighted command. Press the **RETURN** key to indicate your selection. The command is not invoked until you press **RETURN**.

### Cancelling Commands

For most commands, you can press the **ESC** key at any time to cancel the command. This is true only for commands whose completion requires additional keyboard input. For example, when you invoke the Change Values command, the Arborist software guides you through a series of interactive prompts or subcommands to which you must respond before you can complete the Change Values command. Press the **ESC** key to cancel the entire command at any time, and Arborist returns you to the menu from which the command was selected.

The **ESC** key does not cancel commands that execute to completion as soon as they are invoked. For example, the sole purpose of the Subtree command is to display a submenu of associated commands. Once the submenu is displayed, the command has executed to its functional completion, so the **ESC** key has no effect. To cancel a submenu that displays from this type of command, select the `Exit Menu` item from the submenu.

### Selecting Items From Selection Lists

You will occasionally encounter a selectable list of items during the execution of a command. For example, when you load an existing tree structure into memory from disk, a list of tree names from which you can choose appears in the Macro View window. Selection lists always appear in the Macro View window.

Selection of items in selection lists is similar but not identical to command selection. To select an item from such a list, you can either highlight the item with the **Arrow** keys and press **RETURN** (just like commands) or press the character key corresponding to the first letter in the item. This latter method, however, does *not* choose the item until you press the **RETURN** key. When you press the character key, the software highlights the first item in the list whose first letter corresponds to the key. If more than one item corresponds to the key, press the character key again, and the highlight moves to the next one.

## Using Editing Keys

Many Arborist commands require the input of textual information, for example, when you edit node annotations. To simplify this process, certain editing keys are available. The following table lists the editing keys and their respective functions.

| Key/Key Sequence | Function |
|---|---|
| BACKSPACE | Moves the cursor to the left one character, deleting that character. |
| DEL | Deletes the character the cursor is on. |
| INS | Toggles between insert and type-over mode. When the insert mode is active, the cursor is a half character high. |
| Left Arrow | Moves one character to the left. |
| Right Arrow | Moves one character to the right. |
| SHIFT-DEL (not supported on IBM keyboard) | Deletes the character the cursor is on and all characters to the right of the cursor. |
| SHIFT-Left Arrow (CTRL-Left Arrow on IBM) | Moves the cursor to the first character position in the edit field. |
| SHIFT-Right Arrow (CTRL-Right Arrow on IBM) | Moves the cursor to the last character position in the edit field. |

### Help Feature

Arborist includes an online help feature. To use the help feature, press **F9** or **SHIFT-?**. A brief message about the current command or menu item appears in the Macro View window. Press any key after reading the message. Help can be invoked whenever Arborist is waiting for a selection (except when a Macro Browse command is active).

The help feature is not intended as an error recovery system. It is a mechanism to assist you during normal operations.

## Decision Tree Analysis

### Uses

A decision tree is a graphic representation of a problem or decision that involves uncertainty.Decision tree analysis is a decision analysis technique that is useful in structuring and analyzing an uncertain decision in the form of a decision tree.

An uncertain decision may incorporate elements of chance over which you have little control. For example, you face uncertainties when you begin pricing a new product for your company: What is the total market size? What share of that market can you expect to get for your company? What types of pricing actions will your competition take? Decision tree analysis allows you to represent these types of questions as chance points (or nodes) along a tree structure. You then represent the many possible outcomes for each of these nodes.

You do have control over certain elements in your problem. For example, in the pricing problem, you will ultimately make the decision to set an initial price for your product above or below the perceived market price, or you may want to decide from your analysis whether to price your product at all—that is, whether you should enter the market or scrap the project. You can represent these types of decisions as decision nodes in your tree.

Decision tree analysis provides a method for assigning values, probabilities, and other information to nodes and branches as you work your way through the tree structure. The Arborist software allows you to build decision tree structures both systematically and dynamically.

## General Procedure

To perform decision tree analysis, you follow these general steps:

1. Define the decision to be made.

   By carefully defining the decision, you create a logical basis for the decision tree structure. This definition guides you in collecting the information you need for the decision tree.

2. Structure the decision into a decision tree.

   Structuring the decision is important for determining the relationships between decision options and events that affect the decision. By structuring the decision into relationships, you can ensure that no important factors have been overlooked.

3. Quantify the information involved in the decision.

   When you quantify the information in the decision, you assign payoffs and probabilities to decision options and chance events. These assigned values enable you to analyze the tree and evaluate it to determine the best decision.

4. Evaluate the information using various criteria to determine the best decision.

   By evaluating the information in the decision tree, you can determine the best possible decision.

## Decision Tree Building

### Preparation

Before using Arborist to create a decision tree, you analyze the case to determine the answers to these questions:

- Which events require that a choice between alternatives be made?
- Which events are governed by chance?
- Which events are final outcomes?

### Translating the Problem

After you analyze the case to determine the type and sequence of the events, you map the events to the corresponding Arborist elements. Events requiring a choice between alternatives become Arborist decision nodes. Events governed by chance become Arborist chance nodes. Final outcomes become Arborist end nodes.

After you map the case events to the Arborist elements, you can construct the decision tree using one of the following structural approaches to building decision trees.

**Approach 1: One Complete Path at a Time**

In this approach, you build a decision tree one *path* to an end node at a time. That is, you build the tree—a node and branch at a time—until you reach an end node (final outcome), and then you backtrack to each defined node and repeat the process until the tree structure is complete.

You first create the root node of the tree and then assign any associated information to the node. When you define the node type for the root node (or for any node), the Arborist software automatically adds a new undefined node/branch.

In this approach, you again assign any associated information to the new node, and then define its node type. Continue this process until you reach an end node, then go backwards in the tree to the previous branch point (node) and repeat the process. When you have defined all end-node paths for the previous node, then go backwards in the tree to *its* previous node and repeat the process again. Your tree structure is complete when you have traversed every path to all possible end nodes from all possible branch points.

**Approach 2: One Event at a Time**

In this approach, you construct the tree one *decision event* at a time. Like approach 1, you first create the root node of the tree and define its node type. Arborist adds a new undefined node/branch.

Instead of defining the node type of this new node, however, you add undefined nodes to the root node until there is a sufficient number of undefined nodes to enumerate all of the primary decision points needed for the root node. You then go back and define the node type for the first node and add all of its branches. Repeat this process for each primary decision point for the root node (and for every decision point following each primary decision point) until the tree structure is complete.

**Optional Annotations**

In either approach, you can annotate the branches and nodes of your tree as much or as little as you wish. You can fully annotate the tree as you work your way through the tree structure, or you can assign only descriptions to branches (sketch the tree) and wait until later to do the rest.

You are now ready for the tutorial in Chapter 4. The tutorial reinforces and extends the concepts presented in this chapter with the introduction of several commands. When necessary, use Chapter 3 as a reference.

# CHAPTER 4: TUTORIAL GUIDE TO ARBORIST DECISION TREE SOFTWARE

## About the Decision Trees in This Chapter

**Tutorial Trees**

EXAMPLE1 is a decision tree that is used to analyze the decision of whether to lock in at the current interest rate for a loan or to wait. You edit the tree by adding a subtree structure (SUB1) to determine what interest rates do if the decision is made to wait.

LEGAL is a decision tree that you will construct; it is used to determine whether to settle or to litigate a lawsuit.

FINMIN is a decision tree used to evaluate alternative financing plans. It will be used in the last portion of the tutorial to demonstrate the Arborist interface with Lotus 1-2-3.

**Trees Available for Reference**

Both EXAMPLE1 and LEGAL have respective counterparts (RATES and LAWSUIT) that already exist on the diskette for your reference. These reference decision trees are available for you if you have any problems editing or creating the trees during the tutorial.

To view the reference trees, load the tree of interest (see Loading an Example Decision Tree later in this chapter) and use either the Print command with the Tree item (see Chapter 6) or the Browse command (see Chapter 6).

## Starting Arborist Decision Tree Software

### Introduction

If you turned to this chapter directly after reading Chapters 1 (or 2) and 3, the Arborist screen is already displayed. If so, you can skip to step 5 in this section and then continue with the tutorial.

### Loading Arborist

1. Boot your computer and set the default drive (and directory) to A: (C: for an IBM system with a hard-disk drive, E: for a TIPC with a hard-disk drive).

2. If you are using a computer system with a diskette drive, insert the Arborist Master Diskette into drive A.

3. Type ARBORIST and press the **RETURN** key.

   The Arborist loading sequence begins. If you are using a system with a hard-disk drive, skip to step 5. If you are using a system with a diskette drive, the following message is displayed:

   ```
   Please insert Arborist Work Diskette in drive B:
   Press any key to continue
   ```

4. If you have two disk drives, insert your Arborist Work Diskette in drive B and press any key to continue.

   If you have only one disk drive, replace the Arborist Master Diskette with the Arborist Work Diskette when the prompt appears, and press any key to continue. Then press any key when the following prompt appears:

   ```
   Insert diskette for drive B:
   Strike any key when ready...
   ```

After a few moments, the Arborist screen is displayed. See Chapter 3 for details on the Arborist screen and its windows.

5. Press any key, and the Main menu appears in the Menu window.

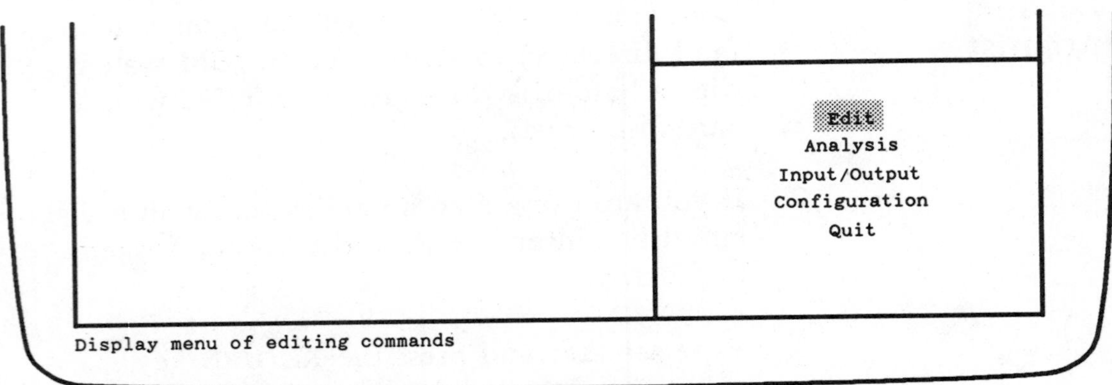


Arborist Decision Tree software is now ready for use. The Arborist software contains several decision trees for use with the tutorial. The next section, Loading an Example Decision Tree, shows you how to load one of these trees.

## Loading an Example Decision Tree

**Introduction**

The tree you are about to load is a graphic display of a decision on whether to lock in at the current 12 percent interest rate or to wait and lock in at some future time. If you wait, one of three events will occur: the rates may rise, remain stable, or fall. Several exercises in this tutorial use this tree. Your first step is to load the tree from disk.

### Selecting the Load Command

**NOTE:** If you select the wrong menu item at any time during the tutorial, you can do several things to get back to the correct menu. You can position the highlight over `Other Menus` or, if appropriate, over `Exit Menu`, and press **RETURN.** You can also press the **ESC** key; this aborts the current command and returns you to the menu from which the command was selected.

1. Using the **Arrow** keys, position the highlight over the `Input/Output` item in the Main menu and press the **RETURN** key.

   The Input/Output menu is displayed in the Menu window.

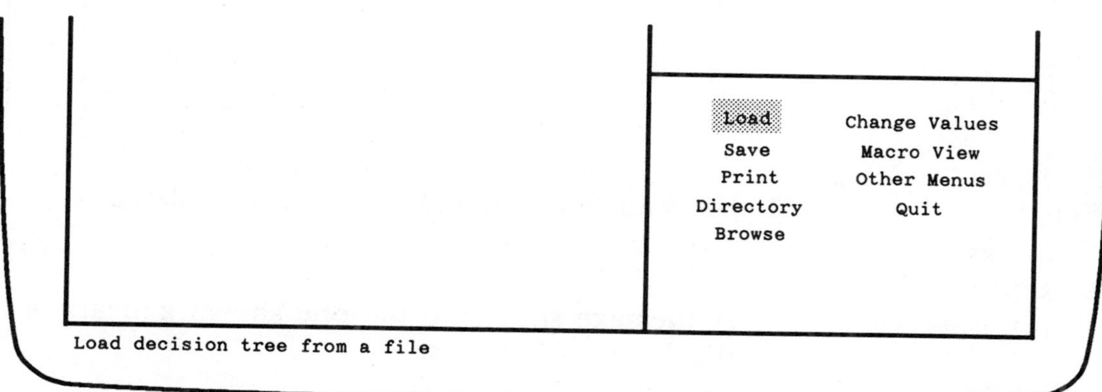


2. Position the highlight over `Load`.

   Note that the Load command is briefly described in the Message window.

3. Press **RETURN**.

   The highlight moves to the Macro View window and is positioned on the first decision tree filename in an alphabetical list of available decision trees. The message `Select file to be loaded` appears in the Message window.

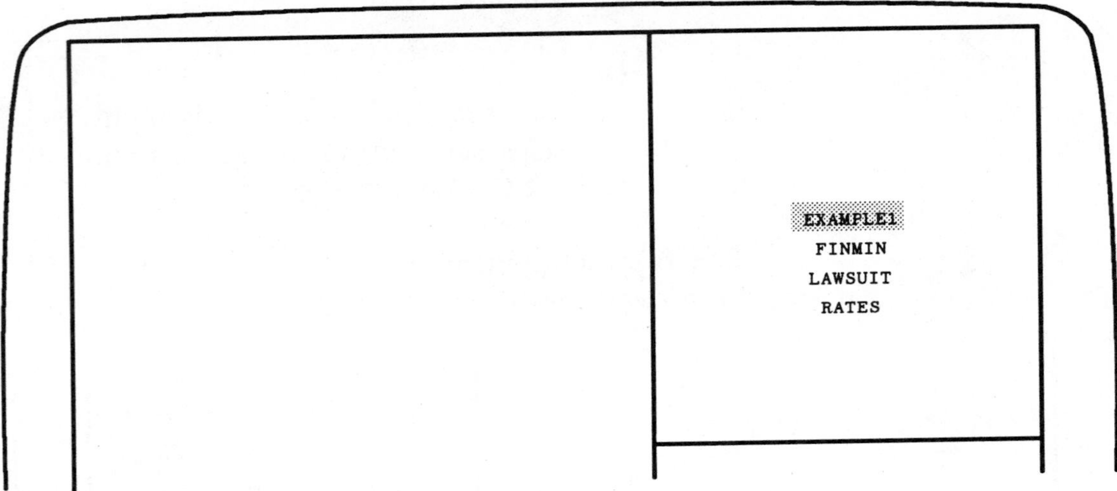


## Selecting the Tree to Load

1. Position the highlight over the tree filename EXAMPLE1 and press **RETURN**.

   A message similar to the one shown appears in the Message window.

Loading file C:\arb2\EXAMPLE1.TRE

Active

The tree is loaded when the `Active` attention bar on the right side of the Message window disappears.

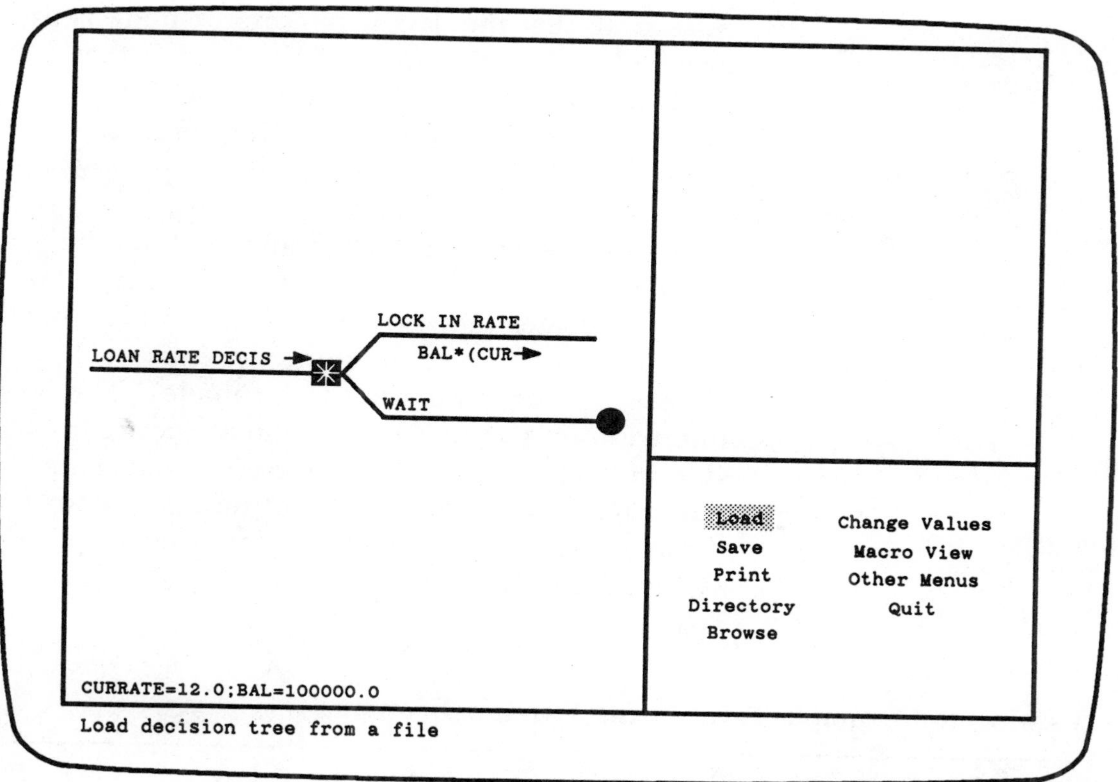


2. Examine the part of the tree that shows on the display and note that LOAN RATE DECISION is the root node, that is, the first node on the left side of the tree. The square indicates that LOAN RATE DECISION is a *decision node*, that is, a point where a decision must be made.

---

**NOTE:** The arrow following LOAN RATE DECIS is a *text overflow arrow*, which indicates that the description or other information is too long to be displayed in its entirety. Refer to Chapter 3, Using Arborist Decision Tree Software, for further explanation of the text overflow arrow.

Also note that the LOAN RATE DECISION node is associated with and named by the branch that leads into it from the left. In general, nodes are associated with their preceding branch.

---

This example tree has two branches extending from the root node: LOCK IN RATE and WAIT. The circle indicates that WAIT is a *chance node* (that is, a point where the outcome depends on chance, not on a decision to be made). The line without a square or a circle at the right side indicates that LOCK IN RATE is an *end node*. Although you cannot see them until you move through the tree, three end nodes follow the WAIT node: RATES RISE, RATES STABLE, and RATES FALL.

## Viewing the Example Tree: Focus Window Browsing

### Focus Browsing

1. Select Browse by pressing the **B** key.

---

**NOTE:** Remember that to *select* a menu item, you can either position the cursor over the item and press **RETURN** or press the first letter of the item.

---

The Select attention bar in the lower-right corner of the Focus window indicates that you are in the Browse mode. The Menu window now displays a list of special keystroke commands available in the Browse mode.

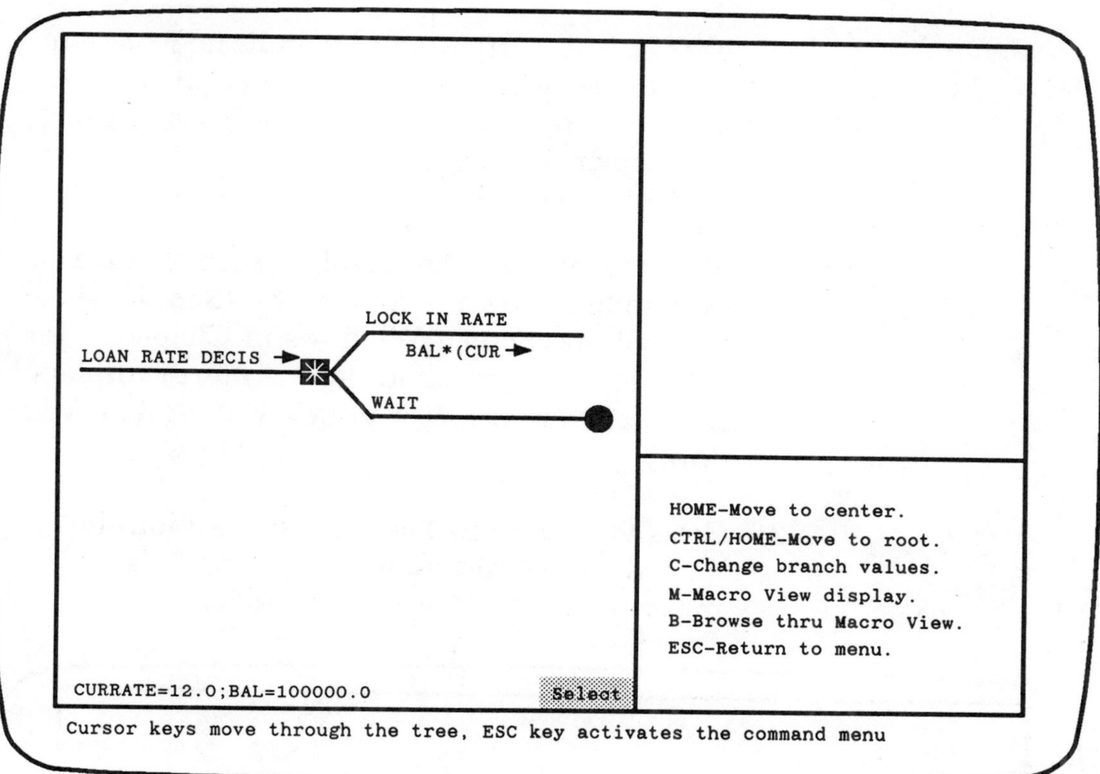


The next four steps show you how to move around in a decision tree in the Focus window. Steps 2 and 3 show how to use the **Arrow** keys to move anywhere you want to go; in particular, you will view the area of the tree at the end node RATES RISE. Steps 4 and 5 demonstrate the use of special keystrokes that allow you to move quickly in the tree directly to a specific location.

2. Press the **Right Arrow** key three times.

   This positions the cursor on RATES STABLE and makes it the *current node* (the node on which you can perform an operation) on the display.

---

**NOTE:** The current node is indicated on your monitor as noted in the section entitled How the Arborist Screen Appears on Your System in Chapter 3.

---

Note that the tree has scrolled such that the WAIT node is now the *focus node* (See the section entitled Screen Windows in Chapter 3 for more information about how Arborist displays the relative position of nodes in the Focus window.)

3. Press the **Up Arrow** key once to position the cursor on the end node RATES RISE. This now makes RATES RISE the current node.

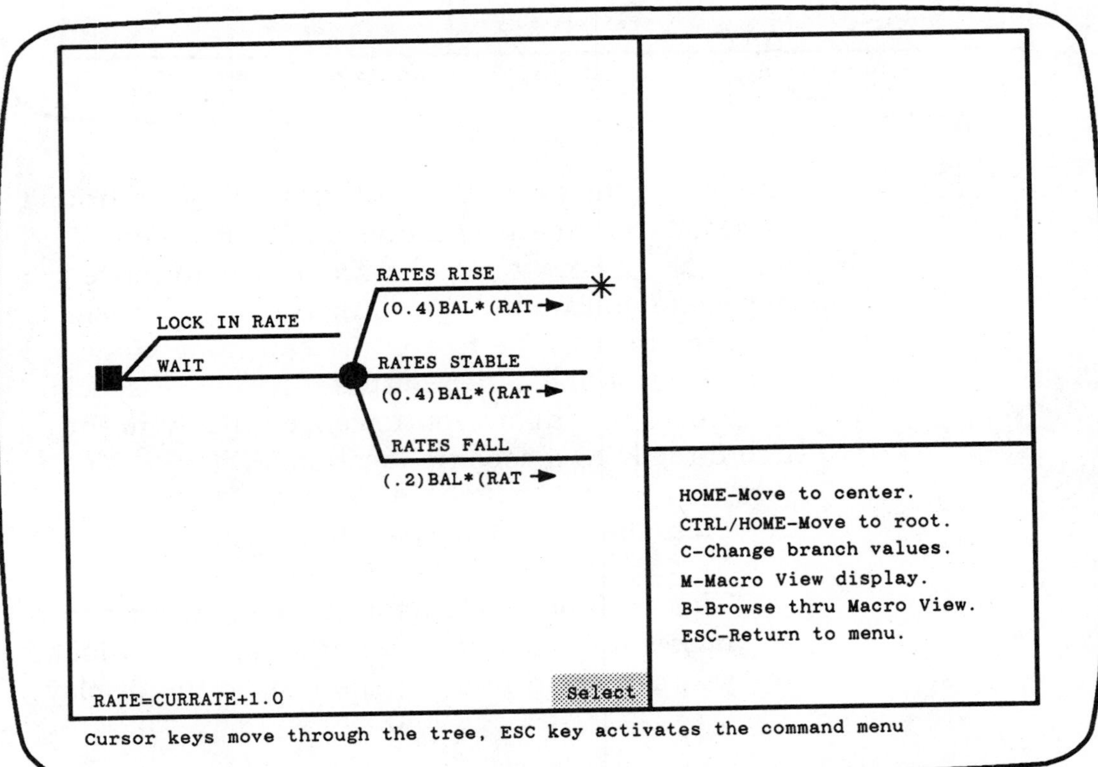

4. Press the **HOME** key.

   The chance node WAIT (the focus node) becomes the current node on the display. While browsing through the Focus window, use the **HOME** key to make the focus node the current node quickly (the **HOME** key works differently when you are macro browsing; see the next section in this chapter).

5. Press the **SHIFT-HOME** (**CTRL-HOME** on an IBM system) keys.

---

**NOTE:** To use two keys that are written with a hyphen between them, press and hold the first key, press the second key, then release both keys.

---

The root node, LOAN RATE DECISION, becomes the current node. You use the **SHIFT-HOME** (**CTRL-** on IBM) key sequence to make the root node the current node quickly.

## Viewing the Example Tree: Macro View

### Generating the Macro Display

1. Press the **M** key to select `Macro View display.`

   A macro display of the decision tree EXAMPLE1 appears in the Macro View window. Because EXAMPLE1 is a relatively simple tree, you can see the entire tree in the Macro View window. For more complex tree structures, the Macro View command displays only the portion of the tree in the vicinity of the focus node.

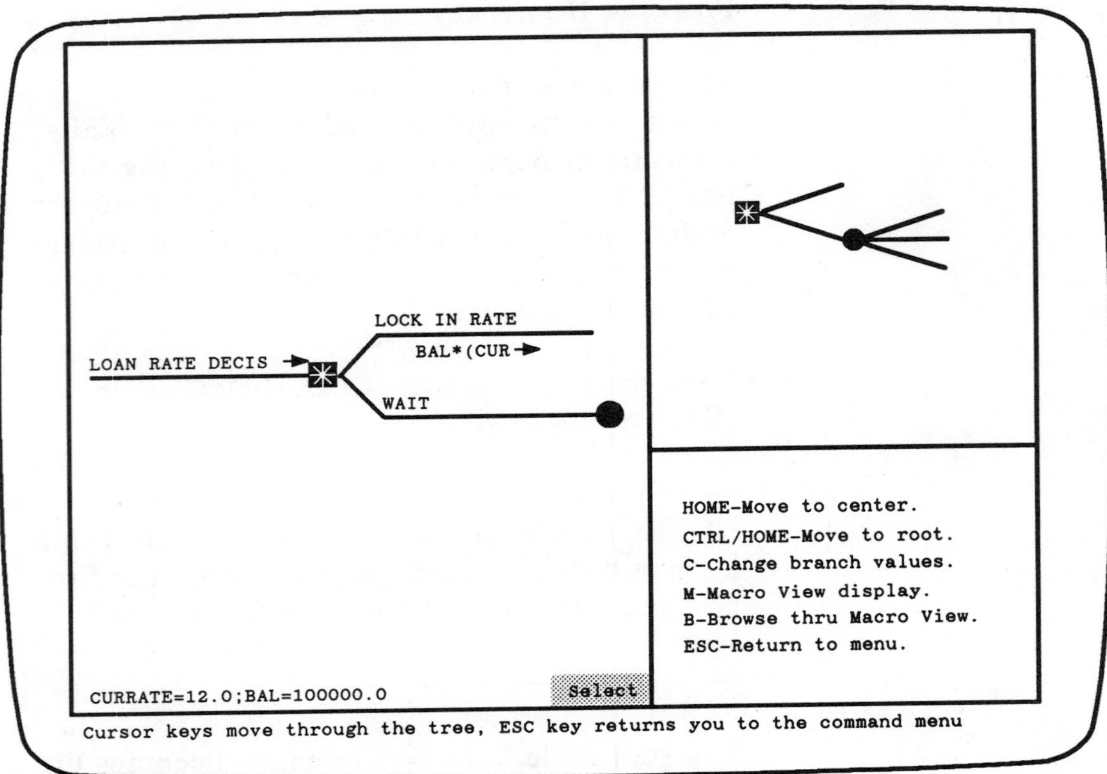


The current node in the Focus window is also highlighted on the macro view of the decision tree. In this case, the root node is highlighted in both the Macro View window and the Focus window.

---

**NOTE:** You can also select the Macro View command from the Edit, Analysis, or Input/ Output menus.

---

## Using Macro Browsing

1. Press the **B** key to select `Browse thru Macro View.`

The Select attention bar moves to the Macro View window to indicate that macro browsing is in progress.

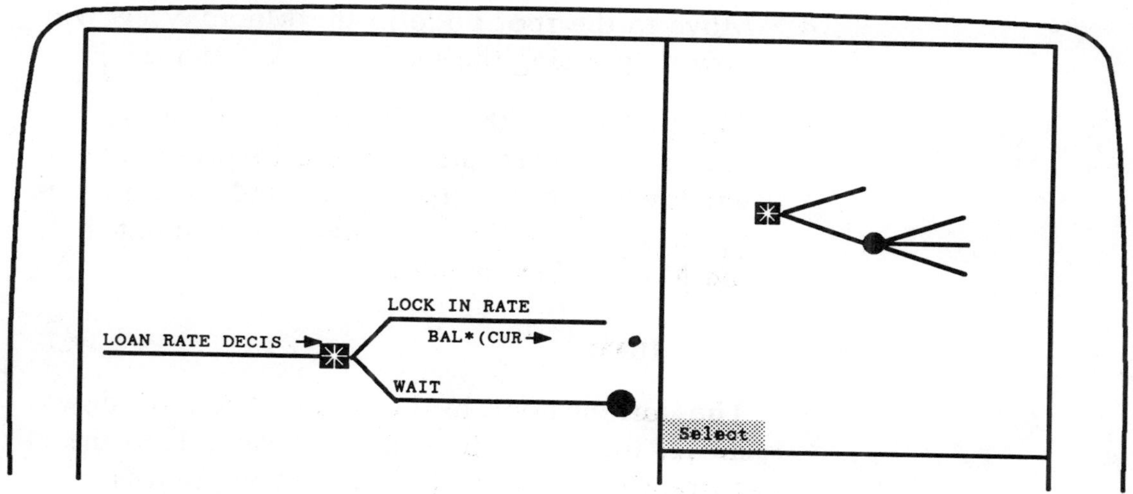


Macro browsing in the Macro View window operates like the Browse command in the Focus window. You control movement with the cursor control keys.

2. Move to an end node by pressing the **Right Arrow** key twice.

   The center end node following the chance node (the node with a circle) is now highlighted—making it the current node—in the Macro View window. Note that the Focus window display is unaffected by this change in the Macro View window.

3. Press **RETURN**.

   The tree in the Focus window disappears and is then redrawn such that the end node RATE STABLE becomes both the current node and the focus node; that is, pressing the **RETURN** key (while macro browsing) synchronizes the Focus window with the Macro View window.

4. Move to the root node in the Macro View window by pressing the **Left Arrow** key twice.

   The root node (the node with a square) becomes the current node in the Macro View window. Note that the Focus window display is again unaffected by this cursor movement in the Macro View window.

5. Press **HOME**.

   The current node in the Macro View window moves to the position that corresponds to the current node in the Focus window; that is, pressing the **HOME** key (while macro browsing) synchronizes the Macro View window with the Focus window.

As you become more familiar with the user interface, you will find that using the **HOME** and **RETURN** keys while macro browsing can make working with complex trees both easier and more efficient. These keys allow you to synchronize the current nodes of the Focus and Macro View windows in order to zoom in on areas that you want to manipulate.

6. Return to the root node in the Macro View window by pressing the **SHIFT-HOME** (**CTRL-HOME** on an IBM PC) keys.

   The highlight in the Macro View window moves to the root node.

**Exiting Focus Browsing**

1. Press the **ESC** key to exit Macro View window browsing.

   This returns you to the Focus window Browse mode. The `Select` attention bar is now displayed in the Focus window.

2. Press **ESC** to exit Focus window browsing.

   This returns you to the Input/Output menu.

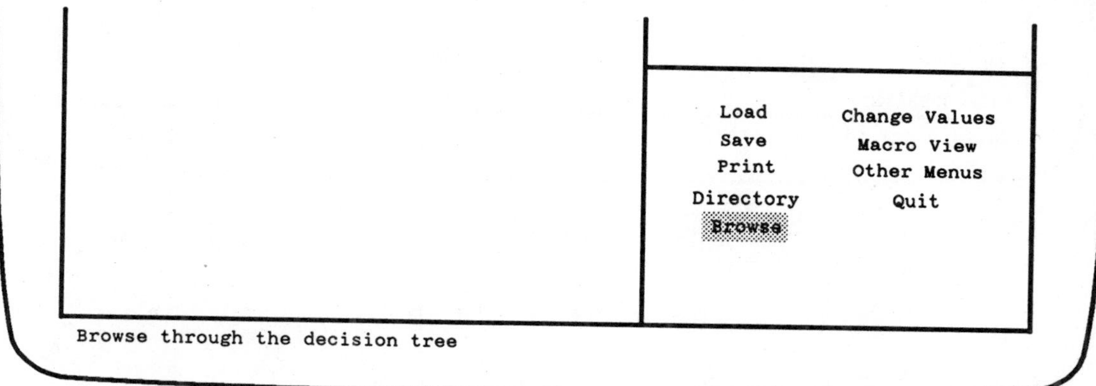


## Modifying the Example Tree: Adding a Subtree

**Selecting the Load Command**

1. Select `Other Menus` by pressing the **O** key.

   You are returned to the Main menu.

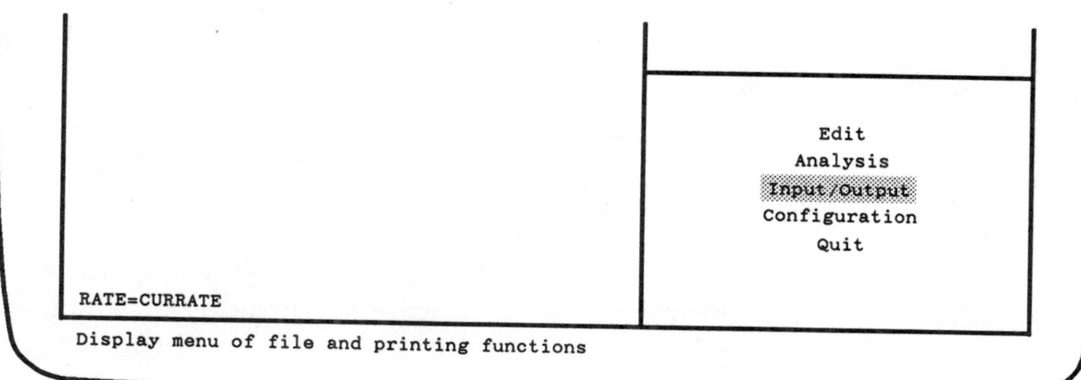

2. Select Edit.

The Edit menu is displayed.

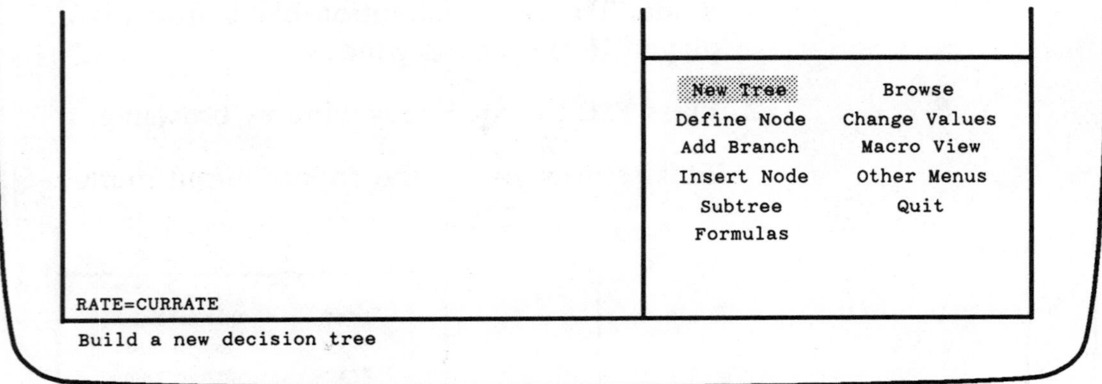


3. Select Subtree by pressing the S key.

The Subtree menu appears.

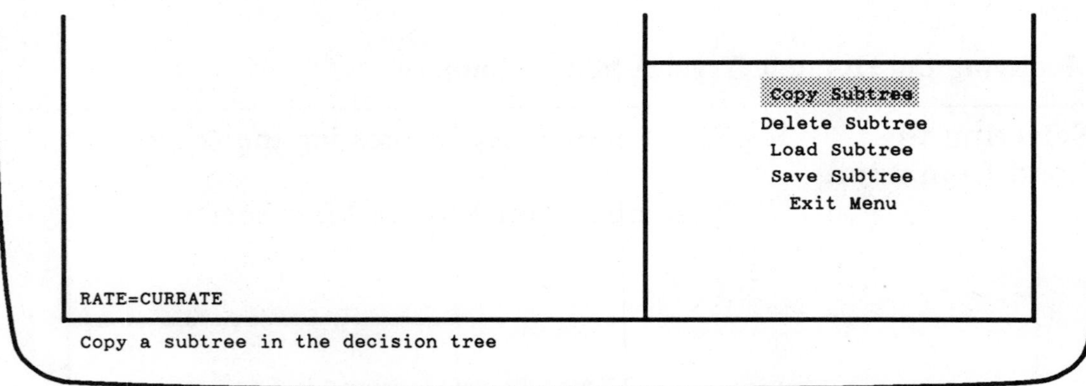


4. Select Load Subtree.

The Select attention bar in the Focus window prompts you to indicate the position at which you wish to add the subtree, as shown in the following figure.

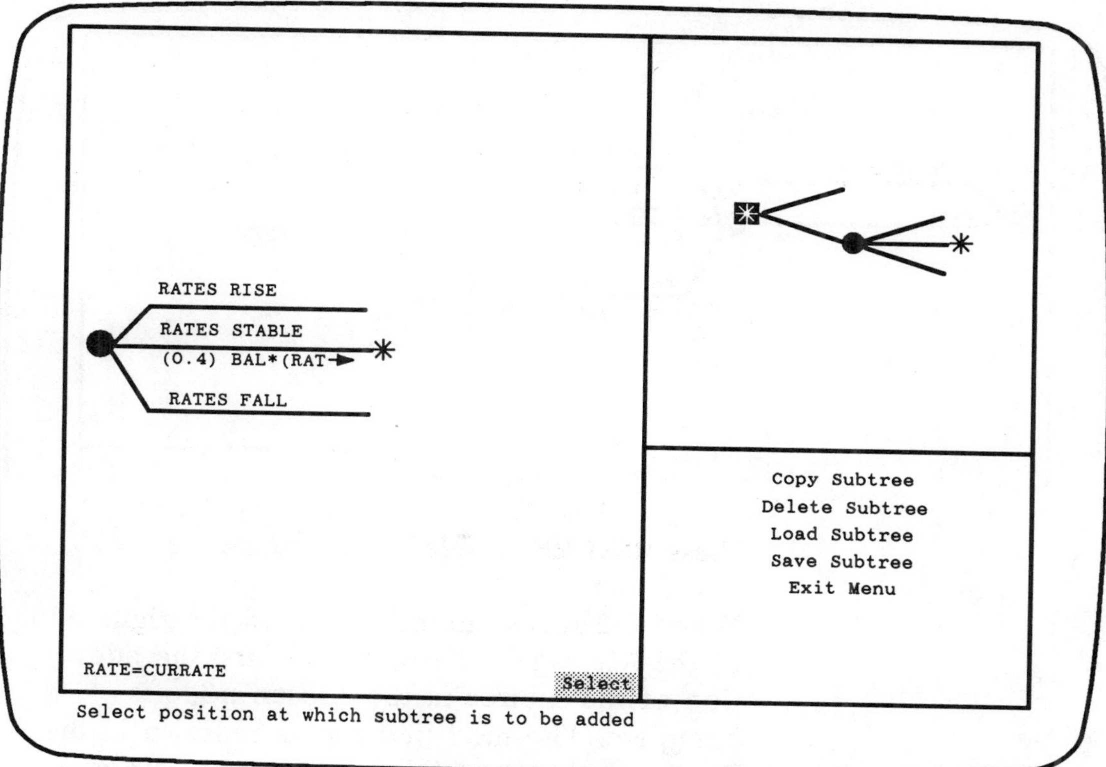


## Selecting the Destination Node

You now load the subtree so that it follows the chance node WAIT.

1. To select the chance node WAIT, press the **Left Arrow** key and press **RETURN**.

   The following message appears in the Message window:

   ```
   Select file to be loaded.
   ```

   A list of all the subtrees available in the current directory is displayed in the Macro View window. In this example, there is only one subtree, SUB1.

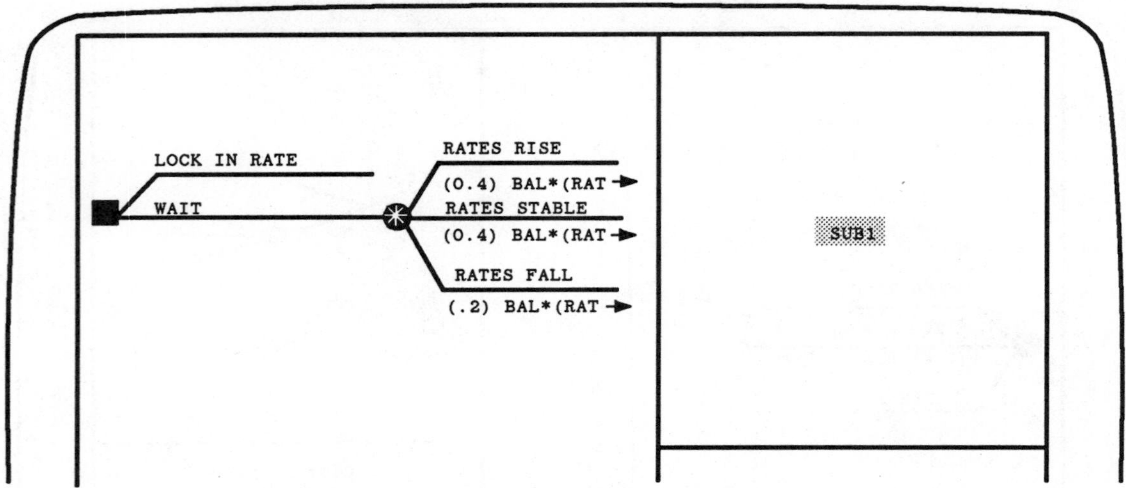


2. Press **RETURN** to select the SUB1 subtree.

   When the Active attention bar on the right side of the Message window disappears, the addition of the subtree at the chosen node is complete. The modified tree is redrawn in the Focus window to reflect the new tree structure.

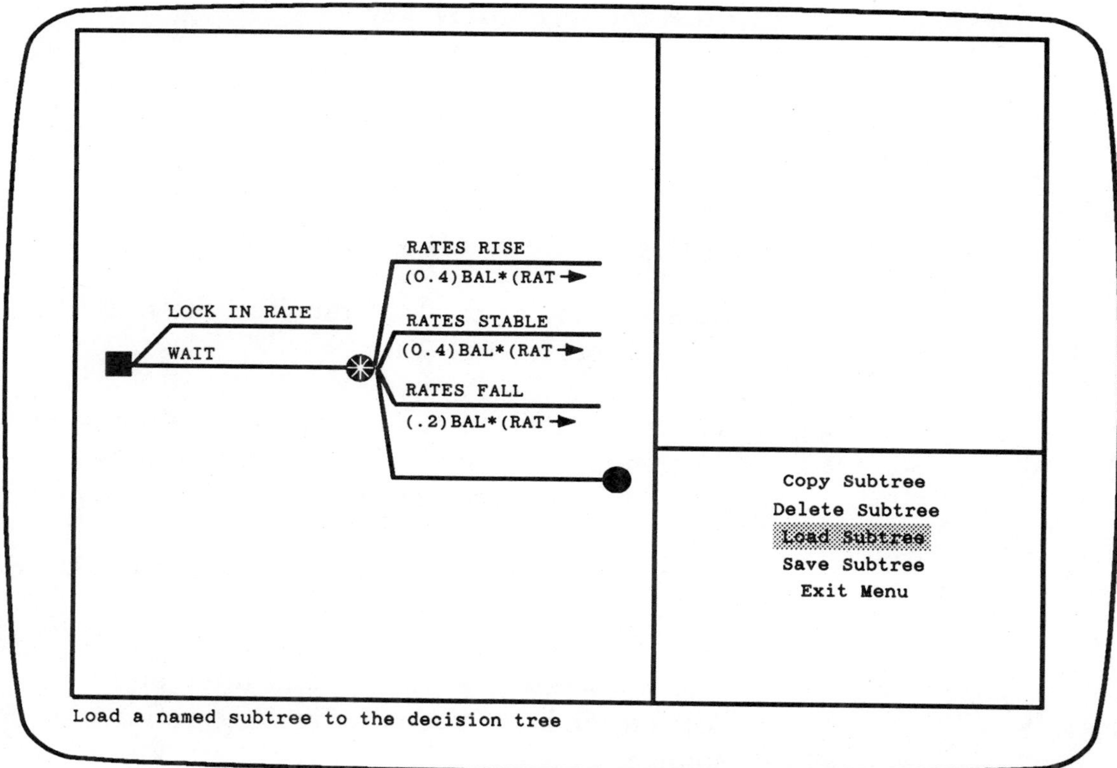


You will use this new chance node structure (subtree) to refine the RATES RISE outcome by specifying three—rather than one—degrees of increase. Your next step is to delete the old RATES RISE end node.

## Modifying the Example Tree: Deleting a Branch

### Deleting a Branch

1. Select Delete Subtree by pressing the **D** key.

   The Select attention bar that appears in the Focus window prompts you to select the node or subtree to be deleted.

2. Press the **Right Arrow** key.

   The cursor moves to the RATES FALL branch.

3. Press the **Up Arrow** key twice.

   RATES RISE is now the current node.

4. To select the RATES RISE branch as the one to be deleted, press **RETURN**.

   The Note attention bar is displayed in the Message window, along with the message shown in the screen on the next page.

5. Respond to the `Are you sure? (Y/N)` prompt by pressing the **Y** (for yes) key.

   The RATES RISE branch and end node are deleted, and the tree is redrawn to reflect the change.

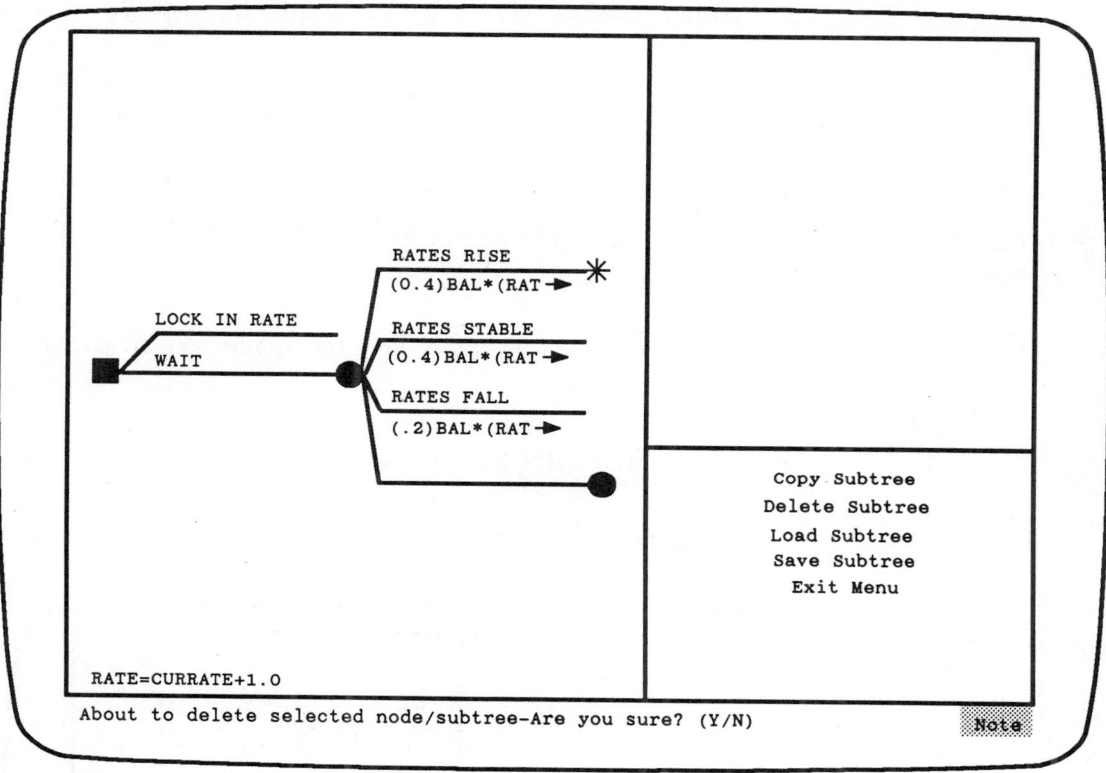


## Modifying the Example Tree: Annotation Editing

**Selecting the Change Values Command**

1. Select `Exit Menu` by pressing the **E** key.

   The Edit menu appears in the Menu window.

| | |
|---|---|
| New Tree | Browse |
| Define Node | Change Values |
| Add Branch | Macro View |
| Insert Node | Other Menus |
| Subtree | Quit |
| Formulas | |

Display menu of subtree commands

2. Select `Change Values` by pressing the **C** key.

   The `Select` attention bar in the Focus window prompts you to select the branch or node you wish to change.

### Selecting the Node

1. Press the **Right Arrow** key to move to the RATES FALL branch.

2. Press the **Down Arrow** key to move to the unnamed branch.

3. Press **RETURN** to select the unnamed branch.

   The Annotate Node menu is displayed.

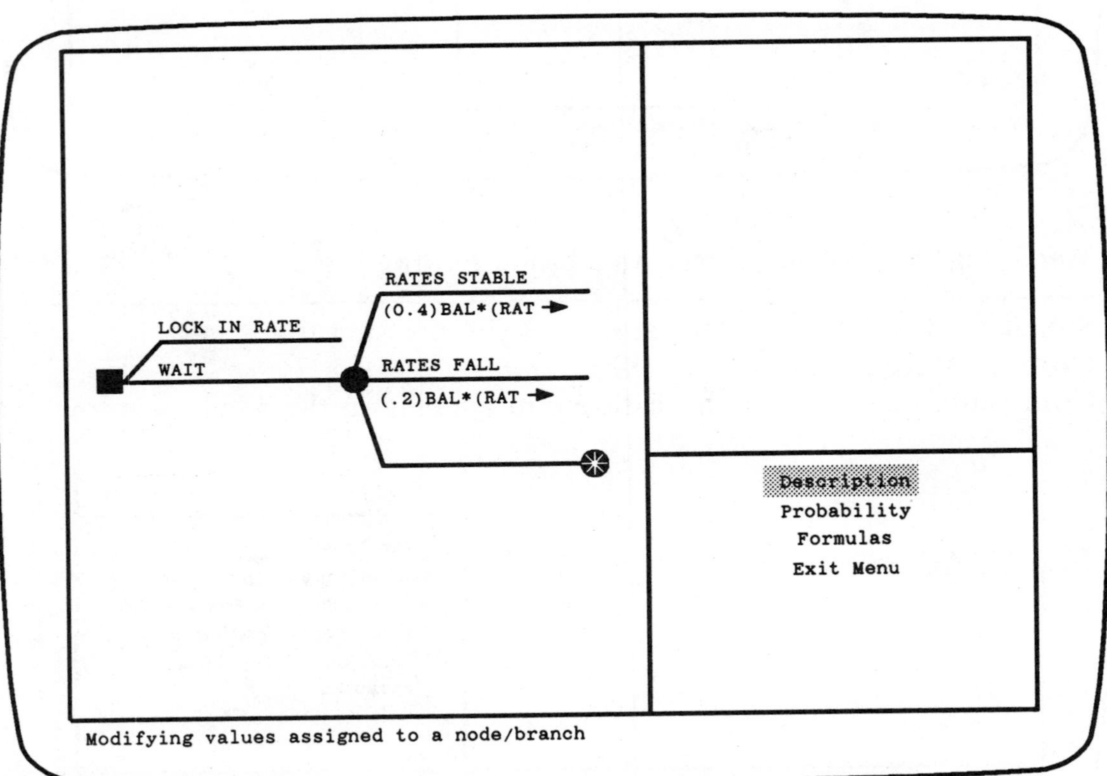

**Specifying the Description**

1. Select Description in order to name the branch.
2. Enter RATES RISE at the cursor in the Menu window and press **RETURN**.

---

**NOTE:** If you notice a typing error before pressing **RETURN**, use the regular editing keys (**Del**, **Ins**, **Left Arrow**, and **Right Arrow** keys, and so on) to correct it. If you notice a typing error after pressing **RETURN**, repeat the two preceding steps.

---

**Specifying the Probability**

1. Press the **P** (for Probability) key to specify the probability.
2. Enter .4 for the node probability and press **RETURN**.
3. Press the **E** key to select Exit Menu.

   The decision tree is redisplayed reflecting the changes you have input using the Change Values command. The Edit menu is redisplayed as shown.

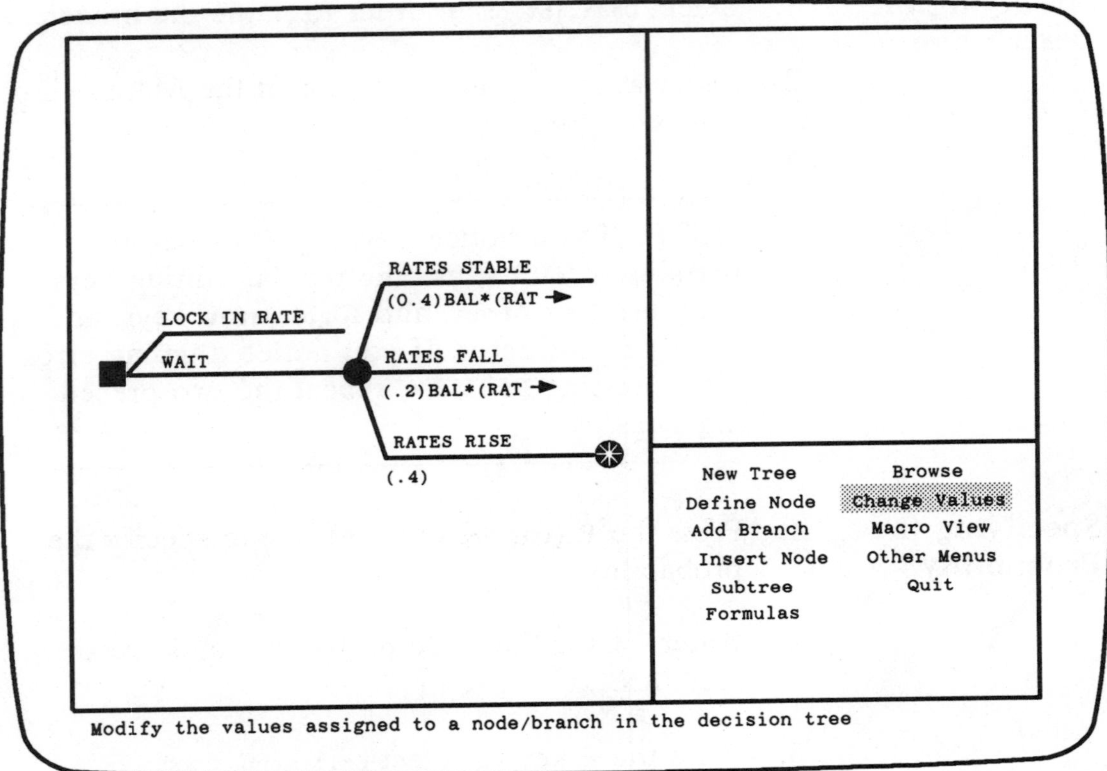


## Analyzing the Example Tree: Expected Value

**Introduction**

The expected value of a decision tree is a numeric value that can be computed for each node in the tree and represents an average payoff at that point. For a decision node, the expected value is simply the value of the alternative with the largest or smallest value, depending on whether you want to maximize profits or minimize losses. For a chance node, the expected value is the sum of the payoff values for each outcome multiplied by the probability that the outcome will occur.

The Arborist software calculates the expected value based on the information you have included in your tree (see Chapter 5 for details about decision variables, formulas, and modeling). In the EXAMPLE1 tree, you will calculate the expected value to minimize losses because the tree is designed to help you minimize the amount you must pay on a loan.

## Performing the Analysis

1. Press the **O** key to select Other Menus.

   The Main menu is displayed.

2. Select Analysis.

   The Analysis menu is displayed.

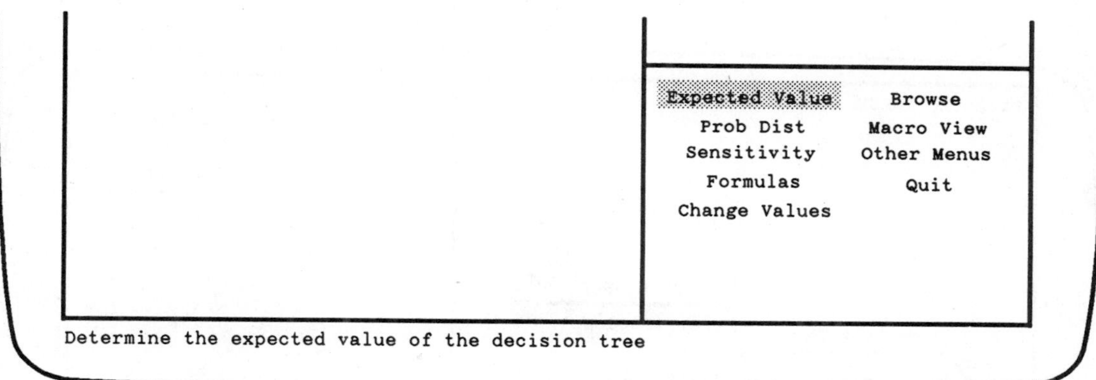


3. Select Expected Value.

   The Gains/Losses menu is displayed.

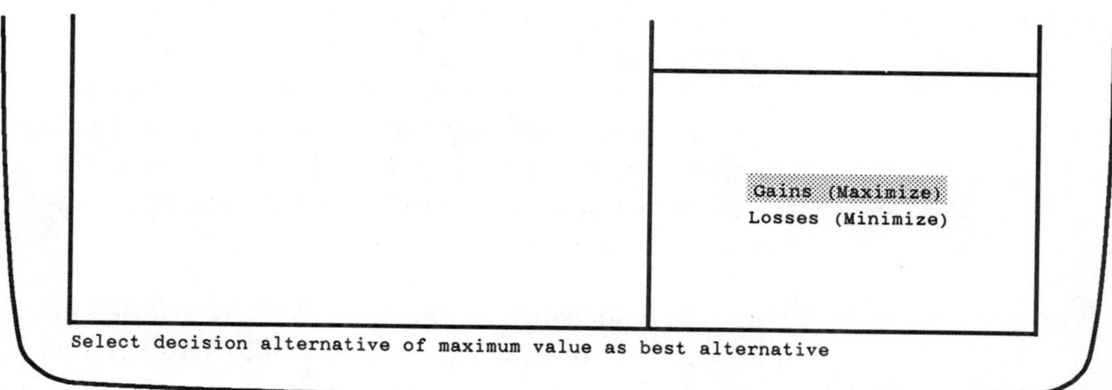

4. Because this particular tree is designed to help you minimize costs, select the `Losses (Minimize)` item.

   The `Active` attention bar appears in the right corner of the Message window, and the message `Calculating expected value of the decision tree` is displayed. When processing is completed, the best path is indicated and the expected value is displayed in the upper-left corner of the Focus window, as shown in the following figure.

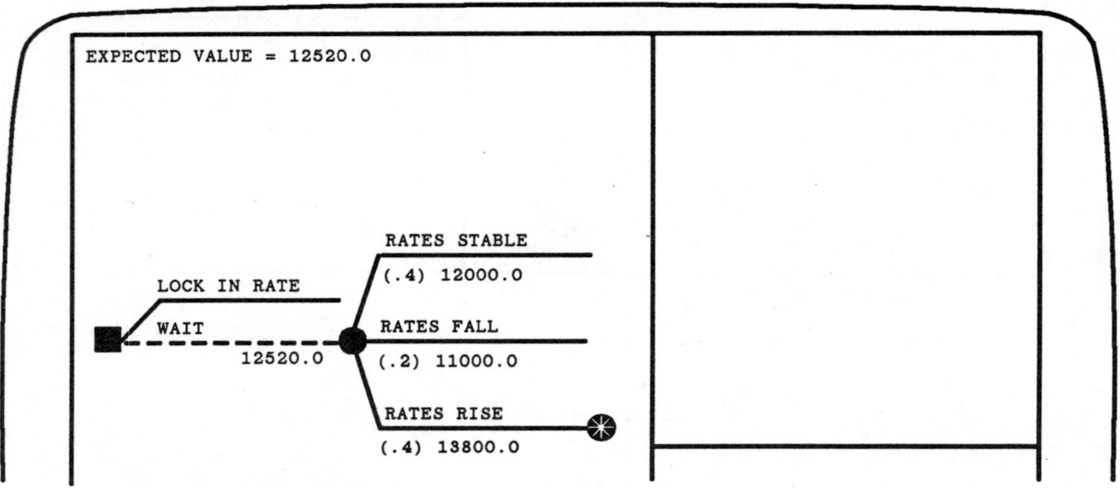


**Interpretation**

As shown at the top-left portion of the Focus window, the expected value for the EXAMPLE1 tree is $12,520. Arborist also displays the alternative at each decision node that has the best expected value (in this tree, it is the WAIT branch). The best paths for chance nodes are not shown because you cannot control the outcomes.

The expected value of the tree ($12,520) does not indicate exactly how much you would pay for one decision based on the EXAMPLE1 tree. The expected value represents an average amount of money you pay if you make this decision over and over. If you lock in at the interest rate several times, you pay $12,750 each time. If you wait on the interest rate several times, you pay an average of $12,520 because 40 percent of the time the rates rise, 40 percent of the time the rates remain stable, and 20 percent of the time the rates fall. The expected value gives you an indication of which alternative is likely to incur the least cost.

## Analyzing the Example Tree: Probability Distribution

### Introduction

The probability distribution in this section displays the five possible outcomes of the best path in this tree along with their respective probabilities of occurring. The outcomes are represented by the five end nodes of the WAIT alternative: RATES STABLE, RATES FALL, and the three end nodes emanating from the chance node RATES RISE—RATES INC 3%, RATES INC 2%, and RATES INC 1%.

### Selecting the Node

1. Select Prob Dist.

   The Select attention bar appears in the Focus window.

2. Use the **SHIFT-HOME** (**CTRL-HOME** on an IBM PC) keys to make the root node the current node, and then press **RETURN**.

   The Select attention bar disappears from the Focus window, and the Cumulative/Noncumulative menu is displayed to enable you to choose either a cumulative or a noncumulative distribution.

Cumulative
Noncumulative

CURRATE=12.0;BAL=100000.0

Output a cumulative probability distribution

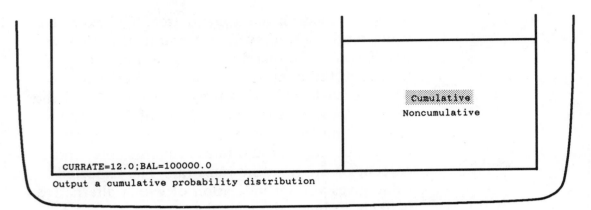

### Selecting the Distribution Type

1. Select Noncumulative.

   The Distribution Range menu is displayed in the Menu window. Note that Lowest Value is highlighted and the number 11000.0 is displayed in the lower-left corner of the Menu window. This is the lower limit of the distribution (smallest outcome) that will be displayed in the histogram.

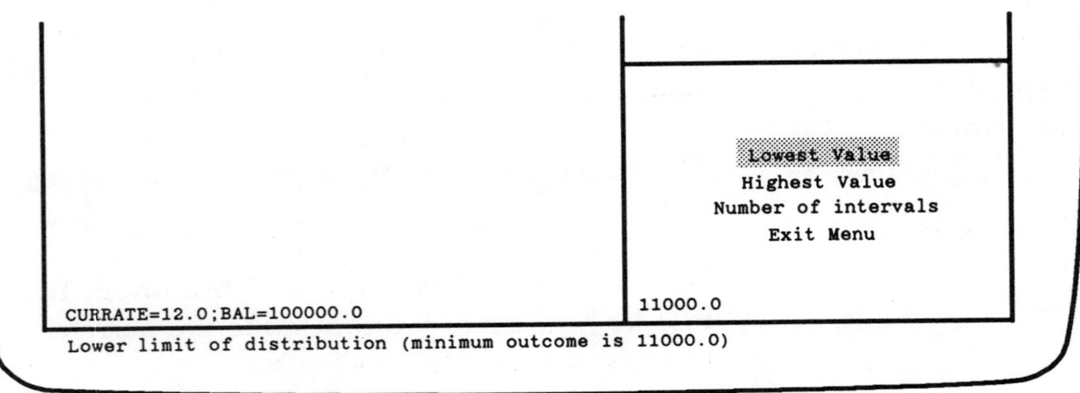


2. You could enter your own values for the lowest value, highest value, and number of intervals here (see the description of the Prob Dist command in Chapter 6); however, to sim-

plify the tutorial, accept the default values for these items (11000.0, 15000.0, and 10, respectively) by pressing the **E** key to select Exit Menu.

The histogram is then displayed in the Focus window (as shown in the following figure).

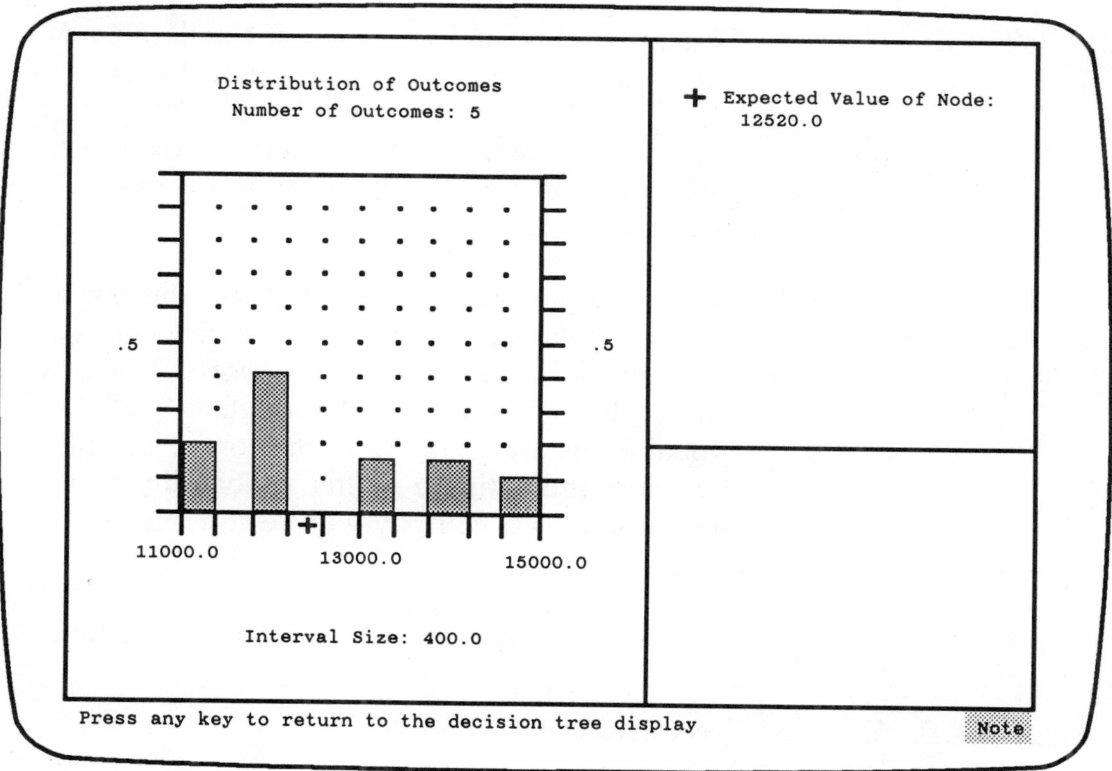


**Interpretation**

This graph shows that there is a 20 percent chance that you will pay an amount between $11,000 and $11,400, a 40 percent chance that you will pay between $11,800 and $12,200, a 16 percent chance that you will pay between $13,000 and $13,400 or between $13,800 and $14,200, and an 8 percent chance that you will pay between $14,600 and $15,000.

Probability distributions are useful analysis tools because they quickly show you the distribution of all possible payoffs. In some distributions, the payoffs may be closely grouped together, indicating little difference in risk between the outcomes. In other distributions, the payoffs are spaced farther apart, indicating higher risks between outcomes. Thus, you may find that the expected value of a tree recommends a preferred path in terms of the highest (or lowest) possible amount, but you may ultimately choose another, less risky, path based on your findings from a probability distribution.

The graph you just generated shows the outcomes evenly spaced, indicating some risk between the upper and lower payoffs. Fortunately, the outcomes with the higher probabilities are grouped at the lower end of the scale, indicating a higher probability that the amount you will pay will be low on the scale.

Press any key to return to the Analysis menu.

## Analyzing the Example Tree: Sensitivity Analysis

**Introduction**

The sensitivity analysis in this section examines the sensitivity of the expected value based on changes in the current interest rate. The current interest rate is represented by the variable CURRATE, which is assigned the value 12.0. You will enter a range of values (9 through 15) for the interest rate, and the Arborist software will use these values to calculate respective expected values.

### Performing the Analysis

1. Select `Sensitivity` by pressing the **S** key.

   The `Select` attention bar is displayed in the Focus window, and `Select the branch where variable values will be applied` is displayed in the Message window.

2. Use the cursor control keys or **SHIFT-HOME** (**CTRL-HOME** on an IBM PC) to make the root node the current node.

3. Press **RETURN** to select the root node.

   The Gains/Losses menu is displayed.

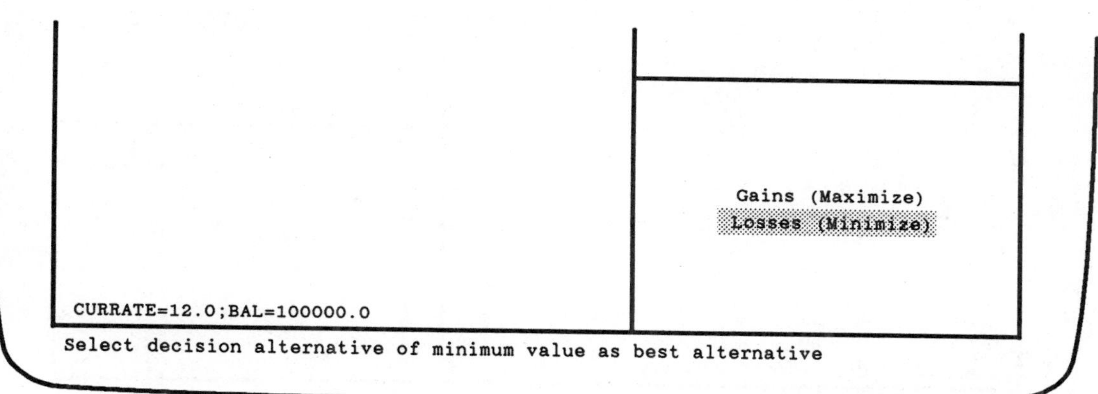


4. Select `Losses (Minimize)`.

   You are prompted for a decision variable name that will be used in the sensitivity analysis for this tree.

Variable Name

CURRATE=12.0;BAL=100000.0 CURRATE

Enter name of variable to perform sensitivity on.

5. Because CURRATE is already displayed, press **RETURN**.

The Values Type menu is displayed.

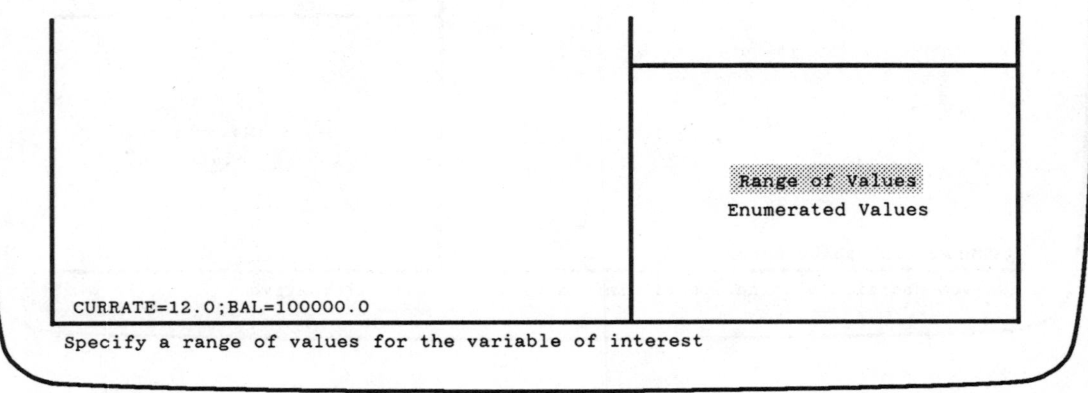


6. Select Enumerated Values.

A cursor appears in the Menu window, and a message in the Message window prompts you to enter a list of values separated by semicolons.

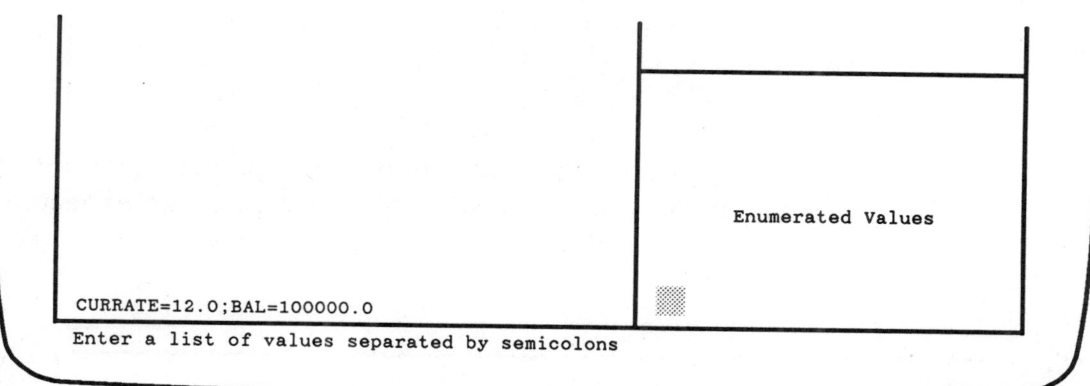


7. Enter `9;10;11;12;13;14;15` and press **RETURN**. (These numbers are the values to be used for the decision variable CURRATE to calculate the expected value.)

   The `Active` attention bar appears in the Message window, and the message `Performing sensitivity analysis` is displayed.

   Arborist calculates the expected value for each value of the variable and then displays the Range of Expected Values menu.

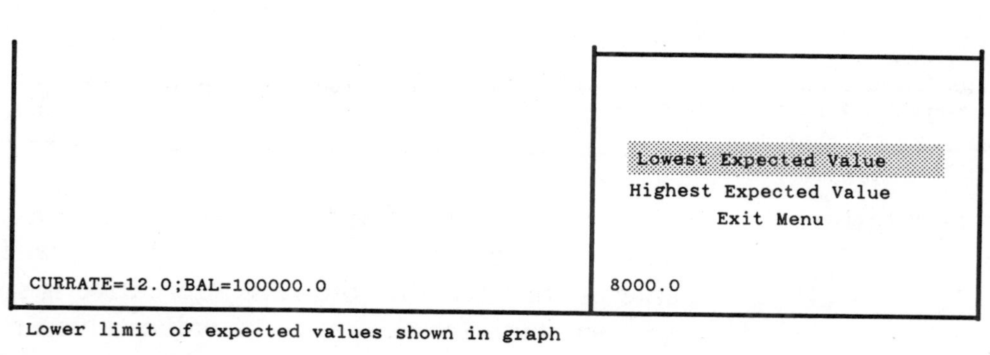

8. Select `Exit Menu` to accept the defaults.

   The sensitivity analysis graph is displayed in the Focus window (as shown in the next figure). The horizontal axis represents variable values, and the vertical axis represents expected values. Plus signs mark the best path.

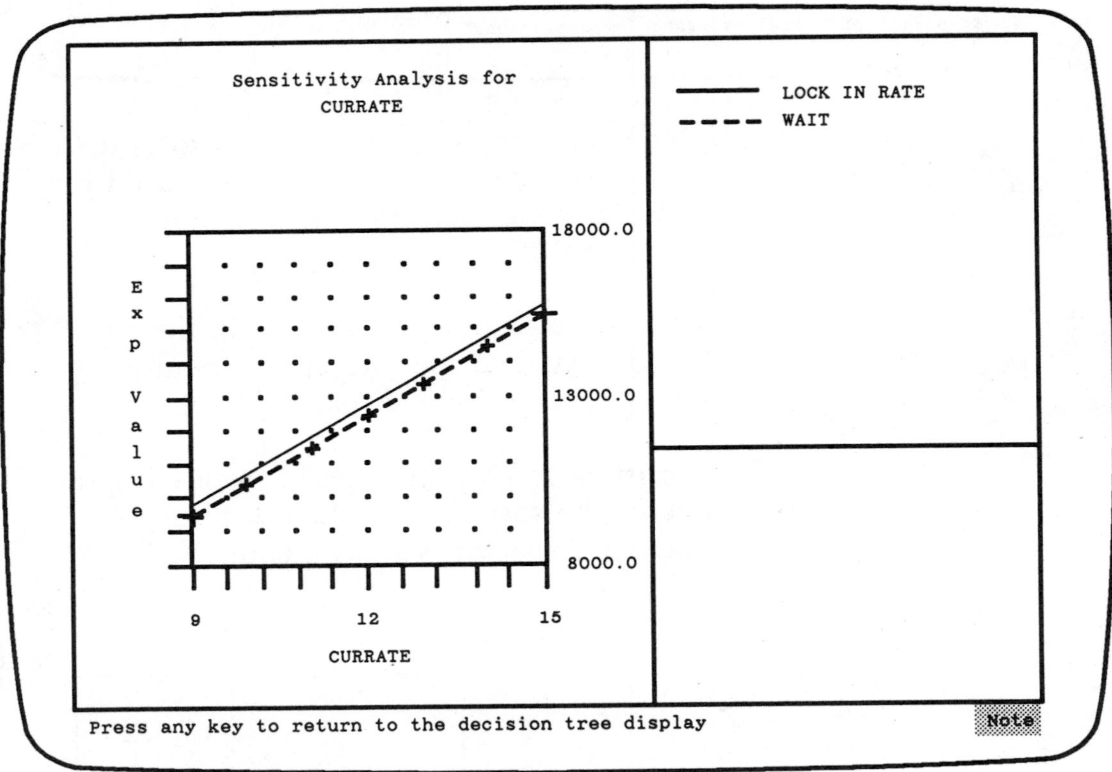


## Interpretation

This graph shows that the expected value is somewhat sensitive to changes in the current interest rate but that the WAIT alternative is still the best path for the range of values given to the interest rate. The best path, however, may not always be marked along only one alternative. Sometimes plus signs mark one alternative as the best path in the graph until a certain point (within the range of values) at which alternatives intersect and another alternative is marked as the best path.

Press any key to return to the Analysis menu.

## Constructing a New Tree: Getting Started

**Introduction**

The decision tree you are going to create, called LEGAL, is used to decide whether to *settle* or to *litigate* a lawsuit. You will create branches for these two possible alternatives and call them SETTLE and LITIGATE. The LITIGATE branch can have two possible outcomes, which you will indicate by adding additional branches and calling them FAVORABLE and UNFAVORABLE.

**General Procedure**

The general procedure you will use for constructing each node of the new tree is as follows:

1. Create the node (using either the New Tree command for the first node or the Add Branch command).

2. Annotate the node (using the Annotate Node menu) by assigning it a name (description) and optional formulas and probabilities.

3. Define the node type for the node (using the Node Type menu).

**Selecting the New Tree Command**

1. Select `Other Menus`.

   The Main menu appears on the display.

2. Select `Edit`.

   The Edit menu appears on the display.

3. Select `New Tree`.

   The `Are You Sure?` prompt appears. This message is a reminder that you are about to delete the current tree.

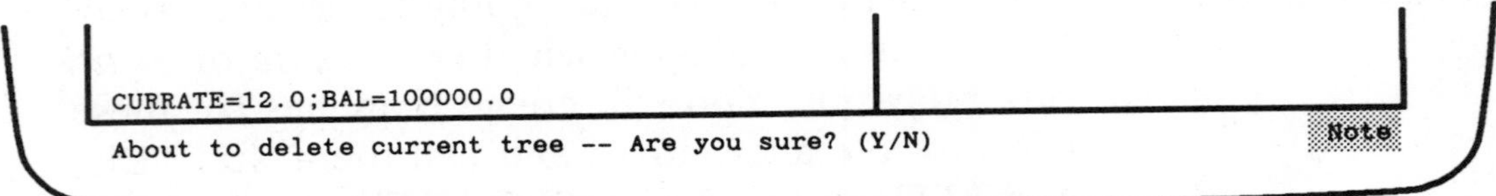


4. Press the `Y` (for yes) key.

   You are then prompted to select the type of modeling.

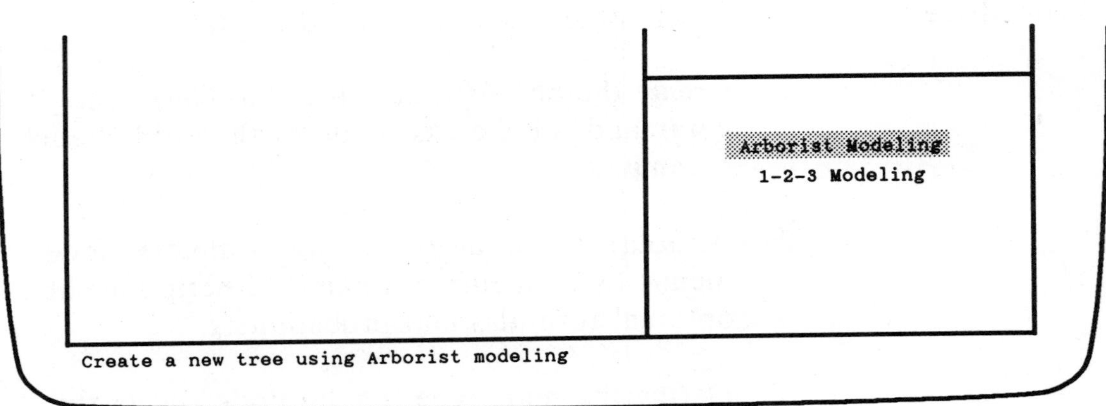


5. Select `Arborist Modeling`.

   A drawing of an undefined root node appears in the Focus window. Note that the node value `0.0` is also displayed. The Annotate Node menu is displayed in the Menu window to enable you to annotate the root node. You are now ready to describe this root node by naming it LEGAL DECISION.

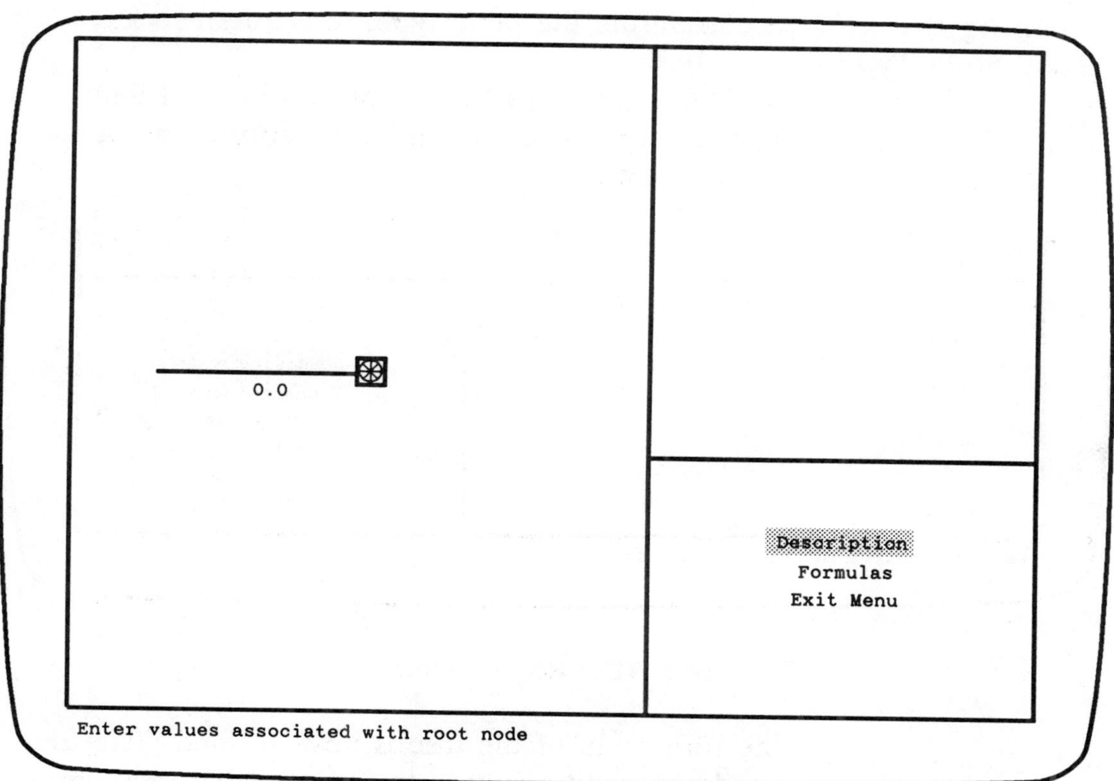


## Describing the Root Node

1. The highlight in the Menu window is positioned on `Description`. Press **RETURN** to select `Description`.

2. Enter LEGAL DECISION and press **RETURN**.

   This is the root node *description*.

3. Select Exit Menu to return to the Edit menu.

   The root node is redrawn with the words LEGAL DECISION above the branch.

## Defining the Root Node Type

1. To define the node type, select Define Node.

   The Node Type menu appears in the Menu window with the highlight positioned on Decision node.

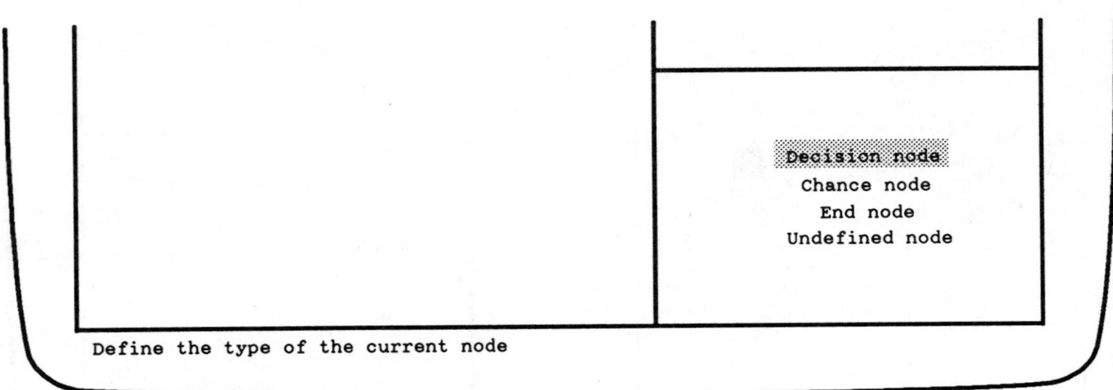


2. Press **RETURN** to select Decision node.

The root node of the tree is now defined. The tree is redrawn with a square to indicate that LEGAL DECISION is a decision node, and another undefined node is displayed.

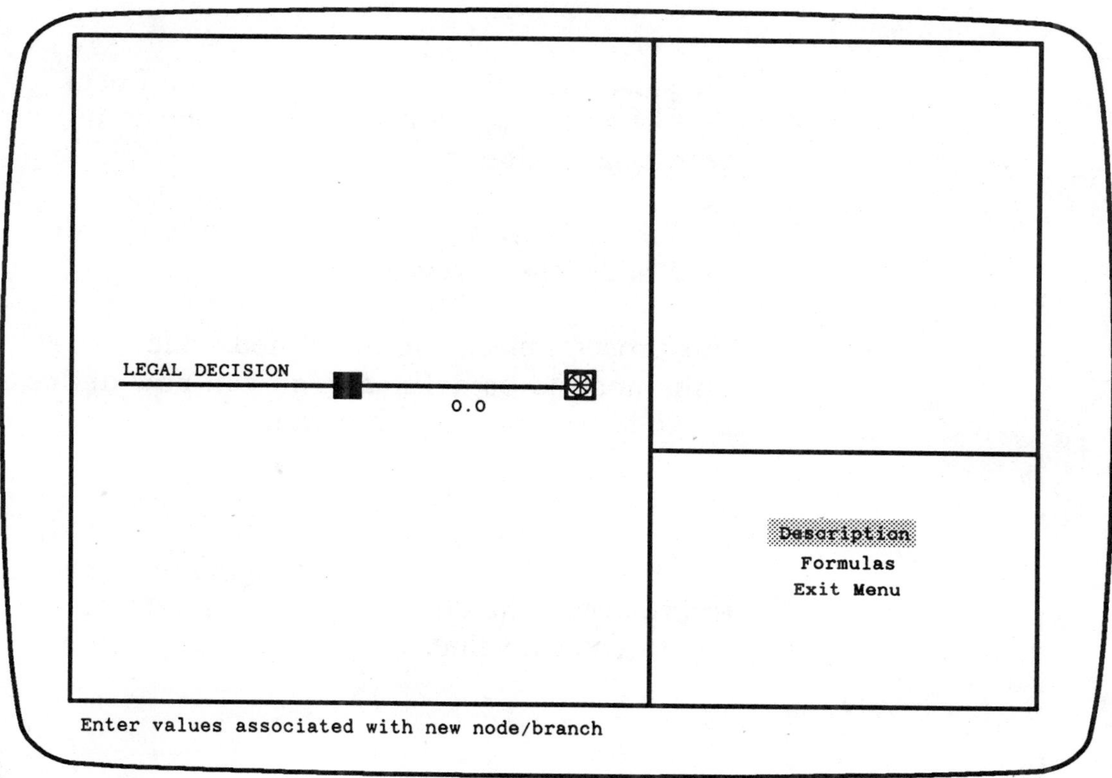


## Constructing a New Tree: Defining Additional Nodes

### Annotating the New Node

The Annotate Node menu is displayed in the Menu window to enable you to annotate the new node in the tree structure. You now describe the new node by naming it SETTLE.

1. Press **RETURN** to select `Description`.

2. Enter SETTLE and press **RETURN**.

3. Select `Exit Menu`.

   The tree is redrawn with SETTLE above the branch leading to the new node.

4. Select Define Node.

   The Select attention bar appears in the Focus window, and Select Node to Define appears in the Message window.

5. Press the **Right Arrow** key to highlight the undefined node, then press **RETURN**.

   This process selects the undefined node SETTLE as the node to be defined. You will now define the node type and give it a value.

6. Select End Node.

   The End Node menu with a single item, Value, is displayed. The cursor appears, prompting you to enter a value.

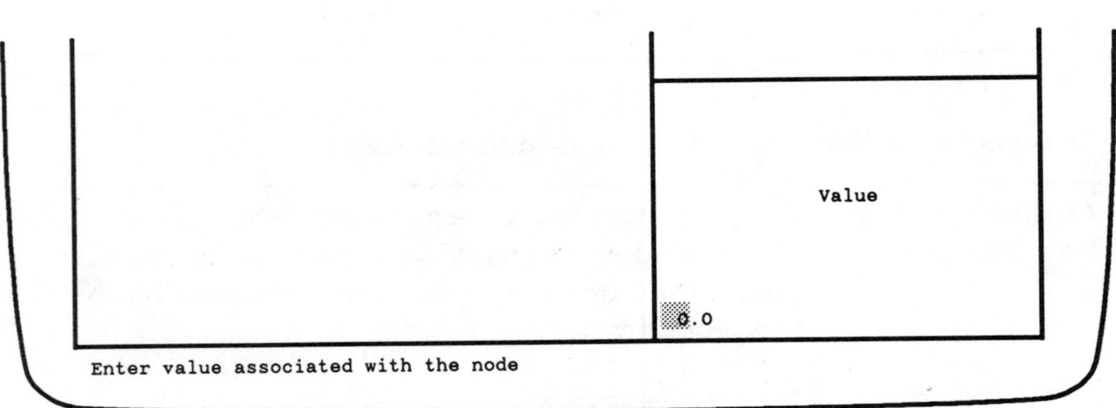


7. Enter the value 250000. and press **RETURN**.

---

**NOTE:** You cannot use commas in numbers. The period is not required.

---

When you press **RETURN**, the value 250000. appears below the SETTLE branch, and the square at the end of the line disappears to indicate that SETTLE is now an end node.

The Edit menu appears in the Menu window. You are now ready to add another branch to the LEGAL DECISION node.

### Adding a Branch

1. Select Add Branch.

   The Select attention bar appears in the Focus window, prompting you to select the node where the new branch is to be added.

2. Press the **Left Arrow** key, and then press **RETURN**, to select the LEGAL DECISION node.

   The Annotate Node menu appears, and the decision tree structure is redrawn in the Focus window to reflect the addition of the new branch. In the next step you will name this branch LITIGATE.

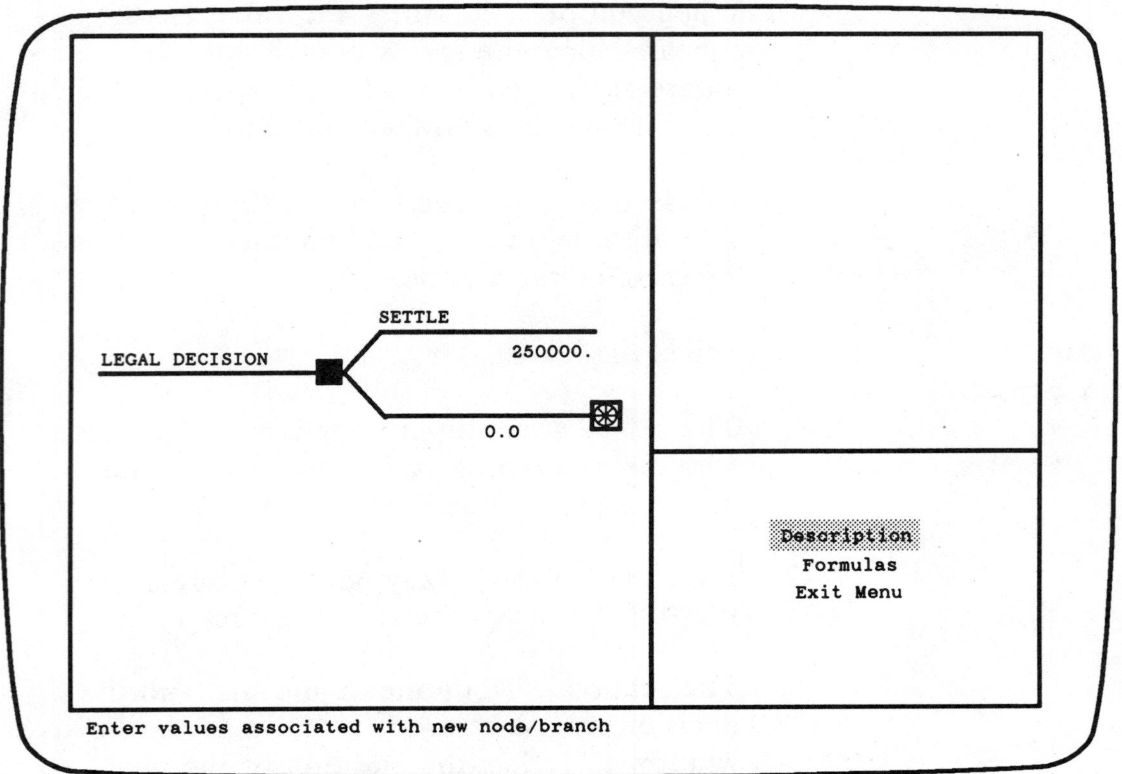


## Annotating the Next New Node

1. Select Description.

2. Enter LITIGATE for the description and press **RETURN.**

3. Select Formulas.

4. Enter COST=50000. and press **RETURN.**

   COST is a decision variable that represents the cost of litigation. This variable will be used in computing the value for all end nodes occurring along the LITIGATE path.

5. Select Exit Menu.

   LITIGATE appears above the new branch, and COST=50000 is displayed briefly in the Focus window. The Edit menu is again displayed.

6. Select Define Node.

   The Select attention bar prompts you to select a node in the Focus window to define or redefine.

7. Press the **Right Arrow** key to highlight the LITIGATE node.

   The formula COST=50000. appears at the bottom left of the Focus window because its associated node (LITIGATE) is now the current node.

8. Press **RETURN** to select the LITIGATE node.

   The Node Type menu is displayed. You are now ready to define the node type for the LITIGATE node.

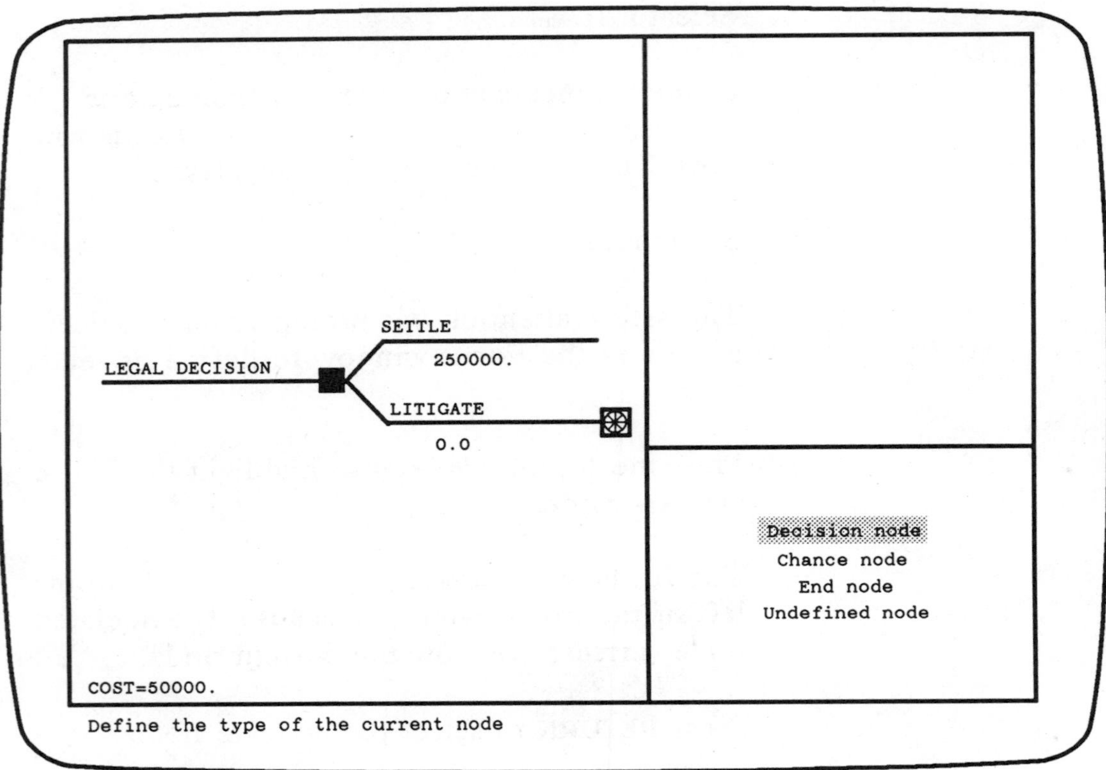


9. Select Chance Node.

The tree is redrawn to reflect the definition of the LITIGATE node as a chance node (displayed as a circle), and a new undefined node is added following the LITIGATE node. The Annotate Node menu is displayed.

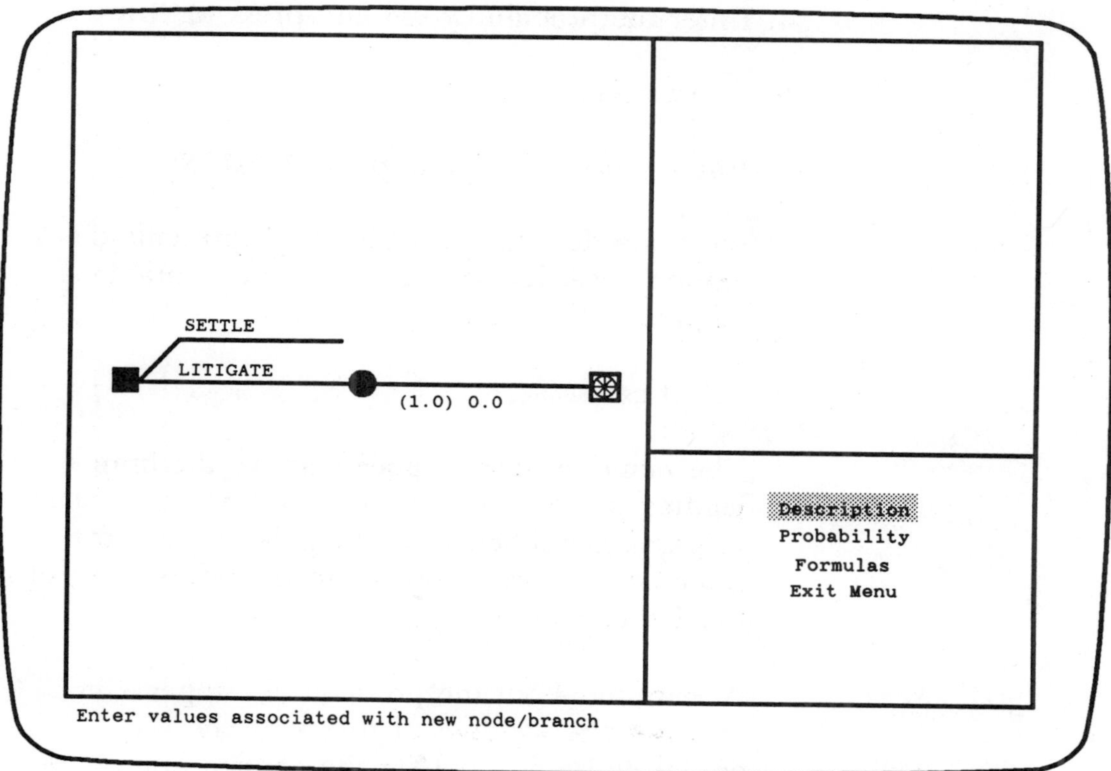


Notice that the Annotate Node menu now includes an item called `Probability`. This is the menu that enables you to annotate a node that branches from a chance node.

## Annotating Another New Node

You will now name the undefined node FAVORABLE and define the probability and formula to be associated with it.

1. Select `Description`.

2. Enter FAVORABLE for the description and press **RETURN**.

3. Select `Probability`.

4. Enter the probability .50 and press **RETURN**.

5. Select Formulas.

6. Enter AWARD=500000. and press **RETURN**.

   AWARD is a decision variable that represents the amount awarded in the case. In a favorable judgment, the award is $500,000.

7. Select Exit Menu.

   The name FAVORABLE appears above the branch leading to the node, the probability .50 appears in parentheses below the branch, and the formula AWARD=500000. appears in the bottom left of the Focus window.

   A warning about the probabilities appears in the Message window. If this were the last branch to be defined for the chance node, you would need to correct the outcome probabilities so that they totaled 1.0 by using the Change Values command.

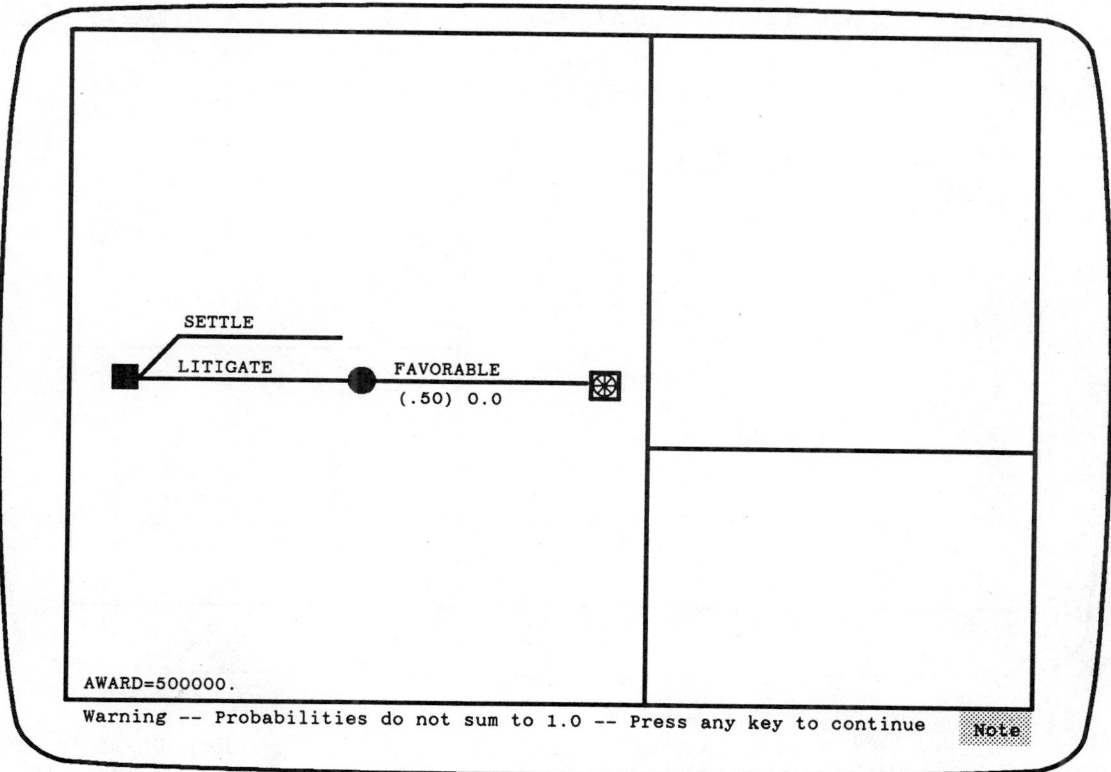


8. Press any key to continue.

Next you will define the node type for the FAVORABLE node.

9. Select Define Node.

   The Select attention bar appears in the Focus window.

10. Press the **Right Arrow** key.

    The FAVORABLE branch is highlighted.

11. Press **RETURN**.

    The Node Type menu appears.

12. Select End Node.

    The End Node menu appears.

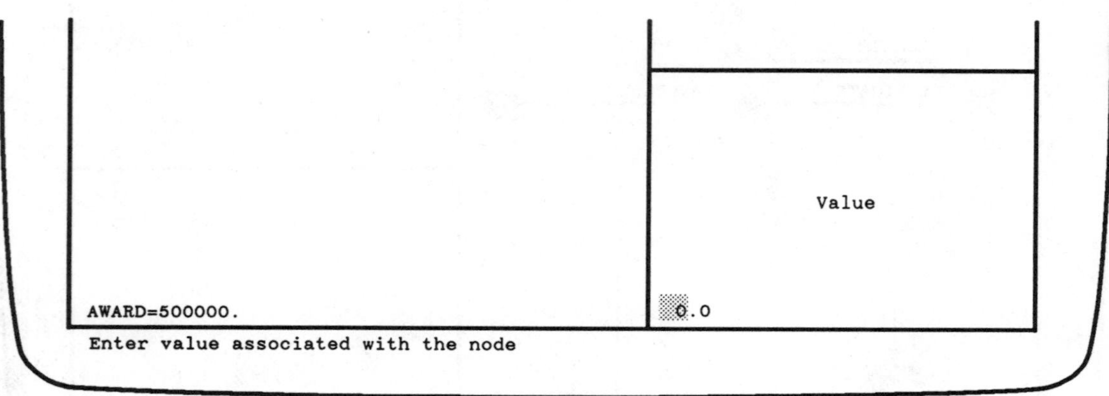


13. Instead of a number, this time enter JUDGMENT and press **RETURN**.

    In the Defining External Formulas section later in this chapter, you will define how the decision variable JUDGMENT is computed from the variables AWARD and COST.

    The display changes to show the new information for the FAVORABLE node of the decision tree, and the Edit menu is displayed.

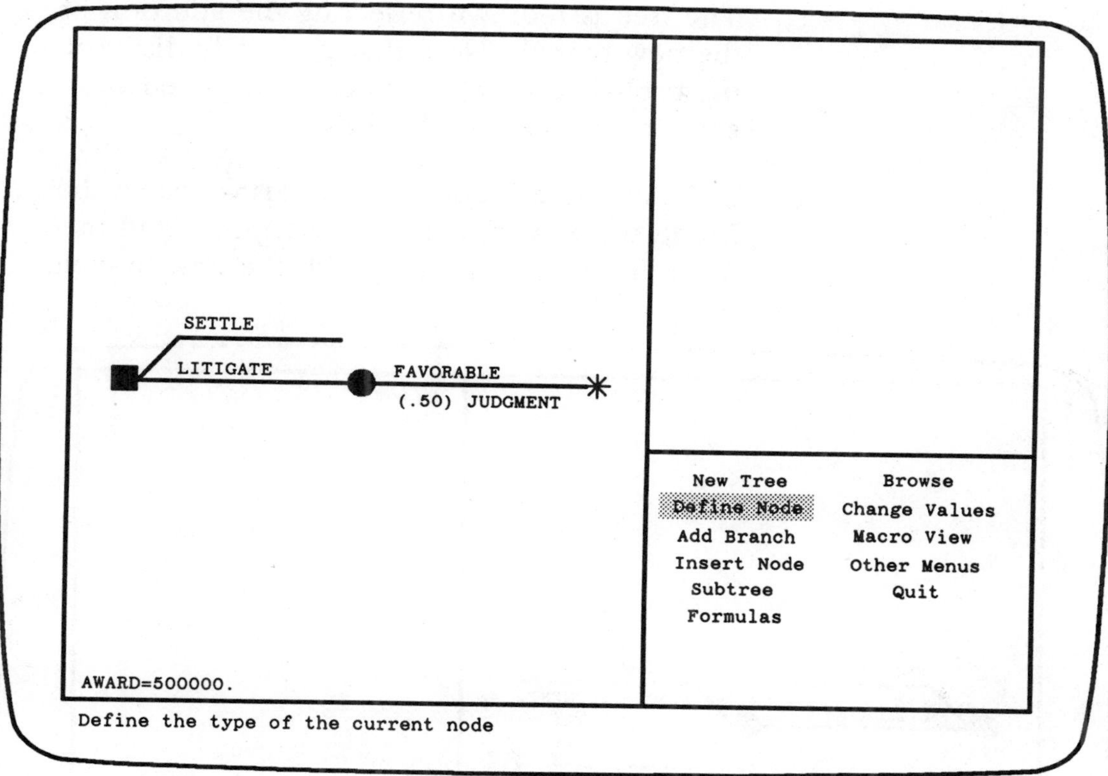


## Adding One More Branch

You will now add the UNFAVORABLE branch at the LITIGATE node.

1. Select Add Branch.

   The Select attention bar prompts you to select the position where you want to add the new branch.

2. To select LITIGATE as the node where the new branch is to be added, press the **Left Arrow** key to highlight the LITIGATE node, and then press **RETURN**.

The tree is redrawn reflecting the addition of the new branch. Note that it already displays the probability (.5), so you do not need to enter a value for probability.

The Annotate Node menu is displayed in the Menu window. Enter the description and the formula to be associated with the new branch.

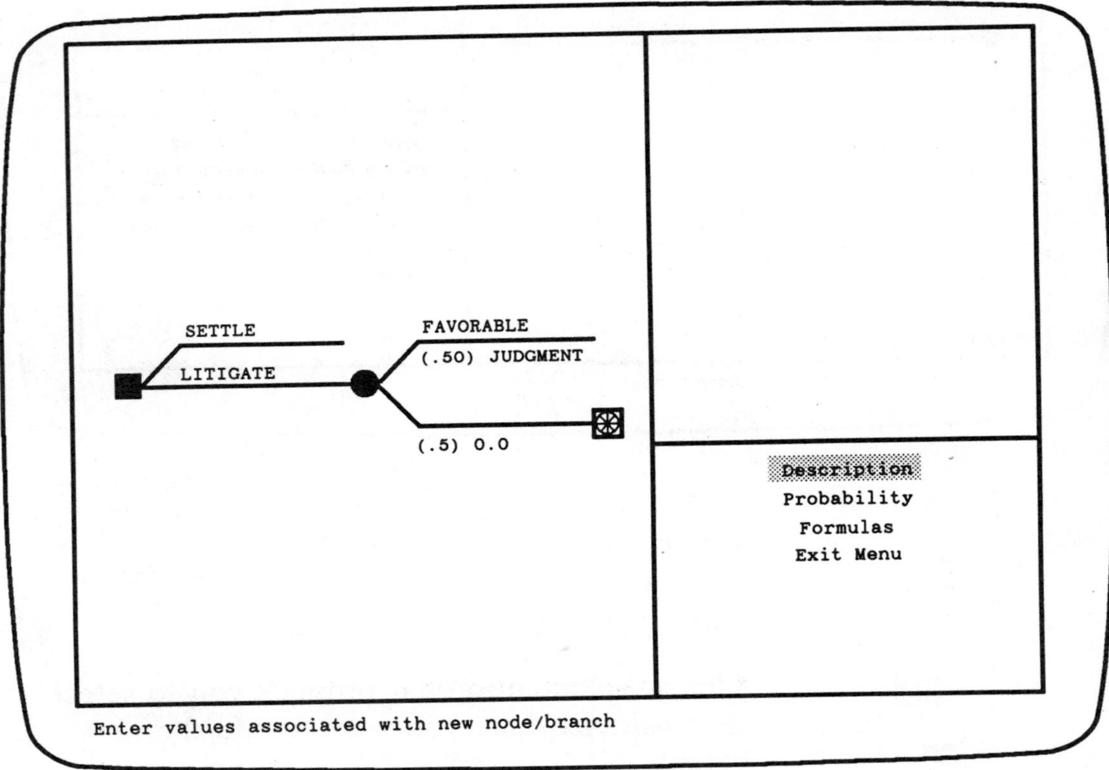


## Annotating the Last Node

1. Select Description.

2. Enter UNFAVORABLE for the description and press **RETURN**.

3. Select Formulas.

4. Enter AWARD=0. and press **RETURN**.

   This formula states that no money will be awarded if the court decision is unfavorable.

5. Select Exit Menu.

   The name UNFAVORABLE is displayed above the new branch.

6. Select Define Node.

7. Press the **Right Arrow** key to highlight the UNFAVORABLE node, and press **RETURN**.

8. Select End Node.

   You are prompted to enter a value for the new node.

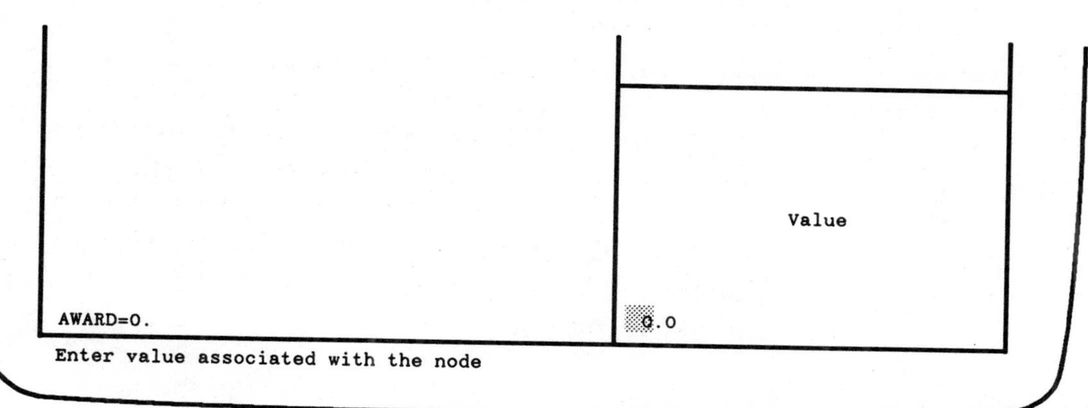


9. Enter the decision variable JUDGMENT—which you will define in the Defining Formulas section next in this chapter—and press **RETURN**.

   The value JUDGMENT appears below the UNFAVORABLE branch.

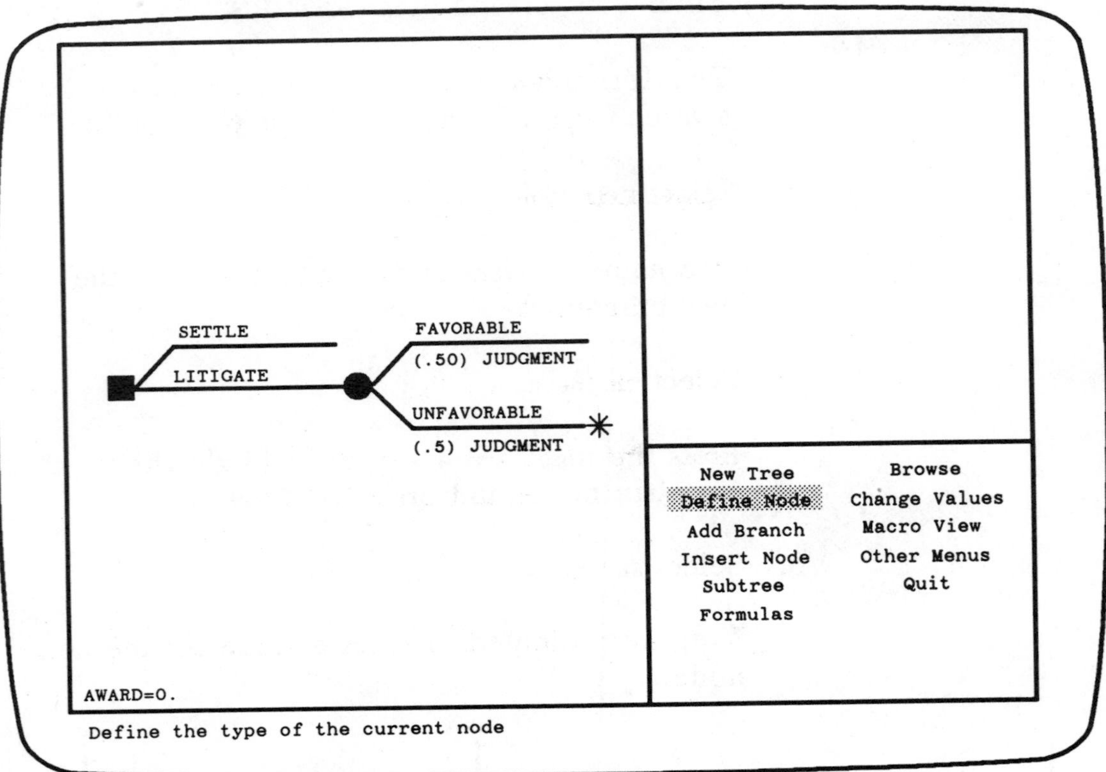


This completes the instructions on constructing a decision tree. (For more information on the steps used to create a tree, see the sections entitled Decision Tree Analysis and Decision Tree Building in Chapter 3.) You are now ready to practice defining external formulas.

## Constructing a New Tree: Defining External Formulas

### Types of Formulas

You can define two types of formulas in trees that use Arborist modeling: annotation formulas and external formulas. Annotation formulas are associated with a specific branch in a particular tree. External formulas are not associated with any particular branch of the tree. You have already defined branch formulas in the tutorial. Now define an external formula for the new tree.

## Defining a Formula

1. Select Formulas from the Edit menu.

   The Formulas menu appears.

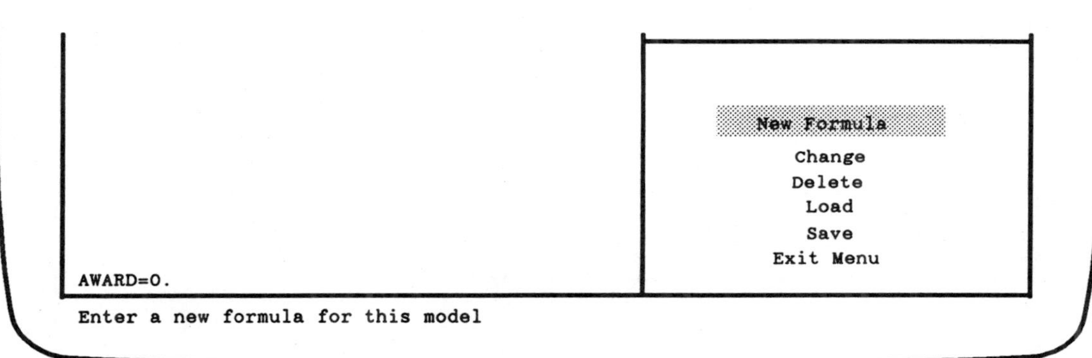


2. Select New Formula.

   The cursor appears in the lower-left corner of the Menu window, waiting for you to enter a formula.

3. Enter JUDGMENT=AWARD-COST and press **RETURN.**

   The name JUDGMENT appears in the Macro View window. When you define external formulas, Arborist uses the first eight characters of the decision variable defined in the formula as the formula name, which is displayed in the

Macro View window. If you use a decision variable name with more than eight characters, Arborist truncates the name in the display.

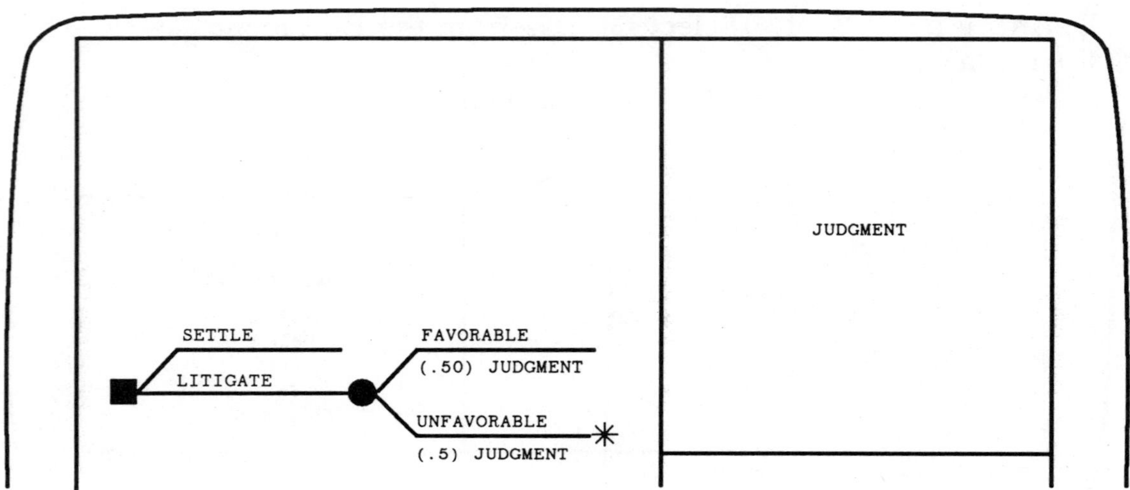


4. Select `Exit Menu`.

You are returned to the Edit menu.

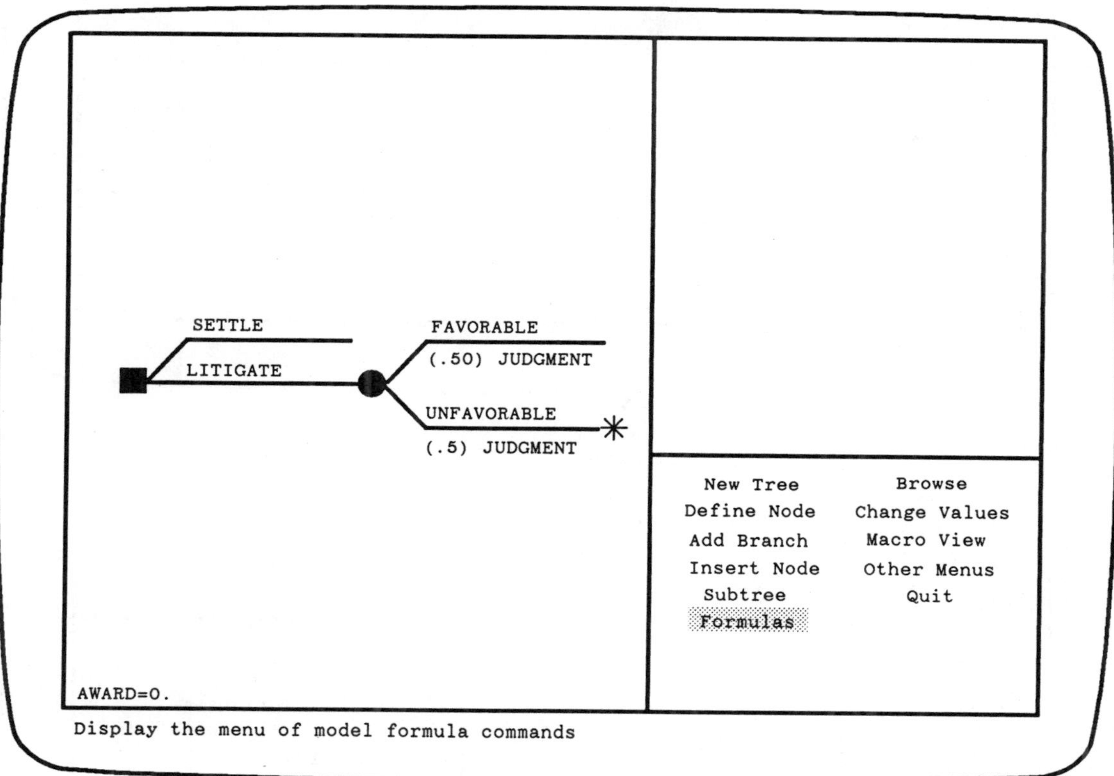


For more information about external formulas and modeling concepts, see Chapter 5, Modeling.

## Saving the New Tree (and Its Associated Formulas)

### Saving the Tree

1. Select `Other Menus`.

   The Main menu appears.

2. Select `Input/Output`.

   The Input/Output menu appears.

```
                                    Load         Change Values
                                    Save         Macro View
                                    Print        Other Menus
                                    Directory    Quit
                                    Browse

AWARD=0.
Display other menus for selection
```

3. Select Save.

The Save menu appears.

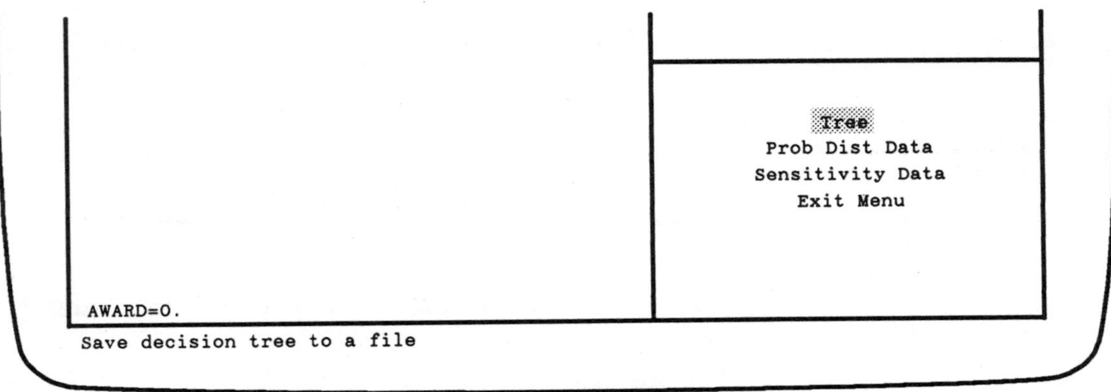


4. Select Tree.

You are prompted for the output filename of the file to which you want to save the tree.

```
                                                  Output filename

AWARD=0.
Save decision tree to a file
```

5. Enter LEGAL (the decision tree filename) and press **RETURN**.

   The Active attention bar is displayed in the Message window, and a message indicates the name of the file to which the tree is being saved.

   Two files are created. The decision tree file is created with the name LEGAL.TRE (all decision tree files have the extension .TRE) and the formulas file is created with the name LEGAL.MDL (all formula definition files have the extension .MDL).

   ---

   **NOTE:** If you have previously saved a tree of the same name, the original file is replaced with the new tree data, and the original file is renamed with the .BAK file extension.

   ---

6. Select Exit Menu to return to the Input/Output menu.

## Analyzing the New Tree: Expected Value

### Performing the Analysis

1. Select Other Menus.

   The Main menu appears.

2. Select Analysis.

   The Analysis menu appears.

3. Select Expected Value.

   The Gains/Losses menu appears.

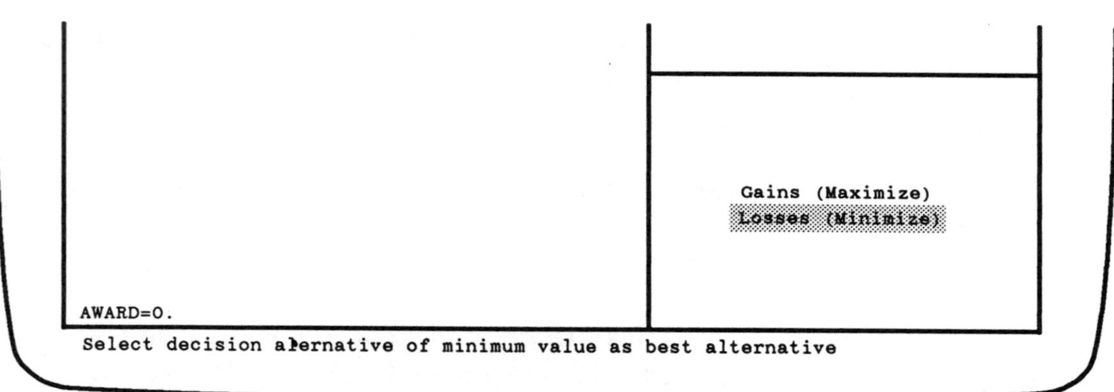


4. Because this particular tree is designed to help you maximize the amount of money you will receive, select Gains (Maximize).

   The Active attention bar is displayed in the Message window while the expected value is being computed. When it has been computed, the SETTLE branch is indicated as the best alternative, and the expected value is displayed in the upper-left corner of the Focus window.

Remember that the expected value is not the value you would realize with certainty in one case. It is the average value you would expect after many instances of the decision.

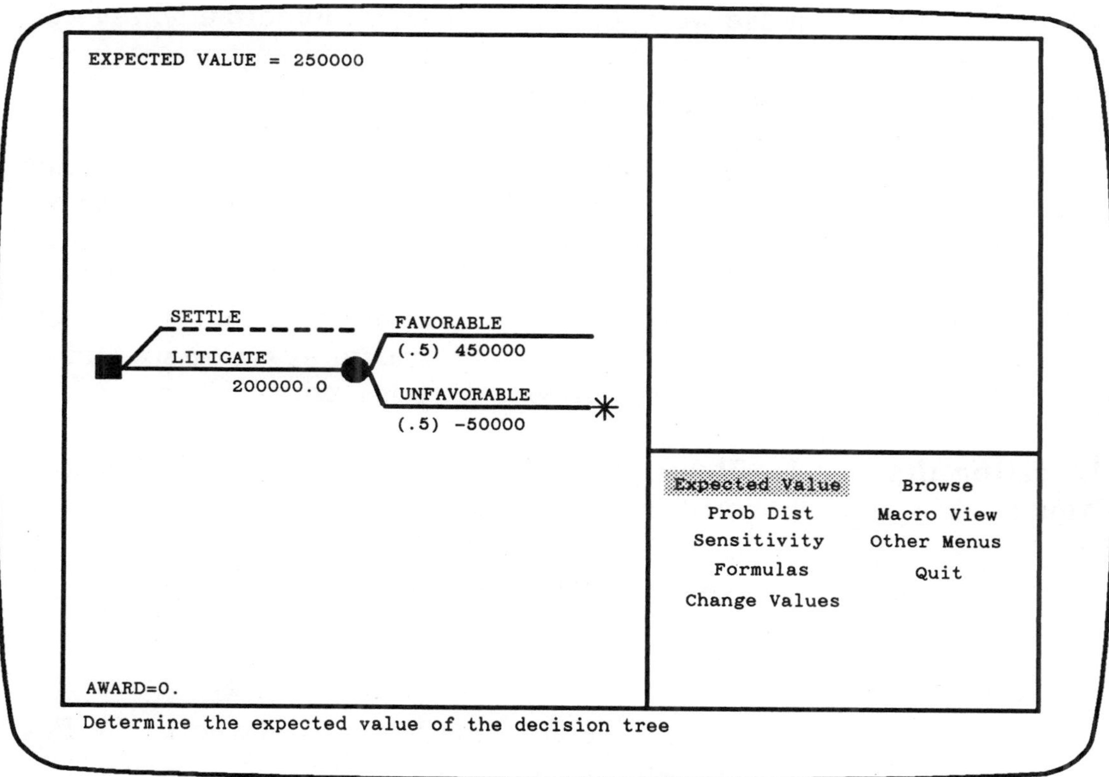


If you wish, you can perform a probability distribution and sensitivity analysis on this tree to practice using what you learned earlier in the tutorial. Otherwise, you can continue reading to learn how to insert a node in your tree.

## Modifying the New Tree: Inserting a Node

### Introduction

For this exercise you will insert a chance node along the LITIGATE subtree prior to the chance node whose end nodes represent a favorable/unfavorable court decision. This new chance node will help determine whether to take the case to court by adding another dimension to the LITIGATE subtree: what would be the impact on your final decision if the judge were to admit (or, more importantly, *not* admit) certain key evidence to your case in the courtroom?

In this section, you will insert the new chance node and—incidentally—use the Copy Subtree command to create two parallel subtrees that emanate from the new node. You will name these subtrees ADMIT EVIDENCE and NOT-ADMIT EVIDENCE, and both will terminate with like end node structures (FAVORABLE and UNFAVORABLE) but with differing probabilities.

**Inserting the New Node**

1. Return to the Edit menu. (To do this, select `Other Menus` and then select `Edit`.)

   The Edit menu is displayed.

2. Select `Insert Node`.

   The `Select` attention bar is displayed in the Focus window, prompting you to select the branch where the node is to be inserted.

3. Press **SHIFT-HOME** (**CTRL-HOME** on an IBM PC) to go to the root node.

   LEGAL DECISION is highlighted.

4. Press the **Right Arrow** key twice to highlight the branch leading into the LITIGATE node, and press **RETURN** to select it as the branch after which the new node will be inserted.

   The Node Type menu is displayed.

5. Select Chance node.

   The display is redrawn with the new node inserted at the end of the LITIGATE branch.

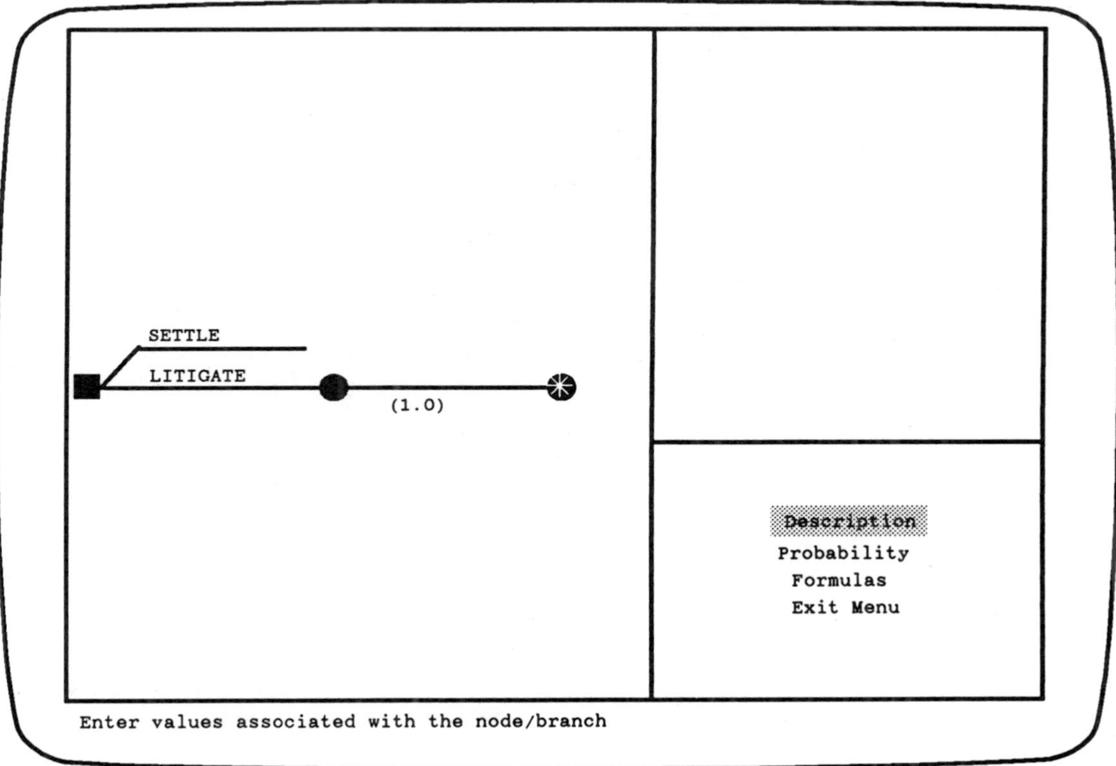


Note that the newly inserted node has actually pushed the FAVORABLE and UNFAVORABLE branches to the right (and off the screen) but that the description LITIGATE remains associated with the branch that originally led into these branches. Arborist automatically assigns the 1.0 probability to the new node branch because the node is a chance node. The Annotate Node menu is displayed in the Menu window to enable you to annotate the branch following the inserted node.

6. Select Description.

7. Type ADMIT EVIDENCE and press **RETURN**.

8. Select Probability.

9. Type .5 and press **RETURN**.

10. Select Exit Menu.

    You are returned to the Edit menu. In the Focus window, the name ADMIT EVIDENCE is displayed over the branch following the inserted node, and the new probability appears beneath the branch. Now that the Insert Node command has completed, the LITIGATE branch is again highlighted as the current node.

    You have now completed enough of the ADMIT EVIDENCE subtree (remember that it already contains the FAVORABLE and UNFAVORABLE end nodes and their associated annotations) to use it as a mold for creating the NOT-ADMIT EVIDENCE subtree, which you will copy and append to the LITIGATE chance node.

**Copying the Subtree**

1. Select Subtree.

   A menu of subtree commands is displayed in the Menu window.

2. Select Copy Subtree.

   The Select attention bar is displayed in the Focus window, prompting you to select the leftmost branch of the subtree that you want to copy.

3. Press the **Right Arrow** key once to highlight the ADMIT EVIDENCE branch, and press **RETURN** to select it.

   The Select attention bar is displayed in the Focus window, prompting you to select the position (destination) in the tree to which the subtree is to be copied.

4. Press the **Left Arrow** key once to highlight the LITIGATE branch and press **RETURN** to select it.

   The subtree is copied to the tree, and the tree is redrawn to show two identical ADMIT EVIDENCE subtrees emanating to the right of the LITIGATE node. Because you already changed the probability to .5, the sum of the probabilities is 1.

   Now you can use the Change Values command to change the description of the new subtree branch to NOT-ADMIT EVIDENCE and to adjust the probabilities of all four end nodes to accommodate the new chance node.

   For example, you might change the probabilities for the FAVORABLE and UNFAVORABLE branches along the ADMIT EVIDENCE subtree to .8 and .2, respectively, and change the probabilities for the FAVORABLE and UNFAVORABLE branches along the NOT-ADMIT EVIDENCE subtree to .3 and .7, respectively.

5. Select `Exit Menu` to return to the Edit menu.

   If you want, you can now use the Save command to save the tree along with your latest modifications. If you need to review this operation, refer to the section entitled Saving the New Tree (and Its Associated Formulas) earlier in this chapter.

# CHAPTER 5: MODELING

## Overview of Modeling

### Why Use Modeling?

In Arborist, *modeling* means to build a formal (mathematical), parameterized description of the problem being analyzed. In simpler terms, modeling is the process of transferring into variables and formulas what you already know about how to calculate a given result. Chapter 4 has already presented some basic modeling techniques.

### An Example

For example, you created a new (modeled) tree called LEGAL DECISION in the middle part of the tutorial. The purpose of the tree was to help you decide which branch (SETTLE or LITIGATE) returns the most money. Recall that the end nodes along the LITIGATE branch were called FAVORABLE and UNFAVORABLE, and both end nodes were assigned a value of JUDGMENT, representing an external formula.

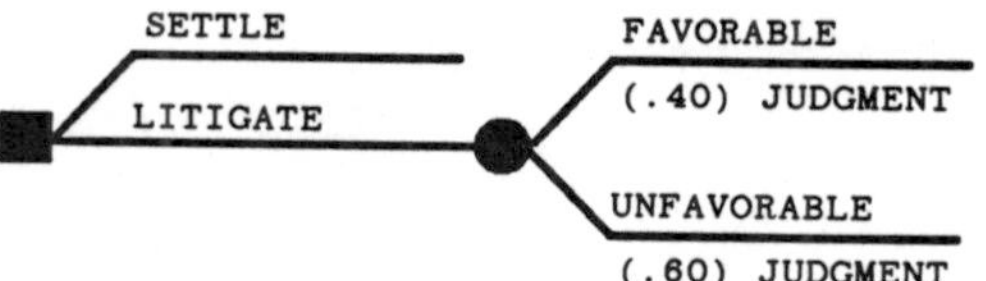


Also recall that you assigned annotation formulas for the LITIGATE, FAVORABLE, and UNFAVORABLE branches (COST=5000, AWARD=500000, and AWARD=0, respectively). You could have assigned numbers as values to the end nodes (as shown in the following figure), and the results would have been just as correct if you were to evaluate the tree.

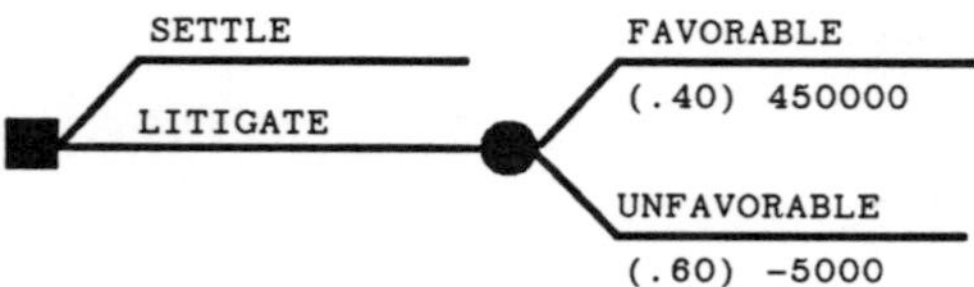


This second tree fragment illustrates how you would approach decision tree analysis *without* modeling. Numeric constants are hard-coded to the tree structure as values for the end nodes. But you had to calculate those end-node values somehow—if not in your head, then on paper.

You know that to calculate the total money received from a court case, you must subtract your total cost from the total amount awarded. In the previous unmodeled tree, the end-node values are the result of this calculation. Thus, your first step into moving from no modeling to building a model into your tree might look like this:

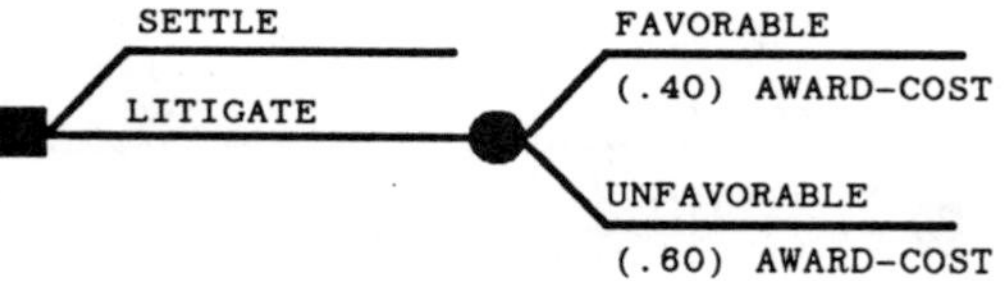


In this step, you assign expressions (AWARD-COST) that represent your calculation in place of the numbers. At the same time, you specify annotation formulas to the LITIGATE, FAVORABLE, and UNFAVORABLE branches (COST=5000, AWARD=500000, and AWARD=0, respectively). These annotation formulas assign the necessary numbers to the decision variables COST and AWARD, which are in turn used in the calculation expressions.

The last step in the modeling process takes you back to the original tree from Chapter 4. To abstract the calculation expressions further, you create one generic calculation formula for this type of problem and make it an external formula: JUDGMENT=AWARD-COST. You can now use this one decision variable (JUDGMENT) as the value for the end nodes FAVORABLE and UNFAVORABLE.

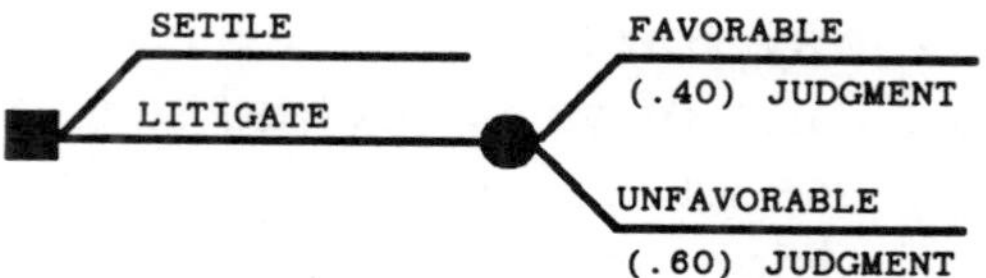


You could extend the modeling process further by using formulas and variables to express probabilities. If, for example, you added a new formula to the LITIGATE branch (PROB=.4), you could replace the numeric constants for the probabilities with expressions on the tree:

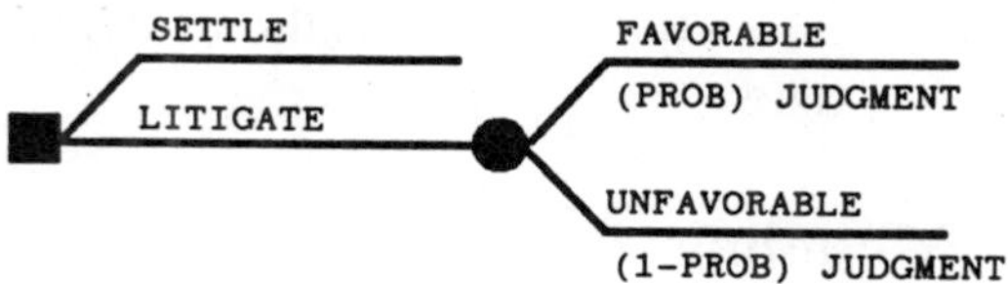


Decision variables, formulas, and expressions are discussed further later in this chapter.

### Advantages of Using Modeling

In Arborist, modeled trees offer several advantages over unmodeled trees:

- Calculative ability — If you use variables and formulas in your trees, Arborist can do calculations for you. This frees you to spend more time building logical decision frameworks rather than doing tedious calculations over and over.

- Flexibility — Variables and formulas make it much easier to change values that ripple throughout a tree structure. If you hard-code value assignments, then you must search through the tree to find them all; also you must recompute the values for branches that could have been represented by formulas.

- Cloning — Because modeling generalizes the way you handle decision-analysis data (in the form of variables and formulas), you can often use an existing tree or subtree for a similar decision problem. You simply copy the tree (or subtree) structure into a new environment and then change a few specific variable values to fit the new problem. The time spent changing values in an unmodeled copied tree would be prohibitive, at best.

- More types of data analysis — Because sensitivity analyses are based on variables, you cannot perform a sensitivity analysis on an unmodeled tree.

Modeling, then, allows you to structure and control your data along the path of a tree, as well as generalize that data so that it can be used (as a model) in similar trees. If you take the time up front to use modeling techniques when designing a tree structure, you can increase the ease and efficiency of your future work.

The next section of this chapter takes a closer look at modeling. You will learn about the types of modeling (Arborist versus Lotus 1-2-3) and some formal definitions of terms.

## Modeling Types and Definitions

**Types of Modeling**

As previously defined, modeling allows you to build a parameterized description of the problem you are analyzing. The type of parameters used is based on whether you are using *Arborist modeling* or *Lotus 1-2-3 modeling*. Both types of modeling use the same concepts of data abstraction, but the Arborist software implements them differently.

You cannot mix Arborist modeling and Lotus 1-2-3 modeling in a single tree. You are prompted to specify the type of modeling when you start to build a new tree. Once specified, Arborist reflects the appropriate command groups—for whichever modeling you are using—in the Menu window.

The primary difference between Arborist modeling and Lotus 1-2-3 modeling is that they are driven by different parameter types: *decision variables* versus *worksheet cells*.

**Decision Variables**

The basic element of Arborist modeling is the decision variable. Most of the variables that you have encountered thus far in the manual were of this type. Each decision variable name must start with an alphabetical character (for example, PRICE or CST1985).

**Worksheet Cells**

The basic element of Lotus 1-2-3 modeling is the worksheet cell. In the tree, worksheet cells are referred to by their range names.

**Formulas**

Formulas are equations that assign values to decision variables (in trees with Arborist modeling) or worksheet cells (in trees with Lotus 1-2-3 modeling). A formula normally applies to a node of the decision tree.

**Expressions**

You create expressions by combining decision variables (or worksheet cells, with Lotus 1-2-3 modeling) with numeric constants, operators, and built-in functions (operators and built-in functions are described at the end of this chapter). You can use these expressions to represent the value of an end node, the probability of a chance outcome, or the value assigned to a decision variable or worksheet cell.

## Arborist Modeling

**Expressions**

With Arborist modeling, expressions used in annotations (formulas, probabilities, and values) can contain any decision variable defined on the path leading from the root node to the node where the expression is used. Expressions can also contain decision variables that are defined in external formulas. Finally, expressions in Arborist modeling can contain any of the operators or built-in functions discussed at the end of this chapter.

**Defining Formulas**

In trees that use Arborist modeling, formulas have the following form:

*decision-variable = expression*

Two types of formulas can be defined in trees that use Arborist modeling: annotation formulas and external formulas.

**Annotation Formulas**

Formulas associated with a specific branch of the tree are called *annotation formulas*. (Recall from the tutorial that an annotation formula is displayed in the lower-left corner of the Focus window when its associated node is the current node.) Annotation formulas allow values to be computed and assigned to a decision variable. You can specify multiple formulas for a branch by separating the formulas with semicolons, as shown in this example:

```
EXPENSES=500;REVENUE=REVENUE+2000
```

The concept of *successive variable assignment* is the key to using annotation formulas. The values assigned to a decision variable depend on the placement of the variable along any given path in a tree—from the root node to an end node. This variable can retain the same value throughout the path and be used to assign values to other variables. The variable can also be assigned new values, depending on how you decide to use it in the tree.

Along a given path, any variable that is assigned a value from a previously assigned variable is thus dependent on that previous assignment; thus, the term successive variable assignment. The point is that you can use variables and annotation formulas to build a logical sequence of branch values without hard-coding numbers to your tree. Look again at the LEGAL DECISION tree:

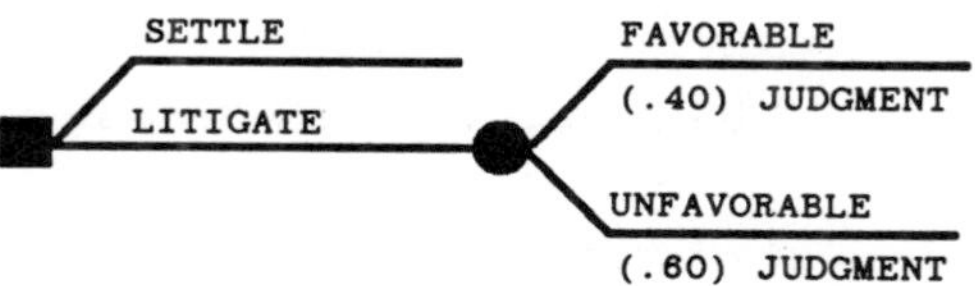


The annotation formulas are not displayed here (they are only displayed in the lower-left corner of the Focus window when their associated node is the current node). If you trace one path (from the root node) to the FAVORABLE end node, you will find the following annotation formulas:

- Root-node branch — No associated formula
- LITIGATE branch — COST=5000
- FAVORABLE branch — AWARD=500000

In this example, the variable assignments along the FAVORABLE path do not affect each other but are instead used in the external formula JUDGMENT. If, however, the FAVORABLE branch were given the annotation formula AWARD=COST+20, then the decision variable AWARD would be dependent on (and assigned by) the variable COST because of COST's previous value assignment. Alternately, giving to the SETTLE branch the annotation formula COST=1000 has no effect on the FAVORABLE annotation formula AWARD=COST+20 because the SETTLE branch does not lie along the FAVORABLE path.

## External Formulas

Formulas that are not associated with a specific branch of the tree are called *external formulas*. These formulas define relationships among decision variables used in the tree. For example, the external formula PROFIT=REVENUE-EXPENSES describes how a value for the decision variable PROFIT is calculated. You can then use PROFIT in other formulas in the tree or as a value at an end node.

Note that external formulas are named by (and assigned to) the decision variable on the left side of the defining formula. In the previous example, the variable PROFIT can stand alone as a value for an end node because it actually represents the expression to which it is assigned (REVENUE-EXPENSES).

To define an external formula, use the Formulas command on either the Analysis menu or the Edit menu. The Formulas command also permits you to load and save sets of external formulas (or models). Formulas are saved with the .MDL extension.

After you have saved an external formula, you can use it to manipulate data in trees for similar problems. For example, you might use an external formula defined for a mutual-fund tree in another tree that analyzes stock information.

The key is to use decision variables and annotation formulas in the tree that correspond to the decision variables in the external formula. The real power of modeling lies in this relationship between successive variable assignments along a tree and their counterparts in external formulas.

## Built-In Functions

**MAX, MIN**

MAX and MIN are standard functions of maximum (the largest numeric value) and minimum (the smallest numeric value). Both functions can take a varying number of arguments. The syntax for these functions are:

MAX(*expr-1*, *expr-2*, ... *expr-n*)
MIN(*expr-1*, *expr-2*, ... *expr-n*)

where *expr* are expressions. For example:

```
MAX(COST1,COST2)
MIN(3,COST1,COST1-COST2)
```

**NPV**

The NPV function returns the net present value of a set of cash flows based on a given discount rate.

This function can take a varying number of arguments. The syntax for the NPV function is:

NPV(*rate*, *flow-1*, *flow-2*, ... *flow-n*)

where *rate* is the discount rate (9.5% is entered as 9.5) and *flow-i* is the cash-flow at time increment *i*. The NPV is computed as:

$$\text{NPV} = \sum_{i=1}^{n} \frac{\text{flow-i}}{(1 + \text{rate}) \ \hat{} \ i}$$

**FV, PV, PMT**

The functions FV (future value), PV (present value), and PMT (loan payment) can be used for situations in which fixed flows occur over a set of periods based on a given interest rate. Each of these functions is discussed in the following paragraphs.

**FV**

The FV (future value) function returns the future value of a series of equal payments occurring with regular frequency at a set interest rate. The syntax for the FV function is:

FV(*payment*, *rate*, *per*)

where *payment* is the amount of the fixed flow, *rate* is the interest rate for the flow period (annual interest rate/the number of payment periods per year), and *per* is the number of payment periods. The FV is computed as follows:

$$\text{FV} = \text{payment} * \frac{((1 + \text{rate}) \ \hat{} \ \text{per}) - 1}{\text{rate}}$$

---

**NOTE:** The value for the argument *per* must be an integer.

---

**PV**

The PV (present value) function returns the present value of a series of future payments of equal value occurring with regular frequency at a set discount rate.

Syntax for the PV function is as follows:

PV(*payment*, *rate*, *per*)

where *payment* is the amount of the fixed flow, *rate* is the discount rate for the payment period (annual discount rate/the number of payment periods per year), and *per* is the number of payment periods. The PV is computed as follows:

$$PV = payment * \frac{1 - ((1 + rate) \wedge -per)}{rate}$$

**PMT**

The PMT (loan payment) function returns the payment amount required for repayment of a principle (prin) at the specified interest rate (adjusted to the payment interval) and a set number of payment periods (per). Syntax for the PMT function is as follows:

PMT(*prin*, *rate*, *per*)

where *prin* is the principle amount of the loan, *rate* is the interest rate (adjusted to the payment period annual interest rate/number of payments per year), and *per* is the number of payments in the life of the loan. PMT is computed as follows:

```
                      rate
PMT = prin * ___________________________
             1 - ((1 + rate) ^ - per)
```

---

**NOTE:** The value for the argument *per* must be an integer.

---

**LOG**

The LOG function returns the base 10 (common) logarithm of the specified number. Syntax for the LOG function is:

LOG(*x*)

where *x* is a real number.

**LN**

The LN function returns the natural logarithm of the specified number. Syntax for the LN function is:

LN(*x*)

where *x* is a real number.

The following in an example of the LN function in a simple expression:

```
LN(1)
```

**IF**

You can use the IF function for conditional expressions in modeling. IF is expressed as follows:

IF(*condition*, *true-value*, *false-value*)

An example of the IF function follows:

```
IF(A<B, A, B)
```

In this example, if *A* is less than *B*, then *A* is used as the value of the expression. Otherwise, *B* is used as the value of the expression.

You can use any of these symbols in the conditional expression of an IF function.

| Symbol | Meaning |
| --- | --- |
| < | Less than |
| > | Greater than |
| < = | Less than or equal to |
| > = | Greater than or equal to |
| = = | Equal to |
| < > | Not equal to |

The following logical operators can be used in the conditional expression of the IF function.

| Operator | Meaning |
| --- | --- |
| & | And |
| \| | Or |
| ~ | Not |

Example 1:

```
IF (A<B & B<C, A, B)
```

In Example 1, the conditional reads: if A is less than B *and* B is less than C.

Example 2:

```
IF (A<B | B<C, A, B)
```

In Example 2, the conditional is: if A is less than B *or* B is less than C.

Example 3:

```
IF (~ (A<B | B<C) & B==3, A, B)
```

In Example 3, the conditional is: if the expression A is less than B **or** B is less than C is not true *and* B equals 3.

# CHAPTER 6: ARBORIST BASIC COMMANDS

## Overview of Commands

### Arborist Main Menu

The Arborist commands are organized into three groups: editing commands, analysis commands, and input/output commands. The editing commands are for creating and modifying decision trees. The analysis commands are for analyzing decision trees. The input/output commands are for loading decision trees and their associated external formulas (models). You can also use the input/output commands to save and print decision trees (including their associated annotation information) and certain analytical data.

Each of these groups of commands is represented by an item in the Arborist Main menu, as follows:

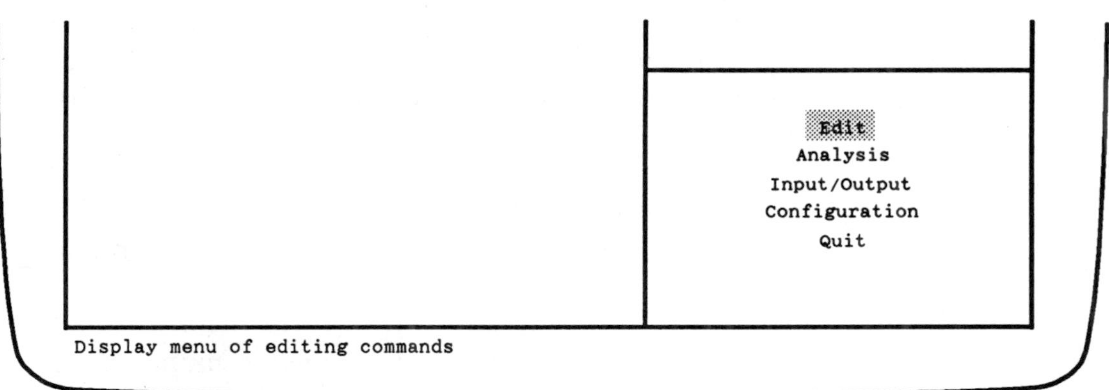


The Configuration command on the Main menu enables you to specify different printer information for your computer, if it changes. If you are using a TI computer, you can also use the Configuration command to change the monitor type. See Appendix B for details on custom printer configuration.

The Quit command exits the Arborist program. When you exit Arborist, all information about the current tree is lost unless you save it first.

## General Commands

The following commands are available from the Edit, Analysis, and Input/Output menus: Browse, Change Values, Macro View, Other Menus, and Quit. The Edit and Analysis menus also provide a Formulas command. When Lotus 1-2-3 modeling is used, the Formulas command in these menus is replaced by the Lotus 1-2-3 command.

The Browse command allows you to move around the decision tree structure; it also provides subcommands to edit annotation information at a specific node or to look at the structure in general.

The Change Values command allows you to change the description and formula assigned to a branch or node. You can also change the probability assigned to a branch following a chance node, or the value assigned to an end node or undefined node.

The Formulas command displays a menu of subcommands to define, change, delete, load, and save formulas.

The Lotus 1-2-3 command displays a menu of subcommands to view cell names, browse in 1-2-3, and change the program and worksheet directories.

The Macro View command displays a larger portion of the tree in the Macro View window.

The Other Menus command displays the Main menu in the Menu window.

## Editing Commands

The Arborist editing commands are for creating and modifying decision trees. The Edit menu provides the following items:

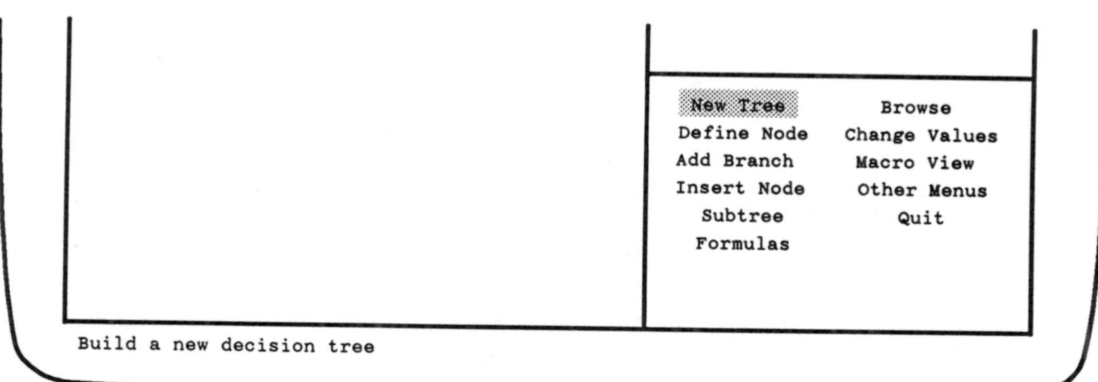


The New Tree command starts a new tree at its root node. If a decision tree is currently loaded when this command is executed, that tree is destroyed.

The Define Node command assigns or modifies the type of a selected node.

The Add Branch command adds a branch at a selected node.

The Insert Node command inserts a node before a selected node.

The Subtree command displays a menu of subcommands to copy, delete, load, and save subtrees.

## Analysis Commands

The Arborist analysis commands are for analyzing decision trees. The Analysis menu provides the following items:

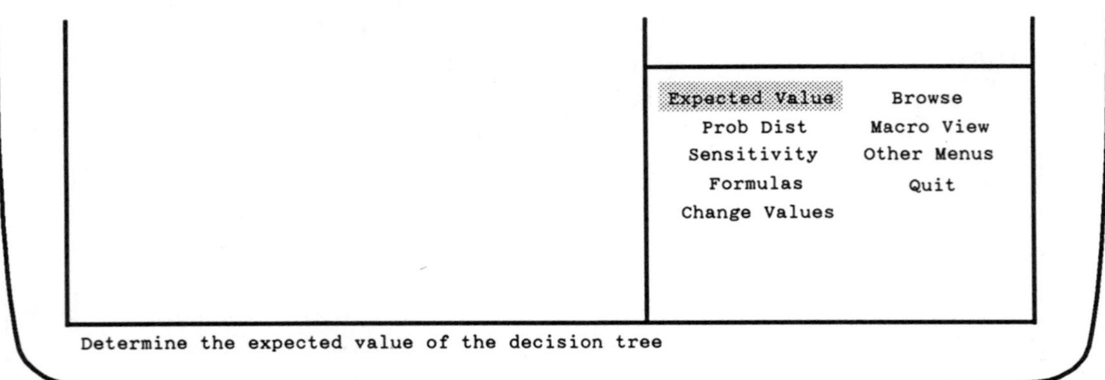


The Expected Value command calculates the expected value of a decision tree.

The Prob Dist command calculates the probability distribution for all outcomes of a selected node.

The Sensitivity command analyzes the sensitivity of the expected value of a decision tree to changes in the value of a selected variable.

**Input/Output Commands**

The Input/Output menu provides the following items:

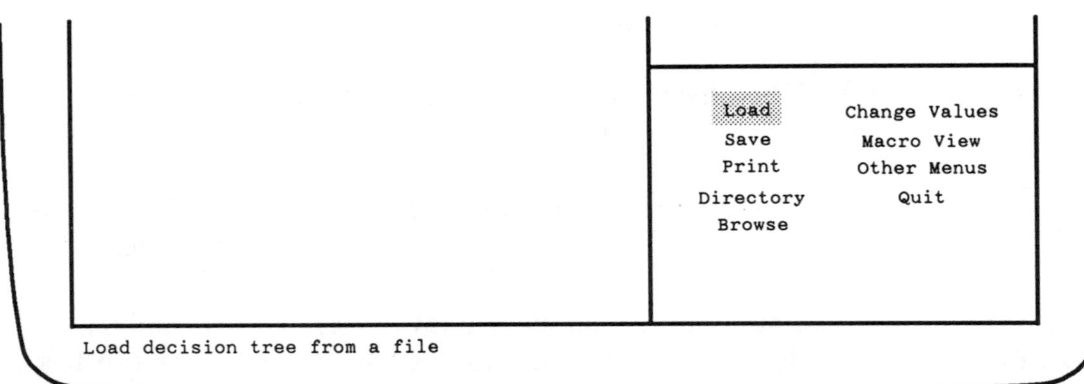


The Load command loads a tree from disk.

The Save command displays a menu of subcommands for saving a tree, probability distribution data, and sensitivity analysis data to a disk file.

The Print command displays a menu of subcommands for printing information about the current tree, probability distribution data, and sensitivity analysis data.

The Directory command changes the current directory.

## Add Branch Command

**Location**

The Add Branch command is located on the Edit menu. Branches can be added only to decision nodes and chance nodes.

**Operation**

Select `Add Branch`, and then select the node to which the branch is to be added. If the selected node is a decision node or a chance node and has fewer than seven branches, an undefined node is added leading from the selected node. Otherwise, the Message window displays an error message.

After the Focus window is redrawn to display the added node, the Menu window displays the Annotate Node menu. If the added node leads from a decision node, the menu contains three items: `Description`, `Formulas`, and `Exit Menu`. If the added node leads from a chance node, the Annotate Node menu contains another item: `Probability`. You can enter a description, formula, and probability for the added node at this time, or you can exit the menu and enter this information later by using the Change Values command. See the section entitled Change Values Command later in this chapter for more information about annotating nodes.

## Browse Command

**Location** The Browse command is located on the Edit, Analysis, and Input/Output menus.

**Operation** Select Browse; Arborist displays the following:

```
HOME - Move to center.
CTRL/HOME - Move to root.
C - Change branch values.
M - Macro View display.
B - Browse thru Macro View.
ESC - Return to menu.
Select
Cursor keys move through the tree, ESC key activates the command menu
```

The Select attention bar appears at the lower-right corner of the Focus window, indicating that you can browse through the tree displayed in the Focus window.

Use the cursor control (**Arrow**) keys to move around the tree. Press the **HOME** key to move to the center node of the Focus window. Press **SHIFT-HOME** (**CTRL-HOME** on an IBM PC) to move to the root node.

Press the **ESC** key to return to the menu from which you selected the Browse command.

Press the **C** key to change the annotation information (description, formulas, probabilities, and value) assigned to the highlighted node.

Press the **M** key to generate the display in the Macro View window. While you browse in the Focus window, your location in the tree is reflected in the Macro View window.

Press the B key to browse through the Macro View window. This subcommand displays the following:

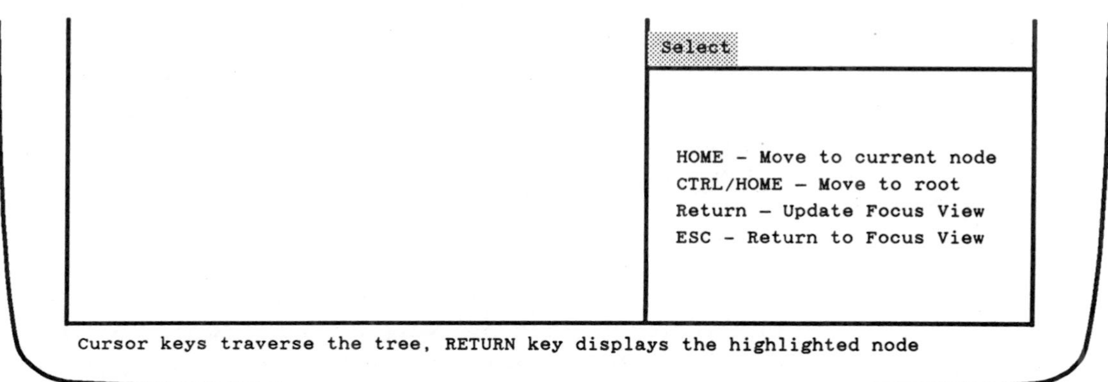


If the macro view is not displayed already in the Macro View window, the display is generated.

The Select attention bar appears in the Macro View window indicating that you can browse through that window. Use the **Arrow** keys to browse through the tree display in the Macro View window.

While you are browsing through the macro display of the tree, the tree display in the Focus window remains static.

Press **HOME** to move to the same node as the current node in the Focus window. Press **SHIFT-HOME** (**CTRL-HOME** on an IBM PC) to make the root node the current node. To update the display in the Focus window so that it reflects the current node in the Macro View window, press **RETURN**. To return to Focus window browsing, press **ESC**.

**Moving Between Windows**

When you work with large and complex decision trees, the Browse command allows you to move quickly between the Focus and Macro View windows using the respective strengths of each. For example, you may be moving around in the Focus window to modify detailed annotations but, because your perspective is limited, you may forget where you are in the tree. Pressing the **B** key activates the Macro View window, where you can continue moving through the tree with a larger view of the structure.

Still in the Macro View window, you find a subtree structure that is parallel to the one you just left in the Focus window; pressing **RETURN** scrolls the Focus window display so that it becomes synchronized with the current node in the Macro View window. Because the Macro View window does not display node names or associated annotations, you might then reactivate the Focus window (by pressing **ESC**) and begin performing detailed operations on the tree.

Thus, the Browse command allows you to zoom in on detailed work, back away to get oriented in the tree structure, and continually keep each window display synchronized as you move around in the decision tree.

## Change Values Command

---

**Location**

The Change Values command is located on the Edit, Analysis, and Input/Output menus.

**Operation**

Select `Change Values`, and then select the node. The Change Values command displays the Annotate Node menu, a menu of items that you can change for the type of node selected. You can change the *description* and *formulas* for all types of nodes. You can also change the *probability* of the branch following a chance node and the *value* of an undefined node or an end node.

When the Annotate Node menu is displayed, select the item to be changed. The current information for the chosen item is displayed at the bottom of the Menu window. Use the edit keys described in Chapter 4, Using Arborist Decision Tree Software, to modify the displayed information.

Press **RETURN** to assign the edited information to a *buffer*, which is a temporary storage location that holds your editing information. Press **ESC** to cancel the edit (leaving the annotation information unchanged). Before you select `Exit Menu`, you can edit the other types of annotations or reedit the previously buffered editing information. When you select `Exit Menu`, all buffered information is reflected in the display of the tree.

Note that when you change the probability on one branch of a two-branch chance node, Arborist adjusts the probability on the other branch to total 1.0. For a tree with more than two branches, you must adjust the probabilities at some time before you evaluate the tree. To update the tree file stored on disk, use the Save command. (See the section entitled Save Command in this chapter.)

## Online Help

Arborist provides special online help for specifying probabilities when you use the Change Values command. When the cursor is positioned on the `Probability` item in the Annotate Node menu, you can press the **F9** key or the **SHIFT-?** keys to invoke a *probability wheel* in the Macro View window:

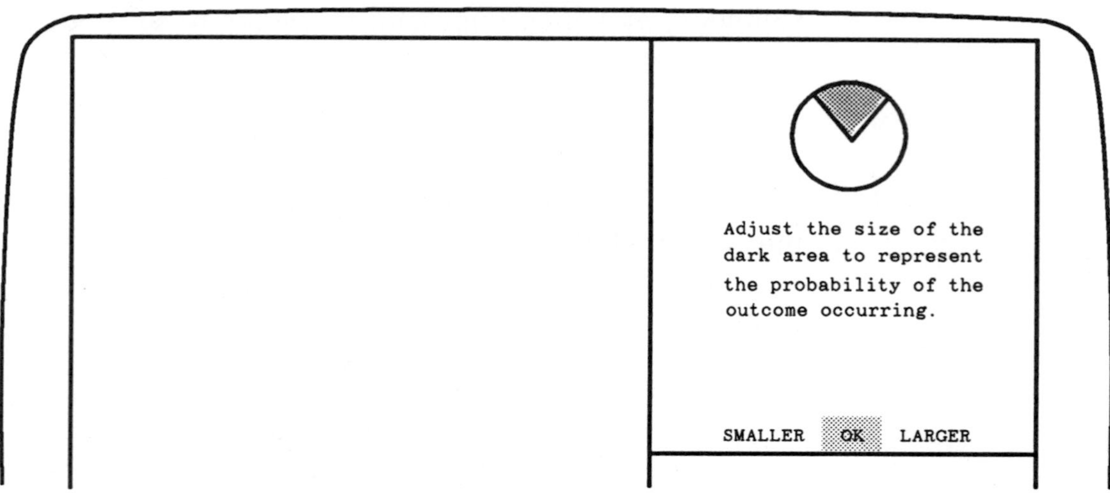
Adjust the size of the
dark area to represent
the probability of the
outcome occurring.
SMALLER
OK
LARGER

The probability wheel is a graphic tool that allows you to choose the percentage of probability for a given branch visually.

Adjust the size of the dark area (indicating the probability) by using the **Left Arrow** and **Right Arrow** keys to position the cursor on SMALLER or LARGER. Once you obtain the appropriate size, press **RETURN**; Arborist supplies the corresponding probability at the bottom of the Menu window.

## Configuration Command

**Location** The Configuration command is located on the Main menu.

**Operation** Select Configuration, and then select the type of printer for your computer. If you have a TI computer, the Configuration command first displays in the Menu window a selection (color versus monochrome) of monitor types. You must select one of these—even if it means reselecting your current monitor type—to access the printer-type selection list.

After you select the printer type, select `Exit Menu`, and you are returned to the Main menu unless your printer supports compressed printing. If you select a preconfigured printer type (anything other than the `Custom` item) and your printer supports compressed printing, the following message is displayed:

```
Use compressed mode to print the tree? (Y/N)
```

Press the **Y** key to activate compressed mode or the **N** key for uncompressed printing, and you are returned to the Main menu. Remember that the compression mode you choose here remains set until you explicitly change it again using the Configuration command.

The `Custom` item on the printer-type selection list allows you to specify special printer configuration options. See Appendix B for details.

The Configuration command does not allow you to change the graphics adapter type for an IBM-compatible computer. Refer to the section entitled Changing the Graphics Adapter Type in Chapter 2 for these instructions.

### Define Node Command

**Location**

The Define Node command is located on the Edit menu.

**Operation**

Select `Define Node`, and then select the node you wish to define or redefine. After you select the node, the Node Type menu is displayed. Valid node types are decision, chance, end, and undefined. What happens next depends on the type of the original node as well as the type you select. The following list describes different actions based on what type of node you start with and the node type you want it to become:

- Undefined node or end node to a decision node — Arborist adds a branch to the decision node and displays the Annotate Node menu so that you can then assign annotations to the new branch.

- Chance node to a decision node — Arborist automatically removes the probabilities from the branches that follow that node.

- Undefined node or end node to a chance node — Arborist adds a branch to the chance node and displays the Annotate Node menu so that you can then assign annotations to the new branch.

- Decision node to a chance node — Arborist automatically assigns equal probabilities to all branches that follow that node.

- Undefined node to an end node (or vice versa) — Arborist displays the Annotate Node menu so that you can then change the value originally assigned to the node.

- Chance node or decision node to an undefined node or end node — The subtree leading from that node is deleted. Arborist first gives you this warning message: `About to delete subtrees` `below current node -- Are you sure? (Y/N)`. If you press the **Y** key, Arborist displays the Annotate Node menu so that you can specify a value for the node.

Changing a node to an undefined node is often useful in the context of creating parallel subtree structures due to the behavior of the Copy Subtree command when the destination node is an undefined node (see the section entitled Subtree Command later in this chapter for details on the Copy Subtree command).

## Directory Command

**Location** The Directory command is located on the Input/Output menu.

**Operation** When you invoke this command, the current drive name and directory are displayed at the bottom of the Menu window, and the Message window prompts you to enter a new drive and directory.

To change the drive or current directory, enter the desired drive or directory and press **RETURN**.

For example, you could enter one of the following:

```
A:

C:\TREES
```

## Expected Value Command

**Location** The Expected Value command is located on the Analysis menu.

**Operation**

When you select this command, a menu of evaluation options is displayed in the Menu window: `Gains (Maximize)` and `Losses (Minimize)`.

Select an evaluation option. Arborist evaluates the decision tree and calculates the expected value. Arborist also annotates the tree with the expected value for each node.

**Display**

The expected value of the decision tree is displayed in the upper-left corner of the Focus window. The best alternative at *each* decision node in the tree is indicated in both the Focus window and the Macro View window. The best alternative is shown even for decision nodes that do not lie along the best path for the entire tree. The Focus window also displays the expected value for each node.

---

**NOTE:** Refer to the section entitled How the Arborist Screen Appears on Your System in Chapter 3 for details on how your computer shows the best alternative path in the Focus and Macro View windows.

---

## Formulas Command

**Location**

The Formulas command is located on the Edit and Analysis menus.

**Operation**

When you select `Formulas`, the Formulas menu is displayed in the Menu window. This menu contains the following items: `New Formula`, `Change`, `Delete`, `Load`, `Save`, and `Exit Menu`.

This section describes how to use the commands on the Formulas menu.

**New Formula**

The New Formula command adds new external formula definitions to the current set of external formulas (model) for the tree.

When you select this command, the cursor appears in the lower-left corner of the Menu window so that you can enter the new external formula definition. After you enter the external formula, press **RETURN** to add the formula to the current model. As each external formula is added to the current model, the decision variable part of the formula is displayed in the Macro View window. The maximum number of external formulas that can be defined for a tree is 39.

Pressing **RETURN** adds the formula definition to only the current model in memory. External formulas are saved to disk when the tree is saved.

---

**NOTE:** An external formula definition file is automatically created when you use the Save command on the Input/Output menu. The formula definition file has the same name as the decision tree file, but with an extension of .MDL.

---

**Change**

The Change command changes an external formula definition in the current model for a specific tree.

When you select this command, the Macro View window displays a list of decision variables that name (are assigned by) external formulas included in the current model. When you select a decision variable from this selection list, the corresponding external formula is displayed at the bottom of the Macro View window for editing. You can edit the formula using the editing keys described in Chapter 3, Using Arborist Decision Tree Software.

After you have changed the formula, press **RETURN** to add the changes to the current model in memory.

**Delete**

The Delete command is used to delete a selected formula from the current model.

When you select this command, the Macro View window displays a list of decision variables that name (are assigned by) external formulas included in the current model. When you select a decision variable from this list by pressing **RETURN**, the corresponding formula is deleted.

**Load**

This command loads a model from a disk file.

When you select this command, the Macro View window displays a list of filenames for model files. Each file contains a set of external formulas. When you select a model file to load, and press **RETURN**, a status message similar to the following is displayed in the Message window:

```
Loading file C:\ARB2\CGSMODEL.MDL      Active
```

When the `Active` attention bar disappears, the model is loaded. External formulas from the file are added to the current model.

---

**NOTE:** If the selected model file contains an external formula for a decision variable that already has a formula in the current model, the formula in the file replaces the current formula. However, this command only replaces external formulas, not annotation (branch) formulas.

---

**Save**

The Save command saves the current model to a disk file for future use (with other decision trees).

When you use this command, a request for the output filename appears in the Menu window.

Enter the filename, which can contain up to eight characters. Press **RETURN** to save the model. Arborist appends the .MDL extension to all model filenames.

**Exit Menu**

When you select `Exit Menu`, you are returned to the menu from which you originally selected the Formulas command.

## Insert Node Command

**Location**

The Insert Node command is located on the Edit menu.

**Operation**

Select `Insert Node`, and then select the node before which the new node is to be inserted. You must then specify the type of the inserted node: decision node or chance node.

After you make this node-type selection, the tree is redrawn with the new node inserted between the branch that originally preceded the selected node and the selected node. The insertion pushes the selected node, its newly-created preceding branch, and anything following the selected node to the right.

Because the inserted node is now associated with the branch originally associated with the selected (original) node, the inserted node assumes the description, formulas, and probability of the selected node. If the selected node is an end node or undefined node, it retains its original value.

When the tree is redrawn, the selected node and its associated new branch are highlighted, and Arborist automatically displays the Annotate Node menu in the Menu window to allow you to annotate the selected node and its associated new branch. You can either enter this information now or use the Change Values command later to specify the annotations. (See the section entitled Change Values Command earlier in this chapter for details on the Annotate Node menu.)

## Load Command

**Location**

The Load command is located on the Input/Output menu.

**Operation**

When you select `Load`, Arborist reads the current directory and displays in the Macro View window a selection list of decision trees (files with the extension .TRE) available.

Select the decision tree to be loaded. If a decision tree is currently displayed, you are notified that loading a new decision tree will delete the current decision tree:

```
Load will delete current tree - Are you sure? (Y/N)
```

Press the **Y** key to delete the current decision tree and replace it with the decision tree you have selected for loading.

Press the **N** key to leave the current decision tree unchanged.

## Macro View Command

**Location** The Macro View command is located on the Edit, Analysis, and Input/Output menus.

**Operation** When you select this command, the decision tree structure is displayed in the Macro View window.

If the structure is large, only a portion of the structure can be shown at a time. If the tree structure is too large to be displayed completely, you can use the Macro Browse command to move through the structure in the Macro View window. Refer to the section entitled Browse Command in this chapter for information about the Macro Browse command.

The Macro View window of the decision tree is synchronized with the Focus window, and the current node is indicated in both windows.

## New Tree Command

**Location** The New Tree command is located on the Edit menu.

**Operation** Select `New Tree`, and then select the type of modeling (Arborist or Lotus 1-2-3). The Annotate Node menu is automatically invoked when the root node is displayed. You can either enter this information now or use the Change Values command later to specify the annotations for the root node. (See the section entitled Change Values Command earlier in this chapter for details on the Annotate Node menu.)

You must define the root node type before adding any branches to it (see the Define Node Command section earlier in this chapter). However, you can load a subtree to the root node without defining it first.

---

**NOTE:** When you execute the New Tree command, Arborist displays a message warning you that you are about to destroy any existing decision tree information. If a decision tree is loaded into Arborist and it has not been saved, you should save it before invoking the New Tree command.

---

## Print Command

**Location**

The Print command is located on the Input/Output menu.

**Operation**

When you select this command, the Menu window displays the Print menu, which contains the following items: `Tree`, `Prob Dist Data`, `Sensitivity Data`, and `Exit Menu`.

When you select an item from the Print menu, you may receive the following message:

```
Printer is not connected
```

If a printer is connected to the computer, this message could indicate that the printer has its power turned off, or is offline.

**Tree**

When you print a decision tree, the printout shows both the tree structure and its associated annotation information. Descriptions are printed above the branch. Formulas, probabilities, and values are printed below the branch.

If formulas, probabilities, or values are too long to fit on a branch, they are represented on the tree as symbols: F*x* for formulas, P*x* for probabilities, and V*x* for values—where *x* is an integer. A separate page for each type of annotation information lists the actual formulas, probabilities, and values using the symbols from the tree as reference. External formulas are also listed on a separate page.

**Prob Dist Data**

When you print probability distribution data, the printout is labeled `Distribution of Outcomes`; this printout shows the raw data used to build the graph that is displayed when you execute the Prob Dist command. Below the title the number of outcomes is indicated, and the interval size is at the bottom of the page.

Three columns in the printout list the following information:

- Origin of each interval
- Sum of the probabilities of all outcomes that fall within the interval
- Cumulative sum of the probabilities of all outcomes that fall within the intervals

Printing raw probability distribution data allows you to examine closely information that cannot always be pinpointed on the screen graph.

**Sensitivity Data**

When you print sensitivity data, the printout is labeled `Sensitivity Analysis for` *<name of decision variable>*; this printout shows the raw data used to build the graph that is displayed when you execute the Sensitivity command. The header gives the name of the variable for which the sensitivity data was developed. Below that are three or more columns that list the following:

- Values assigned to the variable during the sensitivity analysis

- The best expected value for each value of the variable (the data in this column is used to plot the plus signs in the sensitivity graph)
- One column for each alternative that shows the expected value corresponding to the specific variable value

The minimum expected value and the maximum expected value are at the bottom of the page.

**Prob Dist Command**

**Location**

The Prob Dist command is located on the Analysis menu.

**Operation**

When you use this command, you select the node for which the probability distribution is to be computed. The probability distribution includes only those outcomes that can be reached from the node you select.

**Distribution Type**

After you select the node, a menu of distribution types is displayed in the Menu window: `Cumulative` and `Noncumulative`.

**NOTE:** If the tree has not been previously evaluated with the Expected Value command, this screen is preceded by the Expected Value menu, listing evaluation options.

**Range of Values**

After you specify the distribution type, the Menu window displays the Distribution Range menu, containing the following items: `Lowest Value`, `Highest Value`, `Number of Intervals`, and `Exit Menu`.

To accept the default values for these items, select `Exit Menu`. To change the defaults, select the desired item, enter another number, and press **RETURN**.

The Lowest Value and Highest Value set the end points of the horizontal axis of the graph. The default values for the Lowest Value and the Highest Value are the minimum and maximum outcomes in the tree when it is evaluated to find the best expected value.

The default value for the number of intervals is 10. To change the default value, enter an integer from 4 through 20 (the maximum) and press **RETURN**.

You can adjust the end points of the graph (using Lowest and Highest Value) in conjunction with the number of intervals to obtain a specific interval size or to focus on a particular portion of the graph.

When you select `Exit Menu`, the probability distribution is computed and displayed in the Focus window as a histogram.

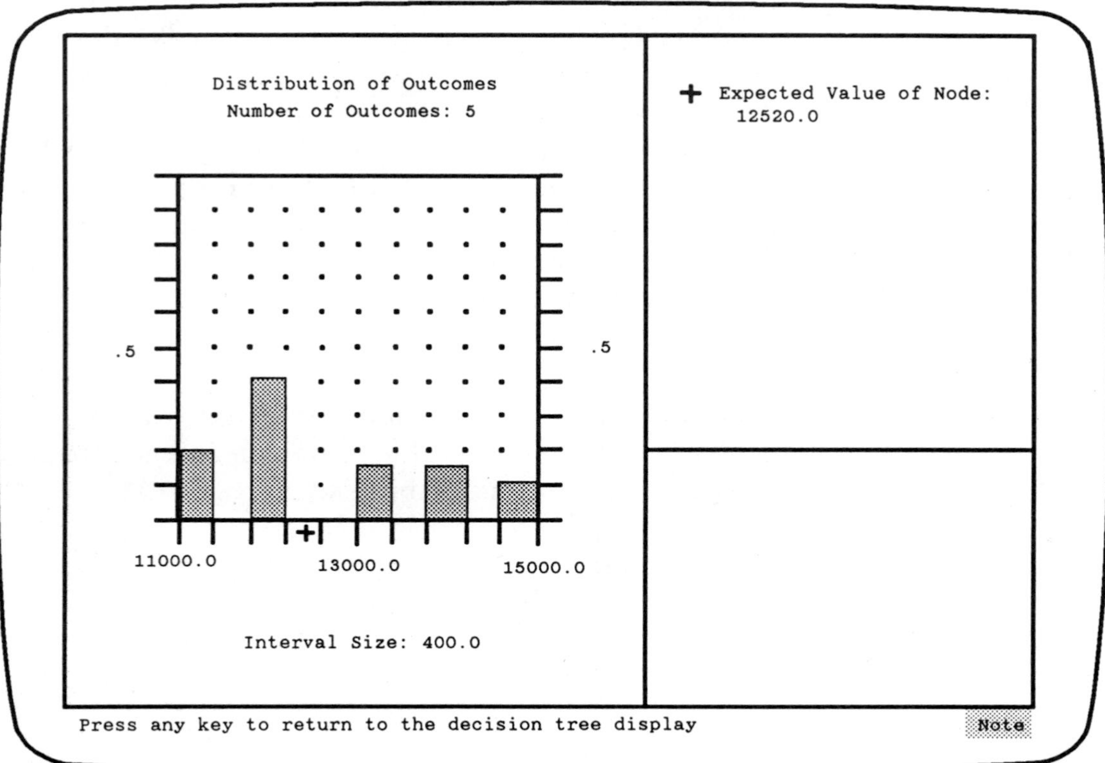


The vertical axis of the histogram is probability. This axis ranges in value from 0.0 to 1.0 in increments of 0.1. The horizontal axis is outcome value. This axis ranges in value from the lowest value specified to the highest value specified (divided into the number of equal intervals specified). If one or more outcomes fall outside the specified range, the Arborist software displays the message `All outcomes not included in distribution -- Press any key to continue`. Press any key to acknowledge the message.

The expected value for the selected node is marked with a plus sign beneath the bottom horizontal line of the histogram.

Note that the number of bars in the graph is less than the number of outcomes if more than one outcome falls in a particular interval. The bar height reflects the *sum* of the probabilities of the outcomes in that interval.

The probability distribution is based on selecting the best alternative at all decision nodes encountered in the decision process. If two (or more) paths (alternatives) yield the same expected value, you will not have a complete probability distribution for the selected node/branch. You must reexecute the Prob Dist command using these alternatives as the selected nodes.

**Printing Prob Dist Data** Use the Print command and select `Prob Dist Data` to print the probability distribution results. (See the section entitled Print Command in this chapter.)

**Saving Prob Dist Data** Use the Save command and select `Prob Dist Data` to save the probability distribution results to a disk file. (See the section entitled Save Command in this chapter.) You can later use this data file with other graphics packages such as Lotus 1-2-3 to print customized, presentation-quality graphs (see Appendix A for details).

**Printing the Graph** See Appendix A for information on printing a screen dump of the graph.

## Save Command

**Location** The Save command is located on the Input/Output menu.

**Operation** When you select this command, the Menu window displays the Save menu, which contains the following items: `Tree`, `Prob Dist Data`, `Sensitivity Data`, and `Exit Menu`.

This section describes how to use the commands on the Save menu.

**Tree Files**

For a decision tree save file, you specify the filename. All filenames must conform to MS-DOS or PC-DOS conventions. Arborist appends the extension .TRE. This file contains only the decision tree structural and annotation information.

The Save command also saves any external formulas to a disk file with the same filename as the tree file but with the extension .MDL.

**Automatic Backup**

When a tree is saved to an existing save file, a backup file with the extension .BAK is created. The backup file contains the original decision tree and the annotation information associated with the tree.

---

**NOTE:** If you use a filename for an existing tree, that file is overwritten without confirmation. However, you can recover the tree by using the .BAK file.

---

**Probability Distribution Data Files**

For probability distribution files, you specify the filename. All filenames must conform to MS-DOS or PC-DOS conventions. Specifying a file extension overrides the default extension. If you do not specify the file extension, Arborist appends the extension .PDA.

The information in a probability distribution data save file is formatted with all text items enclosed in double quotation marks and placed at the beginning of a line. All items associated with the text item follow it and are separated by commas. This format is called Comma Separated Values (CSV).

The CSV format can be used to transfer data to other business software packages to take advantage of the graphing or analysis capabilities of those packages. Refer to Appendix A for information on Lotus 1-2-3 graphing capabilities.

In the probability distribution save file, the first record starts with `"Interval Value"` followed by the interval values separated by commas. The second record in the file starts with `"Probability"` followed by the probabilities associated with the interval values separated by commas. The third record starts with `"Cumulative Probability"` followed by the cumulative probabilities for each interval.

### Sensitivity Analysis Data Files

For sensitivity analysis files, you specify the filename. All filenames must conform to MS-DOS or PC-DOS conventions. Specifying a file extension overrides the default extension. If you do not specify the file extension, Arborist appends the extension .SDA.

The sensitivity analysis file uses the CSV format explained under Probability Distribution Data Files on the preceding page.

In the sensitivity analysis save file, the first record starts with `"Value"` followed by the values for the analysis variable chosen, separated by commas. The second record starts with `"Expected Value"` followed by the best expected value associated with each value of the variable used in the sensitivity analysis. Each value in this second record is separated by commas.

The next group of records consists of a record for each branch from the root node. Each record starts with the branch name followed by the associated expected values, separated by commas, for that branch, given the values of the analysis variable.

The next-to-last record starts with `"Min EV"` followed by the minimum expected value (computed for the decision tree by using the analysis variable values in the first record). The last record starts with `"Max EV"` followed by the maximum expected value (computed for the tree by using the analysis variable values in the first record).

## Sensitivity Command

**Location**

The Sensitivity command is located on the Analysis menu.

**Operation**

When you select this command, you must also select the node at which the variable you will use for sensitivity analysis is assigned a value.

If you use the Sensitivity command on a tree for which sensitivity analysis has been performed, the following message is displayed in the Message window:

```
Redisplay Sensitivity Analysis Results? (Y/N)
```

Press the **Y** key to display the results of the most recently executed sensitivity analysis without waiting for that analysis to be recomputed.

Press the **N** key to perform the sensitivity analysis on a different node or with different parameters.

**Evaluation Options**

After you select the node, the Gains/Losses menu is displayed in the Menu window: `Gains (Maximize)` and `Losses (Minimize)`.

**Variable Selection**

After you select the evaluation option, you are prompted to enter the name of a variable. The variable must be assigned a value at the selected node.

**Variable Value Types**

After you specify the variable, the Values Type menu is displayed in the Menu window: `Range of Values` and `Enumerated Values`. Select the value type.

If you select `Range of Values`, the Menu window displays the Range of Expected Values menu, which contains the following items: `Lowest Value`, `Highest Value`, `Number of Points`, and `Exit Menu`.

Select `Lowest Value`, enter the lower limit of the range of values to be used for the chosen variable, and press **RETURN**.

Select `Highest Value`, enter the upper limit of the range of values to be used for the chosen variable, and press **RETURN**.

Select `Number of Points` and enter the number of points to use in evaluating the decision tree (including the low and high values). The default value for the number of points is 10. To change the default value, enter an integer from 4 through 20 and press **RETURN**.

After you have specified the previous items, select `Exit Menu` to perform the sensitivity analysis. (You can also select `Exit Menu` if you wish to accept the default values.)

If you select `Enumerated Values` from the Value Types menu, the prompt `Enumerated Values` appears in the center of the Menu window. To begin the sensitivity analysis calculations, enter a series of values separated by semicolons, and press **RETURN**.

**Scaling the Graph**

When the sensitivity analysis is completed (by either method of specifying values), the Range of Expected Values menu with the following items appears in the Menu window: `Lowest Expected Value`, `Highest Expected Value`, and `Exit Menu`. These values specify the upper and lower limits of the vertical axis of the graph.

The default values for `Lowest Expected Value` and `Highest Expected Value` are determined by the minimum and maximum outcomes of the tree; these outcomes are computed during the sensitivity analysis. You can adjust the `Lowest Expected Value` and `Highest Expected Value` to focus on the portion of the graph of greatest interest. Enter the values you wish to see displayed and select `Exit Menu`, or simply select `Exit Menu` to accept the defaults.

**Sensitivity Display**

When you select `Exit Menu`, the results are displayed in the Focus window as a graph, as shown.

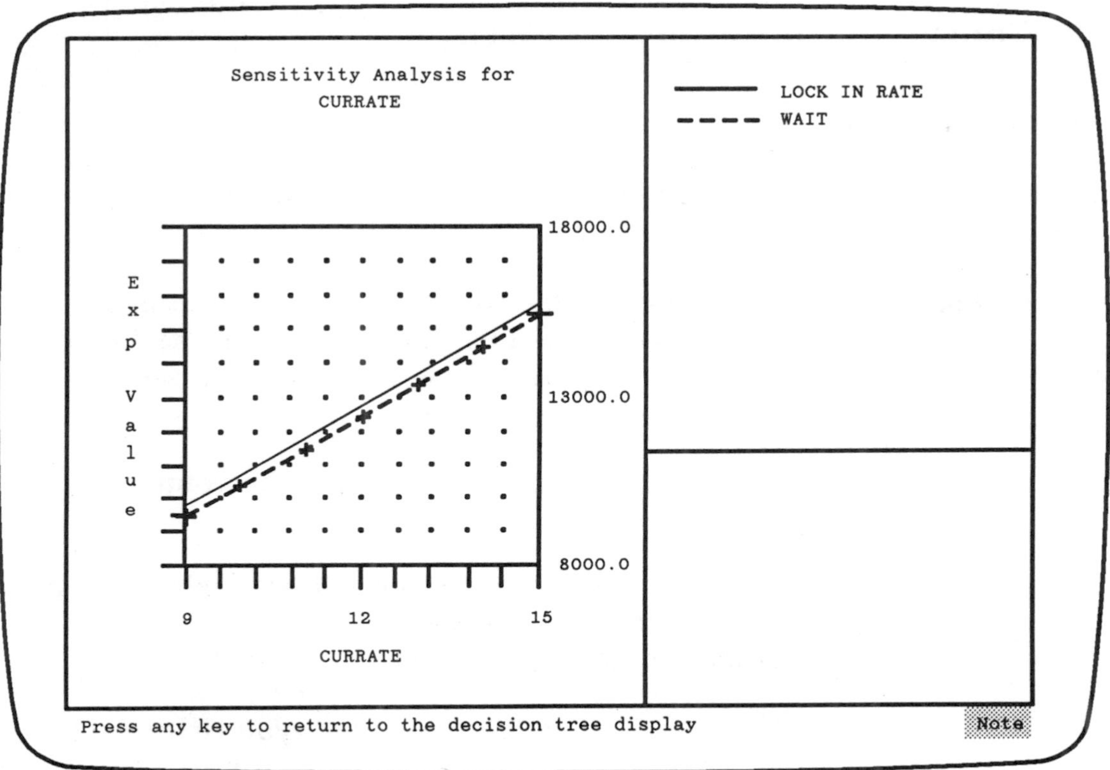


Press any key to return to the Analysis menu.

**Printing Sensitivity Data**

Use the Print command and select `Sensitivity Data` to print the sensitivity analysis results. (See the section entitled Print Command in this chapter.)

**Saving Sensitivity Data**

Use the Save command and select `Sensitivity Data` to save the sensitivity analysis results to a disk file. (See the section entitled Save Command in this chapter.) You can later use this data file with other graphics packages such as Lotus 1-2-3 to print customized, presentation-quality graphs (see Appendix A for details).

**Printing the Graph**

See Appendix A for information on printing a screen dump of the graph.

## Subtree Command

**Location**

The Subtree command is located on the Edit menu.

**Operation**

When you use this command, the Subtree menu with the following items is displayed in the Menu window: `Copy Subtree`, `Delete Subtree`, `Load Subtree`, `Save Subtree`, and `Exit Menu`.

This section describes how to use the commands on the Subtree menu.

**Copy Subtree**

The Copy Subtree command copies a selected subtree structure to a selected destination node. The destination node cannot be an end node.

When you invoke this command, you first select the leftmost node (and its associated preceding branch) of the subtree structure to be copied. You then select the destination node (the node to which the subtree is to be copied), and the tree is redrawn to reflect the addition of the copied subtree.

If the destination is a defined node, the leftmost branch of the copied node is appended to the right side of the destination node and thus becomes a branch of that node. The copied subtree retains all of its original structural and annotation information, including the annotations for its leftmost branch.

If the destination is an undefined node, the copied subtree node *replaces* the undefined node, but the leftmost branch of the copied subtree is not copied.

The leftmost branch of the undefined node retains its original annotations. This behavior can be useful when you want to build parallel subtree structures.

For example, you may have two end nodes that you want to expand equally by adding on parallel decision-node subtrees. Although you cannot copy a subtree to an end node, you can redefine the end nodes as undefined nodes and then copy the subtrees to them. Because of the behavior of the Copy Subtree command when copying to undefined nodes, you can retain the original annotations for the *end nodes* (and their uniqueness) while quickly building tree structures.

After the subtree is copied, you can use the Change Values command to alter the node descriptions, probabilities, values, and formulas in the subtree.

**Delete Subtree**

The Delete Subtree command deletes a node or subtree from a decision tree.

When you invoke this command, you must select the leftmost node of the subtree to be deleted. In the case of a single branch, select the branch. When you select the subtree or branch, the following message appears:

```
About to delete selected node/subtree - Are you sure?
(Y/N)
```

Press the **Y** key to delete the subtree. If you press the **N** key, the current decision tree remains unchanged.

After the subtree is deleted, the new decision tree structure is displayed. The node to which the deleted subtree was connected is now the focus node.

**Load Subtree**

The Load Subtree command loads a subtree chosen from a selection list of available subtrees located on a disk.

When you use this command, you select the node to which the subtree is to be added. A list of subtree filenames in the current directory is displayed in the Macro View window. Select the desired subtree.

If the selected destination node is either a decision node or a chance node, the subtree appears as a branch from the destination node. If the selected destination node is an undefined node, the leftmost node of the subtree replaces the undefined node.

The decision tree display is redrawn to reflect the addition of the new subtree.

After you add the subtree, you can use the Change Values command to alter the node descriptions, probabilities, values, and formulas.

**Save Subtree**

The Save Subtree command saves the chosen subtree structure (and annotation information) to a disk file.

When you invoke this command, you select the leftmost node of the subtree to be saved. The resulting disk file has the extension .STR and is located in the current directory. Arborist ignores any user-specified file extension.

The Save Subtree command saves decision tree structural and annotation information. The Save Subtree command also saves any external formulas to a disk file with the same filename as the subtree file but with the extension .MDL.

When a subtree is saved to an existing save file, a backup file with the extension .BAK is created. The backup file contains the original subtree and the annotation information associated with the subtree.

---

**NOTE:** If you use a filename for an existing subtree, that file is overwritten without confirmation. However, you can recover the subtree by using the .BAK file.

---

# APPENDIX A: PRINTING ARBORIST GRAPHS

## Introduction

This appendix describes two main ways to create presentation-quality printouts of Arborist analysis data:

- Using other graphics packages — You can transfer Arborist data to a package such as Lotus 1-2-3, then generate a graph from the data and make presentation-quality printouts. The first (and largest) portion of this appendix describes an example scenario for creating Lotus graphs using Arborist data.
- Printing screen dumps — You can print hard copies of probability distribution or sensitivity analysis graphs directly from the screen while you are running the Arborist software.

## Using Other Graphics Packages

### Saving Analysis Data

After you do a probability distribution or a sensitivity analysis, follow these steps to save the analysis data for use in other graphics packages.

1. Exit the Analysis menu and enter the Input/Output menu.
2. Select the `Save` function.
3. Select `Prob Dist Data` or `Sensitivity Data`, whichever you want to graph.
4. When you are prompted for an output file, type the filename you wish to use. The extension .PDA for probability distribution data or .SDA for sensitivity data will be added to your filename automatically by Arborist.

5. Select `Exit Menu` and then `Quit` to exit Arborist.

6. At the DOS level, rename the .PDA or .SDA extension of the file to .PRN.

You are now ready to use a graphics package. On the following pages is an example of the steps you can follow in Lotus 1-2-3 to generate a graph.

**Data File Transfer**

1. Erase the old worksheet.

2. Press /.

3. Select `File`.

4. Select `Import`.

5. Select `Numbers`.

6. Select your data file from the choices presented.

---

**NOTE:** If no file is named, you may have to change the directory by typing / and selecting the following: `F(ile) D(irectory)`. Then type the new directory name.

---

**Probability Distribution Data Graph**

Assuming that the number of intervals you specified for the probability distribution data is 10, use the following sequence of commands to generate a graph based on the probability distribution data.

1. Press /.

2. Select `Graph`.

3. Select `Reset`.

4. Select `Graph`.

5. Select `Type`.

6. Select `Bar`.

7. Select `X`.

8. Specify the interval values (for example, B1 through K1.)

9. Select `A`.

10. Specify the probability values (for example, B2 through K2).

11. Select `B`.

12. Specify the cumulative probability values (for example, B3 through K3).

13. Select `Options`.

14. Select `Color` if you have a color monitor.

15. Select `Titles`.

16. Select `X-Axis`.

17. Type `OUTCOMES`.

18. Select `Titles`.

19. Select `Y-Axis`.

20. Type PROBABILITIES.

21. Select Quit to leave the Options menu.

22. Select View to view the graph created by Lotus 1-2-3.

23. Press any key to terminate View.

24. Select Save. This saves the graph as a picture file, which you can print using the Lotus 1-2-3 PrintGraph program. See your associated Lotus 1-2-3 documentation for details on using the PrintGraph program.

**Sensitivity Analysis Data Graph**

Assuming that the decision tree has two initial alternatives and 10 intervals, use the following sequence of commands to generate a graph based on the sensitivity analysis data.

1. Press /.

2. Select Graph.

3. Select Reset.

4. Select Graph.

5. Select Type.

6. Select XY.

7. Select X.

8. Specify the interval values (for example, B1 through K1.)

9. Select A.

10. Specify the probability values (for example, B2 through K2).

11. Select B.

12. Specify the cumulative probability values (for example, B3 through K3).

13. Select C.

14. Specify the second alternative (for example, B4 through K4.)

15. Select `Options`.

16. Select `Color` if you have a color monitor.

17. Select `Titles`.

18. Select `X-Axis`.

19. Type the name of the sensitivity variable.

20. Select `Titles`.

21. Select `Y-Axis`.

22. Type EXPECTED VALUE.

23. Select `Quit` to leave the Options menu.

24. Select `View` to view the graph created by Lotus 1-2-3.

25. Press any key to terminate `View`.

26. Select Save. This saves the graph as a picture file, which you can print using the Lotus 1-2-3 PrintGraph program. See your associated Lotus 1-2-3 documentation for details on using the PrintGraph program.

## Printing Screen Dumps

**TI Set-Up and Operation**

Before you run the Arborist software, install the PRTSCRN device driver.

Enter the following line into your configuration file:

`DEVICE=`[*pathspec*] `PRTSCRN.DEV`

For details on configuration information, refer to your MS-DOS manual.

After you have installed the PRTSCRN device driver, you can print screen dumps of probability distribution or sensitivity analysis graphs any time you wish by pressing **ALT-SHIFT-PRINT**.

**IBM Set-Up and Operation**

Before you run the Arborist software, run the GRAPHICS.COM program from DOS. You might want to install this program directive in your AUTOEXEC.BAT file to enable the screen-dump feature every time you run Arborist. Remember, however, that the GRAPHICS.COM program remains resident in memory until you reboot your system. Keep this in mind if you will be running several software packages and you need to conserve memory space.

After you have run the GRAPHICS.COM program, you can print screen dumps of probability distribution or sensitivity analysis graphs any time you wish by pressing **SHIFT-PRTSC**.

If the screen-dump feature still does not work properly, refer to the mode and configuration command information in your DOS manual.

## APPENDIX B: CUSTOM PRINTER CONFIGURATION

### About Your Printer

Before you configure Arborist for use with your printer, you must know the following information:

- The sequence to reset the printer
- The sequence to specify compressed mode printing (if supported by your printer)
- Whether your printer is a wide-carriage printer
- The character to be used as the node symbol (if your printer supports the printing of mosaic characters)

### Custom Menu

To access the Custom menu, you must first execute the Configuration command from the Arborist Main menu, and then select `Custom` from the menu of printer types. If you are using a TI computer, the Configuration command first prompts you to select (or reselect) the monitor type, and then the menu of printer types is displayed in the Menu window. If you are using an IBM-compatible computer, selecting the Configuration command simply displays the menu of printer types. The following figure shows the Custom menu.

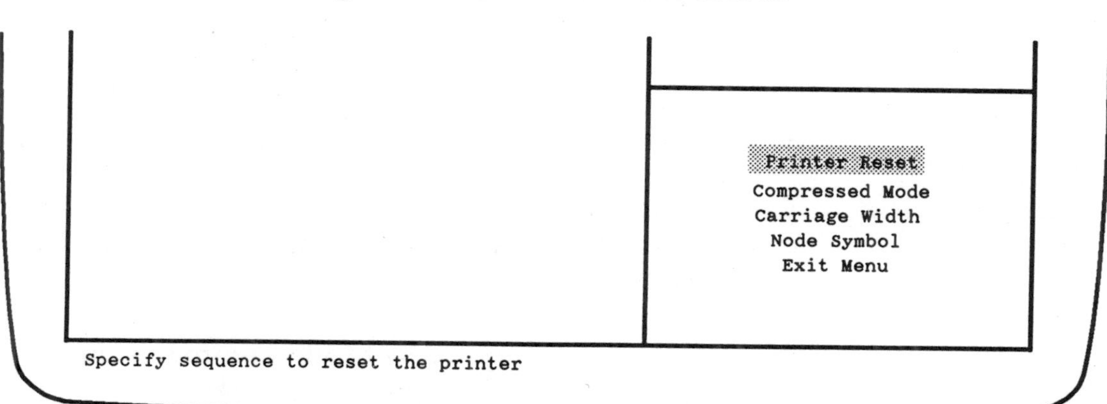

The remainder of this appendix describes the four commands appearing on the Custom menu.

**Printer Reset**

The Printer Reset command must be performed to set the master printer reset escape sequence. The master printer reset is used to reset all special printer modes to their power-up states, including print size and Top Of Form.

To execute the Printer Reset command, move the highlight over the Printer Reset command and press the **RETURN** key. Then enter the decimal byte values of the escape sequence to reset your printer special modes to their power-up states. Separate each decimal byte value with a semicolon.

For example, the escape sequence for the master reset on a Texas Instruments 855 printer is as follows:

```
(ESC) @
```

To enter this escape sequence into Arborist, move the highlight to the Printer Reset command and press the **RETURN** key and then type:

```
27;64
```

This escape sequence is sent to the printer before all printing operations.

**Compressed Mode**

The Compressed Mode command allows you to specify the decimal byte values required to print in compressed mode.

To execute the Compressed Mode command, move the highlight over the Compressed Mode command and press the **RETURN** key. Then enter the decimal byte values of the escape sequence to initiate compressed mode printing. Separate each decimal byte value with a semicolon.

For example, the escape sequence for the master reset on a Texas Instruments 855 printer is as follows:

```
(ESC) P
```

To enter this escape sequence into Arborist, move the highlight to the Compressed Mode command and press the **RETURN** key and then type:

```
27;80
```

This escape sequence is sent to the printer before a tree is printed. Probability distribution and sensitivity analysis data are printed in normal (10 characters per inch) mode.

**Carriage Width**

The Carriage Width command allows you to indicate whether you are using a wide-carriage printer. The Arborist software prints more nodes per page on a wide-carriage printer than on a printer with a standard (8-inch) carriage.

The default carriage width is `Normal`. To indicate that you are using a wide-carriage printer, move the highlight over the Carriage Width command and press the **RETURN** key, and then select `Wide`.

**Node Symbol**

If your printer supports the printing of mosaic characters, the Node Symbol command allows you to specify mosaic characters for decision node representation in Arborist Decision Tree printouts. Specifying mosaic characters overrides the default node characters of D for a decision node and C for a chance node. That is, if you specify mosaic characters to represent decision nodes, no symbol is printed for chance nodes.

To execute the Node Symbol command, move the highlight over the Node Symbol command and press the **RETURN** key. After selecting the command, enter the decimal values of the mosaic characters to be used for the the top and bottom of the decision node symbol.

For example, to specify █ as the top mosaic character and to specify ▬ as the bottom mosaic character on a Texas Instruments 855, enter the following:

```
223;163
```

# IRWIN

## IRWIN Program License Agreement

YOU SHOULD CAREFULLY READ THE FOLLOWING TERMS AND CONDITIONS BEFORE OPENING THIS PACKAGE. THE ENCLOSED COMPUTER PROGRAM AND DOCUMENTATION IS PROVIDED ONLY ON THE CONDITION THAT YOU AGREE TO THE FOLLOWING LICENSE. IF YOU DO NOT AGREE TO THESE TERMS AND CONDITIONS, YOU SHOULD PROMPTLY RETURN THE PACKAGE UNOPENED, AND YOUR MONEY WILL BE REFUNDED.

Irwin provides this program and licenses its use to you. You assume responsibility for the selection of the program to achieve your intended results, and for the installation, use and results obtained from the program.

### License

Under the terms of this license you may use the program on a single machine and copy the program into any machine-readable or printed form for backup or modification purposes in support of your use of the program on the single machine. However, this program may include mechanisms to limit or inhibit copying. If so, it is marked "copy protected."

You may also transfer the program and license to another party who agrees to the terms and conditions of this agreement. If you do transfer it, you must transfer all copies, whether in printed or machine-readable format to the same party, or destroy any copies of the program or its parts that are not transferred. You may not sublicense, assign or transfer the license of the program except as expressly provided in this agreement.

### Limited Warranty

Irwin warrants that the material of the program diskette and user manual are provided free of defect, that the software has been properly recorded on the diskette, and that the user manual is essentially complete and contains all of the information that we deem necessary to use the program; and that the program functions substantially as described in the user manual.

Irwin excludes any and all implied warranties, including warranties of merchantability and fitness for any particular purpose other than those specifically stated herein. Irwin's entire liability and your exclusive remedy shall be the replacement of any diskette not meeting this limited warranty which is returned to Irwin or an authorized dealer with a copy of your receipt.

This warranty gives you specific legal rights and you may also have other rights which vary from state to state. Some states do not allow the exclusion or limitation of implied warranties, so the above limitation may not apply to you.

This warranty is valid for 90 days from the time of your purchase of the program, and is extended only to the first user of the program.

### Term

This license is effective until terminated. It is automatically terminated if you violate any portion of this agreement. When this license is terminated you agree to destroy all copies of the program and its parts.

### General

This agreement will be governed by the laws of the State of Illinois. Should you have any questions concerning this agreement, you may contact Richard D. Irwin, Inc. at 1818 Ridge Road, Homewood, Illinois 60430.

## TEXAS INSTRUMENTS SOFTWARE MEDIA THREE MONTH LIMITED WARRANTY

Customer service and warranty information is applicable only in the United States and Canada. Please refer to local customer service and warranty information where applicable. TEXAS INSTRUMENTS INCORPORATED EXTENDS THIS WARRANTY ONLY TO THE ORIGINAL PURCHASER OF THIS PRODUCT WHO QUALIFIES AS A CONSUMER ("PURCHASER").

---

**WARRANTY DURATION** The media is warranted for a period of three (3) months from the date of original purchase by the Purchaser.

**WARRANTY COVERAGE** This limited warranty covers the media on which the computer program is furnished. It does not extend to the program contained on the media or the accompanying book materials (collectively the "Program"). The media is warranted against defects in material or workmanship. THIS WARRANTY IS VOID IF THE MEDIA HAS BEEN DAMAGED BY ACCIDENT, UNREASONABLE USE, NEGLECT, IMPROPER SERVICE, OR OTHER CAUSES NOT ARISING OUT OF DEFECTS IN MATERIALS OR WORKMANSHIP.

**PERFORMANCE BY TI UNDER WARRANTY** During the above three–month warranty period, defective media will be replaced when it is returned either in person or postage prepaid with a copy of the purchase receipt to TI or to the seller from whom you obtained possession. Defective media will be replaced and you will receive a new Program (including media and associated documentation). The replacement media will be warranted for three months from date of replacement. Other than the postage requirement (where allowed by law), no charge will be made for the replacement. TI strongly recommends that you insure the media for value prior to mailing.

**WARRANTY AND CONSEQUENTIAL DAMAGES DISCLAIMERS**

ANY IMPLIED WARRANTIES ARISING OUT OF THIS SALE INCLUDING, BUT NOT LIMITED TO, THE IMPLIED CONDITIONS OR WARRANTIES OF MERCHANTABILITY AND FITNESS FOR A PARTICULAR PURPOSE, ARE LIMITED IN DURATION TO THE ABOVE THREE-MONTH PERIOD.

IN NO EVENT SHALL TEXAS INSTRUMENTS BE LIABLE TO ANYONE FOR SPECIAL, COLLATERAL, INCIDENTAL OR CONSEQUENTIAL DAMAGES, WHETHER ALLEGED AS A RESULT OF BREACH OF CONTRACT, BREACH OF WARRANTY, OR TORTIOUS CONDUCT. THESE EXCLUDED DAMAGES INCLUDE, BUT ARE NOT LIMITED TO, COST OF REMOVAL OR REINSTALLATION, OUTSIDE COMPUTER TIME, LABOR COSTS, LOSS OF GOODWILL, LOSS OF PROFITS, LOSS OF SAVINGS, OR LOSS OF USE OR INTERRUPTION OF BUSINESS.

Some states do not allow the exclusion or limitation of incidental or consequential damages or limitations on how long an implied warranty lasts, so the above limitations or exclusions may not apply to you.

**LEGAL REMEDIES**

This warranty gives you specific legal rights, and you may also have other rights which vary from state to state.

**TEXAS INSTRUMENTS SERVICE FACILITIES**

To expedite processing, we request that you contact the seller from whom you obtained possession; if you are unable to contact the seller, we recommend you contact the following Austin address:

Texas Instruments Incorporated
12337 Technology Boulevard
Austin, Texas 78759
Attention: Customer Return Area

California:

Texas Instruments Incorporated
DSG Sales
690 Knox St., Suite 100
Torrance, California 90502
Attention: Customer Return Area

Oregon:

Texas Instruments Incorporated
DSG Sales
6700 Southwest 105th
Kristin Square, Suite 110
Beaverton, Oregon 97005
Attention: Customer Return Area

Canadian Residents:

Geophysical Service Incorporated
41 Shelley Road
Richmond Hill, Ontario
Canada L4C 1B1
Attention: Customer Return Area

**IMPORTANT NOTICE OF DISCLAIMER REGARDING THE COMPUTER PROGRAM**

You should read and understand the following before using the software Program. TI does not warrant that the Program will be free from error or will meet your specific requirements. You assume complete responsibility for any decision made or actions taken based on information obtained using the Program. Any statements made concerning the utility of the Program are not to be construed as expressed or implied warranties.

TEXAS INSTRUMENTS MAKES NO WARRANTY, EITHER EXPRESSED OR IMPLIED, INCLUDING BUT NOT LIMITED TO ANY IMPLIED CONDITIONS OR WARRANTIES OF MERCHANTABILITY AND FITNESS FOR A PARTICULAR PURPOSE, REGARDING THE PROGRAM AND MAKES ALL PROGRAMS AVAILABLE SOLELY ON AN "AS IS" BASIS.

IN NO EVENT SHALL TEXAS INSTRUMENTS BE LIABLE FOR SPECIAL, COLLATERAL, INCIDENTAL, OR CONSEQUENTIAL DAMAGES, WHETHER ALLEGED AS RESULT OF BREACH OF CONTRACT, BREACH OF WARRANTY, OR TORTIOUS CONDUCT. THESE EXCLUDED DAMAGES INCLUDE, BUT ARE NOT LIMITED TO, COST OF REMOVAL OR REINSTALLATION, OUTSIDE COMPUTER TIME, LABOR COSTS, LOSS OF GOODWILL, LOSS OF PROFITS, LOSS OF SAVINGS, OR LOSS OF USE OR INTERRUPTION OF BUSINESS. THE SOLE AND EXCLUSIVE LIABILITY OF TEXAS INSTRUMENTS, REGARDLESS OF THE FORM OF ACTION,

SHALL NOT EXCEED THE PURCHASE PRICE OF THE PROGRAM. TEXAS INSTRUMENTS SHALL NOT BE LIABLE FOR ANY CLAIM OF ANY KIND WHATSOEVER BY ANY OTHER PARTY AGAINST YOU.

Some states do not allow the exclusion or limitation of incidental or consequential damages, so the above limitation or exclusion may not apply to you.

## Arborist Decision Tree Software

*Part Number 2240320-0001*

This package represents the fully functional implementation of the Arborist Decision Tree Software, which allows you to build and analyze decision trees for larger, more complex problems (the number of nodes supported by this version is limited only by the amount of system memory).

Arborist combines sophisticated decision analysis techniques and the modeling ("what if") capabilities of Lotus™ 1-2-3™ to provide a powerful decision-making tool for use with personal computers. With Arborist, users can graphically structure and evaluate the numerous alternatives and risks associated with complex decisions. Arborist can work with data from your Lotus 1-2-3 spreadsheet, incorporating uncertain information and graphically displaying the best alternatives and risks involved.

*Computer systems supported:* Texas Instruments Professional Computer, TI Business-Pro™ Professional Computer (TI or AT mode), IBM® Personal Computer, IBM PC/XT®, IBM Personal Computer AT®, IBM Personal System/2™, or true compatibles

*Minimum required configuration:* MS®-DOS 2.*X* or 3.*X*; 512K memory; dual-diskette drive; and TI 3-plane graphics, IBM Color Graphics Adapter (CGA), or Enhanced Graphics Adapter (EGA)

*Recommended options:* 640K memory, hard disk, color monitor, and printer

**FOR ADDITIONAL PRODUCT INFORMATION, CALL TOLL-FREE:**
**1-800-527-3500**

* TI List Price, subject to change without notice.

Trademarks: Arborist and Business-Pro are trademarks of Texas Instruments Incorporated. Lotus and 1-2-3 are trademarks of Lotus Development Corporation. IBM, PC/XT, and Personal Computer AT are registered trademarks and Personal System/2 is a trademark of International Business Machines Corporation. MS is a registered trademark of Microsoft Corporation.

# Index